Readings in DEVELOPMENTAL PSYCHOLOGY

JUDITH KRIEGER GARDNER
Children's Hospital Medical Center, Boston

Readings in DEVELOPMENTAL PSYCHOLOGY

Second Edition

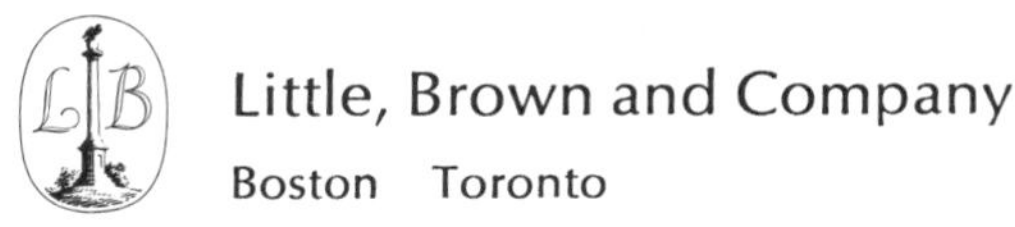

Little, Brown and Company
Boston Toronto

Library of Congress Catalog Card No. 81–85525

ISBN 0–316–303828

9 8 7 6 5 4 3 2 1

MV

Published simultaneously in Canada
by Little, Brown & Company (Canada) Limited

Printed in the United States of America

For my parents

PREFACE

I have sought to collect in this reader some examples of the best writing and thinking in developmental psychology. To give students a provocative yet comprehensive and balanced introduction to this increasingly diverse field of study, I have included selections that capture the principal themes and major differences, both substantive and methodological, among developmental psychologists. Thus, among the selections are articles that emphasize cognitive development as well as ones that stress affective development; some that focus on the individual and his or her capacities and capabilities as well as some that concentrate on society and its influence. By the same token, I have included in roughly equal proportions experimental investigations, theoretical discussions, and case studies, in which one sees a child facing a specific problem.

These basic approaches are reflected in each of the book's sections, which are arranged by stages of development. An introductory section gives an overview of the field and raises the underlying issues with which all developmental psychology is concerned; it is followed by five sections treating infancy, toddlerhood, the early school years, middle childhood, and adolescence. Each part begins with a short introductory essay that presents a brief overview of the developmental stage and discusses each article. The prefatory notes review the design and analysis of experiments, the importance and methodology of empirical works, the scope of the theoretical pieces and their relationship to other research, and the relevance of each case study to the broader issues of the particular stage.

Because the selection includes classic articles which speak to the basic issues of developmental psychology, many of the articles from the first edition remain. New papers have been added to reflect recent movements in the field as well as to update experimental studies. A new emphasis on individual differences is apparent in many of the articles. The relevance of the social milieu to the individual's unique development is receiving more and more attention in the literature.

Since the concerns of children and of developmental psychologists differ at each stage of development, the central issues of each section of the reader are necessarily different. The first section on a developmental stage centers on the infant, who is born and immediately faces the task of constructing a world of physical and social objects. Articles in this section illustrate that infants have control over much of their environment, including the objects they will come to know and the people they will come to care for. The importance of the social environment, the differences between babies in different cultures, the infant's attachment to caretakers, the differences between maternal and paternal interactions, and the unique problems caused by a disability are discussed.

Having built a world and become a part of it, the toddler moves on to a new concern with symbols: toddlers think at a new level, begin to represent the world to themselves, and start to find a niche within the social realm. Included in this section are articles on the development of language and of play as well as pieces describing how society influences children, in particular their sex-role identities.

As the youngster enters school, the socializing influence of the culture becomes more explicit. No longer do parents alone mediate the child's exchange with the environment; now the child must learn to control instinctual patterns. The decline of egocentrism, the growth of effective communication, and the child's general intellectual level are central issues discussed in this section.

Articles in the next section show that during the seemingly quieter years of middle childhood much is accomplished: the youngster develops subtle capacities such as altruism and empathy, forms friendships, and either takes advantage of or is victimized by schooling.

The calm of middle childhood is abruptly changed with the onset of adolescence. In both the cognitive and the affective domains new abilities become apparent as the budding adult seeks to synthesize thoughts and feelings about himself or herself and the world. Through the articles in this section, as throughout the period of adolescence, "finding yourself" or "forging an identity in relation to the environment" is a pervasive theme.

In addition to providing a range of views on the important facets of each life stage, I have included representatives of different theoretical and empirical approaches to developmental psychology. Several major theoretical orientations are presented in the various articles. Reflecting the psychoanalytic position are articles by Erik Erikson and Mary Ainsworth. Jean Piaget's developmental theory is specifically discussed in two selections by Piaget, and represented in others by David Elkind, Lawrence Kohlberg, and Carol Gilligan Two articles by B. F. Skinner present the basic tenets of behaviorism. Other more eclectic theories appear in the articles by Lev Vygotsky, Jerome Bruner, and Martin Hoffman.

A second set of papers consists basically of reviews: either broad reviews of many studies, such as Zick Rubin's article on the development of friendships or Stephen Gould's on the IQ controversy, or more focused reviews synthesizing studies supporting one point of view. Jerome Kagan's paper on attention in infancy, Margaret Donaldson's paper on schooling, and Lawrence Kohlberg's discussion of moral development fit into this category.

Empirical studies constitute the major thrust of the reader. These research reports range from controlled experimental studies in a laboratory to others that adopt a more clinical approach. The range of these empirical works attests to the great variety of techniques and methodologies used by the developmental psychologist. Examples of controlled laboratory experiments include Marc Bornstein, William Kessen, and Sally Weiskopf's investigation of hue discrimination in the infant; Harry Harlow's two studies of social isolation in monkeys; Dedre Gentner's analysis of the development of word meaning; and Laurene Meringoff's probing of the child's differential comprehension of TV and story books. Other experimental studies leave the laboratory, attempting to establish well-controlled conditions in more natural settings.

Yet a third approach to empirical investigation features the analysis of language protocols. Kornei Chukovsky reviews children's spontaneous sayings, Roger Brown and Katherine Nelson pore over detailed transcripts of parent-child verbal interactions, and Lawrence Kohlberg looks for evidence of different stages of moral reasoning in children's responses to dilemmas posed by an experimenter.

The final type of empirical research included in this book is the case study. Selma Fraiberg's blind baby, Clara Park's autistic child, Dorothy Baruch's disturbed little boy, and Hilde Bruch's anorexic teenagers are examples of the pathological; Skinner's baby in the box, Lois Gould's baby X, and Mark Twain's Huckleberry Finn are within the normal range. But each case study speaks implicitly or explicitly to a specific developmental issue and reveals how careful study of a specific individual can yield clues to the course of general development.

This reader reflects the organizational framework used by Howard Gardner in his text, *Developmental Psychology*. However, the book is compatible with other texts, or can be used by itself, as an introduction to developmental psychology as some of its most insightful students see it.

ACKNOWLEDGMENTS

I would like to thank the following people for their help in the preparation of this book: the authors and publishers who allowed their work to be reprinted; Mylan Jaixen and Sally Stickney, my editors at Little, Brown; and the reviewers for their constructive criticism and suggestions. Finally, I would like to express my appreciation to the readers of the first edition, especially those who responded to the revision questionnaire; their reactions have been most gratifying.

J. G.

CONTENTS

Readings in
DEVELOPMENTAL
PSYCHOLOGY

INTRODUCTION

Every field of study requires a background against which its central subject matter can be seen. The routine work of developmental psychology involves devising hypotheses about the behaviors and thought processes of children and planning and executing experiments to test those hypotheses. But the findings and results of these experiments only gain meaning and texture when they are viewed within the broader context of developmental psychology as a whole.

One such context is the life cycle, a backdrop against which descriptions of specific ages and stages can be sketched. The scholar in our time who has thought most deeply — and, in my view, most effectively — about the nature of the human life cycle is Erik Erikson. Building on his vast clinical experience with individuals of different ages, but also on a sensitive knowledge of humanistic literature and of political and social realities of the modern world, Erikson has described eight principal stages of life through which all normal individuals will pass. That all individuals experience each stage is presupposed, but the particular ways in which the crises at each stage are negotiated (or not negotiated) determine in large measure the life each of us leads and the person each of us becomes. Indeed, one beauty of Erikson's view is that, starting from a description which proves applicable to men and women the world over, at the same time we can see how each of us, as individuals, has grown, with our strengths and weaknesses, problems and possibilities.

The study of children can also benefit from a very different context: the history of developmental psychology. Long before there were scientists spinning hypotheses about children, individuals observed children and made careful notes about them. Yet, at one time children were thought of differently than they are now, and, quite possibly, were not viewed as different from adults. That individuals at one time had a very different concept of children is important. It raises the broad questions of what kinds of presuppositions our society makes about children, and how those presuppositions structure the hypotheses that we fashion and the studies that we undertake. Such questions are best approached through an account of the various concepts of childhood and the unique cultural constraints that exist at any time, presented in William Kessen's paper.

These two contexts locate developmental psychology within a cultural-historical frame and provide a humanistic perspective. But developmental psychology is also a science, and an anchor in this perspective is equally important. Heinz Werner was one of the leading proponents of the developmental approach. What we mean by development, how it differs from simple "change," and why it is such a powerful tool in understanding growth are issues discussed in his classic paper. The categories he employs to discuss development have remained basic to all developmental description.

The themes of continuity and change, of flexibility and stability, are echoed again in the final paper of this book, where Zick Rubin asks, "Can personality really change after 20?"

There are many contexts in which to view developmental psychology but those offered here seem particularly appropriate. Armed with some insights into the development of the notion of childhood, as well as an overview of the entire human life cycle, we will be in a far better position to look at the detailed findings about each stage of development — the facts, theories, and generalizations that form the centerpiece of contemporary developmental psychology.

1 Erik H. Erikson
LIFE CYCLE

The observer of life is always immersed in it and thus unable to transcend the limited perspectives of his stage and condition. Religious world views usually evolve pervasive configurations of the course of life: one religion may envisage it as a continuous spiral of rebirths, another as a crossroads to damnation or salvation. Various "ways of life" harbor more or less explicit images of life's course: a leisurely one may see it as ascending and descending steps with a comfortable platform of maturity in between; a competitive one may envision it as a race for spectacular success — and sudden oblivion. The scientist, on the other hand, looks at the organism as it moves from birth to death and, in the larger sense, at the individual in a genetic chain; or he looks at the cultural design of life's course as marked by rites of transition at selected turning points.

The very choice of the configuration "cycle of life," then, necessitates a statement of the writer's conceptual ancestry — clinical psychoanalysis. The clinical worker cannot escape combining knowledge, experience, and conviction in a conception of the course of life and of the sequence of generations — for how, otherwise, could he offer interpretation and guidance? The very existence of a variety of psychiatric "schools" is probably due to the fact that clinical practice and theory are called upon to provide a total orientation beyond possible verification.

Freud confessed only to a scientific world view, but he could not avoid the attitudes (often in contradiction to his personal values) that were part of his times. The original data of psychoanalysis, for example, were minute reconstructions of "pathogenic" events in early childhood. They supported an orientation which — in analogy to teleology — could be called *originology,* i.e., a systematic attempt to derive complex meanings from vague beginnings and obscure causes. The result was often an implicit fatalism, although counteracted by strenuously "positive" orientations. Any theory embracing both life history and case history, however, must find a balance between the "backward" view of the genetic reconstruction and the "forward" formulation of progressive differentiation in growth and development; between the "downward" view into the depth of the unconscious and the "upward" awareness of compelling social experience; and between the "inward" exploration of inner reality and the "outward" attention to historical actuality.

This article will attempt to make explicit those psychosocial insights that often remain implicit in clinical practice and theory. These concern the individual, who in principle develops according to predetermined steps of readiness that enable him to participate in ever more differentiated ways along a widening social radius, and the social organization,

SOURCE: From "Life Cycle" by Erik H. Erikson. Reprinted by permission of the publisher from the *International Encyclopedia of the Social Sciences,* David L. Sills, Editor. Vol. 9, pp. 286–292.

which in principle tends to invite such developmental potentialities and to support the proper rate and the proper sequence of their unfolding.

"Cycle" is intended to convey the double tendency of individual life to "round itself out" as a coherent experience and at the same time to form a link in the chain of generations from which it receives and to which it contributes both strength and weakness.

Strategic in this interplay are developmental crises — "crisis" here connoting not a threat of catastrophe but a turning point, a crucial period of increased vulnerability and heightened potential, and, therefore, the ontogenetic source of generational strength and maladjustment.

THE EIGHT STAGES OF LIFE

Man's protracted childhood must be provided with the psychosocial protection and stimulation which, like a second womb, permits the child to develop in distinct steps as he unifies his separate capacities. In each stage, we assume a new drive-and-need constellation, an expanded radius of potential social interaction, and social institutions created to receive the growing individual within traditional patterns. To provide an evolutionary rationale for this (for prolonged childhood and social institutions must have evolved together), two basic differences between animal and man must be considered.

We are, in Ernst Mayr's terms (1964), the "generalist" animal, prepared to adapt to and to develop cultures in the most varied environments. A long childhood must prepare the newborn of the species to become specialized as a member of a pseudo species (Erikson 1965), i.e., in tribes, cultures, castes, etc., each of which behaves as if it were the only genuine realization of man as the heavens planned and created him. Furthermore, man's drives are characterized by instinctual energies, which are, in contrast to other animals, much less bound to instinctive patterns (or inborn release mechanisms). A maximum of free instinctual energy thus remains ready to be invested in basic psychosocial encounters which tend to fix developing energies into cultural patterns of mutuality, reliability, and competence. Freud has shown the extent to which maladaptive anxiety and rage accompany man's instinctuality, while postulating the strength of the ego in its defensive and in its adaptive aspects (see Freud 1936; Hartmann 1939). We can attempt to show a systematic relationship between man's maladjustments and those basic strengths which must emerge in each life cycle and re-emerge from generation to generation (Erikson 1964).

In Figure 1 . . . , the various psychosocial crises and thus the ontogenetic sources of adaptation and of maladjustment are arranged according to the epigenetic principle. The diagonal signifies a successive development and a hierarchic differentiation of psychosocial strengths.

If a favorable ratio of basic trust over basic mistrust is the first step in psychosocial adaptation, and the second step a favorable ratio of autonomy over shame and doubt, the diagram indicates a number of fundamental facts. Each basic psychosocial trend (1, 2, etc.) meets a crisis (I, 1; II, 2; etc.) during a corresponding stage (I, II, etc.), while *all* must exist from the beginning in some form (broken line) and in later stages (solid lines) must continue to be differentiated and reintegrated with newly dominant trends. An infant will show something like autonomy from the time of birth (I, 2), but it is not until the second year (II, 2) that he is ready to experience and to manage the critical conflict of becoming an autonomous creature while continuing to be dependent. At this time those around him will convey to him a cultural and personal version of the ratio of autonomy and

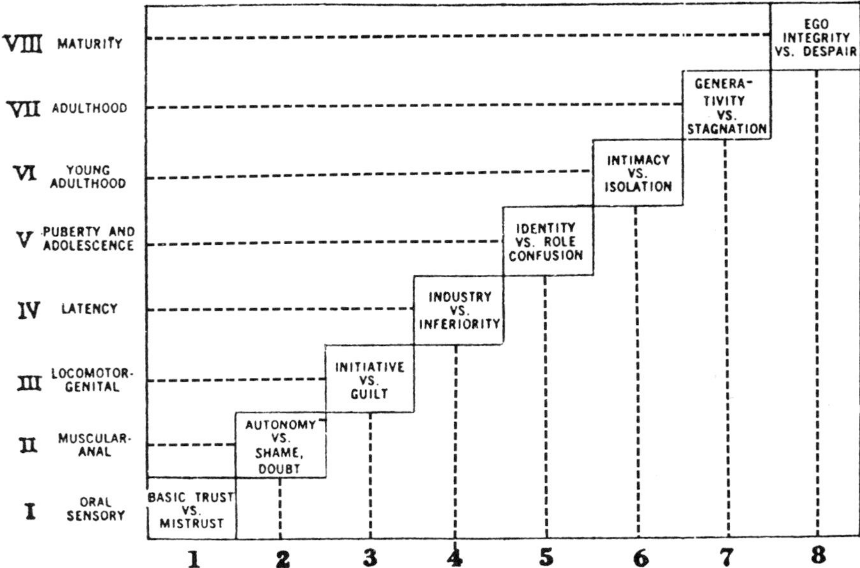

Figure 1. Psychosocial crises in the life cycle. (Adapted from *Childhood and Society*, 2nd Edition, by Erik H. Erikson, with the permission of W. W. Norton & Company, Inc. Copyright 1951, © 1963 by W. W. Norton & Company, Inc.)

dependence. The diagonal thus indicates a necessary sequence of such encounters but leaves room for variations in tempo and intensity.

The epigenetic pattern will have to be kept in mind as we now state for each stage: (*a*) the psychosocial crisis evoked by social interaction, which is in turn facilitated and necessitated by newly developing drives and capacities, and the specific psychosocial strength emanating from the solution of this crisis; (*b*) the specific sense of estrangement awakened at each stage and its connection with some major form of psychopathology; (*c*) the special relationship between all of these factors and certain basic social institutions (Erikson 1950).

Infancy (Basic Trust versus Mistrust — Hope)

The resolution of the first psychosocial crisis is performed primarily by maternal care. The newborn infant's more or less coordinated readiness to incorporate by mouth and through the senses meets the mother's and the society's more or less coordinated readiness to feed him and to stimulate his awareness. The mother must represent to the child an almost somatic conviction that she (his first "world") is trustworthy enough to satisfy and to regulate his needs. But the infant's demeanor also inspires hope in adults and makes them wish to give hope; it awakens in them a strength which they, in turn, are ready and needful to have confirmed in the experience of care. This is the ontogenetic basis of hope, that first and basic strength which gives man a semblance of instinctive certainty in his social ecology.

Unavoidable pain and delay of satisfaction, however, and inexorable weaning make this stage also prototypical for a sense of abandonment and helpless rage. This is the first of the human estrangements against which hope must maintain itself throughout life.

In psychopathology, a defect in basic trust can be evident in early malignant disturbances or can become apparent later in severe addiction or in habitual or sudden withdrawal into psychotic states.

Biological motherhood needs at least three links with social experience — the mother's past experience of being mothered, a method of care in trustworthy surroundings, and some convincing image of providence. The infant's hope, in turn, is one cornerstone of the adult's faith, which throughout history has sought an institutional safeguard in organized religion. However, where religious institutions fail to give ritual actuality to their formulas they may become irrelevant to psychosocial strength.

Hope, then, is the first psychosocial strength. It is the enduring belief in the attainability of primal wishes in spite of the anarchic urges and rages of dependency.

Early Childhood (Autonomy versus Shame, Doubt — Will Power)

Early childhood sets the stage for psychosocial autonomy by rapid gains in muscular maturation, locomotion, verbalization, and discrimination. All of these, however, create limits in the form of spatial restrictions and of categorical divisions between "yes and no," "good and bad," "right and wrong," and "yours and mine." Muscular maturation sets the stage for an ambivalent set of social modalities — holding on and letting go. To hold on can become a destructive retaining or restraining, or a pattern of care — to have and to hold. To let go, too, can turn into an inimical letting loose, or a relaxed "letting pass" and "letting be." Freud calls this the anal stage of libido development because of the pleasure experienced in and the conflict evoked over excretory retention and elimination.

This stage, therefore, becomes decisive for the ratio of good will and willfulness. A sense of self-control without loss of self-esteem is the ontogenetic source of confidence in free will; a sense of overcontrol and loss of self-control can give rise to a lasting propensity for doubt and shame. The matter is complicated by the different needs and capacities of siblings of different ages — and by their rivalry.

Shame is the estrangement of being exposed and conscious of being looked at disapprovingly, of wishing to "bury one's face" or "sink into the ground." This potentiality is exploited in the "shaming" used throughout life by some cultures and causing, on occasion, suicide. While shame is related to the consciousness of being upright and exposed, doubt has much to do with the consciousness of having a front and a back (and of the vulnerability of being seen and influenced from behind). It is the estrangement of being unsure of one's will and of those who would dominate it.

From this stage emerges the propensity for compulsive overcompliance or impulsive defiance. If denied a gradual increase in autonomy of choice the individual may become obsessed by repetitiveness and develop an overly cruel conscience. Early self-doubt and doubt of others may later find their most malignant expression in compulsion neuroses or in paranoiac apprehension of hidden critics and secret persecutors threatening from behind.

We have related basic trust to the institutions of religion. The enduring need of the individual to have an area of free choice reaffirmed and delineated by formulated privileges and limitations, obligations and rights, has an institutional safeguard in the principles of law and order and of justice. Where this is impaired, however, the law itself is in danger of becoming arbitrary or formalistic, i.e., "impulsive" or "compulsive" itself.

Will power is the unbroken determination

to exercise free choice as well as self-restraint in spite of the unavoidable experience of shame, doubt, and a certain rage over being controlled by others. Good will is rooted in the judiciousness of parents guided by their respect for the spirit of the law.

Play Age (Initiative versus Guilt — Purpose)

Able to move independently and vigorously, the child, now in his third or fourth year, begins to comprehend his expected role in the adult world and to play out roles worth imitating. He develops a sense of initiative. He associates with age-mates and older children as he watches and enters into games in the barnyard, on the street corner, or in the nursery. His learning now is intrusive; it leads him into ever new facts and activities, and he becomes acutely aware of differences between the sexes. But if it seems that the child spends on his play a purposefulness out of proportion to "real" purposes, we must recognize the human necessity to simultaneously bind together infantile wish and limited skill, symbol and fact, inner and outer world, a selectively remembered past and a vaguely anticipated future — all before adult "reality" takes over in sanctioned roles and adjusted purposes.

The fate of infantile genitality remains determined by the sex roles cultivated and integrated in the family. In the boy, the sexual orientation is dominated by phallic-intrusive initiative; in the girl, by inclusive modes of attractiveness and "motherliness."

Conscience, however, forever divides the child within himself by establishing an inner voice of self-observation, self-guidance, and self-punishment. The estrangement of this stage, therefore, is a sense of guilt over goals contemplated and acts done, initiated, or merely fantasied. For initiative includes competition with those of superior equipment. In a final contest for a favored position with the mother, "oedipal" feelings are aroused in the boy, and there appears to be an intensified fear of finding the genitals harmed as punishment for the fantasies attached to their excitability.

Infantile guilt leads to the conflict between unbounded initiative and repression or inhibition. In adult pathology this residual conflict is expressed in hysterical denial, general inhibition, and sexual impotence, or in overcompensatory exhibitionism and psychopathic acting-out.

The word "initiative" has for many a specifically American, or "entrepreneur," connotation. Yet man needs this sense of initiative for whatever he learns and does, from fruit gathering to commercial enterprise — or the study of books.

The play age relies on the existence of some form of basic family, which also teaches the child by patient example where play ends and irreversible purpose begins. Only thus are guilt feelings integrated in a strong (not severe) conscience; only thus is language verified as a shared actuality. The "oedipal" stage thus not only results in a moral sense restricting the horizon of the permissible, but it also directs the way to the possible and the tangible, which attract infantile dreams to the goals of technology and culture. Social institutions, in turn, offer an ethos of action, in the form of ideal adults fascinating enough to replace the heroes of the picture book and fairy tale.

That the adult begins as a playing child means that there is a residue of play acting and role playing even in what he considers his highest purposes. These he projects on a larger and more perfect historical future; these he dramatizes in the ceremonial present with uniformed players in ritual arrangements; thus men sanction aggressive initiative, even as they assuage guilt by submission to a higher authority.

Purpose, then, is the courage to envisage

and pursue valued and tangible goals guided by conscience but not paralyzed by guilt and by the fear of punishment.

School Age (Industry versus Inferiority — Competence)

Before the child, psychologically a rudimentary parent, can become a biological parent, he must begin to be a worker and potential provider. Genital maturation is postponed (the period of latency). The child develops a sense of industriousness, i.e., he begins to comprehend the tool world of his culture, and he can become an eager and absorbed member of that productive situation called "school," which gradually supersedes the whims of play. In all cultures, at this stage, children receive systematic instruction of some kind and learn eagerly from older children.

The danger of this stage lies in the development of a sense of inadequacy. If the child despairs of his skill or his status among his tool partners, he may be discouraged from further learning. He may regress to the hopeless rivalry of the oedipal situation. It is at this point that the larger society becomes significant to the child by admitting him to roles preparatory to the actuality of technology and economy. Where he finds, however, that the color of his skin or the background of his parents rather than his wish and his will to learn will decide his worth as an apprentice, the human propensity for feeling unworthy (inferior) may be fatefully aggravated as a determinant of character development.

But there is another danger: If the overly conforming child accepts work as the only criterion of worthwhileness, sacrificing too readily his imagination and playfulness, he may become ready to submit to what Marx called a "craft-idiocy," i.e., become a slave of his technology and of its established role typology.

This is socially a most decisive stage, preparing the child for a hierarchy of learning experiences which he will undergo with the help of cooperative peers and instructive adults. Since industriousness involves doing things beside and with others, a first sense of the division of labor and of differential opportunity — that is, a sense of the technological ethos of a culture — develops at this time. Therefore, the configurations of cultural thought and the manipulations basic to the prevailing technology must reach meaningfully into school life.

Competence, then, is the free exercise (unimpaired by an infantile sense of inferiority) of dexterity and intelligence in the completion of serious tasks. It is the basis for cooperative participation in some segment of the culture.

Adolescence (Identity versus Identity Confusion — Fidelity)

With a good initial relationship to skills and tools, and with the advent of puberty, childhood proper comes to an end. The rapidly growing youths, faced with the inner revolution of puberty and with as yet intangible adult tasks, are now primarily concerned with their psychosocial identity and with fitting their rudimentary gifts and skills to the occupational prototypes of the culture.

The integration of an identity is more than the sum of childhood identifications. It is the accrued confidence that the inner sameness and continuity gathered over the past years of development are matched by the sameness and continuity in one's meaning for others, as evidenced in the tangible promise of careers and life styles.

The adolescent's regressive and yet powerful impulsiveness alternating with compulsive restraint is well known. In all of this, however, an ideological seeking after an inner coherence and a durable set of values can be detected. The particular strength sought is fidelity — that is, the opportunity to fulfill personal potentialities (including erotic vitality or its sublimation) in a context which permits the young person to be true to himself and true to significant others. "Falling in love" also can be an attempt to arrive at a self-definition by seeing oneself reflected anew in an idealized as well as eroticized other.

From this stage on, acute maladjustments due to social anomie may lead to psychopathological regressions. Where role confusion joins a hopelessness of long standing, borderline psychotic episodes are not uncommon.

Adolescents, on the other hand, help one another temporarily through much regressive insecurity by forming cliques and by sterotyping themselves, their ideals, and their "enemies." In this they can be clannish and cruel in their exclusion of all those who are "different." Where they turn this repudiation totally against the society, delinquency may be a temporary or lasting result.

As social systems enter into the fiber of each succeeding generation, they also absorb into their lifeblood the rejuvenative power of youth. Adolescence is thus a vital regenerator in the process of social evolution, for youth can offer its loyalties and energies to the conservation of that which it feels is valid as well as to the revolutionary correction of that which has lost its regenerative significance.

Adolescence is least "stormy" among those youths who are gifted and well trained in the pursuit of productive technological trends. In times of unrest, the adolescent mind becomes an ideological mind in search of an inspiring unification of ideas. Youth needs to be affirmed by peers and confirmed by teachings, creeds, and ideologies which express the promise that the best people will come to rule and that rule will develop the best in people. A society's ideological weakness, in turn, expresses itself in weak utopianism and in widespread identity confusion.

Fidelity, then, is the ability to sustain loyalties freely pledged in spite of the inevitable contradictions of value systems. It is the cornerstone of identity and receives inspiration from confirming ideologies and "ways of life."

Young Adulthood (Intimacy versus Isolation — Love)

Consolidated identity permits the self-abandonment demanded by intimate affiliations, by passionate sexual unions, or by inspiring encounters. The young adult is ready for intimacy and solidarity — that is, he can commit himself to affiliations and partnerships even though they may call for significant sacrifices and compromises. Ethical strength emerges as a further differentiation of ideological conviction (adolescence) and a sense of moral obligation (childhood).

True genital maturity is first reached at this stage; much of the individual's previous sex life is of the identity-confirming kind. Freud, when asked for the criteria of a mature person, is reported to have answered: *"Lieben und Arbeiten"* ("love and work"). All three words deserve equal emphasis.

It is only at this stage that the biological differences between the sexes result in a full polarization within a joint life style. Previously established strengths have helped the two sexes to converge in capacities and values which enhance communication and cooperation, while divergence is now of the essence in love life and in procreation. Thus the sexes first become similar in consciousness, language, and ethics in order then to be maturely different. But this, by necessity, causes ambivalences.

The danger of this stage is possible psychosocial isolation — that is, the avoidance of contacts which commit to intimacy. In psychopathology isolation can lead to severe character problems of the kind which interfere with "love and work," and this often on the basis of infantile fixations and lasting immaturities.

Man, in addition to erotic attraction, has developed a selectivity of mutual love that serves the need for a new and shared identity in the procession of generations. Love is the guardian of that elusive and yet all-pervasive power of cultural and parental style which binds into a "way of life" the affiliations of competition and cooperation, procreation and production. The problem is one of transferring the experience of being cared for in a parental setting to an adult affiliation actively chosen and cultivated as a mutual concern within a new generation.

The counterpart of such intimacy, and the danger, is man's readiness to fortify his territory of intimacy and solidarity by exaggerating small differences and prejudging or excluding foreign influences and people. Insularity thus aggravated can lead to that irrational fear which is easily exploited by demagogic leaders seeking aggrandizement in war and in political conflict.

Love, then, is a mutuality of devotion greater than the antagonisms inherent in divided function.

Maturity (Generativity versus Stagnation — Care)

Evolution has made man the teaching and instituting as well as the learning animal. For dependency and maturity are reciprocal: mature man needs to be needed, and maturity is guided by the nature of that which must be cared for.

Generativity, then, is primarily the concern with establishing and guiding the next generation. In addition to procreativity, it includes productivity and creativity; thus it is psychosocial in nature. From the crisis of generativity emerges the strength of care.

Where such enrichment fails, a sense of stagnation and boredom ensues, the pathological symptoms of which depend on variations in mental epidemiology: certainly where the hypocrisy of the frigid mother was once regarded as a most significant malignant influence, today, when sexual "adjustment" is in order, an obsessive pseudo intimacy and adult self-indulgence are nonetheless damaging to the generational process. The very nature of generativity suggests that the most circumscribed symptoms of its weakness are to be found in the next generation in the form of those aggravated estrangements which we have listed for childhood and youth.

Generativity is itself a driving power in human organization. For the intermeshing stages of childhood and adulthood are in themselves a system of generation and regeneration given continuity by institutions such as extended households and divided labor.

Thus, in combination, the basic strengths enumerated here and the structure of an organized human community provide a set of proven methods and a fund of traditional reassurance with which each generation meets the needs of the next. Various traditions transcend divisive personal differences and confusing conditions. But they also contribute to a danger to the species as a whole, namely, the defensive territoriality of the pseudo species, which on seemingly ethical grounds must discredit and destroy threateningly alien systems and may itself be destroyed in the process.

Care is the broadening concern for what has been generated by love, necessity, or accident — a concern which must consistently overcome the ambivalence adhering to irreversible obligation and the narrowness of self-concern.

Old Age (Integrity versus Despair — Wisdom)

Strength in the aging and sometimes in the old takes the form of wisdom in its many connotations — ripened "wits," accumulated knowledge, inclusive understanding, and mature judgment. Wisdom maintains and conveys the integrity of experience, in spite of the decline of bodily and mental functions. Responding to the oncoming generation's need for an integrated heritage, the wisdom of old age remains aware of the relativity of all knowledge acquired in one lifetime in one historical period. Integrity, therefore, implies an emotional integration faithful to the image bearers of the past and ready to take (and eventually to renounce) leadership in the present.

The lack or loss of this accrued integration is signified by a hidden fear of death: fate is not accepted as the frame of life, death not as its finite boundary. Despair indicates that time is too short for alternate roads to integrity: this is why the old try to "doctor" their memories. Bitterness and disgust mask such despair, which in severe psychopathology aggravates senile depression, hypochondria, and paranoiac hate.

A meaningful old age (preceding terminal invalidism) provides that integrated heritage which gives indispensable perspective to those growing up, "adolescing," and aging. But the end of the cycle also evokes "ultimate concerns," the paradoxes of which we must leave to philosophical and religious interpreters. Whatever chance man has to transcend the limitations of his self seems to depend on his full (if often tragic) engagement in the one and only life cycle permitted him in the sequence of generations. Great philosophical and religious systems dealing with ultimate individuation seem to have remained (even in their monastic establishments) responsibly related to the cultures and civilizations of their times. Seeking transcendence by renunciation, they remain ethically concerned with the maintenance of the world. By the same token, a civilization can be measured by the meaning which it gives to the full cycle of life, for such meaning (or the lack of it) cannot fail to reach into the beginnings of the next generation and thus enhance the potentiality that others may meet ultimate questions with some clarity and strength.

Wisdom, then, is a detached and yet active concern with life in the face of death.

CONCLUSION

From the cycle of life such dispositions as faith, will power, purposefulness, efficiency, devotion, affection, responsibility, and sagacity (all of which are also criteria of ego strength) flow into the life of institutions. Without them, institutions wilt; but without the spirit of institutions pervading the patterns of care and love, instruction and training, no enduring strength could emerge from the sequence of generations.

We have attempted, in a psychosocial frame, to account for the ontogenesis not of lofty ideals but of an inescapable and intrinsic order of strivings, which, by weakening or strengthening man, dictates the minimum goals of informed and responsible participation.

Psychosocial strength, we conclude, depends on a total process which regulates individual life cycles, the sequence of generations, and the structure of society simultaneously, for all three have evolved together.

Each person must translate this order into his own terms so as to make it amenable to whatever kind of trait inventory, normative scale, measurement, or educational goal is his main concern. Science and technology are, no doubt, changing essential aspects of the course of life, wherefore some increased awareness of the functional wholeness of the cycle may be mandatory. Interdisciplinary work will define in practical and applicable terms what evolved order is common to all men and what true equality of opportunity must mean in planning for future generations.

The study of the human life cycle has immediate applications in a number of fields. Paramount is the science of human development within social institutions. In psychiatry (and in its applications to law), the diagnostic and prognostic assessment of disturbances common to life stages should help to outweigh fatalistic diagnoses. Whatever will prove tangibly lawful about the cycle of life will also be an important focus for anthropology insofar as it assesses universal functions in the variety of institutional forms. Finally, as the study of the life history emerges from that of case histories, it will throw new light on biography and thus on history itself.

BIBLIOGRAPHY

Bühler, Charlotte. (1933) 1959. *Der menschliche Lebenslauf als psychologisches Problem.* 2d ed., rev. Leipzig: Hirzel.

Bühler, Charlotte. 1962. *Values in Psychotherapy.* New York: Free Press.

Erikson, Erik H. (1950). 1964. *Childhood and Society.* 2d ed., rev. & enl. New York: Norton.

Erikson, Erik H. 1958. *Young Man Luther.* New York: Norton.

Erikson, Erik H. 1964. *Insight and Responsibility.* New York: Norton.

Erikson, Erik H. 1965. The Ontogeny of Ritualisation in Man. Unpublished manuscript.

Freud, Anna. (1936) 1957. *The Ego and the Mechanisms of Defense.* New York: International Universities Press. First published as *Das Ich und die Abwehrmechanismen.*

Freud, Anna. 1965. *Normality and Pathology in Childhood: Assessment of Development.* New York: International Universities Press.

Hartmann, Heinz. (1939) 1958. *Ego Psychology and the Problem of Adaptation.* Translated by David Rapaport. New York: International Universities Press. First published as *Ich-Psychologie und Anpassungsproblem.*

Mayr, Ernst. 1964. The Evolution of Living Systems. National Academy of Sciences, *Proceedings* 51:934–941.

Werner, Heinz. (1926) 1965. *Comparative Psychology of Mental Development.* Rev. ed. New York: International Universities Press. First published as *Einführung in die Entwicklungspsychologie.*

2

William Kessen

THE AMERICAN CHILD AND OTHER CULTURAL INVENTIONS

The theme of the child as a cultural invention can be recognized in several intellectual and social occasions. Ariès' (1962) commentary on the discovery and transformation of childhood has become common knowledge; there is an agitated sense that American children are being redefined by the present times (Lasch, 1978); there is a renewed appreciation of the complexity of all our children (Keniston, 1977); and ethnographic and journalistic reports tell us of the marvelous departures from our own ways of seeing children that exist in other lands (Kessen, 1975). In simple fact, we have recently seen a shower of books on childish variety across cultures and across the hierarchies of class and race.

We could have just as readily discovered commanding evidence of the shifting nature of childhood by a close look at our own history. Consider just three messages drawn haphazardly from the American past. To the parents of the late 18th century:

> The first duties of Children are in great measure mechanical: an obedient Child makes a Bow, comes and goes, speaks, or is silent, just as he is bid, before he knows any other Reason for so doing than that he is bid. (Nelson, 1753)

Or to our parents and grandparents:

> The rule that parents should not play with their children may seem hard but it is without doubt a safe one. (West, 1914)

Or hear a parent of the 1970s speak of her 6-year-old:

> LuAnn liked the school in California best — the only rules were no chemical additives in the food and no balling in the hallways. (Rothchild & Wolf, 1976)

And we cannot escape the implications of an unstable portrait of the child by moving from folk psychology to the professional sort. On the contrary, a clear-eyed study of what experts have said about the young — from Locke to Skinner, from Rousseau to Piaget, from Comenius to Erikson — will expose as bewildering a taxonomy as the one provided by preachers, parents, and poets. No other animal species has been cataloged by responsible scholars in so many wildly discrepant forms, forms that a perceptive extraterrestrial could never see as reflecting the same beast.

To be sure, most expert students of children continue to assert the truth of the positivistic dream — that we have not yet found the underlying structural simplicities that will reveal the child entire, that we have not yet cut nature at the joints — but it may be wise for us child psychologists in the International Year of the Child to peer into the abyss of the positivistic nightmare — that the child is essentially and eternally a cultural invention and that the variety of the child's definition is not the removable error of an incomplete

SOURCE: From William Kessen, "The American Child and Other Cultural Inventions," *American Psychologist* 34, 1979, pp. 815–820.

science. For not only are American *children* shaped and marked by the larger cultural forces of political maneuverings, practical economics, and implicit ideological commitments (a new enough recognition), *child psychology* is itself a peculiar cultural invention that moves with the tidal sweeps of the larger culture in ways that we understand at best dimly and often ignore.

To accept the ambiguity of our task — to give up debates about the fundamental nature of the child — is not, however, a defeatist or unscientific move. Rather, when we seriously confront the proposition that we, like the children we study, are cultural inventions, we can go on to ask questions about the sources of our diversity and, perhaps more tellingly, about the sources of our agreements. It is surely remarkable that against the background of disarray in our definition of the child, a number of ideas are so widely shared that few scholars question their provenance and warrant. Paradoxically, the unexamined communalities of our commitment may turn out to be more revealing than our disagreements. Within the compass of the next several pages, I point toward disagreements that were present at the beginnings of systematic child study, and then turn in more detail to the pervasive and shared themes of American childhood in our time, themes that may require a more critical review than we have usually given them.

PRESENT AT THE BIRTH

When child psychology was born, in a longish parturition that ran roughly from Hall's first questionary studies of 1880 (Hall, 1883) to Binet's test of construction of 1905 (Binet & Simon, 1916), there were five determining spirits present. Four of them are familiar to us all; the fifth and least visible spirit may turn out to be the most significant. One of the familiars was in the line of Locke and Bain, and it appeared later for Americans as John Broadus Watson; the line has, then and now, represented behavior, restraint, clarity, simplicity, and good news. Paired in philosophical and theoretical opposition was the spirit that derived from Rousseau, Nietzsche, and Freud, the line that represented mind, impulse, ambiguity, complexity, and bad news. The great duel between the two lines has occupied students of children for just under 300 years.

The third magus at the beginning was the most fully American; William James can stand as the representative of the psychologists whose central concern was with sensation, perception, language, thought, and will — the solid, sensible folk who hid out in the years between the World Wars but who have returned in glory. It is of at least passing interest to note that the cognitivists participated lightly in the early development of child study; James and, even more, Munsterberg and, past all measure, Titchener found results from the study of children too messy for the precision they wanted from their methods.

The godfather of child psychology, the solidest spirit of them all, was Charles Darwin, foreshadowing his advocates and his exaggerators. His contemporary stand-in, G. Stanley Hall, was the first in a long and continuing line that has preached from animal analogues, has called attention to the biological in the child, and has produced a remarkably diverse progeny that includes Galton, Gesell, and the ethologists.

I rehearse (and oversimplify) the story of our professional beginnings to call attention to how persistent the lines have been, how little they have interpenetrated and modified one another, and how much their contributions to our understanding of the child rest on a network of largely implicit and undefended assumptions about the basis of human knowledge, social structures, and ethical ascriptions. The lines of the onlooking spirits are themselves historical and cultural constructions that grew, in ways that have rarely been studied analytically or biographically, from the matrix of the larger contemporaneous culture.[1]

And so to the fifth circumnatal spirit, the one that knew no technical psychology. In the middle 50 years of the 19th century, the years that prepared the United States for child psychology, dramatic and persistent changes took place in American society. I could sing the familiar litany of urbanization, industrialization, the arrival of the first millions of European immigrants (another strand of diversity among children that requires a closer look). We know that the Civil War transformed the lives of most American families, white and black (although we still know remarkably little about the daily lives of children during and after the war). The United States developed, and *developed* is the word of choice, from an isolated agricultural dependency to an aggressive and powerful state. Technology and science joined the industrial entrepreneurs to persuade the new Americans, from abroad and from the farm, that poverty was an escapable condition if one worked hard enough and was aggressively independent. But there were other changes that bore more immediately on the lives of American children; let me, as an example of cultural influences on children and child psychology rather than as a worked-through demonstration of my thesis, extract three interwoven strands of the changes that touched children.

The first, and the earliest, was the evolving separation of the domain of work from the domain of home. When women left or were excluded from the industrial work force in the 1830s and 1840s, the boundary marked by the walls of home became less and less penetrable. First for the white, the urban, the middle-class, the northeastern American, but enlisting other parts of the community as time went on, work (or *real work* as contrasted with *homework,* the activity of women and schoolchildren) was carried on in specialized spaces by specialized people, and home became the place where one (i.e., men) did not work (Cott, 1977; Lasch, 1977).

The second and entailed change was the radical separation of what a man was from what a woman was. Colonial and early Federal society, like all other cultures, had stable and divergent visions of the proper sphere of male and female. But in the half century under our present consideration, something of a moral metamorphosis occurred in the United States (and in large measure, in England, too) and one of modern history's most eccentric arrangements of human beings was put in place. The public world of men was seen as ugly, aggressive, corrupting, chaotic, sinful (not an altogether regretted characteristic), and irreligious. The increasingly private world of women was, in inevitable antithesis, sweet, chaste, calm, cultured, loving, protective, and godly. The muscular Christianity of the Mathers and Edwardses became the feminized Christianity of matrons and pastors; the caretaking of culture became the task of women's groups (Douglas, 1978). So dramatic a statement of the contrast is hardly an exaggeration of the facts. And the full story remains to be told; historians of medical practice, for example, are just beginning to reveal the systematic attempt to desex American and British women in the 19th century with methods that ranged from sermons to surgery (Barker-Benfield, 1977).

The third change in American life that set the cultural context for child psychology followed on the first two. Children continued to be cared for by women at home, and in consequence, they took on the coloration of mother, hearth, and heaven. The early American child, who was told, "consider that you may perish as young as you are; there are small Chips as well as great Logs, in the Fire of Hell" (18th-century primer, quoted by Johnson, 1904), became Little Eva, Huckleberry Finn, and eventually Peter Pan. The sentimentalization of children — caught for tombstones and psychology books best by Wordsworth's "Heaven lies about us in our infancy!" — had implications for family structure, education, and the definition of the child in expert writings that we have not yet, nearing the end of the 20th century, fully understood or confronted.

Thus it was that American child psychology began not only under the conflicting attention of Locke, Rousseau, James, and Darwin, but with the progressivist, sexist, and sentimental expectation of the larger culture standing by.

THE COMMON THEMES OF AMERICAN CHILD PSYCHOLOGY

Are we now free of our origins? It would be both unhistorical and undevelopmental to believe so, in spite of all we have learned about research and about children over the last 100 years. The positivist promise of pure objectivity and eternal science has been withdrawn. Therefore, it may be methodologically therapeutic to glance, however briefly, at several common themes of our field that seem dependent, in the usually complicated way of human history, on the story I have sketched thus far. All of the themes may be ready for a thoughtful new evaluation.

The Commitment to Science and Technology

The notable success of the physical sciences in the 19th century, the elation that followed on the Darwinian revolution, and the culture's high hopes for a technological utopia joined at the end of the 19th century to define child psychology as scientific and rational. The vagaries of casual stories about children, the eccentricities of folk knowledge, and the superstitions of grandmothers were all to be cleansed by the mighty brush of scientific method (Jacoby, 1914; Watson, 1928). The conviction that we are scientists remains one of the heart beliefs of child psychology, and in its humane and sensible forms, the commitment to a systematic analytic examination of the lives of children and their worlds is still the unique and continuing contribution of child psychology to American culture.

But some less obvious and perhaps less defensible consequences of the rational scientific commitment were pulled along into child psychology by the high hopes of its founders. Perhaps the one that we have had the most difficulty in handling as a profession is the implication *in all theories of the child* that lay folk, particularly parents, are in need of expert guidance. Critical examination and study of parental practices and child behavior almost inevitably slipped subtly over to advice about parental practices and child behavior. The scientific statement became an ethical imperative, the descriptive account became normative. And along the way, there have been unsettling occasions in which scraps of knowledge, gathered by whatever procedures were held to be proper science at the time, were given inordinate weight against poor old defenseless folk knowledge. Rigorously scheduled feedings of infants, separation of new mothers from their babies, and Mrs. West's injunction against playing with children can stand as examples of scientism that are far enough away not to embarrass us enlightened moderns.

More, I risk the guess that the sentimental view of the child that prevailed at the beginnings of child psychology — a vision which, let it be said, made possible humane and appropriate reforms in the treatment of children — was strongly influential in what can only be called a salvationist view of children. Child psychologists, again whatever their theoretical stripe, have taken the Romantic notion of childish innocence and openness a long way toward the several forms of "If only we could make matters right with the child, the world would be a better place." The child became the carrier of political progressivism and the optimism of reformers. From agitation for child labor reform in the 1890s to Head Start, American children have been saviors of the nation. The romantic inheritance of purity and perfectibility may, in fact, have misled us about the proper unit of developmental study and about the major forces influencing human growth and change. I will return to the consideration of our unit of study shortly.

There has also been a socially hierarchical message in our scientific–normative interactions with the larger culture. Tolstoy said that there is no proletarian literature; there has been no proletarian child psychology either, and the ethically imperative forms of child psychology, our messages to practice, have ranged from pleas for equitable treatment of all children to recipes for forced assimilation to the expected forms of child behavior. Once a descriptive norm has been established, it is an antique cultural principle to urge adherence to it.

Finally, for some eras of child study, there has been an enthusiastic anticipation that all problems are reducible by the science of the moment; intellectual technology can succeed (and imitate) the 19th century's commercial and industrial technology in the progressive and ultimate betterment of humankind. The optimism of the founders of child study and their immediate successors is dimmer today — "The sky's the limit" may be replaced by "You win a few, you lose a few" — and serious questions have been posed even for the basic assumptions underlying the scientific analysis of human behavior (Barrett, 1978). Child psychology may soon have to face anew the question of whether or not a scientific account of human development can be given without bringing in its wake the false claims of scientism and the arrogance of an ethic based on current findings.

The Importance of Mothers, Early Experience, and Personal Responsibility

Strangely at odds with the theme of rational scientific inquiry has been the persistence of the commitment to home and mother in otherwise varying portraits of the child. Some child psychologists have been less than laudatory about the effectiveness of particular mothering procedures (Watson dedicated his directive book on child rearing to the first mother who raises a child successfully), but critics and praisers alike have rarely doubted the basic principle that children need home and mother to grow as they should grow (again, the normative injunction enters). I do not mean to dispute the assumption here; I want only to suggest its connection with the mid-19th-century ideology that long preceded systematic child psychology and to point out several riders on the assumption that have, in the past, been less vividly visible.

Two riders on the home-and-mother position are under active debate and study nowadays — the irrelevance of fathers and the critical role of early experience. The cases represent with the starkness of a line drawing the influence of contemporaneous cultural forces on the definition of psychology's child. It would be difficult to defend the proposition that the recent interest in the place of fathers or the possibilities of out-of-home child rearing grew either from a new theory of development or from striking new empirical discoveries. Rather, for reasons too elaborate to explore here, fewer and fewer American women have been willing or able to devote all of their work time to the rearing of children. It will be instructive to see how much the tasks assigned fathers and day-care centers reflect the old ascriptions to essential maternity. Psychology follows culture, but often at a discreet distance.

The blending of new social requirements into old ideology is precisely demonstrated by the incorporation of fathers and day-care workers into the premise that what happens to the child in the first hours, weeks, months of life holds an especially determining position in human development. Proclaimed on epistemological grounds by Locke, gathered into the American ethos in part because it so well fit the perfectionist argument, elevated to scientific status by evolutionary theory, the doctrine of the primacy of early experience has been an uncontested part of American culture and American child psychology throughout the history of both. Only in the last several years has the premise been called seriously into question (Kagan, Kearsley, & Zelazo, 1978) and, even then, at a time when ever more extravagant claims are being made about the practical necessity of safeguarding the child's first hours (Klaus & Kennell, 1976).

The assumption of essential maternity and the assumption of the determining role of early experience join to support yet another underdebated postulate of child psychology. If something goes wrong in the course of a child's development, it is the primary responsibility of the mother (or whoever behaves as mother), and once more in echo of the salvationist view, if a social problem is not repaired by modification of the child's first years, the problem is beyond repair. The working of the postulate has produced ways of blaming mothers that appear in all theoretical shapes and, more generally, ways of blaming other victims of social injustice because they are not readily transformed by the ministrations of the professionals (Ryan, 1971).

The tendency to assign personal responsibility for the successes and failures of development is an amalgam of the positivistic search for causes, of the older Western tradition of personal moral responsibility, and of the conviction that personal mastery and consequent personal responsibility are first among the goals of child rearing. It is difficult to imagine an American child psychology without a core commitment to the proposition that *someone* is responsible for what happens in the course of development.

The Belief in the Individual and Self-contained Child

Hovering over each of the traditional beliefs mentioned thus far is the most general and, in my view, the most fundamental entanglement of technical child psychology with the implicit commitments of American culture. The child — like the Pilgrim, the cowboy, and the detective on television — is invariably seen as a free-standing isolable being who moves through development as a self-contained and complete individual. Other similarly self-contained people — parents and teachers — may influence the development of children, to be sure, but the proper unit of cultural analysis and the proper unit of developmental study is the child alone. The ubiquity of such radical individualism in our lives makes the consideration of alternative images of childhood extraordinarily difficult. We have never taken fully seriously the notion that development is, in large measure, a social construction, the child a modulated and modulating component in a shifting network of influences (Berger & Luckmann, 1966). The seminal thinkers about children over the past century have, in fact, been almost undeviating in their postulation of the child as container of self and of psychology. Impulses are in the child; traits are in the child; thoughts are in the child; attachments are in the child. In short, almost every major theory of development accepts the premises of individualism and takes the child as the basic unit of study, with all consequences the choice has for decisions that range from selecting a method of research to selecting a therapeutic maneuver.

Uniform agreement on the isolable child as the proper measure of development led to the research paradigms that have dominated child psychology during most of its history; basically, we have observed those parts of development that the child could readily transport to our laboratories or to our testing sites. The use of isolated preparations for the study of development has, happily, been productive of remarkable advances in our knowledge of children, but with the usual cost of uniform dogma, the commitment to the isolable child has occasionally led child psychology into exaggerations and significant omissions.

There are signals now aloft that the dogma of individualism, both in its claim of lifelong stability of personality and in its claim that human action can be understood without consideration of context or history, is under severe stress. The story that Vygotsky (1978) told 50 years ago, the story of the embeddedness of the developing mind in society, has finally been heard. The image of the child as an epigenetic and continuous creation of social and biological contexts is far more ambiguous and more difficult to paint than the relative simplicities of the traditional and culturally justified self-contained child; it may also illuminate our understanding of children and of our science.

THE PRESENT MOMENT

The cultural epigenesis that created the American child of the late 20th century continues, and so does the epigenesis that created child psychology. Necessarily, there is no end of the road, no equilibrium. Rather, the transformations of the past 100 years in both children and child psychology are a startling reminder of the eternal call on us to be scrupulous observers and imaginative researchers; they may also serve to force our self-critical recognition that we are both creators and performers in the cultural invention of the child.

NOTE

1. It has become a cliché to speak of psychoanalysis as an outgrowth of Jewish intellectual culture in turn-of-the-century Vienna (a shallow summary at best), but no corresponding common saying exists for, say, Watson's growing up in postwar Carolina, or Hall's curious combination of *odium sexicum* and *odium theologicum* in Victorian times, or Binet's history as an apostate continental associationist.

REFERENCES

Ariès, P. *Centuries of childhood: A social history of family life* (R. Baldick, Trans.). New York: Knopf, 1962.

Barker-Benfield, G. J. *Horrors of the half-known life.* New York: Harper & Row, 1977.

Barrett, W. *The illusion of technique.* Garden City, N.Y.: Doubleday, 1978.

Berger, P. L., & Luckmann, T. *The social construction of reality: A treatise in the sociology of knowledge.* Garden City, N.Y.: Doubleday, 1966.

Binet, A., & Simon, T. Upon the necessity of establishing a scientific diagnosis of inferior states of intelligence (E. S. Kite, Trans.). In A. Binet & T. Simon, *The development of intelligence in children.* Baltimore, Md.: Williams & Wilkins, 1916. (Originally published, 1905.)

Cott, N. F. *Bonds of womanhood: Women's sphere in New England, 1780–1835.* New Haven, Conn.: Yale University Press, 1977.

Douglas, A. *The feminization of American culture.* New York: Avon Books, 1978.

Hall, G. S. The contents of children's minds. *Princeton Review,* 1883, *11,* 249–272.

Jacoby, G. W. *Child training as an exact science: A treatise based upon the principles of modern psychology, normal and abnormal.* New York: Funk & Wagnalls, 1914.

Johnson, C. *Old-time schools and school-books.* New York: Macmillan, 1904.

Kagan, J., Kearsley, R. B., & Zelazo, P. R. (With the assistance of C. Minton). *Infancy: Its place in human development.* Cambridge, Mass.: Harvard University Press, 1978.

Keniston, K., & Carnegie Council on Children. *All our children: The American family under pressure.* New York: Harcourt Brace Jovanovich, 1977.

Kessen, W. (Ed.). *Childhood in China.* New Haven, Conn.: Yale University Press, 1975.

Klaus, M. H., & Kennell, J. H. *Maternal–infant bonding.* Saint Louis: Mosby, 1976.

Lasch, C. *Haven in a heartless world: The family besieged.* New York: Basic Books, 1977.

Lasch, C. *The culture of narcissism: American life in an age of diminishing expectations.* New York: Norton, 1978.

Nelson, J. *An essay on the government of children under three general heads: Viz., health, manners, and education.* London: (no publisher), 1753.

Rothchild, J., & Wolf, S. B. *The children of the counter-culture.* Garden City, N.Y.: Doubleday, 1976.

Ryan, W. *Blaming the victim.* New York: Random House, 1971.

Vygotsky, L. S. *Mind in society: The development of higher psychological processes* (M. Cole, V. John-Steiner, S. Scribner, & E. Souberman, Eds.). Cambridge, Mass.: Harvard University Press, 1978.

Watson, J. B. *Psychological care of infant and child.* New York: Norton, 1928.

West, M. *Infant care* (Publication No. 8). Washington, D.C.: U.S. Children's Bureau, 1914.

3

Heinz Werner

THE CONCEPT OF DEVELOPMENT FROM A COMPARATIVE AND ORGANISMIC POINT OF VIEW

The field of developmental psychology, as it is conceived here, transcends the boundaries within which the concept of development is frequently applied: development is here apprehended as a concept not merely applicable to delimited areas such as child growth or comparative behavior of animals, but as a concept that proposes a certain manner of viewing behavior in its manifold manifestations. Such a developmental approach to behavior rests on one basic assumption, namely, that wherever there is life there is growth and development, that is, formation in terms of systematic, orderly sequence. This basic assumption, then, entails the view that developmental conceptualization is applicable to the various areas of life science, and is potentially useful in interrelating the many fields of psychology.

The developmental approach has, of course, been clearly of tremendous heuristic value in systematizing certain aspects of biological phenomena in various fields of life science such as comparative anatomy, neurophysiology, and embryology. Analogously, developmental psychology aims at viewing the behavior of all organisms in terms of similar genetic principles. However, this aim of developmental psychology is perhaps even farther reaching than that of developmental biology. Developmental psychology does not restrict itself either to ontogenesis or phylogenesis, but seeks to coordinate within a single framework forms of behavior observed in comparative animal psychology, in child psychology, in psychopathology, in ethnopsychology, and in the general and differential psychology of man in our own culture. Eventually, in linking these variegated observations, it attempts to formulate and systematically examine experimentally testable hypotheses.

In order to clarify and evolve its conceptual framework, developmental psychology has to search for characteristics common to any kind of mental activity in the process of progression or regression. In this comparative venture one has to be wary of the error made by early evolutionists such as Haeckel and G. Stanley Hall, who sought to treat as materially identical various developmental sequences when the data warranted only the assertion of similarity or parallelism. The statement, for instance, that the individual recapitulates in his development the genesis of the species, and the attempt to identify childlike and abnormal forms of behavior, have, in their extreme formulation, aroused just criticism, but criticism which has spread more and more toward undermining comparative developmental psychology as a discipline.

Between the extremes, on the one hand, of viewing as identical various developmental sequences, and on the other, of denying completely any comparability among them, some beginnings toward a theory of development have been made. These beginnings take into

SOURCE: From Dale B. Harris, editor, *The Concept of Development,* the University of Minnesota Press, Minneapolis.

account the formal similarities in these various developmental sequences as well as material and formal differences distinguishing each developmental sequence from another.

THE ORTHOGENETIC PRINCIPLE OF DEVELOPMENT

Developmental psychology postulates one regulative principle of development; it is an orthogenetic principle which states that wherever development occurs it proceeds from a state of relative globality and lack of differentiation to a state of increasing differentiation, articulation, and hierarchic integration.[1] This principle has the status of an heuristic definition. Though itself not subject to empirical test, it is valuable to developmental psychologists in leading to a determination of the actual range of applicability of developmental concepts to the behavior of organisms.[2]

We may offer several illustrations of how this orthogenetic principle is applied in the interpretation and ordering of psychological phenomena.

According to this principle, a state involving a relative lack of differentiation between subject and object is developmentally prior to one in which there is a polarity of subject and object. Thus the young child's acceptance of dreams as external to himself, the lack of differentiation between what one dreams and what one sees, as is found in psychosis, or in some nonliterate societies, the breakdown of boundaries of the self in mescaline intoxication and in states of depersonalization — all of these betoken a relative condition of genetic primordiality compared to the polarity between subject and object found in reflective thinking. This increasing subject-object differentiation involves the corollary that the organism becomes increasingly less dominated by the immediate concrete situation; the person is less stimulus-bound and less impelled by his own affective states. A consequence of this freedom is the clearer understanding of goals, the possibility of employing substitutive means and alternative ends. There is hence a greater capacity for delay and planned action. The person is better able to exercise choice and willfully rearrange a situation. In short, he can manipulate the environment rather than passively respond to the environment. This freedom from the domination of the immediate situation also permits a more accurate assessment of others. The adult is more able than the child to distinguish between the motivational dynamics and the overt behavior of personalities. At developmentally higher levels, therefore, there is less of a tendency for the world to be interpreted solely in terms of one's own needs and an increasing appreciation of the needs of others and of group goals.

Turning to another illustration, one pertaining to concept formation, we find that modes of classification that involve a relative lack of differentiation beween concept and perceptual context are genetically prior to modes of classification of properties relatively independent of specific objects. Thus, a color classification that employs color terms such as "gall-like" for a combination of green and blue, or "young leaves" for a combination of yellow and green, is genetically prior to a conceptual color system independent of objects such as gall or young leaves.

It may be opportune to use this last example as an illustration of the comparative character of the developmental approach. That the color classification attached to specific objects involves a mode of cognition genetically prior to a classification independent of specific objects is, of course, consistent with the main theoretical principle of development. In regard to the comparative character of our discipline, however, it does not suffice for us merely to find this type of classification more typical of the man of lower civilization than of the man of higher. The anthropological data point up the necessity of determining whether there is a greater prevalence of such primitive color conceptualization in areas where cognition can be readily observed in terms of lower developmental levels, e.g., in the early phases of ontogenesis. Experimental studies on young children have demonstrated the greater prevalence of concrete (context-bound) conceptualization with regard not only to color but to many other phenomena as well. Again, to take organic neuropathology as an example, in brain-injured persons we find, as Goldstein, Head, and others have stressed, a concretization of color conceptualization symptomatic of their psychopathology; similar observations have been made on schizophrenics.

At this point we should like to state that a comprehensive comparative psychology of development cannot be achieved without the aid of a general experimental psychology broadened through the inclusion of developmental methodology and developmental constructs. There have appeared on the scene of general psychology beginnings of an extremely significant trend toward the studying of perception, learning, and thinking, not as final products but as developing processes, as temporal events divisible into successive stages. Such "event psychology," as one may call it, introduces the dimension of time as an intrinsic property into all experimental data. It stands thus in contrast to approaches, like that of classical psychophysics, in which the treating of successive trials as repetitive responses eliminates as far as possible sequential effects. European psychologists, particularly in Germany and Austria, have turned to the direct study of emergent and developing mental phenomena (34, 42, 46). For instance, using a tachistoscope, we may study the developmental changes in perception which occur when the time of exposure is increased from trial to trial. In studies of this sort, such developmental changes, or "microgenesis," of percepts are predictable from a developmental theory of the ontogenesis of perception. Some of the ensuing parallels between microgenesis and ontogenesis might be summarized as follows (5): In both microgenesis and ontogenesis the formation of percepts seems, in general, to go through an orderly sequence of stages. Perception is first global; whole-qualities are dominant. The next stage might be called analytic; perception is selectively directed toward parts. The final stage might be called synthetic; parts become integrated with respect to the whole. Initially perception is predominantly "physiognomic." [3] The physiognomic quality of an object is experienced prior to any details. At this level, feeling and perceiving are little differentiated. Again, in the early stages of development imaging and perceiving are not definitely separated.

There is another important technique of studying the emergence and formation of perception. This method was originally utilized in Stratton's well-known experiments in which a person wearing lenses had to adjust to a world visually perceived as upside down. More recently, Ivo Kohler of the Innsbruck Laboratory has utilized this method in extremely significant long-range experiments. He studies stages of perceptual adaptation to a world visually distorted in various ways by prisms or lenses (16, 17, 49). Again, these perceptual formation stages are found to conform to ontogenetic patterns. Ontogenetic studies have made it reasonably certain that the experience of space and spatial objects grows through stages which can be grossly defined. There appears to be an early sensorimotor stage of spatial orientation, succeeded by one in which objects emerge in terms of "things-of-action" (44), where perceptual qualities of things are determined by the specific way these things are handled. For instance, a chair is that object which has a "sitting tone" (Uexküll). A later stage is that of highly objectified or visualized space where the spatial phenomena are perceived in their rather "pure" visual form and form relations.

Keeping these ontogenetic states in mind, it is most enlightening to follow the reports of the subjects used in the Innsbruck Laboratory as they move from level to level in developmental order, adjusting themselves to a disarrayed world. First, they learn to master space on a sensorimotor level; that is, they are able to move about without error. But, though they may be able to ride a bicycle quite skillfully, the visual world as such may, at this stage, still be extremely confused, upside down, or crooked. The further development toward visual adaption shows some remarkable features: the objects seem to fall into two classes, things-of-action and purely visual things. The observer conquers first the things-of-action and only later purely visual things. For instance, observers wearing prisms which invert left and right can see an object already in correct position if it is part of their own actions, but incorrectly — that is, reversed — when purely visually grasped. In a fencing situation, a subject sees his own sword correctly pointing toward the opponent, but at a moment of rest it becomes visually inverted, pointing toward himself. By the same token, a little later in development any object-of-action, such as a chair or a screwdriver, whether it is actually handled or not, is correctly transformed, whereas purely visual objects, such as pictures or printed words, remain reversed. Only at a last stage the differences disappear, and complete transformation of the visual world is achieved.

Another area of general psychology where genetic methodology has been fruitfully applied is that of problem-solving behavior. Whereas Wertheimer's contribution to productive thinking, outstanding as it was, remains essentially agenetic, the signal importance of Duncker's work (7) lies in its genetic methodology. Duncker studied the problem-solving process in terms of genetic stages which follow each other according to developmental laws well established for ontogenesis.[4]

UNIFORMITY VERSUS MULTIFORMITY OF DEVELOPMENT

The orthogenetic law, being a formal regulative principle, is not designed to predict developmental courses in their specificity. To illustrate, it cannot decide the well-known controversy between Coghill's and Windle's conceptions (6, 50) concerning ontogenesis of motor behavior. According to Coghill, who studied the larval salamander, behavior develops through the progressive expansion of a perfectly integrated total pattern, and the individuation within of partial patterns that acquire varying degrees of discreteness. Windle's conception, derived from the study of placental mammals, is that the first responses of the embryo are circumscribed, stereotyped reflexes subsequently combined into complex patterns. It may be possible to reconcile, under the general developmental law, both viewpoints as follows: The development of motor behavior may, depending on the species or on the type of activity, involve either the differentiation of partial patterns from a global whole and their integration within a developing locomotor activity (Coghill) or the integration of originally juxtaposed, relatively isolated global units which now become differentiated parts of a newly formed locomotor pattern (Windle). In both cases there are differentiation and hierarchic integration, although the specific manifestations differ.[5]

Now, it is precisely this polarity between the uniformity of a general regulative principle and the multiformity of specific developmental changes that makes the study of development necessarily a comparative discipline. If we were merely to seek the ordering of changes of behavior in terms of a universal developmental principle, developmental theory might still be of interest to the philosophy of science and theoretical psychology, but it would be of far lesser value to empirical psychology.

In order to get a clearer picture of what is involved here, it might be advantageous to refer to one of our studies, namely, that of the development of the acquisition of meaning, by the use of a word-context test (48).

In this experiment eight- to thirteen-year-old children had the task of finding the meaning of an artificial word which was embedded successively in six verbal contexts. For instance, one such artificial word was "corplum." After each of these six sentences the child was interrogated concerning the meaning of the artificial word.

The six sentences in which "corplum" (correct translation: "stick" or "piece of wood") appears, are as follows: (1) A corplum may be used for support. (2) Corplums may be used to close off an open place. (3) A corplum may be long or short, thick or thin, strong or weak. (4) A wet corplum does not burn. (5) You can make a corplum smooth with sandpaper. (6) The painter used a corplum to mix his paints.

Now, the task confronting the subjects in the word-context test is essentially the synthesis of the cues from a set of six contexts for the purpose of forming a general meaning of the word, that is, a meaning applicable to all six sentences. The success of such an operation is reflected in two kinds of results. The first shows a steady and continuous increase in the achievement of a correct solution with increasing age. The second reflects changes in the underlying patterns of operation. As to the first point, there is a developmental increase in achievement which signifies the increasing capacity for hierarchization, that is, for integrating the various cues within a common name. However, the finding concerning a steady rise in achievement of correctness was, for us, not the most important result. Our main aim was to study the processes underlying such achievement. We were far more concerned with detecting the fact that conceptual synthesis is not achieved by a unitary pattern of operations, but that there are various sorts of processes of synthesis which differ from each other developmentally. The lower forms were found to emerge, to increase, and then to decrease during intellectual growth, yielding finally to more advanced forms of generalization (48, p. 97).

Studies of this sort inform us that the workings of the orthogenetic law as a uniform, regulative principle have to be specified through the ordering and interpretation of the multiform operations. Such a view implies the rejection of a tacit assumption made by many child psychologists that the measured achievement always reflects unequivocally the underlying operations, or that overt achievement is necessarily a true gauge of the developmental stage. This assumption is untenable; the same achievement may be reached by operations genetically quite different (41). An analysis of types of operations rather than measurement merely in terms of accuracy of performance often reveals the truer developmental picture.[6] In fact, a greater accuracy in certain circumstances may even signify a lower developmental level, as in the case of a decorticate frog who shows greater accuracy in catching flies than the normal frog. Gottschaldt (10) presented normal and mentally deficient eight-year-old children with the task of constructing squares or rectangles from the irregular pieces into which these figures had been cut. The normal children had difficulties with the test because they tried to relate the figuratively unrelated pieces to the end form. Operating on a purely mechanical level, the mentally deficient children matched the edges of the same length and thus performed quicker and with fewer errors. Again, a thinker oriented toward and capable of highly abstract thought may be at a disadvantage in certain concrete tasks of concept formation, compared with a concretely thinking person.

CONTINUITY VERSUS DISCONTINUITY OF DEVELOPMENT

The orthogenetic principle of increase in differentiation and hierarchic integration is not meant to imply continuous progress as the exclusive characteristic of developmental change. A good deal of the controversy centering in the continuity-discontinuity problem appears to be due to a lack in clarification of these terms. In particular, there has been considerable confusion about two different aspects of change. One is the quantitative aspect of change. Here the problem of continuity versus discontinuity is related to the measurement — in terms of gradual or abrupt increase with time — of magnitude, of efficiency, of frequency of occurrence of a newly acquired operation in an individual or in a group. The other aspect concerns the qualitative nature of changes. Here the problem of continuity versus discontinuity centers in the question of the reducibility of later to earlier forms — emergence — and the transition between later and earlier forms — intermediacy.

It seems that discontinuity in terms of qualitative changes can be best defined by two characteristics: "emergence," i.e., the irreducibility of a later stage to an earlier; and "gappiness," i.e., the lack of intermediate stages between earlier and later forms. Quantitative discontinuity[7] on the other hand, appears to be sufficiently defined by the second characteristic.

Now it seems that in many discussions, particularly among psychologists, the quantitative and qualitative forms of continuity and discontinuity have not been clearly kept apart. Thus, a change may be discontinuous in terms of quality but may become distinguishable (e.g., measurable) only gradually; i.e., there may be a continuous quantitative increase, such as in frequency of occurrence or in magnitude. For instance, the attempt of the young child to walk on two legs is discontinuous with four-limb locomotion, though the successive actual attempts may show gradual progress toward precision and success.[8] In accordance with our definition given above, two-legged locomotion cannot be reduced to four-limbed locomotion, and, furthermore, there is limitation in regard to intermediate steps.

Another related mistake is that of accepting smallness of change, whether qualitative or quantitative, as an indicator of continuity. For instance, the genetic changes termed "mutation" may be very slight, but there has to be "discontinuity inasmuch as there are no intermediate forms between the unchanged and the changed." [9] This significant fact in mutation, namely, discontinuity, says Schroedinger, "reminds a physicist of quantum theory: no intermediate energies occurring between two neighboring energy levels. He would be inclined to call de Vries's mutation theory . . . the quantum theory of biology." Because of the smallness of change, in developmental psychology as well as in developmental biology, one often will find it possible to argue for discontinuity only on the basis of extensive data accumulated in extensive temporal sequences; discontinuity in change may then be concluded after a trait has become sufficiently distinct in terms of frequency, permanency, and magnitude.

Other factors that are often not clearly recognized for their importance in determining sequences as either continuous or discontinuous are (a) the handling of the data and (b) the nature of the universe of discourse.

Concerning the first factor, it should be realized that discontinuous process changes typical in individual development may be obscured by averaging developmental achievement scores of individuals to secure a composite curve for a group which then suggests continuous growth.[10]

Another fallacy in deriving continuity of behavioral development from group scores has been most recently discussed by Lashley (21) in regard to a particular feature of the usual mental tests, namely, the heterogeneity (discontinuity) of the items which the test patterns comprise. Lashley's criticism implies that discontinuity of processes may be obscured by interpreting developmental data on the assumption that variations in achievement can be based only on variations in a single underlying process. As noted before, the achievement of correctness on our word-context test shows a steady increase with age, whereas underlying processes give a picture of the rise and decline of more or less primitive operations and the abrupt rise of an adult type of generalization around ten or eleven years of age. Reference should be made here to the important study by Nancy Bayley (3) concerning mental development during the first three years. She could show that in terms of accumulated scores there was a steady increase with age; however, a further analysis of the test items in terms of underlying operations revealed a shift from one type of function ("sensorimotor") to a qualitatively different type ("adaptive") occurring at approximately nine months of age.

Secondly, it should be recognized that it is the universe of discourse, the interpretational frame within which the material is grasped, that often determines the ordering in terms of continuity or discontinuity. To illustrate by an analogy, one may represent the relation between color hues in physical terms, i.e., wave length, that change continuously within the range of visibility. Within the psychological frame of reference, however, there is discontinuity. The gradual variation from blue to green is discontinuous with the gradual variation from green to yellow, which, in turn, is discontinuous with the gradual variation from yellow to red.

There is no logical necessity for a concordance in terms of continuity between the quantitative and qualitative aspects of any developmental series. A discontinuous (epigenetic) qualitative change may become distinct gradually; that is, it does not need to be "saltatory" in a quantitative sense, if by that word is meant that a new form or function becomes suddenly overt. Nor does unevenness — spurt versus depression — of any growth curve necessarily point to novel process formation. However, though we have to beware of confusing quantitative discontinuity-continuity with qualitative discontinuity-continuity, quantitative unevenness may, possibly more often than not, point to qualitative discontinuity or emergent evolution. We may illustrate this from Paul Weiss's discussion (40) on embryonic growth: "An obstacle to simple mathematical treatment of growth is its lack of continuity; for embryonic growth advances unevenly, in spurts and jumps, with intermittent depressions. These depressions correspond to phases of intensive histological differentiation" (p. 44). Furthermore, if embryonic growth curves in terms of weight are compared with progress in terms of differentiation and morphogenesis, one finds that both kinds of progressions advance unevenly, but, that "maxima of differentiation coincide with minima of growth." From this, Weiss concludes that "acceleration of differentiating activity is attended by retardation of growth activity, or in other words, that there is some antagonism between differentiation and growth" (p. 134).[11]

Weiss's observations point to an important instance where the saltations and depressions of "accumulating" activity (growth in terms of quantitative discontinuity) appear to be vicariously related to morphogenetic processes directed toward the production of "discrete discontinuous . . . cell types which are not connected by intergradation" — development in terms of qualitative discontinuity (p. 98).

Quite possibly there are analogies to this

vicarious correspondence between quantitative growth and qualitative development on the level of psychological behavior. To illustrate, one such analogy might be found in a frequent observation concerning certain phases of speech development. There appears to occur between the stage of babbling and that of naming, a period during which vocalizing is depressed (22, p. 82). It seems plausible to interpret this period as one during which the awareness of sound patterns as verbal symbols emerges. Once this novel operation has emerged, the child bursts forth with naming, increasing its vocabulary at a swiftly accelerating rate.

In conclusion, it seems to me, that development cannot be comprehended without the polar conceptualization of continuity and discontinuity. Within the "universe of discourse" in which the orthogenetic law is conceived, development, insofar as it is defined as increase in differentiation and hierarchization is, ideally, continuous. Underlying the increase in differentiation and integration are the forms and processes which undergo two main kinds of changes: (a) quantitative changes which are either gradual or abrupt, and (b) qualitative changes which, by their very nature, are discontinuous.[12]

UNILINEARITY VERSUS MULTILINEARITY OF DEVELOPMENT

The orthogenetic law, by its very nature, is an expression of unilinearity of development. But, as is true of the other polarities discussed here, the ideal unilinear sequence signified by the universal developmental law does not conflict with the multiplicity of actual developmental forms. As implied in the conclusion of the preceding section, coexistence of unilinearity and multiplicity of individual developments must be recognized for psychological just as it is for biological evolution. In regard to human behavior in particular, this polarity opens the way for a developmental study of behavior not only in terms of universal sequence, but also in terms of individual variations, that is, in terms of growth viewed as a branching-out process of specialization or aberration.

To illustrate, "physiognomic" perception appears to be a developmentally early form of viewing the world, based on the relative lack of distinction between properties of persons and properties of inanimate things (44, pp. 67f). But the fact that in our culture physiognomic perception, developmentally, is superseded by logical, realistic, and technical conceptualization, poses some paradoxical problems, such as, What genetic standing has adult aesthetic experience? Is it to be considered a "primitive" experience left behind in a continuous process of advancing logification, and allowed to emerge only in sporadic hours of regressive relaxation? Such an inference seems unsound; it probably errs in conceiving human growth in terms of a simple developmental series rather than as a diversity of individual formations, all conforming to the abstract and general developmental conceptualization. Though physiognomic experience is a primordial manner of perceiving, it grows, in certain individuals such as artists, to a level not below but on a par with that of "geometric-technical" perception and logical discourse.

FIXITY VERSUS MOBILITY OF DEVELOPMENTAL LEVEL OF OPERATION

The assumption that all organisms normally operate upon a relatively fixed and rather sharply circumscribed developmental level appears to be tacitly accepted by many psychologists. A contrary view is that all higher organisms manifest a certain range of genetically different operations. This means, for instance, that a child of a certain age or an adult, depending on the task or on inner circumstances, may, qua normal, perform at genetically different levels. Furthermore, there is, so to speak, not only "horizontal" differentiation but also "vertical" differentiation; that is, the more mature compared with the less mature individual has at his disposal a greater number of developmentally different operations.

It should be recognized that these views are not necessarily antagonistic; i.e., fixity as well as mobility of levels of operation coexist as polar principles of development. The principle of fixity is implied in, or can be inferred from, the intrinsic trend of any evolution toward an end stage of maximum stability. Such maximum stability, as the end stage of a developmental sequence, implies the ceasing of growth; that is, implies the permanency, for instance, of specialized reaction patterns, or automatization of response. But the principle of fixity would finally lead to rigidity of behavior if not counterbalanced by the polar principle of mobility. As most generally conceived, mobility implies "becoming" in contrast to "being"; it implies that an organism, having attained highly stabilized structures and operations may or may not progress further, but if it does, this will be accomplished through partial return to a genetically earlier, less stable level. One has to regress in order to progress. The intimate relation of regression to progression appears succinctly expressed in the statement of one of the early evolutionists, Richard Owen (32). On interpreting the resemblance of the embryo to the phylogenetic ancestry, Owen said: "We perceive a return to the archetype in the early embryological phases of development of the highest existing species, or ought rather to say that development starts from the old point" (p. 108).

An impressive illustration of the relation between renewed development and regression on the biological level can be found in the processes of regeneration. Such regeneration, as extensively studied at the amphibian level, consists of two phases, regressive as well as progressive. The progressive phase — analogous to normal embryonic development — starts with the formation of the "blastema" or regenerative bud. But prior to progression there is regression. The regressive phase involves de-differentiation of already specialized cells (26, p. 3). Another probable source for blastema formation is reserve cells, that is, cells that have remained at a low state of differentiation (40, p. 466). It is noteworthy that power of regeneration, being associated with capacity to de-differentiate is, in general, inversely correlated with the organism's ontogenetic or phylogenetic status of differentiatedness (26, p. 62).

In speculating by analogy from biological events of this sort to human behavior one might argue that in creative reorganization, psychological regression involves two kinds of operations: one is the de-differentiation (dissolution) of existing, schematized or automatized behavior patterns; the other consists in the activation of primative levels of behavior from which undifferentiated (little-formulated) phenomena emerge.

The polar conceptualization of normal levels of operation in terms of fixity-mobility appears thus closely linked to another polar distinction, namely, that involved in the relation between lower and higher levels of operation. In regard to this relation, one particular problem among many has aroused considerable interest. It concerns the degree of fixity or mobility of an operation emerging at a certain level, in relation to developmentally later forms of operation.

As mentioned before, development, whether it concerns single functions, complex performances, or the totality of personality, tends toward stabilization. Once a certain stable level of integration is reached, the possibility of further development must depend on whether or not the behavioral patterns have become so automatized that they cannot take part in reorganization. We may refer here to Rapaport's concept of "apparatus" (31, p. 76) or to Piaget's concept of "schema" (30). The individual, for instance, builds up sensorimotor schemata, such as grasping, opening a box, and linguistic patterns; these are the goal of early learning at first, but later on become instruments or apparatuses for handling the environment. Since no two situations in which an organism finds itself are alike, the usefulness of these schemata in adaptive behavior will depend on their stability as well as on their pliability (a paradoxical "stable flexibility")

Furthermore, if one assumes that the emergence of higher levels of operations involves hierarchic integration, it follows that lower-level operations will have to be reorganized in terms of their functional nature so that they become subservient to higher functioning. A clear example of this is the change of the functional nature of imagery from a stage where images serve only memory, fantasy, and concrete conceptualization, to a stage where images have been transformed to schematic symbols of abstract concepts and thought.

DIFFERENTIAL VERSUS GENERAL DEVELOPMENTAL PSYCHOLOGY: INDIVIDUALITY AS A PROBLEM OF DEVELOPMENTAL PSYCHOLOGY

At Clark University we are becoming increasingly impressed with the fruitfulness of the developmental frame of reference for the study of group and individual differences. We may illustrate this approach to the many problems which are in need of investigation by referring to a few studies on cognitive organization.

One problem concerns the over-all maturity status of the individual, that is, his cognitive level of operation under optimal conditions, and the stability of this level under varying internal and external conditions. Friedman, Phillips, and their co-workers at Worcester State Hospital and at Clark University have constructed a genetic scoring system of the Rorschach test founded on developmental theory, and standardized through an ontogenetic study of children. The scoring system is based essentially on the occurrence and frequency of "genetically low" and "genetically high" scores. Restricting ourselves here mainly to the various whole and detail responses, genetically low responses are those which indicate amorphous, diffuse, or confabulatory percepts where little attention is given to part relations and to perception of contours. The genetically high percepts are reflected in the responses whereby the percept is that of a precisely formed unit with integrated parts, where the whole is composed of relatively independent sub-wholes brought together in an integrated fashion. Applying this developmental scoring analysis to the responses of 160 children of from three to eleven years of age, Hemmendinger found the basic principle of development confirmed. That is, with age there is a decrease of the undifferentiated diffuse whole and detail responses along with an increase of the highly articulated, well-integrated whole and detail responses. There is further an interesting shift from the early whole responses toward small detail responses between the ages of about six and eight; later on there is a decline in favor of the integrated whole responses (12).

This genetic scoring method has been utilized for the gauging of developmental levels of cognitive organization in normal and deviant persons in studies carried out at Worcester State Hospital, Clark University, and Boston University.[13] According to the theory, the most severely impaired groups should here show the genetically lowest responses, and there should be a decrease of these responses and an increase in the genetically high responses with less impaired or

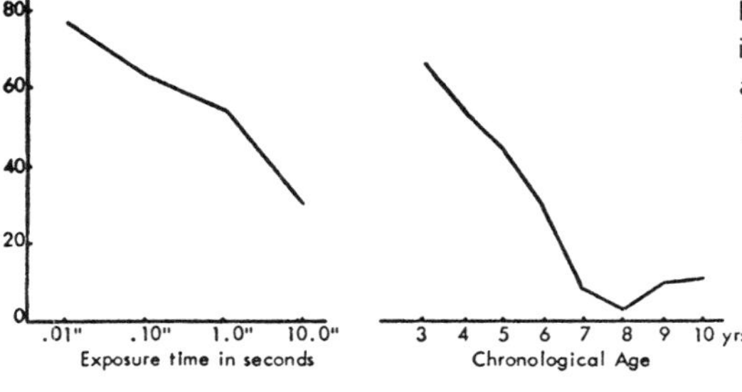

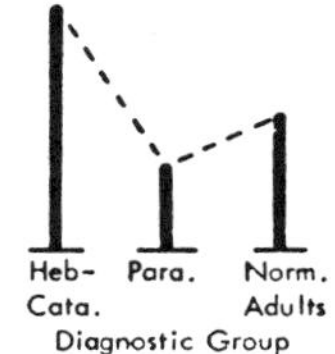

Figure 1. Median percentage of whole responses in normal adults at tachistoscopic exposures, and in children and diagnostic groups at full exposure, of the Rorschach.

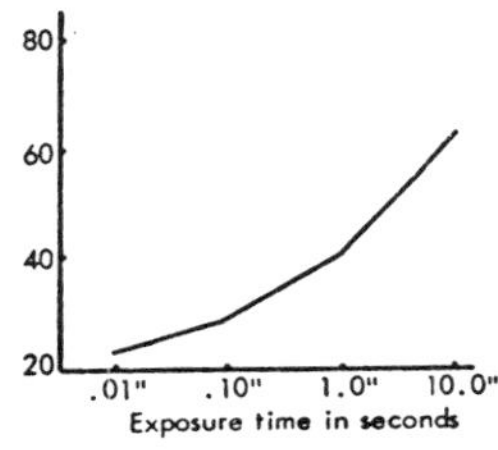

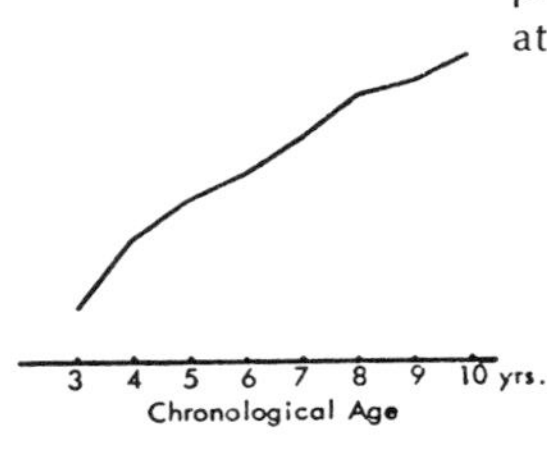

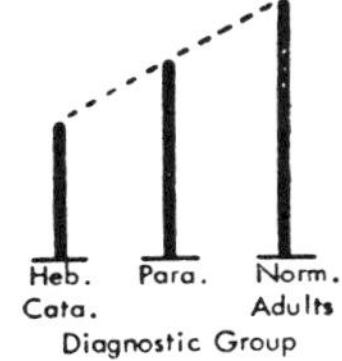

Figure 2. Median percentage of usual detail responses in normal adults at tachistoscopic exposures, and in children and diagnostic groups at full exposure, of the Rorschach.

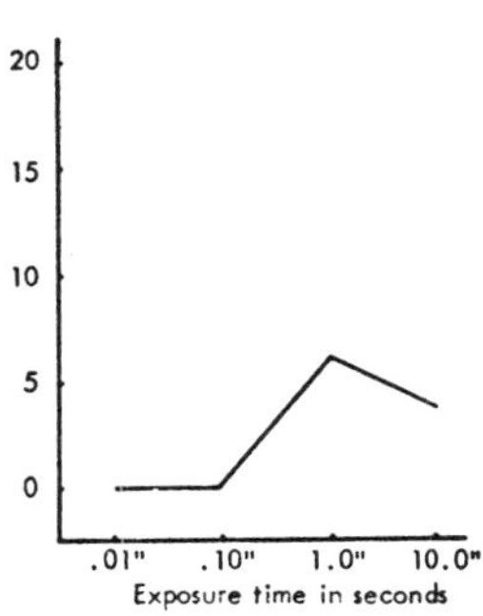

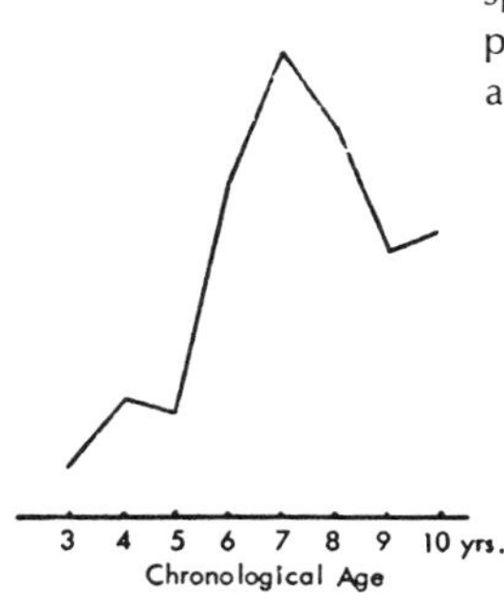

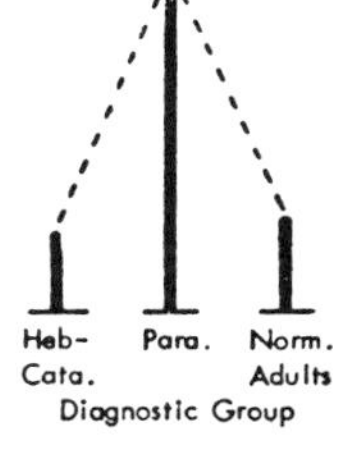

Figure 3. Median percentage of rare detail responses in normal adults at tachistoscopic exposures, and in children and diagnostic groups at full exposure, of the Rorschach.

100
80
60
40
20
.01" .10" 0.1" 10.0"
Exposure time in seconds

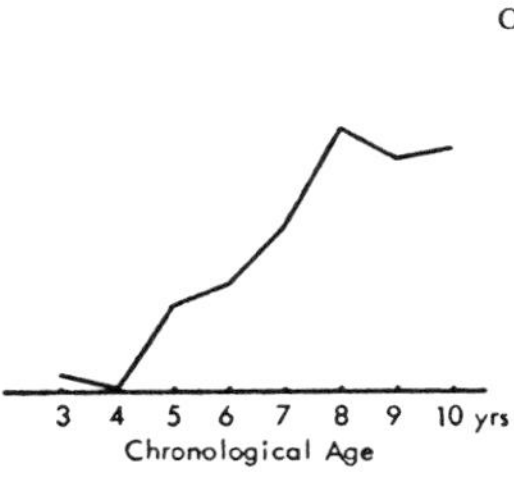

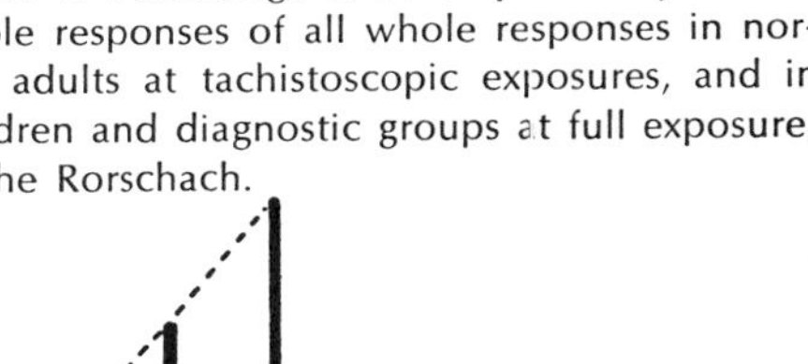

Figure 4. Percentage of developmentally-mature whole responses of all whole responses in normal adults at tachistoscopic exposures, and in children and diagnostic groups at full exposure, of the Rorschach.

Heb-Cata. Para. Norm. Adults
Diagnostic Group

unimpaired groups. The evidence is in good agreement with this expectation (see Figures 1 to 4). It was found that the genetic scores of the hebephrenic-catatonic schizophrenics resembled those of children three to five years of age. The paranoids were similar to children six to ten years of age; the psychoneurotics were intermediate between the ten-year-olds and normal adults (9, 28, 38).

We may add at this point that for the study of individual differences in their developmental aspects, experimental methods other than those based on ontogenesis have become available. Among these, probably the most promising method is that of "microgenesis." This method, already mentioned above, is based on the assumption that activity patterns, percepts, thoughts, are not merely products but processes that, whether they take seconds, or hours, or days, unfold in terms of developmental sequence.

To study microgenesis of perception, Framo presented the Rorschach cards to 80 normals. Twenty subjects in each of four groups viewed the cards at exposures of 0.01 second, 0.1 second, 1 second, and 10 seconds, respectively. A comparison of the responses in this study with the ontogenetic data obtained by Hemmendinger show striking agreements (29).[14]

The over-all conclusion is that the responses of the clinical groups represent various, more or less immature levels of perceptual development as compared to those of normals.

This evidence is supplemented by a study which E. Freed carried out under the direction of Leslie Phillips (29). Freed hypothesized that hebephrenic and catatonic schizophrenics would fail to show increased differentiation with time. Using the same design as Framo, he exposed the Rorschach to a group of 60 hebephrenic-catatonic schizophrenics, 15 at each of four exposure times. At the shortest exposure time their performance was not grossly different from that of the normal adults, but as exposure time was increased these schizophrenics increasingly lagged behind in the development toward perceptually mature responses (see Figure 5). It can be concluded, therefore, that unlike the normal subjects, these schizophrenic groups did not utilize the increases in exposure time to improve their perceptual adequacy and integration.[15]

If we combine the notions and the evidence in terms of ontogenesis, microgenesis, and regression, we may conclude that perceptual processes develop and come to a halt at different levels. At what level the processes stop depends on such conditions as age, experience, and complexity of stimuli, and on the normal or pathologic maturity status of a person. Thus, it might be said that by evaluating the Rorschach responses of a person through genetic scores, one tests the level of perceptual formation to which such a person under optimal time conditions progresses.

Not only has degree of psychiatric intactness been found to correspond to levels of development, but preliminary work at Worcester suggests that forms of symptom expression can also be ordered to the developmental sequence, as indicated by the genetic Rorschach scores. Thus, a number of

Figure 5. Median percentage of developmentally mature whole responses for normals and schizophrenics at four exposure times.

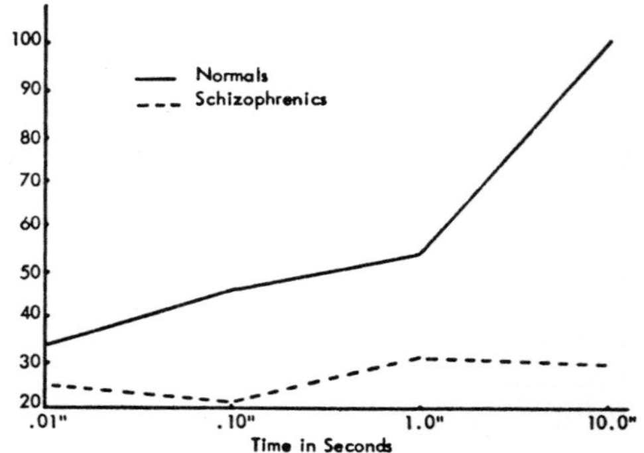

studies have shown that persons whose symptoms are characterized by immediacy of overt reaction function at developmentally lower levels than those whose symptomatology represents displacement to more mediated forms of behavior. This has been shown by Misch, who found that a directly assaultive group is developmentally lower than a group of individuals who only threaten to assault (25). Similar findings have been obtained by Kruger (19) for subjects who demonstrate overt sexual perversion in contrast to those who only fear that they may act in a sexually perverse fashion. In addition, Kruger found that those patients who made a serious suicidal attempt were developmentally lower than those who only threatened to commit suicide.

Another developmental aspect of individuality that is in need of experimental and clinical study concerns what one might call the genetic stratification or the developmental heterogeneity of a person. Developmental stratification means that a person is structured into spheres of operations which differ in regard to developmental level. Still another aspect concerns the flexibility of a person to operate at different levels depending on the requirements of a situation.

In a particular way, it seems to us, this aspect of flexibility is connected with a further problem of individuality, namely, that of creativity. Now creativity, in its most general meaning, is an essential feature of emergent evolution, and this, in turn, implies progression through reorganization. Since we assume that such progress through reorganization cannot be achieved without "starting anew," that is, without regression, it follows that a person's capacity for creativity presupposes mobility in terms of regression and progression. The hypothesis would then be that the more creative the person, the wider his range of operations in terms of developmental level, or in other words, the greater his capacity to utilize primitive as well as advanced operations. This hypothesis is currently being tested at Worcester State Hospital and Clark University by means of the genetic Rorschach scores of relatively creative versus relatively noncreative adults.[16]

It might also be possible to study persons at the other extreme end of mobility, that is, those who, because of their excessive yearning for security, are coping with the environment in terms of rigidly formalized behavior. In this regard the work by the Swedish psychologist Ulf Krogh (18) seems very suggestive. He studied the microgenesis of complex pictures with various groups of people. Among other results he found that persons such as the compulsion-neurotics, whose reaction patterns to the environment are inordinately formalized, are lacking in microgenetic mobility, that is, they are lacking the intermediate steps that are normally present during the unfolding of percepts.

We should like, then, to conclude with this observation: The original aim of developmental theory, directed toward the study of universal genetic changes, is still one of its main concerns; but side by side with this concern, the conviction has been growing in recent years that developmental conceptualization, in order to reaffirm its truly organismic character, has to expand its orbit of interest to include as a central problem the study of individuality.

NOTES

1. This, of course, implies "directiveness." It seems to us, therefore, that one must on logical grounds agree with E. S. Russell (33) that organic development cannot be defined without the construct of "directiveness."

2. In regard to the following discussion, see item 47 in the References.

3. In regard to this term, see item 44 (p. 69) and item 45 (p. 11) of the References.

4. Duncker has also clearly seen one aspect of creative thought processes, hitherto little recognized, namely, the fact that successful problem-solving depends not only on the ability to progress

along new ways, but also on the ability to regress back to a point from which new development can take place. In other words, he has observed a most important genetic principle, that of oscillatory activity in terms of progression and regression. (See the last section of this paper.)

5. Cf. the excellent discussion by Barron, presented at the Chicago Conference on Genetic Neurology (2).

6. It is not accidental that out of the immense field of potentially great significance for developmental psychology, the two main areas emphasized by psychologists in this country were the area of intelligence and the area of learning. They were chosen because they were clearly amenable to rigid quantification on a continuum in terms of more or less. The successes of workers in these fields obtained by statistical treatment of overt behavior and the successes in practical application have reinforced the conviction that outside the rather trivial notion of continuous increase in achievement with increase in age, developmental theory is not needed. In regard to intelligence testing the evaluation of G. Stanley Hall, the father of comparative genetic psychology, still seems to hold: Intelligence tests and measurements, he stated, have done a great work in applying psychology to life and industry but have added scarcely a scintilla to our knowledge of human development (11, p. 450). As to the situation in the area of learning, it seems significant that a man as deeply informed as Hilgard, in a well-balanced evaluation of this field of research, comes to the conclusion that undue stress on quantification may lead to a collapse when underlying processes are not understood (13, p. 328).

7. To facilitate distinction and alleviate confusion, I would suggest substituting "abruptness" for quantitative discontinuity, reserving the term "discontinuity" only for the qualitative aspect of change. It also appears feasible to distinguish between two types of emergence: (a) emergence of a single operation, e.g., abstract function, (b) emergence of a novel pattern of operation. A novel pattern may emerge as a consequence of new operations that enter the pattern, or it may also emerge through a reorganization of the existing characters within a certain pattern, through a changing dominance between these existing characters, etc. One may note here some analogies between psychological emergence and biogenetic emergence coming about (a) through mutant genes, and (b) through changes in local constellations of genes.

8. Such paradoxical coexistence of qualitative discontinuity and gradualness of appearance (progression) seems to pertain to developmental changes of various kinds. For instance, regenerative development of transplanted tissue is either determined according to the domicile within which the transplant is embedded (place-wise) or according to the original extraction of the transplant (origin-wise). This determination is an all-or-none phenomenon; however, visible differentiation is not instantaneously evident but progressive (26, pp. 70f).

9. Schroedinger, p. 34 (37). Schroedinger points out that Darwin was mistaken in regarding the small, continuous chance variations within a species as the basis of evolution by natural selection. These variations (e.g., length of awn in a purebred crop) cannot be formants of a new species because they are not inheritable.

10. Lecomte DuNoüy (8) in his remarkable book, *Biological Time,* takes the extreme view that continuity always is "manufactured" by our treatment of the data: "one of the roles of consciousness is to manufacture continuity from discontinuity."

11. One may note the possibility of discriminating between "growth" as a process of accumulation versus "development" defined by differentiation.

12. For further discussion of the continuity-discontinuity problem, see Bertalanffy, ch. 12 (4); DuNoüy (8); Huxley, ch. 5 (14); Lillie (23); Novikoff (27); Simpson, ch. 14 (39); Schneirla (35, 36).

13. The illustrations given here refer to perceptual organization. For some of our pertinent studies on language behavior, see items 1, 9, 15, 24, 45, and 47 of the References.

14. Figures 1 to 4 show the W. D. and Dd responses and the genetically high responses (Mature W%, Mature D%) for (a) microgenetic changes and (b) ontogenetic changes, and (c) the responses of hebephrenic-catatonic schizophrenics, paranoids, and normals under the usual Rorschach Test conditions.

15. Another area of abnormal behavior to which the microgenetic methodology has been applied is that of speech pathology. Experiments on apprehension of tachistoscopically presented words by normal subjects suggest that paraphrasic naming is related to microgenetically early stages of name formation (46).

16. The study, well advanced, is being carried out by C. Hersch.

REFERENCES

1. Baker, R. W. "The Acquisition of Verbal Concepts in Schizophrenia: A Developmental Ap-

proach to the Study of Disturbed Language Behavior." Unpublished Ph.D thesis, Clark University, 1953.

2. Barron, D. H. "Genetic Neurology and the Behavior Problem," in P. Weiss, ed., *Genetic Neurology*, pp. 223–31. Chicago: University of Chicago Press, 1950.

3. Bayley, N. "Mental Growth during the First Three Years," *Genet. Psychol. Monogr.*, Vol. 14 (1933), No. 1, p. 92.

4. Bertalanffy, L. *Modern Theories of Development*. London: Oxford University Press, 1933.

5. Bruell, J. "Experimental Studies of Temporally Extended Perceptual Processes and the Concept of 'Aktualgenese,'" in symposium on *The Developmental Viewpoint in Perception*, A. P. A. Meetings, Washington, D. C., 1952. Mimeogr. copy, Clark University.

6. Coghill, G. E. *Anatomy and the Problem of Behavior*. New York: Macmillan, 1929.

7. Duncker, K. "On Problem-solving," *Psychol. Monogr.*, Vol. 58 (1945), No. 5, pp. ix + 113.

8. DuNoüy, P. Lecomte. *Biological Time*. New York: Macmillan, 1937.

9. Friedman, H. "Perceptual Regression in Schizophrenia: An Hypothesis Suggested by the Use of the Rorschach Test," *J. Genet. Psychol.*, Vol. 81 (1952), pp. 63–98.

10. Gottschaldt, K. "Aufbau des Kindlichen Handelns," *Schrift. Entwickl. Psychol.*, Vol. 1 (1954), p. 220, Leipzig: Barth.

11. Hall, G. S. *Life and Confessions of a Psychologist*. New York: Appleton, 1923.

12. Hemmendinger, L. "A Genetic Study of Structural Aspects of Perception as Reflected in Rorschach Responses." Unpublished Ph.D. thesis, Clark University, 1951.

13. Hilgard, E. R. *Theories of Learning*. New York: Appleton, 1948.

14. Huxley, J. *Evolution*. London: Allen & Unwin, 1944.

15. Kaplan, B. "A Comparative Study of Acquisition of Meanings in Low-Educated and High-Educated Adults." Unpublished M.A. thesis, Clark University, 1950.

16. Kohler, I. *Über Aufbau und Wandlungen der Wahrnehmungswelt*. Wien: Rudolph M. Rohrer, 1951.

17. ——. "Umgewöhnung im Wahrnehmungsbereich," *Die Pyramide*, Vol. 5 (1953), pp. 92–95, Vol. 6 (1953), pp. 109–13.

18. Krogh, U. "The Actual-Genetic Model of Perception-Personality," *Stud. Psychol. Paedag.*, Series altera, Vol. 7 (1955), p. 394. Lund: Gleerup.

19. Kruger, A. "Direct and Substitute Modes of Tension-Reduction in terms of Developmental Level: An Experimental Analysis by means of the Rorschach Test." Unpublished Ph.D. thesis, Clark University, 1955.

20. Lane, J. E. "Social Effectiveness and Developmental Level," *J. Personal.*, Vol. 23 (1955), pp. 274–84.

21. Lashley, K. S. "Persistent Problems in the Evolution of Mind," *Quart. Rev. Biol.*, Vol. 24 (1949), pp. 28–42.

22. Lewis, M. M. *Infant Speech*. New York: Harcourt, 1936.

23. Lillie, R. S. "Biology and Unitary Principle," *Philos. Sci.*, Vol. 18 (1951), pp.193–207.

24. Mirin, B. "A Study of the Formal Aspects of Schizophrenic Verbal Communication," *Genet. Psychol. Monogr.*, Vol. 52 (1955), No. 2, pp. 149–90.

25. Misch, R. "The Relationship of Motoric Inhibition to Developmental Level and Ideational Functioning: An Analysis by means of the Rorschach Test." Unpublished Ph.D. thesis, Clark University, 1953.

26. Needham, A. E. *Regeneration and Wound Healing*. New York: Wiley, 1952.

27. Novikoff, A. B. "The Concept of Integrative Levels and Biology," *Science*, Vol. 101 (1945), pp. 209–15.

28. Peña, C. "A Genetic Evaluation of Perceptual Structurization in Cerebral Pathology," *J. Proj. Tech.*, Vol. 17 (1953), pp. 186–99.

29. Phillips, L., and J. Framo. "Developmental Theory Applied to Normal and Psychopathological Perception," *J. Personal.*, Vol. 22 (1954), pp. 464–74.

30. Piaget, J. *Play, Dreams, and Imitation in Childhood*. New York: Norton, 1951.

31. Rapaport, D. "The Conceptual Model of Psychoanalysis," *J. Personal.*, Vol. 20 (1951), pp. 56–81.

32. Russell, E. S. *Form and Function*. London: Murray, 1916.

33. ——. *The Directiveness of Organic Activities*. Cambridge: Cambridge University Press, 1945.

34. Sander, F. "Experimentelle Ergebenisse der Gestalt Psychologie," *Bar. ü.d. Kongr. f. Exper. Psychol.*, Vol. 10 (1928), pp. 23–87.

35. Schneirla, T. C. "A Consideration of some Conceptual Trends in Comparative Psychology," *Psychol. Bull.*, Vol. 6 (1952), pp. 559–97.

36. ——. "Problems in the Biopsychology of Social Organization," *J. Abn. and Soc. Psychol.*, Vol. 41 (1946), pp. 385–402.

37. Schroedinger, E. *What is Life?* Cambridge: Cambridge University Press, 1951.

38. Siegel, E. L. "Genetic Parallels of Perceptual Structurization in Paranoid Schizophrenia." Unpublished Ph.D. thesis, Clark University, 1950.

39. Simpson, G. G. *The Meaning of Evolution.* New Haven: Yale University Press, 1950.

40. Weiss, P. *Principles of Development.* New York: Holt, 1939.

41. Werner, H. "Process and Achievement," *Harvard Educ. Rev.,* Vol. 7 (1937), pp. 353–68.

42. ——. "Musical Microscales and Micromelodies," *J. Psychol.,* Vol. 10 (1940), pp. 149–56.

43. ——. "Experimental Genetic Psychology," in P. Harriman, ed., *Encyclopedia of Psychology,* pp. 219–35. New York: Philosophical Library, 1944.

44. ——. *Comparative Psychology of Mental Development,* rev. ed. Chicago: Follet, 1948.

45. ——, ed., *On Expressive Language.* Worcester: Clark University Press, 1955.

46. ——. "Microgenesis in Aphasia," *J. Abn. and Soc. Psychol.,* Vol. 52 (1956), pp. 347–53.

47. ——, and B. Kaplan. "The Developmental Approach to Cognition: Its Relevance to the Psychological Interpretation of Anthropological and Ethnolinguistic Data." Mimeogr. paper, Clark University, 1955.

48. ——. "The Acquisition of Word Meanings: A Developmental Study," *Monogr. Soc. Res. Child Developm.,* Vol. 15 (1952), No. 1, p. 120.

49. ——, and S. Wapner. "The Innsbruck Studies on Distorted Visual Fields in Relation to an Organismic Theory of Perception," *Psychol. Rev.,* Vol. 62 (1955), pp. 130–38.

50. Windle, W. F., and J. E. Fitzgerald. "Development of the Spinal Reflex Mechanism in Human Embryos." *J. Comp. Neurol.,* Vol. 67 (1937), pp. 493–509.

I INFANCY

The infant resembles a stranger entering a vast and entirely new land. The initial challenge is to gain meaning from the world of physical objects as well as from the realm of other people. Research relating to this stage focuses on the equipment the child is born with and on the processes of growth and interaction that the child draws on in coming to know the persons and objects in his or her environment.

As the importance and the complexity of infancy have come to be appreciated, research has proliferated. Considerable attention has been paid to the infant's relations to others, particularly the attachment to the mother. Because it is ethically impossible to conduct experiments manipulating the mother-infant relationship, psychologists have placed great importance on those studies with animals which systematically examine the caretaking relationship between a mother and her child.

Classic studies in this area were conducted with rhesus monkeys by Harry Harlow and his associates. Originally, the Harlow team attempted to determine the extent to which an offspring needs social companionship in order to develop normally. Normal newborn monkeys were isolated from all other monkeys (and humans) for various time periods. They were allowed sensory stimulation including normal laboratory sounds, constant illumination, and surfaces for tactual contact. Six months of such isolation led to extraordinary maladjustments. The monkeys were overly fearful, could not establish any social relations, and were unable to mate or to parent. These experiments suggested a *critical period* for normal social development; monkeys raised for their first six months without any social stimulation were doomed to an abnormal life. Implications were drawn for the rearing of human infants: an extended period of time in an understaffed, ill-equipped institution or in a family that ignored or rejected the child was likely to have profound lifelong effects on the child.

But in the tradition of good scientists, Harlow and his associates probed further. They found that the situation was not so simple. The work of Harlow and Melinda Novak, his student, suggests that the critical period may be less absolute, and the range of possible caretakers and kinds of social stimulation may be much broader than Harlow's original studies suggested. With gradual exposure to younger "therapist" monkeys, isolated monkeys were able to recover many normal social abilities.

We can learn a great deal from experiments using animal subjects, but such experiments can never substitute for the careful study of human subjects. The selection by Mary Ainsworth reviews many studies of attachment and discusses both the choice of the person to whom the infant attaches and the consequences of attachment for subsequent love, care, trust, and autonomy.

Until very recently, the mother-infant dyad was the focus of early social research. Michael Lamb's personal essay speaks to the role of the father and points up what we have found out about father-infant bonding as well as how little we know. The changing social expectations for the father's participation make this area very dynamic and formative.

The social competence of the newborn is highlighted in T. Berry Brazelton's article, in which the infant's attention to the mother is compared with that same infant's behavior with the father. Brazelton discusses the subtle ways in which the caretaker can shape the baby's development and how an infant can affect the caretaker.

A knowledge of attachment and its accompanying feelings is essential to the understanding of subsequent development. But it is equally important to learn about the way in which the infant comes to comprehend the physical world. Jerome Kagan's paper suggests the principles that determine, at least in part, what aspect of the world will command the infant's attention. Kagan introduces the idea of a *schema,* or mental representation, of an experience. He then presents evidence to support his hypothesis that the infant is often attracted to experiences that differ slightly from a schema established by previous experiences.

In addition to wanting to know what objects the child looks at, the psychologist is interested in whether the child sees the world as the adult does. The Bornstein, Kessen, and Weiskopf experiment addresses the longstanding debate over whether infants perceive color as adults do. Some background may be helpful for understanding their elegant study.

The colors we perceive are based on differences in the wavelengths of light, measured in nanometers (1 nanometer or nm equals 10^{-9} meter). A continuum exists from violet (at about 375 nanometers) to red (at 650 nanometers). There are no natural breaks between what we perceive as different colors, yet all of us tend to divide the spectrum at the same points: 450 nm and 480 nm are both "blue," whereas 510 nm is "green." The physical difference between the two blues is the same as that between one of the blues and the green (30 nm). But 450 and 480 are seen as the same color, whereas 480 and 510 appear to be two different colors. The controversy about color perception has revolved around the question of whether we divide the continuous visible spectrum at certain points into red, orange, yellow, green, blue, and violet because we have learned to do so or because our nervous systems are built to so divide the spectrum.

Bornstein, Kessen, and Weiskopf asked just that question. They showed infants three different wavelengths equidistant from one another — for example, 450, 480, and 510 nm. As discussed above, to the normal American adult 450 and 480 are perceived as blue, and 510 is perceived as green. If this perception is something learned (because the child hears the word "blue" when seeing 450 and 480 nm, but "green" when seeing 510 nm), then the infant, who has not yet been taught these labels, should see the three stimuli as all different or all the same. If, on the other hand, the nervous system is so designed that the categories of color are "wired in" and present at birth, then the infant should make the same distinctions that the adult does.

Bornstein, Kessen, and Weiskopf used the technique of habituation to answer this question. They showed a 480 nm stimulus to infants a number of times, and then they showed a stimulus of either 450 or 510 nm. If the infants appeared bored or showed no sign of renewed interest when the second stimulus appeared, it was reasoned that they could not tell the difference between the two stimuli. But if the infants showed increased attentiveness, it was inferred that the second stimulus appeared different.

The infants responded just as adults would: they differentiated between 480 and 510 nm but not between 450 and 480 nm. There is evidence, therefore, that categories of color are *innate*, or already wired into the nervous system at birth. While providing us with important information about the infant's view of the world, these findings have also suggested the answer to a long-debated philosophical issue.

As developmental psychologists investigate different domains, they frequently go to another culture to test the universality of their claims. So Ainsworth went to Uganda and studied mother-infant attachment to gain perspective on the American child. In a rather disarming article, Freedman, a sociobiologist, suggests that ethnic differences in temperament are present at birth and have far-reaching consequences for the subsequent development of children. He turns Erikson's position upside down, suggesting that child-rearing techniques have little or no causative influence on the child's eventual personality.

The findings of the psychological laboratory are rarely applied directly and explicitly to child rearing. Usually a slow filtering process occurs, making it difficult to identify the relationship of scientific data to the actual practices of child raising. B. F. Skinner's article is an exception. On the birth of his second daughter, Skinner designed a practical and ingenious environment to replace the standard baby crib. In his article, Skinner describes the air crib and its use. In the postscript, written in 1977, Skinner tells of the subsequent development of his daughter (now a successful artist in her thirties), and he offers his current thoughts about the air crib.

The case study by Selma Fraiberg, which closes the section on infancy, describes a very special child. Toni, five months old at the start of the study, is totally blind. Fraiberg's sensitive description of Toni's development sets in sharp focus many of the milestones of normal development and forces us to question a number of assumptions. For example, for years crawling was believed to be the result of simple neuromuscular maturation, but Toni does not crawl when we might expect her to. Fraiberg speculates that crawling may depend on the ability to see objects and to want them. Seeing nothing in front of them, blind infants may have no reason to crawl. One can sense from Fraiberg's descriptions the intricate relationship between motor and cognitive development.

A consideration of the different developmental course of a blind child reminds us of the importance of studying the full gamet of subjects. Only by designing and collating studies of animals, normal humans, and humans with specific deficits can we arrive at reliable knowledge about development in the first crucial years of life.

Harry F. Harlow, Robert O. Dodsworth, and Margaret K. Harlow

TOTAL SOCIAL ISOLATION IN MONKEYS

Human social isolation is recognized as a problem of vast importance. Its effects are deleterious to personal adjustment, normal heterosexual development, and control of aggressive and delinquent behaviors. Isolation generally arises from breakdowns in family structures resulting in orphaned or semiorphaned children or in illegitimate children who, for one reason or another, are raised in institutions, inadequate foster homes, or, occasionally, in abnormal homes with relatives.

It is difficult or impossible to study scientifically the impacts of culturally produced social isolation at the human level. The variables are multitudinous and recalcitrant to experimental manipulation and control. Our research has consequently been concerned with the effects of social deprivation in rhesus monkeys. Previously published research has established parallels in the normal social development of human and monkey young.[1-3] There is every reason to believe that the same basic laws operate for these two closely related species and that social conditions which produce abnormality in one species will have comparable effects on the other. Although human behavior is more complex, more variable, and subtler than that of subhuman primates, one should, nevertheless, find insights into the problems created by human social isolation from study of social isolation in monkeys.

For the past ten years we have studied the effects of partial social isolation by raising monkeys from birth onward in bare wire cages such as those shown in Figure 1. These monkeys suffer total maternal deprivation and, even more important, have no opportunity to form affectional ties with their peers. We have already reported the resulting progressively deepening syndrome of compulsive nonnutritional sucking, repetitive stereotyped movements, detachment from the environment, hostility directed outwardly toward others and inwardly toward the animal's own body, and inability to form adequate social or heterosexual attachments to others when such opportunities are provided in preadolescence, adolescence, or adulthood.[4]

More recently, we have initiated a series of studies on the effects of *total* social isolation[5] by housing monkeys from a few hours after birth until 3, 6, or 12 months of age in the stainless-steel chamber illustrated in Figure 2. During the prescribed sentence in this apparatus, the monkey has no contact with any animal, human or subhuman. Al-

This research was supported by a grant from the University of Wisconsin Graduate School and by USPHS grants MH–04528 and FR–0167 from the National Institutes of Health to the University of Wisconsin Department of Psychology Primate Laboratory and Regional Primate Research Center, respectively.

SOURCE: From Harry Harlow, Robert Dodsworth, and Margaret Harlow, "Total Social Isolation in Monkeys," *Proceedings of the National Academy of Sciences* 54 (1965), pp. 90–96.

Figure 1. Semisocial isolation living cage.

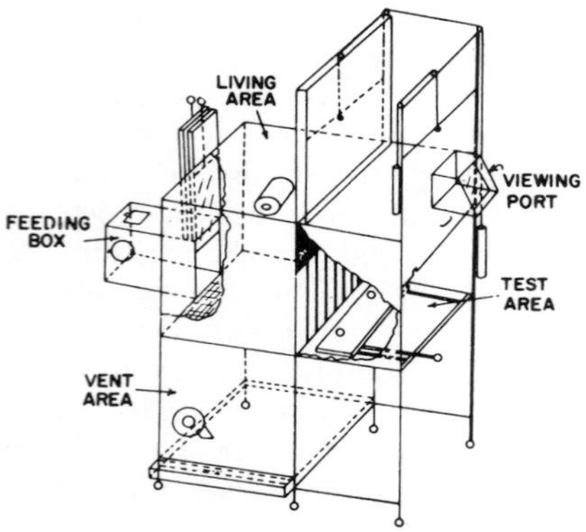

Figure 2. Total social isolation chamber.

though social isolation is total, no attempt is made to maximize *sensory* deprivation. The chamber is constantly illuminated, transmits sounds, and affords relatively adequate opportunities for cutaneous-proprioceptive expression and exploration. The room outside the living cage was sound-masked by a 70-db [decibel] white noise source, but loud sounds from the corridor produced attentive and even freezing responses.

Three groups of newborn monkeys were isolated in individual chambers for 3, 6, and 12 months, respectively. In addition, one group was kept in partial isolation in individual cages in the laboratory nursery for the first 6 months, then placed in the isolation chamber for 6 months. There were six monkeys in the 3-month group and four monkeys in each of the other groups. Isolation effects were measured by comparing the social behavior of pairs of isolated monkeys after release from the chambers with that of pairs of equal-aged monkeys raised in partial isolation. Each experimental pair and its control pair were tested together as a stable group of four in the playroom situation illustrated in Figure 3. The four subjects were released in the room for 30 minutes a day, 5 days a week, for 32 weeks. Long-term effects were subsequently assessed in the playroom from 1 to 2 years after termination of isolation. Two observers recorded the occurrence of selected individual behaviors and social interactions.[6,7] In addition, the effect of isolation on intellectual development has been assessed by means of a comprehensive battery of learning tests, including discrimination, delayed response, and learning-set formation.[8]

No monkey has died during isolation. When initially removed from total social isolation, however, they usually go into a state of emotional shock, characterized by the autistic self-clutching and rocking illustrated in Figure 4. One of six monkeys isolated for 3 months refused to eat after release and died 5 days later. The autopsy report attributed death to emotional anorexia. A second animal in the same group also refused to eat and would probably have died had we not been prepared to resort to forced feeding. This phenomenon of extreme emotional anorexia has not appeared in the 6- or 12-month groups.

Our data indicate that the debilitating effects of 3 months of social isolation are dramatic but reversible. If there is long-term social or intellectual damage, it eludes our measurements. Given the opportunity soon after release to associate with controls of the

Figure 3. Playroom situation.

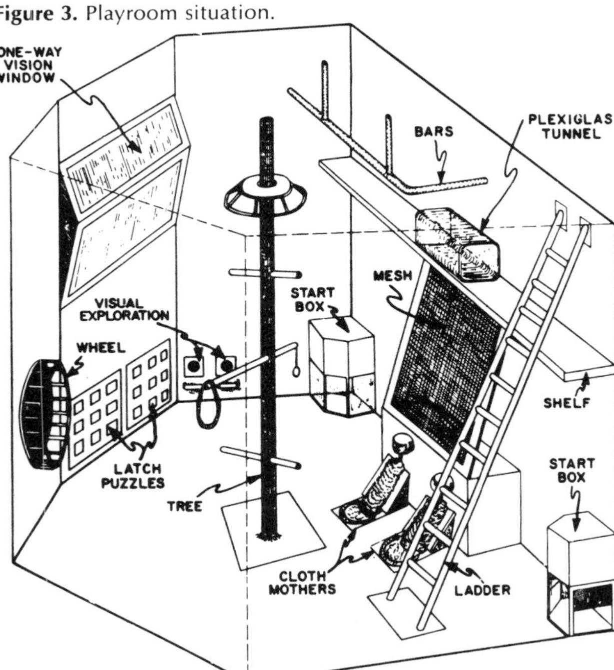

Figure 4. Autistic self-clutching pattern.

same age, these short-term isolates start slowly during the first week and then adapt and show the normal sequence of social behaviors. In human terms they are the children salvaged from the orphanage or inadequate home within the first year of life. Figure 5 presents their postisolation progress in learning-set formation — the most reliable measure we have of relatively complex learning in the rhesus monkey. The performance of both the 3-month isolate group and their controls is indistinguishable from that of equal-aged monkeys tested in other experiments utilizing learning-set problems.

Isolation extending through the first 6 months of life, on the other hand, severely impairs the potentiality for socialization as indicated by playroom data comparing 6-month isolates with their controls and with 3-month isolates and their controls. Of the

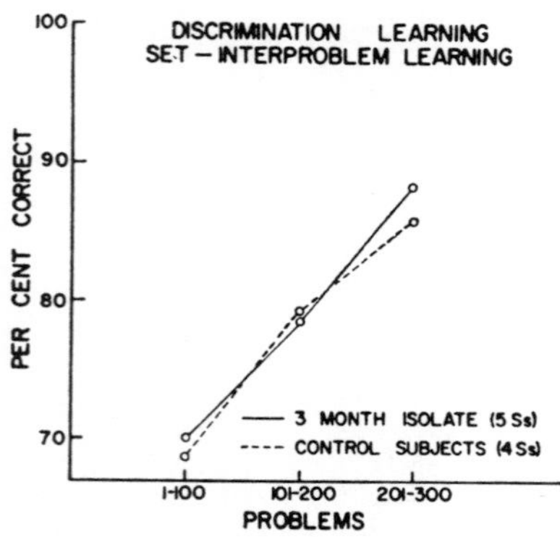

Figure 5. Postisolation learning-set formation.

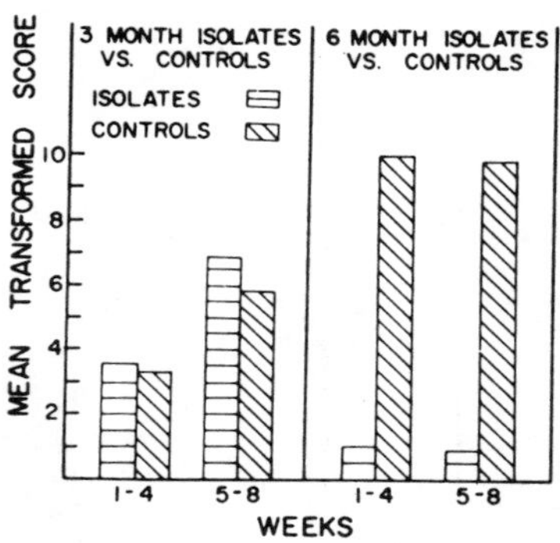

Figure 6. Incidence of social threat in the playroom.

many social measures obtained, only two are shown here for illustrative purposes. Frequency of threat, one of the most reliable social measures, is graphically presented in Figure 6 for both the 3- and 6-month isolates and their appropriate controls during the first 4 weeks and the second 4 weeks after total social isolation. There are no significant differences in frequency of threat between the 3-month isolates and their controls during either test period; there is no reason to believe that the slightly higher frequency of threat by the isolates is other than a chance difference. These data contrast strongly with the differential frequency of threat behavior by the 6-month isolates and their controls during both observational test periods. Transformed scores were used for statistical reasons. The ratio of the actual frequencies of threat for the 6-month isolates and their controls was approximately 1–4. The differences were significant far beyond the 0.05 level. During the next 6 months the 3-month isolates and their controls showed no differential trends in frequency of social threat. The curves for the 6-month isolates and their controls over the 8 months of observation in the playroom are shown in Figure 7. From the 24th week on, frequency of social threat increased somewhat in the 6-month isolates, but these social threats were consistently directed to other isolates.

A comparison of the frequency of contact ("rough-and-tumble") play (Figure 8) for the 3-month isolates and their controls showed no difference during the first 4-week period and no subsequent differential developmental trend. These data differ sharply from those for the 6-month isolates and their controls. Essentially no contact play was observed in the 6-month isolate monkeys during either of the first two 4-week postisola-

Figure 7. Developmental social threat trends.

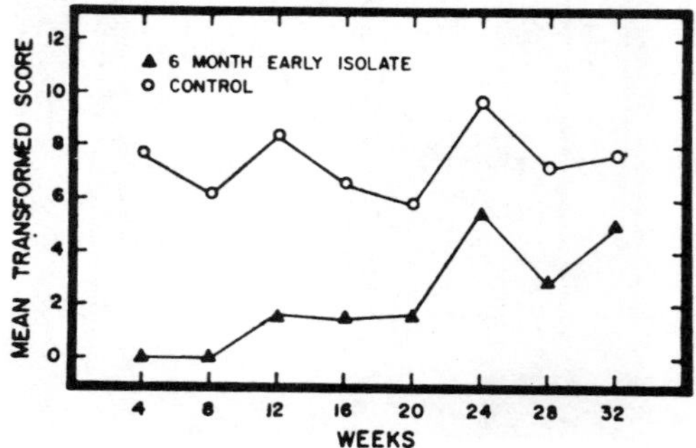

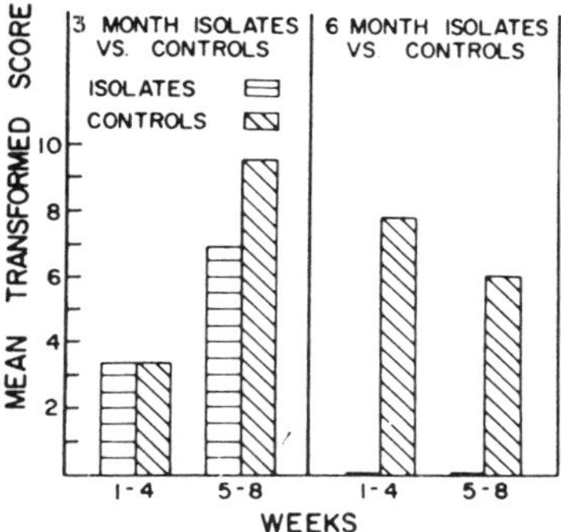

Figure 8. Incidence of contact play.

tion periods, whereas a large amount of such play occurred for the controls. The level of contact play increased materially in the 6-month isolate group (Figure 9) during the course of the 32 weeks of testing, but again the contact play that was exhibited was play between isolates and not between isolates and controls. Actually, social interaction throughout the entire 32-week test period between the 6-month isolate monkeys and their controls was for all practical purposes nonexistent except for bursts of aggression which the controls occasionally directed toward the isolate animals.

The effects of 6 months of total social isolation were so devastating and debilitating that we had assumed initially that 12 months of isolation would not produce any additional decrement. This assumption proved to be false; 12 months of isolation almost obliterated the animals socially, as is suggested by the playroom data for activity play, the simplest form of play, shown in Figure 10.

Activity play was chosen as a prime measure since it represents a primitive play level involving minimal interanimal contact. The 12-month isolates showed practically no activity play, and the trend was a decrease with time. The control monkeys, on the other hand, displayed a relatively constant, high level of activity play. Observation of the 12-month isolated animals and their controls had to be terminated after 10 experimental weeks because the controls became increasingly aggressive toward the helpless isolated animals and might have killed them had we continued social testing.

Figure 9. Developmental trends in contact play.

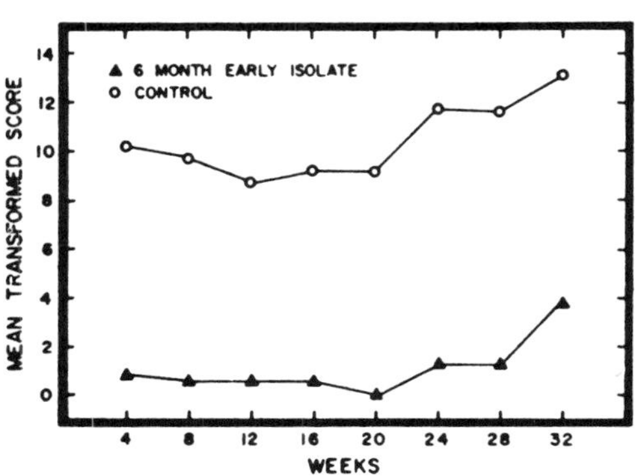

Figure 10. Activity play of 12-month isolates.

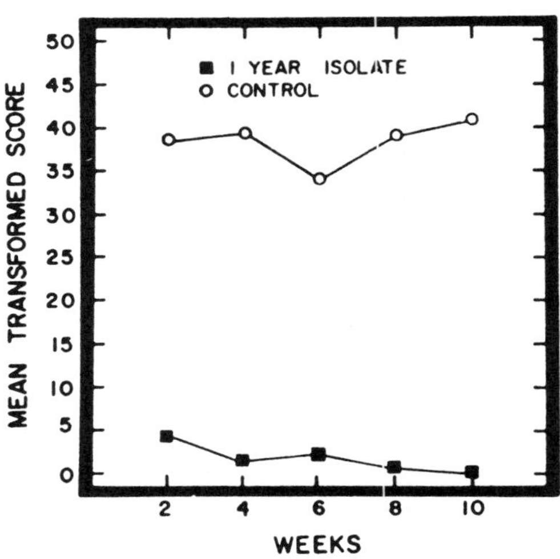

A striking difference between the 6-month and the 12-month socially isolated monkeys occurred in the frequency of autoerotic behaviors. Such behaviors occurred, although with low frequency, in the 6-month isolate group; they were virtually nonexistent in the 12-month socially isolated subjects. Control monkeys, on the other hand, displayed a high level of such behaviors.

Total social isolation during the second half year of life produced a radically different syndrome from that for the first half year. Within a relatively short period of time after release from isolation, the 6-month late isolates adjusted adequately to equal-aged playmates. This finding is indicated in Figure 11 by the frequency of social approach exhibited by these subjects as compared with their controls. Although the differences are not statistically significant, the 6-month late isolates made more approaches than the controls, no doubt reflecting the somewhat greater aggressiveness of the isolates and the consequent caution of the controls. Observational data show that the 6-month late-isolate group was hyper-aggressive compared with its control group whereas both the 6- and 12-month socially isolated subjects were characterized by a marked lack of aggression compared with their controls.

Figure 11. Incidence of social approach in 6-month late isolates.

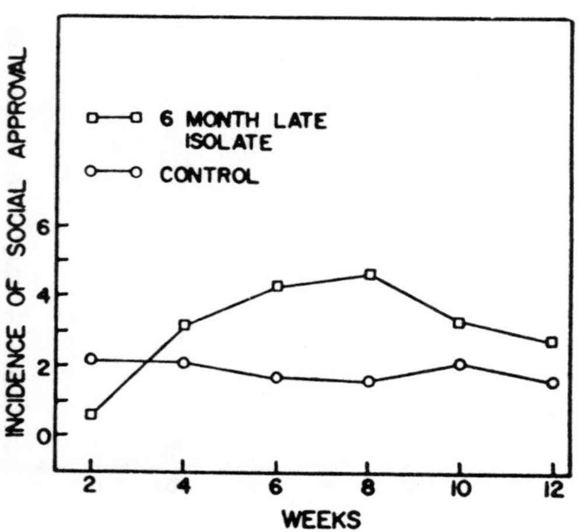

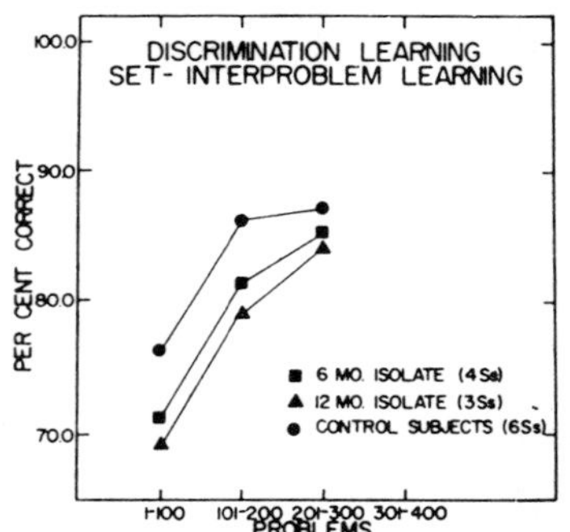

Figure 12. Postisolation learning-set formation.

The effects of 6 and 12 months of total social isolation on learning are confounded in our studies since we attempted, with success in some cases, to measure by remote-control test methods the isolated monkey's ability to solve learning problems during their periods of confinement. Thus, even when the infants failed to progress during isolation, they were being given intellectual stimulation which could have played a significant role in their apparent intellectual normality after release. The learning data obtained on delayed-response and learning-set tasks after removal from total social isolation disclosed no significant differences between 6- and 12-month isolated monkeys and their equal-aged controls, but the consistency of the small differences that did occur suggests the possibility that larger samples might support a difference. The learning-set data are presented in Figure 12. The performance of the control monkeys tends to be higher than that of the 6-month isolates, and the performance of the 6-month isolates tends to be higher than that of the 12-month isolates.

The striking fact, however, is that all the socially isolated monkeys learned effectively after being removed from the social isolation cages. We cannot, at the present time, adequately assess the effect of prolonged total social isolation on the intellectual capabilities of rhesus monkeys. The ultimate appraisal must await experiments in which no training is given during isolation. We can, however, state with confidence that the "intellectual mind" is far less crippled than the "social mind" by prolonged total social deprivation if adequate experience is provided subsequently. Inasmuch as this intellectual sparing is contrary to the current theory of the effects of social deprivation on the intellectual development of human children, a review of the human data may be in order. The so-called intellectual deficits reported for deprived children may well be social deficits in large part rather than intellectual ones.

An experiment presently being prepared for publication by G. D. Mitchell [9] provides data on the social behavior of members of our total-isolation groups toward more normally raised macaque monkeys over long time periods. Eight isolated subjects were assembled, two from the 12-month isolated group, and three each from the 6-month early and 6-month late-isolation groups. They ranged in age from 2 years and 4 months to 3 years and 5 months. The other members of our totally socially isolated groups were not available because of various research commitments. Studies investigating the long-term social behavior of all members of all the groups subjected to total social isolation are presently in progress.

Mitchell tested the social behaviors of individual isolates and normal monkeys toward age mates, adults, and 1-year-old infants. The 12-month isolates showed no play, no aggression, almost no sex behavior, but a high level of fear to adults, to age mates, and even to the infants. Two of the 6-month early isolates showed no play, but one — a female — showed adequate play with adults, age mates, and infants. One of the three showed aggression toward adults, age mates, and infants. One showed aggression only toward adults. The third — the female — showed aggression only toward age mates and infants. Sex behavior was almost nonexistent except for scattered, diffuse sex responses directed toward infants. Two of the three showed extreme fear toward adults but not toward age mates or infants, while the third showed no fear at all.

The 6-month late isolates differed from the 6-month early isolates primarily in only one aspect of behavior: two of the three showed uncoordinated sexual responses toward age mates and one of these showed the same kind of responses to adults. In play, one of the 6-month late group showed essentially normal responsiveness with age mates and also with infants and adults. One showed virtually no play at all, and the third played only with infants. Two of the three showed the same suicidal aggression toward adults as did two of the 6-month early isolates, a behavior rarely seen in normal monkeys. All three showed hostility toward infants, even though two of them were females. This behavior is essentially nonexistent among normal monkeys. Perhaps most surprising was the finding that none showed much hostility toward age mates even though they had been hostile to age mates in the initial observations following isolation. One showed almost no fear to any age range of subjects, while the third showed moderate fear to adults but not to age mates or infants.

In summary, on the follow-up tests, the 12-month isolates were highly fearful and showed almost no positive social behavior and no aggression. Except in sexual behavior, the 6-month early and late isolates were highly similar, as groups, in their social responses. One member of each group showed essentially normal play behavior, and two of each group showed little or no play. Two members of each group showed suicidal aggression toward adults, and five of the six members of the combined groups showed the abnormal phenomenon of aggressing against infants. None of the six was a socially normal animal, for even the two that played with the test animals were hostile to infants and none of the six showed adequate sex behavior. The adjustments of the members of these two groups were highly individual in that a number adapted adequately to specific situations, but none adapted adequately to all or even most types of situations. The effects of isolation in the first year thus were clearly evident 12–24 months (mean, 18 months) after removal from isolation in spite of the prolonged social experience provided the subjects following isolation.

The findings of the various total-isolation and semi-isolation studies of the monkeys suggest that sufficiently severe and enduring early isolation reduces these animals to a social-emotional level in which the primary social responsiveness is fear. Twelve months of total social isolation is apparently sufficient to achieve this result consistently in rhesus monkeys. In contrast, short periods of total social isolation leave no permanent deficits in potentialities or social adjustment. For the rhesus monkey, this period of sparing is at least 3 months. Periods of total isolation somewhere between 3 months and 12 months or prolonged periods of semi-isolation result in different degrees of social damage and permit variable behavioral adaptations, perhaps as a function both of basic individual differences and of social learning experiences. Individuals subjected to the same deprivation conditions can thus emerge as generally fearful or fearless, generally hostile or without aggression, or selectively fearful or selectively hostile. Placed in a free-living situation, most of these animals would be driven off or eliminated before they could have an opportunity to learn to adapt to the group.

NOTES

1. Harlow, H. F., M. K. Harlow, and E. W. Hansen, in *Maternal Behavior in Mammals,* ed. H. L. Rheingold (New York: John Wiley & Sons, Inc., 1963).
2. Harlow, H. F., *Sci. Psychoanalysis, 7,* 93–113 (1964).
3. Seay, B., B. K. Alexander, and H. F. Harlow, *J. Abnorm. Soc. Psychol., 69,* 345–354 (1964).
4. Cross, H. A., and H. F. Harlow, *J. Exptl. Res. Pers., 1,* 39–49 (1965).
5. Harlow, H. F., G. L. Rowland, and G. A. Griffin, *Psychiatric Research Report 19* (American Psychiatric Association, 1964).
6. Rowland, G. L., doctoral dissertation, University of Wisconsin, 1964.
7. Griffin, G. A., M.S. thesis, University of Wisconsin, in preparation.
8. Harlow, H. F., *Am. Scientist, 47,* 459–479 (1959).
9. Mitchell, G. D., M.S. thesis, University of Wisconsin, in preparation.

Melinda A. Novak and Harry F. Harlow

SOCIAL RECOVERY OF MONKEYS ISOLATED FOR THE FIRST YEAR OF LIFE: REHABILITATION AND THERAPY

ABSTRACT: Previous research demonstrated that 12 months of total social isolation initiated at birth produced severe and seemingly permanent social deficits in rhesus monkey subjects. Such monkeys exhibited self-clasping, self-mouthing, and other stereotypic, self-directed responses instead of the appropriate species-typical behaviors. Although early experimentation designed to rehabilitate isolate-reared subjects was not successful, recent research has indicated that 6-month-isolated monkeys could develop social behaviors if exposed to younger, socially unsophisticated "therapist" monkeys. The present experiment demonstrated that 12-month isolate-reared monkeys developed appropriate species-typical behavior through the use of adaptation, self-pacing of visual input, and exposure to younger "therapist" monkeys. Adaptation enabled the isolate monkeys to become familiar with their postisolation environment, while self-pacing facilitated their watching the therapist monkeys' social interactions. So primed, the isolates showed a marked decrease in self-directed behaviors following extensive intimate contact with the therapists. As species-typical behaviors significantly increased during this period, the isolate behavioral repertoire did not differ substantially from the thereapist behavioral repertoire by the end of the therapy period. Such results clearly fail to support a critical period for socialization in the rhesus monkey, and an alternative environment-specific learning hypothesis is proposed.

Lack of social experience during early infancy has been demonstrated to produce severe social deficits in monkey subjects. Monkeys reared in total social isolation from conspecifics develop self-directed patterns of behavior that include self-clasping, self-mouthing, huddling, and stereotypic rocking (Rowland, 1964). After emergence from 6 or more months of isolation, such monkeys fail to exhibit age-appropriate behavior patterns of exploration, play, and social contact. Instead, their behavioral repertoire is characterized by the various self-directed behaviors they adopted in the isolation chamber. Furthermore, these monkeys show few changes with maturity, as the behavioral anomalies

This research was supported by U.S. Public Health Service Grant MH–11894 from the National Institutes of Health to the University of Wisconsin Primate Laboratory. The authors wish to express their appreciation to Sharon Grady and Peggy O'Neill who collected and summarized the data.

persist and species-typical sexual and maternal behaviors remain conspicuously absent (Harlow, Dodsworth, & Harlow, 1965; Harlow & Harlow, 1965; Harlow, Harlow, Dodsworth & Arling, 1966; Mason, 1963; Rowland, 1964; Sackett, 1968a, 1968b; Senko, 1966). Aggressive behaviors do mature in isolate-reared monkeys but these behaviors are either self-directed or inappropriately directed during social encounters. However, isolate-reared monkeys do not differ substantially from control monkeys in their learning set performance, although the period required for adaptation to the test situation is prolonged (Harlow, Schiltz, & Harlow, 1969). Comparisons of the learning set performance of isolate-reared monkeys with monkeys raised in enriched environments indicate that isolated subjects differ from enriched subjects only with regard to the development of oddity learning set (Gluck, Harlow, & Schiltz, 1973).

The effects of isolation rearing are clearly dependent on the duration of the incarceration. For example, 12 months of isolation produces more severe debilitation and disturbance in monkeys than a 6-month isolation period (Rowland, 1964). Isolation rearing effects are also dependent upon the age at which incarceration commences. The syndrome described above is characteristic of animals placed in isolation at birth and has been termed early isolation. If monkeys have had the opportunity to develop social affections prior to incarceration, a subsequent late isolation period produces less marked social deficits (Clark, 1968; Harlow & Novak, 1973; Harlow & Suomi, 1971).

Three major hypotheses have been advanced to account for the early isolation effects. The critical period hypothesis postulates that normal social development is dependent on the reception of specific types of stimulation at specific stages of development (Scott, 1962). Failure to receive such stimulation at the appropriate time results in altered development. According to this theory, the isolation effects stem from the absence of social experience necessary to produce social responsivity. Although this hypothesis can account for the permanent absence of socially appropriate behaviors in 6- or 12-month isolate-reared monkeys, it provides no explanation for the ritualized self-directed behaviors that most of these monkeys exhibit.

The deterioration hypothesis of Lessac (1965) adapted from the earlier perceptual deterioration notions of Hebb (1949) and the sensory deprivation work of Riesen (1960) proposes that normal social responsivity is lost or deteriorates during the isolation period instead of failing to develop in the first place. Such waning of responsivity might be the result of neural deterioration analogous to that found in monkey retinal cells deprived of light. The absence of substantial learning deficits equivalent to the substantive social deficits in isolate-reared monkeys, however, does not support the neural deterioration view; and it is unlikely that deterioration would develop only in those structures related to social behavior and not in those structures related to complex learning processes.

The deterioration hypothesis can be modified and extended so that waning of sociality might be viewed as the result of extinction, where behavior patterns associated with social interaction can only be maintained by means of reinforcement from another monkey. Since extinction is not completely effective in suppressing behavior, this modified deterioration hypothesis does not account for the presumed permanent loss of sociality. This hypothesis, however, might indirectly provide an explanation for the pervasive and widespread development of self-directed behaviors observed in monkeys in isolation. From this perspective, such behaviors as self-clasping, self-mouthing, and rocking are perceived as reinforcing to the monkey. Indeed, it might be argued that these behaviors provide the only possible stimulation to an animal reared in isolation and represent the predictable outcome of such rearing.

The third hypothesis, developed by Fuller and Clark (1966) as a result of their isolation studies in dogs, postulates that the bizarre behavior patterns exhibited by animals removed from isolation are the result of "emergence trauma" associated with the rapid change from a low stimulating environment to an environment of marked complexity. Since the animals should be able to adapt eventually to environments suitable for normally reared conspecifics, *unless* they have suffered permanent neural disabilities, this emergence-stress hypothesis alone does not predict a permanent maintenance of the aberrant behavior. This viewpoint, then, has been accorded only minor importance in the past, first, because the isolation effects did appear to be permanent and second, because attempts to adapt isolate-reared monkeys to the complexities of their postisolation environment were singularly unsuccessful (Clark, 1968). However, it should be noted that the emergence-stress idea is compatible with both of the other major hypotheses, and there is no logical reason to assume that only one general factor operates in the production of the isolation syndrome.

Of all the above hypotheses, the critical period notion was tacitly accepted by primatologists and developmentalists as the explanation for the total isolation effects. Several attempts to adapt or rehabilitate isolate-reared monkeys by employing exposure to socially competent peers, extensive adaptation to the test situation (Clark, 1968) or by training in a conditioning paradigm (Sackett, 1968b) were unsuccessful, thereby strengthening acceptance of the critical hypothesis.

Recent research by Suomi and Harlow (1972), however, has clearly demonstrated that the effects of 6 months of isolation rearing are reversible. Suomi and Harlow proposed that failure to rehabilitate isolate-reared rhesus monkeys by means of exposure to socially competent peers resulted in part from the behaviors manifested by the stimulus monkeys toward the isolate monkeys. In particular, both Rowland (1964) and Clark (1968) reported that age-mate stimulus animals usually aggressed the isolate monkeys, clearly a situation not conducive to social recovery and development.

Therefore, Suomi and Harlow selected 3-month-old female surrogate-peer-reared monkeys as therapists for their isolated monkeys because such therapists, in contrast to 6-month-old monkeys, consistently initiate social contact without manifesting aggressive responses. Also, their behavioral repertoire is much less complex, consisting primarily of clinging responses and unsophisticated play patterns. This method of therapy proved successful, as the isolate-reared monkeys exhibited a marked decrease in self-directed behaviors and a significant increase in social behaviors. Such dramatic results cast doubt on both the critical period and neural deterioration hypotheses as suitable explanations for isolate asociality. Suomi and Harlow also found little evidence for emergence trauma in their isolate-reared monkeys, and their theoretical position was that the capacity for social responsivity is present in all isolated subjects, but social performance is dependent upon exposure to appropriate stimulus animals.

While the study by Suomi and Harlow generated much interest in terms of the possibilities for rehabilitating socially debilitated monkeys, certain questions regarding the generality of these findings remained. First, it could not be ascertained from this study whether reversal of social deficits could be effected with the more severe regimen of rearing monkeys in isolation for 12 months. Not only are the effects of 12 months of isolation more devastating, but Rowland (1964) also reported that 6-month isolate-reared monkeys displayed some slight recovery of locomotion and exploration during exposure to age-mate peers which was never observed in 12-month isolate-reared monkeys. Second, the social competence of their subjects was assessed only by interactions with the therapist monkeys. No rigorous test of social interaction with age-mate mother-peer-reared monkeys following rehabilitation was provided to determine whether recovery generalized to social encounters with other animals. Furthermore, there was no assessment of the effects of this therapy on the maturation of aggression and sexual behavior, behaviors in which isolates are notably deficient.

The present experiment was initiated to determine whether the negative effects of total social isolation rearing for 12 months could be substantially reversed. Three techniques were used in successive stages to produce social recovery in monkeys reared in this manner. First, the isolate-reared monkeys were adapted gradually to their postisolation environment. The second procedure involved a self-pacing of stimulation in which the monkeys were to a limited extent allowed to control their level of visual input. Following the example of Suomi and Harlow, the third procedure involved providing social experience with younger surrogate-peer-reared "therapist" monkeys. It was hypothesized that the combination of techniques described above would provide the most suitable conditions for social recovery of the isolated monkeys. An assessment of both the effectiveness of this therapy as measured by age-mate pairings and the long-term consequences of therapy is reported elsewhere. (Novak, Note *1*).

METHOD

Subjects

Isolates. The isolate subjects were two male and two female rhesus monkeys (*Macaca mulatta*) born within a 2-week period. They were separated from their mothers at birth and reared in the laboratory nursery, according to the procedure described by Blomquist and Harlow (1961), until they were 10 days of age. The isolates were then placed in individual isolation chambers (see Rowland, 1964) which were so constructed as to prevent visual or physical exposure to other monkeys. The isolated subjects remained in their respective chambers until their mean age was 12 months.

Therapists. The therapist monkeys were two male and two female rhesus monkeys, also born within a 2-week period. Their mean age was 10 months *less* than that of the isolate subjects. Like the isolate subjects, these therapist monkeys were separated from their mothers at birth and reared in the laboratory nursery. Unlike the isolate monkeys, they remained in the nursery for the first 30 days of life. At a mean age of 10 days each infant monkey was provided with a simplified surrogate mother (Harlow & Suomi, 1970). Following laboratory rearing the therapist monkeys were placed in individual quadrants of a quad cage, a large rectangular steel mesh cage, 6 × 5 × 3 feet (183 × 152 × 91 cm) that could be divided into 4 equivalent living cages, 3 × 2.5 × 3 feet (91 × 76 × 91 cm), with inner mesh-wall partitions. Thus, the therapist monkeys had visual and some limited physical contact with each other at all times and were permitted 2 hours of social interaction 5 days per week. Three days per week the therapists interacted as pairs within the quad cage, while the remaining 2 days per week they interacted as a group of four in a social playroom previously described in Harlow and Harlow (1965).

Procedure

Postisolation visual adaptation period. When the mean age of the isolate subjects was 12 months, they were removed from their chambers and placed in individual quadrants of a quad cage approximately 3.5 feet (107 cm) from the quad cage of the therapist monkeys. Unlike the therapists' quad cage, the isolates' quad cage had outer walls of Masonite allowing the isolates to see each other but preventing the isolates from seeing the therapist monkeys. This period lasted for 2 weeks.

Self-pacing adaptation period. After the 2-week period the outer Masonite panels were replaced with mesh panels containing half-high Masonite barriers 19 inches (48 cm) high. In this situation the isolate monkeys could actively choose to look at or to avoid the therapist monkeys. Looking behavior, however, was incompatible with the self-directed behaviors of rocking and huddling that would tend to keep the isolate monkey below the top of the barrier. The water bottle spout was placed above the barrier to insure that the isolates would spend at least a small portion of their time exposed to the activity of the therapist monkeys. This period lasted 4 weeks.

Social contact adaptation period. Six weeks after removal from isolation, the isolates were allowed social interaction with each other for 2 hours per day 3 days per week as pairs in the quad cage and for 1 hour per day 2 days per week as a group of four in the social playroom. This period lasted 2 weeks.

Exposure to therapist monkeys — therapy. (a) Weeks 1–4. Immediately after the last adaptation period, the isolate monkeys were allowed physical access to the younger therapist monkeys (now 4 months of age). During the first 4 weeks the isolates were placed in the playroom with the therapists 1 hour per day 2 days per week in groups of four (two isolates and two therapists). The isolates were also exposed to the therapists during quad cage interactions for 2 hours per day 2 days per week in groups of four (two isolates and two therapists in each quad cage). Both isolates and therapists retained one playroom interaction session as an intact group of four for 2 hours per day 1 day per week.

(b) Weeks 5–16. Quad cage interaction was eliminated and playroom interaction was increased to 2 hours per day, 4 days per week. Intragroup interaction continued 1 day per week as described in (a).

(c) Weeks 17–24. The playroom interaction session was changed so that all eight animals (four therapists and four isolates) were placed in the playroom at the same time. Playroom times remained the same. Intragroup interactions continued 1 day per week as described in (a).

Data Collection

All subjects, beginning at 1 month of age, were observed for one 5-minute period per day 5 days per week in their respective home cages. All subjects were also observed for one 5-minute period per day 5 days per week during social interaction periods which were initiated at 1 month of age for the therapist subjects and at 13.5 months of age for the isolate-reared subjects. Data were collected using a modified frequency scoring system such that during every observation period, subject behaviors falling into each of 17 categories were scored for their presence or absence in any of thirty 10-second intervals that comprised the observation period. The following nonsocial categories were used: self-groom (discrete self-directed picking or spreading of the hair), self-mouth (oral contact of any part of own body exclusive of biting), self-bite (vigorous pinching of own body with the teeth), self-clasp (any clutching of own body with hand[s] and/or foot [feet]), huddle (withdrawn posturing with head tucked into chest and lower than the top of the shoulders), rock (repetitive back and forth movement, nonlocomotive), stereotypy (ritualized body movements repeated in a rhythmic manner for at least three cycles), locomotion (change of spatial position by one full step), tactile-oral exploration (manual and/or oral manipulation of environment), vocalization (any sound emitted by the subject), visual exploration (any looking or staring at the environment, scored only if the monkey is doing nothing else). The social categories included: social contact (any physical contact with another monkey excluding grooming or play bouts), social play (rough-and-tumble wrestling, mock biting, chasing, bouncing with another monkey), sexual patterns (thrusting against another monkey, immature mounting), social groom (grooming directed to another monkey), threat (staring facial expression involving open mouth, teeth partially exposed, ears back, eyebrows arched), fear grimace (facial expression involving retraction of lips with fully exposed teeth).

The observations were taken between the hours of 10:10 a.m. and 2:30 p.m. by one of three experienced testers, all of whom had been trained to a rigorous laboratory reliability criterion prior to the beginning of this experiment.

Each subject's daily observation sessions were arranged as indicated below:

Isolate subjects. (a) 6–12 months — one daily observation of subject in isolation chamber, (b) 12–13.5 months — one observation of isolate-reared monkey in individual quadrant of quad cage, (c) 13.5–18 months — one observation of subject in individual quadrant of quad cage and one observation of subject in a social setting (either quad cage or playroom).

Therapist subjects. 1–12 months — one observation of subject in individual quadrant of quad cage and the other observation of the therapist subject in a social setting (either quad cage or playroom).

Data Analysis

The statistical analysis was performed in four parts. First, the behavior of the monkeys in isolation from 6–12 months of age was compared with the homecage behavior of the surrogate-peer-reared monkeys at the same age to assess the effects of isolation rearing during the period of incarceration. Second, a test for emergence trauma was provided by a comparison of the isolate subjects' behavior during a 2-week period immediately following removal from isolation with the behavior manifested during their last 2 weeks in isolation. Third, the isolate-reared subjects' initial social competence was examined by comparing their behavior during initial interactions with one another for a 2-week period with the behavior of the therapist monkeys during social interactions for that same 2-week period. The final analysis was concerned with behavioral changes that occurred during the therapy period in which the isolates interacted with the younger therapist monkeys. The 6-month therapy period was divided into 2-week blocks over which each animal's homecage behaviors were averaged for comparison purposes. Behaviors recorded during quad cage and playroom interactions were treated similarly.

In all cases, behavioral scores for each category were subjected to analyses of variance with group, sex, isolation-postisolation, and time as variables where appropriate. Significant interactions, except for those involving time, were subjected to further analysis by means of the Duncan New Multiple Range Test (Duncan, 1955), while significant time main effects and interactions were analyzed using single *df* orthogonal polynomial trend tests. An alpha level of $p \leq .05$ was accepted as the criterion of statistical significance.

RESULTS

Four general findings were yielded by the data analysis. First, monkeys raised in total social isolation developed significant behavioral anomalies as evidenced by self-clasping, rocking, and huddling responses manifested in isolation. Second, the isolated subjects exhibited a marked emergence trauma upon removal from isolation. Third, isolate-reared subjects were socially incompetent with one another even after a lengthy nonsocial adaptation period. Finally, and most important, the isolated subjects exhibited a highly significant recovery of social behaviors when exposed to younger socially normal peers (therapists).

Isolation Period Behaviors

Figure 1 provides a summary of the behavioral repertoire of the isolated subjects during their last 6 months in isolation and the behavioral repertoire of the therapist monkeys at the same age. Isolate-reared subjects displayed significantly lower levels of locomotion, $F(1, 4) = 7.79$, $p < .05$, and higher levels of self-clasp, $F(1, 4) = 21.23$, $p < .01$, huddle $F(1, 4) = 25.20$, $p < .01$, rock, $F(1, 4) = 12.16$, $p < .05$, and sterotypy, $F(1, 4) = 10.53$, $p < .05$, than the therapist subjects of the same age. Significant time effects were detected for locomotion, $F(17, 72) = 2.20$, $p < .01$, and tactile-oral exploration, $F(17, 72) = 3.83$, $p < .001$, such that both behaviors increased linearly across the 6-month observation period. Significant time with rearing condition interactions were noted for the categories of self-clasp, $F(17, 72) = 4.58$, $p < .001$, and stereotypy, $F(17, 72) = 2.01$, $p < .025$. Isolate but not therapist monkeys displayed a quartic trend in these behaviors over time. There were no differences between the isolate and therapist monkeys with regard to the incidence of self-grooming, vocalization, threat, or fear grimace. Self-biting was never observed in either group during this period. The data clearly indicate that the behavioral repertoire of the isolate-reared monkeys was characterized by the overwhelming presence of self-directed anomalous behavior patterns in contrast to the behaviors of the therapist monkeys of the same age.

Figure 1. Behaviors of isolate and therapist monkeys exhibited during the same age period (the second 6 months of isolation life).

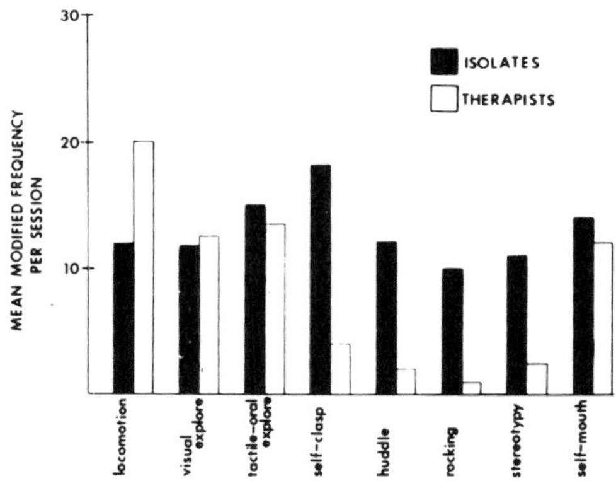

Postisolation Adaptation Behaviors

Figure 2 compares the mean behavioral levels for the 2-week adaptation period for the isolate subjects with the mean behavioral levels for the last two weeks of isolation. The marked changes in behavior provide strong support for the existence of emergence trauma in the isolate monkeys. Following emergence, there were significant decreases in environmentally directed behaviors such as locomotion, $F(1, 4) = 9.25$, $p < .05$, tactile-oral exploration, $F(1, 4) = 20.25$, $p < .025$, and visual exploration, $F(1, 4) = 33.20$, $p < .005$, and marked increases in self-directed withdrawn behaviors such as huddle, $F(1, 4) = 17.79$, $p < .025$, and self-clasp, $F(1, 4) = 60.53$, $p < .001$, as a function of removal from isolation. Stereotypic patterns, predominantly pacing, decreased significantly during the postisolation period, $F(1, 4) = 12.29$, $p < .025$. This change was probably

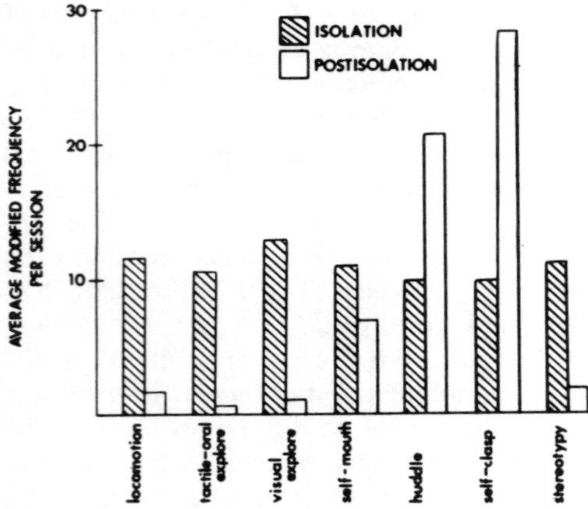

Figure 2. Isolate monkey behavior during the last 2 weeks of isolation compared with behavior exhibited during the first 2 weeks following emergence from isolation.

related to the marked decline in overall activity observed following isolation emergence. Nearly all of these behaviors returned to preemergence levels within a 2–3 week period.

The use of half-high barriers during adaptation was effective in initiating looking behavior in isolate-reared subjects. Measurements of the location of the isolate subjects with respect to the barriers demonstrated that these monkeys spent increasingly more time above the barriers as the early stage of rehabilitation progressed, weekly means: week 1 = .17, week 2 = 2.01, week 3 = 3.74, week 4 = 5.93 intervals; $F(3, 12) = 3.86$, $p < .01$. Furthermore, the isolates spent more time above the barrier when the therapist monkeys were interacting with each other during their 2-hour social sessions than during noninteraction periods: interaction = 4.41, noninteraction = 1.53 intervals; $F(1, 2) = 14.81$, $p < .05$. The initial adaptation period served to reduce emergence trauma, while the half-high barriers appeared to increase visual interaction with the therapist monkeys.

Social Contact Adaptation Period

During the first 2 weeks of social experience, isolate-reared subjects paired with each other were socially incompetent in comparison to therapist subjects paired with each other. As indicated in Figure 3, isolate-reared subjects displayed significantly higher levels of self-clasp, $F(1, 4) = 9.39$, $p < .05$, rock, $F(1, 4) = 16.57$, $p < .025$, and huddle, $F(1, 4) = 33.47$, $p < .005$, and significantly lower levels of social play, $F(1, 4) = 21.24$, $p < .01$, and visual exploration, $F(1, 4) = 10.72$, $p < .05$, than the therapist subjects. Although there were no main effects of sex, there was a significant group by sex interaction for visual exploration, $F(1, 4) = 7.79$, $p < .05$. Female therapist monkeys displayed higher levels of visual exploration than all other subgroups, and male therapist monkeys showed higher levels of visual exploration than any isolate-reared subgroup. No differences between the isolate and therapist monkeys were detected for any other measured behaviors.

It is important to note, however, that there were marked individual differences in the

Figure 3. Behavior of isolate and therapist monkeys exhibited during the social contact adaptation period (isolates paired with isolates, therapists paired with therapists).

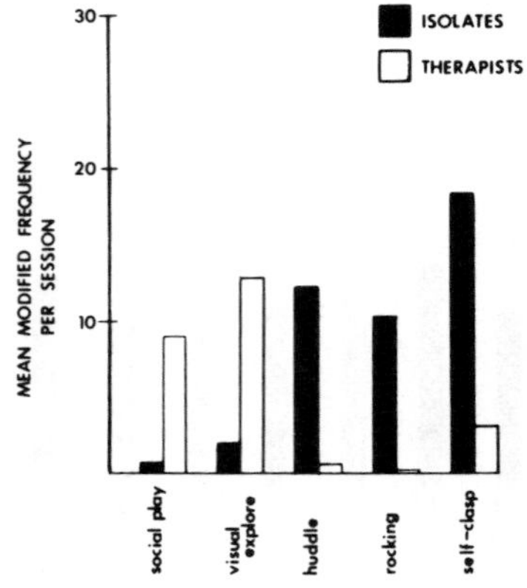

response of the isolate subjects to contact with one another. Two monkeys, a male and female, were quite active during social encounters, while the remaining two monkeys were withdrawn during social interaction. Pairing the two active monkeys with each other resulted in rudimentary play attempts on the very first day of social exposure. Self-directed behaviors occurred less frequently with this pair than with the other pairs. Self-directed responses of huddling and self-clasping occurred with high frequency when the two withdrawn monkeys were paired. When the active male was paired with either withdrawn monkey, his approaches and contact resulted in screeching and crouching by the withdrawn subjects. In most instances the active male continued his contact by mouthing but not biting the back of the crouched monkey. The active female made initial approaches but then ignored the withdrawn monkeys when she was paired with them.

Therapy Period Behaviors

Behaviors in home quadrant of quad cage. Figure 4 illustrates the homecage behaviors of the isolate and therapist monkeys during the 6-month therapy period. Isolate-reared subjects continued to display higher overall levels of self-clasp, $F(1, 4) = 19.25$, $p < .025$, and huddling, $F(1, 4) = 10.02$, $p < .05$), and lower levels of visual exploration, $F(1, 4) = 14.81$, $p < .025$, and tactile-oral exploration, $F(1, 4) = 10.71$, $p < .05$, than the therapist subjects. However, there was some improvement in the isolate behavioral repertoire as indicated by significant group with time interactions for locomotion, $F(17, 72) = 1.95$, $p < .025$, stereotypy, $F(17, 72) = 2.23$, $p < .01$, and rocking, $F(17, 72) = 4.07$, $p < .001$. Figure 5 demonstrates that both rocking and stereotypy declined in the isolated subjects over the therapy period while locomotion increased. There were no differences between isolate-reared and therapist subjects for any other measured behaviors.

The data analysis also revealed two rearing

Figure 4. Homecage behaviors of isolate and therapist monkeys during the therapy period.

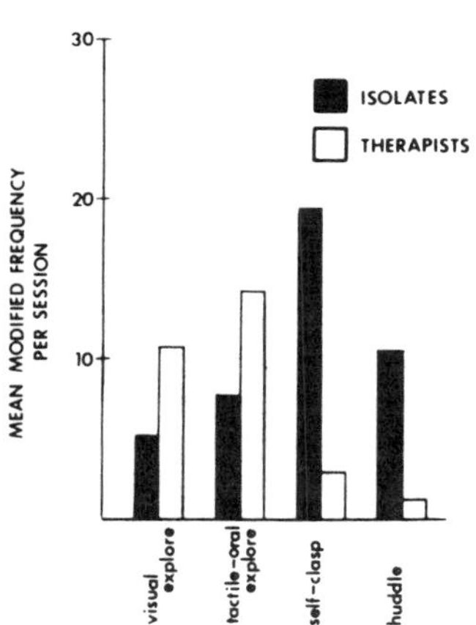

Figure 5. Time-related changes in homecage behaviors of isolate and therapist monkeys during the therapy period.

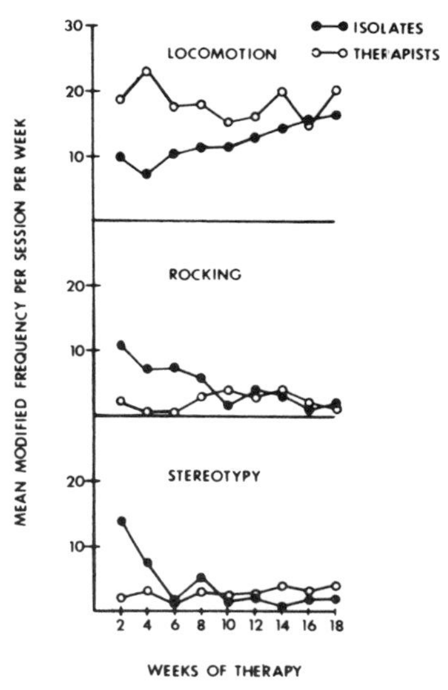

conditions with sex interactions for stereotypy. $F(1, 4) = 24.96$, $p < .01$, and tactile-oral exploration, $F(1, 4) = 17.61$, $p < .025$. The therapist males displayed a significantly lower level of stereotypic behavior patterns than all other subgroups, while the therapist females exhibited higher levels of tactile-oral exploration than all other subgroups. Even though some aberrant isolate homecage behaviors did decrease as a function of the therapy procedure, other self-directed behavior patterns persisted at the levels observed in isolation.

Behaviors in the social playroom. Although the isolate-reared subjects did not display a reduction in most self-directed behaviors during the homecage testing of the therapy period, such a reduction was observed during social interaction with the therapist monkeys. Even though the data analysis revealed significant differences in the levels of self-clasp, $F(1, 4) = 47.79$, $p < .01$, huddle, $F(1, 4) = 10.21$, $p < .05$, rock, $F(1, 4) = 19.47$, $p < .025$, self-mouth, $F(1, 4) = 16.83$, $p < .025$ (mean for isolates = 7.31, for therapists = 2.45), social contact, $F(1, 4) = 16.83$, $p < .025$, social play, $F(1, 4) = 14.27$, $p < .025$), and visual exploration, $F(1, 4) = 21.27$, $p < .025$ (mean for isolates = 8.31, for therapists = 15.20) for the isolate-reared monkeys as compared to the therapist monkeys, evidence for social recovery is provided by several significant rearing conditions with time interactions. Figure 6 indicates that the self-directed behaviors, self-clasp, $F(17, 72) = 3.86$, $p < .001$, rock, $F(17, 72) = 1.96$, $p < .025$, and huddle, $F(17, 72) = 3.30$, $p < .005$, of the isolate-reared subjects decreased to the levels manifested by the therapist subjects at the end of the therapy period. Furthermore, levels of environmentally directed behaviors such as social contact, $F(17, 72) = 1.72$, $p < .05$, tactile-oral exploration, $F(17, 72) = 2.92$, $p < .005$, and social play, $F(17, 72) = 1.98$, $p < .025$, displayed by the isolated subjects increased to those of the therapist subjects by the end of the therapy period. An overall effect of sex on levels of social play was also found in which males played more often than females, $M = 8.71$ versus 4.99, respectively, $F(1, 4) = 10.25$, $p < .05$. There were no differences between isolated-reared monkeys and therapist monkeys for any other measured behaviors.

During playroom sessions the interaction between the isolate and therapist monkeys was characterized by partner preferences. In general, isolates interacted slightly more often with isolates, and therapists interacted more often with therapists. During cross-group encounters the male isolates interacted almost exclusively with a particular male therapist monkey. No such preference for a particular therapist monkey was detected for the female isolates who preferred interacting with each other.

Figure 6. Time-related changes in behaviors of isolate and therapist monkeys exhibited during social therapy sessions.

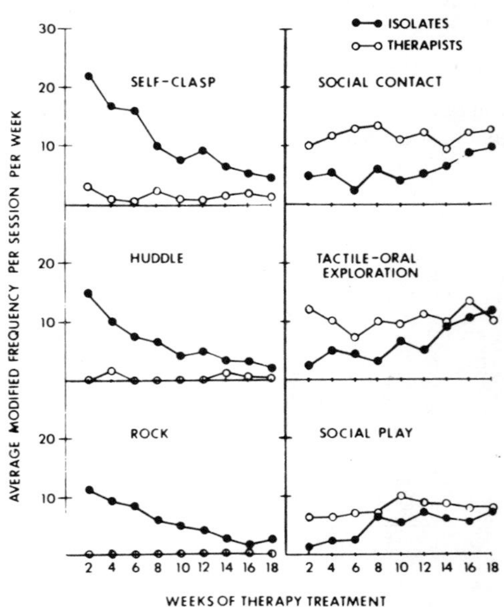

Although there were no differences between isolate-reared and therapist subjects with regard to the incidence of threat or aggressive behaviors, the isolate-reared subjects were clearly dominant over the therapists in the playroom. Dominance was ascertained by both successful displacement of the therapist monkeys from shelves, ledges, and desired objects and actual aggressive responses directed to the therapist monkeys. The therapist monkeys did not displace or aggress the isolate monkeys. The failure to observe group differences was reflected in the fact that the aggressed or displaced therapist animal, if male, often proceeded to aggress or displace another therapist monkey. Although displacement occurred frequently, aggression occurred rarely and was usually instigated by either the active male or female isolate.

Thus, under social therapy conditions, isolated subjects exhibited significant changes in their behavior. Self-directed responses declined steadily to low levels, while social behaviors became prominent in the presence of younger, more socially sophisticated therapist monkeys.

DISCUSSION

Monkeys raised for the first year of life in total social isolation have been characterized as social vegetables which display high levels of self-directed, idiosyncratic behavior both in the presence and absence of social companions. Such debilitating effects of total social isolation have traditionally been considered to be not only pervasive, but also permanent. The findings of the present study, however, clearly demonstrate that monkeys raised without any social experience during the first year of life can learn to be social under appropriate conditions. As in most learning situations, development of social behaviors in isolated monkeys is hypothesized to depend upon techniques that initially reduce anxiety in the new situation, that subsequently reduce interfering behaviors, and that finally promote the desired positive behaviors. Correspondingly, rehabilitation of monkeys raised in isolation for the first year of life was achieved by the use of three such techniques — adaptation, self-pacing of visual input, and exposure to younger therapist monkeys.

Although the present research did not attempt to assess the relative importance of each therapy procedure, nor the order in which the therapies were instituted, it is clear from previous research that exposure to younger therapist monkeys was important for rehabilitation. The need for adaptation and self-pacing of visual input can be measured only indirectly.

The need for adaptation in this study was indicated by the presence of emergence trauma and by playroom adaptation data. According to Fuller and Clark (1966) the presence of emergence trauma in isolated subjects is related to the marked change in complexity from the sterile isolation environment to the complex home cage environment. Since isolated monkeys exhibiting this trauma were extremely withdrawn and fearful, it was important to adapt the monkeys to the new home cage prior to permitting social contact so that such contact would not come to be associated with this heightened fearfulness. Unlike Fuller and Clark, we do not conclude that the lack of sociality in isolate-reared subjects was produced by this emergence trauma, since such trauma dissipated in a 2-week adaptation period, while social behaviors appeared only after extensive exposure to the therapist monkeys.

The importance of adaptation was also indicated by the isolates' initial responses to the brightly colored playroom. During the very first hour of playroom exposure each isolate sat in one corner of the floor and did not move one inch in any direction. After movement commenced two sessions later, the isolates made unusual responses to the apparatus. In one case a male isolate climbed a ladder to a high shelf. Instead of moving onto the shelf, however, he reached out one hand and tentatively touched the shelf in several places. He then backed down the ladder. This particular sequence of behaviors was performed a total of about 40 times over a number of test sessions until the subject finally moved onto the shelf. The sequence disappeared thereafter, demonstrating successful adaptation to these more complex surroundings. Previous research had demonstrated that animals respond positively to moderate changes in their environment and withdraw or fail to respond to extreme environmental alterations (Sackett, 1965). We propose, then, that social contact prior to such adaptation to moderate environmental changes would have slowed the rehabilitation process.

Although the use of half-high barriers was associated with an increase in interest in the therapist monkeys as measured by the isolates' looking behavior, there is no direct evidence to suggest that such interest was produced by these barriers. It is important to note, however, that the two isolates with the highest watching scores were also the same two monkeys that displayed rudimentary play attempts to each other on the very first day of social exposure. In this context, it is possible that the barriers might have facilitated some rudimentary isolate imitation of the therapists' social behaviors.

It was the exposure to the younger therapist monkeys, however, that further reduced isolate self-directed behavior patterns and that accounted almost entirely for the appearance of appropriate social behaviors, including extensive social contact and sophisticated social play. Previous research had already indicated that intimate physical contact was necessary for social recovery, since partial isolates (monkeys raised so that they could see, hear, but not touch other monkeys) failed to acquire appropriate social responsivity (Harlow & Harlow, 1965). The type of contact was crucial as isolates paired with each other after extensive adaptation did not develop sophisticated social patterns (see also Suomi, 1973). Nor, according to previous studies, were such patterns developed by isolates exposed to socially experienced age-mates (Clark, 1968; Rowland, 1964). This is not surprising in light of a learning interpretation, since neither exposure to a socially incompetent partner nor to one which was too socially advanced would be conducive to a gradual acquisition of basic social skills. What is required, then, is a situation in which the animal can learn to be social. We hypothesize that development of social behaviors depends upon exposing the animal to social interactions at their most elementary level followed by increasing levels of complexity. In this regard, the younger therapist monkey is a realized ideal, for its social interactions are initially simple, but gradually increase as a function of experience and age. Pairing newly emerged isolate-reared monkeys with sophisticated age-mate monkeys, with the expectation of observing some social behavior, is equivalent to asking a naive monkey to solve an oddity problem without providing adaptation to the test apparatus or exposure to simpler problems.

With regard to the theoretical models which have been applied to the isolation rearing phenomenon, the present study provides evidence contrary to a critical period interpretation. A similar position was previously outlined by Suomi and Harlow (1972) following their successful rehabilitation of 6-month isolate-reared monkeys. However, a critical period for social development might conceivably last longer than 6 months. The present study therefore offers a compelling argument against the critical period interpretation since a 1-year incarceration period, spanning nearly the entire infancy of the subjects, should be sufficiently long to produce permanent deficits if the critical period theory were applicable. Admittedly our evidence is based on the rather immature social capabilities of monkeys during the second year of life. However, follow-up studies of the grooming and sexual patterns displayed by these isolate-reared subjects essentially support our position.

Since the critical period theory fails to account for the behavior developed as a consequence of isolation, the lack of sociality following removal from isolation, and the subsequent acquisition of sociality following rehabilitation, we propose as an alternative an environment-specific learning hypothesis to explain these findings. According to this hypothesis, an animal acquires a behavioral repertoire reflecting the complex interplay between the animal's basic needs and the ability of the environment to satisfy these needs. Basic needs for an infant rhesus monkey might include nourishment, stimulation, and contact comfort. Depending upon the nature of the environment, satisfaction of a particular need such as stimulation might require the development of different behaviors. For infant monkeys reared with a mother and peers, much stimulation comes from external animate and inanimate objects. For the infant reared in isolation, there is no stimulation from animate objects and only minimal stimulation from the barren walls of the isolation chamber. As a compensation for the low levels of stimulation it appears that the infant redirects its externally oriented activity to itself as is evidenced by the typical isolate patterns of self-clasping, self-mouthing, and stereotypic rocking. Self-clasping responses develop because the infant possesses a strong clasping reflex and clasps the only body available, its own.

Self-mouthing serves as a substitute for suckling. Rocking movements would also seem to provide stimulation, and in this context it is interesting to note that socially restricted infant monkeys reared on moving inanimate surrogates did not display rocking movements (Mason, 1963). Isolate-reared monkeys, then, adopt patterns of behavior that are functional in the isolation chamber, but nonfunctional for social situations.

According to our hypothesis, monkeys newly emerged from isolation do not display complex social behaviors primarily because they did not have the opportunity to learn these behaviors at the time when such learning normally occurs. We do not mean to imply that such behaviors must be learned from older, experienced animals, since monkeys eventually develop these skills even if reared from infancy with only age-mate animals as companions. The infant rhesus monkey appears to be predisposed to develop patterns of play, grooming, and rudimentary sexual behavior, but the maintenance and elaboration of these developmental sequences require the appropriate stimulation (namely, another monkey with which to interact). In the absence of such stimulation the infant fills the void by developing an entirely different sequence of behaviors. However, the present study has strikingly demonstrated that the ability to acquire many normal, species-typical behavior patterns is not lost, but may be suppressed by inappropriate stimulation. Isolate-reared monkeys can learn to be social but only under carefully selected and controlled conditions. In the absence of adaptation procedures and gradually increasing exposure to social stimulation, isolates will never learn to prefer interaction to withdrawal.

REFERENCE NOTE

1. Novak, M. A. *Social recovery of monkeys isolated for the first year of life. II. Test of therapy.* Manuscript in preparation, 1974.

REFERENCES

Bloomquist, A. J., & Harlow, H. F. The infant rhesus monkey program at the University of Wisconsin Primate Laboratory. *Proceedings of the Animal Care Panel,* 1961, *11,* 57–64.

Clark, D. L. *Immediate and delayed effects of early, intermediate, and late social isolation in the rhesus monkey.* Unpublished doctoral dissertation, University of Wisconsin — Madison, 1968.

Duncan, D. B. Multiple range and multiple *F* tests. *Biometrics,* 1955, *11,* 1–42.

Fuller, J. L., & Clark, L. D. Genetic and treatment factors modifying the postisolation syndrome in dogs. *Journal of Comparative and Physiological Psychology,* 1966, *61,* 251–257.

Gluck, J. P., Harlow, H. F., & Schiltz, K. A. Differential effects of early enrichment and deprivation on learning in the rhesus monkey (*Macaca mulatta*). *Journal of Comparative and Physiological Psychology,* 1973, *84,* 598–604.

Harlow, H. F., Dodsworth, R. O., & Harlow, M. K. Total social isolation in monkeys. *Proceedings of the National Academy of Sciences,* 1965, *54,* 90–96.

Harlow, H. F., & Harlow, M. K. Effects of various mother-infant relationships on rhesus monkey behaviors. In B. M. Foss (Ed.), *Determinants of infant behavior* (Vol. 4). London: Methuen, 1965.

Harlow, H. F., Harlow, M. K., Dodsworth, R. O., & Arling, G. L. Maternal behavior of rhesus monkeys deprived of mothering and peer associations in infancy. *Proceedings of the American Philosophical Society,* 1966, *110,* 58–66.

Harlow, H. F., & Novak, M. A. Psychopathological perspectives. *Perspectives in Biology and Medicine,* 1973, *16,* 461–478.

Harlow, H. F., Schiltz, K. A., & Harlow, M. K. Effects of social isolation on the learning performance of rhesus monkeys. In C. R. Carpenter (Ed.), *Proceedings of the Second International Congress of Primatology* (Vol. 1). New York: Karger, 1969.

Harlow, H. F., & Suomi, S. J. The nature of love — simplified. *American Psychologist,* 1970, *25,* 161–168.

Harlow, H. F., & Suomi, S. J. Production of depressive behaviors in young monkeys. *Journal of Autism and Childhood Schizophrenia,* 1971, *1,* 246–255.

Hebb, D. O. *The Organization of Behavior.* New York: Wiley, 1949.

Lessac, M. S. *Effects of early isolation and restriction on the later behavior of beagle puppies.* Unpublished doctoral dissertation, University of Pennsylvania, 1965.

Mason, W. A. Social development of rhesus monkeys with restricted social experience. *Perceptual and Motor Skills,* 1963, *16,* 263–270.

Riesen, A. H. Effects of stimulus deprivation on the development and atrophy of the visual sensory system. *American Journal of Orthopsychiatry,* 1960, *30,* 23.

Rowland, G. L. *The effects of total isolation upon the learning and social behavior of rhesus monkeys.* Unpublished doctoral dissertation, University of Wisconsin — Madison, 1964.

Sackett, G. P. Effects of sensory deprivation level, visual complexity and age upon light contingent responses during rearing. *Animal Behavior,* 1965, *13,* 393–399.

Sackett, G. P. Abnormal behavior in laboratory-reared rhesus monkeys. In M. W. Fox (Ed.), *Abnormal behavior in animals.* Philadelphia: Saunders, 1968. (a)

Sackett, G. P. The persistence of abnormal behavior in monkeys following isolation rearing. In R. Porter (Ed.), *The role of learning in psychotherapy.* London: Churchill, 1968. (b)

Scott, J. P. Critical periods in behavioral development. *Science,* 1962, *138,* 949–958.

Senko, M. G. The effects of early, intermediate, and late experiences upon adult macaque sexual behavior. Unpublished master's thesis, University of Wisconsin — Madison, 1966.

Suomi, S. J. Surrogate rehabilitation of monkeys reared in total social isolation. *Journal of Child Psychology and Psychiatry,* 1973, *14,* 71–77.

Suomi, S. J., & Harlow, H. F. Apparatus conceptualization for psychopathological research in monkeys. *Behavior Research Methods and Instrumentation,* 1969, *1,* 247–250.

Suomi, S. J., & Harlow, H. F. Social rehabilitation of isolate-reared monkeys. *Developmental Psychology,* 1972, *6,* 487–496.

6 Mary D. Salter Ainsworth

INFANT–MOTHER ATTACHMENT

Bowlby's (1969) ethological–evolutionary attachment theory implies that it is an essential part of the ground plan of the human species — as well as that of many other species — for an infant to become attached to a mother figure. This figure need not be the natural mother but can be anyone who plays the role of principal caregiver. This ground plan is fulfilled, except under extraordinary circumstances when the baby experiences too little interaction with any one caregiver to support the formation of an attachment. The literature on maternal deprivation describes some of these circumstances, but it cannot be reviewed here, except to note that research has not yet specified an acceptable minimum amount of interaction required for attachment formation.

However, there have been substantial recent advances in the areas of individual differences in the way attachment behavior becomes organized, differential experiences associated with the various attachment patterns, and the value of such patterns in forecasting subsequent development. These advances have been much aided by a standardized laboratory situation that was devised to supplement a naturalistic, longitudinal investigation of the development of infant–mother attachment in the first year of life. This *strange situation,* as we entitled it, has proved to be an excellent basis for the assessment of such attachment in 1-year-olds (Ainsworth, Blehar, Waters, & Wall, 1978).

The assessment procedure consists of classification according to the pattern of behavior shown in the strange situation, particularly in the episodes of reunion after separation. Eight patterns were identified, but I shall deal here only with the three main groups into which they fell — Groups A, B, and C. To summarize, Group B babies use their mothers as a secure base from which to explore in the preseparation episodes; their attachment behavior is greatly intensified by the separation episodes so that exploration diminishes and distress is likely; and in the reunion episodes they seek contact with, proximity to, or at least interaction with their mothers. Group C babies tend to show some signs of anxiety even in the preseparation episodes; they are intensely distressed by separation; and in the reunion episodes they are ambivalent with the mother, seeking close contact with her and yet resisting contact or interaction. Group A babies, in sharp contrast, rarely cry in the separation episodes and, in the reunion episodes, avoid the mother, either mingling proximity-seeking and avoidant behaviors or ignoring her altogether.

Comparison of Strange-Situation Behavior and Behavior Elsewhere

Groups A, B, and C in our longitudinal sample were compared in regard to their behavior at home during the first year. Stayton and Ainsworth (1973) had identified a security–anxiety dimension in a factor analysis of fourth-quarter infant behavior. Group B infants were identified as securely attached because they significantly more often displayed behaviors characteristic of the secure pole of this dimension, whereas both of the other groups were identified as anxious because their behaviors were characteristic of the anxious pole. A second dimension was clearly related to close bodily contact, and this was important in distinguishing Group A babies from those in the other two groups, in that Group A babies behaved less positively to being held and yet more negatively to being put down. The groups were also distinguished by two behaviors not included in the factor analysis — cooperativeness and anger. Group B babies were more cooperative and less angry than either A or C babies; Group A babies were even more angry than those in Group C. Clearly, something went awry in the physical-contact interaction Group A babies had with their mothers, and as I explain below, I believe it is this that makes them especially prone to anger.

Ainsworth et al. (1978) reviewed findings of other investigators who had compared A–B–C groups of 1-year-olds in terms of their behavior elsewhere. Their findings regarding socioemotional behavior support the summary just cited, and in addition three investigations using cognitive measures found an advantage in favor of the securely attached.

Comparison of Infant Strange-Situation Behavior with Maternal Home Behavior

Mothers of the securely attached (Group B) babies were, throughout the first year, more sensitively responsive to infant signals than were the mothers of the two anxiously attached groups, in terms of a variety of measures spanning all of the most common contexts for mother–infant interaction (Ainsworth et al., 1978). Such responsiveness, I suggest, enables an infant to form expectations, primitive at first, that moderate his or her responses to events, both internal and environmental. Gradually, such an infant constructs an inner representation — or "working model" (Bowlby, 1969) — of his or her mother as generally accessible and responsive to him or her. Therein lies his or her security. In contrast, babies whose mothers have disregarded their signals, or have responded to them belatedly or in a grossly inappropriate fashion, have no basis for believing the mother to be accessible and responsive; consequently they are anxious, not knowing what to expect of her.

In regard to interaction in close bodily contact, the most striking finding is that the mothers of avoidant (Group A) babies all evinced a deep-seated aversion to it, whereas none of the other mothers did. In addition they were more rejecting, more often angry, and yet more restricted in the expression of affect than were Group B or C mothers. Main (e.g., in press) and Ainsworth et al. (1978) have presented a theoretical account of the dynamics of interaction of avoidant babies and their rejecting mothers. This emphasizes the acute approach–avoidance conflict experienced by these infants when their attachment behavior is activated at high intensity — a conflict stemming from painful rebuff consequent upon seeking close bodily contact. Avoidance is viewed as a defensive maneuver, lessening the anxiety and anger experienced in the conflict situation and enabling the baby nevertheless to remain within a tolerable range of proximity to the mother.

Findings and interpretations such as these raise the issue of direction of effects. To what extent is the pattern of attachment of a baby attributable to the mother's behavior throughout the first year, and to what extent is it attributable to built-in differences in potential and temperament? I have considered this problem elsewhere (Ainsworth, 1979) and have concluded that in our sample of normal babies there is a strong case to be made for differences in attachment quality being attributable to maternal behavior. Two studies, however (Connell, 1976; Waters, Vaughn, & Egeland, in press), have suggested that Group C babies may as newborns be constitutionally "difficult." Particularly if the mother's personality or life situation makes it hard for her to be sensitively responsive to infant cues, such a baby seems indeed likely to form an attachment relationship of anxious quality.

CONTEXTS OF MOTHER–INFANT INTERACTION

Of the various contexts in which mother–infant interaction commonly takes place, the face-to-face situation has been the focus of most recent research. By many (e.g., Walters & Parke, 1965), interaction mediated by distance receptors and behaviors has been judged especially important in the establishment of human relationships. Microanalytic studies, based on frame-by-frame analysis of film records, show clearly that maternal sensitivity to infant behavioral cues is essential for successful pacing of face-to-face interaction (e.g., Brazelton, Koslowski, & Main, 1974; Stern, 1974). Telling evidence of the role of vision, both in the infant's development of attachment to the mother and in the mother's responsiveness to the infant, comes from Fraiberg's (1977) longitudinal study of blind infants.

So persuasive have been the studies of interaction involving distance receptors that interaction involving close bodily contact has been largely ignored. The evolutionary perspective of attachment theory attributes focal importance to bodily contact. Other primate species rely on the maintenance of close mother–infant contact as crucial for infant survival. Societies of hunter–gatherers, living much as the earliest humans did, are conspicuous for very much more mother–infant contact than are western societies (e.g., Konner, 1976). Blurton Jones (1972) presented evidence suggesting that humans evolved as a species in which infants are carried by the mother and are fed at frequent intervals, rather than as a species in which infants are left for long periods, are cached in a safe place, and are fed but infrequently. Bowlby (1969) pointed out that when attachment behavior is intensely activated it is close bodily contact that is specifically required. Indeed, Bell and Ainsworth (1972) found that even with the white, middle-class mothers of their sample, the most frequent and the most effective response to an infant's crying throughout the first year was to pick up the baby. A recent analysis of our longitudinal findings (Blehar, Ainsworth, & Main, Note 1) suggests that mother–infant interaction relevant to close bodily contact is at least as important a context of interaction as face-to-face is, perhaps especially in the first few months of life. Within the limits represented by our sample, however, we found that it was *how* the mother holds her baby rather than *how much* she holds him or her that affects the way in which attachment develops.

In recent years the feeding situation has been neglected as a context for mother–infant interaction, except insofar as it is viewed as a setting for purely social, face-to-face interaction. Earlier, mother's gratification or frustration of infant was of interest to both psychoanalytically oriented and social-learning research, on the assumption that a mother's gratification or frustration of infant instinctual drives, or her role as a secondary reinforcer, determined the nature of the baby's tie to her. Such research yielded no evidence that methods of feeding significantly affected the course of infant development, although these negative findings seem almost certainly to reflect methodological deficiencies (Caldwell, 1964). In contrast, we have found that sensitive maternal responsiveness to infant signals relevant to feeding is closely related to the security or anxiety of attachment that eventually develops (Ainsworth & Bell, 1969). Indeed, this analysis seemed to redefine the meaning of "demand" feeding — letting infant behavioral cues determine not only when feeding is begun but also when it is terminated, how the pacing of feeding proceeds, and how new foods are introduced.

Our findings do not permit us to attribute overriding importance to any one context of mother–infant interaction. Whether the context is feeding, close bodily contact, face-to-face interaction, or indeed the situation defined by the infant's crying, mother–infant interaction provides the baby with opportunity to build up expectations of the mother and, eventually, a working model of her as more or less accessible and responsive. Indeed, our findings suggest that a mother who is sensitively responsive to signals in one context tends also to be responsive to signals in other contexts.

PRACTICAL IMPLICATIONS FOR INTERVENTION

What I have so far summarized about research findings pertaining both to contexts of interaction and to qualitative differences in infant–mother attachment has implications for parenting education, for intervention by professionals to help a mother to achieve better interaction with her baby, and for the practices of substitute caregivers. I cannot go into detail here — and indeed such detail would need to be based on much fuller reports of the relevant research than I am able to include here. Among the intervention programs with which I am familiar, some parent–child development centers have reported success in the application of our research findings in improving and sustaining the rate of development of very young children through improving the quality of mother–infant interaction (e.g., Andrews, Blumenthal, Bache, & Wiener, Note 2). Furthermore, the expert clinical interventions of Fraiberg and her associates with families at risk have focused on increasing maternal responsiveness to infant behavioral cues (e.g., Shapiro, Fraiberg, & Adelson, 1976). It may be that such intervention, although obviously expensive, provides the most effective mode of helping dyads in which the difficulty stems from deep-seated difficulties in the mother's personality, such as the aversion to bodily contact characteristic of our Group A mothers.

USING THE MOTHER AS A SECURE BASE FROM WHICH TO EXPLORE

Attachment theory conceives of the behavioral system serving attachment as only one of several important systems, each with its own activators, terminators, predictable outcomes, and functions. During the prolonged period of human infancy, when the protective function of attachment is especially important, its interplay with exploratory behavior is noteworthy. The function of exploration is learning about the environment — which is particularly important in a species possessing much potential for adaptation to a wide range of environments. Attachment and exploration support each other. When attachment behavior is intensely activated, a baby tends to seek proximity/contact rather than exploring; when attachment behavior is at low intensity a baby is free to respond to the pull of novelty. The presence of an attachment figure, particularly one who is believed to be accessible and responsive, leaves the baby open to stimulation that may activate exploration.

Nevertheless, it is often believed that somehow attachment may interfere with the development of independence. Our studies provide no support for such a belief. For example, Blehar et al. (Note 1) found that babies who respond positively to close bodily contact with their mothers also tend to respond positively to being put down again and to move off into independent exploratory play. Fostering the growth of secure attachment facilitates rather than hampers the growth of healthy self-reliance (Bowlby, 1973).

RESPONSE TO SEPARATION FROM ATTACHMENT FIGURES

Schaffer (1971) suggested that the crucial criterion for whether a baby has become attached to a specific figure is that he or she does not consider this figure interchangeable with any other figure. Thus, for an infant to protest the mother's departure or continued absence is a dependable criterion for attachment (Schaffer & Callender, 1959). This does not imply that protest is an invariable response to separation from an attachment figure under all circumstances; the context of the separation influences the likelihood and intensity of protest. Thus there is ample evidence, which cannot be cited here, that protest is unlikely to occur, at least initially, in the case of voluntary separations, when the infant willingly leaves the mother in order to explore elsewhere. Protest is less likely to occur if the baby is left with another attachment figure than if he or she is left with an unfamiliar person or alone. Being left in an unfamiliar environment is more distressing than comparable separations in the familiar environment of the home — in which many infants are able to build up expectations that reassure them of mother's accessibility and responsiveness even though she may be absent. Changes attributable to developmental processes affect separation protest in complex ways. Further research will undoubtedly be able to account for these shifts in terms of progressive cognitive achievements.

Major separations of days, months, or even years must be distinguished from the very brief separations, lasting only minutes, that have been studied most intensively both in the laboratory and at home. Securely attached infants may be able to tolerate very brief separations with equanimity, yet they are likely to be distressed in major separations, especially when cared for by unfamiliar persons in unfamiliar environments. Even so, Robertson and Robertson (1971) showed that sensitive substitute parenting can do much to mute separation distress and avert the more serious consequences of major separations.

Despite a steady increase in our understanding of the complexities of response to and effects of separation from attachment figures in infancy and early childhood, it is difficult to suggest clear-cut guidelines for parents and others responsible for infant and child care. So much depends on the circumstances under which separation takes place, on the degree to which the separation environment can substitute satisfactorily for home and parents, on the child's stage of development and previous experience, and on the nature of his or her relationship with attachment figures. No wonder that the issue of the separations implicit in day care is controversial. Further research is clearly needed. Meanwhile, it would seem wise for parents — if they have a choice — to move cautiously rather than plunging into substitute-care arrangements with a blithe assumption that all is bound to go well.

OTHER ATTACHMENT FIGURES

Many have interpreted Bowlby's attachment theory as claiming that an infant can become attached to only one person — the mother. This is a mistaken interpretation. There are, however, three implications of attachment theory relevant to the issue of "multiple" attachments. First, as reported by Ainsworth (1967) and Schaffer and Emerson (1964), infants are highly selective in their choices of attachment figures from among the various persons familiar to them. No infant has been observed to have many attachment figures. Second, not all social relationships may be identified as attachments. Harlow (1971) distinguished between the infant–mother and peer–peer affectional systems, although under certain circumstances peers may become attachment figures in the absence of anyone more appropriate (see, e.g., Freud & Dann, 1951; Harlow, 1963). Third, the fact that a baby may have several attachment figures does not imply that they are all equally important. Bowlby (1969) suggested that they are not — that there is a principal attachment figure, usually the principal caregiver, and one or more secondary figures. Thus a hierarchy is implied. A baby may both enjoy and derive security from all of his or her attachment figures but, under certain circumstances (e.g., illness, fatigue, stress), is likely to show a clear preference among them.

In recent years there has been a surge of interest in the father as an attachment figure. . . . Relatively lacking is research into attachments to caregivers other than parents. Do babies become attached to their regular babysitters or to caregivers in day-care centers? Studies by Fleener (1973), Farran and Ramey (1977), and Ricciuti (1974) have suggested that they may but that the preference is nevertheless for the mother figure. Fox (1977) compared the mother and the *metapelet* as providers of security to kibbutz-reared infants in a strange situation, but surely much more research is needed into the behavior of infants and young children toward caregivers as attachment figures in the substitute-care environment.

CONSEQUENCES OF ATTACHMENT

A number of investigators, including Main (1973, Note 3), Matas, Arend, and Sroufe (1978), and Waters, Wittman, and Sroufe (in press), having assessed the quality of 1-year-olds' attachment, have followed the children through to ascertain whether this assessment bears a significant relationship to later behavioral measures in the second, third, or even sixth year of life. We (Ainsworth et al., 1978) have reviewed these investigations in some detail; only a brief summary can be given here.

In comparison with anxiously attached infants, those who are securely attached as 1-year-olds are later more cooperative with and affectively more positive as well as less aggressive and/or avoidant toward their mothers and other less familiar adults. Later on, they emerge as more competent and more sympathetic in interaction with peers. In free-play situations they have longer bouts of exploration and display more intense exploratory interest, and in problem-solving situations they are more enthusiastic, more persistent, and better able to elicit and accept their mothers' help. They are more curious, more self-directed, more ego-resilient — and they usually tend to achieve better scores on both developmental tests and measures of language development. Some studies also reported differences between the two groups of anxiously attached infants, with the avoidant ones (Group A) continuing to be more aggressive, noncompliant, and avoidant, and the ambivalent ones (Group C) emerging as more easily frustrated, less persistent, and generally less competent.

CONCLUSION

It is clear that the nature of an infant's attachment to his or her mother as a 1-year-old is related both to earlier interaction with the mother and to various aspects of later development. The implication is that the way in which the infant organizes his or her behavior toward the mother affects the way in which he or she organizes behavior toward other aspects of the environment, both animate and inanimate. This organization provides a core of continuity in development despite changes that come with developmental acquisitions, both cognitive and socioemotional.

This is not to insist that the organization of attachment is fixed in the first year of life and is insensitive to marked changes in maternal behavior or to relevant life events occurring later on. Nor is it implied that attachments to figures other than the mother are unimportant as supplementing or compensating for anxieties in infant–mother attachment — although too little is yet known about how various attachments relate together to influence the way in which infants organize their perception of and approach to the world. Despite the need for further research, however, the yield of findings to date provides relevant leads for policies, education in parenting, and intervention procedures intended to further the welfare of infants and young children.

REFERENCE NOTES

1. Blehar, M. C., Ainsworth, M. D. S., & Main, M. *Mother–infant interaction relevant to close bodily contact.* Monograph in preparation, 1979.

2. Andrews, S. R., Blumenthal, J. B., Bache, W. L., III, & Wiener, G. *Fourth year report: New Orleans Parent–Child Development Center.* Unpublished document, March 1975. (Available from Susan R. Andrews, 6917 Glenn Street, Metairie, Louisiana 70003.)

3. Main, M., & Londerville, S. B. *Compliance and aggression in toddlerhood: Precursors and correlates.* Paper in preparation, 1979.

REFERENCES

Ainsworth, M. D. S. *Infancy in Uganda: Infant care and the growth of love.* Baltimore, Md.: Johns Hopkins Press, 1967.

Ainsworth, M. D. S. Attachment as related to mother–infant interaction. In J. S. Rosenblatt, R. A. Hinde, C. Beer, & M. Busnel (Eds.), *Advances in the study of behavior* (Vol. 9). New York: Academic Press, 1979.

Ainsworth, M. D. S., & Bell, S. M. Some contemporary patterns of mother–infant interaction in the feeding situation. In A. Ambrose (Ed.), *Stimulation in early infancy.* London: Academic Press, 1969.

Ainsworth, M. D. S., Blehar, M. C., Waters, E., & Wall, S. *Patterns of attachment: A psychological study of the strange situation.* Hillsdale, N.J.: Erlbaum, 1978.

Bell, S. M., & Ainsworth, M. D. S. Infant crying and maternal responsiveness. *Child Development,* 1972, *43,* 1171–1190.

Blurton Jones, N. G. Comparative aspects of mother–child contact. In N. G. Blurton Jones (Ed.), *Ethological studies of child behavior.* London: Cambridge University Press, 1972.

Bowlby, J. *Attachment and loss: Vol. 1. Attachment.* New York: Basic Books, 1969.

Bowlby, J. *Attachment and loss: Vol. 2. Separation: Anxiety and anger.* New York: Basic Books, 1973.

Brazelton, T. B., Koslowski, B., & Main, M. The origins of reciprocity: The early mother–infant interaction. In M. Lewis & L. A. Rosenblum (Eds.), *The effect of the infant on its caregiver.* New York: Wiley, 1974.

Caldwell, B. M. The effects of infant care. In M. L. Hoffman & L. W. Hoffman (Eds.), *Review of child development research* (Vol. 1). New York: Russell Sage Foundation, 1964.

Connell, D. B. *Individual differences in attachment: An investigation into stability, implications, and relationships to the structure of early language development.* Unpublished doctoral dissertation, Syracuse University, 1976.

Farran, D. C., & Ramey, C. T. Infant day care and attachment behavior toward mother and teachers. *Child Development,* 1977, *48,* 1112–1116.

Fleener, D. E. Experimental production of infant–maternal attachment behaviors. *Proceedings of the 81st Annual Convention of the American Psychological Association,* 1973, *8,* 57–58. (Summary)

Fox, N. Attachment of kibbutz infants to mother. *Child Development,* 1977, *48,* 1228–1239.

Fraiberg, S. *Insights from the blind.* New York: Basic Books, 1977.

Freud, A., & Dann, S. An experiment in group up-bringing. *Psychoanalytic Study of the Child,* 1951, *6,* 127–168.

Harlow, H. F. The maternal affectional system. In B. M. Foss (Ed.), *Determinants of infant behaviour* (Vol. 2). New York: Wiley, 1963.

Harlow, H. F. *Learning to love.* San Francisco: Albion, 1971.

Konner, M. J. Maternal care, infant behavior, and development among the !Kung. In R. B. Lee & I. DeVore (Eds.), *Kalahari hunter–gatherers.* Cambridge, Mass.: Harvard University Press, 1976.

Main, M. *Exploration, play, and level of cognitive functioning as related to child–mother attachment.* Unpublished doctoral dissertation, Johns Hopkins University, 1973.

Main, M. Avoidance in the service of proximity. In K. Immelmann, G. Barlow, M. Main, & L. Petrinovich (Eds.), *Behavioral development: The Bielefeld Interdisciplinary Project.* New York: Cambridge University Press, in press.

Matas, L., Arend, R. A., & Sroufe, L. A. Continuity of adaptation in the second year: The relationship between quality of attachment and later competence. *Child Development,* 1978, *49,* 547–556.

Ricciuti, H. N. Fear and the development of social attachments in the first year of life. In M. Lewis & L. A. Rosenblum (Eds.), *The origins of fear.* New York: Wiley, 1974.

Robertson, J., & Robertson, J. Young children in brief separation: A fresh look. *Psychoanalytic Study of the Child,* 1971, *26,* 264–315.

Schaffer, H. R. *The growth of sociability.* London: Penguin Books, 1971.

Schaffer, H. R., & Callender, W. M. Psychological effects of hospitalization in infancy. *Pediatrics,* 1959, *25,* 528–539.

Schaffer, H. R., & Emerson, P. E. The development of social attachments in infancy. *Monographs of the Society for Research in Child Development,* 1964, *3* (Serial No. 94).

Shapiro, V., Fraiberg, S., & Adelson, E. Infant–parent psychotherapy on behalf of a child in a critical nutritional state. *Psychoanalytic Study of the Child,* 1976, *31,* 461–491.

Stayton, D. J., & Ainsworth, M. D. S. Individual differences in infant responses to brief, everyday separations as related to other infant and maternal behaviors. *Developmental Psychology,* 1973, *9,* 226–235.

Stern, D. N. Mother and infant at play: The dyadic interaction involving facial, vocal, and gaze behaviors. In M. Lewis & L. A. Rosenblum (Eds.), *The effect of the infant on its caregiver.* New York: Wiley, 1974.

Walters, R. H., & Parke, R. D. The role of the distance receptors in the development of social responsiveness. In L. P. Lipsitt & C. C. Spiker (Eds.), *Advances in child development and behavior.* New York: Academic Press, 1965.

Waters, E., Vaughn, B. E., & Egeland, B. R. Individual differences in infant–mother attachment relationships at age one: Antecedents in neonatal behavior in an urban economically disadvantaged sample. *Child Development,* in press.

Waters, E., Wittman, J., & Sroufe, L. A. Attachment, positive affect, and competence in the peer group: Two studies in construct validation. *Child Development,* in press.

7

Michael E. Lamb

PATERNAL INFLUENCES AND THE FATHER'S ROLE: A PERSONAL PERSPECTIVE

It is by no means easy to review (in international perspective!) research and theory concerning the role of the father in child development. For a start, the limited empirical evidence available has been derived from studies of our own culture, one that cannot be deemed especially representative. Further, the West is currently in flux concerning gender and parental roles. Although I do not foresee an era of androgynous unisexuality, there is little doubt that some long-established assumptions, values, and attitudes concerning children, their care, and their needs are changing. Since I heartily endorse most of these changes, the perspective provided in this essay is unashamedly partisan: It represents my thoughts concerning the father's role — past, present, and future. I have not reviewed the literature systematically, nor have I provided references for most of the findings cited. Those readers who find this frustrating are invited to sample from a smorgasbord of interpretative reviews: Benson (1968), Biller (1971, 1974), Lamb (1976), Lamb and Frodi (1979), Lynn (1974), and Parke (1979) present perspectives so different that the need for further systematic, methodologically sound, and objective research will be apparent to any reader.

FATHERS — PAST AND PRESENT

The Father–Infant Relationship

The past is placed in sharpest relief when we compare it with the present, for the second half of the current decade might well be labeled the era of paternal rediscovery. Not long ago, men in our culture neither sought nor assumed active responsibility for the rearing of their children. This was especially true during the children's earlier years: Infant care was clearly perceived as the province of women. Today, however, increasing numbers of men appear eager to play an active and important role in child rearing, and a growing number of social scientists (both male and female) now recognize that for biological and social reasons, most children have two parents — one of either sex.

The ascendance of paternal consciousness has occurred as a reaction to the presumption (professional and popular) that mothers were the only socializing agents of significance to young children. This presumption of maternal preeminence had developed because mothers traditionally assumed major responsibility for child care — especially in infancy. Since mothers performed most care-

SOURCE: From Michael E. Lamb, "Paternal Influences and the Father's Role: A Personal Perspective," American Psychologist 34, 1979, pp. 938–943.

taking activities, the argument went, they must be the most important influences on their children's development. From the quite plausible conclusion that mothers were *most* important, theorists leapt to the unreasonable inference that mothers were *exclusively* important influences on children's personality development. Confidence in the importance of maternal influences was heightened by the prevailing belief in the special significance of early experiences, since mothers seemed to be involved in an overwhelming proportion of the infant's experiences.[1] By considering only the greater quantity of mother–child than of father–child contact, we neglected to acknowledge that it is the quality (not simply the quantity) of experiences that makes them salient and that fathers may make up in quality some of what they lack in quantity.

Because the presumption of maternal preeminence was so pervasive, empirical investigations of the affective salience of fathers to young infants only began within the last decade, and they have since become popular. To the evident surprise of many investigators, all studies have shown that fathers can be quite as competent and responsive as mothers (Parke, 1979) and that young infants clearly develop attachments to both parents, although most babies preferentially seek comfort from their mothers when they are distressed (see Lamb's, 1978, review). The two parent–infant relationships appear to emerge at roughly the same time in the middle of the first year of life. It is important to note, furthermore, that the babies on whose behavior these conclusions are based came from families that were not atypical in any obvious way, although there has been a marked overrepresentation of middle-class families in the samples. The fathers studied neither sought nor played major roles in the care of their infants, and the absolute amount of father–infant interaction probably averaged less than 10 hours per week.

When parents assume traditionally sex-stereotyped roles in relation to their infants, they engage in different types of interaction with them. From the earliest interactions, mothers are more likely to assume caretaking responsibilities (even when fathers are present and capable), whereas fathers interact in play — particularly, vigorous and stimulating play (Parke & O'Leary, 1976; Yogman, Dixon, Tronick, & Brazelton, Note 1). In later months, father–child interactions are still characterized by play, and mothers retain primary responsibility for caretaking (Lamb, 1978). As a result, I suspect, mothers and fathers come to represent different types of experiences for their babies. The significance of this is that from early in their lives, children are exposed to differentiable and salient models of traditionally masculine and traditionally feminine behavior. From the beginning of the second year, furthermore, we observe the channeling or direction of the child's attention toward the behavior of the same-sex parent (Lamb, 1977). Fathers are primarily responsible for the initiation of this sex-differentiating treatment, since it is they who begin to pay special attention to their sons and apparently withdraw from their daughters. The children — especially boys — respond to this in a predictable fashion: They develop preferences for the same-sex parent. In evaluating this phenomenon, I have suggested elsewhere that it may be one of the major factors in the acquisition of gender identity (Lamb, 1977). Two sources of evidence underscore the plausibility of this notion. First, John Money's experience with sex reassignment has convinced him (Money & Ehrhardt, 1972) that children acquire a sense of gender identity during the first two to three years, and the phenomenon just described is the most readily apparent instance of sex-differentiating treatment during this period. Second, boys raised without fathers tend to manifest gender role deficiencies, and these "effects of father absence" are especially likely when the father is absent during infancy (Biller, 1974). This too suggests the father's behavior during the child's infancy is particularly important, although neither of these arguments is conclusive.

Research on Fathers and Older Children

Inferences about paternal influences on older children are largely dependent on studies of father absence. Unfortunately, as a number of researchers (e.g., Biller, 1974; Herzog & Sudia, 1973; Lamb, 1976) have noted, studies of father absence tend to confuse so many potential influences that it is impossible to differentiate between the direct (those due to the lack of a parent figure and male model) and indirect (e.g., those due to the mother's economic and emotional distress) effects of father absence on the child. As a result, these studies do little to elucidate the nature and process of paternal influence in intact families. For example, the departure of the father is usually a cause of emotional and economic distress for the mother, and it is likely that her behavior will be affected by the stress she experiences. If her children later appear maladjusted, it may be a consequence of her behavior rather than a direct consequence of the father's absence. It would therefore be incorrect to conclude that paternal behavior is a key determinant of personality adjustment from the finding that children raised without fathers are more poorly adjusted than children raised in intact families.

A handful of careful studies do indicate that we can place some credence in the findings of the father-absence literature, however. Especially noteworthy is a study by Blanchard and Biller (1971) which showed that the effects of psychological father absence (which occurs when for professional or attitudinal reasons, fathers seldom spend time with their children) and those of physical father absence were qualitatively similar. Like most studies of father absence, Blanchard and Biller focused on the effects of paternal deprivation on sex role development in boys, and like most other investigations, their research showed deviant or deficient sex role development in at least some boys raised without fathers.

Among girls, father absence appears to predict dissatisfaction with and maladjustment in the female role, as well as difficulties in interaction with males (Hetherington, 1972). These effects are often not evident until adolescence, however, whereas among boys the negative effects of father absence are apparent much earlier.

Confidence in the conclusions of the father-absence literature would be bolstered if studies of intact families showed that identification and interaction with fathers indeed influenced (or were at least correlated with indices of) sex role development. Unfortunately, researchers have failed to find significant father–son similarity — the expectable consequence of filial identification (though see Bronfenbrenner, 1960). The only relatively consistent finding is that paternal masculinity is correlated with daughters' femininity. This finding is consistent with complementary role theory (Lamb, Owen, & Chase-Lansdale, 1979) rather than with the same-sex identification theory that comprises the implicit orientation of most contemporary research on father absence. The results of Mussen's and Biller's research fortunately suggest that the apparent failure of identification theory may be explained rather simply. Mussen and Biller found that the father's nurturance, not simply his masculinity, had to be taken into account when predicting filial masculinity. In other words, fathers are salient models and are (apparently) emulated when they are affectively appealing people whom their children would like to emulate.

This finding underscores what appears to be the single most important reason for our failure to progress further in understanding the nature of paternal (and for that matter, maternal) influences on child development. Quite simply, researchers have regarded relationships as if they were static entities, easily measured along one or a few orthogonal dimensions. It is intuitively obvious, however, that the effects of a father leaving a family will be markedly different depending on the nature of the preceding father–child, mother–father, and mother–child relationships. Greater progress will be made if researchers recognize the multiple determinants of father absence and the heterogeneity of father-absent families. A boy's desire to be like his father is surely influenced by the warmth of the father–son relationship, so why would we even expect boys in general to be like their fathers? We are dealing with complex and dynamic relationships between two personalities; if we are to understand the effect of either individual on the other, it is essential to know something about the nature of their relationship.

It is equally important to acknowledge that the father–child relationship exists within the context of a family system (see Hartup, 1979 . . .). Each member of this system appears likely to influence every other. More specifically, the effects of the father–child relationship probably cannot be understood independent of the mother–child relationship or of the father–mother relationship. It is significant that hostile marital relationships between the parents appear to be as pathogenic as poor parent–child relationships. Indeed, poor relationships between the parents may be more detrimental to healthy personality development than father absence is (Lamb, 1976). Rather than viewing this as evidence minimizing the significance of paternal influences, it can be viewed as an index of the complex nature of the socialization process and of the socializing environment.

Decontextualization of the father–child relationship has thus hampered analytic progress. So, too, has our narrow view of what fathers represent in the lives of their children. In the prototypic family system to which social scientists make implicit and occasionally explicit reference, the father's role is conceived to be that of an instrumental, breadwinning male parent. Because of this, most investigations of paternal influence have (implicitly or explicitly) tested the father's effectiveness as a model of masculinity, career commitment, or achievement orientation. Although I appreciate the value of identificatory/latent learning processes, it seems to me that we have placed too much emphasis on what the father does in front of the child (i.e., what sort of model he provides) and have placed too little emphasis on what he does with or to the child (i.e., what sort of socializing agent and companion he is).

Equally important, we have been so eager to identify the special or unique contributions of the father — the male adult in the family — that we have lost sight of the fact that he is, along with the mother, a major socializing agent in the child's life. He not only models and teaches sex roles, he also models and teaches other values and mores. The father's performance as a transmitter and enforcer of societal rules and expectations surely has implications for more aspects of development than does his role as the male parent. It is likely that the paternal and maternal influences supplement one another to such an extent that it is difficult to identify and quantify the father's unique influence. When both parents affect the same aspect of development in qualitatively similar fashion, however, we should not conclude that the paternal influence is insignificant by virtue of superfluity and redundancy. A socialization system that incorporates redundancy has a greater probability of success than does one that relies on a number of socializing agents each solely responsible for providing specific and necessary information or experiences. From this perspective, father absence can be seen as a circumstance involving both the absence of a male model and the absence of a major socializing agent. Since the father-absent family cannot count on the usual redundancy, its performance as a socializing system can be considered at risk. Minor failures in the socialization process are more likely in such a family, but they are certainly not inevitable, particularly since the family itself is simply one (important) entity amid a complex array of institutions (e.g., school, the peer group) dedicated to the socialization of children.

FATHERS — PRESENT AND FUTURE

I have attempted to explain why we appear to know so little about paternal influences on child development. Even as we investigate the traditional role of the father, however, it is clear that the role itself is changing dramatically. Within contemporary western culture, sex roles are being reevaluated. Although the impetus for change has come largely from women and the major changes have been in female roles, some redefinition of paternal roles appears to be both inevitable and desirable. In the remaining pages of this essay, I consider the implications of moderate and radical changes in gender and parental roles.

Today's children are the first generation to be raised amid doubt about role prescriptions that have long gone unchallenged. This makes their socialization especially difficult. Traditionally, socialization was a process of raising the young to fill major roles in society when the present incumbents vacated them. Yet today we do not know what type of society our children will inherit, nor the roles for which they should be prepared. Even if parents were to presume simply that more egalitarian sex roles will prevail in the future (with men being more involved in child rearing and women more concerned about achievement and the career trajectory than they have been), the process of socialization would still be problematic for two reasons.

First, most parents, both traditional and nontraditional, wish their children to develop secure senses of *gender identity* — that is, confident views of themselves as either male or female. On the other hand, parents who have nontraditional aspirations for their children are not eager to socialize them into traditional *gender roles*. Unfortunately, neither parents nor psychologists know which sex-differentiating aspects of socialization are necessary to ensure the acquisition of gender identity and which simply contribute to the adoption of restrictive traditional sex roles. The likeliest response to this dilemma, I believe, is to adopt the most conservative strategy: Sex type just in case failing to do so will have adverse consequences. Unfortunately, there is no other simple solution.

Second, there are few models of nontraditional masculinity and femininity for the children of today to emulate. As a result, a special burden is borne by contemporary agents of socialization. My colleagues and I (Lamb et al., 1979) have argued that fathers have an enormously important role to play in the socialization of "liberated" daughters. Many contemporary fathers tend to disapprove of nontraditional aspirations (achievement motivation, career commitment) on the part of their daughters. If the fathers of the future instead communicate a belief that career commitment is not incompatible with femininity, we shall see many fewer women experiencing doubt about the compatibility of their social and occupational aspirations.

For somewhat different reasons, paternal attitudes are also destined to facilitate or inhibit changes in the sex-stereotypic behavior and attitudes of sons in contemporary and traditional society. The masculine role is viewed as the most powerful; males surely stand to lose most from any redefinition of sex roles. Consequently, an acknowledgement by fathers of the need for such redefinition is likely to be more persuasive and more salient than similar beliefs on the part of women.

Given the apparent importance of changes in men's attitudes, it is significant that the young fathers of today appear more eager than their predecessors to assume an active role in the rearing and socialization of their children. The majority, of course, seek *some* involvement, without questioning the traditional assumption that women should assume primary responsibility for parenting. This change may not be as far-reaching as I would like, but it does represent a trend toward a more egalitarian social structure. For children, it promises to bring increased exposure to one of the major socializing agents within the family, and this will surely increase the extent of paternal influence even if much of this appears redundant — reduplicative of maternal influences. It will also bring increased exposure to more nurturant models, and this is destined to maximize the propensities of children to emulate their fathers. Finally, the models themselves will represent a more humane brand of masculinity than the contemporary norm does. All of these factors speak for increasing paternal involvement in the processes of socialization.

These changes — the predictable changes — amount to minor modifications of the traditional sex roles. Far less likely (despite the amount of attention they elicit from social reformers and social scientists) are instances of radical role redefinition, as in the cases of role sharing (mother and father equally involved in child rearing and breadwinning) and role reversal (father as caretaker, mother as breadwinner). In collaboration with Frodi, Hwang, and Frodi, I am currently investigating the effects of such family styles on the social and personality development of young children. Space constraints prohibit the elaborate discussion of our predictions. Let me simply note that filial maladjustment is not inevitable; the parents in "alternative families" are not models of pathological roles, however unusual their roles are. Women may be — should be — secure in their femininity and still have occupational aspirations. Similarly, secure masculine identity does not preclude the assumption of major responsibility for child care. It is important not to confuse conformity to traditional sex role prescriptions with the security of gender identity or with mental health. Provided an individual's gender identity is secure, a wide range of gender roles can be assumed. Thus, if children in nontraditional families identify with the same-sex parent and if that parent has a secure gender identity and evinces a coherent, if unusual, sex role, then no untoward consequences need occur.

I am considerably less sanguine about the prospects for the children of single parents. To be sure, deviant outcomes are not inevitable, but they are certainly more likely. When either parent is absent, children are deprived of exposure to a major role model. Further, as Eleanor Maccoby (Note 2) said recently, "Childrearing is something that many people cannot do adequately as single adults functioning in isolation. Single parents need time off from parenting, they need the company of other adults, they need to have other voices joined with theirs in transmitting values and maturity demands to their children" (p. 17). The socialization process need not, of course, fail in all or even most single-parent families. Perhaps the major determinant of success is the extent of social and community support available — support such as substitute care facilities to relieve single parents of the burdens of 24-hour-per-day child-care responsibilities, and financial security sufficient to ensure the health and happiness of the family.

In the eyes of most social scientists, single fathers are in an especially invidious position, for they (typically) have to assume child-care responsibility suddenly without adequate training or supervision. Contrarily, I believe that today's single fathers are more likely than single mothers to succeed in meeting the demands placed on them simply because they are a highly selected and self-motivated group. Societal and judicial prejudices ensure that mothers gain custody by default, whereas fathers who desire custody have to fight for it. As single fatherhood becomes more common, however, failure to cope will likely become as common as among single mothers.

This presumption reflects my belief that the fathers of tomorrow will share in both the joys and the sorrows of parenthood much more than they have in the past. In my view, this represents a wholly admirable evolution within our society. And as the father's role changes, the formative significance of fathers in children's lives is likely to expand greatly. We can only hope for a parallel change in the methodological and conceptual sophistication evinced by social scientists attempting to understand the role of the father in child development.

AUTHOR'S NOTE

1. It is ironic that Freud's emphasis on the formative significance of early experiences should have nurtured the notion of maternal preeminence, since Freud himself placed a major emphasis on the father's role. For Freud, the lack of paternal involvement in child rearing *increased* the father's potential influence.

REFERENCE NOTES

1. Yogman, M., Dixon, S., Tronick, E., & Brazelton, T. B. *Development of infant social interaction with fathers.* Paper presented at the meeting of the Eastern Psychological Association, New York, April 1976.

2. Maccoby, E. E. *Current changes in the family, and their impact upon the socialization of children.* Paper presented at the meeting of the American Sociological Association, Chicago, September 1977.

REFERENCES

Benson, L. *Fatherhood: A sociological perspective.* New York: Random House, 1968.

Biller, H. B. *Father, child, and sex role.* Lexington, Mass.: Heath, 1971.

Biller, H. B. *Paternal deprivation: Family, school, sexuality and society.* Lexington, Mass.: Heath, 1974.

Blanchard, R. W., & Biller, H. B. Father availability and academic performance among third-grade boys. *Developmental Psychology,* 1971, *4,* 301–305.

Bronfenbrenner, U. Freudian theories of identification and their derivatives. *Child Development,* 1960, *31,* 15–40.

Hartup, W. W. The social worlds of childhood. *American Psychologist,* 1979, *34,* 944–950.

Herzog, E., & Sudia, C. Children in fatherless families. In B. M. Caldwell & H. N. Ricciuti (Eds.), *Review of child development research* (Vol. 3). Chicago: University of Chicago Press, 1973.

Hetherington, E. M. Effects of father absence on personality development in adolescent daughters. *Developmental Psychology,* 1972, *7,* 313–326.

Lamb, M. E. *The role of the father in child development.* New York: Wiley, 1976.

Lamb, M. E. The development of parental preferences in the first two years of life. *Sex Roles,* 1977, *3,* 495–497.

Lamb, M. E. The father's role in the infant's social world. In J. H. Stevens & M. Mathews (Eds.), *Mother/child, father/child relationships.* Washington, D.C.: National Association for the Education of Young Children, 1978.

Lamb, M. E., & Frodi, A. M. The role of the father in child development. In R. R. Abidin (Ed.), *Handbook of parent education.* Springfield, Ill.: Charles C Thomas, 1979.

Lamb, M. E., Owen, M. T., & Chase-Lansdale, L. The father–daughter relationship: Past, present, and future. In C. B. Kopp & M. Kirkpatrick (Eds.), *Becoming female.* New York: Plenum, 1979.

Lynn, D. B. *The father: His role in child development.* Monterey, Calif.: Brooks/Cole, 1974.

Money, J., & Ehrhardt, A. *Man and woman,*

boy and girl. Baltimore, Md.: Johns Hopkins University Press, 1972.

Parke, R. D. Perspectives on father–infant interaction. In J. D. Osofsky (Ed.), *Handbook of infant development.* New York: Wiley, 1979.

Parke, R. D., & O'Leary, S. E. Father–mother–infant interaction in the newborn period: Some findings, some observations and some unresolved issues. In K. Riegel & J. Meacham (Eds.), *The developing individual in a changing world: Vol. 2. Social and environmental issues.* The Hague, The Netherlands: Mouton, 1976.

T. Berry Brazelton

BEHAVIORAL COMPETENCE OF THE NEWBORN INFANT

In the past, the newborn infant has been thought of as helpless, insensitive, and ready to be entirely shaped by his environment. This model of helplessness and insensitivity served many purposes in the past. It allowed his caregivers to feel in control and to feel absolutely necessary to him. In the case of sick infants, it allowed medical personnel to feel that their interventions were not as painful as they might have been perceived by a thinking, feeling organism. Finally, in an era when many infants were to die, this contributed to a kind of depersonification that may have protected the infant's parents from investing too early in each infant. Many cultures in which the neonatal death rate is high still institutionalize such practices as not speaking of the newborn as a baby but as a phoenix[1] or of not naming him until he is 3 months old and more likely to survive.[2]

Our concepts of reinforcing parents for early attachment to neonates is a new one. At this time in history, we can afford to urge young parents to attach to a new baby, since very few will die. Even when infants do not survive, we have become convinced that grief reactions will be handled better by parents who have proceeded to attach to the infant than by those who are never allowed to touch or to see the dying infant.[3] If the infant does survive, we feel there is a kind of energy available to new parents to bond to the infant right around delivery and for the new adjustment to parenting.[4] In our society we have depersonalized the delivery process to such an extent that parents feel manipulated and out of control. Hence any effort to give them a feeling of importance around this event will reinforce them for competence and is likely to become a force for earlier and more sensitive attachment to the individual baby. Certainly their joy in achievement of a normal delivery is likely to feed their sense of fulfillment as parents and to reinforce their self-confidence in the adaptation necessary to each new infant. Klaus and Kennell and associates[5] have shown that attention to parents' needs for bonding to the new infant will result in expectable gains in cognitive, linguistic, and affective competence in the infant and child later in his development.

There are other potent and often destructive influences on parenting that make it important that we begin to value the neonate's contribution to his new environment. Since parents' inclination is to nurture the newborn, to value his reactions to their handling, to voice, to vision, it becomes a real putdown to these reactions if we as physicians do not value them in the neonate. If we do attend to them, change neonatal nurseries and lying-in arrangements to value and capture the neo-

Supported in part by grants from Robert Wood Johnson Foundation, Carnegie Foundation, and William T. Grant Foundation.

SOURCE: From T. Berry Brazelton, "Behavioral Competence of the Newborn Infant," *Seminars in Perinatology* 3, 1979, pp. 35–44. Reprinted by permission of Grune & Stratton, Inc. and the author.

nate's best periods of alert responsiveness, we place a stamp of approval both on the parents' attention to the neonate and on the newborn as an important, interactive person from the start. We are providing new, confused parents with a way of communicating with their infants. We are showing them that the neonate can lead them when they are confused.

The demands of a complex, undirected society, coupled with the lack of support (often even negative input) that is provided new parents by our present nuclear family system, leave most parents insecure and at the mercy of tremendous internal and external pressures. They have been told that their infant's outcome is to be shaped by them and their parenting: at the same time there are few stable cultural values on which they can rely for guidance in setting their course as new parents. Most new parents are separated emotionally from their own parents' standards by the generation gap and all that that implies. Our present generation has actively separated itself from the beliefs and mores of the preceding generation. For example, we can cite the ambivalence with which the press and other media are treating Spock's previously accepted ideas.[6] I am not questioning the need for a change in childrearing practices — I certainly endorse many of the revisions — but I want to show how one more potential prop has been eliminated from the young parents' armamentarium for support. Physicians are not readily available to many young parents, and nurse-practitioners are not quite filling the gap yet, although I hope and believe that they will be doing so before long. Pediatricians and physicians in family medicine will be pressed toward a primary care paradigm lest they lose the most rewarding and precious asset a physician has: the feedback from maintaining a supportive, interactive relationship with parents as they foster the development of their children.

Our society's backup for parenting often is a negative one. There is virtually no opportunity for most children as they grow up in small, lonely nuclear family settings to experience how their own or other parents go about raising small brothers and sisters. As a result, they come to parenting with little experience of their own.

The childbirth education groups have shown the importance of preparation for childbirth itself. This preparation points up another missed but powerful potential — that of preparing young couples for their roles as parents.

But an infant is not as helpless as he seems, and there are rewards as well as messages from an infant that can guide a new mother and new father as they become faced with their new roles.

I'd like to begin to point to some of the strengths that are inherent in the parent-infant system, including the guidelines that a reciprocal interactional system between a baby and its parents can produce to guide them and to reward each of them, for the infant comes well equipped to signal his needs and his gratitude to his environment. In fact, he can even make choices about what he wants from his parents, and shut out what he doesn't want in such powerful ways that I no longer see him as a passive lump of clay but as a powerful force for stabilizing and influencing those around him. What I believe we must do is to uncover and expose these infant strengths to parents, to demonstrate the infant's behavior on which they can rely, and to support young parents in their own individualized endeavor to reach out for, attach to, and *enjoy* their new infants! But this is no mean task.

What is the adaptive purpose of prolonged infancy in the human? No other species has as long a period of relative dependency, and I believe that it is important to look for the adaptive advantages in rules of nature, selected over many generations for their survival value. Compared to that of any other species, the human neonate is relatively helpless in the motor sphere and relatively complex, even precocious, in the sensory sphere. This enforces a kind of motoric dependence and a freedom for acquisition of the many patterns of sensory and affective information that are necessary to the child and adult human for mastering and surviving in a complex world. In other words, the prolonged period of infancy allows for early and affective transmission of all the mores and instrumental techniques evolved by society — and a kind of individuality inherent in each culture.

As the potential for early intervention increases, it becomes more and more important that we be able to evaluate infants at risk as early as possible with an eye to more sophisticated preventive and therapeutic approaches. Early intervention may prevent a compounding of problems that occurs all too easily when the environment cannot adjust appropriately to the infant at risk. Premature and minimally brain-damaged infants seem to be less able to compensate in disorganized, depriving environments than are well-equipped neonates, and their problems of organization in development are compounded early.[7] Quiet, nondemanding infants do not elicit necessary mothering from already overstressed parents and are selected by their neonatal behavior for kwashiorkor and marasmus in poverty-ridden cultures such as are found in Guatemala and Mexico.[8,9] Hyperkinetic, hypersensitive neonates may press a mother and father into a kind of desperation that produces childrearing responses from them that reinforce the problems of the child so that he grows up in an overreactive, hostile environment.[10] Parents of children admitted to the wards of the Children's Hospital in Boston for clinical syndromes such as failure to thrive, child abuse, repeated accidents and poisonings, and infantile autism are often successful parents of other children. By history, they associate their failure with the one child to an inability to "understand" him from the neonatal period onward, and they claim a difference from the other children in his earliest reactions to them. If we are to improve the outcome for such children, assessment of the risk in early infancy could mobilize preventive efforts and programs for intervention before the neonate's problems are compounded by an environment that cannot understand him without such help.

We need more sophisticated methods of assessing neonates and for predicting their contribution to the likelihood of failure in the environment-infant interaction. We also need to be able to assess at-risk environments because the impracticality of spreading resources too thin points to the necessity of selecting target populations for our efforts at early intervention. With better techniques for assessing strengths and weaknesses in infants and the environments to which they will be exposed, we might come to better understand the mechanisms for failures in development that result in some of the above-mentioned syndromes. Even desperate socioeconomic conditions produce comparable stresses in many families whose children do not have to be salvaged from the clinical syndromes of child abuse, failure to thrive, and kwashiorkor. Minimally brain-damaged babies do make remarkable compensatory recoveries in a fostering environment. Understanding the infant and the problems he will present to his parents may enhance our value as supportive figures for them as they adjust to a difficult infant.

The Apgar score[11] is the traditional and most universal criterion for assessing the newborn's well-being in the delivery room. Its primary effect has been for the anesthetist and obstetrician to focus attention on the neonate. Its five categories — color, respiratory effort, cardiac effort, body tone, and responsiveness to aversive stimuli — measure the functions necessary to sustain life. The score reflects the neonate's capacity to respond to the stress of labor and delivery. The score is influenced to a certain extent by any perinatal event, such as moderate hypoxia, drugs or anesthesia given the mother, prolonged labor, cesarean section, etc., but since the score is done in the first 5 min after delivery only, it basically measures the immediate capacity of the neonate for an "alarm" reaction. The kind and depth of depression that may follow later and that represents the depleted resources of the baby is in no way predicted by the Apgar score. Subtle effects of insults such as hypoxia or drugs are easily overlooked by the Apgar score, since it is necessary to have a substantial insult to impair the gross functioning of neuromuscular, cardiac, or respiratory systems.

The limited predictive ability of the Apgar score has been a disappointment to pediatricians and pediatric neurologists. However, at an initial screening level, it is important. Drage et al.[12] reported a fourfold increase in neurologic abnormalities at 1 yr in infants with low 5-min Apgar scores compared to those with high scores. However, only 4.3% of those with low 5-min Apgar scores had gross neurologic abnormalities. More subtle effects at outcome were suggested by Lewis et al.,[13] who studied visual attentiveness at 3, 9, and 13 mo of age in babies with normal Apgar scores at 1 min. In this group, they differentiated between those with scores of 7–9 and those with scores of 10 in their capacity to respond to complex visual tasks. Their results suggest that the Apgar score in some way reflects a spectrum of behavior that may predict future functioning, if we use more sensitive tests along with it.

The concept that the newborn functions only at a brain stem level of nervous organization[14] has led to rather stereotyped neurologic examinations that assess reflex behavior with an oversimplified positive-negative approach. Not until recently was it recognized that the higher brain centers serve to modify responses through partial inhibition or facilitation in the neonate and that the intact function of the CNS can be determined by a qualitative assessment of responses in the neonatal period. Brain-damaged infants may have reflex responses available but they may be distortedly exaggerated or partially suppressed, stereotyped or obligatory; the quality of these responses is different from that of the graded ones seen in an intact baby. Hence the more recent neurologic examinations provide scoring systems for these qualitative differences, and the scores become more predictive of good function.

In order to record and evaluate some of the integrative processes evidenced in certain kinds of neonatal behavior, we have developed a behavioral evaluation scale that tests and documents the infant's use of state behavior (state of consciousness) and the response to various kinds of stimulation.[15]

Since the neonate's reactions to all stimuli are dependent on his ongoing "state," any interpretation of them must be made with this in mind. His use of state to maintain control of his reactions to environmental and internal stimuli is an important mechanism and reflects his potential for organization. State no longer need be treated as an error variable but serves to set a dynamic pattern to allow for the full behavioral repertoire of the infant. Specifically, our examination tracks changes in state over the course of the exam, and its lability and direction. The variability of state indicates the infant's capacities for self-organization. His ability to quiet himself as well as his need for stimulation also measures this adequacy.

The behavior exam tests for neurologic adequacy with 20 reflex measures and for 26 behavioral responses to environmental stimuli including the kind of interpersonal stimuli that mothers use in their handling of the infant as they attempt to help him adapt to the new world. Best performance is used to overcome variables. In the exam, there is a graded series of procedures — talking, hand on belly, restraint, holding, and rocking — designed to soothe and alert the infant. His responsiveness to animate stimuli (e.g., voice, face) and to inanimate stimuli (e.g., rattle, bell, red ball, white light, temperature change) is assessed. Estimates of vigor and attentional excitement are measured, and an assessment is made of motor activity and tone and autonomic responsiveness as he changes state. With this examination given on successive days we have been able to outline (1) the initial period of alertness immediately after delivery, presumably the result of stimulation of labor and the new environmental stimuli after delivery, (2) the period of depression and disorganization that follows and that lasts for 24–48 hr in infants with uncomplicated deliveries and no medication effects but for longer periods of 3–4 days if the infants have been compromised from medication given their mothers during labor, and (3) the curve of recovery to "optimal" function after several days. This third period may be the best single predictor of individual potential function, and it seems to correlate well with the neonate's retest ability at 30 days.[16] The shape of the curve made by several examinations may be the most important assessment of the basic CNS intactness of the neonate's ability to integrate CNS and other physiologic recovery mechanisms and of the strength of his compensatory capacities when there have been compromising insults to him during labor and delivery. A condensed list of the behavioral items are indicated in Table 1.

In addition to the 26 items of behavior, assessed on a 9-point scale, there are 20 reflex responses that are also assessed.

We feel that the behavioral items elicit more important evidences of cortical control and responsiveness, even in the neonatal period. The neonate's capacity to manage and overcome the physiologic demands of this adjustment period in order to attend to, to differentiate, and to habituate to the complex stimuli of an examiner's maneuvers may be

Table 1. NEONATAL BEHAVIORAL ASSESSMENT

Behavioral items
1. Response decrement to repeated visual stimuli
2. Response decrement to rattle
3. Response decrement to bell
4. Response decrement to pinprick
5. Orienting response to inanimate visual stimuli
6. Orienting response to inanimate auditory stimuli
7. Orienting response to animate visual stimuli — examiner's face
8. Orienting response to animate auditory stimuli — examiner's voice
9. Orienting response to animate visual and auditory stimuli
10. Quality and duration of alert periods
11. General muscle tone in resting and in response to being handled (passive and active)
12. Motor maturity
13. Traction responses as he is pulled to sit
14. Cuddliness — responses to being cuddled by the examiner
15. Defensive movements — reactions to a cloth over his face
16. Consolability with intervention by examiner
17. Peak of excitement and his capacity to control himself
18. Rapidity of buildup to crying state
19. Irritability during the exam
20. General assessment of kind and degree of activity
21. Tremulousness
22. Amount of startling
23. Lability of skin color (measuring autonomic lability)
24. Lability of states during entire exam
25. Self-quieting activity — attempts to console self and control state
26. Hand to mouth activity

an important predictor of his future central nervous system organization. Certainly, the curve of recovery of these responses over the first neonatal week must be of more significance than the midbrain responses detectable in routine neurologic exams. Repeated behavioral exams on any 2 or 3 days in the first 10 days after delivery might be expected to be sensitive predictors of future CNS function.

In this exam are couched behavioral tests of such important CNS mechanisms as (1) "habituation," or the neonate's capacity to shut out disturbing or overwhelming stimuli, (2) choices in attention to various objects or human stimuli (a neonate shows clear preferences for female versus male voices, and for human versus nonhuman visual stimuli), and (3) control of his state in order to attend to information from his environment (the effort to complete a hand-to-mouth cycle in order to attend to objects and people around him). These are all evidenced in the neonate and even in the premature infant and seem to be more predictive of CNS intactness than are reflex responses.[17]

What are some of the built-in strengths of the human neonate? A few examples will demonstrate how powerful these are as economical determinants of how he will conserve himself in a new overwhelming world and how he can quickly acquire the information he needs to choose to make his caregivers familiar with him and responsive to him in a way that will latch them onto him at a critical period for them both. Right out of the uterus (1) he can and does turn his head to the human voice repeatedly, and his face alerts as he searches for its source; (2) he will attend to and choose a female vocal pitch over any other;[18] (3) humanoid sounds are not only preferred to pure tones in an equivalent range of pitch but when he is tested with continuous sucking as a response system he stops sucking briefly after a pure tone then goes on sucking steadily, whereas after a human tone he stops sucking and then continues in a burst-pause pattern of sucking (as if he were expecting more important information to follow, and as if the pauses in the sucking were designed to allow for attention to this further information);[19] (4) he will attend to and follow with eyes and full 90° head turning a picture of a human face but will not follow a scrambled face, although he will look at it wide-eyed for a long period (in the delivery room and before any caretaking has been instituted);[20] (5) he will turn to and prefer milk smells above those of water or sugar water; and (6) he can taste and respond to with altered sucking patterns the difference between human milk and a cow's milk formula designed to exactly reproduce the contents of breast milk.[21]

There are two questions that might shed light on the potential for recovery and development of neonates. If these complex responses are present, does the neonate learn from experiencing them? If he can learn from the experience of controlling input, from his choices, from his efforts at state control, does his attempt to integrate his CNS in order to respond become an organizing influence? I have been impressed by the efforts to improve the environments for neonates and at-risk infants.

The studies of the effects of stimulation in the neonatal period on the recovery of premature and other high-risk neonates have been limited so far to groups of neonates who are in our present deprivation system, but there is increasing evidence that sensory input that is *appropriate* to the state of physiologic recovery of that neonate may act powerfully to further his weight gain, his sensory integrity, and even his outcome. For example, Pettigrew[22] found that for kittens specific visual input was necessary for the development of the specificity of initially undifferentiated cells, and Blakemore and

Cooper[23] found that visual cortex neurons responded predominantly to stimuli that were equivalent to the environment in which the kittens were reared. However, in both cases these effects were found only after a given level of CNS maturity had been achieved. Prior to that time, exposure had no effect because it did not appropriately fit the organism's level of development.

Most of the studies on early stimulation have not been individualized to the subjects. We have evidence that leads us to feel that each premature or recovering neonate *must* be examined for the possibility of sensory overloading. A premature infant will respond to a soft rattle with head turning away from the rattle (and other evidences of shutting it out), whereas a normal neonate will turn toward the rattle and search for it.[24] We feel that this crude example of the finely defined thresholds for appropriate sensory stimuli, as opposed to those that must be "coped with" or shut out, must be taken as seriously as whether we offer stimulation or not. In the recovery phase, a high-risk baby may be too easily overwhelmed, and "routine" stimulation may force him into an expensive coping model, whereas grading the stimuli to his particular sensory needs may further his recovery as well as his ultimate CNS outcome. How can we tell when he is being overloaded? We can tell by watching his color changes, his kind of respirations, and his state of alertness and accounting for evidences of fatigue. A stressed neonate must be observed for evidences of excessive physiologic demands as he responds to a stimulus for attention; investment in a learning paradigm has its own cost, and this cost must be balanced against his capacity to manage the cost at his stage of physiologic recovery. Using Kearsley's ideas[25] about the relative degree of attention to a stimulus as it is measured against the physiologic demands, we have a clearly defined area of "appropriate" versus "inappropriate" properties of all stimuli that can be applied to each neonate individually and the amount and the quality of stimulation that can be offered to every at-risk neonate without expense.

The studies by Sander et al.[26] show that the infant shapes his motility and his "state" behavior to the environment, *particularly* if it is sensitive to him and to his individual needs. Two models of regulation occurred with the neonates and caretakers they studied. The first related to basic regulation of endogenous bio-rhythmicity and was entrained by specific extrinsic cues in relation to the neonate's endogenous rhythm. Entrainment was most effective when the exogenous cue approximated the point in time at which a shift in the endogenous cycle was occurring. With the repeated establishment of contingent relationships between state changes in the infant and specific configurations in caretaking events, entrainment was favored. The second model depended on the caretaker and infant achieving a regulatory balance based on mutual readiness of states, and with this the stage was set to facilitate initial cognitive development. As the partners appreciated a mutual regulation of states of attention, they began to learn about and from each other, and a kind of reciprocity or affective interaction ensued.

We have shown that as early as 3 weeks there is a clear differentiation between the infant's kind of attention as well as of all of his behaviors when he is attending to an object versus a person,[27] and now we know that he can further differentiate *between persons* — father, mother, and stranger — with a clearly different set of behaviors. If this behavioral attentional set can be shaped as early as this, it denotes a kind of "readiness" for learning that is inexpensive and adaptive for him. Of course, it leads to more and appropriate adult interaction for him. His responses become adaptive in providing him with a feedback source of appropriate stimuli from the adults around him as well as a way of his demonstrating behaviorally to the sensitive adult that now he or she is on target with the infant.

In our laboratory at Children's Hospital Medical Center, we have been looking at this early reciprocal interaction between infants and their parents and, more recently, infants and strangers. We start at 2 weeks and continue with them until 24 weeks in a laboratory situation designed to film and analyze the ingredients of early reciprocity as it develops between infants and familiar adults (Fig. 1). We film the infants in a reclining chair (or baby seat) as the adult comes in to lean over him and enlist his attention in "games" or "play." We first found that as early as we could film it we saw completely different kinds of behavior and attention with a mother and with an attractive object[28] (Fig. 2).

With an attractive object, as it was brought into "reach" space (about 12 inches out in front of him), his attention and face became "hooked" as his extremities and even his fingers and toes pointed out toward it, making brief swipes out toward it, as he attended with a rapt, fixed expression on his face. When he was satiated, his attention broke off abruptly and he averted his eyes or turned his whole head and body away for a brief period before he came back for a further period of "hooked" attention. Thus he established a jagged homeostatic curve of attention, and his arms and legs displayed jerky components of reach behavior as they attended to the object — all at a time when a reach could not be achieved successfully.

Figure 1. Laboratory setting.

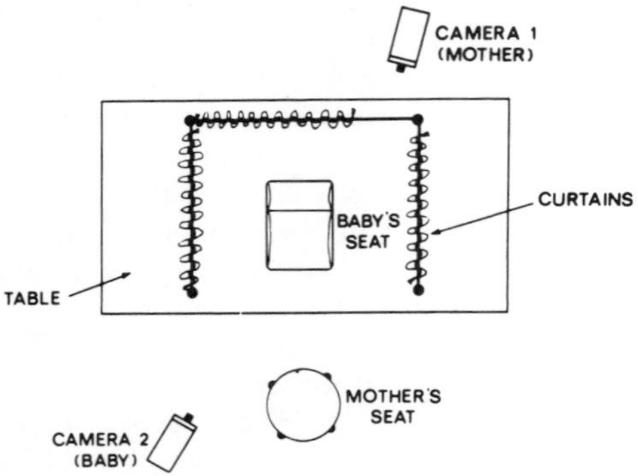

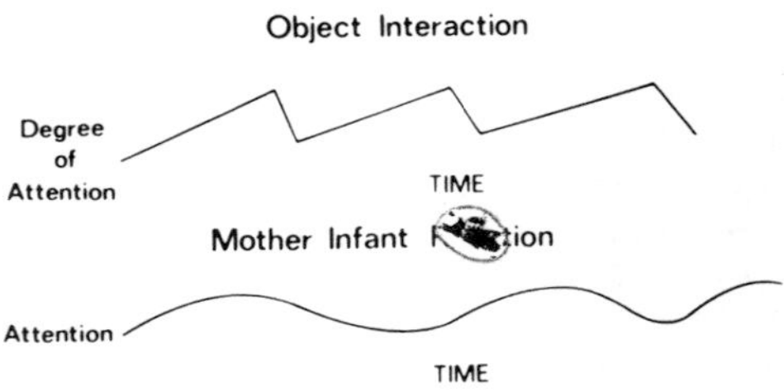

Figure 2. Pattern of change in attention to attractive objects is abrupt and jagged; to mother, smooth and cyclic.

With his mother, his attention and motor behavior were entirely different; movements of his eyes, his face, his mouth, and his extremities all became smooth and cyclic. As he attended, he moved out slightly toward the object with his head, his mouth, his eyes, and even with his legs, arms, fingers, and toes, but almost immediately the approach behavior was followed by smooth, cyclic withdrawal behavior, as if he expected his mother (or father) to come out to him. His attention was cyclic also, and he looked intently at her (his) face, lidded his eyes or turned them slightly to one side, or up and down, still keeping the parent in peripheral view, but alternating between attention and reduced attention, in average cycles of four per minute over a 3-min observation period. This attention-withdrawal cycle within a period of reciprocal interaction looked as if it followed a homeostatic curve of involvement and recovery that was smooth and signaled a period of intense involvement between infant and parent. The parent cycled, too — playing a kind of swan's mating dance as he or she moved in to pass on information or behavior when the infant was looking and withdrew slightly to let up in intensity when the infant withdrew (Fig. 3).

We have been able to characterize the relative reciprocity and amount of affective, and even cognitive, information that a parent can transmit in such a period by the cyclic quality of the interaction. In parents who are too anxious and are insensitive to their infants' homeostatic needs (this parallels the demands of the physiologic systems of an immature organism such as the neonate), the infant necessarily turns off his attention and spends most of the period keeping the tense parent in his peripheral field, checking back from time to time. In failing interactions, the jagged attentional system of the infant resembles a very sparse period of object attention (Fig. 4). One can see from some of the failing interactions that the sparseness of message transmission is in direct contrast to a smooth homeostatic curve of attention in an optimal period of reciprocity. Not only does such a cycle allow for long periods of attention without exhausting the immature physiologic systems of the infant, but it also provides a rich matrix for choices and change in attention at any moment. These cycles also provide a matrix for adaptability of a very sensitive kind to the few caregivers who must become important to the infants.

Figure 3. Interaction in which mother is sensitive to baby's needs to look away and recover.

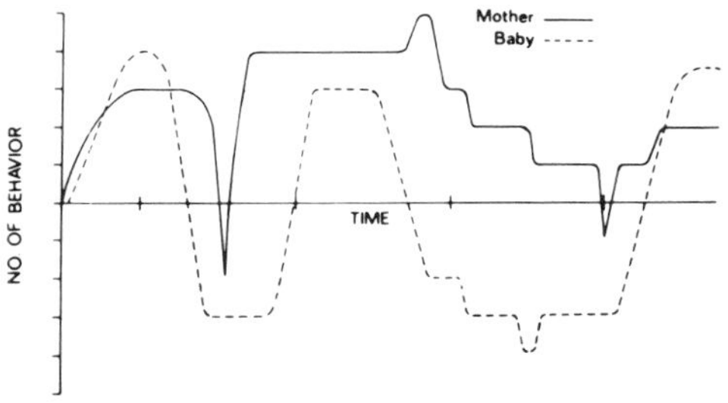

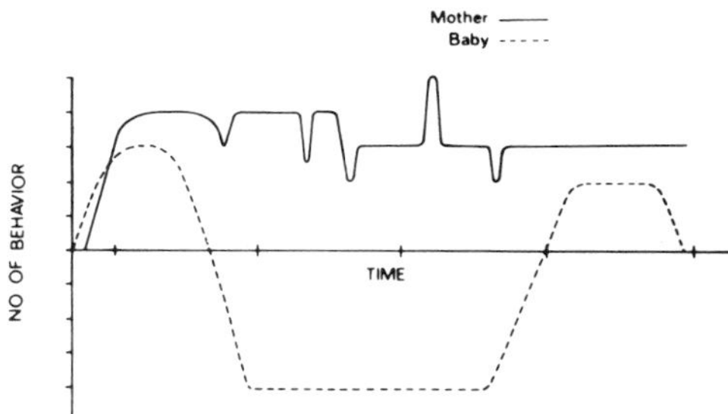

Figure 4. Interaction in which mother is insensitive and baby spends most of time looking away.

We think that we are seeing a reliable difference between mothers and fathers as they perform in this system. Mothers start out and remain smoother, more low-keyed, more cyclic themselves, using other behaviors such as touching, patting, vocalizing, and smiling to "contain" the baby and provide him with a gently containing matrix for early responses such as smiles, vocalizations, and reaches, but they don't seem to be in such a hurry for these to develop, and they are sensitive (often extremely so) to the competing physiologic demands of the infant.[29]

On the other hand, most fathers (and there are notable exceptions) seem to present a more playful, jazzing-up approach (Fig. 5). Their displays are rhythmic in timing and even in quality. As one watches this interaction, it seems that a father is expecting a more heightened, playful response from the baby. And he gets it! Amazingly enough, an infant by 2 or 3 weeks displays an entirely different attitude (more wide-eyed, playful, and bright-faced) toward his father than to his mother. The cycles might be characterized as higher, deeper, and even a bit more jagged. The total period of playful attention may be shorter if the small infant

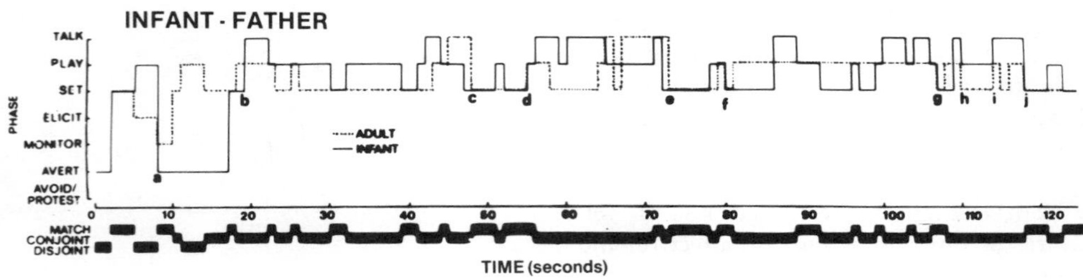

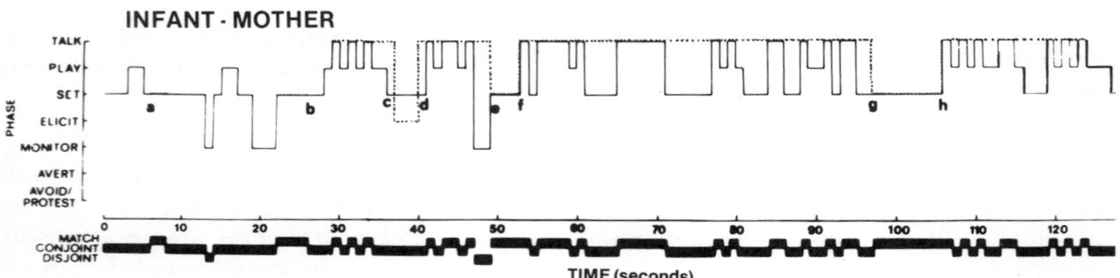

Figure 5. Father keeps baby at higher level of intensity although communication rhythm is comparable to mother-infant rhythm.

gets overloaded, but as he gets older the period of play is maintained for a longer time.[30]

What does this kind of reciprocal "set" mean to the infant? It certainly appears to be basic to the healthy development of infant-parent reciprocity. My own feeling is that we are tuning in on the basic homeostatic systems that govern the physiologic processes as well as the attentional ones in the developing infant. If these are "shaped" by his environment in one way, they may press him toward a psychophysiologic adjustment of one kind or another. Certainly when an environment can tune to the baby's needs for such elegant homeostatic controls, the attention *and* physiologic cycles can be smooth, rich, adjustable. I can easily jump to the kind of tuning up of the CNS cycles that must find regulation as well as input from the environment to proceed toward optimal development of motor and cognitive skills. I think we are looking at the precursors of affective development that are so necessary to the child's total development. We have examples from Harlow's monkeys[31] and from Rene Spitz's and from Provence's later studies of institutionalized infants,[32,33] which show that development did not proceed when there was no such nurturing from the environment.

For the infant, such a reciprocal system, when it is going well, acts as fuel and information for his ongoing development, entertaining the fueling from within that he receives as feedback from learning each new developmental task. Robert White called this latter force a "sense of competence." Both an inner sense of competence and feeling from a gratifying reciprocity with his environment are necessary to the infant's optimal development.

For the parents, the feedback from such a reciprocal system is just as rewarding as it is to the infant and fuels their energy for continuing in such a demanding ongoing relationship as "good" parenting requires. Their awareness of when they are successful must be felt unconsciously when things are going well, and we as supportive experts could and should point out such periods so that they can become consciously aware of their successes as guidelines to their parenting efforts.

For instance, the neonate's behavioral repertoire is eminently fitted for "capturing" a new parent. As he stops crying to turn his head toward her voice, as he "chooses" her voice over a competing male voice, as he turns to root at her breast when she cuddles him, as he nestles his soft head in the corner of her neck when he is placed at her shoulder, a new mother is captivated. We and others[34,35] have found that demonstrating this behavior to parents in the first few days after delivery does indeed alert them to the individual assets of their neonate, and they behave in a significantly more nurturant fashion thereafter.[36] With difficult infants it may be even more critical that we share their difficult behavior with new parents and set up an alliance with them to help them work it out with our supportive help. The behavior of the neonate is certainly designed to capture his parents, but when it is a disappointment to them or when they cannot find a "fit" with him it can turn them away from him. As many mothers of babies who have failed to thrive say when they are asked, "He never reached me," or, "I never could reach him." The behavior of the newborn can be assessed and captured by the professional to foster the parent-child relationship, and, where it predicts to stress in that relationship, as a communication system for professional intervention to alleviate that stress. Sharing the observable behavior and reactions of the neonate with his parents becomes a powerful technique for the professional toward establishing a working relationship with them from the very first.

REFERENCES

1. Blum R, Blum E: Health and Healing in Rural Greece. Palo Alto, Stanford Univ, 1965

2. LeVine RA, LeVine BB: Nyansongo: A Gusii community in Kenya, in Whiting B (ed): Six Cultures: Studies of Child Rearing. New York, Wiley, 1963

3. Klaus MH, Kennell JH: Mothers separated from their newborn infants. Pediatr Clin North Am 17:1015–1037, 1970

4. Klaus MH, Kennell JH, Plumb N, et al: Human maternal behavior at the first contact with her young. Pediatrics 46:187–192, 1970.

5. Ringler NM, Kennell JH, Jarvella R, et al: Mother to child speech at two years — Effects of early postnatal contact. J Pediatr 86:141–144, 1975

6. Spock B: The Common Sense of Baby and Child Care. New York, Duell, Sloan & Pearce, 1946

7. Greenberg NH: A comparison of infant-mother interactional behavior in infants with atypical behavior and normal infants, in Hellmuth J (ed): Exceptional Infant, vol. 2. New York, Brunner Mazel, 1971, p 390

8. Cravioto J, Delcardia ER, Birch HG: Nutrition, growth and neurointegrative development. Pediatrics 38:319–320, 1966

9. Klein RE, Lester BM, Yarbrough C, et al: On malnutrition and mental development: Some preliminary findings, in Chaves A, Borges H, Basta S (eds): Nutrition, vol. 2. Basel, Karger, 1975, pp 315–321

10. Heider GM: Vulnerability in infants and young children. Genet Psychol Monogr 73:1–216, 1966

11. Apgar VA: A proposal for a new method of evaluation of the newborn infant. Anesth Analg 32:260–267, 1953

12. Drage JS, Kennedy C, Berendes H, et al: The Apgar score as an index of infant morbidity: A report from the Collaborative Study of Cerebral Palsy. Dev Med Child Neurol 8:141–148, 1966

13. Lewis M, Bartels B, Campbell H, et al: Individual differences in attention. Am J Dis Child 113:461–465, 1967

14. Peiper A: Cerebral Function in Infancy and Childhood. New York, Consultants Bureau, 1963

15. Brazelton TB: Neonatal Behavioral Assessment Scale. London, National Spastics Society, 1973

16. Horowitz FD, Self PA, Paden LN, et al: Newborn and four week retest on a normative population using the Brazelton newborn assessment procedure. Presented at the Annual Meeting of the

Society for Research in Child Development, Minneapolis, 1971 (unpublished)

17. Tronick E, Brazelton TB: Clinical uses of the Brazelton Neonatal Behavioral Assessment, in Friedlander BZ, Sterritt GM, Kirk GE (eds): Exceptional Infant, vol 3: Assessment and Intervention. New York, Brunner Mazel, 1975

18. Eisenberg RB, Griffin EJ, Coursin DB, et al: Auditory behavior in the human neonate: A preliminary report. J Speech Hear Res 7:245–269, 1964

19. Eimas P, Siqueland E, Lipsitt L: Work in progress. Brown University, 1975 (unpublished)

20. Goren C: Form perception, innate form preferences, and visually mediated head-turning in the human neonate. Presented at the Annual Meeting of the Society for Research in Child Development, Denver, 1975 (unpublished)

21. MacFarlane A: Personal communication (Oxford University, England, 1975)

22. Pettigrew JD: The effect of visual experience on the development of stimulus specificity by kitten cortical neurones. J Physiol 237:49–74, 1974

23. Blakemore C, Cooper GF: Development of the brain depends on the visual environment. Nature 228:477–478, 1970

24. Als H, Tronick E, Brazelton TB: Manual for the behavioral assessment of the premature and at-risk newborn (an extension of the Brazelton Neonatal Behavioral Assessment Scale). Presented at the Annual Meeting of the American Academy for Child Psychiatry, Toronto, 1976 (unpublished)

25. Kearsley RB: The newborn's response to auditory stimulation: A demonstration of orienting and defensive behavior. Child Dev 44:582–590, 1973

26. Sander LW, Chappell PF, Gould SB, et al: An investigation of change in the infant-caretaker system over the first week of life. Presented at the Annual Meeting of the Society for Research in Child Development, Denver, 1975 (unpublished)

27. Brazelton TB, Koslowski B, Main M: The origin of reciprocity in the mother-infant interaction, in Lewis M, Rosenblum L (eds): The Effect of the Infant on Its Caregiver, vol 1. New York, Wiley, 1974

28. Tronick E, Adamson L, Wise S, et al: Mother-infant face-to-face interaction, in Gosh S (ed): Biology and Language. London, Academic, 1975

29. Brazelton TB, Tronick E, Adamson L, et al: Early mother-infant reciprocity. Ciba Found Symp 33, 1975, pp 137–154

30. Yogman M, Dixon S, Adamson L, et al: The development of infant interaction with fathers. Work in progress. Children's Hospital Medical Center, Boston, 1975 (unpublished)

31. Seay B, Hansen E, Harlow HF: Mother-infant separation in monkeys. J Child Psychol Psychiatr 3:123–132, 1962

32. Spitz R: Hospitalization: An inquiry into the genesis of psychiatric conditions in early childhood. Psychoanal Study Child 1:53–74, 1945

33. Provence S, Lipton RC: Infants in Institutions. New York, International Universities, 1962

34. Erikson ML: Assessment and Management of Developmental Changes in Children. St. Louis, Mosby, 1976, pp 67–70

35. Field TM, Dempsey JD, Hallock NH, et al: The mother's assessment of the behavior of her infant. Inf Behav Dev 1:156–167, 1978

36. Parker WB, Als H, Brazelton TB: Neonatal behavior and the attachment process between a mother and her infant. Work in progress. Children's Hospital Medical Center, Boston, 1978 (unpublished)

Jerome Kagan

THE DETERMINANTS OF ATTENTION IN THE INFANT

The evolution of a science is recorded in what are usually gradual but are sometimes abrupt changes in the central question asked, the concepts preferred, and the subject judged convenient for study. Nineteenth-century physiologists asked how sensory events were transferred from receptor surface to brain, conceived of a process requiring energy transmission, and studied animal forms with accessible afferent nerves. Physiologists now believe they know how a flash of light travels from the retina inward but remain puzzled over what happens when afferent nerves release their information at the end of the journey. This question has generated the concepts of inhibition and arousal and has attracted investigators to organisms whose brains are accessible to surgery and electrical recording.

Psychology too has experienced a dramatic shift in preferred question, process, and organism. Until recently behavioral scientists wanted to understand how an animal learned a new habit, be it running a maze or pressing a bar with its paw. The solution seemed to require theoretical and empirical inquiry into the phenomena surrounding motivation, reinforcement, and the hypothetical connections between external stimulus and response. This conception of the problem led naturally to the selection of small mammals which allowed close control of experimental conditions. Psychologists have recently redirected their interest from the puzzle of response acquisition to the mystery of mental processes. This shift is due to several factors. Neurophysiologists have found that the brain's electrical activity covaries more closely with states of attention than with patterns of behavior. The psycholinguists have reminded psychology of the profound chasm between knowing and acting: the young child understands sentences long before he utters them, and all of us possess the competence to generate many more rules than we will ever use. Piaget's lifetime effort to outline a developmental history of the stages of human reasoning has catalyzed inquiry into the structure of thought in the child.

These lines of investigation have been supplemented by events in other sectors. Existentialism, drug experience, and popularizations of psychopathology have aroused interest in the quality of inner feelings at the expense of concern with the pragmatic outcome of action. Public recognition that the majority of school failures are poor children has led public and private institutions to increase their support of scientific exploration of children's thought. And the concept of critical period, an idea

Preparation of this paper was supported in part by research grant HD04299 from NICHD, United States Public Health Service, and a grant from the Carnegie Corporation of New York.

SOURCE: From Jerome Kagan, "The Determinants of Attention in the Infant." Reprinted by permission from the May 1970 issue of *American Scientist,* journal of Sigma Xi, The Scientific Research Society of North America.

born in experimental embryology and nurtured in comparative psychology, has prompted scientists to examine more carefully the early months of human development. These diverse forces have found a common aim in study of the mental processes of the young child.

A six-month-old infant displays a remarkable ability to focus his attention on interesting events, and he will maintain prolonged orientations to the face of a stranger, the movement of a leaf, or a lively conversation. He seems to be quietly absorbing information and storing it for future use. Since acquiring knowledge about the environment depends so intimately upon how the infant distributes his attention, and for how long, it is important to ask what governs these processes. This question has stimulated fruitful research from which an outline of preliminary principles is emerging.

EARLY DETERMINANTS OF FIXATION TIME: CONTRAST AND MOVEMENT

The most obvious index of attentiveness to visual events is the length of orientation to an object — called fixation time. Like any response it has multiple determinants; the relative power of each seems to change as the infant grows. Ontogenetically, the earliest determinant of length of orientation to a visual event derives from the basic nature of the central nervous system. The infant is predisposed to attend to events that possess a high rate of change in their physical characteristics. Stimuli that move or possess light-dark contrast are most likely to attract and hold a newborn's attention. A two-day-old infant is more attentive to a moving or intermittent light than to a continuous light source; to a design with a high degree of black-white contrast than to one of homogeneous hue (Haith 1966; Salapatek and Kessen 1966; Fantz 1966; Fantz and Nevis 1967). These facts come from experiments in which stimuli varying, for example, in degree of black-white contrast (e.g., a black triangle on a white background versus a totally gray stimulus) are presented to infants singly or in pairs while observers or cameras record the length of orientation to each of the stimuli. In general, the newborn's visual search behavior seems to be guided by the following rules: (1) If he is alert and the light is not too bright, his eyes open. (2) Seeing no light, he searches. (3) Seeing light but no edges, he keeps searching. (4) Finding contour edges, his eyes focus on and cross them (Haith 1968).

The attraction to loci of maximal contrast and movement is in accord with knowledge about ganglion potentials in the retinas of vertebrates. Some ganglion cells respond to a light going on; others to its going off; still others to both. Since an object moving across a visual field stimulates a set of cells for a short period, it creates onset and offset patterns similar to those of an intermittent light. Figures that contain dark lines on light backgrounds serve better as onset stimuli than do solid patterns because the change in stimulation created by the border of dark on light elicits more frequent firing of nerve cells, and this phenomenon may facilitate sustained attention (Kuffler 1952, 1953).

The preference for attending to objects with high contrast is dependent, however, on the size of the figure; there seems to be an optimal area that maintains fixation at a maximum. Four-month-old infants shown designs of varying areas (Fig. 1) were most attentive to the moderately large designs (Fig. 2) (McCall and Kagan 1967). Similarly there is a nonlinear relation between the total amount of black-white edge in a figure and attention. Consider a series of black-and-white checkerboards of constant area but varying numbers of squares. The total number of inches at which black borders white increases as the number of squares increases. Karmel (1966) has suggested, on the basis of studies with

Figure 1. One of a set of random designs shown to four-month infants.

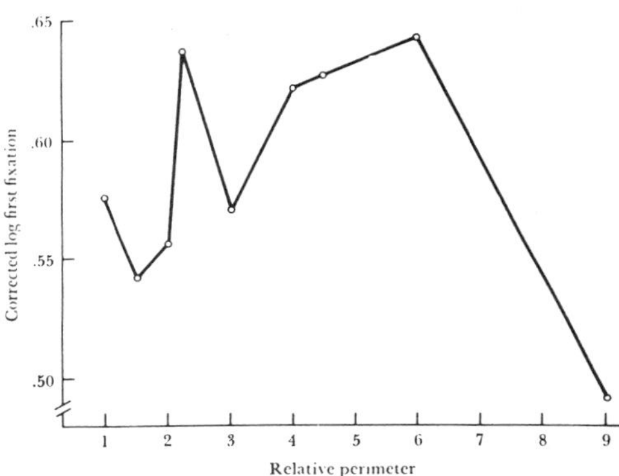

Figure 2. Relation between fixation time and approximate area of random design in four-month infants.

young infants, that the longest fixations are devoted to figures with a moderate amount of edge.

Although indices of attention to auditory events are more ambiguous than those to visual ones, intermittent tones, which have a high rate of change, elicit more sustained interest, as evidenced by motor quieting, than continuous tones (Eisenberg 1964; Brackbill 1966). Nature has apparently awarded the newborn an initial bias in his processing of experience. He does not have to learn what he should examine, as the nineteenth-century empiricists argued. The preferential orientation to change is clearly adaptive, for the source of change is likely to contain the most information about the presence of his mother or danger.

THE ROLE OF DISCREPANCY FROM SCHEMA

The initial disposition to attend to events with a high rate of change soon competes with a new determinant based on experience. The child's encounters with events result, inevitably, in some mental representation of the experience, called a schema. A schema is defined as an abstraction of a sensory event that preserves the spatial or temporal pattern of the distinctive elements of the event. A schema is to be regarded as a functional property of mind that permits an organism to recognize and retrieve information. The schema does not necessarily involve a motor response. It is neither a detailed copy of the event nor synonymous with the language label for the event. An example from a recent experiment may be useful here.

A four-year-old looked through a set of 50 magazine pictures illustrating objects, people, or scenes, many of which he had never seen before and could not name when asked. He spent only a few seconds on each picture and flipped through the 50 in less than three minutes. He was then shown 50 pairs of pictures; one of each pair was the picture he saw earlier, the other was new. He was asked to point to the picture he saw before. Although he could recall spontaneously only three or four, the average four-year-old recognized over 45 of the 50 pictures. Some children recognized them all. Since some of the pictures showed objects the child had never seen (say, a lathe or a slide rule), it is unlikely that his performance can be totally explained by assuming that each picture elicited a language label or a fragmentary motor response. What hypothetical entity shall we invoke to explain the child's ability to recognize over 90 percent of the scenes? If we use the concept schema to refer to the processes that permitted recognition, we can say that each picture contained a unique configuration of salient elements, and the schema preserved that configuration, without necessarily preserving an exact spatial analogue of the event. Some psychologists might use the older term memory engram to convey the meaning we attribute to schema. The schema for a visual event is not a photographic copy, for minor changes in the scenes viewed initially do not produce changes in the child's performance. Nor is the schema synonymous with a visual image, for the child is also able to recognize a series of different melodies or sound patterns after brief exposure to each. Early twentieth-century biologists used the concept of the gene to explain demonstrated properties of cells and nuclear material, though no one knew the gene's structure. We use the concept of schema to account for properties of mind, even though we cannot specify its structure.

The notion of schema helps to explain the older infant's distribution of attention. Toward the end of the second month, fixation time is influenced by the degree to which the child's memory for a particular class of events resembles the specific external event encountered originally. Thus the length of orientation to a picture of a strange face is dependent on the child's schema for the faces he has seen in the past. Events which are moderately discrepant from his schema elicit longer fixations than very familiar events or ones that are completely novel and bear no relation to the schema. The relation of fixation time to magnitude of discrepancy between schema and event is assumed to be curvilinear; this assumption is called the discrepancy hypothesis.

The neurophysiologist describes this attentional phenomenon in slightly different language.

> The prepotent role of novelty in evoking the orienting reflex suggests that this response is not initiated directly by a stimulus, in the customary sense of the term, but rather by a change in its intensity, pattern or other parameters. A comparison of present with previous stimulation seems of prime significance, with an orienting reflex being evoked by each point of disagreement. The concept of a cortical neuronal model . . . accounts for this induction of the orienting reflex by stimuli whose characteristic feature is their novelty. This model preserves information about earlier stimuli, with which aspects of novel stimulation may be compared. The orienting reflex is evoked whenever the parameters of the novel stimulus do not coincide with those of the model [Magoun 1969, p. 180].

Although an orienting reflex can often be produced by any change in quality or intensity of stimulation, duration of sustained attention seems to be influenced by the degree of discrepancy between event and related schema. Consider some empirical support for the discrepancy hypothesis. One- or two-week-old infants look equally long at a black-and-white outline of a regular face (upper right Fig. 3) and a meaningless design, for contrast is still the major determinant of attention at this early age. Even the eight-week-old attends equally long to a three-dimensional model of a head and an abstract three-dimensional form (Carpenter 1969). But four-month-old infants show markedly longer fixations to the two regular faces in Figure 3 than to the design in Figure 1 (McCall and Kagan 1967). The four-month-old has acquired a schema for a human face, and the achromatic illustra-

Figure 3. Achromatic faces shown to infants.

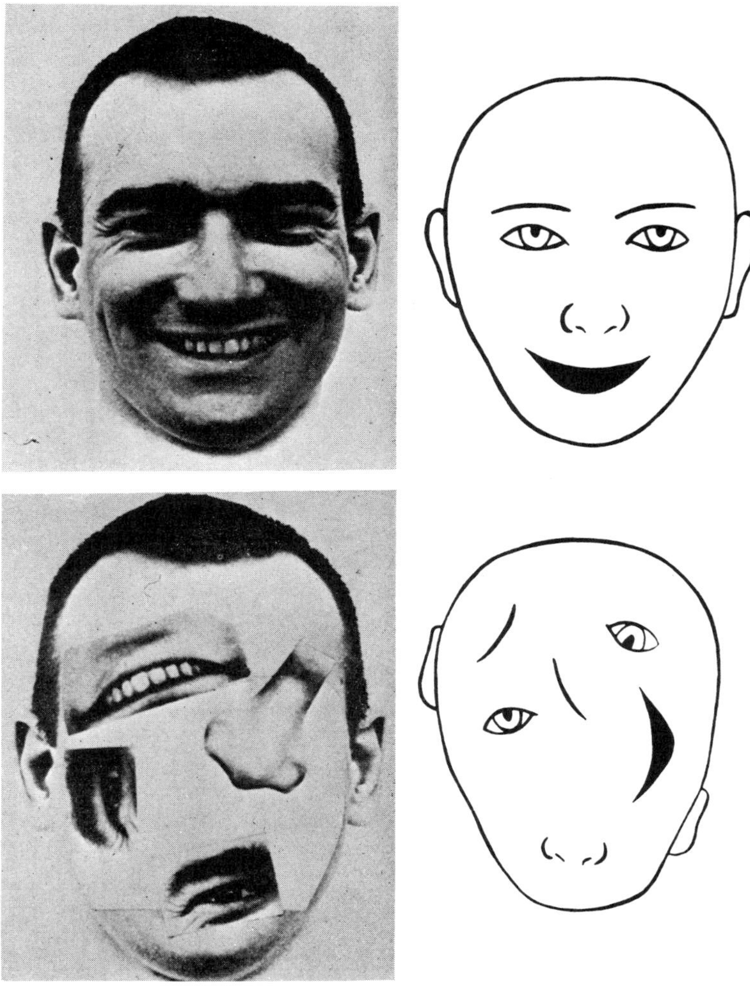

tions are moderately discrepant from that schema. However, if the face is highly discrepant from the schema, as occurs when the components are rearranged (the lower faces in Fig. 3), fixation time is reduced (Wilcox 1969; Haaf and Bell 1967). The moderately discrepant face elicits more sustained attention than the extremely discrepant form at 16 weeks, but not during the first eight weeks of life (Fantz and Nevis 1967; Wilcox 1969; Lewis 1969). The differences in length of fixation to a normal face and to an equally complex but distorted face is greatest between three and six months of age, when infants normally display long fixations to faces. After six months fixation times to photographs of

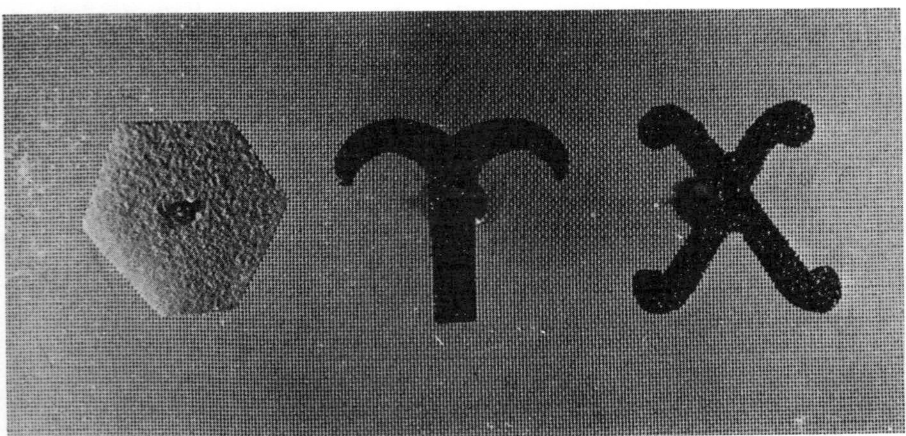

Figure 4. One of the two standard mobiles shown to infants in the laboratory.

faces drop by over 50 percent and are equally long for both regular and irregular faces (Lewis 1969).

This developmental pattern confirms the discrepancy hypothesis. Prior to two months, before the infant has a schema for a human face, photographs of either regular or irregular faces are treated as nonsense designs and elicit equal periods of attention. Between two and four months the schema for a human face is established, and a photograph of a strange face is optimally discrepant from that schema. During the latter half of the first year, the schema for a face becomes so firmly established that photographs of regular or irregular faces, though discriminable, elicit short and equal fixations.

A second source of support for the discrepancy hypothesis comes from experiments in which an originally meaningless stimulus is presented repeatedly (usually 5 to 10 times), and afterward a variation of the original stimulus is shown to the infant. Fixation time typically decreases with repetitions of the first stimulus; but when the variation is presented, fixation times increase markedly (McCall and Melson 1969). In one experiment four-month-old infants were shown a stimulus containing three objects (a doll, a bow, and a flower) for five 30-second presentations. On the sixth trial the infants saw a stimulus in which one, two, or all three objects were replaced with new ones. Most infants showed significantly longer fixations to the changed stimulus than to the last presentation of the original (McCall and Kagan 1970).

The most persuasive support for the curvilinear hypothesis comes from an experiment in which a new schema was established experimentally (Super, Kagan, Morrison, Haith, and Weiffenbach, unpublished). Each of 84 firstborn Caucasian infants, four months old, was shown the same three-dimensional stimulus composed of three geometric forms of different shape and hue for 12 half-minute periods (Fig. 4). Each infant was then randomly assigned to one of seven groups. Six of these groups were exposed at home to a stimulus that was of varying discrepancy from the standard viewed in the laboratory. The mother showed the stimulus, in the form of a

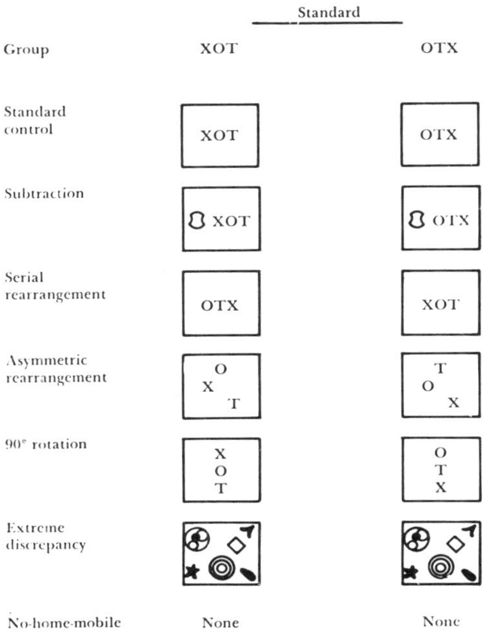

Figure 5. Schematic illustration of the mobiles infants saw at home for 21 days.

mobile, to the child 30 minutes a day for 21 days. The seven experimental groups were as follows (Fig. 5):

Group 1: Control standard. These infants were exposed to the same stimulus they saw in the laboratory at four months.

Group 2: Subtraction. These infants were shown a four-element stimulus constructed by adding a fourth element to the three-element standard seen in the laboratory. ("Subtraction" referred to the later laboratory session [see below], which used only three elements.)

Group 3: Serial rearrangement. Infants exposed to a stimulus in which the three elements of the original standard were rearranged in the horizontal plane.

Group 4: Asymmetric rearrangement. Infants shown the three-element stimulus rearranged in an asymmetric form.

Group 5: Ninety-degree rotation. Infants shown a stimulus in which the three horizontal elements in the standard were rearranged in a vertical plane.

Group 6: Extreme discrepancy. Infants shown a mobile consisting of many more elements of different shapes and colors than those of the standard.

Group 7: No-mobile control. Infants exposed to no stimulus during the 21 day experimental period.

Three weeks later each subject was brought back to the laboratory and shown the same stimulus viewed initially at four months. The major dependent variable was the change in fixation time between the first and second

Figure 6. Relation between fixation time to faces and age of child.

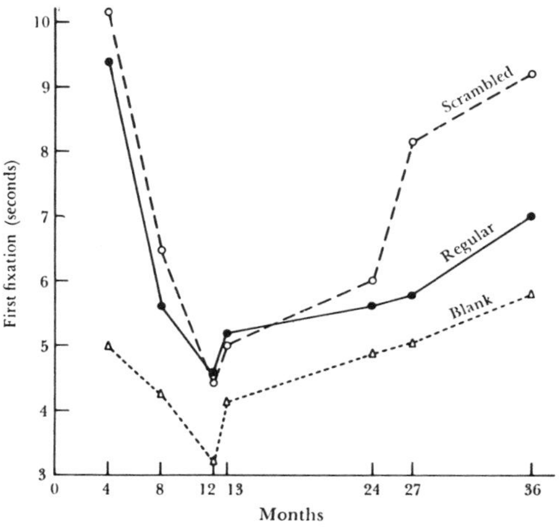

test sessions. Figure 6 illustrates these change scores for total fixation time across the first six trials of each session.

The infants who saw no stimulus at home are the referent group to which all the other groups are to be compared. These infants showed no change in fixation time across the three weeks, indicating that the laboratory stimulus was as attractive on the second visit as on the first. The infants who developed a schema for the asymmetric and vertical rotation mobiles (moderate discrepancy) showed the smallest drop in interest across the three weeks. By contrast, the infants who experienced a minimal (groups 2 and 3) or major discrepancy (group 6) showed the greatest drop in interest. (Analysis of variance for total fixation time across the first six trials yielded an F ratio of 5.29 and a probability value of less than .05.) There was a curvilinear relation between attention and stimulus-schema discrepancy. Although the existing data are still not conclusive, they clearly support the discrepancy hypothesis.

The onset of a special reaction to discrepancy between two and three months is paralleled by other physiological and behavioral changes in the infant. Temporal characteristics of the cortical evoked potential to a visual stimulus approach adult form, growth of occipital neurons levels off, and the alpha rhythm of the electroencephalogram becomes recognizable (Ellingson 1967). The Moro reflex — the spreading and coming together of the arms when the head is suddenly dropped a few inches — begins to disappear, crying decreases, babbling increases, decreased attention to repeated presentations of a visual event becomes a reliable phenomenon (Dreyfus-Brisac 1958; Ellingson 1967), and three-dimensional representations of objects elicit longer fixations than two-dimensional ones (Fantz 1966). Perhaps the infant's capacity to react to discrepancy at this age reflects the fact that the brain has matured enough to permit the establishment of long-term memories and their activation by external events.

THE EFFECT OF THE INFANT'S HYPOTHESES

As the child approaches the end of the first year he acquires a new kind of cognitive structure which we call hypotheses. A hypothesis is an interpretation of some experience accomplished by mentally transforming an unusual event to the form the child is familiar with. The "form he is familiar with" is the schema. The cognitive structure used in the transformation is the hypothesis. Suppose a five-year-old notes a small bandage on his mother's face; he will attempt to find the reason for the bandage and may activate the hypothesis, "She cut her face." A five-month-old will recognize his mother in spite of the bandage but will not try to explain its presence.

To recognize that a particular sequence of sounds is human speech, rather than a telephone, requires a schema for the quality of a human voice. Interpretation of the meaning of the speech, on the other hand, requires the activation of hypotheses, in this case linguistic rules. The critical difference between a schema and a hypothesis resembles the difference between recognition and interpretation. Recognition is the assimilation of an event as belonging to one class rather than another. The performance of the four-year-old in the experiment with 50 pictures illustrates the recognition process. The child requires only a schema for the original event in order to answer correctly. Interpretation involves the additional process of activating hypotheses that change the perception of an event so that it can be understood. It is assumed that the activation of hypotheses to explain discrepant events is accompanied by sustained attention. The more extensive the repertoire of hypotheses — the more knowledge the child has — the longer he can work at interpretation and the more prolonged his attention. The child's distribution of attention at an art museum provides a final analogy. He may be expected to study somewhat unusual pictures longer than extremely realistic ones or surrealistic ones because he is likely to have a richer set of hypotheses for the moderately discrepant scenes. The richer the repertoire of hypotheses, holding discrepancy of event constant, the longer the child will persist at interpretation. There is as yet no body of empirical proof for these ideas, but data that we shall consider agree with these views.

In sum, three factors influence length of fixation time in the infant. High rate of change in physical aspects of the stimulus is primary during the opening weeks, discrepancy becomes a major factor at two months, and activation of hypotheses becomes influential at around 12 months. These three factors supplement each other; and a high-contrast, discrepant event that activates many hypotheses should elicit longer fixation times from an 18-month-old than a stimulus with only one or two of these attributes.

Two parallel investigations attest to the potential usefulness of the complementary principles of discrepancy and activation of hypotheses. In the first, one-, two-, and three-year-old children of middle class families in Cambridge, Massachusetts, and of peasant Indian families from a village in the Yucatan peninsula were shown color prints of male faces — Caucasian for the American children and Indian for the Mexican children (Finley 1967). Fixation time to the faces increased with age. The largest increase between two and three years of age occurred to the discrepant, scrambled face rather than to the nondiscrepant, regular face; the former required the activation of more hypotheses in order to be assimilated.

In the second study 180 white, first-born boys and girls from the Cambridge area viewed the clay faces in Figure 7 repeatedly at 4, 8, 13, and 27 months of age. There was a U-shaped relation between age and fixation time. Fixation decreased from 4 to 13 months but increased between 13 and 27 months. The longer fixations at 4 months reflect the fact that these stimuli were discrepant from the infant's acquired schema for his parents' faces. Fixations decreased at 8 and 13 months because these masks were less discrepant but did not yet activate a long train of hypotheses in the service of assimilation. Between one and two years fixations rose because the child was activating hypotheses to resolve the discrepancy.

As with the first study, the largest increase in fixation time, between 13 and 27 months, occurred to the scrambled face. The children's spontaneous comments indicated that they were trying to understand how a face could be so transformed. "What happened to his nose? Who hit him in the nose?" asked a two-year-old. And, "Who that, Mommy? A monster, Mommy?" said another.

The function resulting from combining the data of the two studies is illustrated in Figure 8. The U-shaped relation between fixation time and age is concordant with the theoretical argument given earlier.

SOCIAL CLASS AND FIXATION TIME

The number of hypotheses surrounding a class of events should covary, in part, with language competence. Hence any experiences that promote acquisition of language should be associated with longer fixation times toward the end of the first year. The positive correlation between parental educational level and the child's linguistic competence is well known and well documented (see, for example, Cazden 1966). Thus a positive relation between parental education and fixation time should appear toward the end of the first

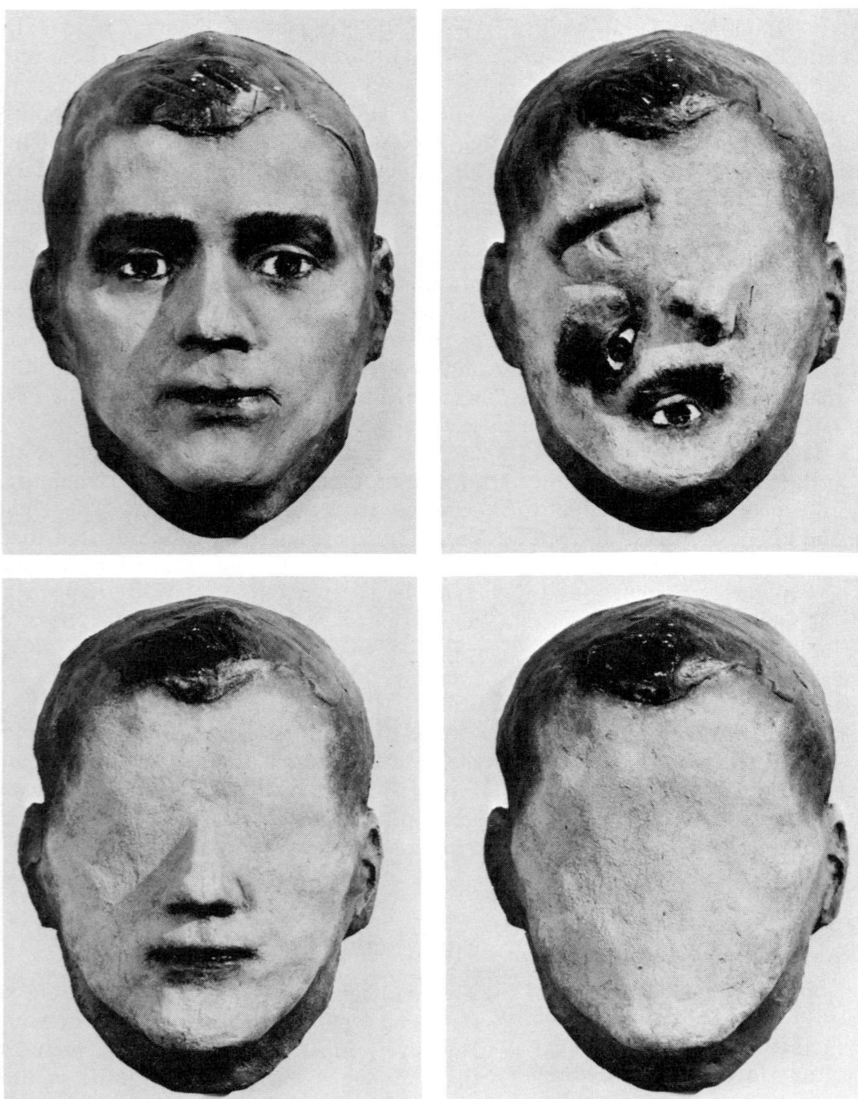

Figure 7. Clay masks shown to children at 4, 8, 13, and 27 months.

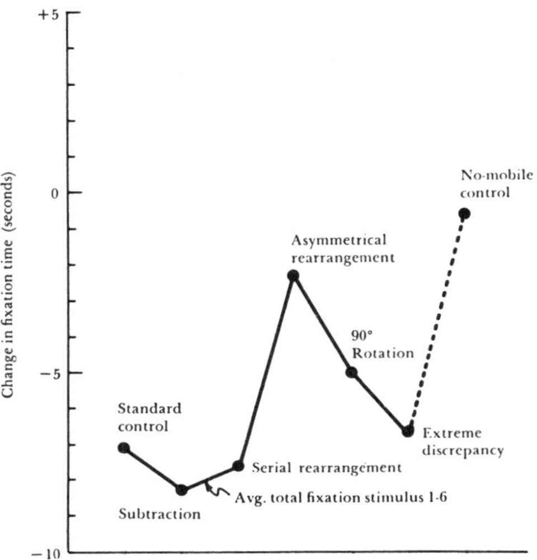

Figure 8. Change in fixation time for each of the experimental groups.

year and grow with time. The data on 180 firstborns indicated that parental education was not highly related to fixation time to faces at 4 and 8 months but was moderately related (correlation coefficient [r] = about 0.4) at 13 and 27 months, and this relation was slightly stronger for girls than for boys. Since the majority of infants either increased in fixation time or showed no essential change between 13 and 27 months, we computed the change in first fixation between 13 and 27 months for each child and correlated that change with parental educational level as well as independent indexes of verbal ability at 27 months. There was a positive relation between increase in fixation time and parents' educational level for the girls (r = .31) but not for boys (r = —.04); 27-month-old girls with the highest vocabulary scores showed the largest increases in fixation time.

It is not clear why the relation between parental education and sustained attention should be stronger for girls than for boys. Other investigators have also reported closer covariation in girls than boys between social class and various indexes of cognitive development including IQ scores and school grades. Moss and Robson (1968) studied the relation between amount of face-to-face interaction mother and infant had in the home and the three-month-old infant's fixation time to photographs of faces in the laboratory. The association was positive for girls (r = .61, $p < .01$) and close to zero for boys. Hess, Shipman, Brophy, and Bear (1968, 1969) and Werner (1969) have reported more substantial correlations for girls than boys between maternal education or verbal ability, on the one hand, and the child's IQ or level of reading achievement on the other. There seems to be a general tendency for indexes of maternal intellectual ability and, by inference, maternal concern with the child's mental development, to be better predictors of cognitive development in daughters than sons.

One interpretation of this puzzling phenomenon rests on the fact that girls are biologically less variable than boys (Acheson 1966). This implies that fewer infant girls would display extreme degrees of irritability, activity, or attentiveness. Let us assume the following principle: the more often the mother attempts to interest her child in an event the stronger the child's tendency to develop a general sensitivity to change and a capacity for sustained attention to discrepancy. This principle is likely to be less valid for infants who temperamentally have a tendency toward apathy or hypervigilance. There are many functional relations in nature that lose their validity when one of the variables assumes an extreme value, and this may be another instance of that phenomenon.

An alternative explanation of the stronger covariation for girls than boys between maternal intelligence and the child's mental development assumes greater differences between well and poorly educated mothers in their treatment of daughters than of sons, especially in maternal actions that promote attention and language acquisition. A mother seems more likely to project her motives, expectations, and self-image on her daughter than on her son, and is more likely to assume that her daughter will come to resemble her. Many poorly educated mothers feel less competent than the college graduate and have greater doubts about their daughters' potential for intellectual accomplishment. Such a mother may set or supply lower standards and less enthusiastic as well as less consistent encouragement to her infant girl to learn new skills. The well educated mother sets higher aspirations and acts as though she held the power to catalyze her child's development.

The situation with sons is somewhat different. Most mothers, regardless of class background, believe their sons will have to learn how to support a family and achieve some degree of independence. Hence mothers of all classes may be more alike in energizing the cognitive development of sons. The restricted range of acceleration of sons, compared with daughters, would result in closer covariation for girls between social class and indexes of cognitive development.

This argument finds support in observations of the mother-child interaction in the home. Well educated mothers are more likely to talk to their four-month-old daughters than mothers with less than a high school education. But this class difference in maternal "talkativeness" does not occur for sons. Observations of an independent sample of 60 mother-daughter pairs at 10 months of age (Tulkin, unpublished) also indicates that middle, in contrast to lower, class mothers spend significantly more time in face-to-face contact with their daughters, vocalize more often to them, and more frequently reward their attempts to crawl and stand. A final source of data is the home observations on some of the 180 children at 27 months. The observer noted each instance in which the mother reproved the child for disobeying a rule. Mothers of all social classes were more likely to reprove sons than daughters. However, reproval for incompetence at a task was most frequently meted out by the well educated mothers of daughters; there was no comparable class difference for mothers of sons.

Thus, independent and complementary evidence supports the idea that differential pressures toward intellectual competence are more likely to covary with social class for mother-daughter than for mother-son pairs. It has usually been assumed that the girl is more concerned with acceptance by parents and teachers than the boy, and that this particular motive for intellectual accomplishment covaries with social class; but intellectual achievement among boys is spurred by more varied motives, including hostility, power, and identification with competent male figures — motives less closely linked to social class. However valid these propositions, they are not operative during the first year of life.

IMPLICATIONS

The influence of contrast, discrepancy, and activation of hypotheses on distribution of attention is probably not limited to the first two years of life. Schools implicitly acknowledge the validity of these principles for older children by using books with contrasting colors and unusual formats and by emphasizing procedures whose aim is to ensure that the child has a relevant hypothesis available when he encounters a new problem. A child who possesses no hypothesis for solution of a problem is likely to withdraw from the task. Many children regard mathematics as more painful than English or social studies because they have fewer strategies to use with a difficult problem in arithmetic than for one in history or composition. The school might well give children more help in learning to generate hypotheses with which to solve problems, and put less pressure on them to accumulate facts.

The principles discussed in this paper are also related to this issue of incentives for acquiring new knowledge. The behaviorist, trying to preserve the theoretical necessity of the concept of reinforcement, has been vexed by the fact that the child acquires new knowledge in the absence of any demonstrable external reward. However, the process of assimilating a discrepant event to a schema has many of the characteristics of a pleasant experience and therefore is in accord with the common understanding of a reward. The central problem in educating children is to attract and maintain focused attention. The central theoretical problem in understanding mental growth is to discern the factors that are continually producing change in schema and hypothesis. Solution of these two problems is not to be found through analyses of the environment alone. We must decipher the relation between the perceiver and the space in which he moves, for that theme, like Ariadne's thread, gives direction to cognitive growth.

REFERENCES

Acheson, R. N. 1966. Maturation of the skeleton. In F. Falkner, ed. *Human development.* Philadelphia: W. B. Saunders, pp. 465–502.

Brackbill, Y., G. Adams, D. H. Crowell, and M. C. Gray. 1966. Arousal level in newborns and preschool children under continuous auditory stimulation. *J. Exp. Child Psychol.* 3:176–88.

Carpenter, G. C. Feb. 1969. Differential visual behavior to human and humanoid faces in early infancy. Presented at Merrill-Palmer Infancy Conference, Detroit, Mich.

Cazden, C. B. 1966. Subcultural differences in child language. *Merrill-Palmer Quart.* 12:185–219.

Dreyfus-Brisac, C., D. Samson, C. Blanc, and N. Monod. 1958. L'électroencéphlograme de l'enfant normal de moins de trois ans. *Etudes néonatales* 7:143–75.

Eisenberg, R. B., E. J. Griffin, D. B. Coursin, and M. A. Hunter. 1964. Auditory behavior in the neonate. *J. Speech and Hearing Res.* 7:245–69.

Ellingson, R. J. 1967. Study of brain electrical activity in infants. In L. P. Lipsitt and C. C. Spiker, eds. *Advances in child development and behavior.* New York: Academic Press, pp. 53–98.

Fantz, R. L. 1966. Pattern discrimination and selective attention as determinants of perceptual development from birth. In A. H. Kidd and J. J. Rivoire, eds. *Perceptual development in children.* New York: International Universities Press.

Fantz, R. L., and S. Nevis. 1967. Pattern preferences in perceptual cognitive development in early infancy. *Merrill-Palmer Quart.* 13:77–108.

Finley, G. E. 1967. Visual attention, play, and satiation in young children: a cross cultural study. Unpublished doctoral dissertation, Harvard Univ.

Haaf, R. A., and R. Q. Bell. 1967. A facial dimension in visual discrimination by human infants. *Child Devel.* 38:893–99.

Haith, M. M. 1966. Response of the human newborn to visual movement. *J. Exp. Child Psychol.* 3:235–43.

Haith, M. M. March 1968. Visual scanning in infants. Paper presented at regional meeting of Society for Research in Child Development. Clark Univ., Worcester, Mass.

Hess, R. D., V. C. Shipman, J. E. Brophy, and R. M. Bear. 1968 and (follow-up phase) 1969. The cognitive environments of urban preschool children. Report to the Graduate School of Education, Univ. of Chicago.

Karmel, B. Z. 1966. The effect of complexity, amount of contour, element size and element arrangement on visual preference behavior in the hooded rat, domestic chick, and human infant. Unpublished doctoral dissertation, George Washington Univ., Washington, D.C.

Kuffler, S. W. 1952. Neurons in the retina: Organization, inhibition, and excitation problems. *Cold Spring Harbor Symposium in Quantitative Biology* 17:281–92.

Kuffler, S. W. 1953. Discharge patterns and functional organization of mammalian retina. *J. Physiol.* 16:37–68.

Lewis, M. 1969. Infants' responses to facial stimuli during the first year of life. *Devel. Psychol.* no. 2, pp. 75–86.

McCall, R. B., and J. Kagan. 1967. Attention in the infant: effects of complexity, contour, perimeter, and familiarity. *Child Devel.* 38:939–52.

McCall, R. B. and J. Kagan. 1970. Individual differences in the infant's distribution of attention to stimulus discrepancy. *Developmental Psychology* 2:90–98.

McCall, R. B., and W. H. Melson. March 1969. Attention in infants as a function of the magnitude of discrepancy and habituation rate. Paper presented at meeting of the Society for Research in Child Development. Santa Monica, Calif.

Magoun, H. W. 1969. Advances in brain research with implications for learning. In K. H. Pribram, ed., *On the biology of learning.* New York: Harcourt, Brace & World, pp. 171–90.

Moss, H. A. 1967. Sex, age and state as determinants of mother-infant interaction. *Merrill-Palmer Quart.* 13:19–36.

Moss, H. A., and K. S. Robson. 1968. Maternal influences on early social-visual behavior. *Child Devel.* 39:401–8.

Salapatek, P., and W. Kessen. 1966. Visual scanning of triangles by the human newborn. *J. Exp. Child Psychol.* 3:113–22.

Super, C., J. Kagan, F. Morrison, and M. Haith. An experimental test of the discrepancy hypothesis. Unpublished.

Tulkin, S. Social class differences in mother-child interaction. Unpublished.

Werner, E. E. 1969. Sex differences in correlations between children's IQs and measure of parental ability and environment ratings. *Devel. Psychol.* 1:280–85.

Wilcox, B. M. 1969. Visual preferences of human infants for representations of the human face. *J. Exp. Child Psychol.* 7:10–20.

Marc H. Bornstein, William Kessen, and Sally Weiskopf

THE CATEGORIES OF HUE IN INFANCY

ABSTRACT: Infant looking time was monitored during habituation to the repeated presentation of a wavelength stimulus selected from one basic adult hue category and after a change in stimulation. Recovery from habituation was greater to a wavelength selected from an adjacent hue category than to a wavelength from the same category even though these two stimuli were equally distant (in nanometers) from the habituation wavelength. Differential responding evidenced infants' categorical perception of hue; that is, infants see the physically continuous spectrum as divided into the hue categories of blue, green, yellow, and red. These results help to resolve the long-standing controversy surrounding the primacy of perception over language in the organization of hue.

We have found that 4-month-old infants respond to differences in wavelength as though they perceived categories of hue — blue, green, yellow, and red. That is, infants responded differently to two wavelengths selected from adjacent adult hue categories (for example, blue at 480 nm and green at 510 nm) but did not respond differently to two wavelengths separated by the same physical distance but selected from a single adult hue category (for example, blues at 450 nm and 480 nm).

Modern school children still paraphrase Newton's original observations on the categories of hue in the spectrum (*1*).

> The Original or primary colours are, *Red, Yellow, Green, Blew,* and a *Violet-purple,* together with *Orange, Indico,* and an indefinite variety of Intermediate gradations.

Substituting narrow monochromatic radiation for prism-dispersed sunlight, and psychophysical techniques for introspection (*2*), modern research has confirmed the relationship between wavelength and color naming given in Newton's original experiments. Wavelengths are usually described by one or two primary hue names (Fig. 1). Color-naming functions are roughly characterized by plateaus — wavelength ranges which form

Supported by grants from the Grant Foundation, Inc., and from the Carnegie corporation of New York; and an NIMH postdoctoral fellowship award 1 F22 MH58197–01 to M. H. B. We thank M. Clemens and N. Kasimer for observing, N. Cox, F. Davis, and C. Zimmer-Hart for technical assistance, and L. E. Marks and H. G. Bornstein for reading the manuscript. . . .

SOURCE: From Marc Bornstein, William Kessen, and Sally Weiskopf, "The Categories of Hue in Infancy," *Science,* Vol. 191, pp. 201–202, 16 January 1976.

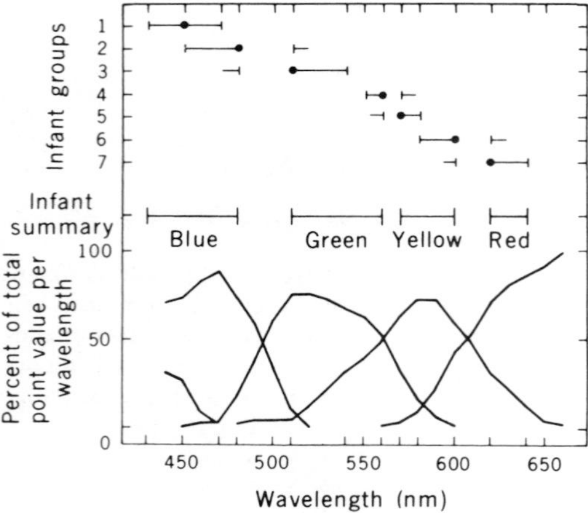

Figure 1. (Upper panel) Results for seven infant experimental groups. Dots stand for habituation stimuli, vertical bars for category and boundary stimuli; a horizontal connection indicates a lack of difference in mean looking times between wavelengths, and a gap indicates, by comparison, a statistically significant difference (see Table 1) (*18*). The summary gives ranges of wavelengths responded to as similar by infants as well as ranges of probable transition between hues. (Lower panel) Adult color-naming functions replotted after Boynton and Gordon (*14*).

categories where a single hue term predominates — and by boundaries between the plateaus. Although the physical dimension is continuous, the psychological structure is discontinuous. Moreover, it has been argued that discrimination is typically poor nearer the center of plateaus (these wavelengths look the same and, hence, tend to be called by the same name), but discrimination is good at boundaries between hues (as chromatic distinctions become clearer, color names change) (*3*). The categorical perception of hue may have a biological basis. De Valois (*4*), for example, has demonstrated that discrimination of wavelength in the macaque (which has demonstrated color vision identical with normal human adult trichromats) is a function of chromatic analysis by thalamic neural tissue. Furthermore, Bornstein (*5*) has matched the results of cross-cultural studies on the designation of hue category centers to the sensitivity maxima of these same neural cells. Finally, the observation that at least two infrahuman species (*6*) see hues categorically makes the assumption of a biological basis for qualitative chromatic distinctions more plausible than the alternative assumptions about learning and language.

These logical, psychological, neurological, and ethological considerations led us to hypothesize that very young human infants would see the physical spectrum in a categorical fashion much like that of adults. To test this hypothesis, we made use of the fact that babies look less and less at a visual stimulus that is repeatedly presented (*7*). At the end of the so-called habituation phase, a test stimulus perceived by the child as dissimilar from the first stimulus produces increased looking (dishabituation); if, however, the child sees the test stimulus as similar to the first stimulus, looking time remains low (continued habituation).

In our experimental situation, infants were shown a given wavelength of light (habituation stimulus, HS (*8*) for fifteen 15-second trials followed by a series of nine 15-second test trials. Intertrial intervals averaged 7.5 seconds. The test series consisted of three blocks each containing three randomized stimuli: HS and two physically different stimuli, one selected from the same category as HS (category stimulus, CS) and one selected from a category adjacent to HS (boundary stimulus, BS). In this design infants serve as their own controls since they are continuously probed in the test series for their responses to HS (*9*).

Our main hypothesis was that the basic hue categories (blue, green, yellow, and red) and the boundaries between categories (blue-green, green-yellow, and yellow-red) common to adults would exist in infants. Consequently, we chose wavelength stimuli to straddle the color-naming boundaries (HS and BS) or to fall wholly within a single adult color-naming category (HS and CS). Moreover, BS and CS in each test sequence were separated by equal physical distances (in nanometers) from HS. Thus, for example, HS for experimental group 2 was a 480-nm light which adults perceive as mostly blue, CS was a 450-nm light perceived by adults also as blue, and BS was a 510-nm light perceived by adults as mostly green. Consequently, if babies look longer at one or another of the test stimuli of 450, 480, and 510 nm, then we would have inferential evidence about the infants' perception of the similarities and qualitative categorization of these wavelengths. Each boundary was explored by two groups of infants — for one group HS and CS were drawn from the category on the short-wavelength side of the boundary (for example, experimental group 2) and for a second group HS and CS were drawn from the category on the long-wavelength side of the boundary (for example, experimental group 3). Thus, HS in group 3 was 510 nm, BS was 480 nm, and CS was 540 nm.

Eight groups of ten healthy, full-term 4-month-old Caucasian infants were seen. Infants looked at the stimuli across the boundaries blue-green, green-yellow, and yellow-red as well as at stimuli expected to fall fully within the four basic adult categories of hue (Table 1). Infants were assigned randomly to groups, with the exception that infants within each group were matched for sex as well as age (*10*).

Table 1. STIMULI AND RESULTS FOR INFANT GROUPS

	N			Mean looking times (seconds) for each stimulus (nanometers) tested						
Group	*M*	*F*	*Age in days (mean ± S.D.)*	*BS*	*Time*	*HS*	*Time*	*CS*	*Time*	P
				Blue plateau						
1	5	5	129 ± 14.0	430	5.0	450	4.2	470	4.5	NS
				Blue-green boundary						
2	5	5	124 ± 9.8	510	7.3	480	5.7	450	5.8	< .001
3	5	5	122 ± 6.8	480	7.0	510	5.0	540	4.0	< .001
				Green-yellow boundary						
4	5	5	129 ± 6.8	570	6.6	560	3.9	550	4.7	< .001
5	5	5	128 ± 6.4	560	6.2	570	3.3	580	4.4	< .001
				Yellow-red boundary						
6	5	5	120 ± 5.9	620	6.0	600	4.6	580	4.2	< .01
7	5	5	118 ± 4.7	600	4.5	620	6.1	640	5.4	< .05
				Control						
8	4	6	129 ± 11.7	630	4.3	630	4.8	630	5.0	NS

Note: N, number of males (*M*) and females (*F*). Mean looking times and individual comparisons are explained in (*18*). Abbreviations: *HS*, habituation stimulus; *CS*, category stimulus; *BS*, boundary stimulus; NS, not significant. *BS* was compared with *HS* and *CS*.

The upper panel of Fig. 1 shows that infants perceived a blue to green boundary between 480 and 510 nm, and parallel patterns of findings indicated hue boundaries for infants from green to yellow and from yellow to red. (*11*). Detailed analysis of these results reveals two additional aspects of the data (Table 1). First, as is common among adults (5), infants (group 1) did not respond to violet (430 nm) as though it were a unitary sensation and wholly different from blue (450 to 470 nm). Second, direction in looking time dishabituation for group 7 is reversed. Long wavelengths have been found to exert a singularly strong influence over infant attention (*12*); it may be, therefore, that sustained looking at 620 nm and 640 nm relative to 600 nm can best be attributed to infants' preference for red. Finally, a control group (experimental group 8) that received the same stimulus throughout both the habituation and test phases (630 nm for 24 consecutive trials) showed no statistical differences among the means of the three test-trial blocks (*13*). In comparison with our observations on infants, the lower panel of Fig. 1 reports Boynton and Gordon's observations of color naming in adults (*14*). In summary, our results indicate that the boundaries and categories for four basic hues are much the same for 4-month-old infants as they are for adults.

The results of this study have several implications. First, human infants group visible wavelengths into hue categories much like the adult's at an earlier age than had been thought in the past and long before the onset of language or formal tuition. These results, then, demonstrate that infants have color vision. Second, the parallel existence of categories in infants and adults, for hue as for speech (*15*), is significant for understanding what organization of the environment the child brings to language. Finally, these results help to resolve an anthropological-linguistic question (*16, 17*) which dates back to Gladstone (*16*): In color, does perception influence language or language influence perception? The fact that the basic hue categories of infants match those of adults strongly favors the primacy of perception.

Department of Psychology,
Yale University,
New Haven, Connecticut 06520

REFERENCES AND NOTES

1. I. Newton, *Philos. Trans. R. Soc. London 80,* 3082 (1671–1672).

2. Recent psychophysical techniques have included naming [A. C. Beare, *Am. J. Psychol. 76,* 248 (1963)], scaling [R. M. Boynton and J. Gordon, *J. Opt. Soc. Am. 55,* 78 (1965)], and similarity estimation [G. Ekman, *Stud. Gen. 16,* 54 (1963)].

3. Wavelength discriminability and hue naming do not coexist in a perfectly correlated way. However, there exist evidence and expert opinion that a high correlation between plateaus and regions of poor discriminability exists in both pigeon [A. A. Wright, *Vision Res. 12,* 1447 (1972)] and man [W. D. Wright, *Researches on Normal and Defective Colour Vision* (Mosby, St. Louis, 1947); L. C. Thomson, *Opt. Acta 1,* 93 (1954); G. Ekman, *ibid.* p. 64; G. Jacobs and H. Gaylord, *Vision Res. 7,* 645 (1967); D. P. Smith, *ibid. 11,* 739 (1971); and B. Graham, M. Turner, D. Hurst, *J. Opt. Soc. Am. 63,* 109 (1973)].

4. R. L. De Valois, I. Abramov, W. R. Mead, *J. Neurophysiol. 30,* 415 (1967); see also A. Cerf-Beare, [*Percept. Psychophys. 13,* 546 (1973)].

5. M. H. Bornstein, *Psychol. Bull. 80,* 257 (1973).

6. Bees [K. von Frisch, *Bees: Their Vision, Chemical Senses, and Language* (Cornell Univ. Press, Ithaca, 1964), pp. 1–24] and pigeons [A. A. Wright and W. W. Cumming, *J. Exp. Anal. Behav. 15,* 7 (1971)] categorize the photic spectrum into hues.

7. L. B. Cohen and E. Gelber, in *Infant Perception,* L. B. Cohen and P. Salapatek, Eds. (Academic Press, New York, in press).

8. Chromatic flux was generated by a monochromator system [M. H. Bornstein and N. Cox, *Behav. Res. Methods Instrum.* 6, 31 (1974)], and calibrations were completed as described by M. H.

Bornstein [*J. Exp. Child Psychol.* *19,* 401 (1975)]. Lights were equated in luminance (3.4 cd/m²) by Judd's modification of International Commission on Illumination (Commission Internationale de l'Eclairage, C.I.E.) Standard Observer luminosity [D. B. Judd, *C.I.E. Proc.* *1,* 11 (1951); for details see G. Wyszecki and W. S. Stiles, Eds., *Color Science* (Wiley, New York, 1967), p. 436]. D. Y. Teller and D. R. Peeples [papers addressed to Association for Research in Vision and Ophthalmology, Sarasota, Fla. (April 1974 and 1975)] have presented evidence that relative spectral sensitivities for infants and adults (CIE) do not differ significantly at medium and long visible wavelengths; our use of Judd's modification of CIE would tend to reduce further potential differences at short wavelengths. Stimuli were circular (88.9 mm diameter), subtended approximately 10° of visual angle at the infant's eye, and were presented against a matte black surround.

9. This technique is a test of coding or categorization and not of discrimination per se, since test stimuli (HS, CS, and BS) and the habituation stimulus (HS) were never simultaneously present.

10. We included in our analysis only children whose looking time (means) on the last three trials of the habituation phase was less than 80 percent of the mean of the highest earlier three-trial period of the habituation phase. That is, we thought some reasonable reduction of looking at HS was requisite to successful testing of the habituation-dishabituation paradigm. Consequently, children who were included showed statistically significant decrements in looking time over the course of habituation ($P < .001$ in all groups).

11. In addition, two infant groups ($HS_s =$ 590 and 600 nm) responded equally to wavelengths between 580 and 610 nm.

12. M. H. Bornstein (*8*). The two reds in group 7 (620 and 640 nm) are predictably, statistically, and reliably separable from 600 nm.

13. This control, along with built-in intraobserver controls, eliminates explanations of these results based on fluctuations of attention.

14. R. M. Boynton and J. Gordon (*2*). In their experiment, subjects were allowed to use one or a combination of two basic color terms — red, yellow, green, or blue — to describe a variety of spectral lights seen in Maxwellian view. Responses were quantified and scaled on the basis of the number of terms used. To derive the percentage functions presented in the lower panel of Fig. 1, we averaged Boynton and Gordon's data at each wavelength and divided the mean number of points for each term by the total number of points for all terms at each wavelength.

15. P. D. Eimas, E. R. Siqueland, P. Jusczyk, J. Vigorito, *Science 171,* 303 (1971).

16. W. E. Gladstone, *Homer and the Homeric Age* (Oxford Univ. Press, Oxford, 1858), vol. 3, pp. 457–499.

17. W. H. R. Rivers, *Br. J. Psychol. 1,* 321 (1905); J. B. Carroll, Ed., *Language, Thought, and Reality: Selected Writings of Benjamin Lee Whorf* (MIT Press, Cambridge, Mass., 1956); M. H. Segall, D. T. Campbell, M. J. Herskovits, *The Influence of Culture on Visual Perception* (Bobbs-Merrill, Indianapolis, 1966), pp. 36–48; B. Berlin and P. Kay, *Basic Color Terms* (University of California Press, Berkeley, 1969); M. Cole and S. Scribner, *Culture and Thought* (Wiley, New York, 1974), p. 44, M. H. Bornstein, *Am. Anthropol.,* in press.

18. Infants' looking was unrestrained, and looking time, the dependent variable, was judged in real time by observers ignorant of both the stimulus wavelength and the infant group. The range of interobserver reliabilities was .932 to .969. Only data from the test phase following habituation are included and represent the means of three trials each for stimuli HS, CS, and BS. Significance of differences among these means was handled within an individual comparisons analysis of variance design [B. J. Winer, *Statistical Principles in Experimental Design* (McGraw-Hill, New York, 1971), pp. 384–388] in which specific, theoretically predicted comparisons (BS versus HS and CS) were tested. No stable sex differences were found.

11

Daniel G. Freedman

ETHNIC DIFFERENCES IN BABIES

The human species comes in an admirable variety of shapes and colors, as a walk through any cosmopolitan city amply demonstrates. Although the speculation has become politically and socially unpopular, it is difficult not to wonder whether the major differences in physical appearances are accompanied by standard differences in temperament or behavior. Recent studies by myself and others of babies only a few hours, days, or weeks old indicate that they are, and that such differences among human beings are biological as well as cultural.

These studies of newborns from different ethnic backgrounds actually had their inception with work on puppies, when I attempted to raise dogs in either an indulged or disciplined fashion in order to test the effects of such rearing on their later behavior.

I spent all my days and evenings with these puppies, and it soon became apparent that the breed of dog would become an important factor in my results. Even as the ears and eyes opened, the breeds differed in behavior. Little beagles were irrepressibly friendly from the moment they could detect me; Shetland sheepdogs were very, very sensitive to a loud voice or the slightest punishment; wire-haired terriers were so tough and aggressive, even as clumsy three-week-olds, that I had to wear gloves while playing with them; and finally, Basenjis, barkless dogs originating in Central Africa, were aloof and independent. To judge by where they spent their time, sniffing and investigating, I was no more important to them than if I were a rubber balloon.

When I later tested the dogs, the breed indeed made a difference in their behavior. I took them, when hungry, into a room with a bowl of meat. For three minutes I kept them from approaching the meat, then left each dog alone with the food. Indulged terriers and beagles waited longer before eating the meat than did disciplined dogs of the same breeds. None of the Shetlands ever ate any of the food, and all of the Basenjis ate as soon as I left.

I later studied 20 sets of identical and fraternal human twins, following them from infancy until they were 10 years old, and I became convinced that both puppies and human babies begin life along developmental pathways established by their genetic inheritance. But I still did not know whether infants of relatively inbred human groups showed differences comparable to the breed differences among puppies that had so impressed me. Clearly, the most direct way to find out was to examine very young infants, preferably newborns, of ethnic groups with widely divergent histories.

Since it was important to avoid projecting my own assumptions onto the babies' behavior, the first step was to develop some sort of objective test of newborn behavior.

SOURCE: From Daniel G. Freedman, "Ethnic Differences in Babies," *Human Nature,* January 1979.

With T. Berry Brazelton, the Harvard pediatrician, I developed what I called the Cambridge Behavioral and Neurological Assessment Scales, a group of simple tests of basic human reactions that could be administered to any normal newborn in a hospital nursery.

In the first study, Nina Freedman and I compared Chinese and Caucasian babies. It was no accident that we chose those two groups, since my wife is Chinese, and in the course of learning about each other and our families, we came to believe that some character differences might well be related to differences in our respective gene pools and not just to individual differences.

Armed with our new baby test, Nina and I returned to San Francisco, and to the hospital where she had borne our first child. We examined, alternately, 24 Chinese and 24 Caucasian newborns. To keep things neat, we made sure that all the Chinese were of Cantonese (South Chinese) background, the Caucasians of Northern European origin, that the sexes in both groups were the same, that the mothers were the same age, that they had about the same number of previous children, and that both groups were administered the same drugs in the same amounts. Additionally, all of the families were members of the same health plan, all of the mothers had had approximately the same number of prenatal visits to a doctor, and all were in the same middle-income bracket.

It was almost immediately clear that we had struck pay dirt; Chinese and Caucasian babies indeed behaved like two different breeds. Caucasian babies cried more easily, and once started, they were harder to console. Chinese babies adapted to almost any position in which they were placed; for example, when placed face down in their cribs, they tended to keep their faces buried in the sheets rather than immediately turning to one side, as did the Caucasians. In a similar maneuver (called the "defense reaction" by neurologists), we briefly pressed the baby's nose with a cloth. Most Caucasian and black babies fight this maneuver by immediately turning away or swiping at the cloth with their hands, and this is reported in most Western pediatric textbooks as the normal, expected response. The average Chinese baby in our study, however, simply lay on his back and breathed through his mouth, "accepting" the cloth without a fight. This finding is most impressive on film.

Other subtle differences were equally important, but less dramatic. For example, both Chinese and Caucasian babies started to cry at about the same points in the examination, especially when they were undressed, but the Chinese stopped sooner. When picked up and cuddled, Chinese babies stopped crying immediately, as if a light switch had been flipped, whereas the crying of Caucasian babies only gradually subsided.

In another part of the test, we repeatedly shone a light in the baby's eyes and counted the number of blinks until the baby "adapted" and no longer blinked. It should be no surprise that the Caucasian babies continued to blink long after the Chinese babies had adapted and stopped.

It began to look as if Chinese babies were simply more amenable and adaptable to the machinations of the examiners, and that the Caucasian babies were registering annoyance and complaint. It was as if the old stereotypes of the calm, inscrutable Chinese and the excitable, emotionally changeable Caucasian were appearing spontaneously in the first 48 hours of life. In other words, our hypothesis about human and puppy parallels seemed to be correct.

The results of our Chinese-Caucasian study have been confirmed by a student of ethologist Nick Blurton-Jones who worked in a Chinese community in Malaysia. At the time, however, our single study was hardly enough evidence for so general a conclusion, and we set out to look at other newborns in other places. Norbett Mintz, who was working among the Navaho in Tuba City, Arizona, arranged for us to come to the reservation in the spring of 1969. After two months we had tested 36 Navaho newborns, and the results paralleled the stereotype of the stoical, impassive American Indian. These babies outdid the Chinese, showing even more calmness and adaptability than we found among Oriental babies.

We filmed the babies as they were tested and found reactions in the film we had not noticed. For example, the Moro response was clearly different among Navaho and Caucasians. This reaction occurs in newborns when support for the head and neck suddenly disappears. Tests for the Moro response usually consist of raising and then suddenly dropping the head portion of the bassinet. In most Caucasian newborns, after a four-inch drop the baby reflexively extends both arms and legs, cries, and moves in an agitated manner before he calms down. Among Navaho babies, crying was rare, the limb movements were reduced, and calming was almost immediate.

I have since spent considerable time among the Navaho, and it is clear that the traditional practice of tying the wrapped infant onto a cradle board (now practiced sporadically on the reservation) has in no way induced stoicism in the Navaho. In the halcyon days of anthropological environmentalism, this was a popular conjecture, but the other way around is more likely. Not all Navaho babies take to the cradle board, and those who complain about it are simply taken off. But most Navaho infants calmly accept the board; in fact, many begin to demand it by showing signs of unrest when off. When they are about six months old, however, Navaho babies do start complaining at being tied, and "weaning" from the board begins, with the baby taking the lead. The Navaho are the most "in touch" group of mothers we have yet seen, and the term mother-infant *unit* aptly describes what we saw among them.

James Chisholm of Rutgers University, who has studied infancy among the Navaho over the past several years, reports that his observations are much like my own. In addition, he followed a group of young Caucasian mothers in Flagstaff (some 80 miles south of the reservation) who had decided to use the cradle board. Their babies complained so persistently that they were off the board in a matter of weeks, a result that should not surprise us, given the differences observed at birth.

Assuming, then, that other investigators continue to confirm our findings, to what do we attribute the differences on the one hand, and the similarities on the other? When we first presented the findings on Chinese and Caucasians, attempts were made to explain away the genetic implications by posing differences in prenatal diets as an obvious cause. But once we had completed the Navaho study, that explanation had to be dropped, because the Navaho diet is quite different from the diet of the Chinese, yet newborn behavior was srikingly similar in the two groups.

The point is often still made that the babies had nine months of experience within the uterus before we saw them, so that cultural differences in maternal attitudes and behavior might have been transferred to the unborn offspring via some, as yet unknown, mechanism. Chisholm, for example, thinks differences in maternal blood pressure may be responsible for some of the differences between Navahos and Caucasians, but the evidence is as yet sparse. Certainly Cantonese-American and Navaho cultures are substantially different and yet the infants are so much alike that such speculation might be dismissed on that score alone. But there is another, hidden issue here, and that involves our own cultural tendency to split apart inherited and acquired characteristics. Americans tend to eschew the inherited and promote the acquired, in a sort of "we are exactly what we make of ourselves" optimism.

MY POSITION on this issue is simple: We are totally biological, totally environmental; the two are as inseparable as is an object and its shadow. Or as psychologist Donald O. Hebb has expressed it, we are 100 percent innate, 100 percent acquired. One might add to Hebb's formulation, 100 percent biological, 100 percent cultural. As D. T. Suzuki, the Zen scholar, once told an audience of neuropsychiatrists, "You took heredity and environment apart and now you are stuck with the problem of putting them together again."

Navaho and Chinese newborns may be so much alike because the Navaho were part of a relatively recent emigration from Asia. Their language group is called Athabaskan, after a lake in Canada. Although most of the Athabaskan immigrants from Asia settled along the Pacific coast of Canada, the Navaho and Apache contingents went on to their present location in about 1200 A.D. Even today, a significant number of words in Athabaskan and Chinese appear to have the same meaning, and if one looks back several thousand years into the written records of Sino-Tibetan, the number of similar words makes clear the common origin of these widely separated peoples.

When we say that some differences in human behavior may have a genetic basis, what do we mean? First of all, we are *not* talking about a gene for stoicism or a gene for irritability. If a behavioral trait is at all interesting, for example, smiling, anger, ease of sexual arousal, or altruism, it is most probably polygenic — that is, many genes contribute to its development. Furthermore, there is no way to count the exact number of genes involved in such a polygenic system because, as geneticist James Crow has summarized the situation, biological traits are controlled by one, two, or *many* genes.

Standing height, a polygenic human trait, can be easily measured and is also notoriously open to the influence of the environment. For this reason height can serve as a model for behavioral traits, which are genetically influenced but are even more prone to change with changing environment.

There are, however, limits to the way that a given trait responds to the environment, and this range of constraint imposed by the genes is called a *reaction range.* Behavioral geneticist Irving Gottesman has drawn up a series of semihypothetical graphs illustrating how this works with regard to human height; each genotype (the combination of genes that determine a particular trait) represents a relatively inbred human group. Even the most favorable environment produces little change in height for genotype A, whereas for genotype D a vast difference is seen as nutrition improves.

When I speak of potential genetic differences in human behavior, I do so with these notions in mind: There is overlap between most populations and the overlap can become rather complete under changing conditions, as in genotypes D and C. Some genotypes, however, show no overlap and remain remote from the others over the entire reaction range, as in genotype A (actually a group of achondroplastic dwarfs; it is likely that some pygmy groups would exhibit a similarly isolated reaction range with regard to height).

At present we lack the data to construct such reaction-range curves for newborn behavior, but hypothetically there is nothing to prevent us from one day doing so.

The question naturally arises whether the group differences we have found are expressions of richer and poorer environments, rather than of genetically distinguishable groups. The similar performance yet substantial difference in socioeconomic status between Navaho and San Francisco Chinese on the one hand, and the dissimilar per-

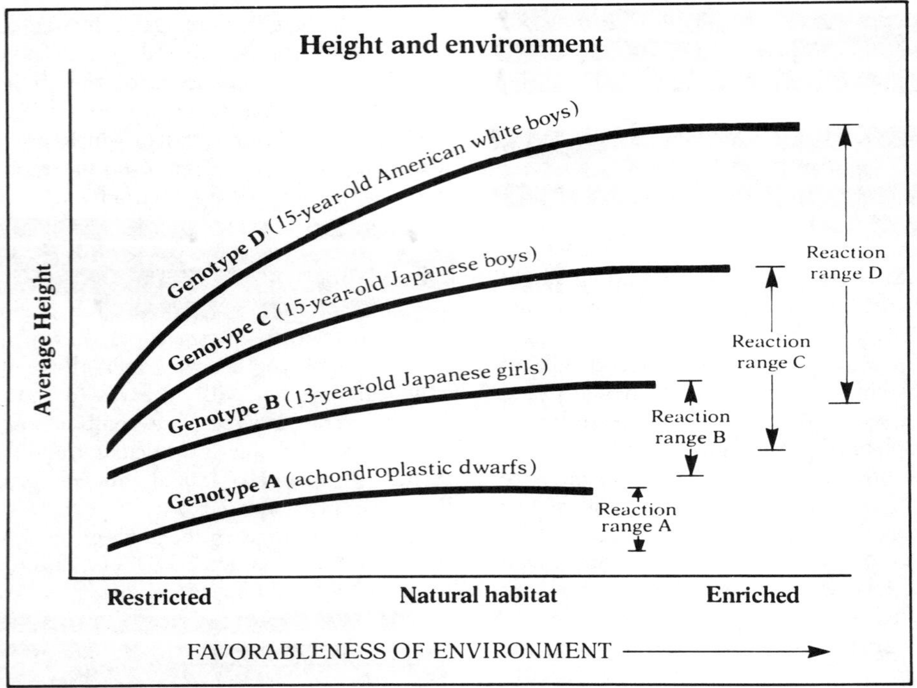

Figure 1. The concept of reaction range shows clearly in this comparison of adolescent groups: the better the environment, the taller the person. Although some groups show considerable overlap in height, no matter how favorable the environment, height cannot exceed the possible reaction range. (© 1974 University of Minnesota. University of Minnesota Press, Minneapolis, MN)

formance yet similar socioeconomic status of San Francisco Chinese and Caucasians on the other favors the genetic explanation. Try as one might, it is very difficult, conceptually and actually, to get rid of our biological constraints.

Research among newborns in other cultures shows how environment — in this case, cultural learning — affects reaction range. In Hawaii we met a Honolulu pediatrician who volunteered that he had found striking and consistent differences between Japanese and Polynesian babies in his practice. The Japanese babies consistently reacted more violently to their three-month immunizations than did the Polynesians. On subsequent visits, the Japanese gave every indication of remembering the last visit by crying violently; one mother said that her baby cried each time she drove by the clinic.

We then tested a series of Japanese newborns, and found that they were indeed more sensitive and irritable than either the Chinese or Navaho babies. In other respects, though, they were much like them, showing a similar response to consolation, and accommodating easily to a light on the eyes or a cloth over the nose. Prior to our work, social anthropologist William Caudill had made an extensive and thorough study of Japanese infants. He made careful observations of Japanese mother-infant pairs in Baltimore, from the third to the twelfth month of life.

Having noted that both the Japanese infants and their mothers vocalized much less to one another than did Caucasian pairs, he assumed that the Japanese mothers were conditioning their babies toward quietude from a universal baseline at which all babies start. Caudill, of course, was in the American environmentalist tradition and, until our publication appeared, did not consider the biological alternative. We believe that the mothers and babies he studied were, in all probability, conditioning each other, that the naturally quiet Japanese babies affected their mothers' behavior as much as the mothers affected their babies'.

With this new interactive hypothesis in mind, one of my students, Joan Kuchner, studied mother-infant interactions among 10 Chinese and 10 Caucasian mother-infant pairs over the first three months of life. The study was done in Chicago, and this time the Chinese were of North Chinese rather than South Chinese (Cantonese) ancestry. Kuchner started her study with the birth of the babies and found that the two groups were different from the start, much as in our study of newborns. Further, it soon became apparent that Chinese mothers were less intent on eliciting responses from their infants. By the third month, Chinese infants and mothers rarely engaged in bouts of mutual vocalizing as did the Caucasian pairs. This was exactly what the Caudill studies of Japanese and Caucasians had shown, but we now know that it was based on a developing coalition between mothers and babies and that it was not just a one-way street in which a mother "shapes" her infant's behavior.

Following our work, Caudill and Lois Frost repeated Caudill's original work, but this time they used third-generation Japanese-American mothers and their fourth-generation infants. The mothers had become "super" American and were vocalizing to their infants at almost twice the Caucasian rate of activity, and the infants were responding at an even greater rate of happy vocalization. Assuming that these are sound and repeatable results, my tendency is to reconcile these and our results in terms of the reaction-range concept. If Japanese height can change as dramatically as it has with emigration to the United States (and with post-World War II diets), it seems plausible that mother-infant behavior can do the same. On a variety of other measures, Caudill and Frost were able to discern continuing similarities to infant and mother pairs in the old country. Fourth-generation Japanese babies, like babies in Japan, sucked their fingers less and were less playful than Caucasian babies were, and the third-generation mothers lulled their babies and held them more than Caucasian American mothers did.

A student and colleague, John Callaghan, has recently completed a study comparing 15 Navaho and 19 Anglo mothers and their young infants (all under six months). Each mother was asked to "get the attention of the baby." When video tapes of the subsequent scene were analyzed, the differences in both babies and mothers were striking. The Navaho babies showed greater passivity than the Caucasian babies. Caucasian mothers "spoke" to their babies continually, using linguistic forms appropriate for someone who understands language; their babies responded by moving their arms and legs. The Navaho mothers were strikingly silent, using their eyes to attract their babies' gaze, and the relatively immobile infants responded by merely gazing back.

Despite their disparate methods, both groups were equally successful in getting their babies' attention. Besides keeping up a stream of chatter, Caucasian mothers tended to shift the baby's position radically, sometimes holding him or her close, sometimes at arm's length, as if experimenting to find the best focal distance for the baby. Most of the silent Navaho mothers used only subtle shifts on the lap, holding the baby at about the same distance throughout. As a result of the intense stimulation by the Caucasian mothers, the babies frequently turned their heads away, as if to moderate the intensity of the encounter. Consequently, eye contact among Caucasian pairs was of shorter duration (half that of the Navaho), but more frequent.

It was clear that the Caucasian mothers sought their babies' attention with verve and excitement, even as their babies tended to react to the stimulation with what can be described as ambivalence: The Caucasian infants turned both toward and away from the mother with far greater frequency than did the Navaho infants. The Navaho mothers and their infants engaged in relatively stoical, quiet, and steady encounters. On viewing the films of these sequences, we had the feeling that we were watching biocultural differences in the making.

Studies of older children bear out the theme of relative unexcitability in Chinese as compared to Anglos. In an independent research project at the University of Chicago, Nova Green studied a number of nursery schools. When she reached one in Chicago's Chinatown, she reported: "Although the majority of the Chinese-American children were in the 'high arousal age,' between three and five, they showed little intense emotional behavior. They ran and hopped, laughed and called to one another, rode bikes and roller-skated just as the children did in the other nursery schools, but the noise level stayed remarkably low, and the emotional atmosphere projected serenity instead of bedlam. The impassive facial expression certainly gave the children an air of dignity and self-possession, but this was only one element effecting the total impression. Physical movements seemed more coordinated, no tripping, falling, bumping, or bruising was observed, nor screams, crashes or wailing was heard, not even that common sound in other nurseries, voices raised in highly indignant moralistic dispute! No property disputes were observed, and only the mildest version of 'fighting behavior,' some good-natured wrestling among the older boys. The adults evidently had different expectations about hostile or impulsive behavior; this was the only nursery school where it was observed that children were trusted to duel with sticks. Personal distance spacing seemed to be situational rather than compulsive or patterned, and the children appeared to make no effort to avoid physical contact."

It is ironic that many recent visitors to nursery schools in Red China have returned with ecstatic descriptions of the children, implying that the New Order knows something about child rearing that the West does not. When the *New Yorker* reported a visit to China by a group of developmental psychologists including William Kessen, Urie Bronfenbrenner, Jerome Kagan, and Eleanor Maccoby, they were described as baffled by the behavior of Chinese children: "They were won over by the Chinese children. They speak of an 'attractive mixture of affective spontaneity and an accommodating posture' by the children: of the 'remarkable control of young Chinese children' — alert, animated, vigorous, responsive to the words of their elders, yet also unnervingly calm, even during happenings (games, classroom events, neighborhood play) that could create agitation and confusion. The children 'were far less restless, less intense in their motor actions, and displayed less crying and whining than American children in similar situations. We were constantly struck by [their] quiet, gentle, and controlled manner . . . and as constantly frustrated in our desire to understand its origins.' "

The report is strikingly similar to Nova Green's description of the nursery school in Chicago's Chinatown. When making these comparisons with "American" nursery schools, the psychologists obviously had in

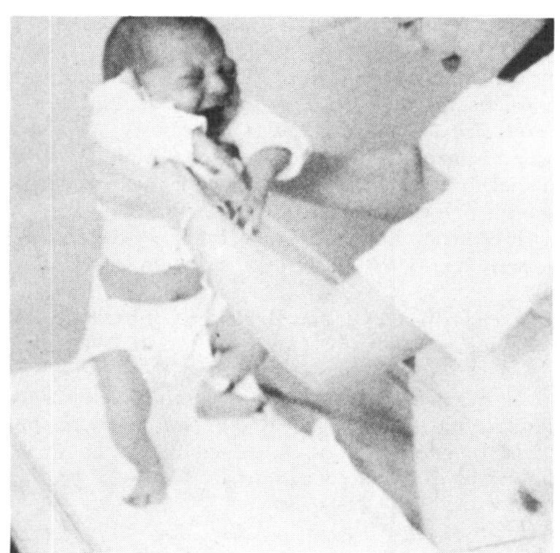

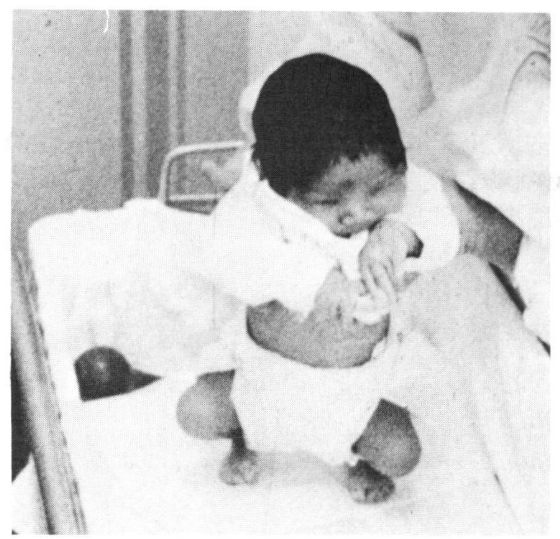

Figure 2. When feet were placed on a flat surface, about eighty percent of Caucasian newborns made stepping movements (left). Ninety-two percent of Navaho newborns did not do so, and most just squatted (right). (Courtesy Daniel Freedman)

mind classrooms filled with Caucasian or Afro-American children.

As they get older, Chinese and Caucasian children continue to differ in roughly the same behavior that characterizes them in nursery school. Not surprisingly, San Francisco schoolteachers consider assignments in Chinatown as plums — the children are dutiful and studious, and the classrooms are quiet.

A reader might accept these data and observations and yet still have trouble imagining how such differences might have initially come about. The easiest explanation involves a historical accident based on different, small founding populations and at least partial geographic isolation. Peking man, some 500,000 years ago, already had shovel-shaped incisors, as only Orientals and American Indians have today. Modern-looking skulls of about the same age, found in England, lack this grooving on the inside of their upper incisors. Given such evidence, we can surmise that there has been substantial and longstanding isolation of East and West. Further, it is likely that, in addition to just plain "genetic drift," environmental demands and biocultural adaptations differed, yielding present-day differences.

Orientals and Euro-Americans are not the only newborn groups we have examined. We have recorded newborn behavior in Nigeria, Kenya, Sweden, Italy, Bali, India, and Australia, and in each place, it is fair to say, we observed some kind of uniqueness. The Australian aborigines, for example, struggled mightily against the cloth over the nose, resembling the most objecting Caucasian babies; their necks were exceptionally strong, and some could lift their heads up and look around, much like some of the African babies we saw. (Caucasian infants cannot do this until they are about one month old.) Further, aborigine infants were easy to calm, resembling in that respect our easygoing Chinese babies. They thus comprised a unique pattern of traits.

Given these data, I think it is a reasonable conclusion that we should drop two long-cherished myths: (1) No matter what our ethnic background, we are all born alike; (2) culture and biology are separate entities.

Clearly, we are biosocial creatures in everything we do and say, and it is time that anthropologists, psychologists, and population geneticists start speaking the same language. In light of what we know, only a truly holistic, multidisciplinary approach makes sense.

REFERENCES

Caudill, W., and N. Frost. "A Comparison of Maternal Care and Infant Behavior in Japanese-American, American, and Japanese Families." *Influences on Human Development,* edited by Urie Bronfenbrenner and M. A. Mahoney. Dryden Press, 1972.

Chisholm, J. S., and M. Richards. "Swaddling, Cradleboards and the Development of Children." *Early Human Development,* in press.

Freedman, D. G. "Constitutional and Environmental Interaction in Rearing of Four Breeds of Dogs." *Science,* Vol. 127, 1958, pp. 585–586.

Freedman, D. G. *Human Infancy: An Evolutionary Perspective.* Lawrence Erlbaum Associates, 1974.

Freedman, D. G., and B. Keller. "Inheritance of Behavior in Infants." *Science,* Vol. 140, 1963, pp. 196–198.

Gottesman, I. I. "Developmental Genetics and Ontogenetic Psychology." *Minnesota Symposia on Child Psychology,* Vol. 8, edited by A. D. Pick. University of Minnesota Press, 1974.

B. F. Skinner

BABY IN A BOX

In that brave new world which science is preparing for the housewife of the future, the young mother has apparently been forgotten. Almost nothing has been done to ease her lot by simplifying and improving the care of babies.

When we decided to have another child, my wife and I felt that it was time to apply a little laborsaving invention and design to the problems of the nursery. We began by going over the disheartening schedule of the young mother, step by step. We asked only one question: Is this practice important for the physical and psychological health of the baby? When it was not, we marked it for elimination. Then the "gadgeteering" began.

The result is an inexpensive apparatus in which our baby daughter has now been living for eleven months. Her remarkable good health and happiness and my wife's welcome leisure have exceeded our most optimistic predictions, and we are convinced that a new deal for both mother and baby is at hand.

We tackled first the problem of warmth. The usual solution is to wrap the baby in half-a-dozen layers of cloth — shirt, nightdress, sheet, blankets. This is never completely successful. The baby is likely to be found steaming in its own fluids or lying cold and uncovered. Schemes to prevent uncovering may be dangerous, and in fact they have sometimes even proved fatal. Clothing and bedding also interfere with normal exercise and growth and keep the baby from taking comfortable postures or changing posture during sleep. They also encourage rashes and sores. Nothing can be said for the system on the score of convenience, because frequent changes and launderings are necessary.

Why not, we thought, dispense with clothing altogether — except for the diaper, which serves another purpose — and warm the space in which the baby lives? This should be a simple technical problem in the modern home. Our solution is a closed compartment about as spacious as a standard crib. The walls are well insulated, and one side, which can be raised like a window, is a large pane

Editors' [*of Ladies' Home Journal*] *Note:* Occasionally an idea appears so new and challenging, so discussion-provoking, that it seems desirable to publish it at once, without the delay attendant on the testing and experimentation which scientists invariably require before giving approval to a new practice. Such is the following article. Child psychologists and health experts, consulted by the *Journal,* agree that Baby Skinner is in excellent health, in no way showing harm from her unusual upbringing. The *Journal* presents the story of how this one baby has been reared, in the belief that mothers everywhere will find it of great interest, will await eagerly the scientists' final verdict.

of safety glass. The heating is electrical, and special precautions have been taken to insure accurate control.

After a little experimentation we found that our baby, when first home from the hospital, was completely comfortable and relaxed without benefit of clothing at about 86° F. As she grew older, it was possible to lower the temperature by easy stages. Now, at eleven months, we are operating at about 78°, with a relative humidity of 50 per cent.

Raising or lowering the temperature by more than a degree or two will produce a surprising change in the baby's condition and behavior. This response is so sensitive that we wonder how a comfortable temperature is ever reached with clothing and blankets.

The discovery that pleased us most was that crying and fussing could always be stopped by slightly lowering the temperature. During the first three months, it is true, the baby would also cry when wet or hungry, but in that case she would stop when changed or fed. During the past six months she has not cried at all except for a moment or two when injured or sharply distressed — for example, when inoculated. The "lung exercise" which is so often appealed to to reassure the mother of a baby that cries a good deal takes the much pleasanter form of shouts and gurgles.

How much of this sustained cheerfulness is due to the temperature is hard to say, because the baby enjoys many other kinds of comfort. She sleeps in curious postures, not half of which would be possible under securely fastened blankets.

When awake, she exercises almost constantly and often with surprising violence. Her leg, stomach and back muscles are especially active and have become strong and hard. It is necessary to watch this performance for only a few minutes to realize how severely restrained the average baby is, and how much energy must be diverted into the only remaining channel — crying.

A wider range and variety of behavior are also encouraged by the freedom from clothing. For example, our baby acquired an amusing, almost apelike skill in the use of her feet. We have devised a number of toys which are occasionally suspended from the ceiling of the compartment. She often plays with these with her feet alone and with her hands and feet in close co-operation.

One toy is a ring suspended from a modified music box. A note can be played by pulling the ring downward, and a series of rapid jerks will produce Three Blind Mice. At seven months our baby would grasp the ring in her toes, stretch out her leg and play the tune with a rhythmic movement of her foot.

We are not especially interested in developing skills of this sort, but they are valuable for the baby because they arouse and hold her interest. Many babies seem to cry from sheer boredom — their behavior is restrained and they have nothing else to do. In our compartment, the waking hours are invariably active and happy ones.

Freedom from clothes and bedding is especially important for the older baby who plays and falls asleep off and on during the day. Unless the mother is constantly on the alert, it is hard to cover the baby promptly when it falls asleep and to remove and arrange sheets and blankets as soon as it is ready to play. All this is now unnecessary.

Remember that these advantages for the baby do not mean additional labor or attention on the part of the mother. On the contrary, there is an almost unbelievable saving in time and effort. For one thing, there is no bed to be made or changed. The "mattress" is a tightly stretched canvas, which is kept dry by warm air. A single bottom sheet operates like a roller towel. It is stored on a spool outside the compartment at one end and passes into a wire hamper at the other. It is ten yards long and lasts a week. A clean section can be locked into place in a few seconds. The time which is usually spent in changing clothes is also saved. This is especially important in the early months. When we take the baby up for feeding or play, she is wrapped in a small blanket or a simple nightdress. Occasionally she is dressed up "for fun" or for her play period. But that is all. The wrapping blanket, roller sheet and the usual diapers are the only laundry actually required.

Time and labor are also saved because the air which passes through the compartment is thoroughly filtered. The baby's eyes, ears and nostrils remain fresh and clean. A weekly bath is enough, provided the face and diaper region are frequently washed. These little attentions are easy because the compartment is at waist level.

It takes about one and one half hours each day to feed, change and otherwise care for the baby. This includes everything except washing diapers and preparing formula. We are not interested in reducing the time any farther. As a baby grows older, it needs a certain amount of social stimulation. And after all, when unnecessary chores have been eliminated, taking care of a baby is fun.

An unforeseen dividend has been the contribution to the baby's good health. Our pediatrician readily approved the plan before the baby was born, and he has followed the results enthusiastically from month to month. Here are some points on the health score: When the baby was only ten days old, we could place her in the preferred face-down position without danger of smothering, and she has slept that way ever since, with the usual advantages. She has always enjoyed deep and extended sleep, and her feeding and eliminative habits have been extraordinarily regular. She has never had a stomach upset, and she has never missed a daily bowel movement.

The compartment is relatively free of spray and air-borne infection, as well as dust and allergic substances. Although there have been colds in the family, it has been easy to avoid contagion, and the baby has completely escaped. The neighborhood children troop in to see her, but they see her through glass and keep their school-age diseases to themselves. She has never had a diaper rash.

We have also enjoyed the advantages of a fixed daily routine. Child specialists are still not agreed as to whether the mother should watch the baby or the clock, but no one denies that a strict schedule saves time. The mother can plan her day in advance and find time for relaxation or freedom for other activities. The trouble is that a routine acceptable to the baby often conflicts with the schedule of the household. Our compartment helps out here in two ways. Even in crowded living quarters it can be kept free of unwanted lights and sounds. The insulated walls muffle all ordinary noises, and a curtain can be drawn down over the window. The result is that, in the space taken by a standard crib, the baby has in effect a separate room. We are never concerned lest the doorbell, telephone, piano or children at play wake the baby, and we can therefore let her set up any routine she likes.

But a more interesting possibility is that her routine may be changed to suit our convenience.

A good example of this occurred when we dropped her schedule from four to three meals per day. The baby began to wake up in the morning about an hour before we wanted to feed her. This annoying habit, once established, may persist for months. However, by slightly raising the temperature during the night, we were able to postpone her demand for breakfast. The explanation is simple. The evening meal is used by the baby mainly to keep itself warm during the night. How long it lasts will depend in part upon how fast heat is absorbed by the surrounding air.

One advantage not to be overlooked is that the soundproofing also protects the family from the baby! Our intentions in this direction were misunderstood by some of our friends. We were never put to the test, because there was no crying to contend with, but it was never our policy to use the compartment in order to let the baby "cry it out."

Every effort should be made to discover just why a baby cries. But if the condition cannot be remedied, there is no reason why the family, and perhaps the neighborhood as well, must suffer. (Such a compartment, by the way, might persuade many a landlord to drop a "no babies" rule, since other tenants can be completely protected.)

Before the baby was born, when we were still building the apparatus, some of the friends and acquaintances who had heard about what we proposed to do were rather shocked. Mechanical dishwashers, garbage disposers, air cleaners and other laborsaving devices were all very fine, but a mechanical baby tender — that was carrying science too far! However, all the specific objections that were raised against the plan have faded away in the bright light of our results. A very brief acquaintance with the scheme in operation is enough to resolve all doubts. Some of the toughest skeptics have become our most enthusiastic supporters.

One of the commonest objections was that we were going to raise a "softie" who would be unprepared for the real world. But instead of becoming hypersensitive, our baby has acquired a surprisingly serene tolerance for annoyances. She is not bothered by the clothes she wears at playtime, she is not frightened by loud or sudden noises, she is not frustrated by toys out of reach, and she takes a lot of pommeling from her older sister like a good sport. It is possible that she will have to learn to sleep in a noisy room, but adjustments of that sort are always necessary. A tolerance for any annoyance can be built up by administering it in controlled dosages, rather than in the usual accidental way. Certainly there is no reason to annoy the child throughout the whole of its infancy, merely to prepare it for later childhood.

It is not, of course, the favorable conditions to which people object, but the fact that in our compartment they are "artificial." All of them occur naturally in one favorable environment or another, where the same objection should apply but is never raised. It is quite in the spirit of the "world of the future" to make favorable conditions available everywhere through simple mechanical means.

A few critics have objected that they would not like to live in such a compartment themselves — they feel that it would stifle them or give them claustrophobia. The baby obviously does not share in this opinion. The compartment is well ventilated and much more spacious than a Pullman berth, considering the size of the occupant. The baby cannot get out, of course, but that is true of a crib as well. There is less actual restraint in the compartment because the baby is freer to move about. The plain fact is that she is perfectly happy. She has never tried to get out nor resisted being put back in, and that seems to be the final test.

Another early objection was that the baby would be socially starved and robbed of the affection and mother love that she needs. This has simply not been true. The compartment does not ostracize the baby. The large window is no more of a social barrier than the bars of a crib. The baby follows what is going on in the room, smiles at passers-by, plays "peek-a-boo" games, and obviously delights in company. And she is handled, talked to and played with whenever she is changed or fed, and each afternoon during a play period which is becoming longer as she grows older.

The fact is that a baby will probably get more love and affection when it is easily cared for, because the mother is not so likely to feel overworked and resentful of the demands made upon her. She will express her love in a practical way and give the baby genuinely affectionate care.

It is common practice to advise the troubled mother to be patient and tender and to enjoy her baby. And, of course, that is what any baby needs. But it is the exceptional mother who can fill this prescription upon demand, especially if there are other children in the family and she has no help. We need to go one step further and treat the mother with affection also. Simplified child care will give mother love a chance.

A similar complaint was that such an apparatus would encourage neglect. But easier care is sure to be better care. The mother will resist the temptation to put the baby back into a damp bed if she can conjure up a dry one in five seconds. She may very well spend less time with her baby, but babies do not suffer from being left alone, only from the discomforts which arise from being left alone in the ordinary crib.

How long do we intend to keep the baby in the compartment? The baby will answer that in time, but almost certainly until she is two years old, or perhaps three. After the first year, of course, she will spend a fair part of each day in a play pen or out-of-doors. The compartment takes the place of a crib and will get about the same use. Eventually it will serve as sleeping quarters only.

We cannot, of course, guarantee that every baby raised in this way will thrive so successfully. But there is a plausible connection between health and happiness and the surroundings we have provided, and I am quite sure that our success is not an accident. The experiment should, of course, be repeated again and again with different babies and different parents. One case is enough, however, to disprove the flat assertion that it can't be done. At least we have shown that a moderate and inexpensive mechanization of baby care will yield a tremendous saving in time and trouble, without harm to the child and probably to its lasting advantage.

Professor Skinner's unusual experiment provoked many questions among the Journal staff. Here are many of them, answered by the author himself. [*Editor,* Ladies Home Journal]

1. How can the mother hear her baby?

The apparatus is only partially soundproofed. With the nursery door open we can hear the baby about as clearly as if she were in an ordinary crib with the nursery door closed. If it were desirable to hear very clearly, the window could be left partly open, with the opening covered by a cloth (say, if the child were sick). The soundproofing has enough advantages from the baby's point of view to make it worth while.

2. Doesn't the discharged sheet have an unpleasant odor?

Not in our experience. There is no noticeable odor in our nursery. Visitors frequently comment on this fact. The reason seems to be that dry urine does not give off a strong odor. Our practice has been to wipe up any traces of bowel movements before moving the sheet along. In case of bad soiling, the sheet could be moved out far enough to permit dipping the soiled section into a pan of water or the whole sheet could be changed, but this has never been necessary.

3. Doesn't the canvas mattress acquire an odor?

Again, not in our experience. The canvas is constantly bathed in warm air, and there is little or no chance for the bacterial action which makes urine smell. The canvas is stretched on a removable frame, and we have a spare to permit cleaning when necessary (every two or three weeks). The canvas could, therefore, be changed in case of vomiting. Or a rubber sheet could be used. (We do use rubber pants at night, to avoid chilling due to evaporation of the wet diaper.)

4. What happens if the current fails?

We have an alarm, operated on dry-cell batteries, which goes off if the temperature deviates more than two degrees from the proper setting. This is wholly independent of the power supply and would tell us of trouble long before the baby had experienced any extreme condition.

5. Don't you believe a baby's daily bath is necessary?

Artificial stimulation of the skin at bathtime may be necessary when the usual clothing and bedding are used, but not in our apparatus. From the very first the fine condition of our baby's skin attracted attention. The skin is soft, but not moist. It is rubbed gently and naturally throughout the day by the under sheet as she moves about. Much of the patting which is advised at bathtime is to make up for the lack of normal exercise of the skin circulation, which is due to clothing. Since our baby's skin is always exposed to the air, a very lively skin reaction to changes in temperature has developed.

6. Don't the mother and child both miss daily bathtime fun?

We have had a lot of fun with our baby — more perhaps than if we had been burdened down with unnecessary chores. We have always played with her when we felt like it, which was often. As for the baby, she has certainly had more than her share of fun. The freedom from clothing and blankets has provided much of it. Her bath is fun, too, though probably not as much as the usual baby's because the contrast is not so great. The advice of the child specialist to "allow the baby to exercise its legs for a few minutes at bathtime" shows what I mean. Our baby exercises her legs all day long. (My wife insists I say that we do bathe our baby twice a week, though once a week is enough.)

The fact that our baby is not only in perfect physical condition but keenly interested in life and blissfully happy is our final answer to any possible charge of neglect.

FURTHER COMMENTS (1977)

The word "box" was put in my title by the editors of the *Journal* and it led to endless confusion because I had used another box in the study of operant conditioning. Many of those who had not read the article assumed that I was experimenting on our daughter as if she were a rat or pigeon. Those who read it, however, viewed it quite favorably. Hundreds of people wrote to say that they wanted to raise their babies in the same way. I sent out mimeographed instructions to help those who proposed to build boxes for themselves. My contacts with potential manufacturers were disappointing but eventually an enterprising man, John Gray, organized the Aircrib Corporation and began production on a modest scale. He contributed much of his own time without remuneration, and when he died his son was unable to carry on. Second-hand Aircribs are now in demand.

Our daughter continued to use the Aircrib for sleeping and naps until she was two and a half, and during that time we all profited from it. The long sheet and canvas "mattress" were replaced by a tightly stretched woven plastic, with the texture of linen, which could be washed and dried instantly, and once her bowel-movement pattern was established she slept nude. Urine was collected in a pan beneath the plastic. Predictions that she would be a bed-wetter were not confirmed. She learned to keep dry in her clothing during the day and when she started to sleep in a regular bed she treated it like clothing. Except for one night when we had been traveling and were all rather tired, she has never wet a bed. She proved remarkably resistant to colds and other infections.

Possibly through confusion with the other box, the venture began to be misunderstood. Stories circulated about the dire consequences of raising a baby in any such way. It was said that our daughter had committed suicide, become psychotic, and (more recently), was suing me. The fact is that she is a successful artist living in London with her husband, Dr. Barry Buzan, who teaches in the field of international studies. My older daughter, Dr. Julie Vargas, used an Aircrib with her two daughters, and she and many others have confirmed the results we reported.

The Aircrib has many advantages for both child and parents. For the child it offers greater comfort, safety, freedom of movement, and an opportunity for the earliest possible development of motor and perceptual skills. For the parent it saves labor and gives a sense of security about the baby's well being. There is no danger of being strangled by bedclothes or becoming uncovered on a cold night. It is somewhat more expensive than an ordinary crib, even including mattress, sheets, blankets and laundry, but the resale value is high. It can often save money by saving space. By drawing a curtain over the window at night it can be closed off from the rest of the room, making it possible for a young couple to stay for another year or two in a one-room apartment or to let a baby share a room with an older child.

I do not expect to see Aircribs widely used in the near future. It is not the kind of thing that appeals to American business. It is impossible to convince a Board of Directors that there is a market that justifies tooling up for mass production to keep the price down, and so long as the price remains high a market will not develop.

Nevertheless, the first two or three years are the most important years in a child's life, and I am sure that much more will eventually be done to make them more enjoyable and productive.

B. F. Skinner
July 1977

13

Selma Fraiberg

TONI

What can we learn from one baby?

When David Freedman and I set out to visit Toni we brought with us a number of hypotheses. We had hypotheses regarding blindness as an impediment to the establishment of human attachments. We had a hypothesis regarding the adaptive substitution of sound for vision. And there were others which are fortunately obliterated by time. In the next 18 months Toni threw out each of our hypotheses one by one, like so many boring toys over the rail of a crib.

We were quite fortunate in our first baby, since she had been selected with no other criteria than her blindness and her age. Toni was a healthy, robust little girl, the youngest of 6 children. Her mother was an experienced mother. In spite of her feelings of guilt and fears for the future of her blind child, she was a woman whose motherliness responded to need, and this baby who needed her in special ways evoked deep tenderness in her.

Toni tossed out one of our hypotheses on the very first visit. She was five months old, making pleasant noises in her crib as we talked with her mother. When her mother went over to her and called her name, Toni's face broke into a gorgeous smile, and she made agreeable responsive noises. I called her name and waited. There was no smile. Dr. Freedman called her name. There was no smile. Mother called her name and once again there appeared the joyful smile and cooing sounds. Her mother said, a little apologetically, "She won't smile for anyone. Not even her sisters and brothers. Only me. She's been smiling when I talk to her since she was three months."

Now in 1961 it was written in all our books (including one of my own) that it is the *visual* stimulus of the human face that elicits smiling in the baby at three months. Toni's smile had just shattered a theory, which shows you what one baby can do. Seven years later I could have given you a long list of blind babies who smiled in response to mother's or father's voice. But that doesn't really matter. If only one blind baby smiles in response to a mother's voice, it demonstrates that there is something wrong with our theory.

In our notes of this session we recorded a number of observations showing the selective response of Toni to her mother, paralleling in all significant ways that of a sighted child at five months. Three months later, at eight months, Toni demonstrated another achievement in the scale of human attachments. Soon after she heard our voices, strange voices, she became sober, almost frozen in her posture. Later, when I held Toni briefly to test her reactions to a stranger, she began to cry, squirmed in my arms, and

All names of children and families . . . are fictitious.

SOURCE: From *Insights from the Blind: Comparative Studies of Blind and Sighted Infants* by Selma Fraiberg. Copyright © 1977 by Selma Fraiberg. Published by Basic Books, Inc., New York. Reprinted by permission.

strained away from my body. It was a classic demonstration of "stranger anxiety." But — in 1961 — we all knew that stranger anxiety appears at eight months on the basis of the *visual* discrimination of mother's face and stranger's face.

Very well. We conceded that under favorable conditions blindness need not be an impediment to the establishment of human attachments. But we still had a lot of other hypotheses tucked away.

One of these had to do with the adaptive substitution of sound for vision. We all knew that around five months of age the sighted child can reach and attain an object on sight. In the case of the blind child we expected that a coordination of sound and grasping would take place at approximately the same time. But at five months of age, at six months, and — astonishingly — even at nine months, Toni made no gesture of reach toward any of the sound objects we presented to her. We sneaked around with jangling keys, rattles, squeaky toys, always in a range where Toni could easily reach them. She looked alert and attentive, but she made no gesture of reach. It did not matter whether we used her own familiar toys or Dr. Freedman's car keys; there was not a gesture of reach. Was the baby deaf? Certainly not. As soon as she heard the sound of the camera motor, for example, she would startle or wince. She could discriminate voices. She could imitate sounds at seven months. What was it then?

At ten months Toni demonstrated for the first time her ability to reach and attain an object on sound cue alone! (Thereafter she became expert in grabbing objects sounded within arm's range.) As we drove back from Toni's house that day we were stunned by the implications of this observation. Toni had given her first demonstration of a direct reach for a sound object at ten months. (The sighted baby coordinates vision and grasping at five months.) But how did Toni solve the problem? We knew perfectly well that no developmental achievement appears overnight. A coordinated action of hand and external stimulus is the result of complex sensorimotor learning. There were antecedents which must have been present for months, unrecognized by us. Now we were obsessed by the problem and its implications. Since memory could not serve us, we went back over hundreds of feet of film, frame by frame, to try to reconstruct the sequence. But the story was not there. And we knew why. Film and film processing are expensive. Since we were financing this research out of pocket we had to be thrifty in our use of film. We had devoted only a small amount of footage to each of the areas we were sampling, and we had thought that our sampling was adequate. In order to pick up our lapse we would have needed generous and unprejudiced samples. The story of Toni's coordinated reach-on-sound cue was lost to us, and we already knew that this story would prove to be a vital clue in the study of the blind baby's development.

To return now to Toni and to go back a bit in the story: At eight months Toni had excellent control of her trunk and was indisputably moving toward an upright posture. She could support her weight on hands and knees, she could elevate herself to a standing position, and she could let herself down easily. There was no question, knowing babies, that Toni was getting ready to creep. As we were leaving Toni's house at the end of the eight-month visit, I said to the mother, "I'll bet when we come back next month Toni will really be into everything!" These were foolish words and I came to regret them.

At nine months Toni was not creeping. Nor at ten months or twelve months. This is what we saw: Toni, with demonstrated postural readiness for creeping, was unable to propel herself forward. On the floor in prone position she executed a kind of radial crawl, navigating in a circle.

Why couldn't Toni propel herself forward? Clearly there needed to be an external stimulus for the initiation of the creeping pattern. What happens in the case of the sighted child? The sighted child at nine months, let us say, is supporting himself ably on hands and knees. He sees an out-of-range object. He reaches for the object. And what we see now is a reach and a collapse, a reach and a collapse, each time moving forward until the object is attained. Within a few days the motor pattern begins to smooth out and becomes a coordinated action of hands and legs in what we call "creeping."

Why didn't Toni creep? Clearly because no external stimulus was present to initiate the creeping pattern. But why shouldn't a sound object provide the lure? We were back to the same problem.

Even years later, I can still remember the stunning impact of that discovery. Toni had brought a brand new insight into the understanding of locomotor development in sighted children. We, all of us, had never had occasion to question the assumption that locomotion in infancy follows maturational patterns that are laid down in a biological sequence. Toni demonstrated that motor maturation follows its biological pattern, but in the absence of an external stimulus for reaching, the creeping pattern will not emerge. We reminded ourselves that in the retrospective histories of all blind children it is common to find that creeping was never achieved, and, in fact, there is a marked delay in the achievement of all locomotor skills from this point on, with independent walking a very late achievement in the second or third years.

Between eight and ten months we began to see something in Toni that roused our own anxieties. At times during the observational session we would see Toni stretch out on the floor, prone on the rug, and for long periods of time lie quite still, smiling softly to herself. The passive pleasure in immobility was chilling to watch. Her mother, watching this with us, looked strained and anxious. "She does that all the time," she told us. She was an experienced mother, you remember, and she knew as well as we did that no healthy baby at nine months will lie on the floor for long periods of time, smiling softly to herself. And when did Toni assume this posture? At any time, we observed, when external sources of stimulation were not available to her, i.e., if no one was talking to her, playing with her, or feeding her. In such moments of non-stimulation she would fall back on this form of self-stimulation in which the ventral surface of her body was in contact with the rug.

Did this mean that the mother was neglecting her? We thought not. During the same period, pleasure in mother's voice and pleasure in being held by mother were clearly seen whenever mother resumed contact with her. But in a normal busy household, where 5 other children must also make their claims upon a mother, there were inevitably periods when Toni was not being played with, talked to, held in mother's arms. It happens to sighted children too. What does a sighted child do at nine months when he is "by himself"? He occupies himself with toys, or if he is creeping, he goes on excursions to visit the underside of the dining room table or the top side of the living room couch, or the inside of the kitchen cupboard. And if he has no toy handy, and if he can't creep, he will occupy himself by looking — just plain looking around. Visual experience creates its own appetite for repetition; the hunger to see and the functional pleasure of vision are among the great entertainments of a baby after the first days of life. Vision keeps the baby "in touch" with his mother and with the world of things, giving continuity to experience. The sighted child at nine months does not have to be continually held by his mother or talked to by his mother in order to be "in touch" with her.

But when Toni could not touch her mother or hear her mother's voice she was robbed of her mother and of a large measure of the sensory experience that linked her to the world outside of her body. In this insubstantial, impermanent world, her own body and body sensations became at times the only certainty, the only continuous source of sensory experience in the otherwise discontinuous experience of darkness. And because proprioceptive experience provides the chief means for "keeping in touch" in the near-void of blindness and the only means for experiencing continuity of self feelings, Toni stretched out on the floor, face down upon the rug. In this posture, which afforded maximal contact between the body surface and the rug, she might obtain feelings of comfort, safety, pleasurable tactile sensations, and a sense of body awareness. We are reminded, too, that the ventral surface of the baby's body is normally stimulated in the posture of being held against the mother's body and that pleasure, intimacy, comfort, and safety are united for a lifetime of love in this posture — the embrace.

What we saw in Toni, face down, nuzzling a rug, was a form of stimulus hunger. Where vision would have insured abundant sources of stimuli and the visual alternatives to contact hunger for the mother, blindness caused this child in periods of external non-stimulation to fall back upon the poverty of body sensations. Like a starving organism that will finally ingest anything where there is not enough food, the stimulus hunger of this child led her to ingest the meager proprioceptive experience of body contact with a rug.

Later, in the University of Michigan study, I was to see variations of this posture in blind children. But when we first saw this in Toni we found it chilling. We had not foreseen such a development in an otherwise healthy child. And remember, too, that during this period, at nine months, we were also sobered by the fact that Toni was unable to locomote in spite of the fact that she had maturational readiness for creeping. In other respects, too, Toni seemed to have reached a developmental impasse. Although she was still lively and responsive to her mother and her sisters and brother, there was almost no interest in toys, and at nine months she was not reaching for objects. Her mother, we observed, seemed anxious and discouraged. For the first time we saw a number of instances in which mother was manifestly out of rapport with her baby.

When we returned at ten months, the entire picture had changed. Toni's mother, entirely on her own, had purchased a walker, and within a short time Toni had become expert in getting around in it. She was still unable to creep, but the walker provided mobility, and Toni was cruising around the house with tremendous energy and making discoveries and rediscoveries at every port. "Did she still want to lie down on the rug?" we asked, concealing our own anxiety. Oh, no, the mother assured us. In fact, she absolutely refused to get into the prone position. Mother took Toni out of her walker and gave us a demonstration. The moment Toni was placed on the floor in the prone position, she yelled in protest and uprighted herself. This was now the posture of immobility — and Toni had found mobility. The moment she was put back in her walker, she stopped crying and took off like a hot-rodder.

We never saw this passive prone posture again in Toni. Within 3 months, at thirteen months of age, she began walking with support — and now also creeping (!). Toni was "into everything," exploring the cupboards and the drawers and getting into mischief. At thirteen months she had a small and useful vocabulary, she was using her hands for fine discriminations, and she was now expert in reaching and attaining objects on sound cue. From this point on, Toni's development progressed without any major impediments. (Only one pathological behavior appeared in the second year, and I will describe this later.)

But now, what about the stereotyped prone behavior which had so alarmed us at eight and nine months? It is clear from the sequence that once Toni acquired mobility she could not even be persuaded to get back into the prone position on the floor. Mobility provided functional motor pleasure, of course, but mobility also put her in touch with a world beyond her body and a world that she could act upon; mobility gave her for the first time a sense of autonomy.

Here, we thought, we had found another clue to the ego deviations encountered among blind children. If we understand that the blind child lives in a near-void for much of his waking day, he can make few discoveries about the world around him until he becomes mobile. And if mobility itself is delayed until well into the second year, he will live for a perilously long time in this near-void in which the presence of the mother or other persons or ministrations to his own body become the only experiences which give meaning to existence. In these periods, when neither sound nor touch, feeding, bath, nor play occur, there is nothing except his own body. Now we began to understand how some blind babies may never find the adaptive routes and remain frozen in the state of body-centeredness, passivity, immobility, and ultimately, non-differentiation.

I mentioned that one pathological trait was observed in Toni beginning in the second year. Let me briefly describe it. When Toni became anxious, when she was separated even briefly from her mother or when a strange person or a strange situation signaled danger to her, she would fall into a stuporous sleep. We observed this ourselves. It was as if a light were switched off. As far as we can reconstruct the onset of this symptom, it was first manifest in connection with a brief separation from her mother. She retained this symptom as late as the fourth year when we obtained reports on her. In all other respects she was a healthy, active little girl, able to ride a trike, play ball, join in children's games. Her speech was good; eating and sleeping were entirely satisfactory. There was only this. We asked ourselves when we would find an otherwise healthy sighted child who defended against danger by falling into a pathological sleep. Never, of course. But then, one should ask, what defenses against danger does a blind child possess?

II TODDLERHOOD

The toddler years, from two to four, encompass some of the most intriguing aspects of development; the child becomes a symbol user as he or she begins to talk and to play. These two activities almost define what is unique about being human. Talking and playing also offer an arena for observing the interaction between the proclivities of different individuals and the effects of the surrounding culture. As soon as the child's abilities appear, the society exerts a pressure that eventually molds the child to conformity. The child comes to master a language with common meanings and grammar, even as he or she learns to play by following agreed-upon rules.

Although psychologists have focused on explanations of how the child develops language skills, they are always guided initially by the child's language itself. The selection by Russian writer Kornei Chukovsky dramatically illustrates the linguistic resources of the young child. This work reveals that when young children explore their world, they do not always have the correct words; but they do see connections between objects, and they do use words (sometimes somewhat idiosyncratically and sometimes with great power and imagination) to tell us what they see. Language is a window to the child's world. By what he or she says, we can begin to understand what the child sees, what the child thinks is important, what the child considers related, and what the child considers unrelated. Most important, we see that the toddlers' world is different from the adults' world. Proceeding from the language itself, we then attempt to explain the process of language development.

Dedre Gentner looks at the process of learning new words. By using artificial or made-up words, she is able to look at the process in isolation and see whether physical perceptual properties or functional attributes are more salient to the early language learner. In so doing, she addresses a question that has long troubled theorists in language acquisition.

Roger Brown summarizes his own monumental study of language acquisition by three children. He examines the function and significance of a child's initial linguistic output — one-word utterances.

He then goes on to describe what the child must eventually master, what mechanisms the child has with which to meet the task, and, finally, how the child comes to learn the language of the community. Brown stresses the importance of learning a system of rules, but indicates how far we still are from being able to answer the question "How is it possible to learn first language at all?"

While Brown is emphasizing the commonalities of all language learning, Katherine Nelson looks at individual differences. She notes that there are different styles of language learning and that these styles permeate many aspects of the child's behavior.

Russian psychologist Lev Vygotsky looks at toddlers' play and discusses pretending, which he believes to be the essence of play. Vygotsky sees play as a major impetus in development, one that enables children to try out new roles which they cannot enact in their daily (non-play) lives. In play, children are forced to articulate the rules involved in particular activities. As a dramatic example, Vygotsky cites two sisters who decide to "play sister." In the course of their play, they make explicit the rules of sisterhood that pass unnoticed in life.

Until very recently, the toddler's cognitive skills were noted only for their absence: what the older child could do was lacking in the toddler. Rochel Gelman's studies of the number concept demonstrate important abilities in preschoolers. Her review article speaks of competencies in numerous areas and has important implications for preschool educational policy.

The role of culture in a toddler's development is usually mediated by the child's parents. Of all the social roles and norms conveyed by the culture, sex role identity is of primary importance. Usually, the child's sex role is suggested by his or her biology and is confirmed by the culture. But what would happen if a child's sex were not known? Lois Gould's provocative piece of fiction about "Baby X" nicely illuminates this issue.

We return to the question of language development in Clara Park's biography of her autistic daughter. What seems so effortless in the development of normal children is placed in sharp perspective as we view the obstacles faced by the autistic child in learning to master even the simplest of linguistic utterances.

Kornei Chukovsky

FROM TWO TO FIVE

I LISTEN . . .

When Lialia was two and a half years old, a man whom she did not know asked her:

"Would you like to be my little daughter?"

She answered haughtily: "I'm only mother's and no other's."

Once when we were taking a walk on the beach, Lialia saw, for the first time, a ship in the distance:

"Mommie, Mommie, the locomotive is taking a bath!" she cried with excitement and amazement.

Enchanting children's speech! It will never cease to give me joy. I once overheard the following delightful dialogue:

"My daddy himself told me this. . . ."

"My mommie herself told me that. . . ."

"But my daddy is himselfer than your mommie — my daddy is much more himselfer. . . ."

And it cheered me up to hear a three-year-old little girl mutter in her sleep:

"Mom, cover my hind leg!"

Another one, when speaking to her father over the telephone, asked:

"Daddy, why do you have such a dusky-dusky voice today?" This was the first time she had heard her father's telephone voice.

It was a pleasure to find out from kids that a bald man had a barefoot head, that a mint candy made a draft in the mouth, that the husband of a grasshopper was a daddyhopper.

And I would be very amused by such childish expressions and exclamations as:

"Daddy, look how your pants are sulking!" . . .

* * *

"Our Granny killed the geese in the wintertime so that they would not catch cold."

* * *

"Mommie, I'm so sorry for the baby horses — they cannot pick their noses." . . .

* * *

George cut a worm in half with his toy spade —

"Why did you do that?"

"The worm was lonesome. Now there are two of them — it is more cheerful for them that way."

* * *

"How dare you pick a fight?" the mother scolded.

"Oh, Mommie, what can I do when the fight just crawls out of me!" . . .

* * *

"I'll get up so early that it will still be late."

* * *

"Don't put out the light, I can't see how to sleep!"

* * *

This child was drawing flowers; around them she drew several dozen dots:

SOURCE: From *From Two to Five* by Kornei Chukovsky, translated and edited by Miriam Morton. Copyright 1963 by Miriam Morton. Reprinted by permission of the University of California Press.

"What are those? Flies?"

"No! They are the fragrance of the flowers."

* * *

HIS SEARCH FOR CERTAINTY

To those who express an absurd opinion we often say, with scorn or indignation:

"You are using a child's logic! You reason like a child!"

To most of us this accusation seems both justifiable and just; indeed, we often hear from small children the most absurd judgments and deductions.

However, we need only think deeper about these "absurdities" of the very young to be forced to reject this hasty opinion; we would then understand that in these absurdities is reflected a burning need for the young mind, no matter how, to take measure of the world and to search out, among the many separate aspects of existence, those elements of coherence whose presence the child strives to find from a very early age.

The following incident occurred at a summer place near Leningrad. A mad dog happened to be shot just at the time when the sun was setting in a flame-red aura; from that day on two-and-a-half-year-old Maia would say, every time she saw a red sky at sundown —

"Again they killed a mad dog!"

It is easy to scoff at this immature thinker who imagined that because of some dying dog the heavens were set afire! But has not this child thus expressed the priceless urge to establish the causal connection between separate facts which constitutes the moving force of all man-created sciences?

This urge frequently leads the child to the most fantastic deductions. This, for instance, was the way four-year-old Tasia mastered the word "trained." She came into contact with this word for the first time in the circus, where she saw an act by trained dogs. As a result, when six months later she heard that the father of one of her little friends was "well trained," she asked, with happy anticipation:

"That means that Kirochka's daddy is — a dog!"

This mistake is, again, quite a "respectable" one; it expresses a splendid ability of the young human mind to adapt to every new complex of unfamiliar phenomena, the results of experience attained in other spheres.

The experience of the young child is inevitably very limited, and for this reason he applies it at times inappropriately.

A train ran over a pig, maimed and killed it. Five-year-old city-bred Zoria witnessed the accident on her vacation in the country. She shed many tears of grief over the unfortunate animal. A few days later she met a frisky live pig.

"The pig glued herself up again," Zoria exclaimed ecstatically.

To such extreme degrees is the child often ignorant of the simplest things he encounters! A newcomer in the world, he meets a dilemma at every step he takes, piling up error upon error.

At the age of two to three every youngster makes an infinite number of similar mistakes based on the deepest ignorance of the most elementary objects and facts.

"Mother, who was born first, you or I?"

* * *

"Daddy, when you were little, were you a boy or a girl?"

* * *

"I like snow better than sun. I can build a fort out of snow but what can I make out of sun?"

* * *

"Put your glasses on or you'll catch cold."

* * *

"I like garlic, it smells like sausage."

* * *

"Mommie, the nettle bites me?"
"Well, in a way . . ."
"Then why doesn't it bark too?"

* * *

"Why do they put a pit in every cherry? We have to throw the pit away anyway."

* * *

"The sea has one shore but the river has two."

* * *

"The sun sets in the sea. Why is there no vapor?"

* * *

"Oh, the moon flew along when we went on the trolley and on the train. She, too, wanted to see the Caucasus!"

* * *

"The ostrich is a giraffe-bird."

* * *

"A turkey is a duck with a bow around its neck."

* * *

Little Olia was feeding bits of cabbage leaves to the chickens:

"Chickens don't eat cabbage," her mother informed her.

"I'm giving it to them so that they may save it for after they become rabbits."

* * *

"What is a knife — the fork's husband?"

* * *

"Daddy, please cut down this pine tree — it makes the wind. After you cut it down the weather will be nice and mother will let me go for a walk."

* * *

Liosha buried a meat bone under his window and watered the spot regularly, to grow a cow. Every morning he ran out to see if the cow's horns had yet sprouted. Valen'ka, observing how her mother watered the flowers, began to water her favorite puppy so that he would grow up sooner.

And I found this in my diary about my little daughter, three and a half:

Mura took off her slipper,
Planted it in the garden —
"Grow, grow, my little slipper,
Grow, little one!
I'll water you every day
And a tree will grow
A miracle tree!

Barefoot children
To the miracle tree
Will hop and skip,
Pretty red booties
They will pick
Saying:
'Oh, you, Murochka,
Oh, you clever one!' "

* * *

The sun and the stars are created in a flash in the child's mind, out of the small fire in the hearth:

"Make a fire, daddy, so that it can fly up into the sky and make the sun and the stars."

* * *

I knew a little boy who would often question his mother about where the night went in the morning. Once, coming across a deep ditch whose bottom was dark, he whispered:

"Now I know where the night hides itself."

* * *

And here is a reason for the arrival of spring:

"The winter got so cold it ran away somewhere."

* * *

A child from the north trying to fall asleep the first evening of his vacation in southern Crimea:

"Mommie, turn off the sun."

* * *

Marina said to her mother one morning:

"Mother, why don't you ever appear in my dreams?"

And in the evening of the same day she said:

"Lie down on my pillow, Mommie, we'll look at my dream together."

* * *

Once when two-year-old Eli felt offended, he threatened:

"I'll make it dark, at once." And, closing his eyes, he was convinced that, as a result, the entire world was plunged into darkness.

In every sentence just quoted, in every childish act, is revealed complete ignorance of the simplest things. Of course, I cite these expressions not to scorn childish absurdities. On the contrary, they inspire me with respect because they are evidence of the gigantic work that goes on in the child's mind which, by the age of seven, results in the conquest of this mental chaos. It is impossible not to be amazed at the brevity of the time during which the child acquires such vast riches of varied knowledge. By the time he enters grade school he is no longer lost in the delusions that were typical of his years "from two to five." By this time his "erudition" is so vast, he is so marvelously well oriented to the world of objects and facts, that he will never again utter any of the phrases quoted in the beginning of this chapter. He knows definitely that chickens do not grow into rabbits, that the fork is not married to the knife. The enormous difference we notice between the scope of knowledge of the young preschool child and of the young school child tells us about the miracle-performing mental activity during this early period of the child's existence.

15

Dedre Gentner

A STUDY OF EARLY WORD MEANING USING ARTIFICIAL OBJECTS: WHAT LOOKS LIKE A JIGGY BUT ACTS LIKE A ZIMBO?

ABSTRACT: Theories of semantic acquisition have differed as to the relative importance of form and function in early word meaning. One reason that the issue has been difficult to resolve is that in everyday life the forms of objects are highly correlated with their normal uses. The present study attempts to circumvent this difficulty by using artificial objects.

Two objects were constructed to differ from one another both in form and in function, and to be quite interesting to children. Children played with these objects and learned their names in a naturalistic setting. One of the objects had an extremely salient function: it delivered jellybeans. Yet, when children were asked to name a hybrid object which had the function (delivering jellybeans) of the jellybean object, but the form of the other original object, the youngest children (aged 2½ to 5 years) named the new object according to form. These and other aspects of the data suggest that the proper resolution of the form-function debate may be more complex than some early accounts had supposed: that functional relevance and salience determine *which words* young children learn, but that the *meanings* stored with the word are based chiefly on form and other perceptual information.

This paper is concerned with the question of what information enters into children's early word meanings. When a child first learns that a word refers to an object, what does the child store as the word's meaning? When the child later applies the word to the same or other objects, on what basis is she doing so? In particular, one focus of concern in recent research is whether perceptual information or functional information is of primary importance in children's early word meanings.

Clark (1973), in her semantic feature theory, proposed that children base their first

This research was supported in part by the National Institute of Education under Contract No. HEW–NIE–C–400–76–0116, and in part by the Psychology Department of the University of Washington. A preliminary account of this research appeared in the Stanford *Papers and Reports on Child Language Development,* No. 15, August 1978.

I would like to thank Louise Carter and Erik Svehaug for their helpful suggestions concerning this research, and Cindy Hunt and Kathy Starr for their help in preparing the manuscript.

SOURCE: From Dedre Gentner, "A Study of Early Word Meaning Using Artificial Objects: What Looks Like a Jiggy but Acts Like a Zimbo?" *Papers and Reports on Child Language Development,* 1978, *15,* 1–6. Reprinted by permission of the author.

word meanings on perceptual information associated with the referent. Her review of parental diaries of children's first word usages suggested that a large number of early noun overextensions were based on similarity of form and other perceptual similarities between the original referent and the new object to which the word was applied. This position is supported by the findings of Anglin (1977) and Bowerman (1974, 1975) and others, whose examinations of overgeneralizations have shown a predominance of perceptually-based overextensions.

Nelson (1973) has put forth an opposing view: that children's initial word meanings are predominantly based on dynamic and functional information, rather than on perceptual information. She points out that children are strongly interested in actions and functional relationships (Piaget, 1954). Questions like "What does it do?" or "What is it for?" seem more important to young children than "What does it look like?". Therefore children are more likely to include in their initial word meanings information about the actions and relationships an object engages in, particularly those that affect the child, than information that merely derives from the perceptual form of the object. As support for this view, Nelson's examinations of early vocabularies showed that children learn first the names of objects that they can operate on and that change and move (Nelson, 1973; Nelson, Rescorla, Gruendel, & Benedict, 1978).

Both theories hold that an object's normal motion is likely to be included in its early meaning, since motion is both perceptually salient and functionally important. Where the two positions differ is on the relative importance of the static form of the object versus the use or function of the object. The Clark theory states that form should predominate over use in early word meaning; the Nelson theory, that use should predominate over form. Both sides have intuitive appeal. The argument for the perceptual view is that at the stage when the child is learning his first words, perceptual regularities may well constitute his main set of dependable cognitive structures; they are therefore likely to be recruited in his attempts to assign meaning to words. The appeal of the functional view is that it seems compelling that children should focus more on the functionally significant aspects of objects than on their mere appearances.

It is difficult to test between these two positions, since form and function are mutually constraining and highly correlated among real objects (Anglin, 1977). Objects designed to float on water generally look a lot like boats; objects that move fast are streamlined, and so on. This correlation makes it hard to resolve the controversy unambiguously using evidence from spontaneous speech, such as patterns of word extension. A further reason that it has been difficult to test between the two views is that Nelson's position has an additional complexity. Nelson states that, while the earliest word meanings are based on functional information, children rapidly learn that perceptual information is correlated with this functional core. Once they learn about this correlation, they may rely on perceptual information rather than functional information in their use of object names. The naming behavior of children whose core meanings were functional, but who used perceptual information when applying words, would of course be indistinguishable in most situations from the behavior of children whose meanings were perceptual. Thus the Nelson theory can yield predictions similar to those of the Clark theory once the child has learned the correlations between form and function for a given object. This makes it all the more difficult to draw evidence from natural usage that can decide between the two positions.

An adequate test between these two theories requires a situation in which static perceptual information and functional information could not have been previously associated by the child. Therefore, to conduct this study, artificial objects were constructed to allow form and function to be independently manipulated. The basic plan was (1) to teach the child, in a naturalistic manner, names for two objects that differed both in form and function; and (2) to then present the child with a hybrid object possessing the form of one object and the function of the other, and ask what this object should be called. If the child thought the original word names referred to the forms of the objects, then the hybrid should have the same name as the object of the same form; and analogously for function. In such a case, Nelson's theory predicts that a child's meaning will center on the functional aspects of the object. Therefore the new object should be named according to shared function. Clark's theory predicts that the child's meaning will be based on perceptual aspects of the object, so that the new object will be named by form.

MATERIALS

Both the forms of the objects and their functions were chosen to be natural and interesting to children. There were two original objects that differed both in form and function, and a hybrid object used as a test object. Figure 1 shows the objects. The *jiggy* was a blue and yellow square box, on the side of which was mounted a bright orange face. There was a lever on the side of the box, connected to the face in such a way that when the child moved the lever back and forth the eyes and nose moved up and down, changing the expression on the face.

The *zimbo* was a modified gumball machine. It had a red base and a clear plastic sphere containing jellybeans. It had a lever similar to that of the jiggy, and operated with the same kind of motion. When the lever was moved back and forth, two or three jellybeans dropped from the machine. Thus, the jiggy and zimbo differed from one another in both form and function.

SUBJECTS

There were 57 subjects, ranging in age from 2½ years to adulthood. The distribution by age and sex is shown in Figure 2.

PROCEDURE

The experiment was conducted in a naturalistic manner. Children encountered the jiggy in a waiting room where other children and adults were playing and talking. Three experimenters, all engaged in different primary studies, joined in treating the jiggy as a natural toy. We would say to the children as they entered the waiting room, "Oh, have you seen the jiggy yet? Here it is. Would you like to make it work?". Then we would ask other children to show the jiggy to the newcomer. When we passed through the room, we made a practice of saying to one or another of the children something like, "Can you remember what this is called?" or "How do you make this work?". In this way, we tried to be sure that all the children were very familiar with both the name and the function of the jiggy, and that they regarded it as a natural toy, and not an experimental device.

The children encountered the *zimbo* in a second room, while participating in an unrelated experiment. Most children spontaneously asked "What's that?", as there were no other objects on its shelf. When this happened (or unprompted, if the child did not inquire) the experimenter said casually "That's a zimbo. Can you see how to work it?". The children, particularly the younger

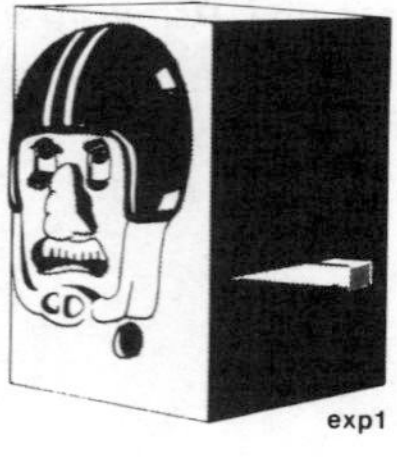

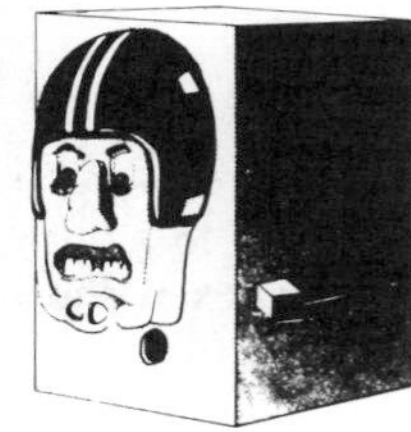

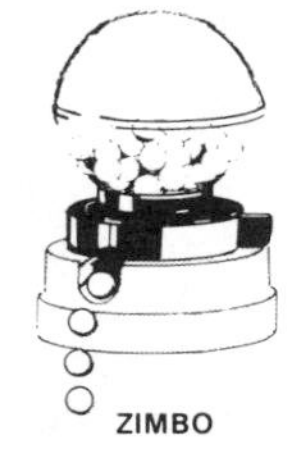

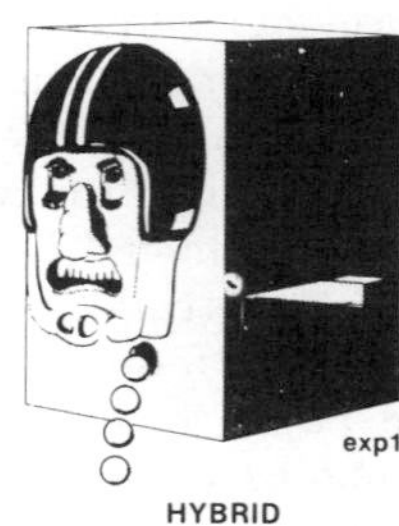

Figure 1. Materials used: *jiggy, zimbo* and hybrid object used in test.

ones, were quite pleased with the zimbo, learned its name very rapidly, and asked to play with it again and again, each time consuming another few jellybeans. By the end of the session, each child had learned the name *zimbo* thoroughly and knew how to operate the machine.

After the other experiment was over, the child and the experimenter went back through the waiting room, again encountering the jiggy. The experimenter casually asked "Do you remember what that is?" to be sure that the child could still remember what the jiggy was called and how it was operated. Finally the child was taken into a third room. The experimenter then unveiled the hybrid object, which looked almost precisely like the jiggy. Before the child could say anything, the experimenter asked, "Can you make this work?". The child stepped forward and moved the handle in the accustomed way. When, instead of changing facial expressions, the machine produced a handful of jellybeans, most children were astonished, often exclaiming to their parents. Then the experimenter asked "What do you think this is?".

RESULTS

Very young children usually responded very readily with one of the original names. Adults and some older children often responded with a combination name, such as *jiggy-zimbo.* In this case, we asked them, "If it had to be called either a *jiggy* or a *zimbo,* which would it be?". The results are shown in Figure 2.

An Age (4 levels) by Sex (2 levels) analysis of variance indicated significant main effects of Age and Sex [$F(3, 49) = 5.15$, $p < .01$ and $F(1, 49) = 14.74$, $p < .01$, respectively]. The Age $\times$ Sex interaction was also significant [$F(3, 49) = 3.65$, $p < .05$].

The pattern of results shows, first, that the youngest children — aged 2½ years to 5 years — responded on the basis of form and not function. For these children, when form and function are put into conflict, it is form rather than function that determines the application of the word to the new object. The second finding is that, while younger and older children responded chiefly on the basis of form, children of middle years responded chiefly on the basis of function. This curvi-

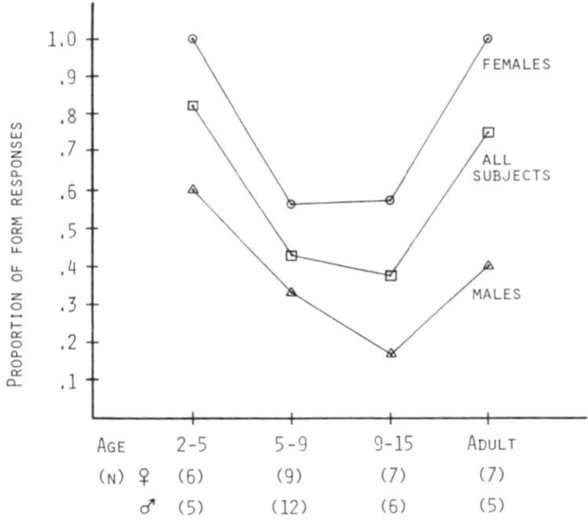

Figure 2. Proportion of responses based on form across age, by sex.

linear pattern raises some interesting possibilities, discussed later in this paper.

DISCUSSION

The fact that the younger children responded on the basis of form rather than function is rather clear counterevidence to the Nelson position, particularly in view of the strong interest that this youngest group displayed in the jellybean function. Almost all the children, particularly the younger ones, asked to play with the zimbo again and again. The young children's learning patterns left no doubt that the functions of the objects, especially that of the zimbo, were important to them. A very consistent informal observation was that young children learned the name of the zimbo considerably faster than the name of the jiggy. For both objects, the children could imitate the name immediately after hearing it. The difference was in retention of the name. After one or two repetitions, almost all the children used the term "zimbo" in spontaneous production for the remainder of the session. Only rarely did a child request a further reminder of its name (e.g., "Can I play with the — uh — what do you call that thing?"). For the jiggy, many more repetitions of the name were required before the child could reliably produce the term non-imitatively.

Thus, the fact that the young children based their responses on form cannot be dismissed with the argument that they found the functional aspects of the situation uninteresting. Moreover, the name *zimbo* was normally produced many more times than the name *jiggy*, because children asked for it repeatedly. Thus any effects of prior frequency of word usage would have increased the likelihood that young children would call the new object a *zimbo*. Yet the children, particularly the youngest, still called it a jiggy according to shared form.

It might be argued, in support of the Nelson theory, that these children had already learned the general correspondence between form and function, and can now apply it in word-learning situations. Perhaps, with still younger children, functional responses would have outweighed form responses. This would require postulating an N-shaped developmental pattern, adding another inflection to the U-shaped pattern found here. Since the youngest children tested gave the highest proportion of perceptual responses, this possibility seems cumbersome and would require considerable defending.

Further experimental evidence that form predominates over function in very early word meanings comes from a series of studies by Tomikawa and Dodd (in press). They constructed a set of nine objects that varied in form and function according to a 3 × 3 matrix: that is, there were three sets of three objects alike in form but different in function, and three different sets of three objects alike in function but different in form. They found that children aged two to four were more likely to categorize these objects on the basis of form than function; and, even more to the point, that two- and three-year-old children readily learned referential names for categories consisting of three perceptually-alike objects, but not for categories of functionally-alike objects.

Here again it appears that children take words as referring to the perceptual object. These results are in accord with the observations of spontaneous extensions (Anglin, 1977; Bowerman, 1977; and Clark, 1973). However, the pattern of results found for the jiggy-zimbo case suggests a finer differentiation of the form-function hypothesis. Young children learned the name of the jellybean-providing zimbo more rapidly than the name of the less functionally interesting jiggy. Yet, when they had to apply a name to the hybrid object, they called it a *jiggy* on the basis of shared form, in spite of the fact that its function was that of the more interesting zimbo. This pattern suggests that we need to distinguish more carefully between *which objects* children learn names for and *what information* about these objects enters into their word meanings. It may well be that function is important in determining which object-names children learn earliest, but that the content of the word meaning, and the basis for applying the word to new instances, is primarily perceptual information.

This proposal, then, is that function determines *which* while form determines *what*. This could account for the seemingly conflicting findings in the literature. Nelson's (1973) findings that early vocabularies are heavily weighted towards small objects with interesting functions can be accounted for, since children should learn first the names of objects whose functions are important to them. On the other hand, Clark's (1973) findings concerning diary overextensions, Bowerman's (1977) observations of spontaneous word usage, and Anglin's (1977) studies of picture-naming, all of which indicate that early word meanings are heavily based on the perceptual form of objects, can also be explained in this framework. Regardless of *which* words a child learns earliest, the claim is that shape of an object, its characteristic movement patterns, and other perceptual information will predominate in the child's representation of the word meaning.

It is perhaps surprising that children fail to base their word meanings on the aspects of the objects that interest them most. One explanation that has been suggested is that children implicitly base their word meanings on information for which they possess relatively well-understood conceptual structures (H. Clark, 1973; Huttenlocher, 1974; Nelson, 1974). The supposition is that completeness of conceptual framework is important even to children. Perceptual regularities, including static perceptual knowledge (that is, knowledge of form) probably constitute the conceptual system that children understand earliest (Bryant, 1974; Piaget, 1954). It is perhaps reasonable, therefore, that they rely on this system in their early word meanings (H. Clark, 1973).

The notion that word meanings are based on well-understood conceptual systems raises some interesting possibilities concerning the U-shaped developmental pattern found here. It is possible that this trend represents children's growing understanding of different kinds of functions. Perhaps at an early age, children think of objects, even mechanical objects, in a simple visual way, since they lack any understanding of mechanical functions. Later, children begin to develop systematic understanding of the kinds of mechanical functions that objects can perform. At this stage they begin to include such information in their word meanings. There may even be a period during which the child relies more exclusively on functional knowledge than an adult would do. Such temporary over-use of a new domain of regularity would be analogous to other instances of over-use of conceptual generalizations in language development; e.g., in acquisition of the past tense, as when *dug* gives way to *digged;* or in acquisition of causative morphology, as when a child who once said "Don't drop it." says instead "Don't fall it." (Bowerman, 1973).

This proposal that children go through a period of temporary over-use of mechanical knowledge in deriving semantics would explain the U-shaped pattern found here. It also might fit with the sex differences found. Girls showed less reliance on functional information throughout than boys. Assuming that the girls in this study had less experience with mechanical devices of this kind than did the boys, they would not have developed as well-elaborated a conceptual system as the boys did. They would therefore have continued to rely more on perceptual information in their word meanings. This account of the sex difference leads to an interesting prediction: that girls should show an earlier shift from perceptual to functional information than boys in cases when the functional knowledge lies in domains more likely to be learned by girls. More generally, for any domain, all else being equal, we would expect non-perceptual information to enter word meanings after the individual has had experience with the relevant system.

In conclusion, the results of the present naturalistic study converge with other experimental findings and observations to suggest that form and function may have different effects on early word learning. While functional relevance appears important in determining which words children learn, the patterns of extension of word use suggest that perceptual information about the referent object predominates in the child's representation of meaning.

REFERENCES

Anglin, J. M. *Word, object and conceptual development.* New York: W. W. Norton & Co., 1977.

Bowerman, M. Semantic factors in the acquisition of rules for word use and sentence construction. In D. Morehead & A. Morehead (Eds.) *Directions in normal and deficient child language.* Baltimore: University Park Press, 1976.

Bowerman, M. The acquisition of word meaning: An investigation of some current conflicts. In N. Waterson and C. Snow (Eds.) *Proceedings of the Third International Child Language Symposium.* New York: Wiley, 1977.

Bryant, P. E. *Perception and understanding in young children: An experimental approach.* New York: Basic Books, 1974.

Clark, E. V. What's in a word: On the child's acquisition of semantics in his first language. In T. E. Moore (Ed.) *Cognitive development and the acquisition of language.* New York: Academic Press, 1973.

Clark, H. H. Space, time, semantics and the child. In T. E. Moore (Ed.) *Cognitive development and the acquisition of language.* New York: Academic Press, 1973.

Huttenlocher, J. The origins of language comprehension. In R. L. Solso (Ed.) *Theories in cognitive psychology: The Loyola Symposium.* Potomac, MD.: Erlbaum, 1974.

Nelson, K. Structure and strategy in learning to talk. *Monographs of the Society for Research in Child Development,* 1973, *38,* 149.

Nelson, K. Concept, word and sentence: Interrelations in acquisition and development. *Psychological Review,* 1974, *81,* 267–285.

Nelson, K., Rescorla, L., Gruendel, J., & Benedict, H. Early lexicons: What do they mean? *Child Development,* 1978, *48,* 960–968.

Piaget, J. *The construction of reality in the child.* New York: Basic Books, 1954.

Tomikawa, S. A., & Dodd, D. H. *Early word meanings: Perceptually or functionally based?* In press.

16

Roger Brown

DEVELOPMENT OF THE FIRST LANGUAGE IN THE HUMAN SPECIES

The fact that one dare set down the above title, with considerable exaggeration but not perhaps with more than is pardonable, reflects the most interesting development in the study of child speech in the past few years. All over the world the first sentences of small children are being as painstakingly taped, transcribed, and analyzed as if they were the last sayings of great sages. Which is a surprising fate for the likes of "That doggie," "No more milk," and "Hit ball." Reports already made, in progress, or projected for the near future sample development in children not only from many parts of the United States, England, Scotland, France, and Germany, but also development in children learning Luo (central East Africa), Samoan, Finnish, Hebrew, Japanese, Korean, Serbo-Croatian, Swedish, Turkish, Cakchiquel (Mayan-Guatemala), Tzeltal (Mayan-Mexico), American Sign Language in the case of a deaf child, and many other languages. The count you make of the number of studies now available for comparative analysis depends on how much you require in terms of standardized procedure, the full report of data, explicit criteria of acquisition, and so on. Brown (in press), whose methods demand a good deal, finds he can use some 33 reports of 12 languages. Slobin (1971), less interested in proving a small number of generalizations than in setting down a large number of interesting hypotheses suggested by what is known, finds he can use many more studies of some 30 languages from 10 different language families. Of course, this is still only about a 1% sample of the world's languages, but in a field like psycholinguistics, in which "universals" sometimes have been postulated on the basis of one or two languages, 30 languages represent a notable empirical advance. The credit for inspiring this extensive field work on language development belongs chiefly to Slobin at Berkeley, whose vision of a universal developmental sequence has inspired research workers everywhere. The quite surprising degree to which results to date support this vision has sustained the researcher when he gets a bit tired of writing

The first five years of Brown's work were supported by Public Health Service Grant MH–7088 from the National Institute of Mental Health, and the second five years by Grant HD–02908 from the National Institute of Child Health and Development. The author is deeply grateful for the generosity of this support and the intelligent flexibility with which both grants have been administered.

This article was delivered as a Distinguished Scientific Contribution Award Address at the annual meeting of the American Psychological Association, Honolulu, September 1972.

SOURCE: From Roger Brown, "Development of the First Language in the Human Species," *American Psychologist* 28, February 1973, pp. 97–106.

down Luo, Samoan, or Finnish equivalents of "That doggie" and "No more milk."

It has, of course, taken some years to accumulate data on a wide variety of languages and even now, as we shall see, the variety is limited largely to just the first period of sentence construction (what is called Stage I). However, the study of first-language development in the preschool years began to be appreciated as a central topic in psycholinguistics in the early 1960s. The initial impetus came fairly directly from Chomsky's (1957) *Syntactic Structures* and, really, from one particular emphasis in that book and in transformational, generative grammar generally. The emphasis is, to put it simply, that in acquiring a first language, one cannot possibly be said simply to acquire a repertoire of sentences, however large that repertoire is imagined to be, but must instead be said to acquire a rule system that makes it possible to generate a literally infinite variety of sentences, most of them never heard from anyone else. It is not a rare thing for a person to compose a new sentence that is understood within his community; rather, it is really a very ordinary linguistic event. Of course, *Syntactic Structures* was not the first book to picture first-language learning as a largely creative process; it may be doubted if any serious linguist has ever thought otherwise. It was the central role Chomsky gave to creativity that made the difference, plus, of course, the fact that he was able to put into explicit, unified notation a certain number of the basic rules of English.

In saying that a child acquires construction rules, one cannot of course mean that he acquires them in any explicit form; the preschool child cannot tell you any linguistic rules at all. And the chances are that his parents cannot tell you very many either, and they obviously do not attempt to teach the mother tongue by the formulation of rules of sentence construction. One must suppose that what happens is that the preschool child is able to extract from the speech he hears a set of construction rules, many of them exceedingly abstract, which neither he nor his parents know in explicit form. This is saying more than that the child generalizes or forms analogies insofar as the generalizations he manifests conform closely to rules that have been made explicit in linguistic science.

That something of the sort described goes on has always been obvious to everyone for languages like Finnish or Russian which have elaborate rules of word formation, or morphology, rules that seem to cause children to make very numerous systematic errors of a kind that parents and casual observers notice. In English, morphology is fairly simple, and errors that parents notice are correspondingly less common. Nevertheless they do exist, and it is precisely in these errors that one glimpses from time to time that largely hidden but presumably general process. Most American children learning English use the form *hisself* rather than *himself* when they are about four years old. How do they come by it? It actually has been in the language since Middle English and is still in use among some adults, though called, for no good reason, a "substandard" form. It can be shown, however, that children use it when they have never heard it from anyone else, and so presumably they make it up or construct it. Why do they invent something that is, from the standard adult point of view, a mistake? To answer that we must recall the set of words most similar to the reflexive pronoun *himself*. They are such other reflexive pronouns as *myself, yourself,* and *herself*. But all of these others, we see, are constructed by combining the possessive pronoun, *my, your,* or *her* with *self*. The masculine possessive pronoun is *his* and, if the English language were consistent at this point, the reflexive would be *hisself*. As it happens, standard English is not consistent at this point but is, rather, irregular, as all languages are at some points, and the preferred form is *himself*. Children, by inventing *hisself* and often insisting on it for quite a period, "iron out" or correct the irregularity of the language. And, incidentally, they reveal to us the fact that what they are learning are general rules of construction — not just the words and phrases they hear.

Close examination of the speech of children learning English shows that it is often replete with errors of syntax or sentence construction as well as morphology (e.g., "Where Daddy went"). But for some reason, errors of word formation are noticed regularly by parents, whereas they are commonly quite unconscious of errors of syntax. And so it happens that even casual observers of languages with a well-developed morphology are aware of the creative construction process, whereas casual observers of English find it possible seriously to believe that language learning is simply a process of memorizing what has been heard.

The extraction of a finite structure with an infinite generative potential which furthermore is accomplished in large part, though not completely, by the beginning of the school years (see Chomsky, 1969, for certain exceptions and no doubt there are others), all without explicit tuition, was not something any learning theory was prepared to explain, though some were prepared to "handle" it, whatever "handle" means. And so it appeared that first-language acquisition was a major challenge to psychology.

While the first studies of language acquisition were inspired by transformational linguistics, nevertheless, they really were not approved of by the transformational linguists. This was because the studies took the child's spontaneous speech performance, taped and transcribed at home on some regular schedule, for their basic data, and undertook to follow the changes in these data with age. At about the same time in the early 1960s, three studies of, roughly, this sort were begun independently: Martin Braine's (1963) in Maryland, Roger Brown's (Brown & Bellugi, 1964) at Harvard with his associates Ursula Bellugi (now Bellugi-Klima) and Colin Fraser (Brown & Fraser, 1963), and Susan Ervin (now Ervin-Tripp) with Wick Miller (Miller & Ervin, 1964) at Berkeley. The attempt to discover constructional knowledge from "mere performance" seemed quite hopeless to the MIT linguists (e.g., Chomsky, 1964; Lees, 1964). It was at the opposite extreme from the linguist's own method, which was to present candidate-sentences to his own intuition for judgment as grammatical or not. In cases of extreme uncertainty, I suppose he may also have stepped next door to ask the opinion of a colleague.

In retrospect, I think they were partly right and partly wrong about our early methods. They were absolutely right in thinking that no sample of spontaneous speech, however large, would alone enable one to write a fully determinate set of construction rules. I learned that fact over a period of years in which I made the attempt 15 times, for three children at five points of development. There were always, and are always, many things the corpus alone cannot settle. The linguists were wrong, I think, in two ways. First, in supposing that because one cannot learn everything about a child's construction knowledge, one cannot learn anything. One can, in fact, learn quite a lot, and one of the discoveries of the past decade is the variety of ways in which spontaneous running discourse can be "milked" for knowledge of linguistic structure; a great deal of the best evidence lies not simply in the child's own sentences but in the exchanges with others on the level of discourse. I do not think that transformational linguists should have "pronounced" on all of this with such discouraging confidence since they had never, in fact, tried. The other way in which I think the linguists were wrong was in their gross exaggeration of the degree to which spontaneous speech is ungrammatical, a kind of hodgepodge of false starts, incomplete sentences, and so on. Except for talk at learned conferences, even adult speech, allowing for some simple rules of editing and ellipses, seems to be mostly quite grammatical (Labov, 1970). For children and for the speech of parents to children this is even more obviously the case.

The first empirical studies of the 1960s gave rise to various descriptive characterizations, of which "telegraphic speech" (Brown & Fraser, 1963) and "Pivot Grammar" (Braine, 1963) are the best known. These did not lead anywhere very interesting, but they were unchallenged long enough to get into most introductory psychology textbooks where they probably will survive for a few years even though their numerous inadequacies are now well established. Bloom (1970), Schlesinger (1971), and Bowerman (1970) made the most telling criticisms both theoretical and empirical, and Brown [1973] has put the whole, now overwhelmingly negative, case together. It seems to be clear enough to workers in this field that telegraphic speech and Pivot Grammar are false leads that we need not even bother to describe.

However, along with their attacks, especially on Pivot Grammar, Bloom (1970) and Schlesinger (1971) made a positive contribution that has turned out to be the second major impetus to the field. For reasons which must seem very strange to the outsider not immersed in the linguistics of the 1960s, the first analyses of child sentences in this period were in terms of pure syntax, in abstraction from semantics, with no real attention paid to what the children might intend to communicate. Lois Bloom added to her transcriptions of child speech a systematic running account of the nonlinguistic context. And in these contexts she found evidence that the child intends to express certain meanings with even his earliest sentences, meanings that go beyond the simple naming in succession of various aspects of a complex situation, and that actually assert the existence of, or request the creation of, particular relations.

The justification for attributing relational semantic intentions to very small children comprises a complex and not fully satisfying argument. At its strongest, it involves the following sort of experimental procedure. With toys that the child can name available to him he is, on one occasion, asked to "Make the truck hit the car," and on another occasion "Make the car hit the truck." Both sentences involve the same objects and action, but the contrast of word order in English indicates which object is to be in the role of agent (hitter) and which in the role of object (the thing hit). If the child acts out the two events in ways appropriate to the contrasting word orders, he may be said to understand the differences in the semantic relations involved. Similar kinds of contrasts can be set up for possessives ("Show me the Mommy's baby" versus "Show me the baby's Mommy") and prepositions ("Put the pencil on the matches" versus "Put the matches on the pencil"). The evidence to date, of which there is a fairly considerable amount collected in America and Britain (Bever, Mehler, & Valian, in press; de Villiers & de Villiers, in press; Fraser, Bellugi, & Brown, 1963; Lovell & Dixon, 1965), indicates that, by late Stage I, children learning English can do these things correctly (experiments on the prepositions are still in a trial stage). By late Stage I, children learning English also are often producing what the nonlinguistic context suggests are intended as relations of possession, location, and agent-action-object. For noncontrastive word orders in English and for languages that do not utilize contrastive word order in these ways, the evidence for relational intentions is essentially the nonlinguistic context. Which context is also, of course, what parents use as an aid to figuring out what their children mean when they speak.

It is, I think, worth a paragraph of digression to point out that another experimental method, a method of judgment and correction of word sequence and so a method nearer that of the transformational linguist himself, yields a quite different outcome. Peter and Jill de Villiers (1972) asked children to observe a dragon puppet who sometimes spoke correctly with respect to word order (e.g., "Drive your car") and sometimes incorrectly (e.g., "Cup the fill"). A second dragon puppet responded to the first when the first spoke correctly by saying "right" and repeating the sentence. When the first puppet spoke incorrectly, the second, tutorial puppet, said "wrong," and corrected the sentence (e.g., "Fill the cup"). After observing a number of such sequences, the child was invited to play the role of the tutorial puppet, and new sentences, correct and incorrect, were supplied. In effect, this is a complicated way of asking the child to make judgments of syntactic well-formedness, supplying corrections as necessary. The instruction is not given easily in words, but by role-playing examples de Villiers and de Villiers found they could get the idea across. While there are many interesting results in their study, the most important is that the children did not make correct word-order judgments 50% of the time until after what we call Stage V, and only the most advanced child successfully corrected wrong orders over half the time. This small but important study suggests that construction rules do not emerge all at once on the levels of spontaneous use, discriminating response, and judgment. The last of these, the linguist's favorite, is, after all, not simply a pipeline to competence but a metalinguistic performance of considerable complexity.

In spite of the fact that the justification for attributing semantic intentions of a relational nature to the child when he first begins composing sentences is not fully satisfactory, the practice, often called the method of "rich interpretation," by contrast with the "lean" behavioral interpretation that preceded it, is by now well justified simply because it has helped expose remarkable developmental universals that formerly had gone unremarked. There are now I think three reasonably well-established developmental series in which constructions and the meanings they express appear in a nearly invariant order.

The first of these, and still the only one to have been shown to have validity for many different languages, concerns Stage I. Stage I has been defined rather arbitrarily as the period when the average length of the child's utterances in morphemes (mean length of utterance or *MLU*) first rises above 1.0 — in short, the time when combinations of words or morphemes first occur at all — until the *MLU* is 2.0, at which time utterances occasionally will attain as great a length as 7 morphemes. The most obvious superficial fact about child sentences is that they grow longer as the child grows older. Leaning on this fact, modern investigators have devised a set of standard rules for calculating *MLU,* rules partially well motivated and partially arbitrary. Whether the rules are exactly the right ones, and it is already clear that they are not, is almost immaterial because their only function is a temporary one: to render children in one study and in different studies initially comparable in terms of some index superior to chronological age, and this *MLU* does. It has been shown [Brown, 1973] that while individual children vary enormously in rate of linguistic development, and so in what they know at a given chronological age, their constructional and semantic knowledge is fairly uniform at a given *MLU*. It is common, in the literature, to identify five stages, with those above Stage I defined by increments of .50 to the *MLU*.

By definition, then, Stage I children in any language are going to be producing sentences of from 1 to 7 morphemes long with the average steadily increasing across Stage I. What is not true by definition, but is true in fact for all of the languages so far studied, is that the constructions in Stage I are limited semantically to a single rather small set of relations and, furthermore, the complications that occur in the course of the Stage are also everywhere the same. Finally, in Stage I, the only syntactic or expressive devices employed are the combinations of the semantically related forms under one sentence contour and, where relevant in the model language, correct word order. It is important to recognize that there are many other things that *could* happen in Stage I, many ways of increasing *MLU* besides those actually used in Stage I. In Stage I, *MLU* goes up because simple two-term relations begin to be combined into three-term and four-term relations of the same type but occurring on one sentence. In later stages, *MLU,* always sensitive to increases of knowledge, rises in value for quite different reasons; for instance, originally missing obligatory function forms like inflections begin to be supplied, later on the embedding of two or more simple sentences begins, and eventually the coordination of simple sentences.

What are the semantic relations that seem universally to be the subject matter of Stage I speech? In brief, it may be said that they are either relations or propositions concerning the sensory-motor world, and seem to represent the linguistic expression of the sensory-motor intelligence which the work of the great developmental psychologist, Jean Piaget, has described as the principal acquisition of the first 18 months of life. The Stage I relations also correspond very closely with the set of "cases" which Charles Fillmore (1968) has postulated as the universal semantic deep structures of language. This is surprising since Fillmore did not set out to say anything at all about child speech but simply to provide a universal framework for adult grammar.

In actual fact, there is no absolutely fixed list of Stage I relations. A short list of 11 will account for about 75% of Stage I utterances in almost all language samples collected. A longer list of about 18 will come close to accounting for 100%. What are some of the relations? There is, in the first place, a closed semantic set having to do with reference. These include the nominative (e.g., "That ball"), expressions of recurrence (e.g., "More ball"), and expression of disappearance or nonexistence (e.g., "All gone ball"). Then there is the possessive (e.g., "Daddy chair"), two sorts of locative (e.g., "Book table" and "Go store") and the attributive (e.g., "Big house"). Finally, there are two-term relations comprising portions of a major sort of declarative sentence: agent-action (e.g., "Daddy hit"); action-object (e.g., "Hit ball"); and, surprisingly from the point of view of the adult language, agent-object (e.g., "Daddy ball"). Less frequent relations which do not appear in all samples but which one would want to add to a longer list include: experiencer-state (e.g., "I hear"); datives of indirect object (e.g., "Give Mommy"); comitatives (e.g., "Walk Mommy"); instrumentals (e.g., "Sweep broom"); and just a few others. From all of these constructions, it may be noticed that in English, and in all languages, "obligatory" functional morphemes like inflections, case endings, articles, and prepositions are missing in Stage I. This is, of course, the observation that gave rise to the still roughly accurate descriptive term *telegraphic speech.* The function forms are thought to be absent because of some combination of such variables as their slight phonetic substance and minimal stress, their varying but generally considerable grammatical complexity, and the subtlety of the semantic modulations they express (number, time, aspect, specificity of reference, exact spatial relations, etc.).

Stage I speech seems to be almost perfectly restricted to these two-term relations, expressed, at the least, by subordination to a single sentence contour and often by appropriate word order, until the *MLU* is about 1.50. From here on, complications which lengthen the utterance begin, but they are, remarkably enough, complications of just the same two types in all languages studied so far. The first type involves three-term relations, like agent-action-object; agent-action-locative; and action-object-locative which, in effect, combine sequentially two of the simple relations found before an *MLU* of 1.50 without repeating the term that would appear twice if the two-term relations simply were strung together. In other words, something like agent-action-object (e.g., "Adam hit ball") is made up *as if* the relations agent-action ("Adam hit") and action-object ("Hit ball") had been strung together in sequence with one redundant occurrence of the action ("hit") deleted.

The second type of complication involves the retention of the basic line of the two-term relation with one term, always a noun-phrase, "expanding" as a relation in its own right. Thus, there is development from such forms as "Sit chair" (action-locative) to "Sit Daddy chair" which is an action-locative, such that the locative itself is expanded as a possessive. The forms expanded in this kind of construction are, in all languages so far studied, the same three types: expressions of attribution, possession, and recurrence. Near the very end of Stage I, there are further complications into four-term relations of exactly the same two types described. All of this, of course, gives a very "biological" impression, almost as if semantic cells of a finite set of types were dividing and combining and then redividing and recombining in ways common to the species.

The remaining two best established invariances of order in acquisition have not been studied in a variety of languages but only for American children and, in one case, only for the three unacquainted children in Brown's longitudinal study — the children called, in the literature, Adam, Eve, and Sarah. The full results appear in Stage II of Brown [1973] and in Brown and Hanlon (1970). Stage II in Brown [1973] focuses on 14 functional morphemes including the English noun and verb inflections, the copula *be,* the progressive auxiliary *be,* the prepositions *in* and *on,* and the articles *a* and *the.* For just these forms in English it is possible to define a criterion that is considerably superior to the simple occurrence-or-not used in Stage I and to the semiarbitrary frequency levels used in the remaining sequence to be described. In very many sentence contexts, one or another of the 14 morphemes can be said to be "obligatory" from the point of view of the adult language. Thus in a nomination sentence accompanied by pointing, such as "That book," an article is obligatory; in a sentence like "Here two book," a plural inflection on the noun is obligatory; in "I running," the auxiliary *am* inflected for person, number, and tense is obligatory. It is possible to treat each such sentence frame as a kind of test item in which the obligatory form either appears or is omitted. Brown defined as his criterion of acquisition, presence in 90% of obligatory contexts in six consecutive sampling hours.

There are in the detailed report many surprising and suggestive outcomes. For instance, "acquisition" of these forms turns out never to be a sudden all-or-none affair such as categorical linguistic rules might suggest it should be. It is rather a matter of a slowly increasing probability of presence, varying in rate from morpheme to morpheme, but extending in some cases over several years. The most striking single outcome is that for these three children, with spontaneous speech scored in the fashion described, the order of acquisition of the morphemes approaches invariance with rank-order correlations between pairs of children all at about .86. This does not say that acquisition of a morpheme is invariant with respect to chronological age: the variation of rate of development even among three children is tremendous. But the order, that is, which construction follows which, is almost constant, and Brown (in press) shows that it is not predicted by morpheme frequency in adult speech, but is well predicted by relative semantic and grammatical complexity. Of course, in languages other than English, the same universal sequence cannot possibly be found because grammatical and semantic differences are too great to yield commensurable data, as they are not with the fundamental relations or cases of Stage I. However, if the 14 particular morphemes are reconceived as particular conjunctions of perceptual salience and degrees of grammatical and semantic complexity, we may find laws of succession which have cross-linguistic validity (see Slobin, 1971).

Until the spring of 1972, Brown was the only researcher who had coded data in terms of presence in, or absence from, obligatory contexts, but then Jill and Peter de Villiers (in press) did the job on a fairly large scale. They made a cross-sectional study from speech samples of 21 English-speaking American children aged between 16 and 40 months. The de Villiers scored the 14 morphemes Brown scored; they used his coding rules to identify obligatory contexts and calculated the children's individual *MLU* values according to his rules.

Two different criteria of morpheme acquisition were used in the analyses of data. Both constitute well-rationalized adaptations to a cross-sectional study of the 90% correct criterion used in Brown's longitudinal study; we will refer to the two orders here simply as 1 and 2. To compare with the de Villiers' two orders there is a single rank order (3) for the three children, Adam, Eve, and Sarah, which was obtained by averaging the orders of the three children.

There are then three rank orders for the same 14 morphemes scored in the same way and using closely similar criteria of acquisition. The degree of invariance is, even to one who expected a substantial similarity, amazing. The rank-order correlations are: between 1 and 2, .84; between 2 and 3, .78; between 1 and 3, .87. These relations are only very slightly below those among Adam, Eve, and Sarah themselves. Thanks to the de Villiers, it has been made clear that we have a developmental phenomenon of substantial generality.

There are numerous other interesting outcomes in the de Villiers' study. The rank-order correlation between age and Order 2 is .68, while that between *MLU* and the same order is .92, very close to perfect. So *MLU* is a better predictor than age in their study, as in ours of morpheme acquisition. In fact, with age partialed out, using a Kendall partial correlation procedure, the original figure of .92 is only reduced to .85, suggesting that age adds little or nothing to the predictive power of *MLU*.

The third sequence, demonstrated only for English by Brown and Hanlon (1970), takes advantage of the fact that what are called tag questions are in English very complex grammatically, though semantically they are rather simple. In many other languages tags are invariant in form (e.g., *n'est-ce pas,* French; *nicht wahr,* German), and so are grammatically simple; but in English, the form of the tag, and there are hundreds of forms, varies in a completely determinate way with the structure of the declarative sentence to which it is appended and for which it asks confirmation. Thus:

"John will be late, won't he?"
"Mary can't drive, can she?"

And so on. The little question at the end is short enough, as far as superficial length is concerned, to be produced by the end of Stage I. We know, furthermore, that the semantic of the tag, a request for confirmation, lies within the competence of the Stage I child since he occasionally produces such invariant and simple equivalents as "right?" or "huh?" Nevertheless, Brown and Hanlon (1970) have shown that the production of a full range of well-formed tags is not to be found until after Stage V, sometimes several years after. Until that time, there are, typically, no well-formed tags at all. What accounts for the long delay? Brown and Hanlon present evidence that it is the complexity of the grammatical knowledge that tags entail.

Consider such a declarative sentence as "His wife can drive." How might one develop from this the tag "can't she?" It is, in the first place, necessary to make a pronoun of the subject. The subject is *his wife,* and so the pronoun must be feminine, third person, and since it is a subject, the nominative case — in fact, *she.* Another step is to make the tag negative. In English this is done by adding *not* or the contraction *n't* to the auxiliary verb *can;* hence *can't.* Another step is to make the tag interrogative, since it is a question, and in English that is done by a permutation of order — placing the auxiliary verb ahead of the subject. Still another step is to delete all of the predicate of the base sentence, except the first member of the auxiliary, and that at last yields *can't she?* as a derivative of *His wife can drive.* While this description reads a little bit like a program simulating the process by which tags actually are produced by human beings, it is not intended as anything of the sort. The point is simply that there seems to be no way at all by which a human could produce the right tag for each declarative without *somehow* utilizing all of the grammatical knowledge described, just how no one knows. But memorization is excluded completely by the fact that, while tags themselves are numerous but not infinitely so, the problem is to fit the one right tag to each declarative, and declaratives are infinitely numerous.

In English all of the single constructions, and also all of the pairs, which entail the knowledge involved in tag creation, themselves exist as independent sentences in their own right, for example, interrogatives, negatives, ellipses, negative-ellipses, and so on. One can, therefore, make an ordering of constructions in terms of complexity of grammatical knowledge (in precise fact, only a partial ordering) and ask whether more complex forms are always preceded in child speech by less complex forms. This is what Brown and Hanlon (1970) did for Adam, Eve, and Sarah, and the result was resoundingly affirmative. In this study, then, we have evidence that grammatical complexity as such, when it can be disentangled, as it often cannot, from semantic complexity, is itself a determinant of order of acquisition.

Of course, the question about the mother tongue that we should really like answered is, How is it possible to learn a first language at all? On that question, which ultimately motivates the whole research enterprise, I have nothing to offer that is not negative. But perhaps it is worth while making these negatives explicit since they are still widely supposed to be affirmatives, and indeed to provide a large part of the answer to the question. What I have to say is not primarily addressed to the question, How does the child come to talk at all? since there seem to be fairly obvious utilities in saying a few words in order to express more exactly what he wants, does not want, wonders about, or wishes to share with others. The more exact question on which we have a little information that serves only to make the question more puzzling is, How does the child come to *improve* upon his language, moving steadily in the direction of the adult model? It probably seems surprising that there should be any mystery about the forces impelling improvement, since it is just this aspect of the process that most people imagine that they understand. Surely the improvement is a response to selective social pressures of various kinds; ill-formed or incomplete utterances must be less effective than well-formed and complete utterances in accomplishing the child's intent; parents probably approve of well-formed utterances and disapprove or correct the ill-formed. These ideas sound sensible and may be correct, but the still-scant evidence available does not support them.

At the end of Stage I, the child's constructions are characterized by, in addition to the things we have mentioned, a seemingly lawless oscillating omission of every sort of major constituent including sometimes subjects, objects, verbs, locatives, and so on. The important point about these oscillating omissions is that they seldom seem to impede communication; the other person, usually the mother, being in the same situation and familiar with the child's stock of knowledge, usually understands, so far as one can judge, even the incomplete utterance. Brown [1973] has suggested the Stage I child's speech is well adapted to his purpose, but that, as a speaker, he is very *narrowly* adapted. We may suppose that in speaking to strangers or of new experiences he will have to learn to express obligatory constituents if he wants to get his message across. And that may be the answer: The social pressures to communicate may chiefly operate outside the usual sampling situation, which is that of the child at home with family members.

In Stage II, Brown [1973] found that all of the 14 grammatical morphemes were at first missing, then occasionally present in obligatory contexts, and after varying and often long periods of time, always present in such contexts. What makes the probability of supplying the requisite morpheme rise with time? It is surprisingly difficult to find cases in which omission results in incomprehension or misunderstanding. With respect to the definite and nondefinite articles, it even looks as if listeners almost never really need them, and yet child speakers learn to operate with the exceedingly intricate rules governing their usage. Adult Japanese, speaking English as a second language, do not seem to learn how to operate with the articles as we might expect they would if listeners needed them. Perhaps it is the case that the child automatically does this kind of learning but that adults do not. Second-language learning may be responsive to familiar sorts of learning variables, and first-language learning may not. The two, often thought to be similar processes, may be profoundly and ineradicably different.

Consider the Stage I child's invariably uninflected generic verbs. In Stage II, American parents regularly gloss these verbs in one of four ways: as imperatives, past tense forms, present progressives, or imminent-intentional futures. It is an interesting fact, of course, that these are just the four modulations of the verb that the child then goes on, first, to learn to express. For years we have thought it possible that glosses or expansions of this type might be a major force impelling the child to improve his speech. However, all the evidence available, both naturalistic and experimental (it is summarized in Brown, Cazden, & Bellugi, 1969), offers no support at all for this notion. Cazden (1965), for instance, carried out an experiment testing for the effect on young children's speech of deliberately interpolated "expansions" (the supplying of obligatory functional morphemes), introduced for a period on every preschool day for three months. She obtained no significant effect whatever. It is possible, I think, that such an experiment done now, with the information Stage II makes available, and expanding only by providing morphemes of a complexity for which the child was "ready," rather than as in Cazden's original experiment expanding in all possible ways, would show an effect. But no such experiment has been done, and so no impelling effect of expansion has been demonstrated.

Suppose we look at the facts of the parental glossing of Stage I generic verbs not, as we have done above, as a possible tutorial device but rather, as Slobin (1971) has done, as evidence that the children already intended the meanings their parents attributed to them. In short, think of the parental glosses as veridical readings of the child's thought. From this point of view, the child has been understood correctly, even though his utterances are incomplete. In that case there is no selection pressure. Why does he learn to say more if what he already knows how to say works quite well?

To these observations of the seeming efficacy of the child's incomplete utterances, at least at home with the family, we should add the results of a study reported in Brown and Hanlon (1970). Here it was not primarily a question of the omission of obligatory forms but of the contrast between ill-formed primitive constructions and well-formed mature versions. For certain constructions, *yes-no* questions, tag questions, negatives, and *wh-* questions, Brown and Hanlon (1970) identified periods when Adam, Eve, and Sarah were producing both primitive and mature versions, sometimes the one, sometimes the other. The question was, Did the mature version communicate more successfully than the primitive version? They first identified all instances of primitive and mature versions, and then coded the adult responses for comprehending follow-up, calling comprehending responses "sequiturs" and uncomprehending or irrelevant responses "nonsequiturs." They found no evidence whatever of a difference in communicative efficacy, and so once again, no selection pressure. Why, one asks oneself, should the child learn the complex apparatus of tag questions when "right?" or "huh?" seems to do just the same job? Again one notes that adults learning English as a second language often do not learn tag questions, and the possibility again comes to mind that children operate on language in a way that adults do not.

Brown and Hanlon (1970) have done one other study that bears on the search for selection pressures. Once again it was syntactic well-formedness versus ill-formedness that was in question rather than completeness or incompleteness. This time Brown and Hanlon started with two kinds of adult responses to child utterances: "approval," directed at an antecedent child utterance, and "disapproval," directed at such an antecedent. The question then was, Did the two sets of antecedents differ in syntactic correctness? Approving and disapproving responses are, certainly, very reasonable candidates for the respective roles, "positive reinforcer" and "punishment." Of course, they do not necessarily qualify as such because reinforcers and punishments are defined by their effects on performance (Skinner, 1953); they have no necessary, independent, nonfunctional properties. Still, of course, they often are put forward as plausible determinants of performance and are thought, generally, to function as such. In order differentially to affect the child's syntax, approval and disapproval must, at a minimum, be governed selectively by correct and incorrect syntax. If they should be so governed, further data still would be needed to show that they affect performance. If they are not so governed, they cannot be a selective force working for correct speech. And Brown and Hanlon found that they are not. In general, the parents seemed to pay no attention to bad syntax nor did they even seem to be aware of it. They approved or disapproved an utterance usually on the grounds of the truth value of the proposition which the parents supposed the child intended to assert. This is a surprising outcome to most middle-class parents, since they are generally under the impression that they do correct the child's speech. From inquiry and observation I find that what parents generally correct is pronunciation, "naughty" words, and regularized irregular allomorphs like *digged* or *goed*. These facts of the child's speech seem to penetrate parental awareness. But syntax — the child saying, for instance, "Why the dog won't eat?" instead of "Why won't the dog eat?" — seems to be set right automatically in the parent's mind, with the mistake never registering as such.

In sum, then, we presently do not have evidence that there are selective social pressures of any kind operating on children to impel them to bring their speech into line with adult models. It is, however, entirely possible that such pressures do operate in situations unlike the situations we have sampled, for instance, away from home or with strangers. A radically different possibility is that children work out rules for the speech they hear, passing from levels of lesser to greater complexity, simply because the human species is programmed at a certain period in its life to operate in this fashion on linguistic input. Linguistic input would be defined by the universal properties of language. And the period of progressive rule extraction would correspond to Lenneberg's (1967 and elsewhere) proposed "critical period." It may be chiefly adults who learn a new, a second, language in terms of selective social pressures. Comparison of the kinds of errors made by adult second-language learners of English with the kinds made by child first-language learners of English should be enlightening.

If automatic internal programs of structure extraction provide the generally correct sort of answer to how a first language is learned, then, of course, our inquiries into external communication pressures simply are misguided. They look for the answer in the wrong place. That, of course, does not mean that we are anywhere close to having the right answer. It only remains to specify the kinds of programs that would produce the result regularly obtained.

REFERENCES

Bever, T. G., Mehler, J. R., & Valian, V. V. Linguistic capacity of very young children. In T. G. Bever & W. Weksel (Eds.), *The acquisition of structure.* New York: Holt, Rinehart & Winston, in press.

Bloom, L. *Language development: Form and function in emerging grammars.* Cambridge: M.I.T. Press, 1970.

Bowerman, M. Learning to talk: A cross-linguistic study of early syntactic development with special reference to Finnish. Unpublished doctoral dissertation, Harvard University, 1970.

Braine, M. D. S. The ontogeny of English phrase structure: The first phase. *Language,* 1963, *39,* 1–14.

Brown, R. *A first language; The early stages.* Cambridge: Harvard University Press, [1973].

Brown, R., & Bellugi, U. Three processes in the acquisition of syntax. *Harvard Educational Review,* 1964, *34,* 133–151.

Brown, R., Cazden, C., & Bellugi, U. The child's grammar from I to III. In J. P. Hill (Ed.), *Minnesota symposium on child psychology.* Vol. 2. Minneapolis: University of Minnesota Press, 1969.

Brown, R., & Fraser, C. The acquisition of syntax. In C. N. Cofer & B. S. Musgrave (Eds.), *Verbal behavior and learning: Problems and processes.* New York: McGraw-Hill, 1963.

Brown, R., & Hanlon, C. Derivational complexity and order of acquisition in child speech. In J. R. Hayes (Ed.), *Cognition and the development of language.* New York: Wiley, 1970.

Cazden, C. B. Environmental assistance to the child's acquisition of grammar. Unpublished doctoral dissertation, Harvard University, 1965.

Chomsky, C. *The acquisition of syntax in children from 5 to 10.* Cambridge: M.I.T. Press, 1969.

Chomsky, N. *Syntactic structures.* The Hague: Mouton, 1957.

Chomsky, N. Formal discussion of Wick Miller and Susan Ervin. The development of grammar in child language. In U. Bellugi & R. Brown (Eds.), The acquisition of language. *Monographs of the Society for Research in Child Development,* 1964, 29(1), 35–40.

De Villiers, J. G., & de Villiers, P. A. A cross-sectional study of the development of grammatical morphemes in child speech. *Journal of Psycholinguistic Research,* 1973, in press.

De Villiers, J. G., & de Villiers, P. A. Development of the use of order in comprehension. *Journal of Psycholinguistic Research,* 1973, in press.

De Villiers, P. A., & de Villiers, J. G. Early judgments of semantic and syntactic acceptability by children. *Journal of Psycholinguistic Research,* 1972, *1,* 299–310.

Fillmore, C. J. The case for case. In E. Bach & R. T. Harms (Eds.), *Universals in linguistic theory.* New York: Holt, Rinehart & Winston, 1968.

Fraser, C., Bellugi, U., & Brown, R. Control of grammar in imitation, comprehension, and production. *Journal of Verbal Learning and Verbal Behavior,* 1963, *2,* 121–135.

Labov, W. The study of language in its social context. *Studium Generale,* 1970, *23,* 30–87.

Lees, R. Formal discussion of Roger Brown and Colin Fraser. The acquisition of syntax. And of Roger Brown, Colin Fraser, and Ursula Bellugi. Explorations in grammar evaluation. In U. Bellugi & R. Brown (Eds.), The acquisition of language. *Monographs of the Society for Research in Child Development,* 1964, *29*(1), 92–98.

Lenneberg, E. H. *Biological foundations of language.* New York: Wiley, 1967.

Lovell, K., & Dixon, E. M. The growth of grammar in imitation, comprehension, and production. *Journal of Child Psychology and Psychiatry,* 1965, *5,* 1–9.

Miller, W., & Ervin, S. The development of grammar in child language. In U. Bellugi & R. Brown (Eds.), The acquisition of language. *Monographs of the Society for Research in Child Development,* 1964, *29*(1), 9–34.

Schlesinger, I. M. Production of utterances and language acquisition. In D. I. Slobin (Ed.), *The ontogenesis of grammar.* New York: Academic Press, 1971.

Skinner, B. F. *Science and human behavior.* New York: Macmillan, 1953.

Slobin, D. I. Developmental psycholinguistics. In W. O. Dingwall (Ed.), *A survey of linguistic science.* College Park: Linguistics Program, University of Maryland, 1971.

17

Katherine Nelson

INDIVIDUAL DIFFERENCES IN LANGUAGE DEVELOPMENT: IMPLICATIONS FOR DEVELOPMENT AND LANGUAGE

ABSTRACT: Differences in characteristics of language development that have been identified in a number of recent studies are reviewed. In these studies, some children have been found to emphasize single words, simple productive rules for combining words, nouns and noun phrases, and referential functions; others use whole phrases and formulas, pronouns, compressed sentences, and expressive or social functions. The evidence for two *styles* of acquisition and their continuity over time is examined. Explanations in terms of hemispheric functions, cognitive maturation, cognitive style, and environmental context are considered, and an explanation in terms of the interaction of individual and environment in different functional contexts is suggested. Implications for development and the mastery of complex systems are discussed.

A new consensus is emerging about the appropriate framework within which to view the important problems of language acquisition. In contrast to the prevailing view a decade ago that language development could only be understood within a linguistic, genetic, rule-testing, individual framework, students of child language today have increasingly accepted the premise of a developing social, cognitive, and communicative system within which language is gradually mastered. The implications of this shift for our view of both language and development are important, as the burgeoning literature in the journals and in such recent edited collections as Collins (1979), K. E. Nelson (1978, 1980), and Lock (1978) indicate. A sense of the richness and interest of the newer approaches can be gleaned from these sources. Here I would like to consider how the study of individual differences in development fits into this new framework and adds to it.

In the older paradigm, individual differences played no part nor could they. A basic assumption of the stance, derived initially from Chomsky's (1965, 1968, 1976) theories, was that grammar was innately given, operating under universal principles. To the extent that this is the case, one could expect to find a similar course of acquisition for all children, and thus variation among individ-

Research reported in this article was supported in part by a grant from the Carnegie Corporation of New York.

I would like to thank Ellen Tanouye for her valuable contribution to data collection and transcription and Joan Lucariello for aid in the analysis.

uals, cultures, and language communities could only be minor and irrelevant. Evidence in favor of this position was found in the fact that similar patterns of early word combinations were found among children from different language communities (Brown, 1973; Slobin, 1973), although differences between languages were also found at later points in development (Slobin, 1973). The latter differences were considered to result from the different cognitive — not linguistic — demands of different languages. A strong argument could be made along similar lines that the similarities found reflected universal cognitive developments (Sinclair-de Zwart, 1973) rather than linguistic ones. In any event, an implicit corollary of the proposition was that any child would be representative of the language acquisition process inasmuch as that process was universal. On these grounds, the prototypical language development research design — the longitudinal study of one, two, or three children — could be justified.[1]

It is not surprising that the first study to call attention to individual differences in language development was also among the first to challenge the prevailing views of syntactic development and to introduce semantics and the method of *rich interpretation*[2] into the study of early word combinations. This was Bloom's (1970) book, based on an earlier dissertation. Bloom suggested in this study that different grammatical representations were developed by different children. Although the grammatical analysis contained in this work was widely acclaimed and debated, its suggestion of different approaches was largely ignored at the time. If anything, the claims of universality grew stronger, culminating in Brown's (1973) analysis of the corpora from 17 children reported in various studies of early multiword utterances that had been completed at that time. Indeed, Brown's compendium stands as a kind of watershed, enshrining the concerns, methods, and achievements of the semantic–syntactic paradigm before the growing impact of cognitive, communicative, and pragmatic concerns had yet been much felt.

The semantic–syntactic paradigm had as its goal the description of the grammar of children's early sentences. Several corollaries followed from this. One was that a single-word utterance was considered irrelevant to the enterprise unless it could be analyzed as a sentence (e.g., Greenfield & Smith, 1976; McNeill, 1970). Another was that two-word utterances were analyzed as sentences, and thus the grammar of 2-year-old children's two-word productions absorbed the attention of the developmental psycholinguistic community for many years. The beginnings of speech in single words or in prelinguistic communication and cognition, the meanings intended and conveyed by children, the uses of language, the development of conversation, the role of mothers and others in the language community in the language-acquisition process, the comprehension of what was said, even later grammatical and metalinguistic development — all topics of intense current interest — were almost totally neglected during this period, except as they might bear on the grammatical enterprise itself (i.e., the use of meaning to interpret syntax). And of course individual differences were, with minor exceptions (e.g., Cazden, 1967), almost completely ignored.

Recently, however, a growing number of studies based on these new concerns have emphasized that important individual differences do exist in both the process and the structure of acquisition and in the speech children produce during the major period of language development, roughly from ages 1 to 5. Since the view of language acquisition as essentially maturational has been largely abandoned, such findings no longer challenge it. It is high time, then, to consider the implications of individual differences for developmental research and theory.

A recent book (Fillmore, Kempler, & Wang, 1979) reviews the nature of individual differences in language abilities and behavior primarily among adults but gives very little attention to developmental differences (except in two chapters on phonological development). In this book, various authors attempt to place in perspective the implications of individual differences for linguistic method and theory, going beyond the competence–performance distinction introduced by Chomsky (1965) to consider variations in peoples' competences. The performance–competence terms were originally used to distinguish between the underlying grammatical rules that were assumed to be the same for all speakers of a language (i.e., competence) and the on-line production and comprehension of utterances in context (performance).

Performance could be expected to vary depending on psychologically relevant factors such as memory, and performance ability could vary from individual to individual in the psychologist's sense of competence. In the linguist's sense, however, competence was assumed to be equivalent across all adult native speakers of a language. In contrast, the consensus view of the Fillmore et al. (1979) book appears to be that linguistic competence itself may vary among adult speakers; that is, different speakers may have different rule systems. Obviously, then, one of the possible implications of individual differences in child language acquisition is that different rule systems are being constructed.

Other alternative or additional implications are possible, however. Of course, individual differences might be only differences in the rate of acquisition of similar rule systems, perhaps reflecting underlying differences in intellectual functioning. (It is important to note in this regard, however, that variations in early language ability do not reliably predict later intelligence test scores.) Individual differences might reflect something like cognitive styles, matters of performance variability but not competence. Such style differences might in turn reflect personality and motivational factors, environmental influences, or both. On the other hand, individual differences in development might suggest different possible learning sequences or strategies.

An additional consideration is that differences in developmental patterns might persist throughout development and into maturity, or they might disappear as the system reached maturity. If these variations were primarily a function of personality or cognitive style or if they reflected the construction of different rule systems, one would in fact expect to see increasing differentiation as the system became more complex. If, however, they reflected learning strategies or sequences, one would expect them to disappear as the system is mastered. Since we know that there is considerable variation in language ability and use among adults, this question can be restated as one of whether developmental variations are functionally related to later variations. Before sorting out these various possible implications, we need to consider first where and what are the differences in question.

THE NATURE OF THE DIFFERENCES

Much of the recent work revealing differences in approach to language can be summarized in a set of polarities: word versus phrase, referential versus expressive, cognitive versus pragmatic, nominal versus pronominal, and analytic versus gestalt. As used here, these are not formal linguistic terms but functional psychological ones. Furthermore, they have not been the starting points of analysis but rather the synthetic outcomes. Their relevance was prefigured in a study focused on the presyntactic stage of learning to talk (K. Nelson, 1973). In that study, 18 children were followed longitudinally from approximately 1 to 2½ years of age. The study utilized records kept by mothers as well as tape recordings of language used by mother and child during monthly visits in the home and periodical probes of such developments as comprehension, imitation, categorization, and reference. A major outcome of the study was the finding of individual approaches to the tasks of learning the language. These approaches were reflected in a number of ways, first in the kinds of words and phrases children learned and used during the single-word period.

For most of the children (called *referential*), early vocabularies consisted of a large proportion of object names (i.e., nouns) with some verbs, proper names, and adjectives. For a large minority (called *expressive*), however, vocabularies were more diverse, with a large number of social routines or formulas (such as "stop it," "I want it," "don't do it") included among the nouns, verbs, and adjectives. Because of these phrases, the vocabularies of the latter children included pronouns and grammatical functors as well as nouns, although whether these terms could be considered "vocabulary items" was problematic, since they were usually embedded in what appeared to be unanalyzed formulas or routines rather than novel constructions. These two primary characteristics, representing content (vocabulary) and form (word or phrase), also appeared to be related to pragmatic factors of use, although this factor was less clear-cut. Expressive children tended more often to be second born and to come from less highly educated families. A plausible case can be made that the conditions of language use are different in the environments associated with these factors (see discussion below), although systematic observations of differences in function were not carried out with this sample.

Nominal–Pronominal

The identification of a child as expressive or referential in the 1973 study was made at approximately 19 months (or when a 50-word vocabulary had been acquired). Differences that persisted until at least 30 months were discovered in later analyses (K. Nelson, 1975, 1976). Although mean length of utterance (MLU) did not differ between the two groups of children at 2 or 2½ years, size of vocabulary did, with the referential children using significantly greater numbers of different words than the expressive children. In addition, the expressive children used pronouns preferentially in sentences, whereas the referential children used primarily nouns in their early multiword utterances. This difference tended to disappear as the referential children began to use more pronouns in more complete sentences at the later age and MLU stage (over 2.5 words).

At about the same time that the first report from the 1973 study was published, Bloom (1973) described variations in the one-word period among the children who had been the subjects of her earlier grammatical analysis of multiword utterances (Bloom, 1970). On the basis of her observations, Bloom proposed that there were two routes to two-word speech and that these were associated with different characteristics of the children's later two-word constructions as well as with differences in later usages and in the use of imitation. She observed that some children seemed to utilize relational terms (such as "all gone") whereas others used more substantive terms (usually nominals such as "dog" or "flowers"). She also found that the relational children produced pivot-open[3] constructions and used more imitations and more pronouns (Bloom, Lightbown, & Hood, 1975). The substantive children used subject–verb–object sentence constructions (or reduced forms of such) and nouns rather than pronouns and did not imitate.

The use of pronouns rather than nouns by expressive[4] children is especially interesting. Its implication is that the child can refer to objects, people, and actions (using the "pro-form" *do*) without specifying them. The semantics involved in the two uses is quite different. First, the lexicon must be less differentiated. "It," to take the simplest case, may refer to any object, whereas "ball" must refer to objects specified by their appropriate properties. To use object terms, the child must have built up concepts appropriate to the words, but to use pronouns the child need only make the general distinction between people and things. It is true that the I–you distinction involves an ability to understand the deictic relationship (i.e., the shift in reference dependent on speaker role), and he–she–they requires differentiation according to sex and number. However, these are very general distinctions compared with the fine-grained analysis required for distinguishing "dog" from "cat," for example, or "truck" from "car." Which is considered to be more difficult depends ultimately on one's notion of complexity (see Anglin, 1977) or on one's notion of whether the child is engaging in feature combining and generalizing or in differentiation. And these in turn depend on knowing where the child starts. The evidence seems to indicate at least that for some children it is easy to learn nouns but less easy to learn pronouns, and for other children the opposite is true. The question is why this is so.

Analytic Versus Gestalt

Table 1 shows a tabulation of some of the many studies that have recently addressed the question of individual differences in language acquisition and the dimensions along which differences from the "standard" account have been identified, including the word–phrase and nominal–pronominal factors just discussed. It is of some interest that many of these investigators commented on their surprise at the appearance of a characteristic previously undocumented in the literature. Brannigan (Note 1) and Peters (1977) have particularly nice accounts, accounts that are understandable given the strong expectation from previous literature that the 15-month-old child may say "doggie," "bow-wow" or "mommy" but will not say "I don't know where it is" (Brannigan, Note 1), "what do you want?" (K. Nelson, 1973), or "I like goodnight moon" (Peters, 1977). Investigators who hear such expressions from 1-year-olds are likely to conclude that they are overinterpreting an unintelligible sound sequence to fit the situation. It is only as these sequences are repeated in similarly appropriate situations that it becomes obvious that the child is using speech meaningfully. But what kind of speech?

Brannigan (Note 1) refers to utterances of this kind as "compressed sentences," which is a good descriptive term for sequences that are executed very rapidly, contain no pauses between words, and have greatly reduced phonological forms. Peters (1977) refers to it as "gestalt language," indicating that it is aiming at whole phrases or sentences rather than single words. I originally (K. Nelson, 1973, p. 25) referred to it in terms of stereotyped units after Lyons's (1969) discussion, units that can be combined into larger units but are not themselves analyzable. Others have referred to formulas and formulaic routines (e.g., Fillmore, Note 2). The criterion for identifying expressive children in my sample included the use of more than six formulas of this kind before reaching the 50-word level. Such use was as typical of expressive speech as object labeling was of referential speech .

Some examples of this type of language are:

Table 1. SUMMARY OF MAJOR STUDIES OF NONREFERENTIAL CHILDREN

				Language characteristics							
					Syntactic						
Study	*n*[a]	*Age*[b]	*Other child characteristics*	*Semantic*	*Formulas*	*Dummy terms*	*Pronouns*	*Other*	*Function*	*Learning strategies*	*Other*
K. Nelson (1973, 1975)	8 (18)	11–30	Less well-educated families or 2nd born; 3M, 5F	Few nominals, smaller vocabularies	X	X	X		Interpersonal, less object naming, more self-reference	Slower rate of vocabulary acquisition, more imitation, whole phrases	Poor articulation
Clark (1974)	1 (1)	27–30	M		X					Whole sentence use and recombination; imitation	
Bloom, Lightbown, & Hood (1975)	2 (5)	24–30 [c]	M				X	Pivot-open sentences		Imitation	
Ramer (1976)	3 (7)	15–23	Middle-class male; 1. firstborn, 2. 2nd born		X	X		Verb-complement relations		Slow	
Lieven (1978)	1 (3)	20–26	F, 2nd born	More "notice" & recurrence; less locative action & attribution	X			Lacked word rules	Get attention		Repetitive
Peters (1977)	1 (1)	7–24	Second-born M	Fewer nominals	X	X	X		Two types: Gestalt, analytic	Whole phrases, intonational contour	Poor articulation
Horgan (in press)	15 (30)	30–48	Academic families	Fewer adjectives				More main verbs; more auxiliaries, lower NP length		Slow learners	Better comprehension, more varied construction
Brannigan (Note 1)	2 (3)	17–20	M		X	X	X	Wh-Q, contractions, do, negatives, articles	Social situations	Phrase targets, compressed sentences	Poor articulation, shift in strategy
Horgan (in press)	1 (1)	15–36	Academic family, F	Few nominals	X			Pivot-open	Tuned to function of questions, not content		

Note. M = male, F = female. NP = noun phrase; Wh-Q = wh question.
[a] Number of nonreferential children in sample; total sample in parentheses.
[b] In months.
[c] Approximate.

"I don't know where it is"
"I'll get it"
"Is it go back" (Jonathan, 17–20 months, from Brannigan, Note 1)

"Open the door"
"I like read *Good Night Moon*"
"Silly isn't it?" (Minh, 14–19 months, from Peters, 1977)

"I don't want it"
"What d'you want"
"Don't do it" (Rebecca, 16 months, from K. Nelson, 1973)

These gestalts have the characteristic of being wholistically produced without pauses between words, with reduced phonemic articulation, and with the effect of slurred or mumbled speech but with a clear intonation pattern enabling the listener to construct the target utterance *in context.* These utterances are representative of anything but clear articulation. An emphasis on intonation and form as opposed to clear phonemic realizations of content was also noted by Dore (1974) between two children whom he designated as "message" and "code" learners, respectively.

Thus far, then, we have noted three recurrent characteristics that frequently appear to go together. On the one hand, learning and use of nouns (object labels) early in the second year, clear articulation of words of one or two syllables, and later two-word substantive combinations; and in the other case the learning and use of pronominals, whole phrases, and poor articulation but clear intonational patterns.

There is at least one other characteristic of early language use that has been associated with these two styles. This is the use of *dummy* terms in early sentences. A much noted example of this was Bloom's (1973) Allison, who produced a form /WIDə/ that she combined with single words during the late one-word and early two-word period but for which there was no clear referent. The use of dummy terms (such as "uh uh" in combinations like "uh-uh down") by some nonreferential speakers was noted by K. Nelson (1973) and has subsequently also been noted by Brannigan (Note 1), Peters (1977), Leonard (1976), and Ramer (1976). These terms seem to be serving the function for the child of filling out the sentence frame. They reinforce the notion suggested by Peters and by Brannigan that some children are aiming at sentence targets rather than single-word targets from the beginning.

Pragmatic Versus Cognitive Functions

Before considering various explanations for these pervasive differences in developing language, it should be noted that they may not be characteristic of individual children at all but of the same children at different times and in different contexts. While the K. Nelson (1973) sample was divided on the basis of the subjects' most characteristic vocabulary, it was not claimed nor was it intended that all children were exclusively one type or the other. Indeed, there appeared to be a continuum from highly referential to highly expressive, and many children appeared to employ aspects of both styles.

Recently, Peters (1977) has given an excellent description of the way in which a single child used the two styles in different contexts. The gestalt style (expressive) was used in social contexts when the child and another were engaged in free play and interactions or in speech contexts that Halliday (1975) would define as pragmatic — instrumental, regulatory, and interpersonal, whereas the analytic style (referential) was used in specifically referential situations such as reading books with mother. The two styles were apparently extremely well differentiated and highly context specific. These findings strongly suggest that there are functional differences between the two types of early speech and that one type may be more appropriate in certain contexts than the other. This in turn suggests why one child might learn one style more readily than another.

Form–Function Relation

Unfortunately, with the exception of Peters's (1977) study, there have been few direct observations of the relation between language function and language form. Some recent evidence from an experiment designed to study the process of word learning (Ross, Nelson, Wetstone, & Tanouye, Note 3) is relevant to this question. In this study, 20-month-old children were taught nonsense labels for unfamiliar objects in a series of four learning sessions carried out in the laboratory in a standard manner. Each object was introduced by the experimenter and named by her at standardized intervals in normal sentence contexts while the child interacted with the toy, experimenter, mother, or observer. The sessions were videotaped for analysis, and the language used by the child was transcribed and coded by a trained assistant skilled in interpreting child language.

The mean MLU of the 20 children whose language use could be analyzed over three or four of the learning sessions was 1.43, with a range from 1.0 to 2.25. Productive language forms were analyzed along a number of dimensions, the most relevant one for the present purpose being the relative use of nouns and pronouns. Such usage has been shown to be a consistent style difference in the various studies reported previously (see Table 1). Among this group there was a very balanced distribution of this variable, with 7 of the children using predominately pronouns (a noun/noun + pronoun ratio of .33 or less), 7 children using predominantly nouns (a noun/noun + pronoun ratio of .67 or more), and 6 children falling in the midrange. (This outcome supports the conclusion to be discussed below that the difference in question reflects a continuum rather than a dichotomy.) Nominal–pronominal status was not related to MLU, amount of verbalization, or the receptive learning of object names, although it was related to amount of labeling, as would be expected.

Language functions in the third learning sessions were coded for the subjects who fell into the two extreme groups and who produced a sufficient number of utterances. There were five nominal users (N) and five pronominal users (P) who met the requirements. Language function was coded from the videotapes according to categories devised for this analysis based on Halliday's (1975) description of pragmatic and mathetic functions (see definitions given in Table 2). Reliability of coding into these categories by two coders showed 85% agreement.

Two categories were identified as primarily referential or object-oriented (name–refer and comment–describe). Two were identified as primarily personal–social in orientation (personal and interactive) and two combined social- and object-oriented functions (instrumental–regulatory and show–give–take). The hypothesis based on previous research was that the pronominal speakers would use primarily personal–social functions and the nominal speakers would use primarily referential functions. Mean scores for the two groups are shown in Table 2. As can be seen, there were large group differences in three of the four categories in question in the predicted direction, whereas there were no differences in the two categories that integrated social and object functions.

When the personal and interactive categories were combined, there was a nonoverlapping distribution between the two groups, with the pronominal speakers using these functions much more frequently on the whole than the nominal group (means of 27.5% and 11.7% respectively). The out-

Table 2. ANALYSIS OF SPEECH FUNCTIONS OF NOMINAL AND PRONOMINAL CHILDREN IN CONCEPT LEARNING SESSION

	% of total utterances	
Functional category	*Nominal*	*Pronominal*
Name–refer (N–R) (Child names or refers to object, e.g., points and says "that")	24.6	13.02
Comment–describe (C) object (Child names a property, action of the object, or state)	9.52	9.44
Instrumental–regulatory (I–R) (Child attempts to regulate the action of another or use another to achieve an end)	33.38	33.03
Show–give–take (S–G–T) (Child engages other in showing or exchanging object)	20.76	17.00
Personal (P) (Child describes own action or state)	11.00	21.81
Interactive (I) (Child establishes or maintains contact with another)	.74	5.70

Note. $n = 5$ for both nominal and pronominal groups.

come for the combined referential functions was less clear, although in the predicted direction. Individual children within the groups showed different patterns, some pronominal children using the name–refer category to a large extent (38%), whereas some nominal children used it relatively little (4%). The group difference was therefore not significant.

The fact that there were not consistent differences between the groups in the use of the referential functions probably reflects situational constraints. That is, the context of the word-learning study was such that the child's attention was constantly directed to the objects to be learned. Thus, naming and referring was the expected or "framed" language use. A child who might not ordinarily choose to talk about objects might feel constrained to do so in this situation. On the other hand, the personal and interactional uses were not specifically called out. The group difference in these functions thus probably reflects a true difference associated with the language form differences. It is interesting to note also that it was only the pronominal children who used negative utterances. For three of the pronominal children, 33% or more of their utterances were negatives (e.g., "no," "I don't want it") whereas only one of the nominal children used any negatives (4%). Negatives in this situation may be an extreme form of personal–social expression.

Thus, under standard conditions of observation, there is evidence that the nominal and pronominal styles are associated with functional preferences. Most children used all functions (although four N and two P children did not use the interactive function). The difference, then, was not one of competence but of what the child preferred to talk about. In turn, what the child talks *about* has implications for *how* he or she talks — that is, the forms used.

It should be emphasized, however, that the nominal form difference was not an artifact of the emphasis on personal–social speech by one group and not the other. Pronouns were used in all functions by pronominal speakers and vice versa, as the following examples from two children illustrate[5]:

Nominal: Want mobol. (P) Mommy get mobol. (I–R) I turn nutty. (P) Put linky back. (I–R)

Pronominal: Put inna box. (I–R) I put back. (P) Cover it. (P) This. (N–R) It's stuck. (C–D)

A partial replication of these results can be found in Furrow's (1980) study of the use of social and asocial speech among 2-year-olds studied in their homes during a free-play session. Using a similar functional analysis, he found that nominal-type speakers engaged in significantly more referential speech ($p < .05$) and pronominal children used more personal functions ($p < .01$). The referential functions difference, however, held only for children at an early level of language mastery (MLU < 2.00).

The results of these exploratory analyses cry out for further replication and for complementary functional analysis of children's speech over a wider range of situations. At this point, they provide preliminary support for the hypothesis that at the beginning of language learning, form and function interact in mutually influential ways.

Consistency and Inconsistency with Later Development

There is evidence from a number of studies that a shift in style of use may take place developmentally. Brannigan (Note 1) traced such a shift from phrases to single words for his subjects, and Horgan (1978) reported a shift from an expressive to a referential strategy at 19 months by her daughter. (However, her daughter apparently retained expressive characteristics throughout the language learning period, as described in Horgan, in press.) Such a shift also fits the pattern of results found in the study of larger groups such as those of K. Nelson (1973, 1975) and Bloom et al. (1975). In the Nelson study, correlations of later language characteristics with early style tended on the whole to be low and nonsignificant at 24 and 30 months, with the exception of vocabulary size and the noun–pronoun use strategy.

In contrast to these apparent shifts, varying strategies have been observed at later periods that seem to be related to the early differences, such as the sentence reconstruction approach reported by Clark (1974) and the variations among toddlers and preschoolers reported by Horgan (in press). Moreover, there are indications in Wolf and Gardner's (1979) work and in Starr's (1975) report, both based on longitudinal studies, that similar stylistic differences persist beyond the second year. Peters's (Note 4) report (discussed below) clearly traces a relation between the early and later strategies that are not apparent in the correlational statistics.

Horgan (in press) reports on differences found among preschoolers that she identified as early "noun lovers" or "noun leavers" (i.e., referential or expressive) in the use of noun phrases in referential communication.[6] Horgan's most interesting and provocative report, however, concerns the longitudinal study of her own daughter, Kelley, an expressive child (or leaver) whose use of language throughout the preschool years was unusual in several respects. She was highly sensitive to language patterns and used language in a playful, social–personal mode. Although she labeled objects, she did not ask for the names of things, preferring to assign her own nonsense names in the Humpty Dumpty mode of making words mean what you want them to. Her production of questions was similarly idiosyncratic. In other words, the specific characteristics that identified her as expressive at the outset did not themselves persist, but apparently related characteristics persisted throughout the language-learning period. As Horgan notes, in line with the observations of Peters (1977), Brannigan (Note 1), and Dore (1974), Kelley was sensitive to the form, the tune (the pattern of the language) and was precocious with respect to manipulating these aspects. On the other hand, she appeared to be indifferent to its content; she did not view it as a particularly useful referential tool.

Thus, although the evidence for the persistence of style differences is rather weak, this may reflect primarily the lack of good longitudinal data following children through the preschool years. To the extent that the differences observed reflect differences in the approach to the learning task itself, we would expect them to disappear. However, to the extent that they reflected individual style differences (as suggested by Horgan, in press), they would be expected to persist over time. And if they reflected on conditions in the environment, they would persist or disappear depending on the persistence of similar conditions. These possibilities are considered next in the context of the various explanations that have been advanced to account for the phenomena.

EXPLAINING INDIVIDUAL DIFFERENCES IN LANGUAGE DEVELOPMENT

In a recent study, Peters (Note 4) cites four factors that may account for the strategy differences discussed above: individual makeup, type of input, type of speech expected by the environment, and perception of speech function. In considering these here, it should be emphasized that, like Peters, I am not attempting to decide among them. Style or strategy differences may be multiply determined. Moreover, different patterns of acquisition-related factors may produce different styles. Although I have spoken of two seemingly coherent "packages" of early language characteristics, it has not yet been shown in any reliable empirical way that these are actually two distinct styles. What may need to be explained are a number of sometimes correlated but logically independent variations. This possibility will be examined further in the section on the language-learning task.

Individual Makeup

In a recent theoretical discussion, Bates (1979) examined some of the data discussed above in terms of a hypothesized three-factor theory of symbolic development displayed phylogenetically as well as ontogenetically. The two cognitive factors are identified as *analytic,* which is related to the means–ends analysis of language and is also essential to tool using, and wholistic or *gestalt* processing, which is associated with imitation. The third factor is *communicative* intent. Bates noted that these three factors may be related to competencies associated differentially with the two hemispheres of the brain, the analytic mode with the left and the wholistic patterning with the right. Similar hemispheric function proposals have been put forth by Peters (1977) and Horgan (in press). Bates made the further suggestion that it is only when the three components become integrated that language — in the species or in the child — emerges. She noted that individual differences may result when there is an asymmetric development in the different components. A child who is relatively more advanced in analytic-type skills may rely on these in early language acquisition, whereas a child whose gestalt processing is relatively advanced may become a skilled user of whole phrases.

Bloom's discussion of individual variation (Bloom & Lahey, 1978) strongly implies also that there are two distinct and regular paths toward language competence, one a pronominal strategy and one a nominal strategy, which she apparently views as matters of cognitive style. Bloom claims that both paths (and individual variations in general) are aimed at the adult target language; that is, they represent one aspect of the language to be learned but do not ordinarily head in a direction that is at odds with the end state. The implication seems to be that there is one adult end state, a position that is not supported by recent evidence (Fillmore et al., 1979). Moreover, it is hard to conceive of convincing evidence that would show that a child was *not* headed in the general direction of adult competence.

Wolf and Gardner (1979) describe individual differences in all aspects of symbolic development that appear to implicate distinct cognitive styles associated with temperamental differences. They distinguish between patterners (similar to the referential–analytic groups described here) who consistently focus their attention on the object world, use other persons largely as means to ends, and use language to pick out physical properties; and *dramatists* (expressive–gestalt) who are socially oriented and use language to establish communication. These differences were displayed by the children they studied in symbolic play as well as in language use, including metaphoric uses, throughout the preschool period.

The emphasis on a social versus object orientation as the basis for early language differences has been suggested in a number of reports, but I have been unable, either in my own studies or in those of others (except Wolf & Gardner, 1979) to find good evidence that expressive speakers are somehow more socially oriented in general. This hypothesis needs further confirmation.

Environmental Conditions

An alternative to the neurological differential, maturation of skill, or style explanation of the differences displayed is that they are determined by environmental conditions of learning. The suggestion that their appearance varies with educational status and sibling order (K. Nelson, 1973) as well as related differences found by Allen (Note 5) in different social class groups point in this direction. Peters (Note 4) also notes differences between the linguistic environments of firstborn and later born children as well as differences in the learning environments of children from different linguistic communities.

A recent analysis of the speech used by mothers to their 2-year-old offspring identified as expressive or referential in the K. Nelson (1973) study reveals a significant relationship between the mother's noun/pronoun ratio and the child's, thus suggesting that there is consonancy between the language the child is exposed to and the language he or she learns along this dimension (Furrow & Nelson, Note 6; see also Wells, 1980).

Despite some variations in this dimension, it appears that most parents in our society (working class as well as middle class according to Miller, Note 7) typically tend to provide children with single words to refer to things in their world. That is, they provide the child with a referential context and a referential language. In contrast, Schiefflin (1979) has described a culture in which mothers try to teach children the appropriate formulas for dealing effectively with peers and older children. Although probably few adults in our culture engage in similar teaching, no doubt many simply assume that the child will learn language without direct tuition and therefore by default provide the environmental conditions for the child to pick up socially useful phrases as well as single words. As an example, Blake (Note 8) has described the close relationship between the pragmatic language used by a black mother–child pair in which the mother used speech primarily to transmit social information and supported the child's similar uses.

As noted earlier, Peters (Note 4) also suggests that what others expect the child to learn affects what the child does learn about the language. For example, whereas mothers in our society "read" books to teach their beginning talkers object labels, children in Vietnam may be expected to learn first the honorific pronoun system.

That the language environment provided by the parent may be significant is suggested also by Lieven (1978), who analyzed the speech of two mothers whose children had quite different speech styles. Beth, a second born, had speech that could be characterized as expressive, whereas Kate, a firstborn, was more clearly referential. Both mothers adjusted their speech to their children along lines found to be generally characteristic of adult language to children, that is, short sentences and more imperatives and interrogatives than found in speech to adults.

The interaction styles of the two mothers differed, however. Kate's mother responded to her utterances 81% of the time, whereas Beth's mother responded only 46% of the time. Kate's mother tended more often to respond with questions; there was more turn-taking in their conversations. Beth's mother more often responded, when she did, with a ready-made word or phrase, with a correction, or with a comment that ignored the child's utterance. In her summary of the two children's styles, Lieven (1978) says:

> These two children appeared to be using language for different ends. Kate talked slowly and coherently about things happening around her and objects in her environment, while Beth devoted more time to using her speech to try and engage her mother's interest. (p. 178)

This description is consonant with the notion that children adopt different strategies and styles because they have different hypotheses about what language is used for. Obviously such hypotheses must be based on their experience with language in use.

Thus, how and why mothers use language may be as important for the child's pattern of acquisition as what kind of language they use. For example, the mother who has a 3- or 4-year-old to cope with, as well as a 1- or 2-year-old, will use characteristically different language in interaction with both children than will the mother who has only one child of 1 or 2 years. A larger percentage of the function of language that the younger sibling hears is likely to be directive and centered around the child's own activities — to be, in effect, pragmatic and expressive. Thus, the child is likely to conclude that language is a pragmatic medium that is useful for social control and social exchange, and this conclusion is likely to be shored up by exchanges with siblings. On the other hand, a child who is exposed to a mother who teaches through relevant questioning is likely to conclude that language is basically a cognitive or referential medium.

Language Function and the Language-Learning Task

Speech in different functional contexts displays different features. As various linguists and sociolinguists have recently pointed out (e.g., Gumperz & Tanner, 1979), an enormous amount of social speech is formulaic in character. Thus, the function of the language that the child is exposed to is reflected in its form. The mother who labels and responds to questions makes it easy for the child to break language into its component parts, to become a word user. Social-control language, on the other hand, is likely to be heard in clumps that are not easily broken up; for example: "D'ya wanna go out?" "I dunno know where it is." "Stop it." Segmentation of such sequences is difficult, but the tune, as Peters (1977) would say, is easy to learn.

Peters's (Note 4) recent analysis of the "units of language acquisition" and Fillmore's (Note 2) description of "preassembled parts" in the adult language are both relevant to this analysis. The language to be learned is traditionally thought of in terms of two basic units, the word and the sentence. In oversimplified but basically correct terms, words are learned as unanalyzed wholes, whereas sentences must be constructed from parts (i.e., words).

Two problems arise with this description. First, words are not readily identifiable as separate parts in the speech stream, and second, many sentences are preassembled and can be used appropriately without further analysis or reconstruction in a new context. In other words, the difference between words and sentences is not as great as traditional accounts have implied. The first problem for language learners is to isolate the parts that they will work with. They next need to learn what occasions of use the parts are appropriate to and finally how to construct new wholes out of old parts. Although the traditional account has children first learning words and then constructing sentences, as we have seen, the process may proceed in a different fashion. There are two accounts in the literature that suggest how children may proceed beyond the early stages using preassembled parts.

Clark (1974) reported a study in depth of her own son's strategy for the acquisition of grammar using a juxtaposition of well-practiced sentence fragments or routines, producing errors that resulted from the failure to make internal adjustments in the unanalyzed fragments. Some examples from her work: "I want *you get a biscuit for me*"; "I don't know *where's Emma gone*"; and "Don't stand *baby's on hand*" — (Clark, 1974, pp. 5–6.) The italicized passages are Clark's identification of the preformed segments. She suggests that "the process of modifying a practiced sequence internally is psychologically more complex than the process of collocating linguistic units" (p. 7). That is, acquiring whole phrases that can be put together in this way may allow children to say more and more completely what they mean than they would if they had to construct an utterance from scratch. The use of formulas appears to be consistent with an imitative approach to language learning as well as with more social contexts of learning and use.

L. Fillmore's (1979) analysis of the learning strategies of second-language learners sheds further light on the social conditions that are important to first-language learning as well as the formulaic strategy. She studied five Spanish-speaking children between 5 and 7 years of age who were learning English as a second language in a natural school setting. They employed both social and cognitive acquisition strategies, and the implementation of the latter was dependent on the success of the former. For example, she gives as the first important social strategy: Join a group of native speakers. If there is no motivation to communicate within a social group, the child's cognitive strategies cannot be utilized. For most first-language learners, the natural group of native speakers are the family members and the motivation to speak in the group is ready-made.

Fillmore (1979) goes on to point out that to be successful learners, children must make the most of what they have and use limited language widely whether it is strictly appropriate or not. In this connection, she observed that each of the children she studied acquired a few formulaic phrases that they made do with for some time in appropriate play situations, for example:

Lookit.
Wait a minute.
Lemme see.
Gimme.
Let's go.
I don't care.
I dunno.
You know what?
I wanna play.
Do you wanna play?

Whaddya wanna do?
I gotta hurry up.
I get 2 turns.
Whose turn is it?
You have to do it this way.
I'm gonna tell on you.
Liar, panzon fire.
It's time to clean up.
OK, you be the X, I'll be the Y.
I'll tell you what to do.
Shaddup your mouth.
Beat it.
Knock it off.

These phrases were then gradually broken apart and recombined with other words or parts of other formulas. For example, "How do you do dese?" (Time 1) was used at Time 2 to produce "How do you do dese in English?" "How do you do dese flower power?" "How do you do dese little tortillas?" This learning and using strategy is, of course, similar to that identified by Clark (1974) and may be used to at least a limited extent by many first-language learners.

This strategy is most useful when the child wishes to *use* language in the ongoing activities of a social group, as emphasized by L. Fillmore (1979), in contrast to *learning* a language as a cognitive object. As noted earlier, intuitively it has seemed that those children whose language is primarily expressive, pragmatic, or gestalt use their language in more purely social contexts for one reason or another. Such children may acquire useful phrases because these phrases are appropriate in group situations. Although parents may sometimes provide the conditions under which such phrases are acquired and used, most frequently it seems that older children and peers provide both the conditions and the ready-made language of this kind. Indeed, most of the relevant examples from my sample come from children with siblings or other close peer relationships.

Thus, the claim is that it is in the framework of social interaction that children learn language, and the nature of the particular kinds of interaction dictates not only the function and content of the language but which parts will be learned first and how those parts will be put together or broken down for reassembly.

Because most children learn language in a variety of contexts for a variety of purposes, most children will exhibit aspects of both formulaic and analytic approaches in their early language. It should also be emphasized that the two approaches to the task both involve analytic and synthetic operations as well as pattern learning. As L. Fillmore (1979) suggests, the mastery of formulas provides the child with the internalized sequences for applying analytic operations, comparing component parts, and reconstructing new wholes from old. For the word learner, the analysis comes first. It appears that children can master language in either way and probably in both at once. Thus far, however, the general research tack has ignored the formula approach almost entirely in favor of the analytic (which is, of course, the favored "scientific" style). What we need is to recognize the importance and function of both alternatives and thereby to construct a balanced account of the acquisition process.

DISCUSSION

In brief, the argument here is that the child does *not* build up language by analyzing its parts in terms of lexicon, syntax, phonology, and pragmatics. Rather, the child acquires the language according to contextually determined parts. The context of language use will determine the function of presented utterances, their relationship to nonlinguistic conditions, the form of sentences, and their relative analyticity in presented form. The child will accumulate language knowledge based on these various exposures. He or she will subject accumulated knowledge (examples) to analysis to determine first units and then combinatory rules (L. Fillmore, 1979; Peters, Note 4).

Because functional contexts are correlated with frequency of particular forms and constructions and because different children are exposed differentially to various types of contexts, different children will begin to put different parts of the language system together initially, and the course of acquisition will look different for different children.

One point that must be emphasized again is that this is not an argument for two distinct patterns, however intriguing such a possibility may be and however prevalent the tendency to dichotomize the data. Certain characteristics seem to go together, as noted throughout this article, but most children present a mixture of these characteristics. They put the parts together bit by bit. The extremes show us more clearly what the bits are.

What remains to be considered in this article are the implications of these variations for developmental theory in general and for the development of the language system in particular. We will consider the former within the context of the latter.

The transition from no language to facile speech is a dramatic one — perhaps the most dramatic one in the development of the child. The various ways that children negotiate this transition do not represent mere oscillations around a mean or spurts and lags in development; rather, it has been shown that different children approach this complex system in different ways and put different parts together in different combinations. In contrast to stage theories that focus on the stable points at which there is similarity among children, the study of transitions is likely to uncover rampant dissimilarity.

It is in fact in transition periods that one must look for the creative, constructive dynamic of development. Minor transitions will show minor variations. Major ones will show major variations, and the move from sensorimotor functioning to language functioning is one of these major transitions that has implications for all aspects of cognitive and social functioning and development. The individual differences displayed here reflect the interaction of system characteristics, child characteristics, and characteristics of the learning context. As the system is mastered, differences can be expected to diminish. What remains will be the residual effects of emphasis or enduring style differences. This, it is suggested, is typical of system development, and language development is therefore a paradigm case within which the complexities of developmental interaction can be viewed (Nelson & Nelson, 1978).

The transition to language involves the mastery of a complex, integrated system that is presented to the child in terms of examples within the context of participatory interactions. Analysts have found it convenient to divide this system into different parts — syntax, semantics, pragmatics, and phonology — but the child cannot divide the language in this manner. Rather, in learning any part of it, children must learn bits of all of these at once. Nonetheless, they must segment the language in some way if they are to master it. I suggest that the naturally occurring differences among children in the way they do this have the potential to reveal important facts about the language as well as about development. Let us consider again briefly the differences we have noted for the clues they offer in this respect.

Substantives Versus Proforms

Probably the most frequent and readily observable difference in early development among English language learners is the noun versus pronoun acquisition strategy. The traditional account claims that the child first acquires words referring to particular entities and events in the world and only later the more abstract and general proforms (pronouns, demonstratives, "do") to stand in place of the more concrete-referring terms. In contrast, the child using a pronoun strategy learns abstract or general terms first and uses them in a wide variety of referential contexts. In some sense it is a highly efficient strategy. On the other hand, it fails when the referents are not obvious.

What does this tell us about the language system children are learning? The noun strategy emphasizes the lexical system, that is, the sense of individual words, in a way that the pronoun strategy does not. The latter allows the child to concentrate on other aspects of the language. Moreover, a successful social here and now language does not require a large repertoire of substantive forms but rather a few formulas and general frames and proforms that can be widely applied. Therefore, the vocabulary can be quite limited, and the learner can concentrate on how to use common syntactic forms — questions and negatives, for example, in addition to imperatives. These effects have been seen in several studies (e.g., Bloom et al., 1975; K. Nelson, 1975).

Does this difference in approach have lasting effects on the child's system? Do children maintain an indifference to precise substantive terminology and thereby slight their vocabulary building and semantic development in general? Here Bernstein's (1970) work on restricted and elaborated codes comes readily to mind, but we do not have any good indications that what is characteristic of the early language period continues to be characteristic of individual children along this dimension if their later experience is conducive to a different emphasis. For example, it not only seems likely but has been observed (K. Nelson, 1973) that a secondborn child from an educated family would begin language in an expressive mode but would quickly catch up on vocabulary when that became salient.

But again, there may be conditions that are conducive to maintaining an emphasis on pragmatic speech and thus that lead the child to continued relative neglect of lexical development. The usual assumption in our culture, and particularly in our schools, is that such neglect reflects low intelligence. This assumption is in turn reflected in intelligence testing that relies heavily on the measurement of vocabulary, but as Horgan (in press) has cautioned in this regard, this may be only a tragic reflection of our own biases.

In developmental terms, variation on this dimension demonstrates that there is no necessary movement from the particular and concrete to the more general and abstract. The child can begin at either end. He or she can choose to call every entity and event "it" (as in "I want it," "Do it") and thus name the most general category possible. Or he or she can make fine distinctions between apples and oranges and dogs and cats. We must conclude that neither possibility is more "natural"; both are available, and the child simply chooses which aspect of the world to emphasize in his or her beginning language. This choice may be conditioned by the model language, and it may have important implications for the development of the semantic system, but we know too little about such development at this point to make any firm predictions about it.

Word Versus Phrase Structure

The analytic–gestalt styles appear to divide the language stream into different-sized clumps. As discussed above, current theories of language development are based on the word strategy that moves from single words to the synthesis of combinations in sentences. In contrast, the child who begins with phrases or whole sentences may subsequently analyze these into smaller parts for the purposes of recombination and may combine parts with other wholes to produce new statements. Most children do some of this. For some children it is a major strategy.

Clearly, both word and sentence approaches are not only possible but occur with some frequency in development, reflecting their dual primacy as linguistic structures. In developmental terms they reveal the intertwined processes of analysis and synthesis working together in various ways to break down the speech stream and build it up again in new productions.

What sort of rules is the gestalt child formulating in this process? At first, these rules must be primarily rules of use. Although little effort has gone into formalizing such rules, they seem obviously to be related to discourse rules such as those specified by Shatz and Gelman (1977), Ervin-Tripp (1977), and others. A major effort in the future must be to show how a system of productive grammatical rules can evolve from a pragmatic system of application rules. The key to this effort is likely to lie in the proposal that pattern analysis along many dimensions simultaneously or sequentially is the basic process mechanism underlying language system mastery.

Such a proposal is central to the recent theorizing of Maratsos and his colleagues (e.g., Maratsos & Chalkley, 1979; Maratsos, Kuczaj, Fox, & Chalkley, 1979), Karmilov-Smith (1978), and Peters (Note 4). It is not feasible to discuss these theories in any detail here as they are necessarily very complex. The kind of rule building that emerges is based on a complex of semantic–distributional and pragmatic–phonological factors, with fairly restricted sets of rules existing side by side until they are eventually combined in a more general system. Similar complexities have been analyzed by Labov and Labov (1978). Gestalt language, in particular formulaic usages as well as imitations, may be particularly useful to the enterprise of pattern analysis in that it enables the language learner to hold onto a bit of language internally (as well as externally), thus allowing it to be subjected to analysis over a period of time. This I take it is L. Fillmore's (1979) point about internalization. Similarly, Peters (Note 4) proposes the term *fission* for this kind of off-line processing. Moreover, if formulaic language is combined with analytic language (as it almost always is), then the latter can serve as a guide to the essential parts that the pattern analyzer needs to extract.

So far these descriptions contain many gaps and much speculation. They do suggest, however, that children who begin with pragmatic formulas do not then have to abandon this route and go back to the beginning to reformulate a grammar along traditional lines. The evidence from Horgan (in press), Clark (1974), L. Fillmore (1979), and Peters (1977) appears quite convincing on this question. Either a single theory of the construction of grammatical rules that will encompass both paths easily must be constructed or it must be shown how different developmental paths converge on similar rule systems. Again, there are hints as to how this might be done, but clearly no coherent theory exists at this point. Existing theories fail to account for all of the data.

Referential Versus Expressive Functions

Halliday's (1975) functional analysis proposed that pragmatic communicative functions appeared first in protolanguage. As we have seen, however, these functions are typical of some language learners in their early speech, whereas for others the language is used from the outset to learn and to share knowledge (Halliday's mathetic, or in my terms referential, function). In effect, these reflect the division between object and social uses of language and might be expected to rest on different systems of knowledge. The now conventional view of language acquisition is that it rests on the cognitive achievements of the sensorimotor period as outlined by Piaget. However, it is important to recognize that the child also comes to understand social relationships during the infancy period (Gelman & Spelke, in press; Kessen & Nelson, 1978; K. Nelson, 1979). The fact that some children begin to use language primarily in a cognitive context, others in the social, indicates that for the language-learning child these systems are to some degree differentiated during this period. Although the correlation of language functions with language forms during development in no sense implies that the forms are derivative of the functions, it is important that when and how the child learns about the language initially is apparently determined to an important degree by what he or she supposes the language to be useful for.

Thus, we have seen that looking at different learning approaches reveals the full range of possibilities at the child's command — the particular and concrete classification as well as the general and abstract, the analytic as well as the gestalt, and the interpersonal as well as the ideational. Moreover, we note that although the child cannot divide the language as we do, learn syntax in terms of abstract markers, master semantics in terms of abstract features, move on to phonology in terms of its distinctive features, and finally master pragmatics in terms of communicative force, still the child can divide up the language in his or her own way and learn the pieces of each that fit together in appropriate contexts. I am convinced that these differential approaches to mastery tell us important things about learning, language, and how to study the developmental process. We ignore them at the risk of continued ignorance.

AUTHOR'S NOTES

1. There is also a practical reason for the small subject design, since such research is extremely demanding in terms of time spent in collecting, transcribing, and analyzing the data. A single researcher can realistically expect to follow only a few children under these conditions. The fact that research must be carried out in this way does not, however, justify the conclusion, too often assumed, that the data so gathered are representative of all children.

2. *Rich interpretation* refers to the use of context to interpret the child's semantic intent in producing an utterance and thus to discern the underlying grammatical relations among its terms.

3. Pivot-open constructions describe the type of sentences many children first produce in which one word (the pivot) occurs in great frequency in fixed positions (first or last) in combination with a variety of other words (the open class). Although this description was originally proposed as a first grammar, it was later abandoned as an explanation in that it failed to fit much of the data, among other reasons (see Brown, 1973).

4. The division of children into two groups is a descriptive convenience. Throughout the article, expressive, pragmatic, pronominal, and gestalt will be considered roughly equivalent terms, in contrast to referential, mathetic, nominal, and analytic (see discussion in text).

5. "Mobol," "Nutty," and "Linky" are names for the object concepts to be learned. Letters in parentheses indicate the functional coding of the utterance as defined in Table 2.

6. These differences are reminiscent of those reported by Bernstein (1970) among boys from different socio-economic classes.

REFERENCE NOTES

1. Brannigan, G. *If this kid is in the one-word period, so how come he's saying whole sentences?* Paper presented at the second annual Boston University Conference on Language Development, Boston, September 30, 1977.

2. Fillmore, C. *Some problems with ungenerated language.* Paper presented at the second annual meeting of the Cognitive Science Society, New Haven, June 1980.

3. Ross, G., Nelson, K., Wetstone, H., & Tanouye, E. *Concept acquisition at 20 months.* Manuscript in preparation, 1980.

4. Peters, A. M. *The units of language acquisition.* Working Papers in Linguistics (Vol. 12, No. 1), University of Hawaii, Department of Linguistics, 1980.

5. Allen, D. A. *The development of propositional speech in young children.* Paper presented at the Society for Research in Child Development, New Orleans, March 20, 1977.

6. Furrow, D., & Nelson, K. *Do nominal kids have nominal mothers?* Manuscript in preparation, 1979.

7. Miller, P. *Dialect instruction in language and speaking: A study of mother-child discourse in a working-class community.* Paper presented at the meeting of the New York Child Language Group, New York, December 1978.

8. Blake, I. K. *Early language use and the black child: A speech-act analysis of mother-child inputs and outputs.* Paper presented at the biennial meeting of the Society for Research in Child Development, San Francisco, March 1979.

REFERENCES

Anglin, J. *Word, object, and conceptual development.* New York: Norton, 1977.

Bates, E. *The emergence of symbols.* New York: Academic Press, 1979.

Bernstein, B. A sociolinguistic approach to socialization: With some reference to educability. In F. Williams (Ed.), *Language and poverty.* Chicago: Markham, 1970.

Bloom, L. *Language development.* Cambridge, Mass.: MIT Press, 1970.

Bloom, L. *One word at a time.* The Hague, The Netherlands: Mouton, 1973.

Bloom, L., & Lahey, M. *Language development and language disorders.* New York: Wiley, 1978.

Bloom, L., Lightbown, P., & Hood, L. Structure and variation in child language. *Monographs of the Society for Research in Child Development,* 1975, *40*(2, Serial No. 160).

Brown, R. *A first language: The early stages.* Cambridge, Mass.: Harvard University Press, 1973.

Cazden, C. On individual differences in language competence and performance. *Journal of Special Education,* 1967, *1,* 135–150.

Chomsky, N. *Aspects of the theory of syntax.* Cambridge, Mass.: M.I.T. Press, 1965.

Chomsky, N. *Language and mind.* New York: Harcourt, Brace & World, 1968.

Chomsky, N. *Reflections on language.* Glasgow, Scotland: Fontana, 1976.

Clark, R. Performing without competence. *Journal of Child Language,* 1974, *1,* 1–10.

Collins, W. A. (Ed.). *Children's language and communication.* Hillsdale, N.J.: Erlbaum, 1979.

Dore, J. A pragmatic description of early language development. *Journal of Psycholinguistic Research,* 1974, *3,* 343–350.

Ervin-Tripp, S. Wait for me roller-skate! In S. Ervin-Tripp & C. Mitchell-Kernan (Eds.), *Child discourse.* New York: Academic Press, 1977.

Fillmore, C., Kempler, D., & Wang, W. S.-Y. (Eds.). *Individual differences in language ability and language behavior.* New York: Academic Press, 1979.

Fillmore, L. W. Individual differences in second language acquisition. In C. J. Fillmore, D. Kempler & W.S.-Y. Wang (Eds.), *Individual differences in language ability and language behavior.* New York: Academic Press, 1979.

Furrow, D. R. *Social and asocial uses of language in young children.* Unpublished doctoral dissertation, Yale University, 1980.

Gelman, R., & Spelke, E. The development of thoughts about animates and inanimates: Implications for research on social cognition. In J. Flavell & L. Ross (Eds.), *The development of social cognition in children,* in press.

Greenfield, P. M., & Smith, J. H. *The structure of communication in early language development.* New York: Academic Press, 1976.

Gumperz, J. J., & Tanner, D. Individual and social differences in language use. In C. J. Fillmore, D. Kempler, & W.S.-Y. Wang (Eds.), *Individual differences in language ability and language behavior.* New York: Academic Press, 1979.

Halliday, M. *Learning how to mean.* London: Edwin Arnold, 1975.

Horgan, D. How to answer questions when you've got nothing to say. *Journal of Child Language,* 1978, *5,* 159–165.

Horgan, D. Rate of language acquisition and noun emphasis. *Journal of Psycholinguistic Research,* in press.

Karmilov-Smith, A. The interplay between syntax, semantics and phonology in language acquisition processes. In R. N. Campbell & P. T. Smith (Eds.), *Recent advances in the psychology of language, A.* New York: Plenum Press, 1978.

Kessen, W., & Nelson, K. What the child brings to language. In B. Z. Presseisen, D. Goldstein, & M. H. Appel (Eds.), *Topics in cognitive development* (Vol. 2). New York: Plenum Press, 1978.

Labov, W., & Labov, T. Learning the syntax of questions. In R. N. Campbell & P. T. Smith

(Eds.), *Recent advances in the psychology of language, B.* New York: Plenum Press, 1978.

Leonard, L. B. *Meaning in child language.* New York: Grune & Stratton, 1976.

Lieven, E. M. Conversations between mothers and young children: Individual differences and their possible implications for the study of language learning. In N. Waterson & C. Snow (Eds.), *The development of communication: Social and pragmatic factors in language acquisition.* New York: Wiley, 1978.

Lock, A. (Ed.). *Action, gesture and symbol: The emergence of language.* New York: Academic Press, 1978.

Lyons, J. *Introduction to theoretical linguistics.* Cambridge, England: Cambridge University Press, 1969.

Maratsos, M., & Chalkley, M. A. The internal language of children's syntax: The ontogenesis and representation of syntactic categories. In K. E. Nelson (Ed.), *Children's language* (Vol. 2). New York: Gardner Press, 1980.

Maratsos, M., Kuczaj, S. A., II, Fox, D. E. C., & Chalkley, M. A. Some empirical studies in the acquisition of transformational relations: Passives, negatives, and the past tense. In W. A. Collins (Ed.), *Children's language and communication.* Hillsdale, N.J.: Erlbaum, 1979.

McNeill, D. *The acquisition of language.* New York: Harper & Row, 1970.

Nelson, K. Structure and strategy in learning to talk. *Monographs of the Society for Research in Child Development,* 1973, *38* (1–2, Serial No. 149).

Nelson, K. The nominal shift in semantic-syntactic development. *Cognitive Psychology,* 1975, *7,* 461–479.

Nelson, K. Some attributes of adjectives used by young children. *Cognition,* 1976, *4,* 13–30.

Nelson, K. The role of language in infant development. In M. H. Bornstein & W. Kessen (Eds.), *Psychological development from infancy.* Hillsdale, N.J.: Erlbaum, 1979.

Nelson, K. E. (Ed.). *Children's language* (Vol. 1). New York: Gardner Press, 1978.

Nelson, K. E. (Ed.). *Children's language* (Vol. 2). New York, Gardner Press, 1980.

Nelson, K. E., & Nelson, K. Cognitive pendulums and their linguistic realizations. In K. E. Nelson (Ed.), *Children's language* (Vol. 1). New York: Gardner Press, 1978.

Peters, A. M. Language learning strategies: Does the whole equal the sum of the parts? *Language,* 1977, *53,* 560–573.

Ramer, A. Syntactic styles in emerging language. *Journal of Child Language,* 1976, *3,* 49–62.

Schiefflin, B. Getting it together: An ethnographic approach to the study of the development of communicative competence. In E. Ochs & B. B. Schiefflin (Eds.), *Developmental pragmatics.* New York: Academic Press, 1979.

Shatz, M., & Gelman, R. Beyond syntax: The influence of conversational constraints on speech modification. In C. E. Snow & C. A. Ferguson (Eds.), *Talking to children: Language input and acquisition.* New York: Columbia University Press, 1977.

Sinclair-deZwart, H. Language acquisition and cognitive development. In T. E. Moore (Ed.), *Cognitive development and the acquisition of language.* New York: Academic Press, 1973.

Slobin, D. I. Cognitive prerequisites for the development of grammar. In C. A. Ferguson & D. I. Slobin (Eds.), *Studies of child language development.* New York: Holt, Rinehart & Winston, 1973.

Starr, S. The relationship of single words to two-word sentences. *Child Development,* 1975, *46,* 701–708.

Wells, G. Apprenticeship in Meaning. In K. E. Nelson (Ed.), *Children's language* (Vol. 2). New York: Gardner Press, 1980.

Wolf, D., & Gardner, H. Style and sequence in symbolic play. In M. Franklin & N. Smith (Eds.), *Early symbolization.* Hillsdale, N.J.: Erlbaum, 1979.

18

Lev Vygotsky

PLAY AND ITS ROLE IN THE MENTAL DEVELOPMENT OF THE CHILD

In speaking of play and its role in the preschooler's development, we are concerned with two fundamental questions: first, how play itself arises in development — its origin and genesis; second, the role of this developmental activity, which we call play, as a form of development in the child of preschool age. Is play the leading form of activity for a child of this age, or is it simply the predominant form?

It seems to me that from the point of view of development, play is not the predominant form of acivity, but is, in a certain sense, the leading source of development in preschool years.

Let us now consider the problem of play itself. We know that the definition of play on the basis of the pleasure it gives the child is not correct for two reasons — first, because we deal with a number of activities which give the child much keener experiences of pleasure than play.

For example, the pleasure principle applies equally well to the sucking process, in that the child derives functional pleasure from sucking a pacifier even when he is not being satiated.

On the other hand, we know of games in which the activity process itself does not afford pleasure — games which predominate at the end of preschool and the beginning of school age and which only give pleasure if the child finds the result interesting; these are, for example, sporting games (not only athletic sports, but also games with an outcome, games with results). They are very often accompanied by a keen sense of displeasure when the outcome is unfavorable to the child.

Thus, defining play on the basis of pleasure can certainly not be regarded as correct.

Nonetheless it seems to me that to refuse to approach the problem of play from the standpoint of fulfillment of the child's needs, his incentives to act, and his affective aspirations would result in a terrible intellectualization of play. The trouble with a number of theories of play lies in their tendency to intellectualize the problem. . . .

Without a consideration of the child's needs, inclinations, incentives, and motives to act — as research has demonstrated — there will never be any advance from one stage to the next. It seems to me that an analysis of play should start with an examination of these particular aspects.

It seems that every advance from one age

Abridged from a stenographic record of a lecture given in 1933 at the Hertzen Pedagogical Institute, Leningrad. [Note: Russian uses a single word, *igra,* where English uses either *play* or *game* (cf. German *Spiel,* French *jeu,* Spanish *juego, et al.*). The resulting potential ambiguity of the original Russian should be borne in mind when encountering the words *play* and *game* in this translation.]

SOURCE: From Lev S. Vygotsky, "Play and Its Role in the Mental Development of the Child," reprinted from *Soviet Psychology,* Spring 1967 by permission of M. E. Sharpe, Inc., Armonk, NY 10504.

stage to another is connected with an abrupt change in motives and incentives to act.

What is of the greatest interest to the infant has almost ceased to interest the toddler. This maturing of new needs and new motives for action is, of course, the dominant factor, especially as it is impossible to ignore the fact that a child satisfies certain needs and incentives in play, and without understanding the special character of these incentives we cannot imagine the uniqueness of that type of activity which we call play.

At preschool age special needs and incentives arise which are highly important to the whole of the child's development and which are spontaneously expressed in play. In essence, there arise in a child of this age large numbers of unrealizable tendencies and immediately unrealizable desires. A very young child tends to gratify his desires immediately. Any delay in fulfilling them is hard for him and is acceptable only within certain narrow limits; no one has met a child under three who wanted to do something a few days hence. Ordinarily, the interval between the motive and its realization is extremely short. I think that if there were no development in preschool years of needs that cannot be realized immediately, there would be no play. Experiments show that the development of play is arrested both in intellectually underdeveloped children and in those with an immature affective sphere.

From the viewpoint of the affective sphere, it seems to me that play is invented at the point when unrealizable tendencies appear in development. This is the way a very young child behaves: he wants a thing and must have it at once. If he cannot have it, either he throws a temper tantrum, lies on the floor and kicks his legs, or he is refused, pacified, and does not get it. His unsatisfied desires have their own particular modes of substitution, rejection, etc. Toward the beginning of preschool age, unsatisfied desires and tendencies that cannot be realized immediately make their appearance, while the tendency to immediate fulfillment of desires, characteristic of the preceding stage, is retained. For example, the child wants to be in his mother's place, or wants to be a rider on a horse. This desire cannot be fulfilled right now. What does the very young child do if he sees a passing cab and wants to ride in it whatever may happen? If he is a spoiled and capricious child, he will demand that his mother put him in the cab at any cost or he may throw himself on the ground right there in the street, etc. If he is an obedient child, used to renouncing his desires, he will go away, or his mother will offer him some candy, or simply distract him with some stronger affect and he will renounce his immediate desire.

In contrast to this, a child over three will show his own particular conflicting tendencies; on the one hand, a large number of long-term needs and desires will appear, which cannot be fulfilled at once but which, nevertheless, are not passed over like whims; on the other hand, the tendency toward immediate realization of desires is almost completely retained.

Henceforth play occurs such that the explanation of why a child plays must always be interpreted as the imaginary, illusory realization of unrealizable desires. Imagination is a new formation which is not present in the consciousness of the very young child, is totally absent in animals, and represents a specifically human form of conscious activity. Like all functions of consciousness, it originally arises from action. The old adage that child's play is imagination in action can be reversed: we can say that imagination in adolescents and schoolchildren is play without action.

It is difficult to imagine that an incentive compelling a child to play is really just the same kind of affective incentive as sucking a pacifier is for an infant. . . .

Play is essentially wish fulfillment, not,

however, isolated wishes but generalized affects. A child at this age is conscious of his relationships with adults, he reacts to them affectively, but in contrast to early childhood he now generalizes these affective reactions (he respects adult authority in general, etc.).

The presence of such generalized affects in play does not mean that the child himself understands the motives which give rise to the game or that he does it consciously. He plays without realizing the motives of the play activity. In this, play differs substantially from work and other forms of activity. On the whole, it can be said that motives, actions, and incentives belong to a more abstract sphere and only become accessible to consciousness at the transitional age. Only an adolescent can clearly account to himself the reason for which he does this or that.

We will leave the problem of the affective aspect for the moment — considering it as given — and will now examine the development of play activity itself.

I think that in finding criteria for distinguishing a child's play activity from his other general forms of activity it must be accepted that in play a child creates an imaginary situation. . . .

. . . What does a child's behavior in an imaginary situation mean? We know that there is a form of play, distinguished long ago and relating to the late preschool period, and considered to develop mainly at school age: namely, the development of games with rules. A number of investigators, although not at all belonging to the camp of dialectical materialists, have approached this area along the lines recommended by Marx when he said that "the anatomy of man is the key to the anatomy of the ape." They have begun their examination of early play in the light of later rule-based play and have concluded from this that play involving an imaginary situation is, in fact, rule-based play. It seems to me that one can go even further and propose that there is no such thing as play without rules and the child's particular attitude toward them.

Let us expand on this idea. Take any form of play with an imaginary situation. The imaginary situation already contains rules of behavior, although this is not a game with formulated rules laid down in advance. The child imagines herself to be the mother and the doll the child, so she must obey the rules of maternal behavior. This was very well demonstrated by a researcher in an ingenious experiment based on Sully's famous observations. The latter described play as remarkable in that children could make the play situation and reality coincide. One day two sisters, aged five and seven, said to each other: "Let's play sisters." Here Sully was describing a case where two sisters were playing at being sisters, i.e., playing at reality. The above-mentioned experiment based its method on children's play, suggested by the experimenter, which dealt with real relationships. In certain cases I have found it very easy to call forth such play in children. It is very easy, for example, to make a child play with its mother at being a child while the mother is the mother, i.e., at what is, in fact, true. The vital difference in play, as Sully describes it, is that the child in playing tries to be a sister. In life the child behaves without thinking that she is her sister's sister. She never behaves with respect to the other just because she is her sister — except perhaps in those cases when her mother says, "Give in to her." In the game of sisters playing at "sisters," however, they are both concerned with displaying their sisterhood; the fact that two sisters decided to play sisters makes them both acquire rules of behavior. (I must always be a sister in relation to the other sister in the whole play situation.) Only actions which fit these rules are acceptable to the play situation.

In the game a situation is chosen which stresses the fact that these girls are sisters:

they are dressed alike, they walk about holding hands — in short, they enact whatever emphasizes their relationship as sisters vis-à-vis adults and strangers. The elder, holding the younger by the hand, keeps telling her about other people: "That is theirs, not ours." This means: "My sister and I act the same, we are treated the same, but others are treated differently." Here the emphasis is on the sameness of everything which is concentrated in the child's concept of a sister, and this means that my sister stands in a different relationship to me than other people. What passes unnoticed by the child in real life becomes a rule of behavior in play.

If play, then, were structured in such a way that there were no imaginary situation, what would remain? The rules would remain. The child would begin to behave in this situation as the situation dictates.

Let us leave this remarkable experiment for a moment and turn to play in general. I think that wherever there is an imaginary situation in play there are rules. Not rules which are formulated in advance and which change during the course of the game, but rules stemming from the imaginary situation. Therefore to imagine that a child can behave in an imaginary situation without rules, i.e., as he behaves in a real situation, is simply impossible. If the child is playing the role of a mother, then she has rules of maternal behavior. The role the child fulfills, and her relationship to the object if the object has changed its meaning, will always stem from the rules, i.e., the imaginary situation will always contain rules. In play the child is free. But this is an illusory freedom.

While at first the investigator's task was to disclose the hidden rules in all play with an imaginary situation, we have received proof comparatively recently that the so-called pure games with rules (played by schoolchildren and late preschoolers) are essentially games with imaginary situations; for just as the imaginary situation has to contain rules of behavior, so every game with rules contains an imaginary situation. For example, what does it mean to play chess? To create an imaginary situation. Why? Because the knight, the king, the queen, and so forth, can only move in specified ways; because covering and taking pieces are purely chess concepts; and so on. Although it does not directly substitute for real-life relationships, nevertheless we do have a kind of imaginary situation here. Take the simplest children's game with rules. It immediately turns into an imaginary situation in the sense that as soon as the game is regulated by certain rules, a number of actual possibilities for action are ruled out.

Just as we were able to show at the beginning that every imaginary situation contains rules in a concealed form, we have also succeeded in demonstrating the reverse — that every game with rules contains an imaginary situation in a concealed form. The development from an overt imaginary situation and covert rules to games with overt rules and a covert imaginary situation outlines the evolution of children's play from one pole to the other.

All games with imaginary situations are simultaneously games with rules and vice versa. I think this thesis is clear.

However there is one misunderstanding which may arise and which must be cleared up from the start. A child learns to behave according to certain rules from the first few months of life. For a very young child such rules, for example, that he has to sit quietly at the table, not touch other people's things, obey his mother, are rules which make up his life. What is specific to rules followed in games or play? It seems to me that several new publications can be of great aid in solving this problem. In particular, a new work of Piaget has been extremely helpful to me. This work is concerned with the development in the child of moral rules. One part is specially devoted to the study of rules of a game, where, I think, Piaget resolves these difficulties very convincingly.

Piaget distinguishes what he calls two moralities in the child — two distinct sources for the development of rules of behavior.

This emerges particularly sharply in games. As Piaget shows, some rules come to the child from the one-sided influence upon him of an adult. Not to touch other people's things is a rule taught by the mother, or to sit quietly at the table is an external law for the child advanced by adults. This is one of the child's moralities. Other rules arise, according to Piaget, from mutual collaboration between adult and child, or between children themselves. These are rules which the child himself participates in establishing.

The rules of games, of course, differ radically from rules of not touching and of sitting quietly. In the first place they are made by the child himself; they are his own rules, as Piaget says, rules of self-restraint and self-determination. The child tells himself: I must behave in such and such a way in this game. This is quite different from the child saying that one thing is allowed and another thing is not. Piaget has pointed out a very interesting phenomenon in moral development — something which he calls moral realism. He indicates that the first line of development of external rules (what is and is not allowed) produces moral realism, i.e., a confusion in the child between moral rules and physical rules. The child confuses the fact that it is impossible to light a match a second time and the rule that it is forbidden to light matches at all, or to touch a glass because it might break: all "don'ts" are the same to a very young child, but he has an entirely different attitude to rules which he makes up himself. (*1*)

Let us turn now to the role of play and its influence on a child's development. I think it is enormous.

I will try to outline two basic ideas. I think that play with an imaginary situation is something essentially new, impossible for a child under three; it is a novel form of behavior in which the child is liberated from situational constraints through his activity in an imaginary situation.

To a considerable extent the behavior of a very young child — and, to an absolute extent, that of an infant — is determined by the conditions in which the activity takes place, as the experiments of Lewin and others have shown. . . . I recall a study by Lewin on the motivating nature of things for a very young child; in it Lewin concludes that things dictate to the child what he must do: a door demands to be opened and closed, a staircase to be run up, a bell to be rung. In short, things have an inherent motivating force in respect to a very young child's actions and determine the child's behavior to such an extent that Lewin arrived at the notion of creating a psychological topology, i.e., to express mathematically the trajectory of the child's movement in a field according to the distribution of things with varying attracting or repelling forces.

What is the root of situational constraints upon a child? The answer lies in a central fact of consciousness which is characteristic of early childhood: the union of affect and perception. At this age perception is generally not an independent feature but an initial feature of a motor-affective reaction; i.e., every perception is in this way a stimulus to activity. Since a situation is always communicated psychologically through perception, and perception is not separated from affective and motor activity, it is understandable that with his consciousness so structured the child cannot act otherwise than as constrained by the situation — or the field — in which he finds himself.

In play, things lose their motivating force. The child sees one thing but acts differently in relation to what he sees. Thus, a situation is reached in which the child begins to act independently of what he sees. Certain brain-damaged patients lose the ability to act independently of what they see; in considering such patients you can begin to appreciate that the freedom of action we adults and more mature children enjoy is not acquired in a flash but has to go through a long process of development.

Action in a situation which is not seen but only conceived on an imagined level and in an imaginary situation teaches the child to guide his behavior not only by immediate perception of objects or by the situation immediately affecting him, but also by the meaning (*2*) of this situation.

Experiments and day-to-day observation clearly show that it is impossible for very young children to separate the field of meaning from the visible field. This is a very important fact. Even a child of two years, when asked to repeat the sentence "Tanya is standing up" when Tanya is sitting in front of him, will change it to "Tanya is sitting down." In certain diseases we are faced with exactly the same situation. Goldstein and Gelb described a number of patients who were unable to state something that was not true. Gelb has data on one patient who was left-handed and incapable of writing the sentence "I can write well with my right hand." When looking out of the window on a fine day he was unable to repeat: "The weather is nasty today," but would say: "The weather is fine today." Often we find in a patient with a speech disturbance that he is incapable of repeating senseless phrases, for example: "Snow is black"; while other phrases equally difficult in their grammatical and semantic construction can be repeated.

In a very young child there is such an intimate fusion between word and object, and between meaning and what is seen, that a divergence between the meaning field and the visible field is impossible.

This can be seen in the process of children's speech development. You say to the child: "clock." He starts looking and finds the clock; i.e., the first function of the word is to orient spatially, to isolate particular areas in space; the word originally signifies a particular location in a situation.

It is at preschool age that we first find a divergence between the fields of meaning and vision. It seems to me that we would do well to restate the notion of the investigator who said that in play activity, thought is separated from objects, and action arises from ideas rather than from things.

Thought is separated from objects because a piece of wood begins to be a doll and a stick becomes a horse. Action according to rules begins to be determined by ideas and not by objects themselves. This is such a reversal of the child's relationship to the real, immediate, concrete situation that it is hard to evaluate its full significance. The child does not do this all at once. It is terribly difficult for a child to sever thought (the meaning of a word) from object. Play is a transitional stage in this direction. At that critical moment when a stick — i.e., an object — becomes a pivot for severing the meaning of horse from a real horse, one of the basic psychological structures determining the child's relationship to reality is radically altered.

The child cannot as yet sever thought from object; he must have something to act as a pivot. This expresses the child's weakness; in order to imagine a horse, he needs to define his actions by means of using the horse in the stick as the pivot. But all the same the basic structure determining the child's relationship to reality is radically changed at this crucial point, for his perceptual structure changes. The special feature of human perception — which arises at a very early age — is so-called reality perception. This is something for which there is no analogy in animal perception. Essentially it lies in the fact that I do not see the world simply in color and shape, but also as a world with sense and meaning. I do not merely see something round and black with two hands; I see a clock and I can distinguish one thing from another. There are patients who say, when they see a clock, that they are seeing something round and white with two thin steel strips, but they do not know that this is a clock; they have lost real relationship to objects. Thus, the structure of human perception could be figuratively expressed as a fraction in which the object is the numerator and the meaning is the denominator; this expresses the particular relationship of object and meaning which arises on the basis of speech. This means that all human perception is not made up of isolated perceptions, but of generalized perceptions. Goldstein says that this objectively formed perception and generalization are the same thing. Thus, for the child, in the fraction object-meaning, the object dominates, and meaning is directly connected to it. At the crucial moment for the child, when the stick becomes a horse, i.e., when the thing, the stick, becomes the pivot for severing the meaning of horse from a real horse, this fraction is inverted and meaning predominates, giving: $\frac{\text{meaning}}{\text{object}}$.

Nevertheless, properties of things as such do have some meaning: any stick can be a horse but, for example, a postcard can never be a horse for a child. Goethe's contention that in play any thing can be anything for a child is incorrect. Of course, for adults who can make conscious use of symbols, a postcard can be a horse. If I want to show the location of something, I can put down a match and say, "This is a horse." And that would be enough. For a child it cannot be a horse: one must use a stick; therefore this is play, and not symbolism. A symbol is a sign, but the stick is not the sign of a horse. Properties of things are retained but their meaning is inverted, i.e., the idea becomes the central point. It can be said that in this structure things are moved from a dominating to a subordinate position.

Thus, in play the child creates the structure $\frac{\text{meaning}}{\text{object}}$, where the semantic aspect — the meaning of the word, the meaning of the thing — dominates and determines his behavior. To a certain extent meaning is emancipated from the object with which it had been directly fused before. I would say that in play a child concentrates on meaning severed from objects, but that it is not severed in real action with real objects.

Thus, a highly interesting contradiction arises, wherein the child operates with meanings severed from objects and actions, but in real action with real objects he operates with them in fusion. This is the transitional nature of play, which makes it an intermediary between the purely situational constraints of early childhood and thought which is totally free of real situations. . . .

Now we can say the same thing about the child's activity that we said about things. Just as we have the fraction $\frac{\text{object}}{\text{meaning}}$, we also have the fraction $\frac{\text{action}}{\text{meaning}}$.

Whereas action dominated before, this structure is inverted, meaning becoming the numerator, while action takes the place of the denominator.

It is important to realize how the child is liberated from actions in play. An action, for example, is realized as finger movements instead of real eating — that is, the action is completed not for the action itself but for the meaning it carries.

At first, in a child of preschool age, action dominates over meaning and is incompletely understood; a child is able to do more than he can understand. It is at preschool age that there first arises an action structure in which meaning is the determinant; but the action itself is not a sideline or subordinated feature; it is a structural feature. Nohl showed that children, in playing at eating from a plate, performed actions with their hands reminiscent of real eating, but all actions that did not designate eating were impossible. Throwing one's hands back instead of stretching them toward the plate turned out to be impossible; that is, such action would have a destructive effect on the game. A child does not symbolize in play, but he wishes and realizes his wishes by letting the basic categories of reality pass through his experience, which is precisely why in play a day can take half an hour, and a hundred miles are covered in five steps. The child, in wishing, carries out his wishes; and in thinking, he acts. Internal and external action are inseparable: imagination, interpretation, and will are internal processes in external action.

The meaning of action is basic, but even by itself action is not indifferent. At an earlier age the position was the reverse: action was the structural determinant while meaning was a secondary, collateral, subordinated feature. What we said about severing meaning from object applies equally well to the child's own actions. A child who stamps on the ground and imagines himself riding a horse has thereby accomplished the inversion of the fraction $\frac{\text{action}}{\text{meaning}}$ to $\frac{\text{meaning}}{\text{action}}$.

Once again, in order to sever the meaning of the action from the real action (riding a horse, without having the opportunity to do so), the child requires a pivot in the form of an action to replace the real one. But once again, while before action was the determinant in the structure "action-meaning," now the structure is inverted and meaning becomes the determinant. Action retreats to second place and becomes the pivot; meaning is again severed from action by means of another action. This is a repetition of the point leading to operations based solely on the meanings of actions; i.e., to volitional choice, a decision, a conflict of motives, and to other processes sharply separated from fulfillment: in short, to the development of the will. Just as operating with the meaning of things leads to abstract thought, in volitional decision the determining factor is not the fulfillment of the action but its meaning. In play an action replaces another action just as an object replaces another object. How does the child "float from one object to another, from one action to another? This is accomplished by movement in the field of meaning — not connected with the visible field or with real objects — which subordinates all real objects and actions to itself.

. . . I have three questions left to answer. First, to show that play is not the predominant feature of childhood but is a leading factor in development. Second, to show the development of play itself; i.e., the significance of the movement from the predominance of the imaginary situation to the predominance of rules. And third, to show the internal transformations brought about by play in the child's development.

I do not think that play is the predominant type of child activity. In fundamental everyday situations a child behaves in a manner diametrically opposed to his behavior in play. In play, action is subordinated to meaning, but in real life, of course, action dominates over meaning.

Thus we find in play — if you will — the negative of a child's general everyday behavior. . . .

As research has shown, play behavior in real life is normally seen only in the type of game when sisters play at "sisters"; i.e., when children sitting at dinner can play at having dinner or (as in Katz's example) when children who do not want to go to bed say, "Let's play that it's nighttime and we have to go to sleep"; they begin to play at what they are in fact doing, evidently creating associations which facilitate the execution of an unpleasant action.

Thus, it seems to me that play is not the predominant type of activity at preschool age. Only theories which maintain that a child does not have to satisfy the basic requirements of life, but can live in search of pleasure, could possibly suggest that a child's world is a play world.

Is it possible to suppose that a child's behavior is always guided by meaning, that a preschooler's behavior is so arid that he never behaves with candy as he wants to simply because he thinks he should behave otherwise? This kind of subordination to rules is quite impossible in life, but in play it does become possible; thus, play also creates the zone of proximal development of the child. In play a child is always above his average age, above his daily behavior; in play it is as though he were a head taller than himself. As in the focus of a magnifying glass, play contains all developmental tendencies in a condensed form; in play it is as though the child were trying to jump above the level of his normal behavior.

The play-development relationship can be compared to the instruction-development relationship, but play provides a background for changes in needs and in consciousness of a much wider nature. Play is the source of development and creates the zone of proximal development. Action in the imaginative sphere, in an imaginary situation, the creation of voluntary intentions and the formation of real-life plans and volitional motives — all appear in play and make it the highest level of preschool development.

The child moves forward essentially through play activity. Only in this sense can play be termed a leading activity which determines the child's development.

The second question is: how does play move? It is a remarkable fact that the child starts with an imaginary situation when initially this imaginary situation is so very close to the real one. A reproduction of the real situation takes place. For example, a child playing with a doll repeats almost exactly what her mother does with her; the doctor looks at the child's throat, hurts him, and he cries, but as soon as the doctor has gone he immediately thrusts a spoon into the doll's mouth.

This means that in the original situation rules operate in a condensed and compressed form. There is very little of the imaginary in the situation. It is an imaginary situation, but it is only comprehensible in the light of a real situation that has just occurred; i.e., it is a recollection of something that has actually happened. Play is more nearly recollection than imagination — that is, it is more memory in action than a novel imaginary situation. As play develops, we see a movement toward the conscious realization of its purpose.

It is incorrect to conceive of play as activity without purpose; play is purposeful activity for a child. In athletic games you can win or lose, in a race you can come first, second, or last. In short, the purpose decides the game. It justifies all the rest. Purpose as the ultimate goal determines the child's affective attitude to play. When running a race, a child can be highly agitated or distressed and little may remain of pleasure because he finds it physically painful to run, while if he is overtaken he will experience little functional pleasure. In sports the purpose of the game is one of its dominant features without which there would be no point — like examining a piece of candy, putting it in one's mouth, chewing it, and then spitting it out.

In play the object, to win, is recognized in advance.

At the end of development rules emerge, and the more rigid they are, the greater the demands on the child's application, the greater the regulation of the child's activity, the more tense and acute play becomes. Simply running around without purpose or rules of play is a dull game that does not appeal to children. . . .

Finally, the third question: what sort of changes in a child's behavior can be attributed to play? In play a child is free, i.e., he determines his own actions, starting from his own "I." But this is an illusory freedom. His actions are in fact subordinated to a definite meaning, and he acts according to the meanings of things.

A child learns to consciously recognize his own actions, and becomes aware that every object has a meaning.

From the point of view of development, the fact of creating an imaginary situation can be regarded as a means of developing abstract thought. I think that the corresponding development of rules leads to actions on the basis of which the division between work and play becomes possible, a division encountered at school age as a fundamental fact.

I would like to mention just one other aspect: play is really a particular feature of preschool age.

As figuratively expressed by one investigator, play for a child under three is a serious game, just as it is for an adolescent, although, of course, in a different sense of the word; serious play for a very young child means that he plays without separating the imaginary situation from the real one.

For the schoolchild, play begins to be a limited form of activity, predominantly of the athletic type, which fills a specific role in the schoolchild's development, but lacks the significance of play for the preschooler.

Superficially, play bears little resemblance to what it leads to, and only a profound internal analysis makes it possible to determine its course of movement and its role in the preschooler's development.

At school age play does not die away but permeates the attitude to reality. It has its own inner continuation in school instruction and work (compulsory activity based on rules). All examinations of the essence of play have shown that in play a new relationship is created between the semantic and visible fields — that is between situations in thought and real situations.

FOOTNOTES

1. I have already demonstrated in an earlier lecture the nature of a very young child's perception of external behavioral rules; all "don'ts" — social (interdiction), physical (the impossibility, for example, of striking a match a second time), and biological (for example, don't touch the samovar because you might burn yourself) — combine to form a single "situational" don't, which can be understood as a "barrier" (in Lewin's sense of the term).

2. [Editor's note: In the following discussion of the role of meaning in relation to objects and actions Vygotsky uses the word *smysl'*, which roughly corresponds to the range of notions covered by the English "meaning," "sense," and "purport." *Smysl'* is uniformly rendered as "meaning" in this translation.]

19

Rochel Gelman

PRESCHOOL THOUGHT

I find it noteworthy that this special issue has provided for a separate essay on preschool thought. Until very recently, almost all researchers of cognitive development have made a habit of contrasting the preschooler with the older child. Preschoolers have been characterized as lacking the classification abilities, communication skills, number concepts, order concepts, memorial skills, and a framework for reasoning about causal relationships between events that older children are granted. Indeed, had one written an essay on preschool thought five years ago, the conclusion might have been that preschoolers are remarkably ignorant. In this essay I review some of the evidence that has begun to pile up against the view that preschoolers are cognitively inept. I then consider why we failed to see what it is that preschoolers can do and possible misinterpretations of the recent findings.

It is commonplace to read about the egocentrism of preschool children. The idea is that the young child either is unable to take the perspective of another child or adult or, worse yet, believes his or her own perspective is the same as that of others. Such general statements derive support from a variety of studies. When asked to describe an abstract shape for another child, a preschooler will sometimes use private labels, for example, "mommy's hat" (Glucksberg, Krauss, & Weisberg, 1966). The child's talk in the presence of others often goes on without any attempt to coordinate this talk with that of other speakers; the child seems not to care who else is speaking, what they say, or whether he or she is being listened to. "He feels no desire to influence his listener nor to tell him anything; not unlike a certain type of drawing room conversation where everyone talks about himself and no one listens" (Piaget, 1955, p. 32). When asked to choose a picture that represents the view of a mountain seen by someone opposite the child, the child selects the representation that matches what the child sees (Piaget & Inhelder, 1956)!

In 1973, Marilyn Shatz and I reported on our studies of the speech used by 4-year-olds when they talked to 2-year-olds, peers, or adults. We found that our subjects generally used short and simple utterances when they described the workings of a toy to their 2-year-old listeners. In contrast, these same 4-year-old children used longer and more complex utterances when describing the same toy to their peers or adults (Shatz & Gelman, 1973). Was it possible that these children, who were presumed to be egocentric speakers

Preparation of this essay was supported in part by National Science Foundation Grant BNS 03327 and National Institute of Child Health and Human Development Grant HD 10965.

by the research community at large, were adjusting their speech in accordance with their perception or conception of their listeners' different abilities and needs? As it turns out, yes. We (Gelman & Shatz, 1977) found that 4-year-olds' speech to a 2-year-old serves different functions and contains somewhat different messages than does their speech to adults. Speech to 2-year-olds serves to show and tell, to focus, direct, and monitor attention; speech to adults includes talk about the child's own thoughts and seeks information, support, or clarification from adults. Adult-directed speech also contains hedges about statements of fact, indicating that the child recognizes that he or she may be wrong and that the adult could challenge his or her statements. The children in our experiments were clearly taking the different needs and capacities of their listeners into account when talking to them. They hardly seem egocentric!

What about the claim that preschoolers think their visual perspective is the same as that of another person? Here again the presumed is contradicted. In an elegant series of experiments with 1–3-year-old children, Lempers, Flavell, and Flavell (1977) demonstrated over and over again that it is simply wrong to deny preschoolers an ability to distinguish their perspective from that of others. In the "show-toy task," 1½–3-year-old children showed toys to adults so that the front side was visible to the adult. This means they turned away from themselves the front of the toy and thereby deprived themselves of their original perspective. When asked to show pictures, almost all the 2- and 3-year-olds turned the front side to the adult and thereby ended up seeing the blank back of the picture. Still younger children showed the picture horizontally rather than egocentrically, that is, they did not simply hold the picture upright and thus show the back to their adult cohort in the task.

More recently, Flavell, Shipstead, and Croft (Note 1) dispelled the rumor that preschoolers believe that the closing of their own eyes deprives others of visual information about them. In fact, there is so much evidence now coming in about the perspective-taking abilities of preschoolers (for reviews, see Gelman, 1978; Shatz, 1978) that I find it hard to understand how I or anyone else ever held the belief that preschoolers are egocentric.

In retrospect one might argue that the perspective-taking abilities of preschoolers make sense. Young children do interact with others and they do talk. If they did not have any perspective-taking abilities, how could they ever communicate (cf. Fodor, 1972)? The argument might continue that we may have been wrong on the perspective-taking front, but surely we were correct in our characterization of other cognitive abilities. After all, number concepts seem much removed from the daily interactions of a preschooler. Besides, they constitute abstract ideas — the kind of ideas that everyone knows are very late in cognitive development. All of this may well be true; nevertheless, preschoolers know a great deal about the nature of number. I and my collaborators have shown that children as young as 2½ years honor the principles of counting and are able to use a counting algorithm to reason numerically, for example, to determine that an unexpected change in the numerical value of a set occurred because of surreptitiously performed addition or subtraction. (See Gelman & Gallistel, 1978, for a review of the arithmetic reasoning abilities of preschoolers.)

Successful counting involves the coordinated application of five principles (Gelman & Gallistel, 1978). These are as follows: (1) The one–one principle — each item in an array must be tagged with one and only one unique tag. (2) The stable-order principle — the tags assigned must be drawn from a stably ordered list. (3) The cardinal principle — the last tag used for a particular count serves to designate the cardinal number represented by the array. (4) The abstraction principle — any set of items may be collected together for a count. It does not matter whether they are identical, three-dimensional, imagined, or real, for in principle, any discrete set of materials can be represented as the contents of a set. (5) The order-irrelevance principle — the order in which a given object is tagged as one, two, three, and so on, is irrelevant as long as it is tagged but once and as long as the stable-order and cardinal principles are honored. Number words are arbitrary tags. The evidence clearly supports the conclusion that preschoolers honor these principles. They may not apply them perfectly, the set sizes to which they are applied may be limited, and their count lists may differ from the conventional list, but nevertheless the principles are used. Thus, a 2½-year-old may say "two, six" when counting a two-item array and "two, six, ten" when counting a three-item array (the one–one principle). The same child will use his or her own list over and over again (the stable-order principle) and, when asked how many items are present, will repeat the last tag in the list. In the present example, the child said "ten" when asked about the number represented by a three-item array (the cardinal principle).

The fact that young children invent their own lists suggests that the counting principles are guiding the search for appropriate tags. Such "errors" in counting are like the errors made by young language learners (e.g., "I runned"). In the latter case, such errors are taken to mean that the child's use of language is rule governed and that these rules come from the child; we are not likely to hear speakers of English using such words as *runned, footses, mouses, unthirsty,* and *two–six–ten*. We use similar logic to account for the presence of idiosyncratic count lists.

Further facts about the nature of counting in young children support the idea that some basic principles guide their acquisition of skill at counting. Children spontaneously self-correct their count errors, and perhaps more important, they are inclined to count without any request to do so. If we accept the idea that the counting principles are available to the child, the fact that young children count spontaneously without external motivation fits well. What's more, the self-generated practice trials make it possible for a child to develop skill at counting.

Still other cognitive domains exist for which it has been possible to reveal considerable capacity on the part of the young child. There are conditions under which preschoolers classify according to taxonomic categories (Rosch, Mervis, Gray, Johnson, & Boyes-Braem, 1976), classify animate and inanimate objects separately (Keil, 1977; Carey, Note 2), and use hierarchical classifications (Keil, 1977; Mansfield, 1977; Markman & Siebert, 1976). They can be taught to use a rule of transitive inference (Trabasso, 1975). They can be shown to be sensitive to temporal order (Brown, 1976). They believe, as do adults, that causes precede their effects (Bullock & Gelman, 1979; Kun, 1978). They use rules to solve problems (Siegler, 1978), and so on. In short, they have considerable cognitive abilities. Why, then, has it taken us so long to see them? I think there are two related reasons.

First, we simply did not look. Indeed, we seemed to choose to ignore facts that were staring us in the face. Consider the case of counting prowess in the young child. It is now clear that preschoolers can and do count. But many of us, myself included, who researched number concepts in children started out with the view that preschoolers were restricted to the use of a perceptual mechanism for number abstraction. The idea was that their representation of number was governed by the same pattern-recognition abilities that are used to distinguish one object from another. Just as they distinguish "cowness" and "treeness," they presumably distinguish "twoness" and "threeness." I don't remember how many times I saw preschoolers counting in my various experiments before I finally recognized they were indeed able to count, no matter what our theories led us to believe. I do remember one 3-year-old telling me that he much preferred one task over another, that being the one in which it was possible to count! And it took us a while to recognize the ubiquitous tendency for 4-year-olds to talk down to 2-year-olds.

The failure to recognize facts that contradict existing theories is not unique to those who study cognitive development. Time and time again we read in the history of science of similar cases. It seems as if we have a general tendency to resist new facts if their recognition means giving up a theory without being able to come up with another that will account for the new as well as the old facts. I believe that we now know enough about the nature of the development of number concepts to be able to deal with the apparent contradictions between the new and old research findings. The young child seems unable to reason about number without reference to representations of specific numerosities, representations obtained by counting. With development, the child's reasoning moves from a dependence on specific representations to an algebraic stage in which specific representations of numerosity are no longer required. In the conservation task, the child has to make inferences about equivalence and nonequivalence on the basis of one-to-one correspondence. It matters not what the particular numbers of items in the two displays are. If they can be placed in one-to-one correspondence, then they are equal by definition. If we are correct, then the abilities we have uncovered can be seen as the beginning understanding of number. In this light their existence need not be seen as contradictory findings. Indeed, once one begins to talk about precursors of later cognitive abilities it is no longer unreasonable to start the search for those concepts and capacities the preschooler must have if he or she is to acquire complex cognitive abilities. We should expect to find domains in which they are quite competent — if only we look.

Recent work on the learning and memorial abilities of young children endorses my belief that there are many cases in which it will suffice to decide to look for competence in order for us to take note of it. As Carey (1978) pointed out, young children perform an incredible task by learning the lexicon of their native language. She estimated that 6-year-old children have mastered to some degree about 14,000 words. To do this, the children need to learn about nine new words a day from the time they start speaking until the time they reach their sixth birthday. This is truly a remarkable accomplishment. So what if the preschooler fails on a task that requires him or her to sort consistently by taxonomic category? The same child has to have some classification abilities in order to learn the lexicon so rapidly. To be sure, the child probably does not learn the full meaning of every new word the first time that word is heard. But as Carey showed, "One or a very few experiences with a new word can suffice for the child to enter it into his or her mental lexicon and to represent some of its syntactic and semantic features." Given this and the continued exposure to that word, it is then possible for a child to learn more about it and to reorganize his or her lexicon and the conceptual framework involved therein.

Nelson (1978) made it clear that young children readily learn the scripts that describe the class of events they encounter. Others (e.g., Mandler, in press) have shown young children to have excellent memories for stories — a fact that really should not surprise us, given the young child's interest in hearing stories.

Although some abilities are so pervasive that simply deciding to attend to them will make them evident, this is not true for a wide variety of cognitive skills, for example, reading and metacognitive skills. This brings me to the second reason for our failure, until recently, to acknowledge the cognitive capacities of preschoolers.

Many of the young child's cognitive abilities are well concealed and require the modification of old tasks or the development of new tasks for their revelation. I return to the question of early number concepts. Young children systematically fail Piaget's number conservation task. With this task, they behave as if they believe that the number of objects in a row changes when items are pushed together or spread apart. They thus begin by agreeing that two rows placed in one-to-one correspondence represent equal amounts; when they see one row lengthened, however, they deny the continued equivalence.

In an effort to control for a variety of variables that might have interfered with the child's possible belief in the invariance of the numerical value of a set despite the application of a lengthening transformation, my colleagues and I developed what we call "the magic task" (Gelman, 1972). The task involves two phases. The first establishes an expectancy for the continued presence of two sets of two given values, say, 3 and 2, despite the repeated covering and uncovering of those sets. To avoid reference to number or the use of ambiguous terms such as *more* or *less,* one of these displays is designated "the winner," and the other "the loser." These are covered and children have to find the winner and tell us why they have or have not done so once they uncover a display. As luck would have it, preschoolers decide on their own that numerical value is the determinant for winning and losing status. They thus establish an expectancy for two particular numerical values. Then, unbeknownst to the child, the second phase of the experiment begins when the experimenter surreptitiously alters one of the expected displays. Across different conditions and experiments, the changes involve addition, subtraction, displacement, change in color of the original objects, and even a change in identity of the original objects. Children who encounter a change in number produced by subtraction or addition say that the expected number has been violated, typically identify the number of elements present and the number that should be present, and make explicit reference to the transformation that must have been performed — even if they did not see it. In contrast, children who encounter the effects of irrelevant transformations say the number of elements is as expected despite the change in length of a display, or in the color, or in the identity of an element in that display.

According to the results of the magic task, preschoolers know full well that lengthening or shortening an array does not alter the numerical value of a display. Still, these same children fail the conservation task. But note how different these tasks are. In the conservation task the child has to judge equivalence on the basis of one-to-one correspondence, correctly interpret questions that are ambiguous, watch the transformation being performed, and then ignore the effect of that transformation. In the magic task the child need not make judgments of equivalence based on one-to-one correspondence, he or she need not (indeed cannot) see the transformation being performed, and there are no ambiguous terms to misinterpret. In other words, the magic task is a very stripped down version of the conservation task. Likewise, many other tasks that show preschoolers in a positive light have downgraded the complexity of the tasks that they fail, altered the instructions, changed the stimuli used, embedded the question of interest in games preschoolers play, provided extensive pretraining before testing on the target task — In short, in many cases it has been necessary to develop tasks and experimental settings to suit the preschool child (Gelman, 1978). This is easier said than done. Consider the magic game which *was* designed to meet our best guesses as to how to elicit the number-invariance rules honored by the young child.

Bullock and Gelman (1977) modified the magic task in order to determine whether preschoolers could compare two number pairs. In particular, the question was whether they would recognize that the number pair 1 and 2 was like 3 and 4 insofar as 1 and 3 were both "less" and 2 and 4 were both "more." Children between the ages of 2½ and 4 were first shown one-item and two-item displays, and they established expectancies for a set of one and a set of two items. Half the children were told that the one-item array was the winner; half were told that the two-item array was the winner. From the experimenter's point of view this was also a more–less comparison task. To determine whether the 2½–4-year-old children in the experiment knew this, we surreptitiously replaced the original displays with three-item and four-item displays and asked which of these was the winner. Many of the older children were confused by this question and said that neither was the winner — an observation which in point of fact was correct. When asked to make the best possible choice, the children then went on to choose the display that honored the relation they were reinforced for during the expectancy training. Apparently the children did not immediately realize that it was all right to make a judgment of similarity, given the fact that neither of the new displays was identical to either of the original displays. Our variation in question format served to tell them that the transfer task called for a similarity judgment. My point here is that we started out with a task that was designed for young children and still we found that the task presented problems.

This example of the subtle ways in which a task can confound the assessment of those early cognitive abilities that are generally buried is not an isolated one. I have discussed others elsewhere (Gelman, 1978), and for me they are very sobering. They make it clear that in many cases, it takes more than a decision to look for early cognitive abilities. It is often exceedingly difficult to know how to design tasks so that they will be suitable for use with young children. I believe this derives in part from the fact that many of the preschoolers' cognitive abilities are fragile and as such are only evident under restricted conditions — at least compared with the conditions under which older children can apply their knowledge. This brings me to my next point.

Some might take the recent demonstrations of early cognitive abilities to mean that preschoolers are miniature adults as far as their cognitions are concerned. This is not what I want people to conclude, and should they so conclude it would not be in the best interests of either those who study cognitive development or the child. The fact remains that despite the recent demonstration of some complex cognitive abilities, young children fail a wide range of tasks that seem so simple for older children. I believe that many of the best insights into the nature of development will come from understanding exactly what conditions interfere with the use and accessibility of those capacities the young child does possess. These insights may also be of the greatest educational relevance. However, these insights can only come after we have uncovered the basic capacities that make cognitive growth a possibility.

What I do want people to realize is that we have been much too inclined to reach conclusions about what preschoolers cannot do, compared with what their older cohorts can do on a variety of tasks. We must cease to approach young children with only those tasks that are designed for older children. The time has come for us to turn our attention to what young children can do as well as to what they cannot do. Without a good description of what young children do know, it's going to be exceedingly difficult, if not impossible, to chart their course as they travel the path of cognitive development. What's worse, we run the serious risk of making unwarranted statements about the nature of preschool curricula. I have had people tell me that there is no point in teaching young children about numbers, since preschoolers cannot conserve numbers. This, I submit, is a non sequitur. The conservation task is but one index of numerical knowledge, and it is beginning to look like it is an index of a rather sophisticated knowledge.

My message is quite straightforward. We should study preschoolers in their own right and give up treating them as foils against which to describe the accomplishments of middle childhood. We have made some progress in recent years, but there is still plenty of room for those who are willing to take on the mind of the young child.

REFERENCE NOTES

1. Flavell, J. H., Shipstead, S. G., & Croft, K. *What young children think you see when their eyes are closed.* Unpublished manuscript, Stanford University, 1978.

2. Carey, S. *The child's concept of* animal. Paper presented at the meeting of the Psychonomic Society, San Antonio, Texas, November 1978.

REFERENCES

Brown, A. L. The construction of temporal succession by preoperational children. In A. D. Pick (Ed.), *Minnesota symposium on child psychology* (Vol. 10). Minneapolis: University of Minnesota Press, 1976.

Bullock, M., & Gelman, R. Numerical reasoning in young children: The ordering principle. *Child Development,* 1977, *48,* 427–434.

Bullock, M., & Gelman, R. Preschool children's assumptions about cause and effect: Temporal ordering. *Child Development,* 1979, *50,* 89–96.

Carey, S. The child as word learner. In M. Halle, J. Bresnan, & G. A. Miller (Eds.), *Linguistic theory and psychological reality.* Cambridge, Mass.: Massachusetts Institute of Technology Press, 1978.

Fodor, J. A. Some reflections on L. S. Vygotsky's *Thought and language. Cognition,* 1972, *1,* 83–95.

Gelman, R. Logical capacity of very young children: Number invariance rules. *Child Development,* 1972, *43,* 75–90.

Gelman, R. Cognitive development. In L. W. Porter & M. R. Rosenzweig (Eds.), *Annual review of psychology* (Vol. 29). Palo Alto, Calif.: Annual Reviews, 1978.

Gelman, R., & Gallistel, C. R. *The child's understanding of number.* Cambridge, Mass.: Harvard University Press, 1978.

Gelman, R., & Shatz, M. Appropriate speech adjustments: The operation of conversational constraints on talk to two-year-olds. In M. Lewis & L. A. Rosenblum (Eds.), *Interaction, conversation, and the development of language.* New York: Wiley, 1977.

Glucksberg, S., Krauss, R. M., & Weisberg, R. Referential communication in nursery school children: Method and some preliminary findings. *Journal of Experimental Child Psychology,* 1966, *3,* 333–342.

Keil, F. *The role of ontological categories in a theory of semantic and conceptual development.* Unpublished doctoral dissertation, University of Pennsylvania, 1977.

Kun, A. Evidence for preschoolers' understanding of causal direction in extended causal sequences. *Child Development,* 1978, *49,* 218–222.

Lempers, J. D., Flavell, E. R., & Flavell, J. H. The development in very young children of tacit knowledge concerning visual perception. *Genetic Psychology Monographs,* 1977, *95,* 3–53.

Mandler, J. M. Categorical and schematic organization. In C. R. Puff (Ed.), *Memory, organization, and structure.* New York: Academic Press, in press.

Mansfield, A. F. Semantic organization in the young child: Evidence for the development of semantic feature systems. *Journal of Experimental Child Psychology,* 1977, *23,* 57–77.

Markman, E. M., & Siebert, J. Classes and collections: Internal organization and resulting holistic properties. *Cognitive Psychology,* 1976, *8,* 561–577.

Nelson, K. How young children represent knowledge of their world in and out of language: A preliminary report. In R. Siegler (Ed.), *Children's thinking: What develops?* Hillsdale, N.J.: Erlbaum, 1978.

Piaget, J. *The language and thought of the child.* London: Routledge & Kegan Paul, 1955.

Piaget, J., & Inhelder, B. *The child's conception of space.* London: Routledge & Kegan Paul, 1956.

Rosch, E., Mervis, C. B., Gray, W. D., Johnson, D. M., & Boyes-Braem, P. Basic objects in natural categories. *Cognitive Psychology,* 1976, *8,* 382–439.

Shatz, M. The relationship between cognitive processes and the development of communication skills. In C. B. Keasey (Ed.), *Nebraska symposium on motivation* (Vol. 26). Lincoln: University of Nebraska Press, 1978.

Shatz, M., & Gelman, R. The development of communication skills: Modifications in the speech of young children as a function of listener. *Monographs of the Society for Research in Child Development,* 1973, *38* (2, Serial No. 152).

Siegler, R. S. The origins of scientific reasoning. In R. S. Siegler (Ed.), *Children's thinking: What develops?* Hillsdale, N.J.: Erlbaum, 1978.

Trabasso, T. R. Representation, memory and reasoning: How do we make transitive inferences? In A. D. Pick (Ed.), *Minnesota symposium on child psychology* (Vol. 9). Minneapolis: University of Minnesota Press, 1975.

20 Lois Gould

X: A FABULOUS CHILD'S STORY

Once upon a time, a baby named X was born. This baby was named X so that nobody could tell whether it was a boy or a girl. Its parents could tell, of course, but they couldn't tell anybody else. They couldn't even tell Baby X, at first.

You see, it was all part of a very important Secret Scientific Xperiment, known officially as Project Baby X. The smartest scientists had set up this Xperiment at a cost of Xactly 23 billion dollars and 72 cents, which might seem like a lot for just one baby, even a very important Xperimental baby. But when you remember the prices of things like strained carrots and stuffed bunnies, and popcorn for the movies and booster shots for camp, let alone 28 shiny quarters from the tooth fairy, you begin to see how it adds up.

Also, long before Baby X was born, all those scientists had to be paid to work out the details of the Xperiment, and to write the *Official Instruction Manual* for Baby X's parents and, most important of all, to find the right set of parents to bring up Baby X. These parents had to be selected very carefully. Thousands of volunteers had to take thousands of tests and answer thousands of tricky questions. Almost everybody failed because, it turned out, almost everybody really wanted either a baby boy or a baby girl, and not Baby X at all. Also, almost everybody was afraid that a Baby X would be a lot more trouble than a boy or a girl. (They were probably right, the scientists admitted, but Baby X needed parents who wouldn't *mind* the Xtra trouble.)

There were families with grandparents named Milton and Agatha, who didn't see why the baby couldn't be named Milton or Agatha instead of X, even it it *was* an X. There were families with aunts who insisted on knitting tiny dresses and uncles who insisted on sending tiny baseball mitts. Worst of all, there were families that already had other children who couldn't be trusted to keep the secret. Certainly not if they knew the secret was worth 23 billion dollars and 72 cents — and all you had to do was take one little peek at Baby X in the bathtub to know if it was a boy or a girl.

But, finally, the scientists found the Joneses, who really wanted to raise an X more than any other kind of baby — no matter how much trouble it would be. Ms. and Mr. Jones had to promise they would take equal turns caring for X, and feeding it, and singing it lullabies. And they had to promise never to hire any baby-sitters. The government scientists knew perfectly well that a baby-sitter would probably peek at X in the bathtub, too.

The day the Joneses brought their baby home, lots of friends and relatives came over to see it. None of them knew about the secret Xperiment, though. So the first thing they asked was what kind of a baby X was. When the Joneses smiled and said, "It's an X!" nobody knew what to say. They couldn't say, "Look at her cute little dimples!" And they couldn't say, "Look at his husky little biceps!" And they couldn't even say just plain "kitchy-coo." In fact, they all thought the Joneses were playing some kind of rude joke.

But, of course, the Joneses were not joking. "It's an X" was absolutely all they would say. And that made the friends and relatives very angry. The relatives all felt embarrassed about having an X in the family. "People will think there's something wrong with it!" some of them whispered. "There *is* something wrong with it!" others whispered back.

"Nonsense!" the Joneses told them all cheerfully. "What could possibly be wrong with this perfectly adorable X?"

Nobody could answer that, except Baby X, who had just finished its bottle. Baby X's answer was a loud, satisfied burp.

Clearly, nothing at all was wrong. Nevertheless, none of the relatives felt comfortable about buying a present for a Baby X. The cousins who sent the baby a tiny football helmet would not come and visit any more. And the neighbors who sent a pink-flowered romper suit pulled their shades down when the Joneses passed their house.

The *Official Instruction Manual* had warned the new parents that this would happen, so they didn't fret about it. Besides, they were too busy with baby X and the hundreds of different Xercises for treating it properly.

Ms. and Mr. Jones had to be Xtra careful about how they played with little X. They knew that if they kept bouncing it up in the air and saying how *strong* and *active* it was, they'd be treating it more like a boy than an X. But if all they did was cuddle it and kiss it and tell it how *sweet* and *dainty* it was, they'd be treating it more like a girl than an X.

On page 1,654 of the *Official Instruction Manual,* the scientists prescribed: "plenty of bouncing and plenty of cuddling, *both.* X ought to be strong and sweet and active. Forget about *dainty* altogether."

Meanwhile, the Joneses were worrying about other problems. Toys, for instance. And clothes. On his first shopping trip, Mr. Jones told the store clerk, "I need some clothes and toys for my new baby." The clerk smiled and said, "Well, now, is it a boy or a girl?" "It's an X," Mr. Jones said, smiling back. But the clerk got all red in the face and said huffily, "In *that* case, I'm afraid I can't help you, sir." So Mr. Jones wandered helplessly up and down the aisles trying to find what X needed. But everything in the store was piled up in sections marked "Boys" or "Girls." There were "Boys' Pajamas" and "Girls' Underwear" and "Boys' Fire Engines" and "Girls' Housekeeping Sets." Mr. Jones went home without buying anything for X. That night he and Ms. Jones consulted page 2,326 of the *Official Instruction Manual.* "Buy plenty of everything!" it said firmly.

So they bought plenty of sturdy blue pajamas in the Boys' Department and cheerful flowered underwear in the Girls' Department. And they bought all kinds of toys. A boy doll that made pee-pee and cried, "Pa-pa." And a girl doll that talked in three languages and said, "I am the Pres-i-dent of Gen-er-al Mo-tors." They also bought a storybook about a brave princess who rescued a handsome prince from his ivory tower, and another one about a sister and brother who grew up to be a baseball star and a ballet star, and you had to guess which was which.

The head scientists of Project Baby X checked all their purchases and told them to keep up the good work. They also reminded the Joneses to see page 4,629 of the *Manual,* where it said, "Never make Baby X feel *embarrassed* or *ashamed* about what it wants to play with. And if X gets dirty climbing rocks, never say 'Nice little Xes don't get dirty climbing rocks.' "

Likewise, it said, "If X falls down and cries, never say 'Brave little Xes don't cry.' Because, of course, nice little Xes *do* get dirty, and brave little Xes *do* cry. No matter how dirty X gets, or how hard it cries, don't worry. It's all part of the Xperiment."

Whenever the Joneses pushed Baby X's stroller in the park, smiling strangers would come over and coo: "Is that a boy or a girl?" The Joneses would smile back and say, "It's an X." The strangers would stop smiling then, and often snarl something nasty — as if the Joneses had snarled at *them*.

By the time X grew big enough to play with other children, the Joneses' troubles had grown bigger, too. Once a little girl grabbed X's shovel in the sandbox, and zonked X on the head with it. "Now, now, Tracy," the little girl's mother began to scold, "little girls mustn't hit little — " and she turned to ask X, "Are you a little boy or a little girl, dear?"

Mr. Jones, who was sitting near the sandbox, held his breath and crossed his fingers.

X smiled politely at the lady, even though X's head had never been zonked so hard in its life. "I'm a little X," X replied.

"You're a *what?*" the lady exclaimed angrily. "You're a little b-r-a-t, you mean!"

"But little girls mustn't hit little Xes, either!" said X, retrieving the shovel with another polite smile. "What good does hitting do, anyway?"

X's father, who was still holding his breath, finally let it out, uncrossed his fingers, and grinned back at X.

And at their next secret Project Baby X meeting, the scientists grinned, too. Baby X was doing fine.

But then it was time for X to start school. The Joneses were really worried about this, because school was even more full of rules for boys and girls, and there were no rules for Xes. The teacher would tell boys to form one line, and girls to form another line. There would be boys' games and girls' games, and boys' secrets and girls' secrets. The school library would have a list of recommended books for girls, and a different list of recommended books for boys. There would even be a bathroom marked BOYS and another one marked GIRLS. Pretty soon boys and girls would hardly talk to each other. What would happen to poor little X?

The Joneses spent weeks consulting their *Instruction Manual* (there were 249½ pages of advice under "First Day of School"), and attending urgent special conferences with the smart scientists of Project Baby X.

The scientists had to make sure that X's mother had taught X how to throw and catch a ball properly, and that X's father had been sure to teach X what to serve at a doll's tea party. X had to know how to shoot marbles and how to jump rope and, most of all, what to say when the Other Children asked whether X was a Boy or a Girl.

Finally, X was ready. The Joneses helped X button on a nice new pair of red-and-white checked overalls, and sharpened six pencils for X's nice new pencilbox, and marked X's name clearly on all the books in its nice new bookbag. X brushed its teeth and combed its hair, which just about covered its ears, and remembered to put a napkin in its lunchbox.

The Joneses had asked X's teacher if the class could line up alphabetically, instead of forming separate lines for boys and girls. And they had asked if X could use the principal's bathroom, because it wasn't marked anything except BATHROOM. X's teacher promised to take care of all those problems. But nobody could help X with the biggest problem of all — Other Children.

Nobody in X's class had ever known an X before. What would they think? How would X make friends?

You couldn't tell what X was by studying its clothes — overalls don't even button right-to-left, like girls' clothes, or left-to-right, like boys' clothes. And you couldn't guess whether X had a girl's short haircut or a boy's long haircut. And it was very hard to tell by the games X liked to play. Either X played ball very well for a girl, or else X played house very well for a boy.

Some of the children tried to find out by asking X tricky questions, like "Who's your favorite sports star?" That was easy. X had two favorite sports stars: a girl jockey named Robyn Smith and a boy archery champion named Robin Hood. Then they asked, "What's your favorite TV program?" And that was even easier. X's favorite TV program was "Lassie," which stars a girl dog played by a boy dog.

When X said that its favorite toy was a doll, everyone decided that X must be a girl. But then X said that the doll was really a robot, and that X had computerized it, and that it was programmed to bake fudge brownies and then clean up the kitchen. After X told them that, the other children gave up guessing what X was. All they knew was they'd sure like to see X's doll.

After school, X wanted to play with the other children. "How about shooting some baskets in the gym?" X asked the girls. But all they did was make faces and giggle behind X's back.

"How about weaving some baskets in the arts and crafts room?" X asked the boys. But they all made faces and giggled behind X's back, too.

That night, Ms. and Mr. Jones asked X how things had gone at school. X told them sadly that the lessons were okay, but otherwise school was a terrible place for an X. It seemed as if Other Children would never want an X for a friend.

Once more, the Joneses reached for their *Instruction Manual.* Under "Other Children," they found the following message: "What did you Xpect? *Other Children* have to obey all the silly boy-girl rules, because their parents taught them to. Lucky X — you don't have to stick to the rules at all! All you have to do is be yourself. P.S. We're not saying it'll be easy."

X liked being itself. But X cried a lot that night, partly because it felt afraid. So X's father held X tight, and cuddled it, and couldn't help crying a little, too. And X's mother cheered them both up by reading an Xciting story about an enchanted prince called Sleeping Handsome, who woke up when Princess Charming kissed him.

The next morning, they all felt much better, and little X went back to school with a brave smile and a clean pair of red-and-white checked overalls.

There was a seven-letter-word spelling bee in class that day. And a seven-lap boys' relay race in the gym. And a seven-layer-cake baking contest in the girls' kitchen corner. X won the spelling bee. X also won the relay race. And X almost won the baking contest, except it forgot to light the oven. Which only proves that nobody's perfect.

One of the Other Children noticed something else, too. He said: "Winning or losing doesn't seem to count to X. X seems to have fun being good at boys' skills *and* girls' skills."

"Come to think of it," said another one of the Other Children, "maybe X is having twice as much fun as we are!"

So after school that day, the girl who beat X at the baking contest gave X a big slice of her prizewinning cake. And the boy X beat in the relay race asked X to race him home.

From then on, some really funny things began to happen. Susie, who sat next to X in class, suddenly refused to wear pink dresses to school any more. She insisted on wearing red-and-white checked overalls — just like X's. Overalls, she told her parents, were much better for climbing monkey bars.

Then Jim, the class football nut, started wheeling his little sister's doll carriage around the football field. He'd put on his entire football uniform, except for the helmet. Then he'd put the helmet *in* the carriage, lovingly tucked under an old set of shoulder pads. Then he'd start jogging around the field, pushing the carriage and singing "Rockabye

Baby" to his football helmet. He told his family that X did the same thing, so it must be okay. After all, X was now the team's star quarterback.

Susie's parents were horrified by her behavior, and Jim's parents were worried sick about his. But the worst came when the twins, Joe and Peggy, decided to share everything with each other. Peggy used Joe's hockey skates, and his microscope, and took half his newspaper route. Joe used Peggy's needlepoint kit, and her cookbooks, and took two of her three baby-sitting jobs. Peggy started running the lawn mower, and Joe started running the vacuum cleaner.

Their parents weren't one bit pleased with Peggy's wonderful biology experiments, or with Joe's terrific needlepoint pillows. They didn't care that Peggy mowed the lawn better, and that Joe vacuumed the carpet better. In fact, they were furious. It's all that little X's fault, they agreed. Just because X doesn't know what it is, or what it's supposed to be, it wants to get everybody *else* mixed up, too!

Peggy and Joe were forbidden to play with X any more. So was Susie, and then Jim, and then *all* the Other Children. But it was too late; the Other Children stayed mixed up and happy and free, and refused to go back to the way they'd been before X.

Finally, Joe and Peggy's parents decided to call an emergency meeting of the school's Parents' Association, to discuss "The X Problem." They sent a report to the principal stating that X was a "disruptive influence." They demanded immediate action. The Joneses, they said, should be *forced* to tell whether X was a boy or a girl. And then X should be *forced* to behave like whichever it was. If the Joneses refused to tell, the Parents' Association said, then X must take an Xamination. The school psychiatrist must Xamine it physically and mentally, and issue a full report. If X's test showed it was a boy, it would have to obey all the boys' rules. If it proved to be a girl, X would have to obey all the girls' rules.

And if X turned out to be some kind of mixed-up misfit, then X should be Xpelled from the school. Immediately!

The principal was very upset. Disruptive influence? Mixed-up misfit? But X was an Xcellent student. All the teachers said it was a delight to have X in their classes. X was president of the student council. X had won first prize in the talent show, and second prize in the art show, and honorable mention in the science fair, and six athletic events on field day, including the potato race.

Nevertheless, insisted the Parents' Association, X is a Problem Child. X is the Biggest Problem Child we have ever seen!

So the principal reluctantly notified X's parents that numerous complaints about X's behavior had come to the school's attention. And that after the psychiatrist's Xamination, the school would decide what to do about X.

The Joneses reported this at once to the scientists, who referred them to page 85,759 of the *Instruction Manual.* "Sooner or later," it said, "X will have to be Xamined by a psychiatrist. This may be the only way any of us will know for sure whether X is mixed up — or whether everyone else is."

The night before X was to be Xamined, the Joneses tried not to let X see how worried they were. "What if — ?" Mr. Jones would say. And Ms. Jones would reply, "No use worrying." Then a few minutes later, Ms. Jones would say, "What if — ?" and Mr. Jones would reply, "No use worrying."

X just smiled at them both, and hugged them hard and didn't say much of anything. X was thinking, What if — ? And then X thought: No use worrying.

At Xactly 9 o'clock the next day, X reported to the school psychiatrist's office. The principal, along with a committee from the Parents' Association, X's teacher, X's classmates, and Ms. and Mr. Jones, waited in the hall outside. Nobody knew the details of the tests X was to be given, but everybody knew they'd be *very* hard, and that they'd reveal Xactly what everyone wanted to know about X, but were afraid to ask.

It was terribly quiet in the hall. Almost spooky. Once in a while, they would hear a strange noise inside the room. There were buzzes. And a beep or two. And several bells. An occasional light would flash under the door. The Joneses thought it was a white light, but the principal thought it was blue. Two or three children swore it was either yellow or green. And the Parents' Committee missed it completely.

Through it all, you could hear the psychiatrist's low voice, asking hundreds of questions, and X's higher voice, answering hundreds of answers.

The whole thing took so long that everyone knew it must be the most complete Xamination anyone had ever had to take. Poor X, the Joneses thought. Serves X right, the Parents' Committee thought. I wouldn't like to be in X's overalls right now, the children thought.

At last, the door opened. Everyone crowded around to hear the results. X didn't look any different; in fact, X was smiling. But the psychiatrist looked terrible. He looked as if he was crying! "What happened?" everyone began shouting. Had X done something disgraceful? "I wouldn't be a bit surprised!" muttered Peggy and Joe's parents. "Did X flunk the *whole* test?" cried Susie's parents. "Or just the most important part?" yelled Jim's parents.

"Oh, dear," sighed Mr. Jones.

"Oh, dear," sighed Ms. Jones.

"Sssh," ssshed the principal. "The psychiatrist is trying to speak."

Wiping his eyes and clearing his throat, the psychiatrist began, in a hoarse whisper. "In my opinion," he whispered — you could tell he must be very upset — "in my opinion, young X here — "

"Yes? Yes?" shouted a parent impatiently.

"Sssh!" ssshed the principal.

"Young *Sssh* here, I mean young X," said the doctor, frowning, "is just about — "

"Just about *what?* Let's have it!" shouted another parent.

". . . just about the *least* mixed-up child I've ever Xamined!" said the psychiatrist.

"Yay for X!" yelled one of the children. And then the others began yelling, too. Clapping and cheering and jumping up and down.

"SSSH!" SSShed the principal, but nobody did.

The Parents' Committee was angry and bewildered. How *could* X have passed the whole Xamination? Didn't X have an *identity* problem? Wasn't X mixed up at *all?* Wasn't X *any* kind of a misfit? How could it *not* be, when it didn't even *know* what it was? And why was the psychiatrist crying?

Actually, he had stopped crying and was smiling politely through his tears. "Don't you see?" he said. "I'm crying because it's wonderful! X has absolutely no identity problem! X isn't one bit mixed up! As for being a misfit — ridiculous! X knows perfectly well what it is! Don't you, X?" The doctor winked. X winked back.

"But what *is* X?" shrieked Peggy and Joe's parents. "*We* still want to know what it is!"

"Ah, yes," said the doctor, winking again. "Well, don't worry. You'll all know one of these days. And you won't need me to tell you."

"What? What does he mean?" some of the parents grumbled suspiciously.

Susie and Peggy and Joe all answered at once. "He means that by the time X's sex matters, it won't be a secret any more!"

With that, the doctor began to push through the crowd toward X's parents. "How do you do," he said, somewhat stiffly. And then he reached out to hug them both. "If I ever have an X of my own," he whispered, "I sure hope you'll lend me your instruction manual."

Needless to say, the Joneses were very happy. The Project Baby X scientists were rather pleased, too. So were Susie, Jim, Peggy, Joe, and all the Other Children. The Parents' Association wasn't, but they had promised to accept the psychiatrist's report, and not make any more trouble. They even invited Ms. and Mr. Jones to become honorary members, which they did.

Later that day, all X's friends put on their red-and-white checked overalls and went over to see X. They found X in the back yard, playing with a very tiny baby that none of them had ever seen before. The baby was wearing very tiny red-and-white checked overalls.

"How do you like our new baby?" X asked the Other Children proudly.

"It's got cute dimples," said Jim.

"It's got husky biceps, too," said Susie.

"What kind of baby is it?" asked Joe and Peggy.

X frowned at them. "Can't you tell?" Then X broke into a big, mischievous grin. *"It's a Y!"*

21

Clara Park

TOWARDS SPEECH — A LONG SLOW CHAPTER

As she grew, the problem of her speech took precedence over all the others. It was through speech that she must join the human race. Kanner had found no better indicator of future development than speech. Five was his year of decision. By her fifth birthday, Elly had in fact begun to develop communicative speech.

. . . According to the count made the month she turned four, Elly had in her life spoken thirty-one different words, fewer than half of which were then in current use. In the course of a week she would speak no more than five or six. She responded to a number of routine commands. That was all.

This situation began to improve that year, the year we spent abroad. There was no sudden change; it happened gradually. Four months after her fourth birthday the word count had reached thirty-eight. More important, when I counted the different words she had spoken in a single week, I found twenty-one. Two months later, although only three new words had been added and she was still using about twenty words a week, they were by and large the same ones. Instead of the frustrating come-and-go of her earlier vocabulary, she was acquiring a core of speech on which we could depend.

Along with this came a new interest in getting us to name things — the letters in her alphabet set, the fruits and vegetables on the pretty curtain I had found for her to darken her bedroom and give us a little more sleep. She would try herself to say "strawberry" or "celery" — the barrier against imitation was at last breaking down. But she mouthed them so clumsily that they were nearly unintelligible even at the time, and totally unrecognizable out of context; they did not get included in the word-count.

All Elly's speech was indistinct; only those who knew her well understood anything she said. She never pronounced a final consonant, and often the initial consonants were ambiguous or wrong. Words of more than one syllable were rare, and tended to turn into Polynesian, so that Becky's name would come out Beh-Beh, recognizable only because Elly would perhaps be looking at her sister's picture. In this indistinctness, as in so much else, there seemed a queer deliberateness. The first time I ever heard her say "all gone" she said it distinctly; I could even hear the terminal "n." I remembered the clear "scissors" she spoke before she was two; I remembered her limpid "El-ly." I smiled; she smiled back mischievously and said the words again, less distinctly. "Ah-gah." It was "ah-gah" for years after that. Her pronunciation did not improve as she began to acquire words more easily; it grew worse. It was as if (*as if*) now she was beginning to talk she had still to maintain her reputation for unintelligibility, to obscure

---

— to herself? to us? — the significance of her entry into the world. At this same time began a new phenomenon which, though unconnected with speech, seemed comparable to her verbal indistinctness. Often, now, she would squint up her eyes, sometimes to the point of actually walking around blind. This would last a few seconds — at most a minute. Her face would have a little smile on it. The action seemed to express a kind of separateness, now she was becoming one of us, and yet it was a game of withdrawal rather than withdrawal itself. She kept it up, with decreasing frequency, over the years — a teasing game which denies withdrawal while affirming it, since it is done with our reaction in mind. We suspect — we cannot know — that the indistinctness of her speech has been similarly functional.

When Elly was two months short of her fifth birthday, the number of words on her vocabulary list was up to fifty-one, more than half in current use. That list was the last I made. That summer she began to learn words rapidly, and by Christmas of that year — the year of our return home — it was clear that there was in effect no limit on the number of common nouns she could acquire. That barrier was down. Anything she could see, actual or pictured, we could name and she could remember and identify. Anything — from aardvark to zebra. Familiarity made no difference. If I had shown her, at bedtime, a unicorn or a hippogriff, she would have known the words next morning. The problem now was no longer to add words to her vocabulary, but to extend the kinds of words she used and to combine them into larger units of meaning.

As she added word to word, her progress seemed astonishing. It hardly seemed that this could be the same Elly who for five years, of all the words we spoke to her, had retained so few. Yet it was. If we had expected that, now Elly had become open to words, everything would be different, our expectations were disappointed. Elly learned new words with the ease of the normal two-year-old she had never been. But she did not learn to talk like a normal two-year-old.

I have just said that there were no limitations on the number of nouns she could acquire. But even among nouns, the easiest words to learn, there were severe limitations on kind. She could learn immediately a word like "igloo" and remember it, although its relevance to her own experience was nonexistent. She could learn and accurately apply the words "oak," "elm," and "maple." Yet words which were, one would think, much closer to her experience she could not understand or learn. Such terms as "home," "sister," "grandmother," "teacher," "friend," or "stranger" were beyond her at five; "friend" and "stranger" are beyond her today. Proper names she acquired with a slowness that seemed clearly related to the weakness of affect. A name, after all, defines the importance of a person, his individual significance. Except for "mama," in occasional use, and "da-da," which made a few rare appearances, Elly got through her first five years without naming a single member of the family. Crude approximations began to appear that fruitful summer of her fifth birthday; in a few months, "Sara," "Becky," "Matt," and "Jill" (the much loved mother's-helper) were semi-intelligible and in frequent use. We could refer to each other by name and Elly would comprehend — "Go to Sara." We could add some of her new nouns: "Take the doll to Jill." People were beginning to be worth naming, although the familiar resistance was still there. At school she hardly looked at the children; she gave no sign that she distinguished them at all. One day, however — she was about five and a half and had been in the class three months — the teacher tried an experiment. Arranging the children in a circle, she asked, "Elly, where's Mark?" Elly, head down, eyes on the floor, jabbed a finger, not at Mark, but in his direction. "Where's Andrea?" Another jab. "Where's Sue?" Another. There were thirteen children. Elly, it turned out, knew them all by name.

It has been speculated that what is impaired in children like Elly is the capacity for abstraction, and it is true that Elly was, and for the most part still is, incapable of giving meaning to words like "love," "hate," "fear," whether used as nouns in their full abstraction or more directly as verbs. But my experience suggests a different formulation — not in terms of abstract and concrete, but in terms of relative and absolute. It is true that an abstract word such as "fun" was beyond her capacity. But she was equally slow to grasp that least abstract of entities, the particularity of a specific individual as manifest to sight and touch and expressed in a name. Moreover, she grasped with especial ease a whole class of word-concepts that are generally considered the product of abstraction, in that the mind in order to arrive at them must proceed from a number of individual experiences, abstract their significant common characteristics, and fix these in a word. Even at two and a half Elly had applied the general term "ball" to objects as different as a flattened rubber oval and a sphere of perforated plastic. This was not very impressive, perhaps — until you reflect that at this time when she had only five or six words, one of them was a product of abstraction. (Balls that *looked* like balls did not elicit the word; Elly was responding to the concept, not the appearance.) At three and a half the idea of a circle was so clear in her mind that she had commandeered music to do duty for the word she did not know. At five and a half, when she was at last ready to learn words in quantity, she learned "triangle," "square," and "rectangle" as easily as at three she had distinguished one block from another. The simple ideas behind the words "Where did Becky go?" or "Do you like candy?" — questions to which an average three-year-old can respond — were beyond her comprehension. But her teachers could say "Draw a red triangle, Elly," and she would do so. When she learned the other words for shape they came so easily it could hardly be called learning. Her sisters showed her them one summer morning, to amuse her: pentagon, hexagon, heptagon, octagon. . . . There was no hesitation, no need for practice or repetition. They spoke the words once; thereafter she simply knew them. Six months later she asked me for "heptagon." I thought she'd said "hexagon"; those we sometimes drew and talked about. Not so. Making a heroic effort at clarity, she said "hep*t*agon — seven sides!" It was as if she had had the concepts for years and had been waiting for the words to describe them. And of course she had; when people had still been invisible to her she had responded to shape and color. Rectangle, a diamond, a square — these words are nothing if not abstract. When ideas were significant to her, Elly had no difficulty with abstraction.

We had not been able to teach her any color words until that fruitful summer of her fifth birthday, although of course we had named colors before, as we had named shapes. As soon as she did learn them, however, she used them to record the niceties of a color sense more acute than even we had suspected.[1] "*Pink*-orange! Green-blue!" This at five — by seven, peacock-green and peacock-blue cars were carefully and enthusiastically distinguished. Color was so important to her that I could use it to call attention to things she would not ordinarily notice. I would say "*purple* mountains," "*brown* horse," and Elly, who had little interest in animals and none in landscape, would see horse or mountain, which had now acquired significance from its color, and learn the word for it. It was not, however, the particular thing which interested her, but the generalized notion of color, which could be applied to any object.

There were many such abstract words she could have learned, but I was concentrating on the human, the ordinary and familiar. Like the Victorian governess whose charge described the shape of the earth as an oblate spheroid, I thought that it was much *nicer* for a little girl to say that it was shaped like an orange. It was more than a year later that it occurred to me to teach her "curved" and "straight." Only one drawing was necessary. Again it had been the word, not the idea, that was lacking. Elly demonstrated that on one of our walks. As we approached a house we had not visited for a year or more, Elly suddenly spoke, loudly and intensely. "*Curved* stairs!" I rang the bell in some excitement. I myself had never noticed the staircase, though I had been here more often than Elly. I might have known I could rely on her. As we entered the hall I saw that it swept up and around in a splendid curve. Certainly her capacity for making this kind of abstraction was not impaired. It was in fact so great that it had been able to sustain itself in her mind over months without the support of any words, to surface when they were supplied.

As we observed Elly's developing speech, it seemed divided into words she could learn instantly once they were pointed out to her, and words she could not learn at all. For a long time there seemed to be no middle ground. What she was able to grasp were absolute terms, whether concrete or abstract — those that reflected concepts that could be defined and understood in themselves. "Box," "cat," "giraffe." "Rectangle," "number," "letter." What she could not understand were relational terms — those that must absorb their full meaning from the situations in which they occur — situations in which the human element plays a part. Elly acquired the word "man" a year before she learned the name of any specific man — "man" is an absolute concept. Once you know the word for a being with short hair and trousers, you need understand no more; from then on, men as such will be recognizable. "Man" is absolute and abstract, but particular men are people, to whom one relates — if one does. "Teacher" is a word which, like "man," is the product of abstraction, but it is first learned in a relational situation: "my teacher." Similarly for "sister," "friend," or "home." It is characteristic of the average child that he learns concepts best in situations in which he can find a personal relation. With Elly, the personal relation seemed at best irrelevant, at worst a hindrance. We wanted to give her words that would enable her to function in the familiar world of a small child. But it was we who defined what a child should find familiar; Elly did not see it our way. Which was more familiar to her, a rectangle or a friend? Her sense of what was important, or unimportant, was simply different from our own.

I recall her, some months past five, looking at a Dick, Jane, and Sally pre-reader with the familiar pictures in series. Dick is painting a chair, in four stages. He has a brush and a can of red paint. I am trying to encourage Elly's new ability to learn names. Pointing to the picture, I say "boy," and meet with comprehension; I then say "Dick." Elly reacts instantly with unusual pleasure; she smiles, she bounces up and down, she repeats the word, she applies it to the succeeding pictures. I am pleased too. For her to learn a personal name so fast is unheard of. But suddenly she gets up and goes to the wall. It is painted blue. "Dick," she says, with emphasis and satisfaction. She moves into another room, goes to another wall, a pink one this time. "Dick." I realize what I should have known; what she has abstracted is not the boy's name, but the concept of "paint," which is also inherent in the picture series, and which to her is both more interesting and more available than the "simple," "direct" idea of a person with a name.

Elly's weakness in understanding human situations was especially marked in her difficulties with personal pronouns. She was six before she used any pronouns at all. This was not as surprising as it might have been; instinctively, in search of sure comprehension, we had spoken of ourselves and her by name, as one does to a two-year-old. But when we did begin, deliberately, to substitute "Would *you*" for "Would Elly like a cookie?" we realized the severity of the problem. The answer, at six, would be, not "yes" (that came much later, not spontaneously, but as a result of careful teaching), or even "I like a cookie," but a simpler echoing: "You like a cookie?" This echolalia, complete to the rising intonation of the question, was, we knew, part of the autistic syndrome; autistic children who, unlike Elly, do speak at a normal age, still speak not flexibly, for communication, but like parrots. Elly had not shown that symptom earlier because she couldn't talk that well. Now she could, and here it was. "Daddy gave you a present," I would say. And as time went on she did more than echo after us; she herself would volunteer the words, with full enjoyment of the fact of the gift. "Daddy give you a present." And now we recognized another specific characteristic of the speech of autistic children. In any statement, "you" is the equivalent of "I" or "me."

There was no confusion or ambiguity in this usage. My experience does not support the conjecture of some psychiatrists that this phenomenon is a sign of the weakness of the ego and the vagueness of its borders. Elly knew who she was. She was "you." The usage was exact, denotative, certain. The whole family understood it. It simply reversed the usual meaning.

It is perfectly logical, when one considers it. Elly thinks her name is "you" because everyone calls her that. No one ever calls her "I." People call themselves "I," and as a further refinement Elly began to call them "I" herself. The reversal of meaning seems nearly impervious to teaching; now, at eight, when Elly says "I like that" it means not that she herself likes it but that her interlocutor does. What can I do? I can tell her to say "kiss me" and reinforce it by kissing her; I can refuse to give her a shove in the swing until she says "push me." But these rare ways of dramatizing the correct usage cannot hold their own against the hundreds of incorrect reinforcements that every day provides. "You made a mistake," I say, and Elly replies, "You made a *mistake!*" "No, *I* didn't make a mistake, *you* made a mistake." "You made a mistake!" Everything one says makes it worse. Twice — on occasions a year apart — Elly has used "me" correctly, to refer to herself. "Becky gave me a book," she said recently, the book in her hands. Hurrying to encourage her, I caught myself saying, "Yes, she did give you a book," thus destroying the effect I had meant to reinforce. I have come to wonder how it is that ordinary two-year-olds can grasp anything so subtle. Yet they do. As mothers know, many of them have this same difficulty as they begin talking, but it rights itself spontaneously in a few weeks. How? As a psychiatrist — not one of ours — remarked to me at a party, the correct use of the first- and second-person pronouns[2] cannot be grasped by logic. The social sense must take over and straighten things out — the sense, or complex of senses, that assesses the relations of people in a given situation, how they think of themselves, and consequently what words they use to identify themselves. Elly's usage is rigidly consistent, severely logical. What it lacks is that social instinct which guides even the dullest of normal children in the labyrinth of personal relations.

This lack affected Elly's acquisition of all the parts of speech. She learned nouns more easily than verbs simply because there are more nouns whose meaning does not depend on surrounding situations. On the veldt, in the zoo, or in an ABC book, a giraffe is a giraffe. "Go" or "come," however, is something else again. It is harder to draw a picture of a verb, as you will find if you try it. Since action requires an actor, and often an object acted upon as well, there is more than one meaning to be abstracted from the simplest verb-picture. Unlike a noun, a verb implies a situation. From it, Elly must draw out the right thing — right not in her terms but in ours. The Dick-paint episode illustrates the ambiguities inherent in pictures — themselves so much simpler than real situations. We soon discovered that the drawing by which we tried to teach "play" might teach "swing" or "girl" instead.

But in spite of this difficulty, verbs slowly followed nouns into Elly's speech. "Walk," indeed, had been one of her first words, used, though not comprehended, before she was two. Four years later it was joined by "look," "jump," and "run," and later, in her seventh year, by such words as "give," "move," "push," "open," "shut," "cut," "hurt" — words easily illustrated in pictures or in action. The children, my good co-therapists, taught her "cough," "laugh," "cry," "scream," and "burp"; she and they took a mischievous delight in testing, usually at the dinner table, her ability to perform these actions on command. "Die," they would say, and Elly, gagging and choking, would collapse onto the floor. Other verbs were more immediately useful. By the time she was eight she responded to "say" — "Say 'butter,' not 'buh-buh,' " — and within a few months she used the verb herself. I found no way of illustrating "see"; Elly was seven before she acquired it, as a kind of tributary of "look," which by that time she could both understand and recognize in print. "Hear" is even worse; I'm not sure she comprehends it even today, and she does not use it. "Know" and "understand" are as yet beyond her grasp, although for three years I have responded to an unintelligible pronunciation with "I don't know" or "I can't understand that." Such nearly indefinable words as "have," "put," "take," and "get" are only now coming into use, and their boundaries overlap in distorted ways. She may suggest, if Daddy is sick, that "Daddy ha' broken arm," using "have" correctly — only to follow it up with "Daddy gi' temperature hundred." And by another strange reversal of normal learning order, these simple words, which children absorb from the environment long before they can manage the symbolic representation of them, Elly has learned only when she was shown them in writing. The visual experience of recognizing letter-combinations has focused her attention on words of which, although she heard them constantly, she seemed unconscious. She had never spoken the word *is* until she was seven, when her kindergarten teacher asked her to write it. Her statements were (and for the most part still are) of the form "Becky *girl,*" "cup *broken.*" Once she saw the word written, however, she began to hear it, and now will use it if she is asked to. The word "equals," however, which functions as a restricted form of "is," she learned with ease and uses freely, volunteering such relatively recondite statements as "seven plus five equals twelve." She has much more difficulty with "seven and five *are* twelve," although "equals" and "plus" come from a set of words proper to age six while "is," like "and," should appear much earlier. The meaning of "equals" is absolute and clear, however, not dependent on the multitudinous shifts of situations.

It is not surprising, then, that Elly made do for years without the verbs that cluster around the ideas of affection, desire, and need. The words "I wanna" characterize the small child, but this child who at two wanted nothing was six before she spoke the word "want" — of course without the "I." In those long intervening years, her desires, never numerous, were conveyed, first by gesture, then — in the expansion of speech at age five — by naming what she wanted. That she should be able to ask for something in words seemed great progress; we hoped — I think we expected — that the realization that language was power would bring with it further appreciation of the joys of communication. And it is true that now, nearing nine, she has a new flexibility in requests; at a single recent mealtime she used four different patterns, not only the primitive "Peanut butter?" but also "Eh' (Elly) ha' vanilla yogurt?" — "Nee[d] egg?" — and "Wan' pie? If words fail to communicate, as with her indistinctness they often do, she will occasionally, if asked, pronounce them better; more likely, she will do as she did at two and a half — lead you to the wanted object, or make your hand approach it. Certainly there is progress here — but the reader who reflects how many ways there are to ask for something, and how often children make use of them, will realize how far there is to go.

And if "want" and "need" came so slowly, what of the verbs whose function it is directly to express emotion? "Love" and "like" lagged behind "want"; although we of course made a point of telling Elly we liked, loved her, she was nearly seven before she herself used the words. Remembering Annie Sullivan, imagining how she made love real to Helen [Keller] in her prison, we had accompanied word with act, and Elly "understood" it. My journal entry records: "'Love' now freely used. Means 'hug,' 'caress.' Will she extend to its full meaning?" Two years later I am still not sure of the answer.

If Elly picked up few words for the positive emotions, for negative ones she acquired fewer still. I remember Becky at eighteen months frightening us with the intensity of her "Go away!" Elly has never said anything like that. To deal with the things she doesn't like she has developed nothing beyond "no" and the anxious, edged voice of her wordless years. I did not think of teaching her "hate," for reasons that, if not wise, are at least obvious. She does use "don't like," but in a way that well illustrates the complex of difficulties confronting us. Beginning with "no like," which though primitive was clear and useful, she progressed to the more conventional expression. But "don't like" is a complex form of words, combining with a contracted negative the irregularities of the verb "do"; its shifts through "doesn't," "don't you," etc., can be reproduced only by a child whose brain has already recorded their patterns. Elly's lazy mouth converts the phrase into "like," preceded by a virtually inaudible "n," thus shearing it of the negative which is its primary indicator of meaning.[3] The words are rendered useless; even to me they are intelligible only in certain contexts and with great good luck. But Elly does not seem to feel the loss; it is a phrase she can do without. Simple avoidance is enough.

The same relational problems affected her acquisition of adjectives — if anything, more severely than nouns and verbs. Her first adjectives have already been described — the color and shape words she learned so readily. "Big" and "little," being relative terms, came less easily. "Long" and "short," "near" and "far," were harder still. She is exploring comparatives now, with a kind of fascination; at bedtime, as I turn off the light, she says "dark, darker, darkest." But she is nearing nine years old. The most striking lack, however, was of course in adjectives that express affect, that should convey her reactions to the world around her. Imagine how important the word "bad" is in the ordinary three-year-old's vocabulary, and then imagine a child with a vocabulary of hundreds of different words who has never needed the idea enough to pull a sound for it out of the environment into her own use. Elly's first use of "bad" (and its companion "good") did not occur until she was six years and four months old; the month before she had learned not only "real" and "pretend" but "left" and "right," concepts which mothers and first-grade teachers know are not easy. The sequence seemed symbolic. I was tempted to elevate it into a definition: an autistic child is one who finds the concepts "left" and "right" more easily available than "good" and "bad." The autistic child is one who, having minimized its interaction with the world, feels no need for words to express opinions about it. When small, it does not request. As it grows, it does not evaluate. "No" is enough.

Elly, at any rate, for years existed in apparent comfort without any value words at all, and though at length she found some uses for "good" and "bad," she has not made much of them. Language for her remains a mode of identification, a means of labeling phenomena; she is as yet not able to use it to express emotion. Small children say "bad" with every gradation of fear and fury; Elly now says "bad" too. But she says it with serene pleasure, to set a phenomenon in its proper category: "Bad can," she says as she collects beer cans from the beach. "Bad dog," she remarks, surveying an overturned garbage can. Elly does not care for dogs. If one comes too close she clings to me; if it jumps up she whimpers. But it would never occur to her to verbalize her emotion. She would not say "bad dog" then.

For all her color sense, she does not say "pretty," "lovely," or "beautiful," all words which she hears often. Nor does she say "ugly." She gets much more mileage out of "dodecagon" and "carnation-pink." She has acquired "right" and "wrong," but only in the unambiguous, objective sense of "correct" and "incorrect" ("Wrong foot," she says, deliberately putting left shoe on right foot). She enjoys using them; she has always been amused by mistakes. The summer she turned seven she acquired "sad" and "happy"; she sang the "don't be sad" song the children made for her, and when I drew a sad face and a happy one, Elly herself volunteered "mouth down" and "mouth up." She knew what sad and happy looked like. Perhaps she had known for a long time, as she had known curved and straight; perhaps not. At any rate, the words had made the ideas usable, and now and then she used them. We and the children would reinforce them by simple dramatics. We'd say "Sara is sad," and Sara would cry crocodile tears, to Elly's amusement. Elly would say "Be happy," and Sara would brighten up. The comprehension of these crude approximations of emotion was light-years beyond her old imperviousness. Yet they bore the same relation to the subtleties of actual emotions as a road map bears to the colors and forms of a living landscape.

"Young/old" and the adverbs "fast/slow" came as she neared eight. "Funny" she got from a word-card; though she laughs a lot, it applies as yet only to clowns. I taught her "tired" and "resting"; she picked up "sick," and "feel better." A skimpy list, and I may have overlooked a word or two that should be on it. But it is virtually complete. If she had said — or shown signs of comprehending — anything like "worried," "friendly," "dangerous," "angry," "mad," "afraid," "scared," or "nice," be sure I would have remembered it.

Prepositions are by definition words that show relationships. As late as six and a half Elly comprehended no prepositions, and of course used none. By this time she was well able to respond to such simple commands as "Bring me the pencil" — but in spite of her uncanny sense of orientation, she was still unable to understand the simple descriptions that answer the question "Where is it?" — a question that she never asked. Where is the pencil? *Under* the bed, *in* the drawer, *behind* the bookcase. Useful words, these; in her seventh year I decided they were too useful to wait for. I couldn't find a set of pictured preposition word-cards,[4] so I made my own. With these, Elly learned the printed words overnight, the spoken ones in a day or two. I taught only four or five of the most useful and easiest to illustrate; she understood them in commands, and gradually began to introduce a few into her own language. Such short words as "in" and "on" are easily slurred, however, and hard for the hearer to recognize. Though Elly's primitive "spoon [is on the] *table*" gave way to "spoon-uh-table," her effective communication had not advanced very far. Later — after seven — when she understood "say," I could ask her to "say it better," but that was in the future. And even then there was a great gulf between speaking intelligibly on request and speaking intelligibly habitually.

But the problems presented by these words were easy compared to the problem of conveying the untidy miscellany of adverbs, articles, and conjunctions, the unsung heroes that give our conversation its preciser meanings. These words are relational in their very nature. But. If. Whether. Maybe. Because. Soon. When. Yet. Like. Except. The words seem unimportant until you try to imagine doing without them, and simple until you try to find ways to teach them. Teach them? No one teaches such words — the small child seems to draw them out of the air. But Elly did not even pick up "and," the simplest connective of them all. She was seven before I thought of a way to convey it, and characteristically it was in terms of color. Our neighbors had a gray house with a blue trim; Elly called it "blue-gray house." Though Elly might verbally confuse blue-gray with blue-and-gray, I knew she was incapable of confusing them in actuality. So I drew two houses, colored them, labeled them, and pronounced the words. From then on she could understand "and," and read it on occasion. When pressed, she could even produce a sound to represent it. But who can draw "if" or "when"? Who can draw "but" itself?

It is words like these that convert vocabulary into langauge. A collection of words — even a large collection — is not equivalent to speech. They must be combined.

The average child begins, like Elly, with isolated words, and sometime between a year and a half and two starts to put these words together. Elly was nearing six before we heard her speak two words in combination. "Laura *girl,*" she said of the small child next door, and this kind of statement, three years later, remains characteristic of her speech. As with a normal child, but much more slowly, two-word combinations gave way to larger aggregates — three, six . . . as the years passed she might sometimes say eight words together, with obvious logical connection. But these were not normal sentences — the almost total absence of articles, conjunctions, prepositions, verb-inflections for tense[5] or person, and the verb "to be" ensures that though her language grows in complexity she is still speaking pidgin. And it is a distorted pidgin at that, for Elly's grasp of word order, in English the most powerful indicator of meaning, is very weak. When a normal child says "Give Becky a green lollipop," we know who is to get the candy; it has been signaled by the word order. When Elly says it, however (dropping, of course, the article), it may mean what it appears to, but may also mean that Becky is doing the giving. "Dr. Mama doll gi' medicine" is meant to mean that Dr. Mama is dosing the doll. The order of the words is scrambled, and the listener must interpret from the context. Elly will say today, "No four find daddy peanut"; it means "I can't find four big peanuts." Responding to a picture of a hat on a table she may get it right — or she may say "table on a hat." She says she will "grow be ten" — I tell her, as I can these days, "Don't forget the 'to' — 'grow *to* be eleven.' " Good-naturedly she does as she is told: "Elly grow *be to* eleven," she says. Her word order is correct more often than not, certainly — but that is not very much to say of the extremely simple speech of an eight-year-old child.

NOTES

1. The most striking confirmation of her color-intelligence occurred when she was six. I had bought several boxes of powder paint for her, and mixed small quantities on demand, so she could paint at home as well as at school. The colors, of course, came out pure — plain red, blue, black — and Elly seemed quite satisfied with them. When we returned to the store for more she asked for white, and we brought a box home and put it on the shelf with the others. A week later she asked

for paint, and when I asked what color replied "pink," "light blue" — colors she had never before requested. It was obvious to her that we could now make these colors, that white was the ingredient needed to produce pastels — something many normal six-year-olds have to be taught.

2. For the record, I should say that Elly did not become conscious of third-person pronouns until she was nearly eight, when she spontaneously picked out "they" from a pile of word-cards as the one she wanted to learn next. The same week added "he" and "she." But though she can recognize them, she has said them only once or twice, and is only beginning to comprehend them securely. Ultimately, it seems plain she will acquire them, but there is nothing natural about the process.

3. We have other indications that she lacks the sense of what sounds carry the burden of communication. Soon after she learned "without" she dropped the "with"; nothing will induce her to put it back. Her indistinct pronunciation drops essential indicators of meaning; she forms no plurals and inflects no verbs because she will not pronounce a final "s" or "d."

4. Later I ran across some by chance. But this is the sort of thing a good counseling service would make available to parents.

5. Her first use of the past tense came the summer she was eight. There have been few since. The two instances in which she has conveyed an idea of futurity are instructive: told I'd come in a minute, she said "Gi' minute Mama come"; in autumn, as we speak of storm-windows, she says "Be winter, ha' 'tor' window." Her comprehension of tenses is limited; asked "Did you have your lunch?" she will reply "Yes" when she hasn't, because she thinks I've asked "Do you want your lunch?" Tense understanding requires situational understanding. "Sara little. Sara grow bigger" can lead to "was" and "grew."

III EARLY SCHOOL YEARS

With the beginning of schooling at about age five, a new form of socializing begins to affect the developing child. To be sure, during infancy and toddlerhood, the culture already exerts pervasive influences on the child — ranging from the styles of parenting to the models of language and play to the presentation of sex-role expectations. But until the child spends a good deal of time each day with teachers and peers, the society's influence is largely mediated by the child's parents. The beginning of schooling marks a real turning point because the child becomes responsible to more people and is increasingly influenced by a larger segment of society — teachers, peers, and the mass media.

Two important issues arise at this age: one in the cognitive realm, the other in the emotional-social area. The cognitive issues have to do with the child's ability to learn — his or her cognitive capacities, native intelligence, and ease with schooling. The emotional-social issue has to do with the acquisition of behaviors, particularly the capacity to control aggressive impulses, that will enable the child to get along with others.

The cognitive issue is addressed by Ellen Markman's study concerned with the child's awareness of his ability to comprehend. Children were given verbal instructions with some crucial information missing. Markman wanted to know at what age children realize that they cannot perform the task with only the information they have. Clear differences exist between first and third graders; Markham attributes early insensitivity to a lack of constructive or active processing.

Margaret Donaldson speaks to the problems faced by children when the demands of the curriculum are not congruent with the abilities of the child. She recasts some of Piaget's classic experiments in terms that are sensible to the child and shows how the child knows both more and less than many psychologists have believed.

A child's success in school depends on certain capacities that eventually evolve in every child, such as the decline of egocentrism and the mastery of language. However, school success is also crucially affected by the child's general intellectual level, which will determine how much the child can eventually learn and at what pace. As a rough and ready measure of this capacity, psychologists and educators have traditionally relied on the IQ (intelligence quotient) test. But whether or not the IQ test measures intelligence and what exactly determines a child's IQ are questions that are far from settled.

Indeed, the most controversial issue in all of developmental psychology may be the relative importance of heredity and environment in the determination of a child's IQ score. Some psychologists believe that a great deal of the child's ultimate development is determined by the child's genes, and it is only a matter of time until his or her unique characteristics appear. Others believe with equal fervor that the child is more malleable, that the culture and the individuals around the child make him or her into what they will. Although it is unlikely that either extreme position is correct, much energy has been devoted to determining the relative plausibility of each. IQ tests are often used in these discussions because our society attributes great importance to the test and because it is believed that the test predicts academic and wordly success.

Stephen J. Gould reviews a recent controversy over the relative contribution by genes to IQ scores. He indicates that the heredity component of the IQ score actually varies in different populations: it is highest in white middle-class groups and low in other racial and socioeconomic groups. He then argues that racial differences in IQ scores are probably not due to genetic differences. It appears that the individual's genetic potential for intellectual achievement cannot be assessed in a vacuum. Rather, it is essential to consider the environment in which that potential will unfold.

Just as intelligence looms in the cognitive realm during these years, so friendships become of prime importance in the social-emotional area. Children begin to understand themselves through the intimate relationships they have with their peers. It is only recently that psychologists have begun to study the development of friendships, and Zick Rubin's article traces the feelings that children have about each other from the preschool child's objective name acknowledgment to the adolescent's sense of what motivates someone else. A decline of egocentrism coupled with a rise of intimacy and a renewed sense of self characterizes the progression of friendships.

In these years the effects of the media become more pervasive as well. Toddlers might well watch TV, but the timing and the program selection are determined by the parent. Now, in the early school years, the child chooses. There has been a great deal of research about television. In the 50s the research had a sociological bent: What effects did this box in every livingroom have on the social behavior of families? Did TV viewing interfere with family outings or with school work? This was followed by a number of studies that looked at the effect of specific content on children's behavior. Vioence and aggression were the primary targets of research; prosocial behavior was examined only slightly. But the difficulty of reproducing "real world" effects in a short-lived experimental setting led to modest results at best. Only very recently have psychologists begun to examine the effects of the media on the child's comprehension of content. Laurene Meringoff's study compares children's understanding of an unfamiliar story when read from a book and when watched on a TV screen. The different reactions have implications for any method of teaching.

The capacity to control aggressive impulses is of great importance during these years. The two case studies closing this section are directly concerned with this particular ability. In the tradition of behaviorism, B. F. Skinner believes that a child's impulses are best controlled by careful reinforcement of correct responses — a technique he terms "behavioral engineering." In the selection from *Walden Two,* a utopian novel, he shows how jealousy is eliminated and self-control is established by means of careful reinforcement of children's behavior and a planned sequence of activity.

The problems of aggressive behavior are vividly portrayed in Dorothy Baruch's case study of a 7-year-old boy who is made sick by pent-up fears and aggression. How he releases his defenses and faces his innermost desires and thoughts is a moving, penetrating, and somewhat extreme picture, but it serves to illuminate aspects of normal development.

Ellen M. Markman

REALIZING THAT YOU DON'T UNDERSTAND: A PRELIMINARY INVESTIGATION

ABSTRACT: This paper raises the question of how people become aware of their own comprehension failure. It is argued that a partial answer to this question can be derived from recent demonstrations that comprehension involves constructive processing. People might detect certain types of problems in their comprehension as a result of information obtained while engaged in constructive processing. To the extent that children are failing to engage in such processing, they would not have this source of information and consequently would be misled into thinking they comprehend material they in fact do not understand. In 2 studies, first through third graders were presented with instructions made obviously incomprehensible by deleting information needed to understand how to perform the task. Third graders noticed the inadequacy of the instructions with minimal probing. In contrast, first graders frequently had to be urged to enact the instructions before becoming aware of the problems. When demonstrations of the tasks accompanied the instructions, children more readily indicated that they had failed to understand. Since demonstrations and enactments both reduce the necessity for mental processing, these results support the hypothesis that children's initial insensitivity to their own comprehension failure is due to a relative lack of constructive processing.

At first sight it might seem that the realization that one has not understood something is an automatic process which requires little effort or complex cognitive processing. In this view, incoming information would be experienced as not understood in much the same more or less automatic way that the unfamiliarity of a word is detected. In the case of a novel word, a sense of unfamiliarity could be sufficient to indicate a failure to comprehend.

This work was supported in part by a Spencer Foundation grant. I would like to express my appreciation to Ms. Mary Ostrom and the staff of Ormondale Elementary School, Portola Valley, California; to Ms. Ethel Mahan and the staff of Montclaire Elementary School, Los Altos, California; and to Mr. Bernie La Casse and the staff of Lincoln Elementary School, Cupertino, California, for their cooperation. I thank C. J. Sengul and Debbie Cornelius for their assistance in running subjects and John Flavell for his comments on this manuscript.

SOURCE: From Ellen M. Markman, "Realizing That You Don't Understand: A Preliminary Investigation," *Child Development* 48, 1977, pp. 986–992.

The unfamiliar-word analogy may be very misleading, however. Certainly not all comprehension is limited to the processes involved in understanding a single word, so it is not likely that all comprehension failure could be signaled by unfamiliarity. In the absence of a theory of comprehension, it is not possible to specify fully the additional mechanisms which could indicate comprehension failure. However, hypotheses regarding one of these mechanisms may be derived from the findings of Bransford, Barclay, and Franks (1972) and Bransford and Franks (1971). These investigators have demonstrated that during prose comprehension people engage in a variety of "constructive" processes which operate upon and transform the original linguistic input. Based on these findings concerning the normal course of comprehension, it seems reasonable to expect that comprehension failure could be signaled by some problem encountered during the constructive processing. An illustration of this hypothetical mechanism as applied to instructions is considered below.

Instructions can be viewed as a series of steps which result in a given goal. To understand instructions fully, one needs to understand how from an initial state the actions to be executed will successively transform the resulting states until the goal is reached. A person who mentally computes these successive transformations is engaging in a type of constructive processing. A person who simply listens to the instructions without mentally applying them is processing the information at a more superficial level. Consider the case in which both of these types of people might fail to understand instructions. Such failure could derive from a large number of problems. To name a few, the individual might not have enough information about how to apply a given transformation; the transformation might seem inapplicable, given the state it has to operate upon; or application of the sequence of steps might not lead to the desired goal. A person who actually confronts one of these problems could presumably be led to the realization that he or she has not understood the instructions. A person who simply listens to the instructions would not have encountered these problems and thus would not realize that he or she had failed to understand.

An implication of this view is that when people take a passive approach to comprehension they may be unaware of their own failure to understand the information. Passive processing might result in a delusion of comprehension. When current work in cognitive development is taken into account (Brown 1975; Flavell 1970; Flavell, Friedrichs, & Hoyt 1970; Paris & Lindauer 1976; Markman, Note 1), this analysis suggests that children in particular may be frequently misled into thinking that they understand material which they have in fact failed to comprehend.

The current work referred to emphasizes two related areas concerned with what might be termed "executive processes" (Miller, Galanter, & Pribram 1960). The first is the view that with development individuals come to take an active, self-directive role in certain areas of cognition. The second, an outgrowth of the first, is that individuals develop the ability to monitor and evaluate their own cognitive processes. The clearest instance of these dual trends can be seen in memory development. Older children utilize a variety of strategies to facilitate the encoding and retrieval of material, while younger children approach memory tasks in a more passive manner (see reviews by Brown [1975] and Flavell [1970]). Information regarding memory monitoring is still limited, but the existing data suggest that older children are more aware of their own memorial capacities and are more likely to engage in metamemorial activities (Flavell & Wellman 1977; Kreutzer, Leonard & Flavell 1975; Markman, Note 1). It is likely that two analogous developmental trends may be taking place with respect to comprehension. Evidence is beginning to appear which indicates that developmental changes in prose comprehension may be a function of the extent and type of processing children engage in (Paris & Lindauer 1976). At present, however, there is no systematic research concerning developmental changes in comprehension monitoring. The purpose of this paper is to provide a preliminary investigation of this topic.

STUDY I

Since the procedures used in this study are new, a brief justification and rationale for the methodology will be provided. In order to avoid problems in assessing individual differences in comprehension, experimental materials were made to be incomprehensible to all subjects. Given the certainty that children could not fully understand the material, the question of interest was whether the children realized that they had not understood. In addition, the tasks were designed to be relatively simple, in that the distortion of the material was made very obvious from an adult perspective. Children were presented with instructions on how to perform a task, and crucial information necessary for executing the task was deleted.

The measure of whether the children realized that they had not understood how to perform the task was whether or not they asked a question or requested more information. Of course failure to ask a question can be due to a variety of factors other than the one of interest. In anticipation of this problem, several precautions were taken. First, the children's participation was enlisted by asking them to serve as consultants to someone who was writing instructions for children. They were told that their advice on the clarity and completeness of the instructions was needed. Thus the children could attribute their failure to comprehend to problems inherent in the material rather than to their own shortcomings. Second, one of the instructions concerned how to perform a magic trick. Magic was selected not just for its motivational advantage but also because a very salient aspect of magic is its incomprehensibility. The enjoyment of magic derives from the fact that it is not understood. Thus magic instructions were expected to maximize the children's realization that they had not understood the instructions and to minimize their reluctance to admit that they had not understood.

Method

Subjects. Twelve children from each of grades 1–3 of a public school in Portola Valley, California, served as subjects. The mean ages of the subjects were 6-2, 7-4, and 8-6 for the three grades, respectively. Half the children in each grade were male.

Procedure. Before the start of the experiment, the experimenter introduced herself to the class and announced that she was attempting to find effective ways to teach children how to play games and perform magic tricks. She emphasized that she needed the students' help in determining the adequacy of her instructions and that students would be asked to suggest improvements in the instructions. Each child was seen individually and administered the two tasks (game and magic trick) in counterbalanced order. Before each task, children were reminded to inform the experimenter if there was anything at all she failed to state clearly enough or forgot to tell them. The procedure for each of the tasks is described below.

GAME. Children were shown alphabet cards which were made by gluing purchased plastic letters onto blank cards with colored borders.

The experimenter explained that equal numbers of cards are dealt to each player, dealt four cards to herself and four to the subject, and emphasized that both the experimenter and child had the exact same number of cards. The following instructions were then given: "We each put our cards in a pile. We both turn over the top card in our pile. We look at cards to see who has the special card. Then we turn over the next card in our pile to see who has the special card this time. In the end the person with the most cards wins the game." There was no mention of what the "special card" might be. The experimenter then went through the following series of probes, recording the subject's comments verbatim. Once the subject asked an adequate question (to be discussed below), the procedure was terminated. Upon termination, the experimenter apologized for not explaining the game very well, agreed with the child that the explanation was faulty, thanked the child for his or her help, and promised to revise and reword the instructions and to return to the class to explain the game when the instructions were revised. The 10 probes were:

1. "That's it. Those are my instructions."
2. "What do you think?"
3. "Do you have any questions?"
4. "Did I tell you everything you need to know to play the game?"
5. "Did I forget to tell you anything?"
6. "Can you tell me how to play?" (The experimenter prompts if necessary.)
7. "Did I tell you everything you need to know to play the game?"
8. "Do you think you can play? Let's play; you go first."
9. "Did I forget to tell you anything?"
10. "Are you sure? Did I tell you everything you need to know?"

MAGIC TRICK. The experimenter first demonstrated the trick as follows: an ordinary cup, plate, penny, and piece of paper were shown to the child. The cup, which was shown to be empty, was placed on the table and the plate placed on top of the cup. The penny was then wrapped in a piece of paper, placed on top of the plate, and pushed through the plate into the cup. (The penny could be heard dropping into the cup.) Then the empty paper and cup which now contained the penny were presented for inspection. While the trick was being performed, the experimenter gave a commentary which simply described what she was doing. After the demonstration, the following instructions were given: "Here's the trick. When you wrap the penny you only pretend to wrap it. It really falls in your lap like this." (The experimenter demonstrates.) The experimenter failed to mention how the penny, now in her lap, could end up in the cup. After the instructions were given, essentially the same 10 probes used in the game were asked. Once the child asked a question, the procedure was stopped, and the experimenter apologized and promised to return to the class to demonstrate the trick.

Scoring. When a child asked a clearly adequate question (or made a relevant statement), the procedure was terminated. A child was given a separate score for the magic and game conditions which indicated at what point in the procedure he or she asked an appropriate question. The scores ranged from 1 to 11. Scores from 1 to 10 corresponded to the 10 probes in the procedure. An 11 indicated that the child never asked a question.

A child's question was considered adequate if it indicated that the child knew he or she did not understand the instructions (in whole or in part) or that the experimenter had omitted information, etc. Examples of questions considered adequate are "I don't get how to play it," "I don't know how it gets into the cup," "How do you know who has the special card?" and "What is the special card?"

Some questions children asked were ambiguous in this respect (and thus the probing procedure continued). Since these children might have been indicating a failure to understand, a second scoring system was devised, giving children credit for these questions. Examples of questions considered adequate under the more liberal criterion but not the conservative are "Is there anything else to this game?" and "Is that all?"

Results and Discussion

Table 1 presents the mean conservative scores for each item by grade. Preliminary analyses revealed no effects of sex or task order, so these variables were omitted from further consideration. Planned comparisons revealed no differences in the scoring criteria at any grade, so the only analyses to be reported involve the conservative criterion. The findings using the liberal criterion are fully comparable.

A grade (3) × item (2) repeated-measures ANOVA was performed on these data. The main effect for grade was significant, $F(2,33) = 10.21$, $p < .01$. Paired comparisons indicated that first graders differed significantly from third graders, $p < .05$. The main effect for item was significant, with the magic task being easier than the game task, $F(1,33) = 12.71$, $p < .01$. There were no significant interactions.

These results clearly indicate that older children realize that the information is incomplete before younger children do. Considerably more probing is necessary before first graders ask a question. However, a more powerful conclusion can be drawn when the qualitative nature of the data is taken into account. Namely, it appears that first graders must be induced to repeat an instruction or even to execute it before they realize anything is wrong.

On the game task, four first graders, two second graders, and no third grader failed to ask a question at all. Of the eight first graders to ask a question, all except one had to attempt to play the game and fail before asking the question (i.e., they received a score of 8, 9, or 10). Five of the 10 second graders and only two of the 12 third graders had to experience failure before asking a question. The difference in frequency between first and third graders is significant by a Fischer's exact probability test, $p < .05$.

The pattern of results was similar but less extreme for the magic task. Only one child from each grade failed to ask a question at all. But fully seven of the 11 first graders who asked a question waited at least until they repeated the instructions. Four of these seven did not ask a question until after observing their failure to perform the trick. In contrast, all of the 11 third graders who asked a question did so before being asked to repeat the instructions, let alone perform the trick. In fact the modal score for third graders was 1. The difference in frequency of first- and third-grade children who had at least to repeat instructions before asking a question was significant by a Fischer's test, $p < .05$. Second graders looked much like third graders on this task, with one child having to fail at performing the trick and

Table 1. MEANS AND STANDARD DEVIATIONS OF SCORES FOR STUDY I BY GRADE AND ITEM

	Item			
	Magic		*Game*	
Grade	*Mean*	*SD*	*Mean*	*SD*
1	5.17	3.93	8.92	2.94
2	2.92	3.63	6.17	4.04
3	1.83	2.87	3.08	2.71

one more needing to repeat the instructions.

These qualitative differences lend support to the hypothesis that young children are processing the material at a relatively superficial level. The findings suggest that the youngest children in this study are failing to execute the instructions mentally, and consequently they do not notice the problems. In contrast, when the children attempt to perform the instructions, they literally confront the problems and then become aware of their failure to understand.

It is possible that the significant item effect also supports this interpretation. Though there are many differences between the two tasks which could contribute to their differential difficulty, there is one difference which may be relevant in this regard.[1] Children actually saw the magic trick demonstrated before they were given instructions on how to perform it. In contrast, verbal instructions constituted the only information children were given concerning the game. A demonstration of a task might serve a function similar to the child's own attempts to follow the instructions. In Study II I examine this possibility by comparing children's performance when the tasks are presented verbally with performance when the verbal instructions are accompanied by a demonstration.

STUDY II

Method

Subjects. Twenty first graders and 20 third graders from an elementary school in Portola Valley, California, served as subjects. Twenty second graders from a comparable population in Cupertino, California, also served as subjects. The mean ages of the first through third graders were 6-5, 7-5, and 8-8, respectively. Half the children in each grade were male.

Procedure. Children were randomly assigned to one of two conditions, "demonstrate" or "verbal," with the restriction that the two groups be equated for grade and sex. Children in both groups received a magic trick and a game task in counterbalanced order. The only difference in the procedure for the groups was in whether or not the tasks were demonstrated for the child. The verbalizations of the experimenter were identical for both groups. Details of the procedure are given below.

Magic trick. In the demonstrate condition, the subject was informed that he or she would see the trick and then be told how to do it. The trick was then performed just as in the previous studies. While performing the trick, the experimenter described what she was doing. This description was identical to that given in the verbal condition described below.

In the verbal condition, the subject was informed he or she would be told what the trick looked like and then how to do it. The description of the trick was: "I have an empty cup and a penny and a piece of paper. I take the plate and put it on top of the empty cup. Then I wrap the penny in the paper and put it on top of the plate. Then I push until the penny goes right through the plate into the cup. But the penny does not break the plate, and there is no hole in the plate at all."

After the trick was demonstrated and described or only described, the instructions on how to perform the trick were given. The instructions for both groups were a slightly expanded version of those used in Study I (see n. 1): "When you wrap the penny, you only pretend to wrap it. It really falls in your lap like this. Then you take the paper and put it on top of the plate and push until the penny falls into the cup." Following the instructions, the probes were given as in Study I.

GAME. In the demonstrate condition, children were told they would first see what the game looked like and then be told how to play. While describing what she was doing, the experimenter held up the cards, dealt them, and put them in a pile. She then said, "The game looks like this." She lifted the top card from each pile, looked at them without letting the child see, and placed both cards face down beside either the child or herself. She continued this procedure for four turns.

In the verbal condition, children were told they would hear what the game looked like and then how to play it. The initial description of the game was the following: "We play with these cards. Each card has a letter on it. We each get one card at a time until all the cards are used up. We each put our cards in a pile. We both have the exact same number of cards in our pile."

After the demonstration and/or description, the instructions on how to play were given. These instructions were identical with those in Study I. The probing procedure was identical with that used in the previous study.

Table 2. MEAN SCORES FOR STUDY II BY GRADE, ITEM, AND CONDITION

		Condition	
Grade	*Item*	*Demonstrate*	*Verbal*
1	Magic	5.40	7.30
	Game	7.60	8.50
2	Magic	3.70	5.50
	Game	6.10	7.60
3	Magic	2.20	3.70
	Game	2.90	4.60

Results and Discussion

The data were coded and scored using the conservative criterion of Study I. The mean scores for each item by condition and grade are presented in Table 2. A grade (3) × condition (2) × item (2) ANOVA was performed on these data. The essential findings of Study I were replicated. There was, as before, a significant main effect of grade, $F(2,54) = 10.93$, $p < .01$. Paired comparisons revealed that the first and second graders were both significantly different from third graders, $p < .05$. As in Study I, the magic task was significantly easier than the game task, $F(1,54) = 7.92$, $p < .01$. There were no significant interactions, all F's < 1.

Furthermore, the qualitative analyses yielded results which were quite comparable to the first study. On the game task, 16 of the 20 first graders asked a relevant question. Thirteen of these 16 did not ask a question until after being asked to execute the instructions. In contrast, only four of the 18 third graders who asked a question had to enact the instructions, $\chi^2(1) = 9.56$, $p < .01$. On the magic task, nine of the 18 first graders who asked a question had to attempt to perform the trick, compared with four out of 20 third graders, $p < .05$ by Fischer's exact probability test.

Since there was no condition × item interaction, the differential difficulty of the items in Study I cannot be attributed to the demonstration of the magic trick. However, the present study does provide support for the hypothesis that superficial processing was preventing children from noticing their failure to comprehend. The main effect of condition was significant, with the demonstration condition producing superior performance, $F(1,54) = 5.22$, $p < .05$.

GENERAL DISCUSSION

In these two studies, first graders gave very little indication of being aware that their comprehension of instructions was faulty. Their failure to ask for more information existed in situations in which information was quite blatantly absent and despite several probes designed to elicit such questions without embarrassment to the child.

Clearly the tasks of the present study are limited, but they were designed to be exceptionally simple. The distortions of material were obvious; they were omissions of material rather than, for example, ambiguity, vagueness, or inconsistency; and they concerned instructions on how to do something, so that the criteria for evaluation with respect to the goal are relatively straightforward. In addition, children were explicitly instructed to check the material for its comprehensibility, an instruction designed to help overcome production deficiencies (Flavell 1970). For these reasons, it is striking that first graders generally performed so poorly. For these same reasons, one should not be overimpressed by the good performance of third graders. On these very simple tasks, they performed well, but it is certainly possible that their performance would deteriorate as the task demands increased.

Though it is fairly clear that the young children in this study had difficulty in realizing that the instructions were inadequate, it is considerably less clear what factors are responsible for their poor performance. The present hypothesis is that it is due to a relative absence of constructive processing. The children appear to be processing material at a relatively superficial level, not really attempting to execute the instructions mentally or determine the relationship between the instructions and goal. As a consequence, they are left unaware of the inadequacy of the instructions.

Two aspects of the data suggest that this interpretation of the children's performance is a reasonable one. Both relate to the argument that, if the child's lack of awareness is due to his or her failure to execute the appropriate mental processing, by removing the necessity for such processing one should be able to facilitate performance. The findings of the second study, that children may be more likely to notice problems in the instructions when the task has been demonstrated, can be fitted into this framework. The actual demonstration of the task can serve as a partial substitute for the mental processes. The child does not have to infer mentally the results of applying each transformation, since he has previously seen some of them enacted.

The second line of evidence is that in both of the studies it was common to find the young children having to enact the instructions before realizing that they were incomplete. When children attempt to perform an instruction, they are forced into processing it more thoroughly. Again, they actually see the results of the transformations and literally confront the problems with the instructions rather than having to infer them. The fact that children are much more likely to notice problems in the instructions when they are forced to process them thoroughly suggests that their initial failure to notice the problems was due to superficial processing.

Although the present explanation for children's insensitivity to their own failure to comprehend must be considered speculative, the implications of this insensitivity seem clear. With an awareness that one has failed to comprehend instructions, for example, an individual might reexamine the series of steps, search for possible misinterpretations, ask for clarification of material, etc., until the problem is resolved. Given the present findings, it is hard to imagine that deficiencies like those evidenced by the first graders would not have an impact on their level of comprehension proper. If individuals are willing to tolerate such gaps in their knowledge, it is unlikely that they would be moved to search for clarification of material. Thus an awareness of one's own comprehension failure provides a basis for initiating appropriate remedial procedures to ensure that comprehension is achieved. Consequently individual and developmental differences in sensitivity to one's comprehension failure will result in differences in the quality of comprehension itself.

AUTHOR'S NOTE

1. One difference between the tasks was that the instructions for the magic trick were briefer than those for the game. It seemed possible that the brevity of the magic instructions might have served as a cue that the instructions were incomplete. This possibility was tested in a separate study by expanding the game instructions and abbreviating the magic instructions. The results of this study were comparable to those of Study I. No differences were found as a consequence of changing the length of the instructions.

REFERENCE NOTE

1. Markman, E. M. Factors affecting the young child's ability to monitor his memory. Unpublished doctoral dissertation, University of Pennsylvania, 1973.

REFERENCES

Bransford, J. D.; Barclay, J. B.; & Franks, J. J. Sentence memory: a constructive versus interpretive approach. *Cognitive Psychology,* 1972, *3,* 193–209.

Bransford, J. D., and Franks, J. J. The abstraction of linguistic ideas. *Cognitive Psychology,* 1971, *2,* 331–350.

Brown, A. L. The development of memory: knowing, knowing about knowing, and knowing how to know. In H. W. Reese (Ed.), *Advances in child development and behavior.* Vol. *10.* New York: Academic Press, 1975.

Flavell, J. H. Developmental studies of mediated memory. In H. W. Reese & L. P. Lipsitt (Eds.), *Advances in child development and behavior.* Vol. *5.* New York: Academic Press, 1970.

Flavell, J. H.; Friedrichs, A. G.; & Hoyt, J. D. Developmental changes in memorization processes. *Cognitive Psychology,* 1970, *1,* 324–340.

Flavell, J. H., & Wellman, H. M. Metamemory. In R. V. Kail, Jr., & J. W. Hagen (Eds.), *Perspectives on the development of memory and cognition.* Hillsdale, N.J.: Erlbaum, 1977.

Kreutzer, M. A.; Leonard, C.; & Flavell, J. H. An interview study of children's knowledge about memory. *Monographs of the Society for Research in Child Development,* 1975, *40* (1, Serial No. 159).

Miller, G. A.; Galanter, E.; & Pribram, K. H. *Plans and the structure of behavior.* New York: Holt, Rinehart & Winston, 1960.

Paris, S. G., & Lindauer, B. K. The role of inference in children's comprehension and memory for sentences. *Cognitive Psychology,* 1976, *8,* 217–227.

23

Margaret Donaldson

THE MISMATCH BETWEEN SCHOOL AND CHILDREN'S MINDS

Visitors to any elementary school would notice that most children in the kindergarten and first-grade classrooms are excited, happy, and eager to learn. But if they were to continue their visit to classrooms of the higher grades, they would find many who are unhappy, unresponsive and bored. Yet from infancy all normal human beings show signs of a keen desire to learn — a desire that does not appear to depend on any reward apart from the satisfaction of achieving competence and control. This desire is still strong in most children when they enter school. How is it that something that starts off so well regularly ends up so badly? Why do many children learn to hate school?

The answer cannot be that most children are stupid after the age of six, nor can it be that teachers enjoy making children miserable. Recent research into the nature of children's language and thinking can help us to see what goes wrong.

It is now clear that we have tended both to underestimate children's competence as thinkers and to overestimate their understanding of language.

The underestimations are in large measure a result of the theories of the most influential of all students of child development, Jean Piaget. From his experiments with young children he concluded that until the age of about seven, though competent in practical skills, children are extremely limited thinkers.

The overestimation of children's understanding of language is, in part, a result of the theories of linguist Noam Chomsky. In the 1960s Chomsky caused a wave of excitement among psychologists by drawing attention to the significance of one simple fact: Children who are only two or three years old can utter complicated sentences *that they have never heard before.*

Since these sentences generally conform to the rules of syntax, the children must, in some sense, know them. And even sentences that are not fully correct by adult standards still show that rules of some kind are at work in their construction. In fact the errors frequently reveal rules, as when "bringed" is used instead of "brought." We can be fairly sure that children who say "bringed" have not heard adults say it. They must have generated the form for themselves by applying the rule for forming past tenses in weak verbs in English.

The implications of these facts presented psychologists with a highly challenging question: How is it possible for a young child to master such a complex system of rules? There seemed to be only two possibilities: The child either has remarkable skills as a thinker, or some very special skills as a language learner. Chomsky argued for the second of these explanations. He proposed that human beings are endowed with a highly specialized faculty for learning language, which he called a language-acquisition de-

SOURCE: From Margaret Donaldson, "The Mismatch Between School and Children's Minds," *Human Nature* 2, March 1979, pp. 60–67. Reprinted by permission of the author.

vice. This idea enjoyed widespread popularity for a while, and at least part of the reason was that the other explanation seemed implausible. There was evidence around — weighty, respectable evidence obtained by careful systematic study and experiment — that appeared to imply that the young child is not much of a thinker.

Yet there was other evidence, freely available but largely neglected, that pointed to a different conclusion. Anyone who talks with young children seriously and attentively knows that they say a great many thoughtful and seemingly intelligent things. The curious thing is that while so much attention was being paid to the grammatical sophistication of children's speech, very little attention was being paid to its meaning.

The following examples are remarks made by very young children (all younger than five, and some barely three years old) as they were listening to stories:

"The nails will tore his trousers." (A prediction about what will happen to a character who is putting nails in his pocket. Uttered in tones of concern.)

"You can't sew a turnip." (A confusion of "sew" and "sow." Uttered with scorn.)

"He's got sharp teeth and sharp claws. He must be a wild cat."

These examples are typical. Yet they are remarkable for the awareness of possibility and impossibility, of contingency and necessity revealed. They establish beyond doubt a well-developed ability to make sense of a highly complex world. And the impression of good sense gleaned from these isolated remarks becomes even greater when we are aware of the context in which they were made.

The problem is to reconcile these observations with experimental evidence that seems to show that children of this age are quite limited in their ability to deal with possibility, to reason inferentially, and to think intelligently in general. Although the evidence comes from diverse sources, the source that has been the most influential over the past few decades is the work of Piaget and his colleagues in Geneva. The reason for Piaget's great influence is not only his ingenious studies of children, but also the fact that he has woven his findings into a theory of great internal consistency and beauty, so that the mind is dazzled.

Once adopted, a theory tends to make us disregard evidence that conflicts with it. This is true even of a theory that is not very impressive, let alone one like Piaget's. But the most entrenched theory can be dislodged in the face of overwhelming evidence that it is wrong.

In the case of our theories about children's thinking, such evidence has been mounting for some time. Recent research, much of it concerned with the comprehension of language, throws new light on the reasons children can seem so limited as thinkers when they are tackling Piaget's tasks, yet so skilled when we watch them and listen to them in their spontaneous behavior.

In the early days after Chomsky's revolution in the field of linguistics, almost all those who were doing research on child language concentrated on studies of what children said. The reason was simply that the evidence needed in order to work out the rules of grammar that the children in some sense knew and used was evidence about language production. As long as this was the main concern, the question of what children could understand was largely ignored. But over the past few years there has been a marked shift of interest from syntax to semantics, and studies of comprehension have come into their own.

My own interest in language comprehension began in 1968 with a study of the ways in which children interpret the words "less" and "more." For this research we built two large cardboard apple trees, each equipped with six hooks on which beautiful red apples could be hung. Putting different numbers of apples on each tree, we asked which tree had more apples, which less. Then the children were asked to put more (or less) on one tree than on the other. The results surprised us. We had thought it likely that they would understand "more" better than they understood "less." What we found was that the two words appeared to be treated as synonyms. No matter which word we used, we tended to get the same responses — and they were the responses that were correct for "more."

This result was provocative in many ways, and it led to a series of further studies. One of these, by David Palermo of Pennsylvania State University, replicated the original results; but others, including research by Susan Carey of M.I.T., used different methods and cast doubt on the interpretation of these first findings.

My own view now is that we were asking the wrong question. Instead of asking how the children understood the words "less" and "more," we should have been looking at their interpretation of the utterances in which these words were used. I was led to see this by the results of a series of further studies, the first of which was still planned as an investigation of the development of word meanings. I wanted to study the children's understanding of words like "all" and "some." Naïvely, as it now seems to me, I hoped to discover the meanings of these words for the children by inserting them in statements like "All the doors are shut" or "All the cars are in the garages," and presenting the statements along with objects that rendered them true or false. What I discovered was that the children seemed to have no single meaning for "all." They judged all the doors to be shut if there was no door open, but often they judged all the cars to be in the garages when one car was sitting in full view outside. In the latter case the question they seemed to be considering was not where the cars were but whether all the garages were occupied. So we tried another configuration. We used two rows of garages, one row having four and the other six; and two rows of cars, one with four and one with five. In this study we again looked at the interpretation of sentences with the word "more" in them.

We were going to ask the children to make a comparison, and we wanted to make it as easy as possible for them, so we arranged the cars one above another on two shelves, with the extra car in one row always projecting on the right-hand side.

When the two rows of cars were presented alone, without garages, most of the children said there were more cars in the row of five than in the row of four. However, we also presented the cars enclosed in garages: four cars in the row of four garages, and five cars in the row of six garages (so that one garage was empty). About one third of the children now changed their judgments, saying there were more cars in the row of four. Again the question the children appeared to be answering was whether all the garages were filled: This was the thing that seemed to stand out, and no matter what we asked, this was the question they answered. Clearly "fullness" was what they expected to be asked about.

An important feature of this last experiment was that the task the children were given was, in its logical structure, the same as a Piagetian conservation test. Of all the tests that Piaget devised to reveal the nature of children's thinking in the preschool and early school years, the conservation tests are probably the best known. There are many such tests — tests of conservation of number, weight, volume, and length — but they all make use of the same key elements. Conservation of number will serve as an example.

First, the experimenter shows the child

two rows of objects, equal in number and laid out opposite one another in one-to-one correspondence. The child is asked whether there is the same number in the two rows. Unless the child agrees that this is so, the test cannot proceed.

In the next step the experimenter destroys the perceptual equivalence of the two rows, by moving the objects in one row closer together, for instance. Usually this action is accompanied by a remark like "Now watch what I do," which ensures that the child is paying attention.

Once the new configuration is in place, the original question is repeated, usually in the same words. Children who continue to say that the two rows are equal are said to conserve and are called conservers. If they claim that one row now has more objects than the other, they are not conserving and are called nonconservers. According to Piaget, a child's ability or inability to conserve is an indication of his or her stage of mental development.

Clearly the task involving two rows of cars, with and without enclosing garages, has the structure of a conservation task, although it is an unorthodox one. First the child is asked a question that calls for a comparison, then something irrelevant to the meaning of the words in the question is changed, then the original question is asked again.

Some may say that many of the children in our study were not conserving. But *what* were they not conserving? The most plausible and generally applicable notion seems to be that what the children were failing to conserve was their interpretation of the words of the experimenter. The same question was put to them twice, but *in a different context.* Adults would have discounted the shift in context. They would have known that in this kind of formal task they were meant to discount it and to base their replies on the meaning of the words. But perhaps the children did not know they were meant to do this, or perhaps they could not do it because the context was too powerful for them. In either event, it looked as though some nonlinguistic feature was strong enough to cause a shift in interpretation of what, for an adult, was a repetition of the same question.

At this stage my attention was drawn to the possibility that part of the reason for the shift in interpretation had to do not with the physical context of the experiment, like fullness of garages or length of rows, but with what the children thought was the intention underlying the experimenter's behavior. I owe this insight to James McGarrigle, who devised an ingenious experiment to test it.

The experiment made use of a number-conservation task and a small teddy bear called Naughty Teddy. The task proceeded in the usual way up to the point where the child agreed that the number in the two rows was the same. But before the experimenter went on to the next stage, Naughty Teddy would emerge from hiding, swoop over one row, and disarrange it. Once the one-to-one correspondence had been destroyed the child was invited to help put Naughty Teddy back in his box (an invitation that was usually accepted with glee) and the questioning was resumed: "Now, where were we? Ah yes, is the number in this row the same as the number in this row?" and so on. What happened was that many more children between the ages of four and six conserved number in the Naughty Teddy version of the task than in the traditional version (50 out of 80, compared with 13 out of 80).

Piaget's account of the reasons for failure cannot deal with this finding. His explanation makes use of several related arguments, putting the emphasis now here, now there. But at the heart of them all is the notion that children fail to conserve because they cannot sufficiently "decenter," that is, they are not flexible about shifting their point of view. Typically nonconservers are held to "center," or concentrate attention, on a particular state or feature, failing to take account either of transformations between states or of other features of the object. They center on the fact that one row of objects is longer than the other and fail to notice that the latter is more dense. In general, they are believed to center on the present moment and to make judgments on the basis of how things *now* appear, with no relation to how they were a moment ago.

It is quite possible to fit these arguments to the finding that children will sometimes change their judgments about the numbers of cars in two rows after the addition of enclosing garages. We have only to say that children who do so "center on fullness." However, there seems to be no way to fit them to the findings of the Naughty Teddy study (and these findings have already been replicated twice, by Julie Dockrell of Stirling University and by Irene Neilson of the Glasgow College of Technology). Nothing in Piaget's theoretical account of conservation suggests that it should matter who changes the arrangement of the objects.

But the Naughty Teddy results do fit very well with the idea that nonconserving children fail to answer the experimenter's question in the same way on the second occasion because, for them, it is not the same question. It seems different because it is not sufficiently detached, or disembedded, from the context of what the child believes the experimenter wants.

So disembedding will explain more of the findings than decentering will. But this does not establish that the decentering argument is false. It is possible that the child has difficulty with both decentering *and* disembedding. We must look at other evidence to see whether children are as limited in their ability to decenter as Piaget would have us believe.

In Piaget's view, inability to decenter is a feature of young minds that shows itself in a wide variety of ways. Some of these have already been considered. Another, perhaps the most fundamental, is the inability to appreciate the relativity of one's own point of view in space and time. A simple example of this is the inability to understand that one's own view of an object is not the same as that of someone looking at it from another side.

In a famous experiment, Piaget established that children presented with a three-dimensional model of a group of mountains have great difficulty choosing a picture of how the model would look to a doll viewing it from another position. For the most part, young children given this task choose the picture that shows exactly what they themselves see. It seems, then, that they are notably lacking in mental flexibility, bound by the egocentric illusion that what they see is the world as it really is. If this were true, it would certainly have far-reaching implications for the ability to think and reason.

Recent research has called this conclusion into question. My own thinking on the subject has been influenced by the work of Martin Hughes. Hughes placed before a group of children a configuration of two walls intersecting to form a cross. At the end of one of the walls he placed a wooden doll, representing a policeman. The children were then given another wooden doll, representing a boy, and were asked to "hide the boy so that the policeman can't see him." (The policeman was not tall enough to look over the walls.)

The arrangement made it easy to tell whether the children were able to escape from the domination of their own point of view, and the results were clear. Even three year olds were highly competent at the task. They showed no sign of a tendency to hide the doll from themselves, as would have been predicted from Piaget's theory, and they showed every sign of understanding what the policeman would be able to see from where he stood. Even when there were two policemen, placed so that the only effective hiding place was one where the boy doll was clearly visible to the child, about 90 percent of the responses from three- and four-year-old children were correct.

THE POLICEMAN TASK differs in many ways from Piaget's mountain task, but one is particularly significant in light of what we now know. In the policeman task there is an interplay of motives and intentions that is entirely comprehensible, even to a child of three. For this reason the task makes *human sense* to the children: They understand instantly what it is all about. The verbal instructions are so well supported by the context that no difficulties of disembedding arise. As soon as the doll is handed over, the children's faces light up, they smile, they latch on.

The mountain experiment on the other hand does not make immediate human sense in this way. There is no interplay of motives and intentions, no intelligible context. The task is as disembedded as the one given the American Indian who was asked to translate into his native tongue the sentence, "The white man shot six bears today." The Indian was baffled. "How can I do that?" he asked. "No white man could shoot six bears in one day."

Now we can reconcile the disparity between children's skills as thinkers in everyday situations and their limitations when confronted with formal tasks. Most formal tasks are geared to minds that are capable of a high degree of disembedding of thought and language — minds that are able to dispense with the support of human sense — and these tasks make demands of a quite special kind.

WHEN WE FIRST LEARN to think and to use language, it is within situations where we have purposes and intentions and where we can recognize and understand similar purposes and intentions in others. These humanly meaningful contexts sustain our thinking.

Precisely how they do this is of the greatest theoretical interest, but it is still mysterious. One thing is clear: When thought and language are functioning smoothly in real-life contexts, we are normally aware of the ends to which our activity is directed but not of the mental means that are needed to get there. We do not stop to think about our thinking or about the words we are using.

A formal task interrupts the flow of life. It demands deliberation, mental awareness, and control. It is by definition a thing to be considered out of context. We must set our minds to it. We must accept the premises, respect the constraints, direct our thought. This activity is difficult and, in a sense, unnatural. But that does not mean it should be avoided or abandoned — only that it will not happen spontaneously. We must recognize this fact so that we do not label our children "stupid" or "backward" if at first they find it hard.

The ability to take a problem out of context and consider it in its own right is the product of long ages of a particular kind of culture. It is closely linked to the development of literacy because written language, unlike speech, is by its very nature disembedded. Speech is transient, elusive, entangled in happenings. A written page, or a clay tablet, is physically separate and permanent: You can take it with you and go back to it. It is scarcely possible to learn to handle written language without becoming aware of it as a system and as a tool of the mind.

Disembedded intellectual skills underlie all our mathematics, all our science, all our philosophy. It may be that we value them too highly in comparison with other human skills and qualities, but we are not at all likely to renounce them. We have come to depend on them. And as schooling progresses, the emphasis on them becomes harder to evade or postpone. The student who can solve problems as problems, divorced from human sense, is the student who will succeed in the educational system. The better a student is at it, the more awards he or she will receive, and the better that student's self-image will be. But large numbers of students never achieve even a moderate level of competence in these skills and leave school with a sense of failure.

Seen in the context of human history, universal compulsory schooling is a new social enterprise, and it is a difficult one. We should not be surprised or ashamed if we do not yet know how to manage it well. At the same time, if we are going to persist in it, there is urgent need for us to learn to manage it better. We must not forget how grave a responsibility we assume when we conscript children for these long, demanding years of service. And when the outcome is not all that we would wish, we must not resort to blaming this on the shortcomings of the children. Since we impose the demands, it is up to us to find effective ways of helping children to meet them.

Many children hate school because it is a hateful thing to be forced to do something at which you fail over and over again. The older children get, the more they are aware that they are failing and that they are being written off as stupid. No wonder many of our children become disheartened and bored.

What are we to do about it? There is no simple formula, but there are a number of guiding principles.

The first takes us back to the topic of decentering. Although research has shown that children are better at this than Piaget claims, it is true that human beings of any age can find it hard. As adults we often fail to understand the child's point of view. We fail to understand what perplexes a child and why. In *Cider with Rosie,* Laurie Lee gives an account of his own first day at school: "What's the matter, Love? Didn't he like it at school, then?"

"They never gave me the present."

"Present? What present?"

"They said they'd give me a present."

"Well, now, I'm sure they didn't."

"They did! They said: 'You're Laurie Lee, aren't you? Well, you just sit there for the present.' I sat there all day but I never got it. I ain't going back there again."

The obvious way to look at the episode is to say that the child didn't understand the adult. But if we are to get better at helping children, it is more profitable to say that the adult failed to make the imaginative leap needed to understand the child. The story carries a profoundly important moral for all teachers and parents: The better you know something yourself, the greater the risk of not noticing that children find it bewildering.

When Jess Reid of the University of Edinburgh studied children who were learning to read, she found that some did not have the least idea of what reading was. They could not say how the postman knew where to deliver a letter. They did not understand the relationship between the sounds of speech and the marks that we make on paper, or that these marks are a means of communication.

It would help greatly if children told teachers when they felt perplexed. Many do not. But if they are explicitly encouraged to ask questions, they can often do so effectively, and the act of asking helps children become conscious of their own uncertainty.

It is also important to recognize how greatly the *process* of learning to read may influence the growth of the mind. Because print is permanent, it offers special opportunities for reflective thought, but they may not be taken if the reading child is not given time to pause. Once children gain some fluency as readers, we can help them notice what they are doing as they extend their skills and begin to grapple with possibilities of meaning; for it is the thoughtful consideration of possibility — the choice of one interpretation among others — that brings awareness and control.

One final principle is implicit in all that has been said: If we want to help children to succeed at school and to enjoy it, it is not enough to avoid openly calling them failures. We must respect them as thinkers and learners — even when they find school difficult.

If we respect them and let them know it, then the experience of learning within a structured environment may become for many more of our children an opening of new worlds, not a closing of prison bars.

REFERENCES

Bruner, J. S. "The Ontogenesis of Speech Acts." *Journal of Child Language,* Vol. 2, 1975, pp. 1–19.

Donaldson, Margaret. *Children's Minds.* W. W. Norton, 1979.

Grieve, R., R. Hoogenraad, and D. Murray. "On the Child's Use of Lexis and Syntax in Understanding Locative Instructions." *Cognition,* Vol. 5, 1977, pp. 235–250.

Lempers, J. D., E. R. Flavell, and J. H. Flavell. "The Development in Very Young Children of Tacit Knowledge Concerning Visual Perception." *Genetic Psychology Monographs,* Vol. 95, 1977, pp. 3–53.

Macnamara, J. "Cognitive Basis of Language Learning in Infants." *Psychological Review,* Vol. 79, 1972, pp. 1–13.

Olson, D. R. "Culture, Technology and Intellect." *The Nature of Intelligence,* edited by L. B. Resnick. Halstead Press, 1976.

Stephen Jay Gould

RACIST ARGUMENTS AND IQ

Louis Agassiz, the greatest biologist of mid-nineteenth-century America, argued that God had created blacks and whites as separate species. The defenders of slavery took much comfort from this assertion, for biblical proscriptions of charity and equality did not have to extend across a species boundary. What could an abolitionist say? Science had shone its cold and dispassionate light upon the subject; Christian hope and sentimentality could not refute it.

Similar arguments, carrying the apparent sanction of science, have been continually invoked in attempts to equate egalitarianism with sentimental hope and emotional blindness. People who are unaware of this historical pattern tend to accept each recurrence at face value: that is, they assume that each statement arises from the "data" actually presented, rather than from the social conditions that truly inspire it.

The racist arguments of the nineteenth century were based primarily on craniometry, the measurement of human skulls. Today, these contentions stand totally discredited. What craniometry was to the nineteenth century, intelligence testing has been to the twentieth. The victory of the eugenics movement in the Immigration Restriction Act of 1924 signaled its first unfortunate effect — for the severe restrictions upon non-Europeans and upon southern and eastern Europeans gained much support from results of the first extensive and uniform application of intelligence tests in America — the Army Mental Tests of World War I. These tests were engineered and administered by psychologist Robert M. Yerkes, who concluded that "education alone will not place the negro [*sic*] race on a par with its Caucasian competitors." It is now clear that Yerkes and his colleagues knew no way to separate genetic from environmental components in postulating causes for different performances on the tests.

The latest episode of this recurring drama began in 1969, when Arthur Jensen published an article entitled, "How Much Can We Boost IQ and Scholastic Achievement?" in the *Harvard Educational Review.* Again, the claim went forward that new and uncomfortable information had come to light, and that science had to speak the "truth" even if it refuted some cherished notions of a liberal philosophy. But again, I shall argue, Jensen had no new data; and what he did present was flawed beyond repair by inconsistencies and illogical claims.

Jensen assumes that IQ tests adequately measure something we may call "intelligence." He then attempts to tease apart the genetic and environmental factors causing differences in performance. He does this primarily by relying upon the one natural experiment we possess: identical twins reared apart — for differences in IQ between genetically identical people can only be environmental. The average difference in IQ

SOURCE: Reprinted from *Ever Since Darwin: Reflections in Natural History* by Stephen Jay Gould, by permission of W. W. Norton & Company, Inc.

for identical twins is less than the difference for two unrelated individuals raised in similarly varied environments. From the data on twins, Jensen obtains an estimate of environmental influence. He concludes that IQ has a heritability of about 0.8 (or 80 percent) *within* the population of American and European whites. The average difference between American whites and blacks is 15 IQ points (one standard deviation). He asserts that this difference is too large to attribute to environment, given the high heritability of IQ. Lest anyone think that Jensen writes in the tradition of abstract scholarship, I merely quote the first line of his famous work: "Compensatory education has been tried, and it apparently has failed."

I believe that this argument can be refuted in a "hierarchical" fashion — that is, we can discredit it at one level and then show that it fails at a more inclusive level even if we allow Jensen's argument for the first two levels:

Level 1: The equation of IQ with intelligence. Who knows what IQ measures? It is a good predictor of "success" in school, but is such success a result of intelligence, apple polishing, or the assimilation of values that the leaders of society prefer? Some psychologists get around this argument by defining intelligence operationally as the scores attained on "intelligence" tests. A neat trick. But at this point, the technical definition of intelligence has strayed so far from the vernacular that we can no longer define the issue. But let me allow (although I don't believe it), for the sake of argument, that IQ measures some meaningful aspect of intelligence in its vernacular sense.

Level 2: The heritability of IQ. Here again, we encounter a confusion between vernacular and technical meanings of the same word. "Inherited," to a layman, means "fixed," "inexorable," or "unchangeable." To a geneticist, "inherited" refers to an estimate of similarity between related individuals based on genes held in common. It carries no implications of inevitability or of immutable entities beyond the reach of environmental influence. Eyeglasses correct a variety of inherited problems in vision; insulin can check diabetes.

Jensen insists that IQ is 80 percent heritable. Princeton psychologist Leon J. Kamin has done the dog-work of meticulously checking through details of the twin studies that form the basis of this estimate. He has found an astonishing number of inconsistencies and downright inaccuracies. For example, the late Sir Cyril Burt, who generated the largest body of data on identical twins reared apart, pursued his studies of intelligence for more than forty years. Although he increased his sample sizes in a variety of "improved" versions, some of his correlation coefficients remain unchanged to the third decimal place — a statistically impossible situation.[1] IQ depends in part upon sex and age; and other studies did not standardize properly for them. An improper correction may produce higher values between twins not because they hold genes for intelligence in common, but simply because they share the same sex and age. The data are so flawed that no valid estimate for the heritability of IQ can be drawn at all. But let me assume (although no data support it), for the sake of argument, that the heritability of IQ is as high as 0.8.

Level 3: The confusion of within- and between-group variation. Jensen draws a causal connection between his two major assertions — that the within-group heritability of IQ is 0.8 for American whites, and that the mean difference in IQ between American blacks and whites is 15 points. He assumes that the black "deficit" is largely genetic in origin because IQ is so highly heritable. This is a *non sequitur* of the worst possible kind — for there is no necessary relationship between heritability within a group and differences in mean values of two separate groups.

A simple example will suffice to illustrate this flaw in Jensen's argument. Height has a much higher heritability within groups than anyone has ever claimed for IQ. Suppose that height has a mean value of five feet two inches and a heritability of 0.9 (a realistic value) within a group of nutritionally deprived Indian farmers. High heritability simply means that short farmers will tend to have short offspring, and tall farmers tall offspring. It says nothing whatever against the possibility that proper nutrition could raise the mean height to six feet (taller than average white Americans). It only means that, in this improved status, farmers shorter than average (they may now be five feet ten inches) would still tend to have shorter than average children.

I do not claim that intelligence, however defined, has no genetic basis — I regard it as trivially true, uninteresting, and unimportant that it does. The expression of any trait represents a complex interaction of heredity and environment. Our job is simply to provide the best environmental situation for the realization of valued potential in all individuals. I merely point out that a specific claim purporting to demonstrate a mean genetic deficiency in the intelligence of American blacks rests upon no new facts whatever and can cite no valid data in its support. It is just as likely that blacks have a genetic advantage over whites. And, either way, it doesn't matter a damn. An individual can't be judged by his group mean.

If current biological determinism in the study of human intelligence rests upon no new facts (actually, no facts at all), then why has it become so popular of late? The answer must be social and political. The 1960s were good years for liberalism; a fair amount of money was spent on poverty programs and relatively little happened. Enter new leaders and new priorities. Why didn't the earlier programs work? Two possibilities are open: (1) we didn't spend enough money, we didn't make sufficiently creative efforts, or (and this makes any established leader jittery) we cannot solve these problems without a fundamental social and economic transformation of society; or (2) the program failed because their recipients are inherently what they are — blaming the victims. Now, which alternative will be chosen by men in power in an age of retrenchment?

I have shown, I hope, that biological determinism is not simply an amusing matter for clever cocktail party comments about the human animal. It is a general notion with important philosophical implications and major political consequences. As John Stuart Mill wrote, in a statement that should be the motto of the opposition: "Of all the vulgar modes of escaping from the consideration of the effect of social and moral influences upon the human mind, the most vulgar is that of attributing the diversities of conduct and character to inherent natural differences."

NOTE

1. I wrote this essay in 1974. Since then, the case against Sir Cyril has progressed from an inference of carelessness to a spectacular (and well-founded) suspicion of fraud. Reporters for the London *Times* have discovered, for example, that Sir Cyril's coauthors (for the infamous twin studies) apparently did not exist outside his imagination. In the light of Kamin's discoveries, one must suspect that the data have an equal claim to reality.

25

Zick Rubin

WHAT IS A FRIEND?

> We're friends now because we know each other's names. — Tony, age three and a half

> Friends don't snatch or act snobby, and they don't argue or disagree. If you're nice to them, they'll be nice to you. — Julie, age eight

> A friend is someone that you can share secrets with at 3 in the morning with Clearasil on your face. — Deborah, age thirteen

> The friendship we have in mind is characterized by mutual trust; it permits a fairly free expression of emotion; it allows the shedding of privacies (although not inappropriately); it can absorb, within limits, conflict between the pair; it involves the discussion of personally crucial themes; it provides occasions to enrich and enlarge the self through the encounter of differences. — Elizabeth Douvan and Joseph Adelson, adults

As these statements illustrate,[1] people have widely differing notions of what a friend is and of the nature of friendship. In his second week at nursery school, three-year-old Dwayne plays with Eddie for the first time and minutes later runs around the yard shouting "We're friends!" Thirteen-year-old Deborah, in contrast, might spend months getting to know a classmate, gradually extending the range and intimacy of their conversations, before deciding that their relationship merits the label of friendship. Some observers may conclude that young children's notions of friendship are so different from the conceptions held by older children, adolescents, and adults that it is misleading to consider them as variations of the same concept. From this point of view, when preschoolers talk about their friends, they are really referring to their playmates, which is a rather different sort of thing. My own view is that the use of the word "friend" by children of different ages nicely reflects the common functions of peer relationships for people of all ages. Both three-year-old Dwayne and thirteen-year-old Deborah are referring to nonfamilial relationships which are likely to foster a feeling of belonging and a sense of identity; it seems quite appropriate that they choose to use the same word. It is clear, however, that the ways in which people reason about friendship change over the course of childhood. Moreover, there appear to be some basic consistencies among people in the nature of this change.

The most systematic research on children's understanding of friendship is being conducted by Robert Selman and his colleagues at the Harvard Graduate School of Education. Selman has patterned both his theoretical approach and his research style on the model of the Swiss psychologist Jean Piaget. He follows Piaget in taking as his central concern the progressively developing mental structures that characterize children's social

SOURCE: Reprinted by permission of the publishers from *Children's Friendships* by Zick Rubin, Cambridge, Mass.: Harvard University Press.

thought. He also follows Piaget in his method of documenting these mental structures — the clinical interview, in which the interviewer probes deeply and resourcefully to capture the child's own understanding of her social world. Selman has adopted this procedure to assess the "friendship awareness" of both normal and emotionally disturbed children, from early childhood through adolescence.[2] On the basis of this work, it is possible for us to identify two sharply contrasting stages of children's conceptions of friendship.

The young child, from about age three to five, characteristically views friends as "momentary physical playmates" — whomever one is playing with at a particular time. Children at this stage do not have a clear conception of an enduring relationship that exists apart from specific encounters. Young children may in fact *have* enduring relationships with others, but they typically conceive of them only in terms of momentary interaction. In addition, children at this stage reflect only on the physical attributes and activities of playmates, rather than on psychological attributes such as personal needs, interests, or traits. In contrast, the older child — by age eleven or twelve — comes to view close friendships as involving "intimate and mutual sharing." Children at this later stage regard friendship as a relationship that takes shape over a period of time. Friends are seen as providers of intimacy and support. The child realizes that, to achieve these ends, close friends need to be psychologically compatible — to share interests and to have mutually agreeable personalities.

To gain a fuller understanding of the contrast between these two stages of reasoning about friendship, let us compare the ways in which younger and older children reflect upon certain central issues: what sorts of people make good friends, how friendships are formed, and the nature of closeness and intimacy.

What sorts of people make good friends? For the young child who views friendship in terms of momentary interactions, the most important qualification for friendship is physical accessibility. When asked what sort of person makes a good friend, preschoolers are likely to provide such answers as "Someone who plays a lot" or "Someone who lives in Watertown." [3] Young children are also likely to focus on specific physical actions. Steven tells me, for example, that Craig is his friend because "he doesn't take things away from me." Conversely, Jake is not his friend because "he takes things away from me." For children at this level, moreover, one's own desires may be seen as a sufficient basis for friendship. When you ask a young child why a certain other child is his friend, the most common reply is "Because I like him." Attempts to probe more deeply are likely to frustrate both the researcher and the child:

ZR: Why is Caleb your friend?
Tony: Because I like him.
ZR: And why do you like him?
Tony: Because he's my friend.
ZR: And why is he your friend?
Tony (speaking each word distinctly, with a tone of mild disgust at the interviewer's obvious denseness): Because . . . I . . . choosed . . . him . . . for . . . my . . . friend.

Children at this stage do not make reference to psychological attributes of friends; at most, they will resort to such stereotypical descriptions as "she's nice" or "he's mean."

Older children are aware of other sorts of qualifications for friendship. Instead of focusing on physical accessibility, they are likely to emphasize the need for psychological compatibility. One aspect of this rapport is the sharing of outlooks and interests. When asked why Jimmy was his friend, thirteen-year-old Jack explained: "We like the same kinds of things. We speak the same language." [4] Children at this level of social awareness also realize that compatibility is not to be equated with similarity. "Good friends sort of fit together," thirteen-year-old Alan said. "They don't have to be exactly alike, but if one is strong in something the other can be weak and he may be good at something else." [5]

How are friendships formed? For children who view friendship in terms of momentary physical interaction, the way to form a friendship is simply to play with the other child. When asked how one should go about making friends, younger children are likely to provide such answers as "Move in next door," "Tell him your name," and "Just go up and ask her to play." From this perspective, the barriers to making friends are physical rather than psychological. A four-year-old interviewed by Selman explained things this way:

Interviewer: Is it easy or hard to make friends?
Child: Hard, because sometimes if you wave to the other person, they might not see you wave, so it's hard to get that friend.
Interviewer: What if they see you?
Child: Then it's easy.[6]

Older children, who view friendships as relationships that continue beyond single encounters, view the process as more complicated. Although they recognize that people may sometimes "hit it off" immediately, these children believe that friendships can best be established gradually, as people find out about one another's traits, interests, and values. "You don't really pick your friends," thirteen-year-old Jack reported. "It just grows on you. You find out that you can talk to someone, you can tell them your problems, when you understand each other." [7]

The nature of intimacy. For the young child, the question of what constitutes closeness translates into the question of what distinguishes a best friend from other friends. And when such a distinction is made, it is in strictly quantitative terms — whatever you do with a friend, you simply do more of it with a best friend: "If you *always* visit, you're best friends." Preschool children may in fact have best friends with whom they interact in ways that seem qualitatively unique to the adult observer. Nevertheless, children who view friendship in terms of momentary physical interactions seem unable to reflect on the special nature of such friendships.

Children who view friendship as a mutual relationship, in contrast, can reflect specifically on the nature of intimacy. Closeness is defined in terms of the degree of understanding that has been built up between two friends, the extent to which they trust each other with personal thoughts and feelings, and the extent to which they are concerned with one another's welfare. A fifteen-year-old boy put it this way:

> A really tight friendship is when you start to really care about the person. If he gets sick, you kind of start worrying about him — or if he gets hit by a car. An everyday friend, you say, I know that kid, he's all right, and you don't really think much of him. But a close friend you worry about more than yourself. Well, maybe not more, but about the same.[8]

This conception of intimacy between friends is remarkably similar to the ways in which philosophers and psychologists have typically defined love.[9] In his discussion of the friendships of late childhood, Harry Stack Sullivan made this equation explicit: "If you will look very closely at one of your children when he finally finds a chum . . . you will discover something very different in the relationship — namely, that your child begins to develop a new sensitivity to what matters to another person. And this is not in the sense of 'what should I do to get what I want,' but instead 'what should I do to contribute to the happiness or to support the prestige and feeling of worth-whileness of my chum' . . . This change represents the beginning of something very like full-blown psychiatrically defined *love*."[10]

Along what path do children progress from a view of friendship as momentary physical interaction to a view of friendship as mutual sharing and intimacy? Is there a sudden flash of social insight, akin to the rapid vocabulary growth of the second year of life or to the height spurt that accompanies puberty? Surely this is not the way it happens. One view of the way it does happen, taken by Selman — with due credit to Piaget — is that social awareness develops in a series of stages, each of which involves a reorganization of mental elements by the child. The two stages of reasoning about friendship that we have examined are labeled "Stage 0" and "Stage 3." To get from Stage 0 to Stage 3, the child progresses through two intermediate stages. In Stage 1, most often characteristic of children between the ages of about six and eight, the child conceives of friendship as "one-way assistance." A friend is a person who does things that please you; accordingly, friends must become aware of one another's likes and dislikes. At this stage, however, there is still no awareness of the reciprocal nature of friendship. This comes at Stage 2, which is most often characteristic of children between the ages of about nine and twelve. For the first time, friendship is understood as a two-way street in which each friend must adapt to the needs of the other. In Stage 2, however, children's awareness of reciprocity remains focused on specific incidents rather than on the friendship itself, as an enduring social relationship. For this reason, Selman labels this the stage of "fairweather cooperation." It is only in the transformation from Stage 2 to Stage 3 that children, by now typically in late childhood or early adolescence, come to reflect on issues of intimacy and mutuality in a continuing relationship.

Thus Selman describes a stepladder progression in children's concepts of friendship. Children climb the ladder, stopping to rest for a while at each rung — in part, presumably, to consolidate the new level of interpersonal awareness that they have achieved — before going on. Other researchers, while confirming this general progression, doubt that the stages are as distinct as Selman's scheme suggests. Whether the progression is like ascending a stepladder or a gradually inclining ramp, however, it involves steady movement along three dimensions of social understanding.

First, there is a progression in the child's ability to take other people's point of view, comparable to the broadening of visual perspective-taking ability that takes place in early childhood.[11] Whereas young children assume that everyone else sees physical objects in precisely the same way that they do, they later come to recognize that different people will see a particular object in different ways, depending on their physical vantage point. An analogous progression takes place in the domain of social understanding. At first, children view friendship in a one-sided and egocentric way, solely in terms of what a friend can do for them. A friend is a friend because "I like him" or "He plays with me" or "I want him to be my friend." Only at later stages do children become capable of figuratively standing back and taking the other person's viewpoint ("She doesn't like it when I act too wild") and, still later, a third-person perspective on their relationships, with an appreciation of interlocking needs and provisions ("We share a lot of the same values"). Thus the developing ability to take another person's point of view can be seen as a mark of both cognitive and social maturing.

Second, there is a shift from viewing people only as physical entities to viewing people as psychological entities as well.[12] When younger children are asked to describe their friends or acquaintances, they concentrate on physical attributes and activities: "Andy's got red hair and he always wears cowboy boots." As children grow older they begin to supplement such concrete descriptions with abstract concepts that refer to behavioral dispositions: "He's a big showoff." [13] Children also become increasingly likely to provide their own psychological explanations of other people's behavior, such as "Because he is black he is very defensive" or "She says bad things about other people so you'll be closer to her." [14] Children, like adults, are everyday psychologists, and their psychologizing becomes more sophisticated — even if not always more accurate — over the course of childhood. In accord with these changes, appraisals of the psychological attributes of others become increasingly important aspects of friendship.

Third, children's conceptions of friendship reflect a shift from viewing social relationships as momentary interactions to viewing them as social systems that endure over some period of time. In terms of a distinction suggested by Erving Goffman, young children conceptualize their commerce with others only as *encounters,* whereas older children become able to conceptualize *relationships.*[15] Following a fight, for example, a young child may be quick to shout "We're not friends!" An older child, like this twelve-year-old, takes a longer view:

> You have known your friend so long and loved him so much, and then all of a sudden you are so mad at him, you say, I could just kill you and you still like each other, because you have always been friends and you know in your mind you are going to be friends in a few seconds anyway.[16]

These three developmental progressions have a basic theme in common: there is a shift in focus from the concrete to the abstract — from observable, here-and-now characteristics of people and their behavior to inferred, underlying characteristics. These progressions in social understandings are made possible, in part, by parallel progressions from concrete to abstract reasoning in a child's intellectual development.[17] But intellectual development alone cannot account for the specific content of children's conceptions of friendship. What is it that causes children to transform their notions of friendship from momentary interaction to one-way assistance, from fair-weather cooperation to shared intimacy? One possibility is that it is chiefly a matter of cultural learning, from the models and formulas provided by adults, older children, and the mass media: "You have to share with your friends," "Mommy's talking on the phone to her best friend," "Batman and Superman are Superfriends — they never let each other down." From this standpoint, the child's changing conceptions of friendship are a series of successively closer approximations to the views of friendship held in a particular culture. It must be acknowledged that Selman and other researchers have derived their descriptions from studies of children in Western societies, usually from middle-class backgrounds. We can safely assume that at least some of the details of these progressions tend to be different among children in non-Western cultures — where, for example, friendship may be based to some degree on formalized arrangements such as blood brotherhood.[18] Even within the United States . . . , there is reason to believe that children from different social backgrounds come to have somewhat different conceptions of friendship.

Without denying the likelihood of such differences, however, most developmental psychologists believe that the principal architect of social understanding is not the child's culture but the child himself. According to this "constructivist" view, as espoused by both Piaget and Sullivan, children work out for themselves what social relationships are all about on the basis of their actual encounters with others. Through their interactions with peers, children discover that other children are similar to them in some respects and different in others. And as children attempt to cooperate with one another, they discover that the coordination of behavior requires an appreciation of the other's capabilities, desires, and values. At first, these "discoveries" remain implicit and unexamined. Gradually, however, children integrate and organize what they have learned, leading to increasingly sophisticated understandings of social relationships. Talking openly about conflicts may be one particularly valuable way to further one's understanding of friendship.

Although the constructivist view is widely held, there is still no systematic research that succeeds in pinning down the ways in which specific experiences lead to transformations in children's social awareness.[19] Even in the absence of such research, however, the constructivist view can help us to make sense out of several observations about children's understandings that might otherwise be puzzling.

First, the constructivist view helps to make clear that there is no inevitable relation between a child's age and his or her level of interpersonal understanding. Whereas almost all children begin to walk within a limited age range — between about nine and fourteen months — there is much greater variation in the ages at which children begin to reason about friendship at particular levels. Unlike walking, the development of social understanding depends on both developing intellectual skills, which may vary widely among individuals, and on specific social experiences, which vary even more widely. As a result, we should be sure not to rely on chronological age as an unfailing index of children's social understanding.

The constructivist view also helps us to see why there are almost always discrepancies between how children answer questions about friendship and how the same children relate to their friends in practice. For example, young children who characteristically view friendship as momentary physical interactions may still demonstrate an ability to work out compromises that suggests a clear practical awareness of the give-and-take of relationships. "I'll live with you there," one preschool boy told a girl who wanted him to play house again, "but I'll work here, and I'm working now" — and he went on building with blocks.[20] As Piaget emphasizes, "Thought always lags behind action and cooperation has to be practiced for a very long time before it can be brought fully to light by reflective thought." [21]

Finally, the constructivist view accommodates the fact that there are often apparent inconsistencies in children's responses to questions about friendship. My nephew Larry, at age twelve, explained why Mark was his best friend in terms of the sharing of outlooks and interests: "We're both short, we're the same smartness, and we like the same sports." Such awareness of the psychological bases of compatibility is characteristic of Stage 3 reasoning in Selman's scheme. But when I asked Larry what would lead people who were best friends not to be friends any more, he could think only of the possibilities that one of them moved away or transferred to another school, reflecting a physicalistic conception of friendship that is more characteristic of Selman's Stage 0. The notion that friends can grow apart because of changing outlooks or interests did not occur to Larry, who had not yet had much experience with the ending of friendships. Such "inconsistencies" are to be expected, once we recognize that the child's conceptions are derived from interpretations of concrete experiences rather than from logical analysis of friendships in the abstract.

This discussion of children's progression toward increasingly "advanced" conceptions of friendship may seem to imply that, by the time we become adults, we all reason about friendship in thoroughly sophisticated, humane, and logical terms. The conception of friendship by two psychologists that I quoted at the start of this chapter — with its mutual trust, absorption of conflict, and opportunity for self-enrichment — is one definition of this ideal endpoint. It is worthwhile to ask, however, whether most adults typically conceive of friendship in such terms. The fact is that they do not. When adults of varying ages are asked to explain the basis of their close friendships, they mention a wide range of factors, including physical proximity ("Because we're neighbors"), likability ("He is a good companion"), similarity of outlooks ("We have the same interests . . . in religion and the way we look at things"), trust ("She listens and you know it is not going any further"), and reciprocal help and support ("I know that if I ever needed help with anything I could always go to her").[22] The reasoning behind these descriptions runs the gamut from Stage 0 to Stage 3 and beyond. Adults' descriptions of an "ideal close relationship" reflect almost the same range and diversity.

My point is not that adults frequently reason like children about friendship. It is, rather, that people do not in fact progress toward more advanced levels of social awareness in an ever-upward climb toward an ideal endpoint, with each "higher" level, once attained, replacing the lower levels already passed. Instead, as Selman and others have noted, lower stages are not discarded but are built upon and remain available for future use in specific situations. It is interesting to note, in this connection, that both children and adults tend to reason in more sophisticated ways about their deepest friendships and loves than about casual relationships. Indeed, one's view of any close relationship, as it progresses from first meetings to intimacy, may have to go through the very same stages — albeit in a shorter time period — as do conceptions of friendship through the course of childhood.[23]

What, then, is a friend? Philosophers and psychologists can provide their own definitions, but these are not entirely adequate to our purposes. Friendship, in the sense that it matters to us, is what a child makes it out to be. Whether Billy views Sean as "someone I play with in school" or as "someone I can trust — and who can trust me" will inevitably have a major impact on the way in which Billy proceeds to conduct his relationship with Sean. And these conceptions contain important clues about how Billy is likely to navigate relationships with other children as well. If we are interested in understanding a child's friendships, therefore, we must do our best to understand them in the child's own terms.

NOTES

1. From William Damon, *The Social World of the Child* (San Francisco: Jossey-Bass, 1977), pp. 160, 164. Elizabeth Douvan and Joseph Adelson, *The Adolescent Experience* (New York: Wiley, 1966), p. 176.

2. Robert Selman, "Toward a Structural Analysis of Developing Interpersonal Relations Concepts: Research With Normal and Disturbed Preadolescent Boys," in Anne D. Pick, ed., *Minnesota Symposium on Child Psychology,* vol. 10 (Minneapolis: University of Minnesota Press, 1976). Robert Selman and Dan Jaquette, "Stability and Oscillation in Interpersonal Awareness: A Clinical-Developmental Analysis," in Charles B. Keasey, ed., *Nebraska Symposium on Motivation, 1977* (Lincoln: University of Nebraska Press, 1978).

3. Robert Selman and Dan Jaquette, "The Development of Interpersonal Awareness" (working draft of manual, Harvard-Judge Baker Social Reasoning Project, 1977).

4. Damon, *The Social World of the Child,* p. 163.

5. Selman and Jaquette, "The Development of Interpersonal Awareness," p. 132.

6. Selman and Jaquette, "The Development of Interpersonal Awareness," p. 118.

7. Damon, *The Social World of the Child,* p. 164.

8. Selman and Jaquette, "The Development of Interpersonal Awareness," p. 144.

9. See, for example, Zick Rubin, *Liking and Loving: An Invitation to Social Psychology* (New York: Holt, Rinehart and Winston, 1973), chap. 10 ("The Nature of Love").

10. Harry Stack Sullivan, *The Interpersonal Theory of Psychiatry* (New York: Norton, 1953), p. 245.

11. See John H. Flavell, "The Development of Knowledge About Visual Perception," in Keasey, ed., *Nebraska Symposium on Motivation, 1977.*

12. W. J. Livesley and D. B. Bromley, *Person Perception in Childhood and Adolescence* (London: Wiley, 1973).

13. Helaine H. Scarlett, Allan N. Press, and Walter H. Crockett, "Children's Descriptions of Peers: A Wernerian Developmental Analysis," *Child Development,* 1971, *42,* 439–453.

14. Barbara Hollands Peevers and Paul Secord, "Developmental Change in Attribution of Descriptive Concepts to Persons," *Journal of Personality and Social Psychology,* 1973, *27,* 120–128.

15. Erving Goffman, *Encounters* (Indianapolis: Bobbs-Merrill, 1961).

16. Selman and Jaquette, "The Development of Interpersonal Awareness," p. 165.

17. See Thomas J. Berndt, "Relations Between Social Cognition, Nonsocial Cognition, and Social Behavior: The Case of Friendship," in Lee Ross and John H. Flavell, eds., *New Directions in the Study of Social-Cognitive Development,* in press.

18. For description of friendships in non-Western cultures, see, for example, Robert Brain, *Friends and Lovers* (New York: Basic Books, 1976). Yehudi A. Cohen, "Patterns of Friendship," in Cohen, ed., *Social Structure and Personality* (New York: Holt, Rinehart and Winston, 1961).

19. For an impressive beginning along these lines, see William A. Corsaro, "Friendship in the Nursery School: Social Organization in a Peer Environment," in Steven R. Asher and John M. Gottman, eds., *The Development of Children's Friendships* (Cambridge University Press, in press).

20. Katherine H. Read, *The Nursery School,* 6th ed. (Philadelphia: Saunders, 1976), p. 347.

21. Jean Piaget, *The Moral Judgment of the Child* (Glencoe, Ill.: Free Press, 1948), p. 56; originally published in 1932.

22. Lawrence Weiss and Marjorie Fiske Lowenthal, "Life Course Perspectives on Friendship," in Lowenthal, Majda Turner, David Chiriboga, et al., *Four Stages of Life* (San Francisco: Jossey-Bass, 1975).

23. For a discussion of the development of adult social relationships that parallels the stages we have been discussing, see George Levinger and J. Diedrick Snoek, *Attraction in Relationship: A New Look at Interpersonal Attraction* (Morristown, N.J.: General Learning Press, 1972).

Laurene Krasny Meringoff

INFLUENCE OF THE MEDIUM ON CHILDREN'S STORY APPREHENSION

ABSTRACT: This study compared children's apprehensions of an unfamiliar story either read to them from an illustrated book or presented as a comparable televised film. There were 48 children, 24 of whom were younger (M age = 7.6) and 24 of whom were older (M age = 9.6), who were randomly assigned to one medium condition and individually presented the story. Response measures examined recall of story content as well as inferences about characters and events. Children exposed to the televised story remembered more story actions, offered estimates of shorter elapsed time and distance traveled for carrying out a repeated story event, and relied more on visual content as the basis for inferences. In comparison, children who were read the story in picture book form recalled more story vocabulary, based their inferences more on textual content, general knowledge, and personal experience, and made more use of the storytelling situation as an opportunity to ask questions and make comments about the story. To the extent that children have repeated experience with specific media, such differential medium effects on apprehension suggest important implications for children's cognitive development.

Throughout history stories have been used to teach children as well as to entertain them. Yet the media or material forms in which stories are communicated have shifted and proliferated over the years. With the development of electronic technology, television has emerged as one of the dominant media in which stories are presented to children. The "same" storyline now routinely crosses media boundaries, more books are selected and written for screen adaptation, and more stories originally produced for tele-

This article is based on the author's doctoral dissertation submitted to Harvard Graduate School of Education. The research was supported by grants from the John and Mary R. Markle Foundation and National Institute of Education Grant NIE-G-78-0031.

The author wishes to thank Courtney Cazden, Gerald Lesser, and especially Howard Gardner for their support and encouragement throughout this project. The assistance of Barbara Flagg and David Pillemer in data analysis is gratefully acknowledged. Sincere thanks are also expressed to Frank Peros, Francis Manzelli, and participating teachers and children at the Watertown Public Schools.

---

vision are subsequently rendered into print (Duke, 1979). Increasingly, a child's initial exposure to a story is as likely to come from seeing it on television as it is from reading it in a book.

It was well over 10 years ago that McLuhan (1962) popularized the observation that the medium itself contributes to the quality of the message it transmits. Other writers have since offered theoretical perspectives sensitive to distinctions between media and the nature of symbolization. For example, Gardner, Howard, and Perkins (1974) observed that the same medium (television) may be a vehicle for different symbol systems (language, visual imagery), and the same symbol system (language) may occur in different media (book, television).

The role that experience with different symbol systems may play in cognitive development has also been discussed. Salomon (1979) pointed out that differences in the symbol systems used by media to represent content, and not media per se, influence cognition and learning. Symbol systems differ with respect to the kinds of information they are best suited to convey. Moreover, Salomon (1979) asserted that "if their *unique* symbolic capabilities are capitalized upon, each medium addresses itself to different . . . mental skills, thus benefits learners of different aptitudes and serves different educational ends" (p. 144). In similar spirit, Olson and Bruner (1974) suggest possible educational implications for such differences: "Each form of experience, including the various symbol systems tied to the media, produces a unique pattern of skills for dealing with or thinking about the world" (p. 149). According to Olson and Bruner, one may define intelligence by these media-related skills.

Knowledge about the unique strengths and limitations of media seems essential to know how each medium can best be used and how learning can be maximized. Yet little research has examined the specific effects that different media presentations may have on children's understanding and appreciation of stories. As Schramm (1977) has noted, "There is almost a complete lack of studies intended to ascertain under what conditions and for what purposes one medium may be superior to another" (p. 33).

For example, a substantial body of research has focused on children's reproduction of orally presented story material. Some researchers have devised analytic systems or grammars for parsing simple stories into elements hypothesized to have certain structural importance for the listener and have used these systems to analyze the content of children's retold stories (Brown & Smiley, 1977; Mandler & Johnson, 1977; Stein, Note 1). Although this research allows predictions to be made about children's recall of specific kinds of story content, its applicability is limited by presentation of stories within a single medium, use of artificially spare story materials, and reliance on verbal recall to the exclusion of other response measures.

Similar limitations pertain to research examining children's learning of television narratives. For example, studies indicate that younger viewers exhibit less ability to draw inferences about the meaningful relationships among discrete events (Collins, 1970, 1979), and they base inferences about film story content more on behavior viewed than on inferred psychological states (Flapan, 1968). However, without comparison to other formats, it is uncertain to what extent age differences are attributable to limits in cognitive skills and to what extent they are due to particular demands imposed by the form in which the story is presented. Collins (1979) raises a similar question by suggesting that younger children's difficulty with television plots is likely to involve factors beyond the sources of difficulty that occur in comprehension of prose (e.g., certain dramatic and cinematic features peculiar to audiovisual narratives).

The present research was designed as an initial attempt to investigate whether the expression of stories in two different media materially affects the ways in which their content is remembered and understood by children. It also examines whether such medium effects have differential impacts on children of various ages. To address these questions, the study compares children's apprehension of a story either read to them from a picture book or presented as a televised film.

Questions and Hypotheses

Medium differences. Does the medium in which a story is communicated to children influence their apprehension of it? Are different kinds of story information conveyed more effectively to children by a picture book or by television?

Hypotheses about such differences follow from analysis of the material features of these media. By comparing one medium's rendering of a story against the other, certain of the properties of each become more clearly articulated. Once differences are identified between media as sources of story content, one can begin to predict how such differences might be reflected in children's responses.

Illustrated storybooks and television are both media equipped to deliver narrative content via the symbol systems of verbal language and visual images ordered over time. However, one evident difference between the way these media treat visual imagery is their relative ability to depict movement. Book illustrations can suggest or imply movement by such means as the position in which objects or characters are placed in a single picture (Friedman & Stevenson, 1975) or by changes indicated in this positioning from one picture to the next. Nevertheless, each image remains discrete and static. In contrast, the illusion of movement is inherent in the display of television images. Although the present study compares media, the difference noted here between static and moving imagery also describes a contrast between two related but distinct symbol systems.

The direct consequence of this difference is that film animates a story's images and renders a more highly illustrated version of the text than its book counterpart. However, the extent of a film's illustration tends to vary with the nature of story content. Some narrative elements lend themselves more readily than others to both visualization and movement. A story's actions are particularly accessible to direct illustration, that is, what characters do (their movements, gestures, the changing physical relationships among characters and objects). In contrast, dialogue between characters is often accompanied by displaying the speakers rather than the content of their conversation.

It was hypothesized that television's ability to depict story actions dynamically and concomitantly to visually reinforce the corresponding text would tend to make more salient the visible and behavioral features of story characters. As an outcome, does the television presentation as opposed to book presentation of a story result in children's greater recall of the actions and greater reliance on visualized content (character's appearance, depicted behavior) in drawing inferences about the story? Does television engender more physical gesturing during the recounting of the story?

On the other hand, the book's provision of more limited and static pictorial information may allow for greater auditory attention to the text. In comparison to television, does the picture book delivery of a story lend itself to children's greater recall of story language (especially more formal expressive language that usually eludes visual illustration), greater use of textual content (like dialogue), and more outside-story knowledge as the bases for inferences?

A related difference between these media is the greater visual and temporal discontinuity in the book's treatment of events. Are there medium differences in children's spatial and temporal perceptions of story events? Does exposure to the book encourage estimates of longer duration and greater distances for story events, for example, or simply more variable estimates than those generated by the television version?

Age differences. What difference does age make in children's apprehension of stories? Are children differentially sensitive to medium effects depending on their age?

Given the usual trajectory of development, recall and understanding of stories should increase with age, although appearance of these age differences is expected to vary with the specific task demands. In fact, simple age differences in children's story recall (Mandler & Johnson, 1977; Stein & Glenn, Note 2), comprehension of television dramas (Collins, 1979), and varying influences of tasks on children's narrative performance (Brown, 1975) are well documented. Regarding an interaction between age and medium, preoperational children may be more influenced by perceptual differences between a book's rendering of a story and that of television. In contrast, older children (and adults) who are read a storybook or shown a television story would be more likely to extract the meaningful content shared by the two presentations and to overlook or transcend differences in the mediating form.

METHOD

Subjects

There were 48 children, 24 of whom were 6- to 8-years-old and 24 of whom were 9- to 10-years-old, who were recruited from an ethnically heterogeneous public school in Watertown, Massachusetts. Children were selected across classrooms within the school and pooled into a younger and older subsample. Mean chronological age of the younger group was 7 years 6 months; mean chronological age of the older group was 9 years 6 months. Equal numbers of boys and girls at each age level were then randomly assigned to one of the two media conditions, picture book or television.

Materials

The issue of comparability. The design of the study required that enough similarity exist in the story's content as presented in each medium and yet that some characteristic use be made of each format. Only then, it was reasoned, was a meaningful and interesting comparison possible wherein differences found in the children's responses could appropriately be attributed to the specific nature of each medium.

Consideration of what might constitute a suitable level of comparability was facilitated by imagining a continuum along which the formal characteristics of different audiovisual renderings of a given storybook vary. At one end there was a high degree of similarity between the presentation in each medium. As Metz (1974) observed, "The film can transform the non-cinematic structures it takes up, but it can also be content with merely adopting them as they are, i.e., inscribing them in a new material while preserving their original form" (p. 98). In iconographic films, for example, although the camera can direct the viewer's visual attention around the book's pictures in prescribed ways, absence of movement within the image limits the representativeness of such films. At the opposite end are films characterized by low similarity to their book counterparts because the story's verbal text and/or visual content have been appreciably altered. In such cases, attempts to examine differences in treatment at a formal level are confounded by blatant changes in content. Within the range bounded by these two ends of the continuum are films with an optimal level of comparability for this research.

Description. An unfamiliar folktale entitled *A Story A Story,* which already existed in both formats, was used. In picture book form (Haley, 1970), the story was 32 pages long and illustrated with 17 woodcuts. The televised format (Schindel, 1973) consisted of an animated film adopting the same graphic style as the book; that is, the book's images appeared in the film but now moved. The story's visual treatment was also subject to other filmic modifications. For example, length of shots, location of cuts, and use of such editing techniques as *dissolves* or *fades* structured the temporal and spatial dimensions of the story differently than the book. In terms of overall comparability, the story was visualized with similar images in both media; what varied was the amount of visual information, its dynamic quality, and the resulting degree of visual and temporal continuity.

A new soundtrack was prepared for the film using the experimenter's voice so that the voice-over narration of the verbal text would be the same in the two formats. Soft background music made with wood instruments was retained in the film. A ¾-inch (2 cm) video cassette of the film was used in the study.

The story tells how "once . . . there were no stories on earth to hear. All the stories belonged to Nyame, the Sky God." The story's hero, a spider man named Ananse, spins a web up to the sky and asks the Sky God for his stories. The Sky God demands, "Bring me Osebo the leopard-of-the-terrible-teeth, Mmboro the hornet-who-stings-like-fire, and Mmoatia the fairy-whom-men-never-see." In three subsequent episodes, Ananse captures these creatures and brings them back up to the Sky God, who, in return, proclaims the stories to belong to Ananse. In the end, the spider man takes the golden box of stories back to earth, letting them scatter to the corners of the world.

Procedure

The children were individually tested in an unused classroom in the school. Daily scheduling of the children for testing was alternated across classrooms and media treatments. The experimenter introduced the study as follows: "I'd like to share a story with you today. It's name is *A Story A Story.* First we'll look at and listen to the story. Then, afterwards, we can talk about the story and do some picture games about it." The story was presented to each child a single time. The book was held equidistant between child and reader so the child could easily see each page spread while the experimenter read the story aloud. In the video presentation, the child sat the same distance from the experimenter, but both faced the television monitor that stood equidistant in front of them at the children's eye level. Oral delivery of the story was well standardized with practice and approximated the 10-minute length of the film. (Any verbal interaction initiated by a child in the course of the story was recorded and responded to succinctly.) A series of tasks lasting approximately 45 minutes was administered to each child immediately following the story.

Measures

In an attempt to tap the myriad ways in which children experience story materials, response measures were designed to elicit various kinds of learning and understanding. Presentation of stories in different media also emphasized the need to obtain responses across different modalities, particularly those used by each medium. (For a complete list of response measures, see Meringoff, 1978.) They included the following.

Story recall. To determine what objective information children remembered about the story, children's verbal recall of the story was tested on both a spontaneous and an aided basis. In free recall, procured just following the story presentation, children were instructed to "tell the story back as close as you can remember it to the way it was told to you." For aided recall, a series of open-ended probes were administered about the story content (e.g., what was said and done in each major segment of the story).

Picture ordering. This task served as an alternate, nonverbal measure of children's grasp of the storyline — in particular, their ability to reconstruct the narrative sequence of events. Seven illustrations were selected that sampled major events in the story. To abstract the images from both media, a schematized line drawing of each illustration was prepared. These drawings were laid out in random order, and the children were asked to rearrange them into the correct order "so that they tell the story just the same way it happened."

Inference making. To discern learning beyond the explicit story content, diverse inferences were sampled: physical features of characters (size, strength), character affect, and attributes of story events (duration, distance, and difficulty). Two types of information were solicited from children: the specific inference drawn (weak or strong?) and the source of evidence used to substantiate each inference (how do you know?). In the case of temporal (duration) and spatial (distance) inferences, children estimated the duration and distance traveled for a repeated story event.

Viewing behaviors. Two story-related behaviors generated spontaneously by children during the session were monitored: physical gesturing (i.e., any clearly visible body movements used to illustrate the verbal recounting of the story) and conversation initiated by children during the story presentation.

Scoring

Story recall. Three kinds of content were identified for medium differences: actions, dialogue, and figurative language. An action was defined as an independent clause containing an active verb (except verbs introducing dialogue). Instances of dialogue were defined as independent clauses of speech directed between characters, often preceded by verbs like *said* or *asked*. Figurative language was defined by use of words for their formally expressive properties, aside from any referential meaning; these included phonetic refrains (e.g., *sora sora sora*), repeated words and phrases (e.g., "It is raining, raining, raining"), and the African titles and descriptive terms used to name each of the main characters (e.g., "Osebo, the leopard-of-the-terrible-teeth").

One of the three parallel episodes comprising the middle of the story was randomly selected for inclusion in analysis, and the other two were omitted. The remainder of the story was retained in analysis. One point was assigned if in the child's spontaneous or probed retelling, the gist or approximate content of each of 24 actions, 13 bits of dialogue, and 17 instances of figurative language were included. To test for reliability, a random sample of protocols (drawn anew for each of the three content scores) was independently scored by a reader who was blind to condition. Based on the total scorable units, initial agreement with the experimenter's ratings was 97% for actions, 95% for dialogue, and 97% for figurative language.

Inference making. A coding system was developed to describe sources of information on which children based their inferences. Two general categories were defined: reasons using explicit story content and those applying to information not included in the given story content. Each of these was further articulated. Within-story content could have (a) a visual source (e.g., the appearance of characters or depiction of their actions) or (b) a textual source (e.g., in dialogue or other exclusively verbal content). Outside-story information could be based on (a) inferred story content (e.g., "Ananse was smart"), (b) general beliefs or knowledge about the world (e.g., "Skinny people are usually bigger"), or (c) a personal association with a character or situation (e.g., "I would have got mad too").

For example, in assessing the difficulty of hanging the tied leopard up in the tree, the text provided the following reference: "So Ananse tied the leopard by his foot, by his foot, by his foot, by his foot, with the vine creeper." The accompanying book illustration shows the event's outcome: Ananse leans away from the tree, one end of the rope held taut in hand, the other tied around the suspended leopard. In the film, this hanging is animated in four distinct pulls, each synchronized with one "by his foot," ending in the same position assumed in the book. Responses coded as relying on visual content consisted primarily of action descriptions (e.g., "the way he was pulling the rope," "It looked like he was struggling"). Reasons coded as textual took into account dialogue (e.g., "The leopard would let him 'cause he said they were playing a game"). Responses were allocated to outside-story sources when children applied such general knowledge as "leopards are heavy."

Each distinctive reason provided by the children was tallied as one. To test for reliability, an independent judge scored all protocols blind to condition. Percentage of agreement was based on the total number of scored responses for each inference. An average of 89% agreement was achieved across the four items between the judge's and author's scores. Each analysis addressed the question of whether differences were present in the extent to which children drew on visual information in making inferences about the story.

Elapsed time and distance traveled. Most of the older children offered estimates in standard units of measurement. (The younger children's estimates were too idiosyncratic to be included in the analysis.) Time-duration responses were categorized as less than 1 hour, 1 or more hours, or 1 day or more. Reported distances were coded into number of feet ($<$1,000 or $\geq$1,000) or number of miles ($<$1,000 or $\geq$1,000).

RESULTS

Table 1 provides a summary of significant effects of medium and age on each dependent variable.

Story Recall

Each of the three content scores — actions, dialogue, and figurative language — was subjected to an analysis of variance with two between-subjects factors — medium and age.

As predicted, children shown the television version exhibited significantly higher recall of the story actions than those presented the story in picture book form, $F(1, 44) = 4.12$, $p < .05$. Conversely, exposure to the picture book elicited greater recall of the story's figurative language than did the televised rendering, $F(1, 44) = 7.53$, $p < .01$. With regard to recall of dialogue, however, the advantage accrued to children in the book condition occurred primarily among the younger children and is not significant,

Table 1. SUMMARY OF SIGNIFICANT EFFECTS OF MEDIUM AND AGE ON EACH DEPENDENT VARIABLE

	Significant independent variables	
Dependent variable	*Medium advantage*	*Age advantage*
Verbal recall [a]		
Actions	Television*	9–10 (older)**
Figurative language	Book**	9–10*
Dialogue	*ns*	9–10**
Narrative sequence[b]	*ns*	9–10***
Visual basis for inference[b]		
Character size	Television*	*ns*
Character affect	Television*	*ns*
Difficulty of action	Television**	*ns*
Nonvisual basis[b]		
Character strength	Book**	*ns*
Estimates for story events[b]		
Shorter elapsed time	Television*	—
Shorter distance traveled	Television	—
Physical gesturing[b]	Television	9–10*
Initiating verbalization[b]	Book***	*ns*

Note. Only those effects with $p < .10$ are shown.
[a] Uses F test. [b] Uses chi-square or Fisher exact probability test.
* $p < .05$. ** $p < .01$. *** $p < .001$.

$F(1, 44) = 2.19$. The age effect is significant in all cases, with the older children recalling more of the actions, $F(1, 44) = 17.20$, $p < .01$, figurative language, $F(1, 44) = 5.09$, $p < .05$, and dialogue $F(1, 44) = 38.68$, $p < .01$ than the younger children. There were no interaction effects.

Picture Ordering

This measure was scored on the basis of whether or not the entire sequence of seven pictures was correctly reconstructed. The chi-square test was used for analysis of this and remaining data, except when an expected cell value fell below 5.0, in which case the Fisher exact probability test was substituted. In all cases, the data were laid out in 2 × 2 contingency tables ($df = 1$).

Whereas more of the younger children in the picture book condition correctly reordered the story sequence than those exposed to the television format ($p = .07$), the older children's responses suggest the opposite tendency ($p = .14$). With regard to age differences, the older children were significantly more successful than the younger children in handling this sequencing task ($\chi^2 = 14.10$, $p < .001$), due primarily to the large gap in performance between the two age groups of children who were presented the television story (correct ordering of the seven picture sequence: 11 of 12 older children, 1 of 12 younger children). When errors were defined more precisely as the number of misplaced pictures within each constructed sequence, the same performance patterns appeared: The younger children in the video condition committed the greatest number of individual errors, and the older children in the video condition committed the fewest.

Inference Making

As hypothesized, rendering of this story in each medium is correlated with children's use of different kinds of information as the basis for making story-related inferences. Exposure to the television story is associated with significantly greater use of visual information as a basis for drawing inferences about character's size ($\chi^2 = 4.74$, $p < .05$), affect ($\chi^2 = 5.36$, $p < .05$), and the difficulty of performing a story event ($\chi^2 = 6.76$, $p < .01$). The explanations generated by children in the book condition suggest a complementary preference for strictly textual content and outside-story references. In the case of character strength, most children use some visual information as a basis for their inferences. However, when their remaining responses were analyzed, the children who were presented with the book were found to make significantly more use of other kinds of information (i.e., the unillustrated story text and outside-story data) than those exposed to the video format ($\chi^2 = 6.72$, $p < .01$).

Interestingly, there were no systematic differences in the inferences themselves, only in the evidence offered to explain them. Thus, these findings highlight the variation in approaches to inference making that may underlie superficially similar solutions.

In terms of age differences, there was a tendency — in one case significant ($\chi^2 = 5.36$, $p < .05$) — for the older children to bring more outside-story knowledge to bear than younger ones in substantiating their inferences.

Elapsed time and distance traveled. Analysis of these items pertains only to older children. A significant relationship was found between children's time estimates for this event and the story medium; estimates of shorter duration (< 1 hour) are significantly associated with exposure to the video version, and those of longer duration (≥ 1 hour) are significantly associated with the picture book presentation ($\chi^2 = 6.18$, $p < .02$). With regard to distance traveled, there was a tendency for children in the television treatment to offer estimates of less distance ($< 1{,}000$ feet) and for children experiencing the story in its picture book format to report perceptions of greater distance ($p = .07$).

Further analysis indicated that two thirds of the children who estimated either the least or the most distance for the character to travel also cited the correspondingly shortest or longest times for this trip to take. This suggests some internal consistency in children's perceptions of the event and also builds confidence in the reliability and validity of their responses.

Spontaneous Behavior

Gesturing. Children receiving the television story tended to use physical gestures to illustrate their verbal retelling of the story more often than those who were presented with the book ($\chi^2 = 3.08$, $.05 < p < .10$). The story content illustrated was almost always actions (as defined in verbal recall). For example, "Mmoatia the fairy . . . came dancing, dancing, dancing" was enacted by two fingers "dancing" on the table top. The older children were significantly more likely than younger children to accompany their recounting with illustrative gestures ($\chi^2 = 5.48$, $p < .02$). Among those children who gestured, the older 9- to 10-year-olds also tended to gesture more than their younger counterparts ($M = 5.0$ older; $M = 2.5$ younger).

Initiating conversation. Children were significantly more likely to initiate story-relevant verbalization (either comments or questions) when the story was presented in its picture book format than when communicated as a television story ($\chi^2 = 11.12$, $p < .001$). The two age groups behaved similarly.

DISCUSSION

Medium Differences

The findings of this research offer evidence of significant differences in children's responses to comparable story material presented in two different media — picture book and television. The media differences observed provide support for the hypothesis that structural differences in these media — in particular, differences in their relative visualization of a story — influence which content is conveyed more effectively to children.

The film's provision of more visual information may well bring this content to the foreground of children's attention. Children who experienced the televised story recalled more story actions (usually depicted) and more often used information judged to have its source in visual content to explain their story-related inferences. The suggested tendency toward more frequent gesturing among these children may be another expression of television's emphasis on behavioral content. That is, the film's animation of characters may provide a more ready stimulus for reenactment than the book's still images. This interpretation is certainly consistent with social learning theory and research on observational learning (Bandura, 1969; Friedrich & Stein, 1973).

Conversely, the lesser visual information offered in the book seems to permit greater attention to the verbal text. Children who were read the story in book form remembered more figurative language, which (having no visual counterpart) relies solely on being heard. The book audience also sought more of their explanations for inferences from nonvisual sources.

However, this explanation does not account for the nonsignificant medium difference observed in the recall of dialogue or for variation in recall within each of the three content categories. Consideration of several factors should help future research make better predictions about medium differences in story recall.

Visual reinforcement of text. Television does illustrate some kinds of story content more than others; for example, actions tend to be visualized more often than dialogue. However, there are also instances in which television does not directly illustrate a story action (e.g., "and filled a calabash with water" shows a calabash shaking in limbo on the screen) and does depict the content of dialogue (e.g., Ananse sprinkles water over the hornet nest and cries, "It is raining, raining, raining"). Close analysis of the variation in visual treatment of story content will enable researchers to generate finer predictions about recall.

Importance of story content. Content elements vary in their importance to the plot. More important story content tends to be better remembered by children and adults (Brown & Smiley, 1977; Johnson, 1970). In the present study, what appear to be more important actions tend to be better remembered by children in both medium conditions. If story elements are rated for importance a priori, this variation could be incorporated into predictions about recall. (Interestingly, to the extent that illustrators and film producers intuitively choose to illustrate the more important content, importance and visual reinforcement of content may be "confounded" in effective story materials.)

Redundancy of story content. Taking into account the sequential and cumulative nature of narrative content, differences exist in the extent to which content elements introduce new information (Paul, 1959). Although repetitive story content may not necessarily be better remembered, children's retention of repetitive figurative language also suggests that a story's text does not function homogeneously to convey objective information. Rather, a story's use of language needs to be closely studied, for words may work as sounds as well as symbols with referential meaning (Arnheim, 1969).

Space and time. The differences in spatial and temporal estimates reported provide supportive evidence for the premise that the different treatment of space and time by each medium influences not only *what* but *how* story content is perceived. The finding that children experiencing the televised story estimate shorter distances and elapsed time for story events suggests that television's more continuous rendering of story events, as compared with the book's rendering, may tend to compress these physical dimensions in the viewer's perception.

Alternatively, however, it would seem more accurate to base such predictions on the specific ways each medium handles events. For example, film's potential ability to lengthen as well as shorten the duration of an event is well documented (Burch, 1973; Eisenstein, 1949; Millar & Reisz, 1968). In advancing hypotheses, it is important to consider how much of given events is shown and the degree of spatial and temporal continuity with which they are represented.

The striking difference observed in children's conversation during the story presentation is consonant with their potential control over the flow of each story in time. Television stories are not typically subject to the stop and start control of the viewer; if you do not want to miss anything, you need to be fairly quiet and attentive. In comparison, children can interrupt a storybook delivery with their questions or comments in a one-to-one exchange with the narrator. In naturalistic storytelling settings, this difference in interaction and the resulting variation in story renderings would probably be even greater.

Format of measures. In the case of the picture-ordering task, the tendency toward better performance among younger children exposed to the book may be due to their better grasp of the storyline. Alternatively, however, there may be an interaction between task and medium. Children in the storybook condition have been exposed to fewer "intermediate" images. Relatedly, the format of the task may be more readily comprehensible to children whose initial experience of the story included viewing a similar sequence of individual pictures. In future research, it will be important to incorporate dependent measures with care as to their degree of similarity to or difference from the form in which the story content is presented.

Age Differences

The extent to which differences appear in the performance of the two age groups varied with the nature of the task. For example, older children consistently outperformed younger children on tasks requiring verbal recall of the story or picture reconstruction of the narrative sequence. The frequency with which gesturing accompanied children's story retelling was also significantly related to age. The greater occurrence of gesturing among older children may reflect greater command over both the story content and the task of retelling so that they have "energy left over" to embellish their speech. Future research should provide children, especially younger children, with other opportunities to physically reenact stories. Recording and analysis of this measure also need to be refined to identify the nature (e.g., imitativeness or novelty) and extent of this behavioral response. In contrast, there was virtually no difference in the extent to which both age groups initiated conversation during the story telling. That the children behaved similarly in each age group suggests the consistency with which this ascribed difference in medium context may influence children's behavior.

Implications

This research needs to be replicated using different story materials and drawing from different populations of children. If a given medium brings specific story content to the foreground of children's attention (that content emphasized being a function of its own material properties), then children repeatedly exposed to this medium may accumulate experience with some kinds of information more than others. They may attend to it, recognize it, remember it, interpret it, use it in problem solving, perhaps even prefer it to other information. Moreover, they may be cultivating the particular cognitive skills required to extract this information from the symbol systems in which it is represented (Salomon, 1979).

A possible consequence is that children raised on television stories may develop a strong visual memory for and sensitivity to stories, whereas story experience with books, radio, and other less visual media may foster greater listening skills and the application of more self-generated knowledge in interpreting their meaning. Conceivably, development of specific perceptual skills may be affected by the balance of visual and auditory information available in the media to which children are exposed. To the extent that experiences with different media activate and develop specific kinds of skills and learning, delineation of these media effects will inform us about the development of intelligence.

REFERENCE NOTES

1. Stein, N. L. *The effects of increasing temporal disorganization on children's recall of stories.* Paper presented at the meeting of the Psychonomic Society, St. Louis, November 1976.

2. Stein, N. L., & Glenn, C. G. *A developmental study of children's recall of story material.* Paper presented at the meeting of the Society for Research in Child Development, Denver, April 1975.

REFERENCES

Arnheim, R. *Visual thinking.* London: Faber & Faber, 1969.

Bandura, A. Social-learning theory of identificatory processes. In D. A. Goslin (Ed.), *Handbook of socialization theory and research.* Chicago: Rand McNally, 1969.

Brown, A. L. Recognition, reconstruction, and recall of narrative sequences by pre-operational children. *Child Development,* 1975, *46,* 156–166.

Brown, A. L., & Smiley, S. Rating the importance of structural units of prose passages: A problem of metacognitive development. *Child Development,* 1977, *48,* 1–8.

Burch, N. *The theory of film practice.* New York: Praeger, 1973.

Collins, W. A. Learning of media content: A developmental study. *Child Development,* 1970, *41,* 1133–1142.

Collins, W. A. Children's comprehension of television content. In E. Wartella (Ed.), *Development of children's communicative behavior.* Beverly Hills, Calif.: Sage, 1979.

Duke, J. S. *Children's books and magazines: A market study.* White Plains, N.Y.: Knowledge Industry Publications, 1979.

Eisenstein, S. *Film form.* New York: Harcourt, Brace, 1949.

Flapan, D. *Children's understanding of social interaction.* New York: Teachers College Press, 1968.

Friedman, S., & Stevenson, M. Developmental changes in the understanding of implied motion in two-dimensional pictures. *Child Development,* 1975, *46,* 773–778.

Friedrich, L. K., & Stein, A. H. Aggressive and prosocial television programs and the natural behavior of preschool children. *Monographs of the Society for Research in Child Development,* 1973, *38* (4, Serial No. 151).

Gardner, H., Howard, V., & Perkins, D. Symbol systems: A philosophical, psychological and educational investigation. In D. Olson (Ed.), *Media and symbols: The forms of expression, communication and education.* Chicago: National Society for the Study of Education, 1974.

Haley, G. *A story a story.* New York: Atheneum, 1970.

Johnson, R. Recall of prose as a function of the structural importance of the linguistic units. *Journal of Verbal Learning and Verbal Behavior,* 1970, *9,* 12–20.

Mandler, J., & Johnson, N. Remembrance of things parsed: Story structure and recall. *Cognitive Psychology,* 1977, *9,* 111–151.

McLuhan, M. *The Gutenberg galaxy.* Toronto, Canada: University of Toronto Press, 1962.

Meringoff, L. K. *A story a story: The Influence of the medium on children's apprehension of stories* (Doctoral dissertation, Harvard University, 1978). *Dissertation Abstracts International,* 1978, *39,* 06A-3476. (University Microfilms No. 78-23681)

Metz, C. *Language and cinema.* The Hague, Netherlands: Mouton, 1974.

Millar, G., & Reisz, K. *The technique of film editing.* New York: Hastings House, 1968.

Olson, D., & Bruner, J. Learning through experience and learning through media. In D. Olson (Ed.), *Media and symbols: The forms of expression, communication and education.* Chicago: National Society for the Study of Education, 1974.

Paul, I. H. Studies in remembering: The reproduction of connected and extended verbal material. *Psychological Issues,* 1959, *1* (2).

Salomon, G. Media and symbol systems as related to cognition and learning. *Journal of Educational Psychology,* 1979, *71,* 131–148.

Schindel, M. (Producer). *A story a story.* Weston, Conn.: Weston Woods, 1973. (Film)

Schramm, W. *Big media, little media.* Beverly Hills, Calif.: Sage, 1977.

B. F. Skinner

from WALDEN TWO

EDITOR'S NOTE: Published in 1948, *Walden Two* is B. F. Skinner's novel depicting a utopian community based on the principles of behavioristic psychology. A group of people from a nearby university have come to spend a few days visiting Walden Two. T. E. Frazier, one of the community's founders, is their host. In the following selection Frazier has brought the visitors to the children's quarters where Mrs. Nash, a children's caretaker, explains how the community raises its children. The guests, especially Professor Burris and Mr. Castle, discuss the problems of developing self-control in children.

The quarters for children from one to three consisted of several small playrooms with Lilliputian furniture, a child's lavatory, and a dressing and locker room. Several small sleeping rooms were operated on the same principle as the baby-cubicles. The temperature and the humidity were controlled so that clothes or bedclothing were not needed. The cots were double-decker arrangements of the plastic mattresses we had seen in the cubicles. The children slept unclothed, except for diapers. There were more beds than necessary, so that the children could be grouped according to developmental age or exposure to contagious diseases or need for supervision, or for educational purposes.

We followed Mrs. Nash to a large screened porch on the south side of the building, where several children were playing in sandboxes and on swings and climbing apparatuses. A few wore "training pants"; the rest were naked. Beyond the porch was a grassy play yard enclosed by closely trimmed hedges, where other children, similarly undressed, were at play. Some kind of marching game was in progress.

As we returned, we met two women carrying food hampers. They spoke to Mrs. Nash and followed her to the porch. In a moment five or six children came running into the playrooms and were soon using the lavatory and dressing themselves. Mrs. Nash explained that they were being taken on a picnic.

"What about the children who don't go?" said Castle. "What do you do about the green-eyed monster?"

Mrs. Nash was puzzled.

"Jealousy. Envy," Castle elaborated. "Don't the children who stay home ever feel unhappy about it?"

"I don't understand," said Mrs. Nash.

"And I hope you won't try," said Frazier, with a smile. "I'm afraid we must be moving along."

We said good-bye, and I made an effort to thank Mrs. Nash, but she seemed to be puzzled by that too, and Frazier frowned as if I had committed some breach of good taste.

"I think Mrs. Nash's puzzlement," said Frazier, as we left the building, "is proof enough that our children are seldom envious or jealous. Mrs. Nash was twelve years old when Walden Two was founded. It was a little late to undo her early training, but I think we were successful. She's a good example of the Walden Two product. She could probably recall the experience of jealousy, but it's not part of her present life."

"Surely that's going too far!" said Castle. "You can't be so godlike as all that! You must be assailed by emotions just as much as the rest of us!"

"We can discuss the question of godlikeness later, if you wish," replied Frazier. "As to emotions — we aren't free of them all, nor should we like to be. But the meaner and more annoying — the emotions which breed unhappiness — are almost unknown here, like unhappiness itself. We don't need them any longer in our struggle for existence, and it's easier on our circulatory system, and certainly pleasanter, to dispense with them."

"If you've discovered how to do that, you are indeed a genius," said Castle. He seemed almost stunned as Frazier nodded assent. "We all know that emotions are useless and bad for our peace of mind and our blood pressure," he went on. "But how arrange things otherwise?"

"We arrange them otherwise here," said Frazier. He was showing a mildness of manner which I was coming to recognize as a sign of confidence.

"But emotions are — fun!" said Barbara. "Life wouldn't be worth living without them."

"Some of them, yes," said Frazier. "The productive and strengthening emotions — joy and love. But sorrow and hate — and the high-voltage excitements of anger, fear, and rage — are out of proportion with the needs of modern life, and they're wasteful and dangerous. Mr. Castle has mentioned jealousy — a minor form of anger, I think we may call it. Naturally we avoid it. It has served its purpose in the evolution of man; we've no further use for it. If we allowed it to persist, it would only sap the life out of us. In a cooperative society there's no jealousy because there's no need for jealousy."

"That implies that you all get everything you want," said Castle. "But what about social possessions? Last night you mentioned the young man who chose a particular girl or profession. There's still a chance for jealousy there, isn't there?"

"It doesn't imply that we get everything we want," said Frazier. "Of course we don't. But jealousy wouldn't help. In a competitive world there's some point to it. It energizes one to attack a frustrating condition. The impulse and the added energy are an advantage. Indeed, in a competitive world emotions work all too well. Look at the singular lack of success of the complacent man. He enjoys a more serene life, but it's less likely to be a fruitful one. The world isn't ready for simple pacifism or Christian humility, to cite two cases in point. Before you can safely train out the destructive and wasteful emotions, you must make sure they're no longer needed."

"How do you make sure that jealousy isn't needed in Walden Two?" I said.

"In Walden Two problems can't be solved by attacking others," said Frazier with marked finality.

"That's not the same as eliminating jealousy, though," I said.

"Of course it's not. But when a particular emotion is no longer a useful part of a behavioral repertoire, we proceed to eliminate it."

"Yes, but how?"

"It's simply a matter of behavioral engineering," said Frazier.

"Behavioral engineering?"

"You're baiting me, Burris. You know perfectly well what I mean. The techniques have been available for centuries. We use them in education and in the psychological management of the community. But you're forcing my hand," he added. "I was saving that for this evening. But let's strike while the iron is hot."

We had stopped at the door of the large children's building. Frazier shrugged his shoulders, walked to the shade of a large tree, and threw himself on the ground. We arranged ourselves about him and waited.

* * *

"Each of us," Frazier began, "is engaged in a pitched battle with the rest of mankind."

"A curious premise for a Utopia," said Castle. "Even a pessimist like myself takes a more hopeful view than that."

"You do, you do," said Frazier. "But let's be realistic. Each of us has interests which conflict with the interests of everybody else. That's our original sin, and it can't be helped. Now, 'everybody else' we call 'society.' It's a powerful opponent, and it always wins. Oh, here and there an individual prevails for a while and gets what he wants. Sometimes he storms the culture of a society and changes it slightly to his own advantage. But society wins in the long run, for it has the advantage of numbers and of age. Many prevail against one, and men against a baby. Society attacks early, when the individual is helpless. It enslaves him almost before he has tasted freedom. The 'ologies' will tell you how it's done. Theology calls it building a conscience or developing a spirit of selflessness. Psychology calls it the growth of the super-ego.

"Considering how long society has been at it, you'd expect a better job. But the campaigns have been badly planned and the victory has never been secure. The behavior of the individual has been shaped according to revelations of 'good conduct,' never as the result of experimental study. But why not experiment? The questions are simple enough. What's the best behavior for the individual so far as the group is concerned? And how can the individual be induced to behave in that way? Why not explore these questions in a scientific spirit?

"We could do just that in Walden Two. We had already worked out a code of conduct — subject, of course, to experimental modification. The code would keep things running smoothly if everybody lived up to it. Our job was to see that everybody did. Now, you can't get people to follow a useful code by making them into so many jacks-in-the-box. You can't foresee all future circumstances, and you can't specify adequate future conduct. You don't know what will be required. Instead you have to set up certain behavioral processes which will lead the individual to design his own 'good' conduct when the time comes. We call that sort of thing 'self-control.' But don't be misled, the control always rests in the last analysis in the hands of society.

"One of our Planners, a young man named Simmons, worked with me. It was the first time in history that the matter was approached in an experimental way. Do you question that statement, Mr. Castle?"

"I'm not sure I know what you are talking about," said Castle.

"Then let me go on. Simmons and I began by studying the great works on morals and ethics — Plato, Aristotle, Confucius, the New Testament, the Puritan divines, Machiavelli, Chesterfield, Freud — there were scores of them. We were looking for any and every method of shaping human behavior by imparting techniques of self-control. Some techniques were obvious enough, for they had marked turning points in human history. 'Love your enemies' is an example — a psychological invention for easing the lot of an oppressed people. The severest trial of oppression is the constant rage which one suffers at the thought of the oppressor. What Jesus discovered was how to avoid these inner devastations. His technique was to *practice the opposite emotion.* If a man can succeed in 'loving his enemies' and 'taking no thought for the morrow,' he will no longer be assailed by hatred of the oppressor or rage at the loss of his freedom or possessions. He may not get his freedom or possessions back, but he's less miserable. It's a difficult lesson. It comes late in our program."

"I thought you were opposed to modifying emotions and instincts until the world was ready for it," said Castle. "According to you, the principle of 'love your enemies' should have been suicidal."

"It would have been suicidal, except for an entirely unforeseen consequence. Jesus must have been quite astonished at the effect of his discovery. We are only just beginning to understand the power of love because we are just beginning to understand the weakness of force and aggression. But the science of behavior is clear about all that now. Recent discoveries in the analysis of punishment — but I am falling into one digression after another. Let me save my explanation of why the Christian virtues — and I mean merely the Christian techniques of self-control — have not disappeared from the face of the earth, with due recognition of the fact that they suffered a narrow squeak within recent memory.

"When Simmons and I had collected our techniques of control, we had to discover how to teach them. That was more difficult. Current educational practices were of little value, and religious practices scarcely any better. Promising paradise or threatening hell-fire is, we assumed, generally admitted to be unproductive. It is based upon a fundamental fraud which, when discovered, turns the individual against society and nourishes the very thing it tries to stamp out. What Jesus offered in return for loving one's enemies was heaven *on earth,* better known as peace of mind.

"We found a few suggestions worth following in the practices of the clinical psychologist. We undertook to build a tolerance for annoying experiences. The sunshine of midday is extremely painful if you come from a dark room, but take it in easy stages and you can avoid pain altogther. The analogy can be misleading, but in much the same way it's possible to build a tolerance to painful or distasteful stimuli, or to frustration, or to situations which arouse fear, anger or rage. Society and nature throw these annoyances at the individual with no regard for the development of tolerances. Some achieve tolerances, most fail. Where would the science of immunization be if it followed a schedule of accidental dosages?

"Take the principle of 'Get thee behind me, Satan,' for example," Frazier continued. "It's a special case of self-control by altering the environment. Subclass A 3, I believe. We give each child a lollipop which has been dipped in powdered sugar so that a single touch of the tongue can be detected. We tell him he may eat the lollipop later in the day, provided it hasn't already been licked. Since the child is only three or four, it is a fairly diff ——— "

"Three or four!" Castle exclaimed.

"All our ethical training is completed by the age of six," said Frazier quietly. "A simple principle like putting temptation out of sight would be acquired before four. But at such an early age the problem of not licking the lollipop isn't easy. Now, what would you do, Mr. Castle, in a similar situation?"

"Put the lollipop out of sight as quickly as possible."

"Exactly. I can see you've been well trained. Or perhaps you discovered the principle for yourself. We're in favor of original inquiry wherever possible, but in this case we have a more important goal and we don't hesitate to give verbal help. First of all, the children are urged to examine their own behavior while looking at the lollipops. This helps them to recognize the need for self-control. Then the lollipops are concealed, and the children are asked to notice any gain in happiness or any reduction in tension. Then a strong distraction is arranged — say, an interesting game. Later the children are reminded of the candy and encouraged to examine their reaction. The value of the distraction is generally obvious. Well, need I go on? When the experiment is repeated a day or so later, the children all run with the lollipops to their lockers and do exactly what Mr. Castle would do — a sufficient indication of the success of our training."

"I wish to report an objective observation of my reaction to your story," said Castle, controlling his voice with great precision. "I find myself revolted by this display of sadistic tyranny."

"I don't wish to deny you the exercise of an emotion which you seem to find enjoyable," said Frazier. "So let me go on. Concealing a tempting but forbidden object is a crude solution. For one thing, it's not always feasible. We want a sort of psychological concealment — covering up the candy by paying no attention. In a later experiment the children wear their lollipops like crucifixes for a few hours."

"Instead of the cross, the lollipop,
About my neck was hung,"

said Castle.

"I wish somebody had taught me that, though," said Rodge, with a glance at Barbara.

"Don't we all?" said Frazier. "Some of us learn control, more or less by accident. The rest of us go all our lives not even understanding how it is possible, and blaming our failure on being born the wrong way."

"How do you build up a tolerance to an annoying situation?" I said.

"Oh, for example, by having the children 'take' a more and more painful shock, or drink cocoa with less and less sugar in it until a bitter concoction can be savored without a bitter face."

"But jealousy or envy — you can't administer them in graded doses," I said.

"And why not? Remember, we control the social environment, too, at this age. That's why we get our ethical training in early. Take this case. A group of children arrive home after a long walk tired and hungry. They're expecting supper; they find, instead, that it's time for a lesson in self-control: they must stand for five minutes in front of steaming bowls of soup.

"The assignment is accepted like a problem in arithmetic. Any groaning or complaining is a wrong answer. Instead, the children begin at once to work upon themselves to avoid any unhappiness during the delay. One of them may make a joke of it. We encourage a sense of humor as a good way of not taking an annoyance seriously. The joke won't be much, according to adult standards — perhaps the child will simply pretend to empty the bowl of soup into his upturned mouth. Another may start a song with many verses. The rest join in at once, for they've learned that it's a good way to make time pass."

Frazier glanced uneasily at Castle, who was not to be appeased.

"That also strikes you as a form of torture, Mr. Castle?" he asked.

"I'd rather be put on the rack," said Castle.

"Then you have by no means had the thorough training I supposed. You can't imagine how lightly the children take such an experience. It's a rather severe biological frustration, for the children are tired and hungry and they must stand and look at food; but it's passed off as lightly as a five-minute delay at curtain time. We regard it as a fairly elementary test. Much more difficult problems follow."

"I suspected as much," muttered Castle.

"In a later stage we forbid all social devices. No songs, no jokes — merely silence. Each child is forced back upon his own resources — a very important step."

"I should think so," I said. "And how do you know it's successful? You might produce a lot of silently resentful children. It's certainly a dangerous stage."

"It is, and we follow each child carefully.

If he hasn't picked up the necessary techniques, we start back a little. A still more advanced stage" — Frazier glanced again at Castle, who stirred uneasily — "brings me to my point. When it's time to sit down to the soup, the children count off — heads and tails. Then a coin is tossed and if it comes up heads, the 'heads' sit down and eat. The 'tails' remain standing for another five minutes."

Castle groaned.

"And you call that envy?" I said.

"Perhaps not exactly," said Frazier. "At least there's seldom any aggression against the lucky ones. The emotion, if any, is directed against Lady Luck herself, against the toss of the coin. That, in itself, is a lesson worth learning, for it's the only direction in which emotion has a surviving chance to be useful. And resentment toward things in general, while perhaps just as silly as personal aggression, is more easily controlled. Its expression is not socially objectionable."

Frazier looked nervously from one of us to the other. He seemed to be trying to discover whether we shared Castle's prejudice. I began to realize, also, that he had not really wanted to tell this story. He was vulnerable. He was treading on sanctified ground, and I was pretty sure he had not established the value of most of these practices in an experimental fashion. He could scarcely have done so in the short space of ten years. He was working on faith, and it bothered him.

I tried to bolster his confidence by reminding him that he had a professional colleague among his listeners. "May you not inadvertently teach your children some of the very emotions you're trying to eliminate?" I said. "What's the effect, for example, of finding the anticipation of a warm supper suddenly thwarted? Doesn't that eventually lead to feelings of uncertainty, or even anxiety?"

"It might. We had to discover how often our lessons could be safely administered. But all our schedules are worked out experimentally. We watch for undesired consequences just as any scientist watches for disrupting factors in his experiments.

"After all, it's a simple and sensible program," he went on in a tone of appeasement. "We set up a system of gradually increasing annoyances and frustrations against a background of complete serenity. An easy environment is made more and more difficult as the children acquire the capacity to adjust."

"But *why?*" said Castle. "Why these deliberate unpleasantnesses — to put it mildly? I must say I think you and your friend Simmons are really very subtle sadists."

"You've reversed your position, Mr. Castle," said Frazier in a sudden flash of anger with which I rather sympathized. Castle was calling names, and he was also being unaccountably and perhaps intentionally obtuse. "A while ago you accused me of breeding a race of softies," Frazier continued. "Now you object to toughening them up. But what you don't understand is that these potentially unhappy situations are never very annoying. Our schedules make sure of that. You wouldn't understand, however, because you're not so far advanced as our children."

Castle grew black.

"But what do your children get out of it?" he insisted, apparently trying to press some vague advantage in Frazier's anger.

"What do they get out of it!" exclaimed Frazier, his eyes flashing with a sort of helpless contempt. His lips curled and he dropped his head to look at his fingers, which were crushing a few blades of grass.

"They must get happiness and freedom and strength," I said, putting myself in a ridiculous position in attempting to make peace.

"They don't sound happy or free to me, standing in front of bowls of Forbidden Soup," said Castle, answering me parenthetically while continuing to stare at Frazier.

"If I must spell it out," Frazier began with a deep sigh, "what they get is escape from the petty emotions which eat the heart out of the unprepared. They get the satisfaction of pleasant and profitable social relations on a scale almost undreamed of in the world at large. They get immeasurably increased efficiency, because they can stick to a job without suffering the aches and pains which soon beset most of us. They get new horizons, for they are spared the emotions characteristic of frustration and failure. They get — " His eyes searched the branches of the trees. "Is that enough?" he said at last.

"And the community must gain their loyalty," I said, "when they discover the fears and jealousies and diffidences in the world at large."

"I'm glad you put it that way," said Frazier. "You might have said that they must feel superior to the miserable products of our public schools. But we're at pains to keep any feeling of superiority or contempt under control, too. Having suffered most acutely from it myself, I put the subject first on our agenda. We carefully avoid any joy in a personal triumph which means the personal failure of somebody else. We take no pleasure in the sophistical, the disputative, the dialectical." He threw a vicious glance at Castle. "We don't use the motive of domination, because we are always thinking of the whole group. We could motivate a few geniuses that way — it was certainly my own motivation — but we'd sacrifice some of the happiness of everyone else. Triumph over nature and over oneself, yes. But over others, never."

"You've taken the mainspring out of the watch," said Castle flatly.

"That's an experimental question, Mr. Castle, and you have the wrong answer."

Frazier was making no effort to conceal his feeling. If he had been riding Castle, he was now using his spurs. Perhaps he sensed that the rest of us had come round and that he could change his tactics with a single holdout. But it was more than strategy, it was genuine feeling. Castle's undeviating skepticism was a growing frustration.

"Are your techniques really so very new?" I said hurriedly. "What about the primitive practice of submitting a boy to various tortures before granting him a place among adults? What about the disciplinary techniques of Puritanism? Or of the modern school, for that matter?"

"In one sense you're right," said Frazier. "And I think you've nicely answered Mr. Castle's tender concern for our little ones. The unhappinesses we deliberately impose are far milder than the normal unhappinesses from which we offer protection. Even at the height of our ethical training, the unhappiness is ridiculously trivial — to the well-trained child.

"But there's a world of difference in the way we use these annoyances," he continued. "For one thing, we don't punish. We never administer an unpleasantness in the hope of repressing or eliminating undesirable behavior. But there's another difference. In most cultures the child meets up with annoyances and reverses of uncontrolled magnitude. Some are imposed in the name of discipline by persons in authority. Some, like hazings, are condoned though not authorized. Others are merely accidental. No one cares to, or is able to, prevent them.

"We all know what happens. A few hardy children emerge, particularly those who have got their unhappiness in doses that could be swallowed. They become brave men. Others become sadists or masochists of varying degrees of pathology. Not having conquered a painful environment, they become preoccupied with pain and make a devious art of it. Others submit — and hope to inherit the earth. The rest — the cravens, the cowards — live in fear for the rest of their lives. And that's only a single field — the reaction to pain. I could cite a dozen parallel cases. The optimist and the pessimist, the contented and the disgruntled, the loved and the unloved, the ambitious and the discouraged — these are only the extreme products of a miserable system.

"Traditional practices are admittedly better than nothing," Frazier went on. "Spartan or Puritan — no one can question the occasional happy result. But the whole system rests upon the wasteful principle of selection. The English public school of the nineteenth century produced brave men — by setting up almost insurmountable barriers and making the most of the few who came over. But selection isn't education. Its crops of brave men will always be small, and the waste enormous. Like all primitive principles, selection serves in place of education only through a profligate use of material. Multiply extravagantly and select with rigor. It's the philosophy of the 'big litter' as an alternative to good child hygiene.

"In Walden Two we have a different objective. We make every man a brave man. They all come over the barriers. Some require more preparation than others, but they all come over. The traditional use of adversity is to select the strong. We control adversity to build strength. And we do it deliberately, no matter how sadistic Mr. Castle may think us, in order to prepare for adversities which are beyond control. Our children eventually experience the 'heartache and the thousand natural shocks that flesh is heir to.' It would be the cruelest possible practice to protect them as long as possible, especially when we *could* protect them so well."

Frazier held out his hands in an exaggerated gesture of appeal.

"What alternative *had* we?" he said, as if he were in pain. "What else could we do? For four or five years we could provide a life in which no important need would go unsatisfied, a life practically free of anxiety or frustration or annoyance. What would *you* do? Would you let the child enjoy this paradise with no thought for the future — like an idolatrous and pampering mother? Or would you relax control of the environment and let the child meet accidental frustrations? *But what is the virtue of accident?* No, there was only one course open to us. We had to *design* a series of adversities, so that the child would develop the greatest possible self-control. Call it deliberate, if you like, and accuse us of sadism; there was no other course." Frazier turned to Castle, but he was scarcely challenging him. He seemed to be waiting, anxiously, for his capitulation. But Castle merely shifted his ground.

"I find it difficult to classify these practices," he said. Frazier emitted a disgruntled "Ha!" and sat back. "Your system seems to have usurped the place as well as the techniques of religion."

"Of religion and family culture," said Frazier wearily. "But I don't call it usurpation. Ethical training belongs to the community. As for techniques, we took every suggestion we could find without prejudice as to the source. But not on faith. We disregarded all claims of revealed truth and put every principle to an experimental test. And by the way, I've very much misrepresented the whole system if you suppose that any of the practices I've described are fixed. We try out many different techniques. Gradually we work toward the best possible set. And we don't pay much attention to the apparent success of a principle in the course of history. History is honored in Walden Two only as entertainment. It isn't taken seriously as food for thought. Which reminds me, very rudely, of our original plan for the morning. Have you had enough of emotion? Shall we turn to intellect?"

Frazier addressed these questions to Castle in a very friendly way and I was glad to see that Castle responded in kind. It was perfectly clear, however, that neither of them had ever worn a lollipop about the neck or faced a bowl of Forbidden Soup.

Dorothy Baruch

from ONE LITTLE BOY

"You can even call me Dorothy," I said to Kenneth. "But it doesn't matter. And I'm not the kind of doctor who gives vaccinations and such. I've got a playroom around the corner with clay and paints and puppets and lots of other things to play with. Let's go in there now."

He looked toward his mother. Neither seeking nor demanding. Neither quizzical nor protesting. He just looked.

"She'll wait here," I offered. And I held my hand out and led the way.

He did not take my hand.

I wondered: Would he accept friendliness from me? Would he be able to? How long would it be before he could discard the unchildlike apathy and dare trust me even a little? How long would he remain folded back into himself?

He followed me down the hall without protest, and I kept my hand extended behind me. I thought of children much younger who, even while refusing a proffered hand, still found a minute measure of comfort in knowing that it was there to reach for and cling to should one wish.

We turned the corner and I opened the playroom door.

Brown floor. Good and hardy with its covering of linoleum tile. Green-blue walls that could be washed down. A sink with running water. A stool to sit on. Nothing more. Only a closet door half ajar giving promise of playthings to explore.

I wondered if he felt as I did the comfort of this small, bare room with its lean look of sparseness and space. No demanding clutter of things to be done with. A room where a child, strengthened by the therapist's support, could gain courage to explore what lay in his mind. A room where feelings that had towered inside him like overwhelming ogres could be whittled down to manageable size. Where fantasies that had brought dread and confusion could be looked at without too grave fear that their faces would turn real. Where wishes that had seemed too close to the border of terror could be transformed into shapes that might soundly approach promised lands. Where yearnings born in the lost years and now become hopeless might return to past seekings and move on with new hope. In this room, events that had been distorted by disappointment or by misapprehension, fear and fantasy could be depicted and dramatized. They could be given form so solid that a child might finally reach a place where imagination could still communicate with horizons beyond reality while effort and action remained compatibly geared in with the real world about.

Kenneth went with me into the playroom.

He looked toward the door of the closet that stood slightly ajar. But he said nothing.

I followed his look. "Perhaps you'd like to see what's in there?"

He stood wheezing.

He needed to find out that I was available to him as a therapist is always available to a patient; that I would be beside him steadily, helping him to explore into himself. This he

---

could do through playing out his feelings, in the way that children reveal themselves, in contrast to adults who talk out what is inside. There would be no restriction on his bringing out the ugly, the absurd, the fearful. To this end he needed to discover that he could feel and say anything, and, for the most part, do what he wanted. I would try to tell him simply.

"This is a place where you can do just about anything you wish. You don't have to ask me."

He moved to the closet. Wheezing. Saying nothing.

When I opened the door he fingered the box with the doll-puppets in it. Still silent.

"Perhaps you'd like to see it?" I asked. "Shall I get it out?"

He shook his head slowly. And with voice held in and almost tearful, he said, "I'd rather not."

I thought his eyes moved to another box. "There are crayons in there. See?" I lifted it. "Would you like them?"

And again, pulling breath in, he whispered, "I'd rather not."

I realized then that to him my asking seemed like pushing. I was being too much like a teacher prodding him toward doing. Or like mother seeking accomplishment through him? Or like father?

I moved the stool over to where he stood and sat down beside him. Both of us silent.

He continued standing there in front of the toy closet, his shoulders slack, his arms at his sides. He kept on wheezing. I sat and he stood until finally he turned his head slowly, his body unturning, and he looked at me. Without wish or question. Without expression. Not staring. Merely looking.

I said very softly, "Some people would rather do nothing." He needed to find out that I would not push him.

He nodded almost imperceptibly and stood a while longer. Then he turned and moved to the window and looked out. Wheezing.

I moved my stool up quietly beside him and looked out with him. The two of us looked out together in silence. I, not intruding; just being there with him.

After a while my ear caught a sound. He had spoken scarcely above a whisper. One word — "Dorothy" — out into space.

Gently I put an arm about him to let him know more surely in the early body-language of a mother with her baby that I was with him. My arm around his shoulder could say it better and more convincingly than my tongue could.

He leaned toward me and looked at me piteously, as if he wished to cry and couldn't.

"Please, Dorothy, I don't want to do anything." He hadn't believed me. Almost tearful, but without tears coming, he went on, beseeching me not to force him. "Please don't make me."

A lump rose in my throat.

"No, dear, I shan't."

After another span of silence shared between us, I added, "This is a place where you can do what you want. You can do nothing if that's what you want. You don't have to live up to anything here. You don't have to be a big boy. You can be a baby, even, if you wish . . ." and very low, "you can play you're my baby, if you wish . . ."

He sighed and the tightness seemed suddenly to loosen a bit.

And then, for all his seven-year-old bigness, he climbed into my lap and curled up like a Great Dane puppy, knuckle-boned and gangly and yet almost soft in his helplessness.

Still saying nothing, he lay there. And I saw that he breathed a little more quietly until our allotted time was up. . . .

* * *

As Kenneth worked on, a major stream of thought crossed the horizon into clearer view and etched its way through time: Things went into holes and hollows.

Bombs fell into craters. Rain streamed into

boats and barrels. Water ran into mouths. And wee-wee squirted into this and that and "any old hole."

In turn questions came bubbling up from crevices and ran as tributaries from the main current: "What happens *in* there after the water goes in?" pointing to a water-drenched hole in a mound of clay . . . "What comes out?" In his mind there was a picture of something going in, of its being transformed, and of its coming out. "When the food goes in the mouth, what happens in here?" touching his stomach. "It grows into big jobs and brother big jobs. It changes. And it comes out the big job hole."

And still another question: "Do some things burst when some things come out?"

He drew a picture with crayons of a father plane flying overhead. Underneath was a house where a mother lived. The father plane dropped a brown bomb right into the mother's chimney. Only, as it touched the chimney it turned into a great big fire-bomb. Red and burning. Once inside the house it started a conflagration. Flames filled the house. The steam in the house grew bigger and had to get out some way. And finally, with a tremendous blast, the house exploded into a million bits.

Something going in. Something being transformed. Something coming out. How?

I was not surprised when Kenneth tied these questions together one day, showing that they had in truth been fantasies and wonderings about impregnation and birth.

His guppies, he said, had too many babies.

"The babies come out from the mother guppies' stomachs. From their stomachs somewhere. But I don't know from just where. I've never examined a guppy that close."

He drew his eyebrows together and sat as if trying to solve some great riddle. "I wonder what hole they come out of, those baby guppies?" And quickly another question hit its toes on the heels of this last. "I wonder," more slowly, "I wonder where *we* come out of? What hole?"

"What would be your guess?" I asked him.

"What hole?" figuring. "Now what hole could it be? Let me see. Could it be the wee-wee hole?" His hand moved toward his own body as if he were trying to solve the question in terms of himself. "No! The wee-wee hole isn't big enough. Could it be the big job hole? Let me see. No! The big job hole, that's bigger but it still isn't big enough. Not for a real live baby to come out of. No hole's big enough." And then, quizzically, "Is there another hole?"

I knew from way back that he knew it, but he needed me to put it into words for him now.

"Not on a man," I said. "But there is on a woman."

"Oh!" he exclaimed, with the light breaking through in the brilliance of discovery. "She's got a *baby* hole! Oh, I see!"

He repeated the cherished finding. "She's got three holes! A wee-wee hole. A big job hole. And a baby hole. That's what that other hole's for."

Then again thoughtful, "I'd like to know, Dorothy, how does the baby come out of the baby hole? Does the mother come apart?"

It was near the end of the session so I told him that we could have a clay mother and make her have a baby next time. Then he could see how the baby got out.

"Make her be a real fat mother," he requested. "With a baby inside."

I nodded and we both chuckled in anticipation.

He started to leave, well satisfied.

Suddenly, however, half-way to the door, an important thought struck him. "But how about the father? And how does the baby get *in?* Babies need fathers, too, don't they?"

"Yes, of course babies need fathers, and we can have a father here too next time!"

"That's good!" He beamed satisfaction. "We'll have a father, too. And then we can see what *he* does."

When he came in for his next session the ripely rounded mother was waiting for him. Inside her body lay a cardboard baby, curved, head down, waiting to be born. The father, beside the mother, looked sturdily possessive.

Kenneth eyed them, smiling. Presently he picked up the mother and nodded approvingly, "She surely is big and fat."

He examined her in detail. "Oh, yes, I see the wee-wee hole, that's this one. And I see the big job hole, that's this one. I guess, then, that this one here is the baby hole. Is that where she's going to have the baby from?" And without waiting for an answer, "I wonder will it be a boy or a girl?"

"Which do you think?"

"Me? I don't know. I'm no mind reader. Come on, we'd better make her have it and see."

So without more ado, we had the father get her to the hospital and with me as doctor, and him as chief assistant, we readily helped the baby come out.

He picked it up, looked it over, and muttered, disgustedly, "Oh, it's a boy."

But his main concern was for the mother. He was manipulating her, changing her form, thinning her down.

"There," with a satisfied air, "there she is now. She hasn't got that big monster tummy any more. But she has got big things for the baby to stick his face into and drink from."

The baby was at last in the mother's arm, its face at her breast.

"See, Mister," turning to the father. "You've got a baby boy."

Then to me, "What did the father do? How did he help?"

Inadvertently or intentionally, I did not know which, his hand touched the clay man's genitals.

I nodded. "You're showing me the right thing just at the right moment. I think you knew what the father helps with to make the baby."

He nodded slyly, grinning broadly, very pleased. Then, almost garrulously, he rattled off what his mother had read to him earlier from one of the books she had gotten. "The father has a seed. It's very, very, very tiny. And he plants it in the mother. And first it looks like a seed and then a pollywog and then a fish and then a monkey and then it gets bigger and looks like a real baby after a long long time."

We took tiny bits of clay and made mother seeds and father seeds and welded them together to get the idea that mother and father each contribute half the seed for the new baby to grow from. "They weld together all in one and the baby starts." And with a kind of defiant decisiveness, "The mother *does* need the father to get a baby."

Then his eyebrows puckered. "But tell me, Dorothy, where does the father get his seed from? Does he keep it in his stomach? Or in his penis? Or where?"

"From quite near there," I commenced. But before I could finish, he anticipated me, "Oh, from here!" pointing down at himself. "From those balls."

"Yes."

"Oh, dear." His face fell. "Oh, dear." His voice trailed dejectedly, "Oh, dear, that's too bad!"

"Why?" I queried.

"Because," he answered, disconsolate, "I wanted a *lot* of children, but if they come from there *I can only have two*."

I assured him that even though there were only two balls, there were millions and millions of baby seeds in each.

"Millions and millions!" he exclaimed, very pleased. "Then I could have millions and millions of babies. That is, if I lived long enough."

"And you would have to live a very long time," I said. "Each baby, you know, takes nine months to grow."

"I know. And besides, millions would be too expensive. Children *are* expensive, by the time you get them chops and stew and suits and shoes."

We pondered for some minutes on the economic problems of raising a family. And then Kenneth, glancing at the father, went back to biological concerns. "Now, how does the father's seed get out of the father?"

"How would you guess?"

He looked knowing. "Through here. Through the wee-wee hole?"

"Yes, you knew it."

He nodded. "I guess I'm kind of a good guesser," self-satisfied. "I think it comes up from the seed bag in the balls here and out the wee-wee hole."

"Yes," I nodded. "And then? What do you think?"

"I think, then it goes into the mother's baby hole. Here," pointing. And half to himself, wonderingly, "How does it get there? Well, I guess the father has to bring it there with his penis."

I nodded again.

"O.K. Let's play the baby they had is two years old now and they want another baby. You show me how the father gets it there." As he talked he pushed the cardboard baby back up inside the mother, then seriously handed the father to me, and laid the mother on her back. "Now you show me."

Just as seriously I laid the father on the mother with his arms around her and hers around him in mutual embrace, body to body in the way of man and woman since the time of Adam and Eve.

Kenneth's face was beatific. "They love each other, that father and mother."

Then he peered under the father so as to see all the better. He regarded them from every possible angle and smiled as if he, like Pippa, felt that all was right with the world.

"The father puts his penis right in the baby hole and now the baby's started and they're loving each other."

"And sometimes," I said, "they do it just for love because too many babies would be too expensive, as we said."

"This time, though, they're doing it for a baby," he decided. "There, now it's done."

He lifted the father off.

"Lady, you're going to have a baby," he announced.

To me he said, "Now he's done it and the baby's starting." And then he voiced a strange request which I did not immediately comprehend.

"Dorothy, now you say, 'One month.' "

"One month," I said.

He put a small chunk of clay on the mother's abdomen and smoothed it over. "Now say two months."

"Two months," I said.

He put another chunk of clay on and smoothed it.

"Now three months."

"Three months!" And more clay.

By the time we got to nine months the lady was monstrous. "She got big in front and on her sides, too." And presently, "Now the baby's going to come. I'll be the doctor this time and," offhandedly, "you can be the nurse. Take her to the hospital, father. Here she is. Out comes the baby. Hm. What do you know? It's another boy. See, you people. You've got two boys. One's three and the other's just a baby. You can go home in a few days. But I want you to be careful. That's enough babies for a while. Remember now to do it just for love."

But after the mother arrived home where the big brother had been waiting, there transpired a curious turn of events.

Scowling fury stormed into Ken's face. "You should have known," addressing the mother, "it was much too soon to have another baby." And grimly wordless, he pounded a shower of bombs down on the baby until it was buried under the heap.

His intent came out even more clearly in the following session. He went through the baby scene again and at the end he exclaimed, "We'll bomb the father for asking the mother to have another baby. They already have one. That's enough. Brothers are nuisances. They're bad." And, turning to the father, he shook a warning finger at him. "Next time, you're not to have a baby brother. Next time you do it just for love."...

* * *

At last, after two years of therapy, Kenneth had shown the ultimate intent that had lain covered for so long: the wish to get rid of the mean mother and to possess the good mother. At last he could avow that this double wish applied to his own mother, not just to *a* mother; not to *any* mother but to *his*.

This is every child's wish, though the push and pull of it may be less violent. This was our wish, too, in the forgotten time behind the curtain of available memories.

Every mother is two mothers to a child. The mother who denies, the mother who grants less than a child yearns for — this mother he wants to eradicate. The mother who gives, who is loving, who understands and cherishes — this mother he wants to own for himself. To her he wants to be "onliest." The onliest to suckle and nuzzle when he is tiny; the onliest to be held in sheltering arms. The onliest, later, if he is a son, to possess in the fantasy of marrying, just as the small daughter turns, if all goes well, to the father and murmurs wishfully, "We'll get married, Daddy, when I get big." Since the parent can never give himself to the child as fully as wishes demand, the child inevitably in his mind sees the parent as partly mean.

In his mind a child makes a mother more mean or less mean according to his fantasied wishes and needs as well as according to what he has actually known. The same with a father.

Again and again Kenneth had approached the conscious facing of his wish to get rid of his "mean" mother and the bigness of his demands. Again and again he had backed away. But through the repeated attempts, he had at last gained courage enough to look at his feelings for what they meant in their ultimate intent. The repetition of his *theme and variations* had been a necessary part of his therapy, as in most people's, in order to work through to the point where he could take the conscious impact of his wish's aim. Even though we had very gradually approached the ultimate baring of his unconscious desire to get rid of his mean mother, the fear of what killing her might portend in terms of actually losing his good mother along with the mean mother, had struck him after he was home. This became clear in his next session.

He came in with the very slightest whisper of a wheeze, barely perceptible but a wheeze no less. He slumped down onto the floor of the playroom without getting anything from the closet with which to play.

He didn't want to talk. He couldn't remember what he had done in the last session. "What was it?" he wondered, looking puzzled. No, he couldn't recall any of it. And nothing had happened at home to upset him either. He didn't want to do anything, say anything, remember anything. No, he declared, nothing was wrong. He reminded me of the little-boy-pulled-into-himself who had come in two years before.

"If you ask me, I think you scared yourself last time into the wheezes!" I ventured.

He regarded me stonily. Then anger flared. "Well, if you *have* to pull my thoughts out, I've been mad at Brad. I wanted to punch him in the nose. Only I couldn't, because I was afraid of being scolded by YOU."

"Then you're really mad at me."

"Yes," emphatically, with all trace of the wheeze gone. "I'd like to tell you off. Bawl you out. Why do you have to butt in and disturb things?"

"You blame me for having disturbed your thoughts. Mad because you would have liked to keep on thinking way down inside you that you were having that baby with mother. And I disturbed the idea!"

He nodded. "And so I feel like bawling you out. That's all."

"Nothing more violent?"

"If I did, then you . . . No, *she* . . . she wouldn't take care of me. She'd guess or find out somehow, and she'd send me away."

At last this fear was out and in the open — this old fear so terrible that it had played a big part in making Kenneth block his hostility and keep it in. This fear had sprung up stark before Brad's birth when his mother had screamed that she did not want another boy, when he had seen what he had sensed much earlier, that she had not wanted him. His muscles had caught this fear from her muscles' tensions when he had nuzzled and found her breasts dry and when, despite the meticulous care that she gave him, he had apprehended her essential inability to give of herself and her love. This fear had spelled loss and desertion. A fear that no child can bear.

His eyes now were wide and frightened.

"That idea makes you terribly scared!"

He did not move. He did not answer. But as I watched him I saw the slow tears creep into his eyes. Down his cheeks they trickled. They were the first tears I'd seen him shed.

There he sat on the bare brown floor of the play-room, alone with his sorrow. Not tight or cringingly backing away. Not wheezing. But meeting his thoughts and fears with a natural, full sorrow. Strong enough not to seek refuge in me. Strong enough to bear his sorrow himself.

After a little while, he pulled a dirty handkerchief from his pocket and wiped his face, streaking it with grime. A smile came slowly, and in a low voice he began to muse. "I can't club her. I can't poke her. But I *can* do other things. And I just will. When I'm mad I'll do different things to annoy her. I won't eat what she wants me to. I'll turn on the washing machine while she's not looking and I'll plug the lights in her bedroom so they won't light when she wants them. And then later when she's trying to go to sleep, I'll turn the lights on. And I'll go cut the clothes line. And I'll wheeze."

"And that will irritate her?"

"You guessed it."

"And it will hurt you also!"

"Yes, you've said it. I guess it's a no-good idea. But . . ."

"But," I picked up the wishful note in his voice, "it's an idea you still sort of like."

He looked relieved and easy as he rose from the floor and went to the play closet. He brought out the mother he had made the time before and the baby.

"Here's the baby who was born last week," he said. "I'll make him grow bigger." He got out clay and fashioned a boy. "He's a day old and a week old and a month old and a year." He kept making him bigger. "And now he's about four or five, I don't know exactly, maybe just three. But he wants to go into his mother. Only he can't. That's the daddy's job."

He took more clay and fashioned a father. "Now the daddy and the mother, they'll have a baby in the proper way."

Thus Kenneth gave his mother back to his father. Thus he stepped off his magic carpet and set foot on the ground.

IV MIDDLE CHILDHOOD

The years of middle childhood are the ones that developmental psychologists have examined the least. But development does not stop at this time; rather, quiet and subtle changes occur as the child gains skills and retrenches emotions in preparation for adolescence. One profitable approach to middle childhood is to contrast the development of certain natural cognitive capacities and the specific learning that takes place in schools.

An introduction to cognitive development, Piaget's paper discusses how the child spontaneously comes to make sense out of his or her world. In Piaget's view, the development of knowledge should be considered within the context of an individual's biological development and as occurring naturally as the person interacts in the physical and social realms. Piaget contrasts this form of cognition with learning, which he views as a discrete event, provoked by environmental stimuli. What is learned (such as a fact or a rule) can be forgotten; but the development of knowledge results in new mental structures, which are permanent and come to control how all new information is encountered, interpreted, and stored.

Mandler, Scribner, Cole, and DeForest bridge the area between the spontaneous developmental processes in cognition and the conventional forms of learning. They show that certain tasks will be performed similarly by children in different cultures regardless of schooling. But they also suggest that it is fallacious to assume (as many psychologists do) that the environment in which most American children are raised is the same as the environment in which *all* children have grown up. Observations document that school is a rarefied "special" environment, which promotes linguistic sophistication and abstract thought. In contrast, most of the world's children learn in context — they learn to cook, to sew, to weave, to navigate, to build, to trade, while their elders are engaged in these activities — and thus it becomes unnecessary to formulate general rules and verbal statements of what is happening. As a result, those who grow up with informal education have different cognitive skills than those who attend school. But, as this study shows, even certain "school-like" skills, such as memorizing, are not limited to schools and often are demonstrated in contextual situations.

Standing back even further, Jerome Bruner conjectures about the relationship between pedagogy and human development, and in the process he tries to unravel some questions about the growth of the mind. Bruner views the culture as providing "amplifiers" for the individual's skills: amplifiers of action (hammer and wheel), amplifiers of the senses (pictures, diagrams, and microscopes), and amplifiers of thought processes (mathematics and logic). Each culture transmits these amplifiers to its children, but each culture differs in how the amplifiers are transmitted. Technically oriented societies do so in schools and use verbal, abstract concepts; "indigenous" societies do so in the context of action. Drawing implications for education, Bruner also examines how a curriculum might be devised in light of these considerations.

Middle childhood has traditionally been viewed as a quiet time in the emotional area — a latent period, with the establishment of sex-role identity and the control of aggression on one side and the turbulent crises of adolescence on the other. In fact, however, there *are* changes in the emotional-social realm, such as the development of empathy and altruism. Emotional behaviors are now highly interrelated with cognitive considerations. Take, for example, the emerging ability to understand the feelings of another or to act on someone else's behalf — the appearance of altruism. Martin Hoffman's article argues that even an apparently emotional capacity such as altruism is rooted in cognitive capacities and that altruism actually represents a synthesis of affect and cognition.

In school as well, affect and cognition interweave as the child's self-esteem has an effect on his or her ability to achieve. Carol Dweck and Therese Goetz write about learned helplessness — a condition in which a child believes that personal failures are caused by his or her own lack of ability and cannot be remedied. The authors contrast these "helpless" children with "mastery-oriented" children, who believe they will succeed if they simply try harder. Sources of these attributes — including society, teachers, and parents — are discussed, as well as the differential effects of these characteristics on boys and girls and the implications for children's development.

Armed with cognitive sophistication, declining egocentrism, the ability to go beyond literal interpretation, and the capacity to empathize with others, the school-age child is a sensitive and complex individual. He or she now reacts deeply and lastingly to pivotal events. In Rudyard Kipling's autobiographical short story "Baa Baa Black Sheep," we watch the disintegration of the hero, Punch, as he leaves his parents in India and goes to England to be educated. The insensitivity of others to the nature of his attachments and to his early caretaking, his own mourning at the loss of his parents, and his submersion in an alien culture lead to his complete inability to function. His experience is contrasted with that of his younger sister, who was too young to remember much of her past in India and therefore is able to adapt to the new environment much more easily. In Punch and his sister we again see the inextricable links between emotional and cognitive factors.

Finally, in an excerpt from Mark Twain's *Huckleberry Finn,* we watch Huck argue with himself about turning in Jim, the runaway slave. This is a fine example of a conflict between two levels of thought — a situation that is a major impetus to development. The part of the selection in which Tom Sawyer and Huck plan Jim's escape is a humorous but authentic portrayal of a child's concern with rules and proper behavior.

Jean Piaget

DEVELOPMENT AND LEARNING

First I would like to make clear the difference between two problems: the problem of *development* in general, and the problem of *learning*. I think these problems are very different, although some people do not make this distinction.

The development of knowledge is a spontaneous process, tied to the whole process of embryogenesis. Embryogenesis concerns the development of the body, but it concerns as well the development of the nervous system, and the development of mental functions. In the case of the development of knowledge in children, embryogenesis ends only in adulthood. It is a total developmental process which we must re-situate in its general biological and psychological context. In other words, development is a process which concerns the totality of the structures of knowledge.

Learning presents the opposite case. In general, learning is provoked by situations — provoked by a psychological experimenter; or by a teacher, with respect to some didactic point; or by an external situation. It is provoked, in general, as opposed to spontaneous. In addition, it is a limited process — limited to a single problem, or to a single structure.

So I think that development explains learning, and this opinion is contrary to the widely held opinion that development is a sum of discrete learning experiences. For some psychologists development is reduced to a series of specific learned items, and development is thus the sum, the cumulation of this series of specific items. I think this is an atomistic view which deforms the real state of things. In reality, development is the essential process and each element of learning occurs as a function of total development, rather than being an element which explains development. I shall begin, then, with a first part dealing with development, and I shall talk about learning in the second part.

To understand the development of knowledge, we must start with an idea which seems central to me — the idea of an *operation*. Knowledge is not a copy of reality. To know an object, to know an event, is not simply to look at it and make a mental copy, or image, of it. To know an object is to act on it. To know is to modify, to transform the object, and to understand the process of this transformation, and as a consequence to understand the way the object is constructed. An operation is thus the essence of knowledge; it is an interiorized action which modifies the object of knowledge. For instance, an operation would consist of joining objects in a class, to construct a classification. Or an operation would consist of ordering, or putting things in a series. Or an operation would consist of counting, or of measuring. In other words, it is a set of actions modifying the object, and enabling the knower to get at the structures of the transformation.

SOURCE: Jean Piaget, "Development and Learning," from *Piaget Rediscovered*, a report on the Conference on Cognitive Studies and Curriculum Development (March 1964), edited by Richard E. Ripple and Verne N. Rockcastle. Reprinted by permission.

An operation is an interiorized action. But in addition, it is a reversible action; that is, it can take place in both directions, for instance, adding or subtracting, joining or separating. So it is a particular type of action which makes up logical structures.

Above all, an operation is never isolated. It is always linked to other operations, and as a result it is always a part of a total structure. For instance, a logical class does not exist in isolation; what exists is the total structure of classification. An asymmetrical relation does not exist in isolation. Seriation is the natural, basic operational structure. A number does not exist in isolation. What exists is the series of numbers, which constitute a structure, an exceedingly rich structure whose various properties have been revealed by mathematicians.

These operational structures are what seem to me to constitute the basis of knowledge, the natural psychological reality, in terms of which we must understand the development of knowledge. And the central problem of development is to understand the formation, elaboration, organization, and functioning of these structures.

I should like to review the stages of development of these structures, not in any detail, but simply as a reminder. I shall distinguish four main stages. The first is a sensory-motor, preverbal stage, lasting approximately the first 18 months of life. During this stage is developed the practical knowledge which constitutes the substructure of later representational knowledge. An example is the construction of the schema of the permanent object. For an infant, during the first months, an object has no permanence. When it disappears from the perceptual field it no longer exists. No attempt is made to find it again. Later, the infant will try to find it, and he will find it by localizing it spatially. Consequently, along with the construction of the permanent object there comes the construction of practical, or sensory-motor, space. There is similarly the construction of temporal succession, and of elementary sensory-motor causality. In other words, there is a series of structures which are indispensable for the structures of later representational thought.

In a second stage, we have pre-operational representation — the beginnings of language, of the symbolic function, and therefore of thought, or representation. But at the level of representational thought, there must now be a reconstruction of all that was developed on the sensory-motor level. That is, the sensory-motor actions are not immediately translated into operations. In fact, during all this second period of pre-operational representations, there are as yet no operations as I defined this term a moment ago. Specifically, there is as yet no conservation which is the psychological criterion of the presence of reversible operations. For example, if we pour liquid from one glass to another of a different shape, the pre-operational child will think there is more in one than in the other. In the absence of operational reversibility, there is no conservation of quantity.

In a third stage the first operations appear, but I call these concrete operations because they operate on objects, and not yet on verbally expressed hypotheses. For example, there are the operations of classification, ordering, the construction of the idea of number, spatial and temporal operations, and all the fundamental operations of elementary logic of classes and relations, of elementary mathematics, of elementary geometry and even of elementary physics.

Finally, in the fourth stage, these operations are surpassed as the child reaches the level of what I call formal or hypothetic-deductive operations; that is, he can now reason on hypotheses, and not only on objects. He constructs new operations, operations of propositional logic, and not simply the operations of classes, relations, and numbers. He attains new structures which are on the one hand combinatorial, corresponding to what mathematicians call lattices; on the other hand, more complicated group structures. At the level of concrete operations, the operations apply within an immediate neighborhood: for instance, classification by successive inclusions. At the level of the combinatorial, however, the groups are much more mobile. These, then, are the four stages which we identify, whose formation we shall now attempt to explain.

What factors can be called upon to explain the development from one set of structures to another? It seems to me that there are four main factors: first of all, *maturation*, in the sense of Gesell, since this development is a continuation of the embryogenesis; second, the role of *experience* of the effects of the physical environment on the structures of intelligence; third, *social transmission* in the broad sense (linguistic transmission, education, etc.); and fourth, a factor which is too often neglected but one which seems to me fundamental and even the principal factor. I shall call this the factor of *equilibration* or, if you prefer it, of self-regulation.

Let us start with the first factor, maturation. One might think that these stages are simply a reflection of an interior maturation of the nervous system, following the hypotheses of Gesell, for example. Well, maturation certainly does play an indispensable role and must not be ignored. It certainly takes part in every transformation that takes place during a child's development. However, this first factor is insufficient in itself. First of all, we know practically nothing about the maturation of the nervous system beyond the first months of the child's existence. We know a little bit about it during the first two years but we know very little following this time. But above all, maturation doesn't explain everything, because the average ages at which these stages appear (the average chronological ages) vary a great deal from one society to another. The ordering of these stages is constant and has been found in all the societies studied. It has been found in various countries where psychologists in universities have redone the experiments but it has also been found in African peoples, for example, in the children of the Bushmen, and in Iran, both in the villages and in the cities. However, although the order of succession is constant, the chronological ages of these stages varies a great deal. For instance, the ages which we have found in Geneva are not necessarily the ages which you would find in the United States. In Iran, furthermore, in the city of Teheran, they found approximately the same ages as we found in Geneva, but there is a systematic delay of two years in the children in the country. Canadian psychologists who redid our experiments, Monique Laurendeau and Father Adrien Pinard, found once again about the same ages in Montreal. But when they redid the experiments in Martinique, they found a delay of four years in all the experiments and this in spite of the fact that the children in Martinique go to a school set up according to the French system and the French curriculum and attain at the end of this elementary school a certificate of higher primary education. There is then a delay of four years, that is, there are the same stages, but systematically delayed. So you see that these age variations show that maturation does not explain everything.

I shall go on now to the role played by experience. Experience of objects, of physical reality, is obviously a basic factor in the development of cognitive structures. But once again this factor does not explain everything. I can give two reasons for this. The first reason is that some of the concepts which appear at the beginning of the stage of concrete operations are such that I cannot see how they could be drawn from experience. As an example, let us take the conservation of the substance in the case of changing the shape of a ball of plasticene. We give this ball of plasticene to a child who changes its shape into a sausage form and we ask him if there is the same amount of matter, that is, the same amount of substance as there was before. We also ask him if it now has the same weight and thirdly if it now has the same volume. The volume is measured by the displacement of water when we put the ball or the sausage into a glass of water. The findings, which have been the same every time this experiment has been done, show us that first of all there is conservation of the amount of substance. At about eight years old a child will say, "There is the same amount of plasticene." Only later does the child assert that the weight is conserved and still later that the volume is conserved. So I would ask you where the idea of the conservation of substance can come from. What is a constant and invariant substance when it doesn't yet have a constant weight or a constant volume? Through perception you can get at the weight of the ball or the volume of the ball but perception cannot give you an idea of the amount of substance. No experiment, no experience, can show the child that there is the same amount of substance. He can weigh the ball and that would lead to the conservation of weight. He can immerse it in water and that would lead to the conservation of volume. But the notion of substance is attained before either weight or volume. This conservation of substance is simply a logical necessity. The child now understands that when there is a transformation something must be conserved because by reversing the transformation you can come back to the point of departure and once again have the ball. He knows that something is conserved but he doesn't know what. It is not yet the weight, it is not yet the volume; it is simply a logical form — a logical necessity. There, it seems to me, is an example of a progress in knowledge, a logical necessity for something to be conserved even though no experience can have led to this notion.

My second objection to the sufficiency of experience as an explanatory factor is that this notion of experience is a very equivocal one. There are, in fact, two kinds of experience which are psychologically very different and this difference is very important from the pedagogical point of view. It is because of the pedagogical importance that I emphasize this distinction. First of all, there is what I shall call physical experience, and secondly, what I shall call logical-mathematical experience.

Physical experience consists of acting upon objects and drawing some knowledge about the objects by abstraction from the objects. For example, to discover that this pipe is heavier than this watch, the child will weigh them both and find the difference in the objects themselves. This is experience in the usual sense of the term — in the sense used by empiricists. But there is a second type of experience which I shall call logical-mathematical experience where the knowledge is not drawn from the objects, but it is drawn by the actions effected upon the objects. This is not the same thing. When one acts upon objects, the objects are indeed there, but there is also the set of actions which modify the objects.

I shall give you an example of this type of experience. It is a nice example because we have verified it many times in small children under seven years of age, but it is also an example which one of my mathematician friends has related to me about his own childhood, and he dates his mathematical career from this experience. When he was four or five years old — I don't know exactly how old, but a small child — he was seated on the ground in his garden and he was counting pebbles. Now to count these pebbles he put them in a row and he counted them one, two, three, up to ten. Then he finished counting them and started to count them in the other direction. He began by the end and once again he found ten. He found this marvelous that there were ten in one direction and ten in the other direction. So he put them in a circle and counted them that way and found ten once again. Then he counted them in the other direction and found ten once more. So he put them in some other direction and found ten once more. So he put them in some other arrangement and kept counting them and kept finding ten. There was the discovery that he made.

Now what indeed did he discover? He did not discover a property of pebbles; he discovered a property of the action of ordering. The pebbles had no order. It was his action which introduced a linear order or a cyclical order, or any kind of an order. He discovered that the sum was independent of the order. The order was the action which he introduced among the pebbles. For the sum the same principle applied. The pebbles had no sum; they were simply in a pile. To make a sum, action was necessary — the operation of putting together and counting. He found that the sum was independent of the order, in other words, that the action of putting together is independent of the action of ordering. He discovered a property of actions and not a property of pebbles. You may say that it is in the nature of pebbles to let this be done to them and this is true. But it could have been drops of water, and drops of water would not have let this be done to them because two drops of water and two drops of water do not make four drops of water as you know very well. Drops of water then would not let this be done to them, we agree to that.

So it is not the physical property of pebbles which the experience uncovered. It is the properties of the actions carried out on the pebbles and this is quite another form of experience. It is the point of departure of mathematical deduction. The subsequent deduction will consist of interiorizing these actions and then of combining them without needing any pebbles. The mathematician no longer needs his pebbles. He can combine his operations simply with symbols and the point of departure of this mathematical deduction is logical-mathematical experience and this is not at all experience in the sense of the empiricists. It is the beginning of the coordination of actions, but this coordination of actions before the stage of operations needs to be supported by concrete material. Later, this coordination of actions leads to the logical mathematical structures. I believe that logic is not a derivative of language. The source of logic is much more profound. It is the total coordination of actions, actions of joining things together, or ordering things, etc. This is what logical-mathematical experience is. It is an experience of the actions of the subject, and not an experience of objects themselves. It is an experience which is necessary before there can be operations. Once the operations have been attained this experience is no longer needed and the coordinations of actions can take place by themselves in the form of deduction and construction for abstract structures.

The third factor is social transmission — linguistic transmission or educational transmission. This factor, once again, is fundamental. I do not deny the role of any one of these factors; they all play a part. But this factor is insufficient because the child can receive valuable information via language or via education directed by an adult only if he is in a state where he can understand this information. That is, to receive the information he must have a structure which enables him to assimilate this information. This is why you cannot teach higher mathematics to a five-year-old. He does not yet have structures which enable him to understand.

I shall take a much simpler example, an example of linguistic transmission. As my very first work in the realm of child psychology, I spent a long time studying the relation between a part and a whole in concrete experience and in language. For example, I used Burt's test employing the sentence, "Some of my flowers are buttercups." The child knows that all buttercups are yellow, so there are three possible conclusions: the whole bouquet is yellow, or part of the bouquet is yellow, or none of the flowers in the bouquet is yellow. I found that up until nine years of age (and this was in Paris, so the children certainly did understand the French language) they replied, "The whole bouquet is yellow or some of my flowers are yellow." Both of those mean the same thing. They did not understand the expression, "some *of* my flowers." They did not understand this *of* as a partitive genitive, as the inclusion of some flowers in my flowers. They understood some of my flowers to be my several flowers as if the several flowers and the flowers were confused as one and the same class. So there you have children who until nine years of age heard every day a linguistic structure which implied the inclusion of a sub-class in a class and yet did not understand this structure. It is only when they themselves are in firm possession of this logical structure, when they have constructed it for themselves according to the developmental laws which we shall discuss, that they succeed in understanding correctly the linguistic expression.

I come now to the fourth factor which is added to the three preceding ones but which seems to me to be the fundamental one. This is what I call the factor of equilibration. Since there are already three factors, they must somehow be equilibrated among themselves. That is one reason for bringing in the factor of equilibration. There is a second reason, however, which seems to me to be fundamental. It is that in the act of knowing, the subject is active, and consequently, faced with an external disturbance, he will react in order to compensate and consequently he will tend towards equilibrium. Equilibrium, defined by active compensation, leads to reversibility. Operational reversibility is a model of an equilibrated system where a transformation in one direction is compensated by a transformation in the other direction. Equilibration, as I understand it, is thus an active process. It's a process of self-regulation. I think that this self-regulation is a fundamental factor in development. I use this term in the sense in which it is used in cybernetics, that is, in the sense of processes with feedback and with feedforward, of processes which regulate themselves by a progressive compensation of systems. This process of equilibration takes the form of a succession of levels of equilibrium, of levels which have a certain probability which I shall call a sequential probability, that is, the probabilities are not established a priori. There is a sequence of levels. It is not possible to reach the second level unless equilibrium has been reached at the first level, and the equilibrium of the third level only becomes possible when the equilibrium of the second level has been reached, and so forth. That is, each level is determined as the most probable given that the preceding level has been reached. It is not the most probable at the beginning, but it is the most probable once the preceding level has been reached.

As an example, let us take the development of the idea of conservation in the transformation of the ball of plasticene into the sausage shape. Here you can discern four levels. The most probable at the beginning is for the child to think of only one dimension. Suppose that there is a probability of 0.8, for instance, that the child will focus on the length, and that the width has a probability of 0.2. This would mean that of ten children, eight will focus on the length alone without paying any attention to the width, and two will focus on the width without paying any attention to the length. They will focus only on one dimension or the other. Since the two dimensions are independent at this stage, focusing on both at once would have a probability of only 0.16. That is less than either one of the two. In other words, the most probable in the beginning is to focus only on one dimension and in fact the child will say, "It's longer, so there's more in the sausage." Once he has reached this first level, if you continue to elongate the sausage, there comes a moment when he will say, "No, now it's too thin, so there's less." Now he is thinking about the width, but he forgets the length, so you have come to a second level which becomes the most probable after the first level, but which is not the most probable at the point of departure. Once he has focused on the width, he will come back sooner or later to focus on the length. Here you will have a third level where he will oscillate between width and length and where he will discover that the two are related. When you elongate you make it more thin, and when you make it shorter, you make it thicker. He discovers that the two are solidly related and in discovering this relationship, he will start to think in terms of the transformation and not only in terms of the final configuration. Now he will say that when it gets longer it gets thinner, so it's the same thing. There is more of it in length but less of it in width. When you make it shorter it gets thicker; there's less in length and more in width, so there is compensation — compensation which defines equilibrium in the sense in which I defined it a moment ago. Consequently, you have operations and conservation. In other words, in the course of these developments you will always find a process of self-regulation which I call equilibration and which seems to me the fundamental factor in the acquisition of logical-mathematical knowledge.

I shall go on now to the second part of my lecture, that is, to deal with the topic of learning. Classically, learning is based on the stimulus-response schema. I think the stimulus-response schema, while I won't say it is false, is in any case entirely incapable of explaining cognitive learning. Why? Because when you think of a stimulus-response schema, you think usually that first of all there is a stimulus and then a response is set off by this stimulus. For my part, I am convinced that the response was there first, if I can express myself in this way. A stimulus is a stimulus only to the extent that it is significant and it becomes significant only to the extent that there is a structure which permits its assimilation, a structure which can integrate this stimulus but which at the same time sets off the response. In other words, I would propose that the stimulus-response schema be written in the circular form — in the form of a schema or of a structure which is not simply one way. I would propose that above all, between the stimulus and the response there is the organism, the organism and its structures. The stimulus is really a stimulus only when it is assimilated into a structure and it is this structure which sets off the response. Consequently, it is not an exaggeration to say that the response is there first, or if you wish at the beginning there is the structure. Of course we would want to understand how this structure comes to be. I tried to do this earlier by presenting a model of equilibration or self-regulation. Once there is a structure, the stimulus will set off a response, but only by the intermediary of this structure.

I should like to present some facts. We have facts in great number. I shall choose only one or two and I shall choose some facts which our colleague, Smedslund, has gathered. . . . Smedslund arrived in Geneva a few years ago convinced (he had published this in one of his papers) that the development of the ideas of conservation could be indefinitely accelerated through learning of a stimulus-response type. I invited Smedslund to come to spend a year in Geneva to show us this, to show us that he could accelerate the development of operational conservation. I shall relate only one of his experiments.

During the year that he spent in Geneva he chose to work on the conservation of weight. The conservation of weight is, in fact, easy to study since there is a possible external reinforcement, that is, simply weighing the ball and the sausage on a balance. Then you can study the child's reactions to these external results. Smedslund studied the conservation of weight on the one hand, and on the other hand, he studied the transitivity of weights, that is, the transitivity of equalities if A = B and B = C, then A = C, or the transitivity of the equalities if A is less than B, and B is less than C, then A is less than C.

As far as conservation is concerned, Smedslund succeeded very easily with five- and six-year-old children in getting them to generalize that weight is conserved when the ball is transformed into a different shape. The child sees the ball transformed into a sausage or into little pieces or into a pancake or into any other form, he weighs it, and he sees that it is always the same thing. He will affirm it will be the same thing, no matter what you do to it; it will come out to be the same weight. Thus Smedslund very easily achieved the conservation of weight by this sort of external reinforcement.

In contrast to this, however, the same method did not succeed in teaching transitivity. The children resisted the notion of transitivity. A child would predict correctly in certain cases but he would make his prediction as a possibility or a probability and not as a certainty. There was never this generalized certainty in the case of transitivity.

So there is the first example, which seems to me very instructive, because in this problem in the conservation of weight there are two aspects. There is the physical aspect and there is the logical-mathematical aspect. Note that Smedslund started his study by establishing that there was a correlation between conservation and transitivity. He began by making a statistical study on the relationships between the spontaneous responses to the questions about conservation and the spontaneous responses to the questions about transitivity, and he found a very significant correlation. But in the learning experiment, he obtained a learning of conservation and not of transitivity. Consequently, he was successful in obtaining learning of what I called earlier physical experience (This is not surprising; it is simply a question of noting facts about objects.) but he was not successful in obtaining a learning in the construction of the logical structure. This doesn't surprise me either, since the logical structure is not the result of physical experience. It cannot be obtained by external reinforcement. The logical structure is reached only through internal equilibration, by self-regulation, and the external reinforcement of seeing the balance did not suffice to establish this logical structure of transitivity.

I could give many other comparable examples, but it seems to me useless to insist upon these negative examples. Now I should like to show that learning is possible in the case of these logical-mathematical structures, but on one condition — that is, that the structure which you want to teach to the subjects can be supported by simpler, more elementary, logical-mathematical structures. I shall give you an example. It is the example of the conservation of number in the case of one-to-one correspondence. If you give a child seven blue tokens and ask him to put down as many red tokens, there is a preoperational stage where he will put one red one opposite each blue one. But when you spread out the red ones, making them into a longer row, he will say to you, "Now, there are more red ones than there are blue ones."

Now how can we accelerate, if you want to accelerate, the acquisition of this conservation of number? Well, you can imagine an analogous structure but in a simpler, more elementary, situation. For example, with Mlle. Inhelder, we have been studying recently the notion of one-to-one correspondence by giving the child two glasses of the same shape and a big pile of beads. The child puts a bead into one glass with one hand and at the same time a bead into the other glass with the other hand. Time after time he repeats this action, a bead into one glass with one hand and at the same time a bead into the other glass with the other hand and he sees that there is always the same amount on each side. Then you hide one of the glasses. You cover it up. He no longer sees this glass but he continues to put one bead into it while putting at the same time one bead into the other glass which he can see. Then you ask him whether the equality has been conserved, whether there is still the same amount in one glass as in the other. Now you will find that very small children, about four years old, don't want to make a prediction. They will say, "So far, it has been the same amount, but now I don't know, I can't see anymore, so I don't know." They do not want to generalize. But the generalization is made from the age of about five and one-half years.

This is in contrast to the case of the red and blue tokens with one row spread out, where it isn't until seven or eight years of age that children will say there are the same number in the two rows. As one example of this generalization, I recall a little boy of five years and nine months who had been adding the beads to the glasses for a little while. Then we asked him whether, if he continued to do this all day and all night and all the next day, there would always be the same amount in the two glasses. The little boy gave this admirable reply, "Once you know, you know for always." In other words, this was recursive reasoning. So here the child does acquire the structure in this specific case. The number is a synthesis of class inclusion and ordering. This synthesis is being favored by the child's own actions. You have set up a situation where there is an iteration of one same action which continues and which is therefore ordered while at the same time being inclusive. You have, so to speak, a localized synthesis of inclusion and ordering which facilitates the construction of the idea of number in this specific case, and there you can find, in effect, an influence of this experience on the other experience. However, this influence is not immediate. We study the generalization from this recursive situation to the other situation where the tokens are laid on the table in rows, and it is not an immediate generalization but it is made possible through intermediaries. In other words, you can find some learning of this structure if you base the learning on simpler structures.

In this same area of the development of numerical structures, the psychologist Joachim Wohlwill, who spent a year at our Institute at Geneva, has also shown that this acquisition can be accelerated through introducing additive operations, which is what we introduced also in the experiment which I just described. Wohlwill introduced them in a different way but he too was able to obtain a certain learning effect. In other words, learning is possible if you base the more complex structure on simpler structures, that is, when there is a natural relationship and development of structures and not simply an external reinforcement.

Now I would like to take a few minutes to conclude what I was saying. My first conclusion is that learning of structures seems to obey the same laws as the natural development of these structures. In other words, learning is subordinated to development and not vice-versa as I said in the introduction. No doubt you will object that some investigators have succeeded in teaching operational structures. But, when I am faced with these facts, I always have three questions which I want to have answered before I am convinced.

The first question is, "Is this learning lasting? What remains two weeks or a month later?" If a structure develops spontaneously, once it has reached a state of equilibrium, it is lasting, it will continue throughout the child's entire life. When you achieve the learning by external reinforcement, is the result lasting or not and what are the conditions necessary for it to be lasting?

The second question is, "How much generalization is possible?" What makes learning interesting is the possibility of transfer of a generalization. When you have brought about some learning, you can always ask whether this is an isolated piece in the midst of the child's mental life, or if it is really a dynamic structure which can lead to generalizations.

Then there is the third question, "In the case of each learning experience what was the operational level of the subject before the experience and what more complex structures has this learning succeeded in achieving?" In other words, we must look at each specific learning experience from the point of view of the spontaneous operations which were present at the outset and the operational level which has been achieved after the learning experience.

My second conclusion is that the fundamental relation involved in all development and all learning is not the relation of association. In the stimulus-response schema, the relation between the response and the stimulus is understood to be one of association. In contrast to this, I think that the fundamental relation is one of assimilation. Assimilation is not the same as association. I shall define assimilation as the integration of any sort of reality into a structure, and it is this assimilation which seems to me fundamental in learning, and which seems to me the fundamental relation from the point of view of pedagogical or didactic applications. All of my remarks today represent the child and the learning subject as active. An operation is an activity. Learning is possible only when there is active assimilation. It is this activity on the part of the subject which seems to me underplayed in the stimulus-response schema. The presentation which I propose puts the emphasis on the idea of self-regulation, on assimilation. All the emphasis is placed on the activity of the subject himself, and I think that without this activity there is no possible didactic or pedagogy which significantly transforms the subject.

Finally, and this will be my last concluding remark, I would like to comment on an excellent publication by the psychologist Berlyne. Berlyne spent a year with us in Geneva during which he intended to translate our results on the development of operations into stimulus-response language, specifically into Hull's learning theory. Berlyne published in our series of studies of genetic epistemology a very good article on this comparison between the results of Geneva and Hull's theory. In the same volume, I published a commentary on Berlyne's results. Now the essence of Berlyne's results is this: our findings can very well be translated into Hullian language, but only on condition that two modifications are introduced. Berlyne himself found these modifications quite considerable, but they seemed to him to concern more the conceptualization than the Hullian theory itself. I'm not so sure about that. The two modifications are these. First of all, Berlyne wants to distinguish two sorts of responses in the S-R schema. First, responses in the ordinary, classical sense, which I shall call "copy responses," and secondly, what Berlyne called "transformation responses." Transformation responses consist of transforming one response of the first type into another response of the first type. These transformation responses are what I call operations, and you can see right away that this is a rather serious modification of Hull's conceptualization because here you are introducing an element of transformation and thus of assimilation and no longer the simple association of stimulus-response theory.

The second modification which Berlyne introduces into the stimulus-response language is the introduction of what he calls internal reinforcements. What are these internal reinforcements? They are what I call equilibration or self-regulation. The internal reinforcements are what enable the subject to eliminate contradictions, incompatibilities, and conflicts. All development is composed of momentary conflicts and incompatibilities which must be overcome to reach a higher level of equilibrium. Berlyne calls this elimination of incompatibilities internal reinforcements.

So you see that it is indeed a stimulus-response theory, if you will, but first you add operations and then you add equilibration. That's all we want!

Jean M. Mandler, Sylvia Scribner, Michael Cole, and Marsha DeForest

CROSS-CULTURAL INVARIANCE IN STORY RECALL

ABSTRACT: A comparison was made of recall of stories by Liberian nonschooled children, nonliterate adults, nonschooled literate adults, and schooled literate adults. These data were then compared to similar data from American children and adults. Highly similar patterns of recall were found for all groups, although there was improvement in performance from childhood to adulthood. The data were used to support a hypothesis of the universality of certain kinds of schematic organization and their control of memorial processes.

Most cross-cultural comparisons of memory performance have used tasks and materials taken from traditional American and European laboratory studies, typical paradigms being the free recall of lists of words or of paired associates and the serial recall of unrelated items. Children and peoples of nonindustrialized cultures have not fared too well in these studies. In general their recall is poor, and they show few signs of using the variety of organizational strategies which characterize the recall of college students.

The bias of these studies might be described as a reliance on categorical and associative forms of organization of stimulus materials to the exclusion of the common schematic forms of organization that govern much of our daily perception, comprehension, and remembering. Typically in daily life we must understand and remember familiar scenes and common sequences of events rather than supermarket shelves and shopping lists. The latter are frequently organized in a categorical fashion, in which the principles of grouping are taxonomic, based on function or similarity and class membership. In contrast, most scenes and events are organized into schemata on the basis of spatiotemporal contiguities; they may be characterized as sets of expectations about what will be experienced together in space or time.

Schematically organized materials differ in a number of ways from categorically organized ones; not surprisingly, therefore, a number of principles of memory for the two kinds of materials differ (Mandler, in press). Categorical organizations, at least as they have typically been studied, consist of atemporally connected sets of items from unrelated sets of taxonomic categories. When studying such

This research was supported in part by National Institutes of Health grant MH 24492 and by the Ford Foundation. We wish to thank Barbara Vance for data analysis and Bai Paasewe and Mambu Sambolah for collecting and transcribing data.

SOURCE: From Jean M. Mandler, Sylvia Scribner, Michael Cole, and Marsha DeForest, "Cross-cultural Invariance in Story Recall," *Child Development* 51, 1980, pp. 19–26.

lists, subjects may spontaneously categorize each item as it is presented in terms of some superordinate category, but the overall structure of the list must be discovered: it is not automatically activated. If a categorical organization is found, it is often used to organize storage and/or retrieval of the list; words from within categories are typically clustered in recall. However, the order in which categories, or items within categories, are retrieved is indeterminate. For example, both start and stop rules for category search have usually been specified in terms of unknown strength of individual items or as a function of words already recalled in relation to category size.

Schematic organizations, on the other hand, are automatically activated. The sets of expectations we have formed about what rooms look like, or what happens when we go to a restaurant, or what general sorts of events are apt to occur in a story, are an inherent part of our processing of these situations. Not only is our comprehension of the scene or event sequence structured by those sets of expectations (schemata), but our retrieval is guided by them as well. An event schema, for example, provides a determinate retrieval mechanism, providing a start point, a temporally organized search sequence, and a stop point.

Experiments on free recall of categorized lists have shown that American college students typically, although not always, use the categorical structure to order their recall. Young children and nonschooled populations from other cultures usually do not. It has been suggested that the particular experience of Western schooling is implicated in these differences (Brown 1977; Cole & Scribner 1977). It is certainly not lack of knowledge of taxonomic categorical organization that accounts for its absence as a retrieval mechanism in young school children or nonschooled adults (Scribner 1974; Worden 1974). It is more likely a question of the extent to which this type of organization has been practiced and used over an extended period of time and thus has become an accustomed means of remembering.

Hierarchically arranged taxonomic classifications are slowly developing forms of organization. Preschool children have difficulty verbalizing hierarchical classificatory relationships (Anglin 1977; Macnamara 1972), and errors about the relations between superordinate and subordinate classes continue into the elementary school years (Inhelder & Piaget 1964). Even very young children, however, seem to have acquired well-organized representations of common event sequences, such as eating in a restaurant or going shopping (Nelson 1978; Schank & Abelson 1977). Many simple perceptual and action-based schemata develop rapidly in infancy (Piaget 1952). Other, more abstract, schemata are probably formed more slowly, although a number of impressively abstract schemata are found in quite young children. For example, if one examines the stories generated by 2–5-year-old children in the corpus collected by Pitcher and Prelinger (1963), one can see the gradual growth of a story schema, the reflection of the canonical form in which simple stories are told in many cultures (Mandler & Johnson 1977).

Schank and Abelson (1977) contend that our knowledge base is primarily structured in terms of the episodes represented by various types of schemata. In a similar vein, Nelson (1974, 1977) suggests that concepts are originally learned in the context of such episodes; only gradually are they generalized from these contexts and reorganized into "context-free" hierarchically organized categorical structures. Although these notions are still speculative and will require a great deal more specification, they do suggest that some kinds of schematic organization, such as our knowledge of common scenes and event sequences, may be universal and acquired at an early age. If this is the case, then memory for scenes, stories, and other schematically organized stimuli should not be expected to show the extensive qualitative variations among ages and populations that have so often been found for taxonomically organized stimuli (cf. Brown 1977).

The finding of developmental and cultural differences in memory for categorized lists is well documented. However, there are few relevant studies on memory for schematically organized materials. A few developmental studies have found similar patterns of responding in recognition of scenes and recall of stories from the first grade to adulthood (Mandler 1978; Mandler & Johnson 1977; Mandler & Robinson 1978). However, there have been virtually no cross-cultural comparisons of memory for scenes and stories, especially between schooled and unschooled populations. Not only have stories rarely been used as stimulus materials, but, as Cole and Scribner (1977) have pointed out, most attempts to make materials culturally relevant have been concerned with their content, not their organization.

The present study is concerned with the extent to which materials having a common type of schematic organization lead to similar ways of organizing and retrieving information among various groups. Stories should provide ideal material for this kind of cross-cultural comparison, since similar types of organization of stories are found in folktales from around the world. The structure of folktales may even be a cultural universal, perhaps reflecting a universal structuring of human memory. Presumably stories that survive in an oral tradition are either optimally structured for memorability in the first place or else have attained such structure through repeated tellings (Mandler & Johnson 1977).

The present study is an initial test of the notions discussed above. We made a working assumption that the organization of simple stories is a cultural universal and, furthermore, that it is consistent with daily modes of comprehension and remembering that are also universal, regardless of type of culture or amount of schooling. Therefore, we expected to find recall of stories by nonschooled children and adults in a nonliterate society to be more similar to American performance than has typically been found in memory studies using lists of words and other nonschematically organized materials. Specifically, we expected qualitatively similar performance among all groups. Quantitative differences between children and adults might still be expected, however, due to the growth in elaborateness and extensiveness of schematic knowledge that takes place during childhood. These predictions were tested by asking several literate and nonliterate groups of Vai-speaking people in Liberia to recall the same stories used by Mandler and Johnson in their study of American school children and college students.

METHOD

Subjects

Subjects were 80 native Vai-speaking people from Cape Mount County in Liberia. The Vai are a rural farming society, most of whose people live in small villages. They have a tradition of involvement in commercial trade and have invented a syllabic writing system which is known and used by aproximately 20% of the male population. During the nineteenth century, the Vai were heavily influenced by Muslim missionaries, and virtually all Vai espouse the Muslim faith; some of the male population can read Arabic in order to recite from the Qur'an, and a small number understand enough Arabic to read and write other materials. There are some government and missionary schools in the area, so that a growing number of children and some adults are literate in English, the official language of Liberia.

The 80 subjects were divided into four groups of 20 each. All ages given are approximate since in some cases exact age was unknown. The first group was nonschooled children ranging in age from 6 to 11 years. This group was further subdivided into younger and older children. Ten children ranged in age from 6 to 8 years; the other 10 ranged from 9 to 11 years. The second group was schooled literate adults, ranging in age from 14 to 50 years, mean age 21. Number of years of schooling varied between 4 and 12, with a mean of 6.5. The third group was nonschooled literate adults, ranging in age from 18 to 51, mean age 31 years. These subjects had no formal schooling in the Western sense of the term, but eight had learned to read Vai, nine to read Arabic, two to read English, and one to read both Vai and Arabic. The fourth group was nonschooled nonliterate adults, ranging in age from 17 to 55, mean age 34 years. It can be seen that the two nonschooled adult groups were on the average older than the schooled group. It is rare to find schooled literate adults among the older members of this society. The sample was also somewhat imbalanced in terms of sex, there being more males than females in each group.

Materials

Five stories were used. Four were the same stories used by Mandler and Johnson (1977). Two of these were taken from Rumelhart (1977) — one was a summarized version of an old Russian folktale, consisting of 18 propositions ("The Czar and His Daughters"), and the other was one of Aesop's fables, consisting of 10 propositions ("The Dog and His Shadow"). The other two stories were modified versions of stories used by Piaget (1926/1960). One of these is the story of Niobe (10 propositions); the other is a variant of the Greek tale about Epaminandas (17 propositions). The fifth story ("The Bet"), consisting of 25 propositions, was taken from a collection of Vai tales (Ellis 1914/1970). The four "foreign" stories were translated into Vai, with only minor changes to make the terminology compatible with Vai traditions. For example, dragons and princesses were converted to water people and chief's daughters. All five stories were judged by the subjects to be "real" Vai stories.

Design and Procedure

Subjects were recruited as part of a larger investigation into the consequences of learning one of the three literacy systems existing in the area (see Scribner & Cole, in press). The study was conducted in an area that contained an elementary and junior high school and was the home of the experimenter, a native Vai speaker who had completed high school. The sessions were conducted individually on the porch of a house or in an isolated part of the village. Recall was tape-recorded for later transcription and translation. The experimenter memorized the stories and then, with the written versions in hand, told each subject as naturally as possible from two to five stories; recall was requested after each story was told. Based on spontaneous comments by a number of adult subjects, the experimenter felt confident that subjects understood that they were to produce verbatim recall. Subjects were included in the data analyses on the basis of equalizing the number of subjects and stories per group. Half of the subjects in each group contributed two stories; the other half contributed three. Protocols were selected so that each of the five stories was recalled by 10 subjects in each group.

Scoring Procedures

Scoring was carried out in the same manner as in Mandler and Johnson (1977). The Vai protocols were translated into English and scored for presence or absence of each proposition. Two criteria were used: a strict criterion, in which there was agreement between two scorers familiar with the stories and the grammar that the recalled proposition expressed the essential meaning of the relevant statement; and a loose criterion, in which the scorers agreed that only a subsidiary part of a proposition was recalled or there was disagreement among the scorers. It was originally planned to use the loose criterion for analysis to lessen the impact of any distortions that might arise in translation of the protocols. However, there was little difficulty in applying the strict criterion, and analyses carried out with both the strict and loose criteria were the same in all important respects. Therefore, the strict criterion was used for the analyses reported here.

The story propositions were grouped according to the basic units (nodes) of the story grammar described by Mandler and Johnson (1977). Each story consisted of a "setting" followed by one to three "episodes." Each episode had one to three propositions ($\overline{X} = 1.6$) representing each of the following five nodes: beginning, complex reaction, attempt, outcome, and ending. The number of propositions recalled from each of these nodes was calculated for each subject and expressed as a proportion of the total number of propositions presented in each node in the particular stories that subject heard.

RESULTS

An analysis of variance was carried out on the proportion of propositions recalled in each node, summed across stories, for subjects in the four groups. Children recalled 48% of the story propositions; their performance was significantly poorer than the three adult groups, $F(3,76) = 11.09$, $p < .001$. Nonliterate adults recalled slightly less (62%) than unschooled literate adults (69%) or schooled literate adults (73%), but Newman-Keuls tests indicated that none of these differences was significant.

As found in previous studies (Mandler 1978; Mandler and Johnson 1977; Stein and Glenn 1979), recall of the six nodes varied markedly, $F(5,380) = 64.35$, $p < .001$. Of greater interest, however, was the lack of a significant interaction between story node and group, $F(15,380) = 1.52$, $p \approx .10$. This result indicates that the pattern of recall of various parts of the stories was similar for all four groups.

Separate analyses were carried out on the children's data, comparing the younger to the older children. Somewhat surprisingly, there was no significant improvement in recall from the 6–8-year-old group to the 9–11-year-old group, $F < 1$. Separate analyses were also carried out on the three adult groups. These analyses, which eliminated the children's generally lower scores, were slightly more sensitive than the overall analysis. In this analysis the interaction between adult group and story node was significant, $F(10,285) = 2.12$, $p < .05$. A Newman-Keuls breakdown of this interaction indicated that the nonliterate adults were significantly poorer in recall of reactions and endings than the other two groups. No other differences were significant.

These various results are illustrated in figure 1, with the adult data in the left panel and the children's data in the right. The data from first and fourth graders and college students from the Mandler and Johnson (1977) study have been included for comparison purposes. Because of the procedural and translation differences, as well as the inclusion of a new story in the present study, it was not reasonable to make a statistical comparison. On the other hand, it is not really necessary, because the striking simi-

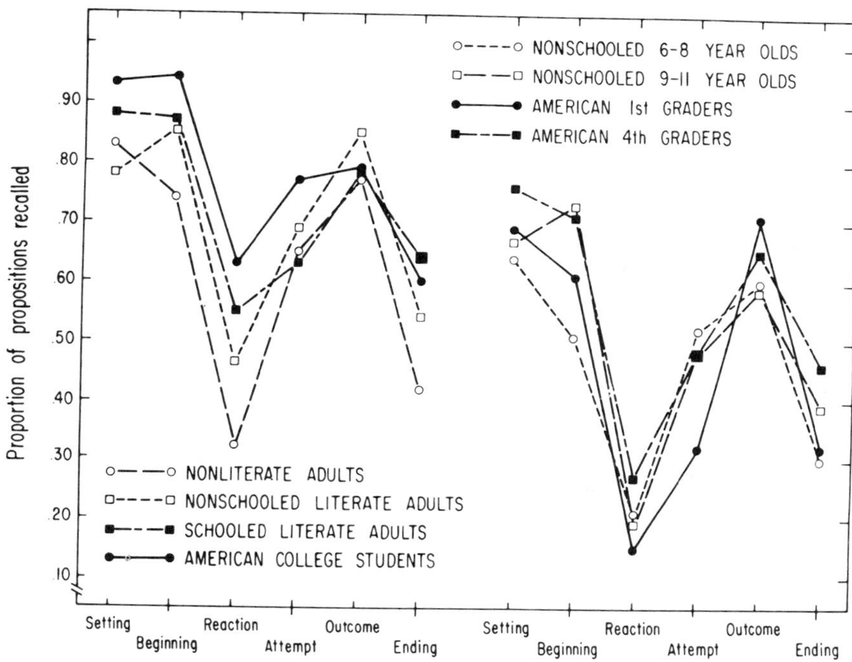

Figure 1. Proportion of propositions recalled from each story node by eight groups of subjects. Adult data are in the left panel, children's data in the right panel. The three American groups' data were taken from Mandler and Johnson (1977).

larity in patterns of recall for all the groups is readily apparent.

It will be recalled that the nonschooled literate adults had learned to read in various languages, predominantly Vai or Arabic. Although the samples were small (eight and nine subjects, respectively), their data were analyzed separately to see if literacy in these two languages differentially affected recall. Some suggestive differences were found: the Arabic nonschooled literate subjects recalled 72%, whereas the Vai nonschooled literate subjects recalled 64%. These differences are almost comparable to those between the schooled literate and nonliterate adults. There are too many unknown factors involved in acquiring literacy in these languages outside the school situation to interpret the difference, but it should be reemphasized that the range of variation under discussion is quite small.

One of the five stories used in this study was a Vai story not used in the previous Mandler and Johnson experiment. Since subjects and stories were confounded variables, it was not possible to make a statistical comparison of this story with the others. Nevertheless, it is possible to compare the range of variation across stories. Table 1 shows the mean proportion of propositions recalled in each node for each of the stories. It can be seen that recall of the Vai tale ("The Bet") is comparable to the recall of the others. Overall, 62% of its propositions were recalled, compared with a mean of 63% for the other stories. The fairly wide range in recall of individual nodes across stories is

Table 1. PROPORTION OF PROPOSITIONS RECALLED FROM EACH STORY CATEGORY FOR EACH STORY

Story	*Setting*	*Beginning*	*Reaction*	*Attempt*	*Outcome*	*Ending*
Dog	.86	.76	.64	.30	.88	.41
Czar	.93	.73	.33	.53	.68	.25
Niobe	.82	.88	.38	.95	.65	.59
Epaminandas	.68	.86	.10	.61	.82	.46
Bet	.66	.75	.41	.61	.76	.43

due to saliency of particular statements above and beyond their category membership and also to redundancies either expressed or implied across some nodes. For example, both "The Bet" and Epaminandas setting nodes contain two statements, one introducing the protagonist and the other a minor statement about locale. Typically, such minor statements are poorly recalled. Similarly, reaction statements are usually obvious and redundant with the following attempt and outcome and are often omitted from recall protocols. In the Dog story, however, the reaction is unusual and necessary to explain the following events: not surprisingly, it is more often verbalized.

A final analysis was made of the temporal sequencing of recall. Two types of sequence inversions were scored: inversions between nodes of the story schema and inversions within nodes. In well-structured stories few between-node inversions should occur in recall since the schema provides the correct ordering. Within-node statements are not ordered by a story schema, but as a rule there are either custom-based orderings (a character is typically introduced in a setting before stating where he or she lives) or causal orderings (one picks up the sword before wielding it). In some cases, there is no apparent ordering, and sequence inversions in recall are somewhat more likely.

As found in previous studies (Mandler 1978; Mandler & Johnson 1977), there were very few inversions of propositions between nodes. Fifteen percent of the subjects in each adult group made one such inversion each; 40% of the children made one inversion (and one child made two). These differences in proportions were not significant, however, $\chi^2(3) = 7.32$, $p < .10$. The frequency of within-node inversions was greater, although absolute numbers were small. Thirty-five percent of the children made one or two within-node inversions. Percentages for the adults were 30% for both schooled and nonschooled literate adults and 70% for the nonliterate adults. The latter proportion differs significantly from the others, $\chi^2(3) = 11.11$, $p < .001$. We have no explanation for this finding. In general, however, the patterning of recall in terms of output ordering is similar among the groups, as well as to other studies of story recall; sequencing of recall almost always respects the schematic order.

DISCUSSION

The conclusion from these data is simple. Nonschooled children and adults from a generally nonliterate society recalled stories in a fashion very similar to schooled children and adults from a literate industrialized society. In this study, as in many others, there were improvements in recall as a function of age. Such improvements are to be expected due to an increasing knowledge base and the elaboration of schemata that take place during childhood (see Botvin & Sutton-Smith [1977] for a discussion of the increasing complexity of self-generated stories during this period). However, there were few qualitative differences between child and adult performance. As for the adults, the effects of literacy were minimal. There were slight improvements in recall due to literacy and/or schooling, primarily in recall of reactions and endings. These small differences may be due to "conversational postulates" for telling stories: don't state the obvious and don't be redundant. Reactions in these simple tales are usually obvious, and endings are often partially redundant with outcomes. Possibly the small effects of literacy and schooling reflect an increased tendency to take recall instructions literally, or reflect more experience in verbatim recall.

The data from this study stand in marked contrast to many cross-cultural studies which have found highly different patterns of recall among schooled and nonschooled populations. Although our conclusion is simple, fitting the disparate findings from story and list recall into a general theory of memory will be a complex task. The introductory comments at the beginning of this paper only sketch an outline of what we presume to be some of the crucial variables. Nevertheless, a few broad comments can be made.

First, it should be noted that these recall data were taken from an ordinary sample of children and adults. These are not the epic singers of a nonliterate society who have learned special skills (Havelock 1971; Lord 1965). Second, it seems unlikely that the differences so often found in memory between schooled and nonschooled populations are due to a general difficulty nonschooled populations have in deliberate remembering tasks. Although this suggestion has frequently been made, in the present study subjects were engaging in deliberate memorization. They were not retelling stories as a by-product of some everyday activity, but were asked specifically to listen to and reproduce them as exactly as possible. Deliberate mnemonic strategies may well vary as a function of age and/or schooling, but this factor is more apt to be important when unfamiliar or nonschematically organized materials are used. Although it is likely, as Cole and Scribner (1977) have suggested, that societies differ in the extent to which they require deliberate memorization, this difference seems not to be important to memory for materials that reflect the familiar structures of everyday life.

Third, these data both confirm and restrict Bartlett's (1932) view of memory as schematically determined. For Bartlett, schemata reflect particular social and cultural interests. Although there is ample evidence cultural differences in recall determined by differences in experience, training, and interests (e.g., Deregowski 1970), the type of schematic remembering demonstrated here is not culture specific, but seems to reflect universal ways of structuring experience. The cultural content of a story is in some sense less important in determining how that story is remembered than the form in which it is told.

Undoubtedly cultural familiarity with plots and social themes also influences recall. One of the conventions for storytelling is that the motivation and goals of a protagonist can be omitted. In folktales most of these are well known to a given society and are easily "filled in" by a listener. To a member of another culture who is unfamiliar with a particular theme, such an omission of the complex reaction node is apt to be disastrous to both comprehension and recall. But, barring such unfamiliarity accompanied by omission of the relevant information, people should have little difficulty recalling the tales of another cultural group.

Finally, our hypothesis that the type of story schema we have studied is universal is different from that recently proposed by

Kintsch and Greene (1978). These investigators found that American college students had more trouble recalling an Apache Indian story than a Grimm fairy tale. They suggest that story schemata are culture specific, that the typical form of Western folktales may not be found in other cultures, and that therefore people can be expected to have difficulty remembering stories from cultures other than their own. Their data indeed illustrate that recall is a function of story structure. The structure of the Apache story was "then-connected" (Mandler & Johnson 1977), a story form in which episodes are only loosely temporally connected. The Grimm tale had a tighter structure, consisting of causally connected episodes. However, within any given culture, both kinds of stories are found, and, in general, people recall less of then-connected stories because they tend to forget whole episodes (Mandler 1978). Therefore, we must be cautious about equating structural differences and their associated differences in recall with cultural differences in story schemata.

Cross-cultural comparisons of the typical structures of stories from the oral tradition will not be easy. Many Western folktales have been fashioned by literary authors such as the Grimms and Anderson. Stories from other cultures, on the other hand, have often been recorded as fragments collected by anthropologists from a variety of informants. Characters may suddenly change because one informant recalls a particular protagonist by one name and another by a different one, or each informant may recall a separate set of adventures of a common type of protagonist which are then collected into a single "story." This does not imply that stories from other cultures are in general differently structured than ours, even though they may contain culture-specific content and conventions. The present data were obtained from only two cultures, but nevertheless they suggest that at least some kinds of story formats are widespread and perhaps universal. In any case, when stories have the kind of schematic form studied here, they are recalled by peoples of different ages and different backgrounds in highly similar ways.

REFERENCES

Anglin, J. *Word, object, and conceptual development.* New York: Norton, 1977.

Bartlett, F. C. *Remembering.* Cambridge: Cambridge University Press, 1932.

Botvin, G. J., & Sutton-Smith, B. The development of complexity in children's fantasy narratives. *Developmental Psychology,* 1977, *13,* 377–388.

Brown, A. L. Development, schooling and the acquisition of knowledge: comments on chapter 7 by Nelson. In R. C. Anderson, R. J. Spiro, & W. E. Montague (Eds.), *Schooling and the acquisition of knowledge.* Hillsdale, N.J.: Erlbaum, 1977.

Cole, M., & Scribner, S. Cross-cultural studies of memory and cognition. In R. V. Kail & J. W. Hagen (Eds.), *Perspectives on the development of memory and cognition.* Hillsdale, N.J.: Erlbaum, 1977.

Deregowski, J. B. Effect of cultural value of time upon recall. *British Journal of Social and Clinical Psychology,* 1970, *9,* 37–41.

Ellis, G. *Negro culture in West Africa.* New York: Johnson, 1970. (Originally published 1914.)

Havelock, E. A. *Prologue to Greek literacy.* Cincinnati: University of Cincinnati Press, 1971.

Inhelder, B., & Piaget, J. *The early growth of logic in the child.* New York: Harper, 1964.

Kintsch, W., & Greene, E. The role of culture-specific schemata in the comprehension and recall of stories. *Discourse Processes,* 1978, *1,* 1–13.

Lord, A. B. *Singer of tales.* New York: Atheneum, 1965.

Macnamara, J. Cognitive basis of language learning in infants. *Psychological Review,* 1972, *79,* 1–13.

Mandler, J. M. A code in the node: the use of a story schema in retrieval. *Discourse Processes,* 1978, *1,* 14–35.

Mandler, J. M. Categorical and schematic organization in memory. In R. C. Puff (Ed.), *Memory, organization, and structure.* New York: Academic Press, in press.

Mandler, J. M., & Johnson, N. S. Remembrance

of things parsed: story structure and recall. *Cognitive Psychology,* 1977, *9,* 111–151.

Mandler, J. M., & Robinson, C. A. Developmental changes in picture recognition. *Journal of Experimental Child Psychology,* 1978, *26,* 122–136.

Nelson, K. Concept, word and sentence: interrelations in acquisition and development. *Psychological Review,* 1974, *81,* 267–285.

Nelson, K. Cognitive development and the acquisition of concepts. In R. C. Anderson, R. J. Spiro, & W. E. Montague (Eds.), *Schooling and the acquisition of knowledge.* Hillsdale, N.J.: Erlbaum, 1977.

Nelson, K. How young children represent knowledge of their world in and out of language: a preliminary report. In R. Siegler (Ed.), *Children's thinking — what develops?* Hillsdale, N.J.: Erlbaum, 1978.

Piaget, J. *The origins of intelligence in children.* New York: Norton, 1952.

Piaget, J. *The language and thought of the child.* London: Routledge & Kegan Paul, 1960. (Originally published 1926.)

Pitcher, E. G., & Prelinger, E. *Children tell stories: an analysis of fantasy.* New York: International Universities Press, 1963.

Rumelhart, D. E. Understanding and summarizing brief stories. In D. LaBerge & S. J. Samuels (Eds.), *Basic processes in reading: perception and comprehension.* Hillsdale, N.J.: Erlbaum, 1977.

Schank, R. C., & Abelson, R. P. *Scripts, plans, goals, and understanding.* Hillsdale, N.J.: Erlbaum, 1977.

Scribner, S. Developmental aspects of categorized recall in a West African society. *Cognitive Psychology,* 1974, *6,* 475–494.

Scribner, S., & Cole, M. *The consequences of literacy: a case study among the Vai.* Cambridge, Mass.: Harvard University Press, in press.

Stein, N. S., & Glenn, C. G. An analysis of story comprehension in elementary school children. In R. Freedle (Ed.), *New directions in discourse processing.* Hillsdale, N.J.: Ablex, 1979.

Worden, P. E. The development of the category-recall function under three retrieval conditions. *Child Development,* 1974, *45,* 1054–1059.

Jerome Bruner

THE GROWTH OF MIND

These past several years, I have had the painful pleasure — and it has been both — of exploring two aspects of the cognitive processes that were new to me. One was cognitive development, the other pedagogy. I knew, as we all know, that the two were closely related, and it was my naive hope that, betimes, the relation would come clear to me. Indeed, 2 years ago when I first knew that in early September 1965 I would be standing here, delivering this lecture, I said to myself that I would use the occasion to set forth to my colleagues what I had been able to find out about this vexed subject, the relation of pedagogy and development. It seemed obvious then that in 2 years one could get to the heart of the matter.

The 2 years have gone by. I have had the privilege of addressing this distinguished audience (Bruner, 1964) on some of our findings concerning the development of cognitive processes in children, and I have similarly set forth what I hope are not entirely unreasonable ideas about pedagogy (Bruner, in press). I am still in a very deep quandary concerning the relation of these two enterprises. The heart of the matter still eludes me, but I shall stand by my resolve. I begin on this autobiographical note so that you may know in advance why this evening is more an exercise in conjecture than a cataloguing of solid conclusions.

What is most unique about man is that his growth as an individual depends upon the history of his species — not upon a history reflected in genes and chromosomes but, rather, reflected in a culture external to man's tissue and wider in scope than is embodied in any one man's competency. Perforce, then, the growth of mind is always growth assisted from the outside. And since a culture, particularly an advanced one, transcends the bounds of individual competence, the limits for individual growth are by definition greater than what any single person has previously attained. For the limits of growth depend on how a culture assists the individual to use such intellectual potential as he may possess. It seems highly unlikely — either empirically or canonically — that we have any realistic sense of the furthest reach of such assistance to growth.

The evidence today is that the full evolution of intelligence came as a result of bipedalism and tool using. The large human brain gradually evolved as a sequel to the first use of pebble tools by early near-man. To condense the story, a near-man, or hominid, with a slightly superior brain, using a pebble tool,

Address of the President to the Seventy-Third Annual Convention of the American Psychological Association, Chicago, September 4, 1965.

SOURCE: From Jerome S. Bruner, "The Growth of Mind," *American Psychologist* 20, 1965, pp. 1007–1017.

could make out better in the niche provided by nature than a near-man who depended not on tools but on sheer strength and formidable jaws. Natural selection favored the primitive tool user. In time, thanks to his better chance of surviving and breeding, he became more so: The ones who survived had larger brains, smaller jaws, less ferocious teeth. In place of belligerent anatomy, they developed tools and a brain that made it possible to use them. Human evolution thereafter became less a matter of having appropriate fangs or claws and more one of using and later fashioning tools to express the powers of the larger brain that was also emerging. Without tools the brain was of little use, no matter how many hundred cubic centimeters of it there might be. Let it also be said that without the original programmatic capacity for fitting tools into a sequence of acts, early hominids would never have started the epigenetic progress that brought them to their present state. And as human groups stabilized, tools became more complex and "shaped to pattern," so that it was no longer a matter of reinventing tools in order to survive, but rather of mastering the skills necessary for using them. In short, after a certain point in human evolution, the only means whereby man could fill his evolutionary niche was through the cultural transmission of the skills necessary for the use of priorly invented techniques, implements, and devices.

Two crucial parallel developments seem also to have occurred. As hominids became increasingly bipedal, with the freed hands necessary for using spontaneous pebble tools, selection also favored those with a heavier pelvic bony structure that could sustain the impacting strain of bipedal locomotion. The added strength came, of course, from a gradual closing down of the birth canal. There is an obstetrical paradox here: a creature with an increasingly larger brain but with a smaller and smaller birth canal to get through. The resolution seems to have been achieved through the immaturity of the human neonate, particularly cerebral immaturity that assures not only a smaller head, but also a longer period of transmitting the necessary skills required by human culture. During this same period, human language must have emerged, giving man not only a new and powerful way of representing reality but also increasing his power to assist the mental growth of the young to a degree beyond anything before seen in nature.

It is impossible, of course, to reconstruct the evolution in techniques of instruction in the shadow zone between hominids and man. I have tried to compensate by observing contemporary analogues of earlier forms, knowing full well that the pursuit of analogy can be dangerously misleading. I have spent many hours observing uncut films of the behavior of free-ranging baboons, films shot in East Africa by my colleague Irven DeVore with a very generous footage devoted to infants and juveniles. I have also had access to the unedited film archives of a hunting-gathering people living under roughly analogous ecological conditions, the !Kung Bushman of the Kalahari, recorded by Laurance and Lorna Marshall, brilliantly aided by their son John and daughter Elizabeth.[1] I have also worked directly but informally with the Wolof of Senegal, observing children in the bush and in French-style schools. Even more valuable than my own informal observations in Senegal were the systematic experiments carried out later by my colleague, Patricia Marks Greenfield (in press).

Let me describe very briefly some salient differences in the free learning patterns of immature baboons and among !Kung children. Baboons have a highly developed social life in their troops, with well-organized and stable dominance patterns. They live within a territory, protecting themselves from predators by joint action of the strongly built, adult males. It is striking that the behavior of baboon juveniles is shaped principally by play with their peer group, play that provides opportunity for the spontaneous expression and practice of the component acts that, in maturity, will be orchestrated into either the behavior of the dominant male or of the infant-protective female. All this seems to be accomplished with little participation by any mature animals in the play of the juveniles. We know from the important experiments of Harlow and his colleagues (Harlow & Harlow, 1962) how devastating a disruption in development can be produced in subhuman primates by interfering with their opportunity for peer-group play and social interaction.

Among hunting-gathering humans, on the other hand, there is *constant* interaction between adult and child, or adult and adolescent, or adolescent and child. !Kung adults and children play and dance together, sit together, participate in minor hunting together, join in song and story telling together. At very frequent intervals, moreover, children are party to rituals presided over by adults — minor, as in the first haircutting, or major, as when a boy kills his first Kudu buck and goes through the proud but painful process of scarification. Children, besides, are constantly playing imitatively with the rituals, implements, tools, and weapons of the adult world. Young juvenile baboons, on the other hand, virtually never play with things or imitate directly large and significant sequences of adult behavior.

Note, though, that in tens of thousands of feet of !Kung film, one virtually never sees an instance of "teaching" taking place outside the situation where the behavior to be learned is relevant. Nobody "teaches" in our prepared sense of the word. There is nothing like school, nothing like lessons. Indeed, among the !Kung children there is very little "telling." Most of what we would call instruction is through showing. And there is no "practice" or "drill" as such save in the form of play modeled directly on adult models — play hunting, play bossing, play exchanging, play baby tending, play house making. In the end, every man in the culture knows nearly all there is to know about how to get on with life as a man, and every woman as a woman — the skills, the rituals and myths, the obligations and rights.

The change in the instruction of children in more complex societies is twofold. First of all, there is knowledge and skill in the culture far in excess of what any one individual knows. And so, increasingly, there develops an economical technique of instructing the young based heavily on *telling* out of context rather than *showing* in context. In literate societies, the practice becomes institutionalized in the school or the "teacher." Both promote this necessarily abstract way of instructing the young. The result of "teaching the culture" can, at its worst, lead to the ritual, rote nonsense that has led a generation of critics from Max Wertheimer (1945) to Mary Alice White (undated) of Teachers' College to despair. For in the detached school, what is imparted often has little to do with life as lived in the society except insofar as the demands of school are of a kind that reflect *indirectly* the demands of life in a technical society. But these indirectly imposed demands may be the most important feature of the detached school. For school is a sharp departure from indigenous practice. It takes learning, as we have noted, out of the context of immediate action just by dint of putting it into a school. This very extirpation makes learning become an act in itself freed from the immediate ends of action, preparing the learner for the chain of reckoning remote from payoff that is needed for the formulation of complex ideas. At the same time, the school (if successful) frees the child from the pace setting of the round of daily activity. If the school succeeds in avoiding a pace-setting round of its own, it may be one of the great agents for promoting reflectiveness. Moreover, in school, one must "follow the lesson" which means one must learn to follow either the abstraction of written speech — abstract in the sense that it is divorced from the concrete situation to which the speech might originally have been related — or the abstraction of language delivered orally but out of the context of an ongoing action. Both of these are highly abstract uses of language.

It is no wonder, then, that many recent studies report large differences between "primitive" children who are in schools and their brothers who are not: differences in perception, abstraction, time perspective, and so on. I need only cite the work of Biesheuvel (1949) in South Africa, Gay and Cole (undated) in Liberia, Greenfield (in press) in Senegal, Maccoby and Modiano (in press) in rural Mexico, Reich (in press) among Alaskan Eskimos.

What a culture does to assist the development of the powers of mind of its members is, in effect, to provide amplification systems to which human beings, equipped with appropriate skills, can link themselves. There are, first, the amplifiers of action — hammers, levers, digging sticks, wheels — but more important, the programs of action into which such implements can be substituted. Second, there are amplifiers of the senses, ways of looking and noticing that can take advantage of devices ranging from smoke signals and hailers to diagrams and pictures that stop the action or microscopes that enlarge it. Finally and most powerfully, there are amplifiers of the thought processes, ways of thinking that employ language and formation of explanation, and later use such languages as mathematics and logic and even find automatic servants to crank out the consequences. A culture is, then, a deviser, a repository, and a transmitter of amplification systems and of the devices that fit into such systems. We know very little in a deep sense about the transmission function, how people are trained to get the most from their potential by use of a culture's resources.

But it is reasonably clear that there is a major difference between the mode of transmission in a technical society, with its schools, and an indigenous one, where cultural transmission is in the context of action. It is not just that an indigenous society, when its action pattern becomes disrupted, falls apart — at a most terrifying rate — as in uncontrolled urbanization in some parts of Africa. Rather, it is that the institution of a school serves to convert knowledge and skill into more symbolical, more abstract, more verbal form. It is this process of transmission — admittedly very new in human history — that is so poorly understood and to which, finally, we shall return.

There are certain obvious specifications that can be stated about how a society must proceed in order to equip its young. It must convert what is to be known — whether a skill or a belief system or a connected body of knowledge — into a form capable of being mastered by a beginner. The more we know of the process of growth, the better we shall be at such conversion. The failure of modern man to understand mathematics and science may be less a matter of stunted abilities than our failure to understand how to teach such subjects. Second, given the limited amount of time available for learning, there must be a due regard for saving the learner from needless learning. There must be some emphasis placed on economy and transfer and the learning of general rules. All societies must (and virtually all do) distinguish those who are clever from those who are stupid — though few of them generalize this trait across all activities. Cleverness in a particular activity almost universally connotes strategy, economy, heuristics, highly generalized skills. A society must also place emphasis upon how one derives a course of action from what one has learned. Indeed, in an indigenous society, it is almost impossible to separate what one does from what one knows. More advanced societies often have not found a way of dealing with the separation of knowledge and action — probably a result of the emphasis they place upon "telling" in their instruction. All societies must maintain interest among the young in the learning process, a minor problem when learning is in the context of life and action, but harder when it becomes more abstracted. And finally, and perhaps most obviously, a society must assure that its necessary skills and procedures remain intact from one generation to the next — which does not always happen, as witnessed by Easter Islanders, Incas, Aztecs, and Mayas.[2]

Unfortunately, psychology has not concerned itself much with any of these five requisites of cultural transmission — or at least not much with four of them. We have too easily assumed that learning is learning is learning — that the early version of what was taught did not matter much, one thing being much like another and reducible to a pattern of association, to stimulus-response connections, or to our favorite molecular componentry. We denied there was a problem of development beyond the quantitative one of providing more experience, and with the denial, closed our eyes to the pedagogical problem of how to represent knowledge, how to sequence it, how to embody it in a form appropriate to young learners. We expended more passion on the part-whole controversy than on what whole or what part of it was to be presented first. I should except Piaget (1954), Köhler (1940), and Vygotsky (1962) from these complaints — all until recently unheeded voices.

Our neglect of the economy of learning stems, ironically, from the heritage of Ebbinghaus (1913), who was vastly interested in savings. Our nonsense syllables, our random mazes failed to take into account how we reduce complexity and strangeness to simplicity and the familiar, how we convert what we have learned into rules and procedures, how, to use Bartlett's (1932) term of over 30 years ago, we turn around on our own schemata to reorganize what we have mastered into more manageable form.

Nor have we taken naturally to the issue of knowledge and action. Its apparent mentalism has repelled us. Tolman (1951), who bravely made the distinction, was accused of leaving his organisms wrapt in thought. But he recognized the problem and if he insisted on the idea that knowledge might be organized in cognitive maps, it was in recognition (as a great functionalist) that organisms go somewhere on the basis of what they have learned. I believe we are getting closer to the problem of how knowledge affects action and vice versa, and offer in testimony of my conviction the provocative book by Miller, Galanter, and Pribram (1960), *Plans and the Structure of Behavior.*

Where the maintenance of the learner's interest is concerned, I remind you of what my colleague Gordon Allport (1946) has long warned. We have been so concerned with the model of driven behavior, with drive reduction and the *vis a tergo* that again, until recently, we have tended to overlook the question of what keeps learners interested in the activity of learning, in the achievement of competence beyond bare necessity and first payoff. The work of R. W. White (1959) on effectance motivation, of Harlow and his colleagues (Butler, 1954; Harlow, 1953) on curiosity, and of Heider (1958) and Festinger (1962) on consistency begins to redress the balance. But it is only a beginning.

The invention of antidegradation devices, guarantors that skill and knowledge will be maintained intact, is an exception to our oversight. We psychologists have been up to our ears in it. Our special contribution is the achievement test. But the achievement test has, in the main, reflected the timidity of the educational enterprise as a whole. I believe we know how to determine, though we have not yet devised tests to determine, how pupils use what they learn to think with later in life — for there is the real issue.

I have tried to examine briefly what a culture must do in passing on its amplifying skills and knowledge to a new generation and, even more briefly, how we as psychologists have dealt or failed to deal with the problems. I think the situation is fast changing — with a sharp increase in interest in the conversion problem, the problems of economy of learning, the nature of interest, the relation of knowledge and action. We are, I believe, at a major turning point where psychology will once again concern itself with the design of methods of assisting cognitive growth, be it through the invention of a rational technology of toys, of ways of enriching the environment of the crib and nursery, of organizing the activity of a school, or of devising a curriculum whereby we transmit an organized body of knowledge and skill to a new generation to amplify their powers of mind.

I commented earlier that there was strikingly little knowledge available about the "third way" of training the skills of the young: the first being the play practice of component skills in prehuman primates, the second the teaching-in-context of indigenous societies, and the third being the abstracted, detached method of the school.

Let me now become highly specific. Let me consider a particular course of study, one given in a school, one we are ourselves constructing, trying out, and in a highly qualitative way, evaluating. It is for schools of the kind that exist in Western culture. The experience we have had with this effort, now in its third year, may serve to highlight the kinds of problems and conjectures one encounters in studying how to assist the growth of intellect in this "third way."

There is a dilemma in describing a course of study. One begins by setting forth the intellectual substance of what is to be taught. Yet if such a recounting tempts one to "get across" the subject, the ingredient of pedagogy is in jeopardy. For only in a trivial sense is a course designed to "get something across," merely to impart information. There are better means to that end than teaching. Unless the learner develops his skills, disciplines his taste, deepens his view of the world, the "something" that is got across is hardly worth the effort of transmission.

The more "elementary" a course and the younger its students, the more serious must be its pedagogical aim of forming the intellectual powers of those whom it serves. It is as important to justify a good mathematics course by the intellectual discipline it provides or the honesty it promotes as by the mathematics it transmits. Indeed, neither can be accomplished without the other. The content of this particular course is man: his nature as a species, the forces that shaped and continue to shape his humanity. Three questions recur throughout:

What is human about human beings?
How did they get that way?
How can they be made more so?

In pursuit of our questions we explore five matters, each closely associated with the evolution of man as a species, each defining at once the distinctiveness of man and his potentiality for further evolution. The five great humanizing forces are, of course, tool making, language, social organization, the management of man's prolonged childhood, and man's urge to explain. It has been our first lesson in teaching that no pupil, however eager, can appreciate the relevance of, say, tool making or language in human evolution without first grasping the fundamental concept of a tool or what a language is. These are not self-evident matters, even to the expert. So we are involved in teaching not only the role of tools or language in the emergence of man, but, as a necessary precondition for doing so, setting forth the fundamentals of linguistics or the theory of tools. And it is as often the case as not that (as in the case of the "theory of tools") we must solve a formidable intellectual problem ourselves in order to be able to help our pupils do the same. I should have said at the outset that the "we" I employ in this context is no editorial fiction, but rather a group of anthropologists, zoologists, linguists, theoretical engineers, artists, designers, camera crews, teachers, children, and psychologists. The project is being carried out under my direction at Educational Services, Incorporated, with grants from the National Science Foundation and the Ford Foundation.

While one readily singles out five sources of man's humanization, under no circumstances can they be put into airtight compartments. Human kinship is distinctively different from primate mating patterns precisely because it is classificatory and rests on man's ability to use language. Or, if you will, tool use enhances the division of labor in a society which in turn affects kinship. So while each domain can be treated as a separate set of ideas, their teaching must make it possible for the children to have a sense of their interaction. We have leaned heavily on the use of contrast, highly controlled contrast, to help children achieve detachment from the all too familiar matrix of social life: the contrasts of man versus higher primates, man versus prehistoric man, contemporary technological man versus "primitive" man, and man versus child. The primates are principally baboons, the prehistoric materials mostly from the Olduvai Gorge and Les Eyzies, the "primitive" peoples mostly the Netsilik Eskimos of Pelly Bay and the !Kung Bushmen. The materials, collected for our purposes, are on film, in story, in ethnography, in pictures and drawings, and principally in ideas embodied in exercises.

We have high aspirations. We hope to achieve five goals:

1. To give our pupils respect for and confidence in the powers of their own minds
2. To give them respect, moreover, for the powers of thought concerning the human condition, man's plight, and his social life
3. To provide them with a set of workable models that make it simpler to analyze the nature of the social world in which they live and the condition in which man finds himself
4. To impart a sense of respect for the capacities and plight of man as a species, for his origins, for his potential, for his humanity
5. To leave the student with a sense of the unfinished business of man's evolution

One last word about the course of study that has to do with the quality of the ideas, materials, and artistry — a matter that is at once technological and intellectual. We have felt that the making of such a curriculum deserved the best talent and technique available in the world. Whether artist, ethnographer, film maker, poet, teacher — nobody we have asked has refused us. We are obviously going to suffer in testing a Hawthorne effect of some magnitude. But then, perhaps it is as well to live in a permanent state of revolution.

Let me now try to describe some of the major problems one encounters in trying to construct a course of study. I shall not try to translate the problems into refined theoretical form, for they do not as yet merit such translation. They are more difficulties than problems. I choose them, because they are vividly typical of what one encounters in such enterprises. The course is designed for 10-year-olds in the fifth grade of elementary school, but we have been trying it out as well on the fourth and sixth grades better to bracket our difficulties.

One special point about these difficulties. They are born of trying to achieve an objective and are as much policy bound as theory bound. It is like the difference between building an economic theory about monopolistic practices and constructing policies for controlling monopoly. Let me remind you that modern economic theory has been reformulated, refined, and revived by having a season in policy. I am convinced that the psychology of assisted growth, i.e., pedagogy, will have to be forged in the policy crucible of curriculum making before it can reach its full descriptive power as theory. Economics was first through the cycle from theory to policy to theory to policy; it is happening now to psychology, anthropology, and sociology.

Now on to the difficulties. The first is what might be called *the psychology of a subject matter.* A learned discipline can be conceived as a way of thinking about certain phenomena. Mathematics is one way of thinking about order without reference to what is being ordered. The behavioral sciences provide one or perhaps several ways of thinking about man and his society — about regularities, origins, causes, effects. They are probably special (and suspect) because they permit man to look at himself from a perspective that is outside his own skin and beyond his own preferences — at least for awhile.

Underlying a discipline's "way of thought," there is a set of connected, varyingly implicit, generative propositions. In physics and mathematics, most of the underlying generative propositions like the conservation theorems, or the axioms of geometry, or the associative, distributive, and commutative rules of analysis are by now very explicit indeed. In the behavioral sciences we must be content with more implicitness. We traffic in inductive propositions: e.g., the different activities of a society are interconnected such that if you know something about the technological response of a society to an environment, you will be able to make some shrewd guesses about its myths or about the things it values, etc. We use the device of a significant contrast as in linguistics as when we describe the territoriality of a baboon troop in order to help us recognize the system of reciprocal exchange of a human group, the former somehow provoking awareness of the latter.

There is nothing more central to a discipline than its way of thinking. There is nothing more important in its teaching than to provide the child the earliest opportunity to learn that way of thinking — the forms of connection, the attitudes, hopes, jokes, and frustrations that go with it. In a word, the best introduction to a subject is the subject itself. At the very first breath, the young learner should, we think, be given the chance to solve problems, to conjecture, to quarrel as these are done at the heart of the discipline. But, you will ask, how can this be arranged?

Here again the problem of conversion. There exist ways of thinking characteristic of different stages of development. We are acquainted with Inhelder and Piaget's (1958) account of the transition from preoperational, through concrete operational, to propositional thought in the years from preschool through, say, high school. If you have an eventual pedagogical objective in mind, you can translate the way of thought of a discipline into its Piagetian (or other) equivalent appropriate to a given level of development and take the child onward from there. The Cambridge Mathematics Project of Educational Services, Incorporated, argues that if the child is to master the calculus early in his high school years, he should start work early with the idea of limits, the earliest work being manipulative, later going on to images and diagrams, and finally moving on to the more abstract notation needed for delineating the more precise idea of limits.

In "Man: A Course of Study," (Bruner, 1965) there are also versions of the subject appropriate to a particular age that can at a later age be given a more powerful rendering. We have tried to choose topics with this in mind: The analysis of kinship that begins with children using sticks and blocks and colors and whatnot to represent their own families, goes on to the conventional kinship diagrams by a meandering but, as you can imagine, interesting path, and then can move on to more formal and powerful componential analysis. So, too, with myth. We begin with the excitement of a powerful myth (like the Netsilik Nuliajik myth), then have the children construct some myths of their own, then examine what a set of Netsilik myths have in common, which takes us finally to Lévi-Strauss's (1963) analysis of contrastive features in myth construction. A variorum text of a myth or corpus of myths put together by sixth graders can be quite an extraordinary document.

This approach to the psychology of a learned discipline turns out to illuminate another problem raised earlier: the maintenance of interest. There is, in this approach, a reward in understanding that grows from the subject matter itself. It is easier to engineer this satisfaction in mathematics, for understanding is so utter in a formal discipline — a balance beam balances or it does not; therefore there is an equality or there is not. In the behavioral sciences the payoff in understanding cannot be so obviously and startlingly self-revealing. Yet, one can design exercises in the understanding of man, too — as when children figure out the ways in which, given limits of ecology, skills, and materials, Bushmen hunt different animals, and then compare their predictions with the real thing on film.

Consider now a second problem: *how to stimulate thought in the setting of a school.* We know from experimental studies like those of Bloom and Broder (1950), and of Goodnow and Pettigrew (1955), that there is a striking difference in the acts of a person who thinks that the task before him represents a problem to be solved rather than being controlled by random forces. School is a particular subculture where these matters are concerned. By school age, children have come to expect quite arbitrary and, from their point of view, meaningless demands to be made upon them by adults — the result, most likely, of the fact that adults often fail to recognize the task of conversion necessary to make their questions have some intrinsic significance for the child. Children, of course, will try to solve problems if they recognize them as such. But they are not often either predisposed to or skillful in problem finding, in recognizing the hidden conjectural feature in tasks set them. But we know now that children in school can quite quickly be led to such problem finding by encouragement and instruction.

The need for this instruction and encouragement and its relatively swift success relates, I suspect, to what psychoanalysts refer to as the guilt-ridden oversuppression of primary process and its public replacement by secondary process. Children, like adults, need reassurance that it is all right to entertain and express highly subjective ideas, to treat a task as a problem where you *invent* an answer rather than *finding* one out there in the book or on the blackboard. With children in elementary school, there is often a need to devise emotionally vivid special games, story-making episodes, or construction projects to reestablish in the child's mind his right not only to have his own private ideas but to express them in the public setting of a classroom.

But there is another, perhaps more serious difficulty: the interference of intrinsic problem solving by extrinsic. Young children in school expend extraordinary time and effort figuring out what it is that the teacher wants — and usually coming to the conclusion that she or he wants tidiness or remembering or to do things at a certain time in a certain way. This I refer to as extrinsic problem solving. There is a great deal of it in school.

There are several quite straightforward ways of stimulating problem solving. One is to train teachers to want it and that will come in time. But teachers can be encouraged to like it, interestingly enough, by providing them and their children with materials and lessons that *permit* legitimate problem solving and permit the teacher to recognize it. For exercises with such materials create an atmosphere by treating things as instances of what *might* have occurred rather than simply as what did occur. Let me illustrate by a concrete instance. A fifth-grade class was working on the organization of a baboon troop — on this particular day, specifically on how they might protect against predators. They saw a brief sequence of film in which six or seven adult males go forward to intimidate and hold off three cheetahs. The teacher asked what the baboons had done to keep the cheetahs off, and there ensued a lively discussion of how the dominant adult males, by showing their formidable mouthful of teeth and making threatening gestures had turned the trick. A boy raised a tentative hand and asked whether cheetahs always attacked together. Yes, though a single cheetah sometimes followed behind a moving troop and picked off an older, weakened straggler or an unwary, straying juvenile. "Well, what if there were four cheetahs and two of them attacked from behind and two from in front. What would the baboons do then?" The question could have been answered empirically — and the inquiry ended. Cheetahs *do not* attack that way, and so we do not know what baboons *might* do. Fortunately, it was not. For the question opens up the deep issues of what might be and why it is not. Is there a necessary relation between predators and prey that share a common ecological niche? Must their encounters have a "sporting chance" outcome? It is such conjecture, in this case quite unanswerable, that produces rational, self-consciously problem-finding behavior so crucial to the growth of intellectual power. Given the materials, given some background and encouragement, teachers like it as much as the students.

I should like to turn now to the *personalization of knowledge.* A generation ago, the progressive movement urged that knowledge be related to the child's own experience and brought out of the realm of empty abstractions. A good idea was translated into banalities about the home, then the friendly postman and trashman, then the community, and so on. It is a poor way to compete with the child's own dramas and mysteries. A decade ago, my colleague Clyde Kluckhorn (1949) wrote a prize-winning popular book on anthropology with the entrancing title *Mirror for Man.* In some deep way, there is extraordinary power in "that mirror which other civilizations still hold up to us to recognize and study . . . [the] image of ourselves [Lévi-Strauss, 1965]." The psychological bases of the power are not obvious. Is it as in discrimination learning, where increasing the degree of contrast helps in the learning of a discrimination, or as in studies of concept attainment where a negative instance demonstrably defines the domain of a conceptual rule? Or is it some primitive identification? All these miss one thing that seems to come up frequently in our interviews with the children. It is the experience of discovering kinship and likeness in what at first seemed bizarre, exotic, and even a little repellant.

Consider two examples, both involving film of the Netsilik. In the films, a single nuclear family, Zachary, Marta, and their 4-year-old Alexi, is followed through the year — spring sealing, summer fishing at the stone weir, fall caribou hunting, early winter fishing through the ice, winter at the big ceremonial igloo. Children report that at first the three members of the family look weird and uncouth. In time, they look normal, and eventually, as when Marta finds sticks around which to wrap her braids, the girls speak of how pretty she is. That much is superficial — or so it seems. But consider a second episode.

It has to do with Alexi who, with his father's help, devises a snare and catches a gull. There is a scene in which he stones the gull to death. Our children watched, horror struck. One girl, Kathy, blurted out, "He's not even human, doing that to the seagull." The class was silent. Then another girl, Jennine, said quietly: "He's got to grow up to be a hunter. His mother was smiling when he was doing that." And then an extended discussion about how people have to do things to learn and even do things to learn how to feel appropriately. "What would you do if you had to live there? Would you be as smart about getting along as they are with what they've got?" said one boy, going back to the accusation that Alexi was inhuman to stone the bird.

I am sorry it is so difficult to say it clearly. What I am trying to say is that to personalize knowledge one does not simply link it to the familiar. Rather one makes the familiar an instance of a more general case and thereby produces awareness of it. What the children were learning about was not seagulls and Eskimos, but about their own feelings and preconceptions that, up to then, were too implicit to be recognizable to them.

Consider finally the problem of *self-conscious reflectiveness*. It is an epistemological mystery why traditional education has so often emphasized extensiveness and coverage over intensiveness and depth. We have already commented on the fact that memorizing was usually perceived by children as one of the high-priority tasks but rarely did children sense an emphasis upon ratiocination with a view toward redefining what had been encountered, reshaping it, reordering it. The cultivation of reflectiveness, or whatever you choose to call it, is one of the great problems one faces in devising curriculum. How lead children to discover the powers and pleasures that await the exercise of retrospection?

Let me suggest one answer that has grown from what we have done. It is the use of the "organizing conjecture." We have used three such conjectures — what is human about human beings, how they got that way, how they could become more so. They serve two functions, one of them the very obvious though important one of putting perspective back into the particulars. The second is less obvious and considerably more surprising. The questions often seemed to serve as criteria for determining where they were getting, how well they were understanding, whether anything new was emerging. Recall Kathy's cry: "He's not human doing that to the seagull." She was hard at work in her rage on the conjecture what makes human beings human.

There, in brief, are four problems that provide some sense of what a psychologist encounters when he takes a hand in assisting the growth of mind in children in the special setting of a school. The problems look quite different from those we encounter in formulating classical developmental theory with the aid of typical laboratory research. They also look very different from those that one would find in an indigenous society, describing how children picked up skills and knowledge and values in the context of action and daily life. We clearly do not have a theory of the school that is sufficient to the task of running schools — just as we have no adequate theory of toys or of readiness building or whatever the jargon is for preparing children to do a better job the next round. It only obscures the issue to urge that some day our classical theories of learning will fill the gap. They show no sign of doing so.

I hope that we shall not allow ourselves to be embarrassed by our present ignorance. It has been a long time since we have looked at what is involved in imparting knowledge through the vehicle of the school — if ever we did look at it squarely. I urge that we delay no longer.

But I am deeply convinced that the psychologist cannot alone construct a theory of how to assist cognitive development and cannot alone learn how to enrich and amplify the powers of a growing human mind. The task belongs to the whole intellectual community: the behavioral scientists and the artists, scientists, and scholars who are the custodians of skill, taste, and knowledge in our culture. Our special task as psychologists is to convert skills and knowledge to forms and exercises that fit growing minds — and it is a task ranging from how to keep children free from anxiety and how to translate physics for the very young child into a set of playground maneuvers that, later, the child can turn around upon and convert into a sense of inertial regularities.

And this in turn leads me to a final conjecture, one that has to do with the organization of our profession, a matter that has concerned me greatly during this past year during which I have had the privilege of serving as your President. Psychology is peculiarly prey to parochialism. Left to our own devices, we tend to construct models of a man who is neither a victim of history, a target of economic forces, or even a working member of a society. I am still struck by Roger Barker's (1963) ironic truism that the best way to predict the behavior of a human being is to know where he is: In a post office he behaves post office, at church he behaves church.

Psychology, and you will forgive me if the image seems a trifle frivolous, thrives on polygamy with her neighbors. Our marriage with the biological sciences has produced a cumulation of ever more powerful knowledge. So, too, our joint undertakings with anthropology and sociology. Joined together with a variety of disciplines, we have made lasting contributions to the health sciences and, I judge, will make even greater contributions now that the emphasis is shifting to the problems of alleviating stress and arranging for a community's mental health. What I find lacking is an alignment that might properly be called the growth sciences. The field of pedagogy is one participant in the growth sciences. Any field of inquiry devoted to assisting the growth of effective human beings, fully empowered with zest, with skill, with knowledge, with taste is surely a candidate for this sodality. My friend Philip Morrison once suggested to his colleagues at Cornell that his department of physics grant a doctorate not only for work in theoretical, experimental, or applied physics, but also for work in pedagogical physics. The limits of the growth sciences remain to be drawn. They surely transcend the behavioral sciences cum pediatrics. It is plain that, if we are to achieve the effectiveness of which we as human beings are capable, there will one day have to be such a field. I hope that we psychologists can earn our way as charter members.

NOTES

1. I am greatly indebted to Irven DeVore and Educational Services Incorporated for the opportunity to view his films of free-ranging baboons, and to Laurance and Lorna Marshall for the opportunity to examine their incomparable archives. DeVore and the Marshalls have been generous in their counsel as well.

2. I have purposely left out of the discussion the problems of impulse regulation and socialization of motives, topics that have received extended treatment in the voluminous literature on culture and personality. The omission is dictated by emphasis rather than evaluation. Obviously, the shaping of character by culture is of great importance for an understanding of our topic as it bears, for example, upon culture-instilled attitudes toward the uses of mind. Since our emphasis is upon human potential and its amplification by culturally patterned instrumental skills, we mention the problem of character formation in passing and in recognition of its importance in a complete treatment of the issues under discussion.

REFERENCES

Allport, G. Effect: A secondary principle of learning. *Psychological Review,* 1946, *53,* 335–347.

Barker, R. On the nature of the environment. *Journal of Social Issues,* 1963, *19,* 17–38.

Bartlett, F. *Remembering.* Cambridge, England: Cambridge Univer. Press, 1932.

Biesheuvel, S. Psychological tests and their application to non-European peoples. *Yearbook of Education.* London: Evans, 1949. Pp. 87–126.

Bloom, B., & Broder, L. Problem solving processes of college students. *Supplementary Educational Monograph, No. 73*. Chicago: Univer. Chicago Press, 1950.

Bruner, J. The course of cognitive growth. *American Psychologist,* 1964, *19,* 1–15.

Bruner, J. Man: A course of study. *Educational Services Inc. Quarterly Report,* 1965, Spring–Summer, 3–13.

Bruner, J. *Toward a theory of instruction.* Cambridge: Harvard Univer. Press, in press.

Butler, R. A. Incentive conditions which influence visual exploration. *Journal of Experimental Psychology,* 1954, *48,* 19–23.

Ebbinghaus, H. *Memory: A contribution to experimental Psychology.* New York: Teachers College, Columbia University, 1913.

Festinger, L. A theory of cognitive dissonance. Stanford: Stanford Univer. Press, 1962.

Gay, J., & Cole, M. Outline of general report on Kpelle mathematics project. Stanford: Stanford University, Institute for Mathematical Social Studies, undated. (Mimeo)

Goodnow, Jacqueline, & Pettigrew, T. Effect of prior patterns of experience on strategies and learning sets. *Journal of Experimental Psychology,* 1955, *49,* 381–389.

Greenfield, Patricia M. Culture and conservation. In J. Bruner, Rose Olver, & Patricia M. Greenfield (Eds.), *Studies in cognitive growth.* New York: Wiley, in press. Ch. 10.

Harlow, H., & Harlow, Margaret. Social deprivation in monkeys. *Scientific American,* 1962, November.

Harlow, H. F. Mice, monkeys, men, and motives. *Psychological Review,* 1953, *60,* 23–32.

Heider, F. *The psychology of interpersonal relations.* New York: Wiley, 1958.

Inhelder, Bärbel, & Piaget, J. *The growth of logical thinking.* New York: Basic Books, 1958.

Kluckhorn, C. *Mirror for man.* New York: Whittlesey House, 1949.

Köhler, W. *Dynamics in psychology.* New York: Liveright, 1940.

Lévi-Strauss, C. The structural study of myth. *Structural anthropology.* (Trans. by Claire Jacobson & B. Grundfest Scharpf) New York: Basic Books, 1963. Pp. 206–231.

Lévi-Strauss, C. Anthropology: Its achievements and future. Lecture presented at Bicentennial Celebration, Smithsonian Institution, Washington, D.C., September 1965.

Maccoby, M., & Modiano, Nancy. On culture and equivalence. In J. Bruner, Rose Olver, & Patricia M. Greenfield (Eds.), *Studies in cognitive growth.* New York: Wiley, in press. Ch. 12.

Miller, G., Galanter, E., & Pribram, K. *Plans and the structure of behavior.* New York: Holt, 1960.

Piaget, J. *The construction of reality in the child.* New York: Basic Books, 1954.

Reich, Lee. On culture and grouping. In J. Bruner, Rose Olver, & Patricia M. Greenfield (Eds.), *Studies in cognitive growth.* New York: Wiley, in press. Ch. 13.

Tolman, E. Cognitive maps in rats and men. *Collected papers in psychology.* Berkeley & Los Angeles: Univer. California Press, 1951. Pp. 241–264.

Vygotsky, L. *Thought and language.* (Ed. & trans. by Eugenia Hanfmann & Gertrude Vakar) [Cambridge, Mass.: M.I.T. Press, 1962].

Wertheimer, M. *Productive thinking.* New York & London: Harper, 1945.

White, Mary A. The child's world of learning. Teachers College, Columbia University, undated. (Mimeo)

White, R. W. Motivation reconsidered: The concept of competence. *Psychological Review, 1959, 66,* 297–333.

Martin L. Hoffman

DEVELOPMENTAL SYNTHESIS OF AFFECT AND COGNITION AND ITS IMPLICATIONS FOR ALTRUISTIC MOTIVATION

ABSTRACT: This article presents an argument, based on psychological research and inferences about human evolution, for the plausibility of an intrinsic altruistic motive, following which a theoretical model for the development of such a motive is outlined. The central idea of the model is that a person's empathic response to another person's distress, interacting with his cognitive sense of the other person, provides the basis for a motive independent of egoistic motivation to help the other person. Empathic distress and three steps in the development of a sense of the other are discussed, along with empirical evidence for the approximate ages at which they occur. A theoretical account of the interaction between these affective and cognitive processes is then presented, followed by an attempt to assess the evidence for the theory.

A type of moral encounter of increasing interest to psychology is that in which an individual witnesses another person in distress. Whether or not the individual attempts to help is presumably the net result of altruistic and egoistic forces. The source of egoistic forces requires no explanation, since they have long been the focus of motivation theories (e.g., Cofer & Appley, 1964). The primary objective of this article is to present a developmental theory of altruistic motivation that may provide an integrative framework for ordering the available knowledge about people's reactions to others in distress. The theoretical argument focuses on the contribution of empathy to the motive to help as a function of various facets of cognitive development. A secondary objective, necessary for the first, is to pull together diverse reasearch findings that suggest a certain developmental progression in the child's cognitive construction of others. A third objective, which for purposes of coherence will be presented first, is to present a case for the plausibility of at least a component of the motive to help others in distress that may be independent of the observer's egoistic motive system.

INDEPENDENT ALTRUISTIC MOTIVE

The doctrinaire view in psychology has been that altruism can ultimately be explained in terms of egoistic, self-serving motives. Al-

This article was prepared in conjunction with Grant HD–02258 from the National Institute of Child Health and Human Development. It is an expansion of a paper presented initially at the NICHHD workshop, 'The Development of Motivation in Childhood," in Elkridge, Maryland, in 1972.

SOURCE: From Martin Hoffman, "Developmental Synthesis of Affect and Cognition and Its Implications for Altruistic Motivation," *Developmental Psychology* 11, 1975, pp. 607–622. Copyright 1975 by the American Psychological Association. Reprinted by permission of the publisher and author.

though widespread, this assumption remains untested — perhaps a reflection of Western philosophical thought — with no more empirical support behind it than the assumption that there is an independent, constitutional basis for the motive to help others. The issues are complex, and clear support for one position or the other is unavailable. Several convergent lines of evidence, however, seem to suggest that the assumption of an independent motive to help others may be somewhat more reasonable than the assumption that an egoistic motive base underlies all such behavior.

A first crude line of evidence for an independent motive to help others is the burgeoning research showing that — contrary newspaper accounts notwithstanding — people of all ages do tend to offer help, at least when they are the only witness present and the need is clear (see reviews by Bryan & London, 1970; Krebs, 1970; Staub, 1974). Furthermore, the percentage of those who help is quite high. Children 8–10 years of age, for example, were found to attempt to help others in about half the opportunities to help that occurred in a naturalistic setting (Severy & Davis, 1971). This is consistent with Staub's (1970, 1971a) findings in a laboratory experiment: Half the second-to-fourth graders left what they were doing to help a crying child in the next room — which is particularly interesting in view of the usual restraint shown by young children in laboratory studies. Although fewer sixth graders offered help in the same situation, half of those who had been given prior permission to enter the room did so, as did over 90% of a seventh-grade sample. The findings for adults are sometimes quite dramatic, both in terms of the frequency and the speed with which the subjects aid the victim. Darley and Latané (1968) found that 85% of their subjects attempted to help someone they thought was having an epileptic fit, 90% of them acting within 60 sec. Piliavin and Piliavin (1972) and Piliavin, Rodin and Piliavin (1969) also found helping response rates of nearly 100%, and median reaction times of 5 and 10 sec, in two experimental studies in which a subway rider carrying a cane collapsed on the floor of the train. Clark and Word (1972) report that all their subjects rushed to help a man they heard fall and cry out in pain; the average reaction time was less than 9 seconds. The fact that people normally help when they are the only witness suggests that they are not acting for purposes of gaining social approval. Furthermore, although their behavior might reflect an internalized norm of social responsibility (Berkowitz & Connor, 1966), the quick reaction times, which suggest an element of impulsiveness in the behavior, would seem to argue in favor of a more basic action tendency triggered by the awareness of another's distress rather than, or perhaps in addition to, a social responsibility norm.

More convincing support for an independent altruistic motive component may be found in research that relates the observer's egoistic, social, and emotional needs to his helping behavior. If egoism underlies altruism we would expect people to be more likely to help others when their own needs for approval are aroused and unmet. The research findings are exactly the opposite. People are more apt to help when their approval needs are satisfied. For example, children who are popular, emotionally secure, and self-confident are more apt to help than children who lack social approval (Murphy, 1937; Staub & Sherk, 1970). Children who receive a great deal of affection at home are more likely to help than children who receive little affection (Hoffman, 1975; Mussen, Harris, Rutherford, & Keasy, 1970; Yarrow, 1973). Furthermore, the tendency to help is increased by the experimental arousal of positive moods and feelings of success and decreased by the arousal of such deprived need states as feelings of failure (Berkowitz & Connor, 1966; Isen, 1970; Isen, Horn, & Rosenhan, 1973; Moore, Underwood, & Rosenhan, 1973).

Perhaps egoistic need fulfillment reduces preoccupation with one's own concerns and thus leaves one more open and responsive to the needs of others. Also pertinent is the evidence that altruistic action may be self-rewarding, that is, the opportunity to terminate an aversive stimulus delivered to another person can serve as a reinforcer for a learned response in the absence of any conventional egoistic reinforcer; furthermore, the latency of the response is reduced when the number of distress cues from the victim is increased (Weiss, Boyer, Lombardo, & Stich, 1973). It thus appears that helping is often not a self-serving act, which lends credence to the existence of an altruistic motive system that may operate to some degree independently of the egotistic.

A final argument bears on man's evolution, with which any theory of intrinsic motivation must be in accord. Two lines of evidence are potentially relevant: observation of higher mammals and inferences about human nature based on knowledge of the circumstances in which man evolved. Systematic animal studies have unfortunately not been made, and the evidence for altruism in animals is scanty, anecdotal, and often subject to alternative interpretations (Hebb, 1971; Krebs, 1970, 1971), although some reasonably clear-cut examples can be found.[1] The theoretical issues bearing on human evolution are too complex to be given full treatment here (see Alexander, 1971; Campbell, 1972), but a brief summary seems in order. First, there is general agreement among the theorists, based on evidence from fossil remains (bones, tools, weapons), that during most of man's evolutionary history he lived in a highly adverse environment under constant threat from starvation and predators. He faced this adverse environment not alone but by banding together with others in small nomadic hunting groups. The obviously greater survival value of cooperative and social life over solitary life has led some writers to take the view that natural selection must have favored altruism and other prosocial traits rather than a crude, unbridled egoism alone (e.g., Wynne-Edwards, 1962). Others, however, claim this is impossible: Since the unit of reproduction is the individual, natural selection must have favored egoistic traits that maximize the fitness of the individual (e.g., Williams, 1966).[2] Both points of view seem to have merit. So does Campbell's (1965) notion that the joint presence of both egoistic and altruistic tendencies would have had the greatest survival value; the varied and multiply contingent nature of the environment makes it seem likely that egoistic behavior was more adaptive at certain times and altruistic behavior at other times.

One obvious solution is to find evidence for some type of prosocial tendency that may also contribute to individual fitness. Such a conception has been advanced by Trivers (1971), who uses a rescue model to show that natural selection had to favor altruistic behavior because of its long-run benefit to the organism performing it. In the model, individual A encounters another person, B, whose life is in danger (e.g., from drowning). It is assumed that (a) the probable cost to A of rescuing B is far less than the gain to B, and (b) there is a high likelihood of a role reversal in the future. Both assumptions seem valid. The first appears to be an accurate portrayal of most such encounters even today; the second is entirely consistent with the known conditions of man's existence during the long period of evolution — small face-to-face groups, long interaction between the same specific others, and frequent exposure to danger. Trivers shows mathematically that if the entire population is sooner or later exposed to the same danger, the two who make the attempt to save the other will be more apt to survive than two who face these dangers on their own. It follows that the tendency to help others in distress is very likely a part of man's biological inheritance, despite the fact that his contemporary social and physical environment differs markedly from that of his remote ancestors and may no longer support one-to-one reciprocity.

Recent research on the limbic system, an ancient part of the brain which humans share with all mammals, offers further support for the evolutionary argument. According to MacLean (1958, 1962, 1967, 1973), the research shows that whereas one part of the limbic system is concerned with feelings, emotions, and behavior that insures self-preservation, another part appears to be involved in expressive and feeling states that are conducive to sociability and preservation of the species. MacLean (1962) concludes that the research suggests that "in the complex organization of the phylogenetically old and new structures under consideration we presumably have a neural ladder for ascending from the most primitive sexual feelings to the highest level of altruistic sentiments" (p. 300).

Although by no means conclusive, the available evidence thus appears to be more in keeping with the conception of independent altruistic and egoistic motive systems than with the view that all altruism derives from egoistic motives. This is not to deny that man is also by nature selfish and aggressive (e.g., Tinbergen, 1968) nor that helping others may often be selfishly motivated or fostered by such essentially irrelevant personality characteristics as courage and independence (London, 1970). Indeed, as noted earlier, the acquisition of both egoistic and altruistic structures would appear to have been most adaptive in man's evolution. Our argument does suggest, however, that a built-in mechanism for direct mediation of helping behavior is a tenable hypothesis, however fragile it may at times appear in individualistic societies such as our own.

What might this mechanism be? An obvious candidate is man's capacity for empathy. MacLean's research (1973) indicates that the primitive limbic cortex has strong neural connections both with the hypothalamus, which plays a basic role in integrating emotional expression with viscerosomatic behavior, and with the prefrontal cortex, a newer formation of the brain. The prefrontal cortex functions in "helping us to gain insight into the feelings of others . . . [and] receives part of this insight — the capacity to see with feeling — through its connection with the limbic brain" (MacLean, 1973, p. 58). In other words, the brain structures required for affective involvement with objects in the external world, including people, were apparently present early in man's evolution. The more recent addition of newer brain structures along with the acquisition of connective neural circuits have made it possible for such affect to be experienced in conjunction with a cognitive, increasingly sophisticated social awareness or insight into others — and all of this appears to be independent of the neural base for egoistic, self-preserving behavior. In brief, the neural basis for a primitive empathy was apparently present early in man's evolution. Empathy could thus have served man and continued to evolve into increasingly complex forms as his brain developed and grew.

Empathy has been defined in many ways, most of which fall into two general rubrics, one pertaining to the cognitive awareness of another person's feelings or thoughts (e.g., Borke, 1971; Dymond, 1949) and the other to the affective reaction to another's feelings (e.g., Feshbach & Roe, 1968; Stotland, 1969). The latter conception is used here.

The idea that empathy may provide a motive for altruism is not new. It was suggested two centuries ago by Adam Smith (1759/1948) and David Hume (1751/1957) and has appeared frequently in the recent psychological literature (e.g., Freud, 1937; Hoffman, 1963, 1970; Hoffman & Saltzstein, 1967; Isaacs, 1933; Piliavin & Piliavin, 1972; Stern, 1924; Aronfreed & Paskal, Note *3*; Hoffman & Saltzstein, Note *4*). These writers have typically stressed the affective aspects of empathy, however, and neglected cognitive factors, which "appear to be indispensable to any formulation of emotion" (Schachter & Singer, 1962). Since cognition determines how even simple emotions like joy and fear are experienced (Hunt, Cole, & Reis, 1958; Ruckmick, 1936; Schachter & Singer, 1962), we may presume that cognition also determines how one experiences a complex emotion like empathy. The central idea of the theory to be presented here is that since a fully developed empathic reaction is an internal response to cues about the affective states of someone else, the empathic reaction must depend heavily on the actor's cognitive sense of the other as distinct from himself, which undergoes dramatic changes developmentally. The development of a sense of the other will now be examined, followed by a discussion of how this cognitive development interacts with the individual's early empathic responses to lay the basis for altruistic motivation.

DEVELOPMENT OF A COGNITIVE SENSE OF OTHERS

To delineate the broad stages in development of a sense of the other requires bringing together several different strands of research — that pertaining to object or person permanence, role taking, and personal identity.

Person Permanence

Person permanence pertains to the awareness of another's existence as a separate physical entity. The young infant apparently lacks this awareness; objects, events, and people are not experienced as distinct from the self. Not until about 6 months, according to Piaget (1954), does the infant organize the fleeting images making up his world into discrete objects and experience them as separate from his own biologically determined sensations. The main empirical evidence comes from studies of object displacement (e.g., Bell, 1970; Décarie, 1965; Escalona, Corman, Galenson, Schecter, Schecter, Golden, Leoi, & Barax, Note 5; Uzgiris & Hunt, Note 6). If a desired object is hidden behind a screen before the infant's eyes, he loses interest in it as though it no longer existed. By 6 months he removes the screen to get the object, which shows that he can then internally reproduce the image of an object and use the image as a guide to the object. His sense of the object is still limited, however, since it is short lived and the screen's presence is necessary as a sign of the object. We know this because until about 18 months the infant does not seek the object if the experimenter first places it in a container that he then hides behind a screen and brings out empty after releasing the object. At that age the child retrieves an object after a succession of such invisible displacements, indicating that he can then evoke an object's image even when there is nothing in sight to attest to its existence. Piaget sees this as the beginning of object permanence — a stable sense of the separate existence of physical objects even when outside the individual's immediate perceptual field. Recent research by Bell (1970) and Saint-Pierre (Note 7), however, suggests that "person" permanence occurs several months earlier; that is, by 1 year children can retain a mental image of a person.

Although not stressed in the literature, there is evidence that the process of acquiring a sense of the object, hence person permanence, is gradual (Bell, 1970; Uzgiris & Hunt, Note 6). Children may also regress to the global level because of fatigue and emotional arousal, which lessen the ability to "utilize available cues" (Easterbrook, 1959). Only later may person permanence be expected to become stable enough for self and other to be sharply differentiated throughout the normal course of daily events.

Role Taking

The child's sense of the separate existence of persons is for some time highly limited. Although aware of people's existence as physical entities, he does not yet know that they have inner states of their own, and he tends to attribute to them characteristics that belong to him. Piaget (1932) believes it is not until about 7 or 8 years that this egocentrism begins to give way to the recognition that others have their own perspective. The role-taking research is generally supportive although its emphasis has been heavily cognitive, dealing with the other person's perceptions and thoughts, and ignoring affect.[8] Furthermore, the experimental tasks often require cognitive and verbal skills. For example, the task might involve predicting how objects would look to people in different positions around a room (Flavell, 1968; Lovell, 1959; Piaget & Inhelder, 1948/1967; Selman, 1971), selecting appropriate gifts for males and females of different ages (Flavell, 1968), or communicating a message to someone whose perspective is lacking in some respect, that is, he is blindfolded, very young, or enters the situation late and consequently lacks certain necessary information (Chandler & Greenspan, 1972; Flavell, 1968). These skills may mask the child's actual role-taking competence. To estimate how early in life the child can take another's role requires evidence from studies employing cognitively less complex measures. Three recent studies approach this ideal. In two, some of the children as young as 2 years 6 months were able to perform simple visual role-taking tasks (Fishbein, Lewis, & Keiffer, 1972; Masangkay, McCluskey, McIntyre, Sims-Knight, Vaughn, & Flavell, 1974). In another, 4-year-olds showed that they could take the cognitive and motivational perspective of younger children by using simpler and more attention-getting language (Shatz & Gelman, 1973).

It seems likely that even younger children are capable of role taking in highly motivating, natural settings: two examples follow. In one, which the writer observed, Marcy, aged 20 months, was in the playroom of her home and wanted a toy that her sister Sara was playing with. She asked Sara for it, but Sara refused vehemently. Marcy paused, as if reflecting on what to do, and then began to rock on Sara's favorite rocking horse (which Sara never allowed anyone to touch), yelling "Nice horsey! Nice horsey!" and keeping her eyes on Sara all the time. Sara came running angrily, whereupon Marcy immediately ran directly to the toy and grabbed it. Without analyzing the full complexity of Marcy's behavior, it is clear that she deliberately set about to lure her sister away from the toy. Though not yet 2 years, she showed awareness of another's inner states that differed from her own. Although her behavior was more Machiavellian than altruistic, Marcy demonstrated that she could take another's role, even though she probably could not have understood the instructions in a typical role-taking experiment.

In the second incident, Michael, aged 15 months, and his friend Paul were fighting over a toy and Paul started to cry. Michael appeared disturbed and let go, but Paul still cried. Michael paused, then brought his teddy bear to Paul but to no avail. Michael paused again, and then finally succeeded in stopping Paul's crying by fetching Paul's security blanket from an adjoining room. Several aspects of this incident deserve comment. First, it is clear that Michael initially assumed that his own teddy bear, which often comforts him, would also comfort Paul. Second, Paul's continued crying served as negative feedback that led Michael to consider alternatives. Third, Michael's final, successful act has several possible explanations: (a) He simply imitated what he had observed in the past; this is unlikely since his parents were certain he had never seen Paul being comforted with a blanket. (b) He may have remembered seeing another child soothed by a blanket, which reminded him of Paul's blanket (more complex than it first appears, since Paul's blanket was out of Michael's perceptual field at the time). (c) He was somehow able to reason by analogy that Paul would be comforted by something he loved in the same way that Michael loved his own teddy bear. Whatever the correct interpretation, this incident, as well as a strikingly similar one reported by Borke (1972), suggests that a child not yet 1 year and 6 months can, with the most general kind of feedback, assess the specific needs of another person which differed from his own.

If we may generalize tentatively from these two instances, it would appear that role taking in familiar, highly motivating natural settings may precede laboratory role taking by several years. That is, the rudiments of role-taking competence may be present in some children by age 2 years or earlier, although performance varies with the setting and cognitive complexity of the particular task.[9]

Personal Identity

The third broad step in the development of a sense of the other pertains to the view of the other as having his own personal identity — his own life circumstances and inner states beyond the immediate situation. This developmental stage has been ignored in the literature. The closest to it is Erikson's (1950) conception of ego identity, which pertains in part to the individual's sense of his own sameness through time. In support of Erikson, it seems reasonable that at some point the child develops the cognitive capacity to integrate his own discrete inner experiences over time and to form a conception of himself as having different feelings and thoughts in different situations but being the same continuous person with his own past, present, and anticipated future. There is little relevant research. Kohlberg (1966) suggests that during the preoperational period (2–7 years) children not only lack the concept of conservation with respect to mass, weight, and number (Piaget, 1954) but also with regard to qualitative attributes such as gender. He found, for example, that it is not until 6 or 7 years that children firmly assert that a girl could not be a boy even if she wanted to or even if she played boys' games or wore boys' haircuts or clothes, thus demonstrating a sense of stabilization and continuity regarding gender. There is also evidence that a firm sense of one's own racial identity may not be established until about 7 or 8 years (Proshansky, 1966). (Although younger children use racial terms and show racial preferences, their racial conception appears to reflect verbal fluency rather than a stable attainment of racial concepts.) Finally, in a developmental study by Guardo and Bohan (1971), 6- and 7-year-olds recognized their identity as humans and as males or females mainly in terms of their names, physical appearance, and behaviors — which is consistent with the gender and racial identity research. Their sense of self-continuity from past to future was hazy, however, until 8 or 9 years when more covert and personalized differences in feelings and attitudes began to contribute to self-recognition, although even then their names and physical characteristics were the main anchorage points of identity.

It appears, then, that somewhere between 6 and 9 years marks the beginning of the child's emerging sense of his own continuing identity. By early adolescence, this may be expected to expand considerably. Furthermore, once the child can see that his own life has coherence and continuity despite the fact that he reacts differently in different situations, he should soon be able to perceive this in others. He can then not only take their role and assess their reactions in particular situations but also generalize from these and construct a concept of their general life experience. In sum, his awareness that others are coordinate with himself expands to include the notion that they, like him, have their own person identities that go beyond the immediate situation.

To summarize, the research suggests that by about the age of 1 year children are capable of recognizing others as separate physical entities; by about 2–3 years they have a rudimentary awareness that others have inner states independent of their own; and by about 6–9 years they are beginning to be aware that others have their own identities outside the immediate situation.

DEVELOPMENT OF ALTRUISTIC MOTIVES

A theory of altruistic motivation aroused by distress cues from another will now be presented. It is essentially a developmental account of the synthesis of the above three levels of a cognitive sense of the other with the affect experienced when witnessing another person in distress. The sharing of positive emotions like joy and excitement may also contribute to helping behavior, but the connection is probably less direct because the empathic response to another's distress must be presumed to be primarily unpleasant.

Empathic Distress

Empathic distress refers to the involuntary, at times forceful experiencing of another person's painful emotional state. It may be elicited by expressive cues that directly reflect the other's feelings or by other cues that convey the impact of external events on him. The most parsimonious explanation of empathic distress as a learned response in early childhood is the classical conditioning paradigm in which cues of pain or displeasure from another or from his situation evoke associations with the observer's own past pain, resulting in an empathic affective reaction. A simple example is the child who cuts himself, feels the pain, and cries. Later, on seeing another child cut himself and cry, the sight of the blood, the sound of the cry, or any other distress cue or aspect of the situation having elements in common with his own prior pain experience can now elicit the unpleasant affect initially associated with that experience.

There is also suggestive evidence for a rudimentary, possibly isomorphic distress response shortly after birth. Thus Simner (1971) reports that 2-day-old infants cried vigorously and intensely at the sound of another infant's cry. He also gives evidence that this was not merely a response to a noxious stimulus; that is, the infants reacted in a more subdued manner to equally loud nonhuman sounds including computer-simulated infant cries. Nor did the subjects' cries appear to be due to imitation, since they appeared to be genuinely upset and agitated by the other's cry (Simner, Note *10*). Regardless of the process involved, the resulting co-occurrence of the infant's own cry, his distress, and the other's cry — given the fusion of self and other in the infant's mind — may contribute to his eventually learning that others experience distress just as he does. Simner's finding may thus signify an innate mechanism that contributes to the early learning of empathic distress.

Such an innate mechanism is consistent but not crucial to the present thesis. What is crucial is that conditioning is possible in the early weeks of life (Kessen, Haith, & Salapatek, 1970). This together with the inevitable distress experiences in infancy makes it highly likely that humans are capable of experiencing empathic distress long before acquiring a cognitive sense of the other, the early manifestations of which, as already noted, appear at about 1 year or later. For much of the first year at least, then, it follows that distress cues from others probably elicit a global empathic distress response in the infant — presumably a fusion of unpleasant feelings and stimuli from his own body, the dimly perceived "other," and the situation. The infant cannot yet differentiate himself from the other, and there is evidence that he also has difficulty differentiating the other from the other's situation (Burns & Cavey, 1957; Deutsch, 1974). Consequently, he must often be unclear as to who is experiencing any distress that he witnesses, and he may at times be expected to behave as though what happened to the other person was happening to him. That is, the cues associated with another person's distress evoke an upset state in him, and he may then seek comfort for himself. Consider a colleague's 11-month-old daughter who, on seeing another child fall and cry, first stared at the victim, appearing as though she were about to cry herself, and then put her thumb in her mouth and buried her head in her mother's lap — her typical response when she has hurt herself and seeks comfort.

This appears to be a primitive, involuntary response, that is, a response based mainly on the "pull" of surface cues and minimally on higher cognitive processes, attention, and effort. If the child acts, his motive may in a sense be egoistic: to eliminate discomfort in the "self." It is not entirely egoistic, however, since the "self" at this stage is not in opposition to the other but rather a fusion (self/other/situation) that includes the other. Perhaps the more fundamental reason for viewing this empathic distress as basic in the development of altruistic motivation despite its egoistic components is that it shows that we may involuntarily and forcefully experience emotional states pertinent to another person's situation rather than to our own — that we are built in such a way that our own feelings of distress will often be contingent not on our own but on someone else's misfortune.

Sympathetic Distress and the Role of Cognition

As noted earlier, the meaning of an emotion is determined by appropriate cognitions. Schachter and Singer's (1962) formulation seems pertinent:

> One labels, interprets, and identifies this stirred-up state in terms of the characteristics of the situation and one's apperceptive mass. . . . The cognition, in a sense, exerts a steering function [and] determines whether the state of arousal will be labeled as "anger," "joy," "fear" or whatever. (p. 380)

In like fashion, one's cognitive sense of the other may be presumed to determine the meaning of his affective response to cues about the other's inner states. A major change may therefore be expected when the child begins to discriminate between the stimuli from his own body and those from without, acquiring a sense of the other as separate from himself. When confronted with someone in pain, he now knows that it is the other and not he who is actually in distress. Consequently, it seems reasonable to assume that the earlier empathic distress, a parallel affective response, is gradually transformed into a more reciprocal, sympathetic concern for the victim, here called sympathetic distress. This transformation is hypothesized to occur in three stages, which correspond to the three cognitive levels described earlier.

1. It seems reasonable to suppose that along with the gradual emergence of a sense of the other as distinct from the self, the affective portion of the child's global empathic distress — the feeling of distress and desire for its termination — is extended to the separate self and other that emerge. Early in this process the child may be only vaguely and momentarily aware of the other as distinct from the self; the image of the other, being transitory, may often slip in and out of focus. Consequently, he probably reacts to another's distress as though his dimly perceived self and other were somehow simultaneously, or alternately, in distress. Consider a child known

to the writer whose typical response to his own distress, beginning late in the first year, was to suck his thumb with one hand and pull his ear with the other. At 12 months, on seeing a sad look on his father's face, he proceeded to look sad and suck his thumb, while pulling his father's ear. The co-occurrence of distress in the emerging self and other may be an important factor in the transition from the simple empathic distress, discussed above, to the first stage of sympathetic distress which includes an affective response, awareness of the fact that another person is the victim, and desire to terminate his distress.

The child's response at this stage may continue to have a purely empathic component, including the desire to terminate his own distress, and perhaps an element of fear that the undesired event may happen to him. The important thing, however, is that the quasi-egoistic concern for his "own" discomfort gives way, at least in part, to the feeling of concern for another. This is a new addition to the child's repertoire which enables him for the first time to behave in what appears to be a truly altruistic manner, that is, to attempt to relieve the distress of another person who is perceptually distinct from the self. The response of a colleague's 20-month-old son is illustrative. When a visiting friend who was about to leave burst into tears, complaining that her parents were not home (they were away for 2 weeks), his immediate reaction was to look sad, but then he offered her his beloved teddy bear to take home. His parents reminded him that he would miss the teddy if he gave it away, but he insisted — possibly because his sympathetic distress was greater than the anticipated unpleasantness of not having the teddy, which would be indicative of the strong motivational potential of sympathetic distress.

Although the child now knows that the other is a separate physical entity and therefore that the other is the victim, he cannot yet distinguish between his own and the other's inner states (thoughts, perceptions, needs); without thinking about it, he automatically assumes that they are identical to his own. Consequently, although he can sense the other's distress, he does not understand what caused it nor does he know the other's needs in the situation (except when they happen to coincide with his own as in the preceding example). This lack of understanding is often evidenced in the child's efforts to help, which consist chiefly of giving the other what he himself finds most comforting. Examples are Michael's initial attempt to placate his friend Paul; the action of another child, 13 months old, who brought his own mother to comfort a crying friend even though the friend's mother was equally available; and still another child who offered his beloved doll to comfort an adult who looked sad.

Despite the limitation of this initial level of sympathetic distress, it is a significant advance; for the first time the child experiences a feeling of concern for the other as distinct from the self, although his actual attempts to help may be misguided due to limited understanding of the nature of the distress and the type of action needed to relieve it.

2. At about 2 years, according to our earlier role-taking discussion, the child has begun to acquire a sense of others not only as physical entities but also as sources of feelings and thoughts in their own right, that is, as persons who have inner states that at times differ from his own, as well as perspectives based on their own needs and interpretations of events. He does not know what their perspectives are, however, and is in general no longer certain that the real world and his perception of it are the same thing.

Perhaps at this point a clarification is in order. Although the role-taking research stresses development of the capacity to grasp another's perspective when it differs from one's own, this is only to expose the nature of the child's progress away from egocentrism. In real life, the child usually finds the perspective of others is similar to his own, since all children have the same basic nervous system as well as many experiences in common during the long period of socialization. This was true in the earlier example: Although Michael discovered he and Paul had different specific preferences in the situation, his assumption that Paul's basic emotional need was the same as his was confirmed. Thus while moving away from the automatic, egocentric assumption that the other's inner states are identical to his, the child discovers that his feelings resemble the feelings experienced independently by others in similar situations. The other's feelings are independent of his, but not basically different. This must inevitably contribute to a sense of "oneness," which preserves and may even enhance the motivation to alleviate the other's distress which he acquired earlier.

At this second level the child's empathic proclivity continues to direct his attention away from himself and toward others, and he may still have a tendency to attribute his own feelings to the victim. But now, because of the emerging awareness that others have independent inner states, the affect aroused in him by another's distress may be presumed to motivate more active efforts to put himself in the other's place and find the true source of his distress.[11] He is also very likely more aware of the tentative and hypothetical nature of his resulting inferences. Consequently, his motivation to relieve the other's distress is less egocentric and based to a greater degree on veridical assessment of the other's needs, trial and error, and response to corrective feedback. With increased role-taking ability, he can also detect more subtle cues of distress (e.g., those reflecting such inferred inner states as disappointment and longing). These too may then stimulate his concern and motivate efforts to discern the source of the other's discomfort.

3. Despite the obvious progress, the child's response is still confined to the other's immediate distress. This limitation is overcome at the third cognitive level, around 6 to 9 years according to our previous discussion, at which stage the child has an emerging conception of himself and others as continuous persons each with his own history and identity. By early adolescence he is fully aware not only that others feel pleasure and pain in situations but also that these feelings occur in the context of their larger pattern of life experiences. Consequently, although he may continue to react to their situational distress, his concern is intensified when he knows this reflects a chronic condition. That is, being aware that others have inner states and a separate existence beyond the situation enables him to respond not only to their transitory, situation-specific distress but also to what he imagines to be their general condition. Although the situational may often reflect the general, this is not always true and there at times may be a discrepancy between the two. On these occasions the observer will ordinarily be expected to respond in terms of the general since it is the more inclusive, hence compelling index of the victim's welfare.

This third level, then, consists of the synthesis of empathic distress and a mental representation of the other's general plight — his typical day-to-day level of distress or deprivation, the opportunities available or denied to him, his future prospects, and the like. If this representation falls short of what the observer conceives to be a minimally acceptable standard of well-being (and if the observer's own life circumstances place him substantially above this standard), a sympathetic distress response may be expected, regardless of the other's apparent momentary state.

To summarize, the individual who progresses through these three stages becomes capable of a high level of sympathetic distress. He can process various types of information — that gained through his own empathic reaction, immediate situational cues, and general knowledge about the other's life. He can act out in his mind the emotions and experiences suggested by this information and introspect on all of this. He may thus gain an understanding of the circumstances, feelings, and wishes of the other and have feelings of concern and the wish to help while maintaining the sense that this is a separate person from himself.

With further cognitive development the person may also be able to comprehend the plight not only of an individual but also of an entire group or class of people — such as the economically impoverished, politically oppressed, socially outcast, victims of war, or mentally retarded. Because of his different background, his own specific distress experiences may differ from theirs. All distress experiences may be presumed to have a common affective core, however, and this together with the individual's cognitive capabilities at this age provides the requisites for a generalized empathic distress. (Possible exceptions are people rendered incapable of empathy by their socialization or people whose status in life has permitted only the most superficial contact with less fortunate people; consider as an example Marie Antoinette's apocryphal "Let them eat cake" response to the people who were clamoring for bread.) The synthesis of empathic distress with the perceived plight of an unfortunate group may result in what would seem to be the developmentally most advanced form of sympathetic distress.

Sympathetic Distress as Egoistic or Altruistic Motive

Since sympathetic distress has an empathic component, the act of helping another person should contribute to reduction of the actor's distress as well as that of the other. The question may be asked, does this mean that sympathetic distress is really an egoistic motive? The writer suggests that all motives may prompt action that is potentially gratifying to the actor but this must not obscure certain fundamental differences among them. Sympathetic distress differs from the usual egoistic motives (e.g., sensual pleasure, material gain, social approval, economic success) in three significant ways: It is aroused by distress in another person rather than oneself; a major goal of the ensuing behavior is to help the other, not just oneself; and, the potential for gratification in the observer is contingent on his acting to reduce the other's distress. In brief, the arousal condition, aim of the ensuing action, and basis of gratification in the actor are all dependent on someone else's welfare. It therefore seems appropriate to designate sympathetic distress as an altruistic motive and distinguish it from more directly self-serving, egoistic motives.

SUMMARY OF EVIDENCE FOR THE THEORY

The attempt will now be made to show that the theoretical model advanced here may provide an integrative framework for ordering existing knowledge on helping and related behavior, as well as generating hypotheses for further research.

Several predications about sympathetic distress and its relation to helping behavior follow from the theory: (a) People should generally respond to another's distress with an affective response as well as a tendency to help. (b) The intensity of the affect and the speed of the helping response should increase with the salience of the pain cues. (c) The affect should tend to subside more quickly when the observer engages in helping behavior than when he does not. First, there is abundant evidence, noted earlier, that people of all ages tend to help. More importantly, affect seems to accompany the helping behavior. That is, witnessing another person in physical pain or failing in a task typically results in an affective reaction as measured physiologically and is usually followed by an overt attempt to help (Berger, 1962; Craig & Weinstein, 1965; Geer & Jarmecky, 1973; Lazarus, Speisman, Mordkoff, & Davison, 1962; Murphy, 1937; Stotland, 1969; Tannenbaum & Gaer, 1965; Tomes, 1964; Weiss et al., 1973).[12] Second, the intensity of the affect and the speed of the overt response have been found to increase as the number and intensity of distress cues from the victim increase (Geer & Jarmecky, 1973; Weiss et al., 1973). And third, there is evidence that the affect continues at a high level of intensity in adult subjects who do not go to the aid of the victim but declines for those who do (Latané & Darley, 1970). A similar finding was obtained in Murphy's (1937) classic nursery school study: When children overtly helped others, their affective response diminished; when they did not help, the affect was prolonged.

The theory would also lead to the expectation that young children, even before acquiring the necessary cognitive skills, would nevertheless experience empathic or sympathetic distress, although at times they may do nothing or engage in inappropriate action. Evidence for this can be found in the nursery school observations reported by Bridges (1931) and Murphy (1937) in which the younger children usually reacted to another's distress with a worried, anxious look but did nothing, whereas the older children typically engaged in an overt helpful act. Further evidence is provided by the several anecdotes mentioned earlier in this article describing an affective response followed by an overt act that was clearly designed to help but inappropriate. (Reinforcement and imitation theories might have difficulty explaining these findings, since the child's socialization agents are not often likely to reward or to provide models of inaction or inappropriate action.)

Other findings and their possible relevance to the theory follow: (a) The evidence that helping correlates positively with role-taking ability (Rubin & Schneider, 1973) and is increased by role-taking training (Clore & Jeffrey, 1972; Staub, 1971b) is clearly in keeping with the theory. (b) The evidence, cited earlier, that people are more apt to help another when their emotional needs are satisfied also fits the theory, since sympathetic distress requires the observer to pay attention to the needs of others, which is more apt to happen if he is not preoccupied with his own emotional needs. (c) Since the theory implies a general human readiness to help others in distress, it would lead to the general expectation that little effort is ordinarily required to instigate helping behavior in children. Thus the evidence that helping behavior in children may result from exposure to altruistic models — both experimentally (see review by Bryan & London, 1970) and in the home (Rosenhan, 1969; Hoffman, 1970, 1975) can be readily encompassed by the theory, although it may not be a logical deduction from it. (d) Finally, the assumed synthesis between the affect aroused and the observer's cognitive sense of the other is, as discussed earlier, in agreement with the recent research both on emotions and on the structure of the brain.

The theory thus seems to provide a broad integrative framework that encompasses much of what is known about people's responses to others in distress. A true assessment of the model, however, awaits the test of predictions derived specifically from it. Here are some possible examples. The presumed interaction between empathic distress and cognition suggests that training in role taking, or exposure to information regarding the life condition of others, should be especially effective in producing helping behavior when it directs the subject's attention to feelings and when the subjects are empathic to begin with (although there may be a ceiling effect); and similarly, the arousal of empathic distress should result in more helping in children who are cognitively able to take the other's role than in those who are not. The theory would also predict that certain socialization experiences would enhance the child's naturally developing motivation to help others in distress. For example, altruism should be more prevalent in children whose empathic proclivities have been strengthened by being allowed the normal run of distress experiences, rather than being shielded from them, since this would help provide a broad base for empathic and sympathetic distress in the early years. (We refer here to mild distress experiences that the child can readily resolve on his own or with parental help when necessary; frequent, severe distress may lead to a building up of frustration and subsequent egoistic self-preoccupation that could interfere with the child's sensitivity and openness to the needs of others.) It would also follow from the theory that when a discrepancy exists between the various cues indicating another person's distress (e.g., when the cues indicating the victim's immediate distress are at odds with the available information regarding his general life condition), the observer will ordinarily react in terms of the more inconclusive distress index.

CONCLUDING REMARKS

Although the focus of this article has been on sympathetic distress as a motive, the evidence cited suggests that it is typically accompanied by helping behavior. The relation between the arousal of the motive and relevant behavior is not guaranteed, however, any more than it is for other motives. In addition to the strength and developmental level of the motive, which have been stressed here, other factors presumably have an effect. Evidence was cited earlier, for example, which suggests that level of intensity of the distress cues and extent of the observer's well-being may be important considerations. Other factors found to influence the observer's response are the extent to which the observer has the cognitive and coping skills required for appropriate action (Bridges, 1931; Murphy, 1937; Latané & Darley, 1970) and the extent to which the situation points up his individual responsibility to act rather than indicating, for example, that the responsibility is diffused (Geer & Jarmecky, 1973; Latané & Darley, 1970; Schwartz, 1970; Tilker, 1970).

In individualistic societies, the motive to help will also often be overridden by more powerful egoistic motives, as evidenced by the negative relation obtained between helping others and competitiveness (Rutherford & Mussen, 1968). As noted by Hoffman (1970) and Staub (1970), American middle-class children are often socialized both to help others and to respect authority and follow the rules, but in some situations one cannot do both. Perhaps the best known instance of the way authority attitudes may serve as a deterrent to prosocial behavior is Milgram's (1963) finding that adult males will administer high levels of electric shock on instruction from the experimenter, despite strong feelings of compassion for the victim — a finding that must make us less sanguine about the altruistic potentialities of at least American men. It should be noted, however, that in a partial replication of Milgram's experiment, Tilker (1970) found that when the subject was placed in the role of observer he not only showed an increasing sympathetic distress response as the shock levels were increased but often intervened to stop the experiment, despite the instructions to the contrary and the continuing opposition from the person administering the shock.

The evidence that sympathetic distress may continue when the observer does not act has been cited. We would also expect the observer at times to engage in some sort of defense or cognitive restructuring of the situation so as to justify inaction (e.g., by derogating the victim or seeing him as deserving his fate). There is some evidence that this may happen, at least when it is physically impossible for the observer to help (Chaikin & Darley, 1973; Lincoln & Levinger, 1972; Stokols & Schopler, 1973). Whether this restructuring reduces the observer's distress is not known.

Pending further research, the following relationship between altruistic motives and action seems in keeping with current knowledge: (a) Distress cues from another person trigger the sympathetic distress response in the observer; (b) his initial tendency is to act; (c) if he does not act, he will typically continue to experience sympathetic distress or cognitively restructure the situation to justify inaction.

REFERENCE NOTES

1. A chimpanzee in the wild who discovers a new food source will, before having his own fill, typically call out to the others who immediately join him (Lawick-Goodall, 1968). As for chimpanzee behavior in captivity, Nissen (Nissen & Crawford, 1936) describes a female who, upon seeing Nissen taunt and strike her cagemate, attempted to pull the cagemate to safety; a week later, when Nissen next appeared and the cagemate approached him, she tried strenuously and continuously to pull the cagemate back until Nissen left. Finally, porpoises are known to aid wounded adults and newborn infants whose mothers are unavailable — and also drowning humans — by raising them to the surface for needed air (Kellogg, 1961; McBride, 1940, McBride & Hebb, 1948).

2. It should perhaps be noted that evolutionists do not regard maternal sacrifice or any form of action in the service of a kin's well-being as altruistic, since such action benefits one's own genetic line.

3. Aronfreed, J., & Paskal, V. *Altruism, empathy, and the conditioning of positive affect.* Unpublished manuscript, University of Pennsylvania, 1965.

4. Hoffman, M. L., & Saltzstein, H. D. Parent practices and the development of children's moral orientations. In W. E. Martin (Chair), *Parent behavior and children's personality development: Current project research.* Symposium presented at the meeting of the American Psychological Association, Chicago, September 1960.

5. Escalona, S., Corman, H., Galenson, E., Schecter, D., Schecter, E., Golden, M., Leoi, A., & Barax, E. *Albert Einstein scales of sensori-motor development.* Unpublished manuscript, Department of Psychiatry, Albert Einstein School of Medicine, 1967.

6. Uzgiris, I., & Hunt, J. McV. *Ordinal scales of infant development.* Paper presented at the 18th International Congress of Psychology, Moscow, August 1966.

7. Saint-Pierre, J. *Etude des differences entre la récherché active de la personne humaine et celle de l'object inanimé.* Unpublished master's thesis, University of Montreal, 1962.

8. Research like Borke's (1971, 1973), which seems to show that young children can infer emotional states of others, is plagued by the problem that the subjects may simply be attributing their own emotional reactions to others rather than demonstrating awareness of their independent inner states.

9. The fact that role-taking competence may occur so early in life suggests an interesting analogy with Chomsky's (1965) "language acquisition device." Perhaps children have the capacity to take others' perspectives at an earlier age than usually assumed, and all it takes to be manifested in performance is the appropriate social context, along with the necessary feedback. If so, the years of social interaction often thought to be necessary for role-taking competence may instead serve the function of providing exercise for a preexisting capacity.

10. Simner, M.: Personal communication, 1973.

11. Although this discussion stresses the effect of cognitive role taking, it is also intended to illustrate the importance of empathic distress. That is, in the absence of empathic distress role taking may serve other more egoistic needs.

12. A major exception is Lerner's (Note *13*) finding that adults lowered their esteem of perceived victims. This was, however, apparently due to an empathy-inhibiting set created by the experimental instructions (Aderman & Berkowitz, 1970; Aderman, Brehm, & Katz, 1974; Stotland, 1969).

13. Lerner, M. J. *The effect of a negative outcome on cognitions of responsibility and attraction.* Unpublished manuscript, University of Kentucky, 1968.

REFERENCES

Aderman, D., & Berkowitz, L. Observational set, empathy, and helping. *Journal of Personality and Social Psychology,* 1970, *14,* 141–168.

Aderman, D., Brehm, S. S., & Katz, L. B. Empathic observation of an innocent victim: The just world revisited. *Journal of Personality and Social Psychology,* 1974, *29,* 342–347.

Alexander, R. D. The search for an evolutionary philosophy of man. *Proceedings of the Royal Society of Melbourne,* 1971, *84,* 99–120.

Bell, S. M. The development of the concept of the object as related to infant-mother attachment. *Child Development,* 1970, *41,* 291–311.

Berger, S. M. Conditioning through vicarious instigation. *Psychological Review,* 1962, *69,* 450–466.

Berkowitz, L., & Connor, W. H. Success, failure and social responsibility. *Journal of Personality and Social Psychology,* 1966, *4,* 664–669.

Borke, H. Interpersonal perception of young children: Ego-centrism or empathy? *Developmental Psychology,* 1971, *5,* 263–269.

Borke, H. Chandler and Greenspan's "Ersatz ego-centrism": A rejoinder. *Developmental Psychology,* 1972, *7,* 107–109.

Borke, H. The development of empathy in Chinese and American children between three and six years of age. *Developmental Psychology,* 1973, *9,* 102–108.

Bridges, K. M. B. *The social and emotional development of the preschool child.* London: Kegan Paul, 1931.

Bryan, J. H., & London, P. Altruistic behavior by children. *Psychological Bulletin,* 1970, *73,* 200–211.

Burns, N., & Cavey, L. Age differences in empathic ability among children. *Canadian Journal of Psychology,* 1957, *11,* 227–230.

Campbell, D. T. Ethnocentric and other altruistic motives. In D. Levine (Ed.), *Nebraska Symposium on Motivation* (Vol. 13). Lincoln: University of Nebraska Press, 1965.

Campbell, D. T. On the genetics of altruism and the counter-hedonic components in human culture. *The Journal of Social Issues,* 1972, *28,* 21–38.

Chaikin, A. L., & Darley, J. M. Victim or perpetrator: Defensive attribution of responsibility and the need for order and justice. *Journal of Personality and Social Psychology,* 1973, *25,* 268–275.

Chandler, M. J., & Greenspan, S. Ersatz egocentrism: A reply to H. Borke. *Developmental Psychology,* 1972, *7,* 104–106.

Chomsky, N. A. *Aspects of the theory of syntax.* Cambridge: M.I.T. Press, 1965.

Clark, R. D., & Word, L. E. Why don't bystanders help? Because of ambiguity? *Journal of Personality and Social Psychology,* 1972, *24,* 392–400.

Clore, G. L., & Jeffery, K. M. Emotional role playing, attitude change, and attraction toward a disabled person. *Journal of Personality and Social Psychology,* 1972, *23,* 105–111.

Cofer, C., & Appley, M. *Motivation: Theory and research.* New York: Wiley, 1964.

Craig, K. D., & Weinstein, M. S. Conditioning vicarious affective arousal. *Psychological Reports,* 1965, *17,* 955–963.

Darley, J. M., & Batson, C. D. From Jerusalem to Jericho: A study of situational and dispositional variables in helping behavior. *Journal of Personality and Social Psychology,* 1973, *27,* 100–108.

Décarie, T. G. *Intelligence and affectivity in early childhood.* New York: International Universities Press, 1965.

Deutsch, F. Female preschoolers' perceptions of affective responses and interpersonal behavior in videotaped episodes. *Developmental Psychology,* 1974, *10,* 733–740.

Dymond, R. A scale for the measurement of empathic ability. *Journal of Consulting Psychology,* 1949, *13,* 127–133.

Easterbrook, J. A. The effect of emotion on cue utilization and the organization of behavior. *Psychological Review,* 1959, *66,* 183–201.

Erikson, E. H. *Childhood and society.* New York: Norton, 1950.

Feshbach, N. D., & Roe, K. Empathy in six and seven year olds. *Child Development,* 1968, *39,* 133–145.

Fishbein, H. D., Lewis, S., & Keiffer, K. Children's understanding of spatial relations. *Developmental Psychology,* 1972, *7,* 21–33.

Flavell, J. H. *The development of role-taking and communication skills in children.* New York: Wiley, 1968.

Freud, A. *Ego and the mechanisms of defense.* London: Hogarth Press, 1937.

Geer, J. H., & Jarmecky, L. The effect of being responsible for reducing another's pain on subject's response and arousal. *Journal of Personality and Social Psychology,* 1973, *26,* 232–237.

Guardo, C. J., & Bohan, J. B. Development of a sense of self-identity in children. *Child Development,* 1971, *42,* 1909–1921.

Hebb, D. O. Comment on altruism: The comparative evidence. *Psychological Bulletin,* 1971, *76,* 409–410.

Hoffman, M. L. Parent discipline and the child's consideration for others. *Child Development,* 1963, *34,* 573–588.

Hoffman, M. L. Conscience, personality, and socialization techniques. *Human Development,* 1970, *13,* 90–126.

Hoffman, M. L. Altruistic behavior and the

parent-child relationship. *Journal of Personality and Social Psychology,* 1975, *31,* 937–943.

Hoffman, M. L., & Saltzstein, H. D. Parent discipline and the child's moral development. *Journal of Personality and Social Psychology,* 1967, *5,* 45–57.

Hume, D. *An inquiry concerning the principles of morals.* New York: Liberal Arts Press, 1957. (Originally published, 1751.)

Hunt, J. McV., Cole, M., & Reis, H. Situational cues distinguishing anger, joy, and sorrow. *American Journal of Psychology,* 1958, *71,* 136–151.

Isaacs, S. S. *Social development in young children.* London: Routledge, 1933.

Isen, A. M. Success, failure, and reaction to others: The warm glow of success. *Journal of Personality and Social Psychology,* 1970, *15,* 294–301.

Isen, A. M., Horn, N., & Rosenhan, D. L. Effects of success and failure on children's generosity. *Journal of Personality and Social Psychology,* 1973, *27,* 239–247

Kellogg, W. N. *Porpoises and sonar.* Chicago: University of Chicago Press, 1961.

Kessen, W., Haith, M. M., & Salapatek, P. H. Infancy. In P. Mussen (Ed.), *Carmichael's manual of child psychology.* New York: Wiley, 1970.

Kohlberg, L. A cognitive-developmental analysis of children's sex-role concepts and attitudes. In E. Maccoby (Ed.), *The development of sex differences.* Stanford, Calif.: Stanford University Press, 1966.

Krebs, D. L. Altruism: An examination of the concept and a review of the literature. *Psychological Bulletin,* 1970, *73,* 258–303.

Krebs, D. L. Infrahuman altruism. *Psychological Bulletin,* 1971, *76,* 411–414.

Latané, B., & Darley, J. Bystander intervention in emergencies. In J. Macaulay & L. Berkowitz (Eds.), *Altruism and helping behavior.* New York: Academic Press, 1970.

Lawick-Goodall, J. V. The behavior of free-living chimpanzees in the Gombe Stream Reserve. *Animal Behavior Monographs,* 1968, *1,* 161–311.

Lazarus, R. S., Speisman, J. C., Mordkoff, A. M., & Davison, L. A. A laboratory study of psychological stress produced by a motion picture film. *Psychological Monographs,* 1962, 76 (34, Whole No. 553).

Lincoln, H., & Levinger, G. Observer's evaluations of the victim and the attacker in an aggressive incident. *Journal of Personality and Social Psychology,* 1972, *22,* 202–210.

London, P. The rescuers: Motivational hypotheses about Christians who saved Jews from the Nazis. In J. Macaulay & L. Berkowitz (Eds.), *Altruism and helping behavior.* New York: Academic Press, 1970.

Lovell, K. A follow-up of some aspects of the work of Piaget and Inhelder on the child's conception of space. *British Journal of Educational Psychology,* 1959, *29,* 107–117.

MacLean, P. D. The limbic system with respect to self-preservation and the preservation of the species. *Journal of Nervous Mental Disease,* 1958, *127,* 1–11.

MacLean, P. D. New findings relevant to the evolution of psychosexual functions of the brain. *Journal of Nervous Mental Disease,* 1962, *135,* 289–301.

MacLean, P. D. The brain in relation to empathy and medical education. *Journal of Nervous Mental Disease,* 1967, *144,* 374–382.

MacLean, P. D. *A triune concept of the brain and behavior.* Toronto, Canada: University of Toronto Press, 1973.

McBride, A. F. Meet Mister Porpoise. *National History Magazine,* 1940, *45,* 16–29.

McBride, A. F., & Hebb, D. O. Behavior of the captive bottle-nose dolphin, *tursiops truncatus.* *Journal of Comparative Physiological Psychology,* 1948, *41,* 111–123.

Masangkay, Z., McCluskey, K., McIntyre, C.; Sims-Knight, J., Vaughn, B., & Flavell, J. The early development of inferences about the visual percepts of others. *Child Development,* 1974, *45,* 357–366.

Milgram, S. A behavioral study of obedience. *Journal of Abnormal and Social Psychology,* 1963, *67,* 371–378.

Moore, B. S., Underwood, B., & Rosenhan, D. L. Affect and altruism. *Developmental Psychology,* 1973, *8,* 99–104.

Murphy, L. B. *Social behavior and child personality.* New York: Columbia University Press, 1937.

Mussen, P., Harris, S., Rutherford, E., & Keasey, C. B. Honesty and altruism among preadolescents. *Developmental Psychology,* 1970, *3,* 169–194.

Nissen, H. W., & Crawford, M. P. A preliminary study of food-sharing behavior in young chimpanzees. *Journal of Comparative Psychology,* 1936, *22,* 383–419.

Piaget, J. *The moral judgment of the child.* New York: Harcourt, Brace, & World, 1932.

Piaget, J. *The construction of reality in the child.* New York: Basic Books, 1954.

Piaget, J., & Inhelder, B. *The child's conception of space.* New York: Norton, 1967. (Originally published, 1948.)

Piliavin, I. M., Rodin, J., & Piliavin, J. A. Good

samaritanism: An underground phenomenon. *Journal of Personality and Social Psychology,* 1969, *13,* 289–299.

Piliavin, J. A., & Piliavin, I. The effect of blood on reactions to a victim. *Journal of Personality and Social Psychology,* 1972, *23,* 353–361.

Proshansky, H. M. The development of intergroup attitudes. In L. W. Hoffman & M. L. Hoffman (Eds.). *Review of Child Development Research* (Vol. 2). New York: Russell Sage Foundation, 1966.

Rosenhan, D. Some origins of concern for others. In P. H. Mussen, J. Langer, & M. Covington (Eds.). *Trends and issues in developmental psychology.* New York: Holt, Rinehart & Winston, 1969.

Rubin, K. H., & Schneider, F. W. The relationship between moral judgment, egocentrism, and altruistic behavior. *Child Development,* 1973, *44,* 661–665.

Ruckmick, C. A. The psychology of fear and emotion. New York: McGraw-Hill, 1936.

Rutherford, E., & Mussen, P. Generosity in nursery school boys. *Child Development,* 1968, *39,* 755–765.

Schachter, S., & Singer, J. E. Cognitive, social and physiological determinants of emotional state. *Psychological Review,* 1962, *69,* 379–399.

Schwartz, S. Moral decision making and behavior. In J. Macaulay & L. Berkowitz (Eds.), *Altruism and helping behavior.* New York: Academic Press, 1970.

Selman, R. L. Taking another's perspective: Role-taking development in early childhood. *Child Development,* 1971, *42,* 1721–1734.

Severy, L. J., & Davis, K. E. Helping behavior among normal and retarded children. *Child Development,* 1971, *42,* 1017–1031.

Shatz, M., & Gelman, R. The development of communication skills: Modifications in the speech of young children as a function of listener. *Monographs of the Society for Research in Child Development,* 1973, *38* (5, Serial No. 152).

Simner, M. L. Newborn's response to the cry of another infant. *Developmental Psychology,* 1971, *5,* 136–150.

Smith, A. *Moral and political philosophy.* New York: Hafner, 1948. (Originally published, 1759.)

Staub, E. A child in distress: The influence of age and number of witnesses on children's attempts to help. *Journal of Personality and Social Psychology,* 1970, *14,* 130–140.

Staub, E. Helping a person in distress: The influence of implicit and explicit "rules" of conduct on children and adults. *Journal of Personality and Social Psychology,* 1971, *17,* 137–144. (a)

Staub, E. The use of role-playing and induction in children's learning of helping and sharing behavior. *Child Development,* 1971, *42,* 805–816. (b)

Staub, E. Helping a distressed person. In L. Berkowitz (Ed.), *Advances in experimental social psychology* (Vol. 7). New York: Academic Press, 1974.

Staub, E., & Sherk, L. Need for approval, children's sharing behavior, and reciprocity in sharing. *Child Development,* 1970, *41,* 243–253.

Stern, W. *Psychology of early childhood up to the sixth year of age.* New York: Holt, 1924.

Stokols, D., & Schopler, J. Reactions to victim under conditions of situational detachment: The effects of responsibility, severity, and expected future interaction. *Journal of Personality and Social Psychology,* 1973, *25,* 199–209.

Stotland, E. Exploratory investigations of empathy. In L. Berkowitz (Ed.), *Advances in experimental social psychology* (Vol. 4). New York: Academic Press, 1969.

Tannenbaum, P. H., & Gaer, E. P. Mood changes as a function of stress of protagonist and degree of identification in a film-viewing situation. *Journal of Personality and Social Psychology,* 1965, *2,* 612–616.

Tilker, H. A. Socially responsible behavior as a function of observer responsibility and victim feedback. *Journal of Personality and Social Psychology,* 1970, *14,* 95–100.

Tinbergen, N. On war and peace in animals and man: An ethologist's approach to the biology of aggression. *Science,* 1968, *160,* 1411–1418.

Tomes, H. The adaption, acquisition, and extinction of empathically mediated emotional responses. *Dissertation Abstracts,* 1964, *24,* 3442–3443.

Trivers, R. L. The evolution of reciprocal altruism. *Quarterly Review of Biology,* 1971, *46,* 35–57.

Weiss, R. F., Boyer, J. L., Lombardo, J. P., & Stich, M. H. Altruistic drive and altruistic reinforcement. *Journal of Personality and Social Psychology,* 1973, *25,* 390–400.

Williams, G. C. *Adaptation and natural selection.* Princeton, N.J.: Princeton University Press, 1966.

Wynne-Edwards, V. C. *Animal dispersion in relation to social behavior.* Edinburgh, Scotland: Oliver & Boyd, 1962.

Yarrow, M. R., Scott, P. M., & Waxler, C. Z. Learning concern for others. *Developmental Psychology,* 1973, *8,* 240–260.

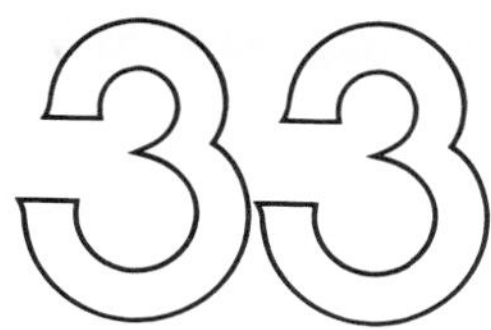

Carol S. Dweck and Therese E. Goetz

ATTRIBUTIONS AND LEARNED HELPLESSNESS

Learned helplessness in achievement situations exists when an individual perceives the termination of failure to be independent of his responses. This perception of failure as insurmountable is associated with attributions of failure to invariant factors, such as a lack of ability, and is accompanied by seriously impaired performance. In contrast, mastery-oriented behavior — increased persistence or improved performance in the face of failure — tends to be associated with attributions of failure to variable factors, particularly to a lack of effort. One would think that persistence following failure would be related to one's level of ability or to one's history of success in that area. Yet our research with children has shown that, compared to achievement cognitions, these variables are relatively poor predictors of response to failure.

In this chapter we examine the role of attributions in determining the response to failure of learned helpless and mastery-oriented children. First we review research that establishes the link between attributions and reactions to failure and that documents the nature of the performance change occasioned by failure. Next we explore the generality of individual differences in helplessness, specifically sex differences, and present findings that indicate how these individual differences develop. In addition, we show how attributions can mediate the generalization of failure effects to novel achievement and academic situations and demonstrate how this phenomenon can account for individual differences in particular academic areas such as sex differences in verbal and mathematical achievement. We then describe current research on the applicability of this learned helplessness analysis, developed in intellectual-achievement failure situations, to children's responses to failure in social situations. Finally, we present evidence that helpless and mastery-oriented children differ not only in the attributions they report when asked, but also in less structured situations, in the timing of their achievement-related cognitions and, indeed, in the role played by causal attributions.

The research reported here was supported in part by Grant NE G-00-3-0088 from the National Institute of Education to the first author and by Grant ND 00244 from the U.S. Public Health Service.

SOURCE: From Carol Dweck and Therese Goetz, "Attributions and Learned Helplessness," in J. Harvey, W. Ickes, and R. Kidd, editors, *New Direction in Attribution Research,* Volume II, 1978, pp. 157–179, Hillsdale, New Jersey: Lawrence Erlbaum Associates, Inc. Reprinted by permission of the publisher.

ATTRIBUTIONS, HELPLESSNESS, AND RESPONSE TO FAILURE

Learned helplessness was first investigated systematically in animals by Seligman and Maier (1967), who found that subjects who were pretreated with unavoidable, inescapable shock in one situation subsequently failed to avoid or escape from shock in a different situation in which control animals readily learned the avoidance contingency. In contrast to the normal animals, whose behavior following shock was characterized by intense activity, these animals tolerated extreme amounts of shock passively. Few attempts were made to prevent its recurrence. Even with forced exposure to the contingency between responding and shock termination, many trials were required before all of the animals began responding reliably on their own (Seligman, Maier, & Geer, 1968). The authors proposed that the animals exposed to prior, inescapable shock learned that the probability of shock termination given a response was equal to the probability of shock termination given no response — or, that shock termination and responding were independent. In other words, in the same way that organisms can learn about contingencies, they can learn about the absence of contingencies. Moreover, this learning can generalize to similar situations, seriously decreasing the probability of attempting instrumental responses and therefore of recognizing the presence of a contingency when one in fact exists.

Analogous divergent behavioral patterns are apparent when children are confronted with failure in intellectual problem-solving situations. Some children tend actively to pursue alternative solutions when they encounter failure, often to a greater extent than prior to failure. The performance of others, however, undergoes marked deterioration, with some children becoming literally incapable of solving the identical problems they solved with relative ease only shortly before. Our first question, then, was whether this behavioral parallel between the experimental animals in the Seligman and Maier studies and the children in problem-solving situations is accompanied by parallel cognitions. Do children who tend to give up in the face of failure tend to see the remedy as beyond their control, to see the probability of success following failure as negligible whether they respond or not? To answer this question, a study was conducted (Dweck & Reppucci, 1973) in which a series of problems was administered to children by two experimenters, one of whom gave soluble problems, the other insoluble ones.[1] Problems from the success and the failure experimenters were randomly interspersed. After a number of trials, however, the failure experimenter began to administer soluble problems, ones that were virtually identical to some that had been administered by the success experimenter earlier. A surprisingly large number of children failed to solve these problems, despite the fact that they were motivated to solve as many problems as they possibly could (they earned tokens, redeemable for highly attractive prizes, for correct solutions), despite the fact that they had solved similar problems from the success experimenter, and despite the fact that they continued to show a rather large practice effect on problems administered by the success experimenter.

On the basis of their performance on the soluble problems from the failure experimenter compared to the analogous problems from the success experimenter, the children were split at the median into two groups: those who failed to solve the problems or who showed the greatest increases in solution times versus those who tended to maintain or improve their performance. It should be emphasized that these two groups had not differed on initial performance. If anything, among the females, those who subsequently showed the most deterioration had shown superior performance under success. What did distinguish the two groups were their attributional patterns, that is, their characteristic ways of explaining their intellectual academic successes and failures (see Weiner, 1972, 1974).

Children's attributions were assessed by means of the Intellectual Achievement Responsibility Scale (Crandall, Katkovsky, & Crandall, 1965), a forced-choice attribution questionnaire in which achievement situations with positive and negative outcomes are depicted and the child selects the one of two alternatives that best describes how he would explain that outcome. One of the alternatives always presents an external factor as the cause of the success or failure, whereas the other alternative presents an internal factor, either one's ability or one's effort, as the cause.

We found that children who persisted in the face of failure placed significantly more emphasis on motivational factors as determinants of outcomes. Attributions of failure to lack of motivation imply that failure is surmountable through effort, a factor that is generally perceived to be under the control of the individual. Children whose performance deteriorated tended more than persistent children to place the blame for their failures on largely uncontrollable external factors rather than effort. When they did take responsibility for failures, they were relatively more likely than the persistent children to blame their lack of ability. Both attributions to external factors and attributions to lack of ability imply that failure is difficult to overcome, particularly within a given situation where transformations in, say, the teacher's attitude or in one's aptitude are highly unlikely. This pattern of helpless attributions — minimizing the role of effort — was more characteristic of girls than boys.

Given that helpless children emphasize the unchangeable nature of failure and deemphasize the role of effort in overcoming failure, it is not surprising that their performance suffers. But terms like "decreased persistence," "reduced effort," or "impaired performance" can encompass a multitude of behaviors. What then is the precise nature of the performance decrement that takes place when failure occurs? We know that helpless children do not merely slow down and take greater care, since their error rate, as well as their response latency, increases with failure. Do they simply withdraw when failure occurs and begin to respond randomly? Do they at first attempt sophisticated alternative solutions but abandon them more quickly than the more persistent children? Do they, under the pressure, slip a notch or two to less mature problem-solving strategies that are easier to execute but less efficient and less likely to yield correct answers? Or, does the sophistication of their strategies undergo a gradual erosion as they experience successive failures until they become incapable of problem solving? By the same token, one might ask what accounts for the often improved performance of mastery-oriented children following failure. Again, citing an undifferentiated construct like "effort" is somewhat unsatisfying as an explanation. After all, one would hardly expect a knotty intellectual problem to yield to the same kind of exertion as a demanding physical task. Clearly, "heightened effort" must be broadened to include alterations in task strategy in addition to increases in speed, concentration, force, and the like.

In order to examine the precise nature of the performance change exhibited by helpless and mastery-oriented children under failure, children were given a task that allowed us to monitor moment-to-moment changes in their problem-solving strategies (Diener & Dweck, 1978, Study I). Children, categorized as helpless or mastery-oriented on the basis of their tendency to neglect or emphasize effort as a determinant of failure, were first trained on eight soluble discrimination-learning problems. For each problem they were shown pictures on cards, two at a time, that differed in three respects: the shape of the form depicted (e.g., circle or triangle), the color of the form (e.g., red or green), and the symbol that appeared in the center of the form (e.g., star or dot). One of the six stimulus values (e.g., red) was correct for the whole problem, and the child's task was to discover which one by utilizing the feedback ("correct" or "wrong") that was provided. On the first training problem feedback was given after every choice, but by the seventh problem children received feedback only after every fourth response. From the child's choices in the block of four trials before feedback was given, we could infer his hypothesis. From the sequence of hypotheses over blocks of trials, we could infer his problem-solving strategy. Strategies could be ordered in terms of maturity, the most sophisticated being the one that on the average yields the solution most quickly and the least sophisticated being one that can never lead to problem solution and that is exhibited most often by the youngest children.

All children in the study were able to employ problem-solving strategies that were successful in reaching the correct solutions on the training problems. On all measures of performance on the training problems — sophistication of strategy, trials to criterion on each problem, number of hints required to reach criterion on the training problems, efficiency of feedback utilization — helpless and mastery-oriented children were virtually identical.

When children reached criterion on the eighth training problem, four insoluble test problems were administered. In essence, every fourth trial the child was told that his choice was incorrect. (The number of trials administered on the test problems was limited, so that the feedback could conceivably be veridical.) Changes in problem-solving strategy over the four failure problems were monitored. The mastery-oriented children not only were able to maintain the sophistication of the problem-solving strategy they had displayed earlier, but, to our surprise, an appreciable proportion (26.3%) of them actually began using even more mature strategies — those typical of older children. It would appear that in response to the limited number of trials they were now allowed, they attempted and perfected a more advanced form of problem solving than they appeared capable of before failure. Helpless children, in contrast, showed a steady regression in strategy across the failure problems. By the second trial, 37.9% had already abandoned strategies that could lead to solution, and by the fourth trial, 68.9% were failing to show any sign of a useful strategy. Of these, two-thirds showed the repeated choice of a single stimulus value regardless of feedback and one-third showed alternating choice of the left and right stimulus, regardless of its nature. Although some girls displayed a sudden dramatic decline in strategy use near the beginning, most of the children displayed a more gradual regression over the course of the failure trials. None showed any evidence of attempting more sophisticated strategies.

After the test problems, children were asked to generate attributions for their failures: "Why do you think you had trouble with these problems?" Over half of the helpless children cited a lack of ability (e.g., "I'm not smart enough") as the cause. None of the mastery-oriented children offered this explanation. Instead they tended to cite effort and other potentially surmountable factors. Again, despite the equivalent initial proficiency and successes of the helpless and mastery-oriented children, the cognitions they entertained about their failures differed and their performance over failure trials became progressively divergent. In fact, by the time helpless children made their postfailure attributions to lack of ability, they could perhaps find evidence for this in their performance on the later trials.

Thus helplessness, the perception of failure as uncontrollable, does indeed predict responses to failure. But does it cause them? If so, we reasoned, then it should be possible to alter children's responses to failure by altering their attributions for failure (Dweck, 1975). Specifically, helpless children taught to attribute their failures to a lack of effort — as mastery-oriented children do — should become more able to cope with failure effectively. To test this possibility, a number of extremely helpless children were identified and were assigned to one of two relatively long-term treatment procedures. All of the children showed the attributional pattern indicative of helplessness on the Intellectual Achievement Responsibility Scale, and, on a questionnaire that directly pitted attributions of failure to lack of effort against attributions of failure to lack of ability, all showed a strong tendency to endorse the lack of ability alternative. Moreover, every one evidenced severely impaired performance following the occurrence of failure, with some being unable to recover baseline performance for several days after a relatively mild failure experience.

In order to assess precisely the effects of failure on the problem-solving performance of the helpless children before and after treatment, stable baselines of speed and accuracy were established on math problems. When the baseline performance had stabilized, failure trials were interpolated between the sets of problems the children had been solving daily. The decrease in the speed and accuracy on the problems that followed the failure problems (compared to the identical problems on the previous day) was used as the index of the disruptive effects of failure.

Following this assessment of their reactions to failure, the children were given one of two treatment procedures in a different situation. Half of the children received only success experiences in the treatment situation, a procedure recommended by advocates of what might be called the "deprivation theory" of maladaptive responses to failure. This position holds that poor reactions to failure stem from a lack of confidence in one's abilities, which in turn stems from a scarcity of success experiences in a given area. If such children, then, could be supplied with the missing success, their confidence would rise and would bolster them against the negative effects of failure. Indeed, there is evidence to suggest that reported expectations of success are correlated with persistence in the face of failure (e.g., Battle, 1965; Feather, 1966). Moreover, the treatment was one that highlighted the contingency between the child's efforts and his successes.

The other half of the children received attribution retraining. Although here, too, success predominated, several failure trials were programmed each day. On the occasions when failure occurred the child's actual performance was compared to criterion performance and the failure was explicitly attributed by the experimenter to a lack of effort. Thus the children in this group received direct instruction in how to interpret the causes of their failures. Both treatments were carried out for 25 daily sessions. At the middle and the end of training, children were returned to the original situation, and the effects of failure on their performance were again assessed.

By the middle of training, all of the children in the attribution retraining condition showed improvement in their response to failure, although all still showed some impairment when their postfailure performance was compared to that of the previous, prefailure day. However, by the end of training, none of the children showed any appreciable impairment, and unexpectedly most of them showed improvement in performance as a result of failure. According to the investigator (Dweck), who tended to eavesdrop during the testing, several of the children, upon encountering failure, were heard to mutter such things as "I missed that one. That means I have to try harder." In addition, when the effort versus ability attribution measure was readministered by an individual unconnected with the study, children in the attribution retraining treatment showed significant increases in their tendency to emphasize effort over ability as a determinant of failure.

The children in the success-only treatment, as well as the proponents of the "deprivation model," fared far more poorly. This group showed no improvement on the midtraining and posttraining failure tests and no change on the attribution measures. Some of the children even showed a tendency to react somewhat more adversely to failure than they had before the start of this treatment. (Of course, children in this group were subsequently given attribution retraining.) Thus even though the performance of these children had been showing steady improvement during training and during the nonfailure days of testing, failure remained a cue for continued failure, and they remained incapable of dealing with it competently. Just as level of proficiency did not predict mastery-oriented responses to failure, a history of success did not do so either. In contrast, intervention at the level of failure attributions can essentially eliminate the deleterious effects of failure.

Why does prior mastery fail to predict future mastery attempts? Why is success not enough? To begin to answer this question, we turn to the issue of how helplessness develops.

THE DEVELOPMENT OF HELPLESSNESS

We have studied the development of helplessness in the context of sex differences in children's attributions for and responses to failure — a context in which an intriguing paradox exists. It is often assumed that girls learn to blame their abilities for failure because teachers and other adults view them as less competent than boys and somehow convey this to them. This seems to be far from the case. If anything, in grade school it is the girls who are receiving the information that they are the ones who possess the ability; hence, the paradox.[2]

Girls, on the average, are far more successful than boys in the academic arena during the elementary school years. They receive consistently higher grades (e.g., McCandless, Roberts, & Starnes, 1972) and regularly outscore boys on tests of reading achievement (see Asher & Markel, 1974). In addition, they receive less criticism from teachers (see Brophy & Good, 1974) and are, in fact, more highly regarded by teachers on almost every conceivable dimension: skills, motivation, personal characteristics, conduct, and more (Coopersmith, 1967; Digman, 1963; Stevenson, Hale, Klein, & Miller, 1968). One would hardly call this discrimination against females. What is more, girls themselves think that teachers believe them to be smarter, that teachers believe they work harder, and that teachers like girls better (Dweck, Goetz, & Strauss, 1977).

Yet despite this record of success and this largely benign environment, girls show far greater evidence of helplessness than boys when they receive failure feedback from adult evaluators. Girls place less emphasis than boys on motivational factors as determinants of failure and are more likely than boys to attribute failure feedback to a lack of ability (Dweck & Reppucci, 1973; Nicholls, 1975). In line with this, they are also more likely than boys to show decreased persistence or impaired performance when failure occurs, when the threat of failure is present, or when the evaluative pressure on a difficult task is increased (Butterfield, 1965; Crandall

& Rabson, 1960; Dweck & Gilliard, 1975; Nicholls, 1975; Veroff, 1969). This occurs even on tasks at which girls have demonstrated their ability or have even outperformed boys.

Boys, in spite of their poorer grades and the greater criticism they receive, and despite the lower esteem in which they are held by teachers, respond quite differently to failure feedback from adults. They tend to attribute it to controllable or variable factors. In line with this, they tend to confront failure with improved performance or increased persistence and to seek out tasks that present a challenge. Boys have also been found to credit success to their abilities more readily than girls (Nicholls, 1975).

Some have argued that this differential response to failure stems from boys' and girls' discrepant socialization histories (e.g., Barry, Bacon, & Child, 1957; Crandall, 1963; Veroff, 1969). Boys, it is said, have been trained to be independent and to formulate their own standards of excellence against which to judge the adequacy of their performance. Thus, this line of reasoning continues, when a boy receives negative feedback, he can accept it or reject it depending on how it matches his own assessment. Girls, however, are believed not to develop independent standards and therefore to remain more dependent upon external evaluation. They consequently look to the feedback of others to assess their performance and evaluate their abilities.

If this position were correct, one would expect the typical sex differences in responses to failure to have wide generality. For example, although the research showing the sex differences has always been conducted with adult evaluators, one would expect the difference to remain relatively constant regardless of who delivered the feedback. Boys' internal standards, after all, should withstand variations of this sort. Yet we know that in the late grade-school years, peers become increasingly important to boys as sources of evaluative feedback (Bronfenbrenner, 1967; Hollander & Marcia, 1970). Perhaps, then, boys do not view adult criticism as indicative of their abilities, but would view such feedback from peers as reflecting their level of competence.

In research designed to test this hypothesis (Dweck & Bush, 1976), children attempted several trials of a task and received failure feedback from either a male or female, adult or peer evaluator. As in past research, when feedback was provided by an adult evaluator, particularly a female adult, girls showed greater helplessness than boys; they were more likely to attribute their failures to a lack of ability and to show impaired performance in the face of failure. Interestingly, there was a tendency for boys to blame the female adult evaluator more than girls did and for those who did so to show impaired performance. However, most boys attributed their failures to a lack of effort and persisted under failure. With peer evaluators (and particularly the male peer), the pattern was essentially reversed. Boys were the ones who saw the failure feedback as indicative of their abilities and the ones whose performance suffered. In fact, boys receiving negative feedback from male peers showed the most impairment of any group. Girls in this condition tended to ascribe the feedback to a lack of effort and to show significant improvement in their performance under failure.

These findings suggest that it is not boys' and girls' general socialization histories that determine response to failure, but rather their specific histories with particular agents. This, in turn, implies that in order to learn how feedback acquires different meanings for the two sexes, one should analyze the pattern of evaluative feedback they experience from the various evaluators. Because adults are the major evaluators in all academic environments, this analysis was undertaken in grade-school classrooms and the findings were then corroborated in a laboratory experiment (Dweck, Davidson, Nelson, & Enna, in press).

Of particular interest were the ways in which negative feedback was used — how much it was used compared to positive feedback, what it was typically used for, the specificity with which it was used — and the attributions teachers made for children's intellectual failures. It would be expected, for example, that negative feedback from an evaluator who is typically more negative than positive, whose feedback typically refers to nonintellectual aspects of behavior, whose criticism is used diffusely for a wide variety of referents, and who attributes failure to lack of motivation, would *not* be interpreted as indicating a lack of ability. It would be expected that negative feedback from an agent who is generally positive, who uses feedback quite specifically to refer to intellectually inadequate aspects of performance, and who does not attribute failure to a lack of effort, would more readily be attributed to a lack of ability. These, basically, were the patterns hypothesized to occur for boys and girls in the classroom.

Trained observers coded every instance of evaluative feedback given by fourth- and fifth-grade teachers to their students during academic subjects. The observers noted whether the feedback was positive or negative and recorded the class of behavior for which the feedback was given — either conduct, nonintellectual aspects of academic work (e.g., neatness), or intellectual aspects of academic work (e.g., correctness of answer). Observers also noted when teachers made explicit attributions for children's successes or failures.

The results have helped to resolve the paradox of how the more favorable treatment of girls can lead to their denigration of their competence, to helplessness, and to lessened ability to cope with failure. They also show how boys can learn to discount failures or see them as unrelated to their abilities. But first a brief indication of ways in which girls and boys did not differ. They did not differ in the absolute amount of feedback for *intellectual aspects of work* (i.e., average per boy and average per girl within classroom) or in the portion of this feedback that was positive, negative, or absent. Therefore, sex differences do not appear to be related to the amount or proportion of success and failure feedback for intellectual performance.

However, when one looks at the feedback in general and at the feedback for intellectual quality of work within the context of all feedback, striking sex differences become apparent. First, negative feedback to boys was, overall, far more frequent. Since negative outcomes that are in accord with environmental forces can plausibly be attributed to them (see Enzle, Hansen, & Lowe, 1975; Kelley, 1971), boys may attribute failure feedback to the teacher's attitude. Second, negative feedback was used in a more diffuse and a more ambiguous fashion vis-á-vis the intellectual quality of boys' work. Past research has clearly shown that feedback used in a nonspecific manner to refer to a wide variety of nonintellectual behaviors comes to lose its meaning as an assessment of the intellectual quality of the child's work (Cairns, 1970; Eisenberger, Kaplan, & Singer, 1974; Warren & Cairns, 1972). In fact, negative feedback for boys was used *more often* for conduct and nonintellectual aspects of work than it was for the intellectual quality of their academic performance (67.5% and 32.5%, respectively).

One might argue that although conduct feedback may convey to the child something about the teacher's values or attitudes toward him or her, such feedback can easily be discriminated from feedback for work-related matters and would not seriously affect the information value of feedback addressed to the child's work. In contrast, intellectual and nonintellectual aspects of work occur simultaneously and if feedback is typically used for both, then the basis for the feedback or its referent on any given occasion is more likely to be ambiguous. However, even if conduct is excluded from the analysis and we look only at work-related feedback, still 45.6% of the feedback for boys' work referred to intellectually irrelevant aspects of their performance. That means that almost half of the criticism that boys got for their work had nothing to do with its intellectual adequacy. Instead this feedback referred to such things as neatness, instruction-following, and style of response delivery — "form" rather than "content." Finally, looking at the explicit attributions teachers made for children's intellectual failures, we find that teachers attributed boys' failures to lack of motivation eight times more often than they did girls'. In short, when boys are given failure feedback by adults they can easily view it as reflecting something about the evaluators' attitude toward them or as being based on an assessment of some nonintellectual aspect of their work. When they do see it as referring to the intellectual quality of their work, they can attribute the failure to a lack of motivation.

In striking contrast, girls received relatively little negative feedback for conduct, and the vast majority (88.2%) of the negative feedback they received for their work referred specifically to its intellectual aspects. Thus, since the teacher is generally positive toward girls (they also got more praise than boys), they are less apt to see criticism as reflecting a negative attitude toward them. Second, since feedback is used for them in a very specific fashion for intellectual aspects of work, girls are not as likely to see the assessment as being based on an evaluation of nonintellectual qualities. Finally, since teachers view girls as highly motivated and girls themselves concur in this assessment, they cannot attribute their failures to a lack of motivation. They may have little choice but to view the negative feedback as an objective evaluation of their work and to attribute their intellectual failures to a lack of ability.

Thus the two sexes differ widely in the degree to which negative feedback serves as a valid indicant of the intellectual ability displayed in their academic performance. The results for positive feedback, although not as striking, were essentially the opposite. For work-related praise, 93.8% was contingent upon the intellectual quality of work for boys, but only 80.9% for girls, suggesting that positive evaluation for boys may be more indicative of competence than it is for girls.

These patterns of negative and positive feedback to the two sexes were both consistent across classrooms and rather general across children within classrooms. Are teachers simply reacting to the different behavior of the two sexes, or are they instead reacting differentially to similar behavior from the two sexes? The answer is probably a bit of both. Although it is clear that boys are often more disruptive, less neat in their work, and less motivated to perform well in the elementary school years, there is also some evidence that they tend to be scolded more often and more severely than girls for similar transgressions (Etaugh & Harlow, 1973).

In terms of trying to understand how the use of negative feedback determines its meaning for boys and girls, however, this question may not be critical. We have shown (Dweck et al., in press) that any child exposed to the contingencies that boys and girls are exposed to in the classroom will interpret the feedback accordingly. These contingencies can serve as direct and powerful causes of children's attributions. We have taken the "teacher–girl" and the "teacher–boy" contingencies of negative feedback that we observed in the classroom and have programmed them in an experimental situation.

Specifically, on an initial anagram task

with mixed success and failure trials, children received negative feedback that either: (1) referred exclusively to the correctness of their answers (like girls in the classroom), or (2) referred sometimes to correctness and sometimes to neatness (like boys in the classroom). There were two teacher–girl groups — one matched to the teacher–boy group on number of intellectual (correctness) criticisms and the other matched on total number of criticisms. All children next performed a second task (a digit–symbol substitution task) at which they failed on the initial trials and received standardized feedback from the same experimenter. They were then given a written question that asked them to attribute the failure feedback on this second task to one of the three factors described: ability, effort, or the experimenter.

As predicted, most of the children in the teacher–boy condition (75%) did *not* view the failure feedback on the second task as reflecting a lack of ability. Instead, insufficient effort was the alternative that was most frequently endorsed. Although an attempt was made to assure the children of the anonymity of their choices, only two of the 60 children in the study cited the evaluator as the cause of their failure. However, both of these children were in the teacher–boy condition.

In sharp contrast, children in both the teacher–girl conditions overwhelmingly interpreted the failure feedback they received as indicating a lack of ability. Only 25% of these children ascribed their failures to a lack of effort. There were no differences between male and female subjects in their attribution choices in any of the conditions.

These findings clearly indicate that regardless of sex, children who receive failure feedback that is solution-specific (and for which no alternative explanation is provided) are far more likely to regard subsequent failure feedback from that agent as indicative of their ability than are children who receive failure feedback that is often solution-irrelevant. It appears then that the pattern of feedback observed in the classroom for teacher–boy versus teacher–girl interactions can have direct effects on children's interpretations of their failures.

THE GENERALIZATION OF HELPLESSNESS

What are the implications of these individual differences in attributions for the generalization of failure experiences to new situations? To the extent that one's perceived cause of failure remains in effect in a new situation, then one will view past outcomes as predictive of future ones (cf. Brickman, Linsenmeier, & McCareins, 1976). In this way, an individual's causal attributions might serve as mediators of failure effects from one situation to others involving new tasks or new evaluators.

For girls, attributions of failure to a lack of ability on a task or in an academic area imply that when presented with a similar task in the future, the past outcome is relevant to subsequent ones and, in this case, would presage a poor future. To the extent that one encounters similar academic subjects throughout school, girls' earlier condemnations of their ability will continue to be applicable. Thus girls' attributions of failure to ability may discourage continued "testing" of the environment in future grades both because similar tasks may mediate generalization of the effects of past failures and because it is unpleasant to conclude that one lacks ability despite renewed effort.

For boys, however, although blaming the teachers' attitudes or biases may impair motivation and performance in the immediate situation, by blaming the evaluator they can maintain their belief in their ability to succeed. Therefore, when the agent changes, as when they are promoted to the next grade or attend a new school, they can discount their past failures and can approach the situation with renewed effort. Thus boys' attributions of past failures to the agent may encourage testing of the environment when the agent changes. Moreover, attributions of past failures to a lack of effort imply that when in the future one cares to succeed one can at that time begin to apply oneself.

When one considers success feedback, the picture becomes even clearer. To the extent that girls' successes are not viewed by them as indicative of their ability but are attributed to the beneficence of the agent or to intellectually irrelevant aspects of their work, then past successes should not be seen by them as predictive of future success with a new agent. For boys, however, past successes have been achieved despite an "inhibitory" environmental force (Kelley, 1971) — the teacher — and are therefore more apt to be chalked up to their abilities. Thus in new school situations with a new teacher, boys will see their successes more than their failures as indicative of ability and as predictive of future performance.

This analysis — postulating attributions as mediators of the effects of past outcomes — provides a mechanism with which to explain the commonly found sex differences in expectancy of success. Crandall (1969) presents a good deal of evidence that girls underestimate their chances for success relative to what their past performance in similar situations would warrant. Boys, on the other hand, are more likely to overestimate their chances of future success relative to their past accomplishments. For example, girls have been found to predict lower grades for themselves than boys do for themselves, even when they have received equal or higher grades than boys in the past. This effect does not appear to be due to sex typing or social desirability of responses. It is plausible to assume that in formulating an expectancy, one will focus on those past outcomes that are most indicative of what is likely to occur in the situation at hand. If boys focus on their successes and girls on their failures, this would yield overestimation and underestimation, respectively. In fact, Crandall presents data to suggest that when feedback is mixed or inconsistent, girls tend to weight the negative aspects and boys the positive.

This analysis further predicts that the sex discrepancy in achievement expectancies would be maximal at the beginning of a school year, when the subject matter (ability areas) remain roughly constant but the teacher (evaluator) has changed. Under these circumstances one would expect boys' expectancies to rise dramatically, but girls' perhaps to decline. However, as the year progresses and both boys and girls learn that this year's teacher is similar to last year's — for example, in attitudes, criteria, grading practices, and feedback patterns — the gap in expectancy should diminish.

Two studies were designed to investigate the hypothesis that sex differences in attributions mediate the generalization of prior failure experiences to new situations. Essentially, one would predict that no change in the situation or changes in factors perceived to be irrelevant to past failures should lead to persistence of failure effects, whereas changes in factors that are viewed as causes of failure should encourage recovery from failure.

In the first laboratory study, children worked on a task (on which both neatness and accuracy were said to be important) and received failure feedback from an adult female experimenter after each of the first four trials. Expectancy of success was monitored prior to each trial. For the fifth trial, children experienced one of four conditions: a new task, a new evaluator, both a new task and a new evaluator, or no change from the previous four trials.[3] The recovery of the child's expectancy on the fifth trial served as the index of the perceived relevance of the change to his future outcomes. This procedure is analogous to that employed in studies of habituation, in which a stimulus is repeatedly presented until the response to it has diminished. The original stimulus and the novel stimulus are then administered during testing. The magnitude of the recovery of the response reflects the perceived novelty of the testing stimulus.

In the present study, it was predicted that changes in only those factors to which boys and girls attribute their failures would promote a recovery of expectancy by creating the perception of the situation as a new one. Specifically, since boys tend to attribute failure to teacher-like agents more than girls do, it was expected that boys' expectancies would recover significantly more than girls' when the evaluator was changed. This prediction was confirmed. Not only did girls show no recovery, but their expectancies declined from Trial 4 to Trial 5 much as they did in the condition in which nothing was altered.

Since girls tend to attribute their failures to a lack of ability more than boys do, it was predicted that their expectancies would recover more than boys' when a new task was introduced. The perception of oneself as lacking ability should no longer be valid if the task on which one failed has been eliminated — provided that the ability one blamed was task-specific. Boys' recovery should be limited by the continued presence of the same evaluator. The results indicated that although both sexes recovered significantly in this condition, girls by no means regained their initial level of confidence and in fact did not recover any more than boys did. More striking, however, was our finding that even when both the evaluator and the task were varied — making it a largely new situation — girls' expectancies did not show complete recovery. Boys', naturally, did.

Of course it is possible that girls were simply more reluctant to state high expectancies again given the fate of their original predictions. However, these findings suggest that perhaps failure feedback leads girls to consider themselves lacking in an intellectual ability that goes beyond the particular task at hand. In this way, they may be transferring a failure experience from one domain to another by applying a general label to their perceived deficit. It is interesting to note that we started with a situation in which boys and girls confronted a new task with equivalent expectancies and ended with a situation in which boys and girls confronted a new task with the typical sex difference in expectancy.

The second study tested the hypothesis that sex differences in academic achievement expectancies would be maximal at the beginning of a school year at which time the ability areas remain similar but the evaluator is different. Prior to their first and second report cards of the year, over 300 fourth-, fifth-, and sixth-grade children were given questionnaires that assessed how well they expected to do on their upcoming report cards. Although girls had received significantly higher grades than boys on their final report cards the previous year, girls predicted significantly poorer performance for themselves than boys predicted for themselves on their first report cards. Needless to say, girls then received higher grades on their first (and second) report cards. By the second report card the gap had closed, but girls still did not give higher predictions than boys, which is what accurate estimates from both would yield.

The results from these studies provide strong support for the view that individual differences in attributions result in differences in the generalization of failure effects. The results also suggest that failure effects may have more of a long-term and cumulative effect for girls than for boys and provide a way of understanding why, despite their early advantage, girls begin to lag behind boys in many achievement areas later on. Even more interesting is the fact that this analysis can account for the development of differential performance by the two sexes in different subject areas.

It has long been a source of curiosity that although girls fairly typically have outperformed boys on tests of verbal achievement, starting at around the junior high or early high school years boys begin to outscore girls on tests of mathematical achievement (Maccoby & Jacklin, 1974). If one analyzes the characteristics of math versus verbal skills as they are acquired over the school years and considers this in conjunction with responses to and generalization of failure experiences, an explanation for the emerging achievement differences becomes clear (although, of course, it does not rule out other potential contributing factors). Once the basic verbal skills — reading, spelling, vocabulary — are acquired, increments in difficulty are gradual. Never again, or rarely, is the child confronted in school with a new unit that puts him at a complete loss or for which a totally new set of concepts and skills must be mastered. Learning to read a new word or to spell it or define it involves fundamentally the same process one has gone through before with old words. New learning is, in a sense, assimilated into a larger, pre-existing body of knowledge.

With math, however, a new unit may involve totally new concepts, the relevance of which to past learning may not be immediately, or ever, clear. New units in math often involve quantum leaps as from arithmetic to algebra to geometry to calculus and so on. For a young child even the links between addition and multiplication or between multiplication and division may not be readily apparent. This characteristic of the acquisition of mathematical skills provides numerous opportunities for initial failures and, if one is so inclined, for concluding that one lacks ability. To the extent that one blames a lack of general mathematical ability, the effects of the failures may generalize to all future tasks subsumed under the label "math," resulting in: (1) lowered persistence in the face of difficulties, which are inevitably encountered even by those accomplished in mathematics; (2) avoidance of math courses when that option becomes possible; and (3) perhaps interference with new learning, which in math often requires sustained attention and the maintenance of systematic problem-solving strategies, both of which are hampered by helplessness. Thus, it may be the case that two children who start out with equivalent skills and equivalent "aptitude" in elementary school end up with divergent skills later on. This possibility — that differential achievement can be accounted for by how well the nature of skill acquisition coincides with attributional tendencies — is currently under investigation (by Carol Dweck and Barbara Licht).

Although this research has focused on sex differences in helplessness, the variable "sex," like many demographic variables, simply serves as a convenient way of summarizing a particular learning history. In this case the histories of the two sexes favor different attributional tendencies. However, there are important within-sex differences in these tendencies and one would expect the relationships elaborated here to apply to these individual differences as well.

In the same vein, most of the research to date relating perceptions of causality to responses to outcomes has focused on intellectual achievement situations; yet similar relationships should hold for situations involving social interaction.

HELPLESSNESS AND SOCIAL INTERACTIONS

In the same way that intellectual failures can be met with a variety of responses, so, too, can social rejection. One may attempt a variety of strategies designed to reverse the rejection, or one may respond with behavior that represents a marked deterioration from the previous interaction. For instance, a normally socially facile person may withdraw or resort to hostile retaliatory measures. Do attributions guide selection of coping patterns in social situations in the same way that they appear to in academic–intellectual ones?

The importance of this question is highlighted when it is viewed in the context of past work on children's interpersonal coping and peer relationships. Most previous investigations have virtually ignored the role of perceptions of control and have concentrated instead on cognitive and social skills, with the assumption that problems in coping must be primarily a result of deficits in these skills (Allen, Hart, Buell, Harris, & Wolf, 1964; Baer & Wolf, 1970; Keller & Carlson, 1974; O'Connor, 1969, 1972; Spivack & Shure, 1974). Yet those programs that have focused on skill or overt behavior alone have not reliably promoted or maintained effective peer relationships (see Gottman, 1977). The most effective programs have been the ones that appear to be teaching the contingency between the child's actions and the social outcomes he experiences (see Gottman, Gonso, & Schuler, 1976: Oden & Asher, 1977).

Focusing on perception of control over aversive outcomes brings to the fore a number of important possibilities not addressed by earlier approaches. Past researchers have considered only rejected and isolated children, implicitly assuming the more popular ones to be free of potentially serious problems in interpersonal coping. However, just as learned helplessness in achievement situations appears to be unrelated to competence, responses to negative social outcomes may be relatively unrelated to social skills; popular as well as unpopular individuals may have coping problems. For instance, some popular children may interpret their few experiences with social rebuff as indications of permanent rejection not open to change by their actions, paralleling the instance of the "A" student who attributes a low grade to a lack of ability despite all previous evidence to the contrary. Moreover, it may be that some individuals are isolated *not* because they lack social skills or the knowledge of appropriate behavior, but because they fear or have experienced social rejection and view it as insurmountable.

We are currently conducting an investigation to establish the relationship between perceptions of control and causal attributions for rejection.[4] In order to tap causal attributions for social rejection, we have developed a questionnaire depicting a series of hypothetical social situations in which children are either rejected or accepted by same-sex peers. Responses on this measure are being related to responses in a situation in which each child must cope with potential social rejection by a peer of the same sex. In this way, we can determine whether causal attributions that imply difficulty in surmounting rejection are in fact associated with deterioration of social behavior in the face of rejection.

In the questionnaire, children are presented with an instance of rejection and are asked to evaluate a list of reasons the rejection may have occurred. Both the situations and their causes were selected as the most representative of those generated by children in the course of extensive interviews. For example: "Suppose you move into a new neighborhood. A girl you meet does not like you very much. Why would this happen to you?" The reasons include such factors as personal ineptitude, a characteristic of the rejector, chance, misunderstandings, and a mutual mismatch of temperaments or preferences.

Just as failure attributions to some factors, like effort, imply surmountability, so too do rejection attributions to misunderstanding. Similarly, attributing rejection to one's lack of ability (e.g., "It happened because it's hard for me to make friends") implies a relatively enduring outcome, as would an ability attribution for academic failure. Blaming the rejector for interpersonal rejection has the same implications as blaming the evaluator for academic failure. Given the parallel implications of interpersonal and intellectual attributions, one would also expect parallel reactions and generalization effects.

The data from over 100 children tested thus far indicate that individuals differ in consistent ways from one another in the causes to which they ascribe social rejection. In order to test the hypothesized relationships between attributions and responses to rejection, a method of sampling each child's interpersonal strategies both before and after social rejection has been devised. Children try out for a pen pal club by communicating a sample getting-to-know-you letter (conveying the "kind of person" they are) to a peer evaluator. The experimenter then relays to the child the evaluator's decision — in this case, not to admit the child into the club. To assess the effect the evaluation has on subsequent responses, the child is told he has a chance to try again, to send another message to the same evaluator.[5] After a short wait, enthusiastic acceptance is relayed to the child, and his home address is recorded to place on file for the club (which has actually been set up for this project).

These communications are currently being rated by trained, independent judges along a number of dimensions designed to reflect the child's strategy for attaining acceptance and to reveal alterations in strategy across situations. As with the attribution measure, the data thus far indicate that there are striking differences in strategies for coping with interpersonal rejection. Responses range from mastery-oriented patterns, with more and different strategies used after rejection, to complete withdrawal — about 10% of the children could not come up with a second message to the rejecting evaluator, even after gentle prodding and prompting. Only after the experimenter explicitly attributed the rejection to an idiosyncracy of the committee member would these children produce a message for a different evaluator, which enabled us to provide acceptance feedback.

The initial data indicate that those children who either gave up or were extremely reluctant to send a message to the rejecting committee member also favored attributions that emphasized the insurmountability of rejection. Those children who were notable for their self-confident responses to the rejection and thoughtful approaches to their second communication emphasized the role of surmountable factors like misunderstandings. Thus, preliminary analysis of the attribution and coping measures suggests that individual differences in attribution are indeed systematically related to responses following rejection in the predicted ways.

HELPLESSNESS AND THE OCCURRENCE OF ATTRIBUTIONS

Researchers in the area of attributions assume that following some discrete event, such as the delivery of evaluative feedback, an attribution is always made (see Dweck & Gilliard, 1975). Individual differences are assumed to occur only in the nature of the attribution that is made at that point. However, we have recently completed research that shows there are also clear individual differences in the timing or occurrence of causal attributions when the situation is less structured (Diener & Dweck, 1978).

When attributions were measured at a prespecified time — either on a preexperimental attribution questionnaire or on a task-specific, postfailure attribution probe — we obtained the typical helpless versus mastery-oriented differences in attributions and task persistence. However, when children's spontaneous, ongoing reports of achievement-cognitions were monitored, we found that attributions were made primarily by helpless children and not by mastery-oriented ones. In this research, described in part earlier, children were trained to criterion on a discrimination-learning task. Following the training problems, failure feedback ("wrong") was begun, and chances in problem-solving strategies were tracked. As noted above, helpless children showed a steady decline in the sophistication of the strategies they employed, whereas nearly all of the mastery-oriented children maintained their strategies and a number even began using more mature strategies than they had before. These results were replicated in a second study, which was identical in all respects but one: prior to the seventh training trial, children were requested to verbalize what they were thinking, if anything, while performing the task. The instructions gave them license to report anything — from justification for their stimulus selection to plans for their lunch. This procedure allowed us to monitor differences in not only the nature of particular achievement-related cognitions but also in the presence, the timing, and the relative frequency of various cognitions.

All children verbalized freely; and, prior to failure, the verbalizations of the helpless and mastery-oriented children were virtually identical. Almost all of the statements pertained to task strategy and almost none reflected achievement-related cognitions. Following the onset of failure, however, a dramatic shift took place. Both groups of children began to report many more achievement cognitions, but what they emphasized differed markedly. The helpless children rather quickly began to make attributions for their failures, attributing them to a lack or loss of ability, and to express negative affect about the task. The mastery-oriented children, in contrast, did not make attributions for failure. Instead they engaged in self-instruction and self-monitoring designed to bring about success. They continued to express a positive prognosis for future outcomes (e.g., "One more guess and I'll have it") and to express positive affect toward the task (e.g., "I love a challenge"). It would appear that despite the feedback of the experimenter, the mastery-oriented children did not consider themselves to have failed. They were making mistakes, to be sure, but they seemed certain that with the proper concentration and strategy they could get back on the track. Thus they dwelled on prescription rather than diagnosis, remedy rather than cause.

One might argue that although mastery-oriented children did not verbalize effort attributions, they were implied by their self-instructions. However, the few attributions that were explicitly verbalized did not seem to fall into any one category. Moreover, when one considers the nature of the task, it is clear that identifying the cause of failure is in this case irrelevant to achieving success. Whether the cause is thought to be insufficient effort, bad luck, increased task difficulty, or lower ability than previously believed, the remedy still would be sustained concentration and the use of sophisticated strategies.

This observed difference in the tendency of helpless and mastery-oriented children to attend to the cause of failure raises a number of interesting questions. Would the mastery-oriented children have attended to the causes of failure sooner if a diagnosis were necessary for the prescription of a remedy? Or, is there among them a subset of children who are too "action oriented" to analyze causal factors systematically? Although helpless children readily concede that they have failed soon after negative feedback begins, at what point do mastery-oriented children define themselves as having failed, when do they attribute, and at what point do they consider terminating their efforts? Are there those among the mastery-oriented who suffer from what may be termed the "Nixon syndrome" — unusually prolonged persistence designed to forestall the admission of failure (cf. Bulman & Brickman, 1976)? For such children, as for helpless children, failure may have highly negative connotations for their competence; yet rather than surrender to it prematurely, they persist past the point of diminishing returns in the belief that, as expressed by Richard Nixon, "You're never a failure until you give up."

In short, in past research, experimenters have typically at a predetermined point defined failure for the subject and asked him to make a causal attribution. The current results suggest that there are also important differences in the timing or even the occurrence of attributions. The implications of these differences have yet to be explored.

NOTES

1. In this and in subsequent studies the participants were late grade-school-age children (grades four to six). Throughout the research great care was taken to ensure that every child left the experimental situation feeling that his performance had been commendable. For example, in a typical study following the failure trials, children were given mastery experiences, were assured that they had conquered a difficult task more quickly than most, and were told they had done so well there was no need to complete the remaining problems. Thus the procedure incorporated what is essentially persistence training.

2. This is not to deny that later in their academic careers girls may indeed encounter these attitudes.

3. Pilot work had ensured that both tasks employed elicited identical mean initial expectancies, that boys and girls did not differ in their initial expectancies, and that ability, effort, and evaluator attributions for failure were all perceived as plausible candidates.

4. This research is the second author's dissertation.

5. A test for generalization to a new evaluator is also included.

REFERENCES

Allen, K. E., Hart, B., Buell, J. S., Harris, F. R., & Wolf, M. M. Effects of social reinforcement of isolate behavior of a nursery school child. *Child Development,* 1964, *35,* 511–518.

Asher, S. R., & Markel, R. A. Sex differences in comprehension of high- and low-interest material. *Journal of Educational Psychology,* 1974, *66,* 680–687.

Baer, D. M., & Wolf, M. M. Recent examples of behavior modification in pre-school settings. In C. Neuringer & J. L. Michael (Eds.), *Behavior modification in clinical psychology.* New York: Appleton–Century–Crofts, 1970.

Barry, H., Bacon, M. C., & Child, I. L. A cross-cultural survey of some sex differences in socialization. *Journal of Abnormal and Social Psychology,* 1957, *55,* 327–332.

Battle, E. Motivational determinants of academic task persistence. *Journal of Personality and Social Psychology,* 1965, *2,* 209–218.

Brickman, P., Linsenmeier, J. A. W., & McCareins, A. Performance enhancement by relevant success and irrelevant failure. *Journal of Personality and Social Psychology,* 1976, *33,* 149–160.

Bronfenbrenner, U. Response to pressure from peers versus adults among Soviet and American school children. *International Journal of Psychology,* 1967, *2,* 199–207.

Brophy, J. E., & Good, T. L. *Teacher–student relationships.* New York: Holt, 1974.

Bulman, R. J., & Brickman, P. *When not all problems are soluble, does it still help to expect success?* Unpublished manuscript, 1976.

Butterfield, E. C. The role of competence motivation in interrupted task recall and repetition choice. *Journal of Experimental Child Psychology,* 1965, *2,* 354–370.

Cairns, R. B. Meaning and attention as determinants of social reinforcer effectiveness. *Child Development,* 1970, *41,* 1067–1082.

Coopersmith, S. *The antecedents of self-esteem.* San Francisco: Freeman, 1967.

Crandall, V. C. Sex differences in expectancy of intellectual and academic reinforcement. In C. P. Smith (Ed.), *Achievement-related motives in children.* New York: Russell Sage Foundation, 1969.

Crandall, V. C., Katkovsky, W., & Crandall, V. J. Children's beliefs in their own control of reinforcements in intellectual–academic situations. *Child Development,* 1965, *36,* 91–109.

Crandall, V. J. Achievement. In H. W. Stevenson (Ed.), *Child psychology.* The sixty-second yearbook of the National Society for the Study of Education. Chicago: NSSE, 1963.

Crandall, V. J., & Rabson, A. Children's repetition choices in an intellectual achievement situation following success and failure. *Journal of Genetic Psychology,* 1960, *97,* 161–168.

Diener, C. I., & Dweck, C. S. An analysis of learned helplessness: Continuous changes in performance, strategy, and achievement cognitions following failure. *Journal of Personality and Social Psychology,* in press.

Digman, J. M. Principal dimensions of child personality as inferred from teachers' judgments. *Child Development,* 1963, *34,* 43–60.

Dweck, C. S. The role of expectations and attributions in the alleviation of learned helplessness. *Journal of Personality and Social Psychology,* 1975, *31,* 674–685.

Dweck, C. S., & Bush, E. S. Sex differences in learned helplessness: (I) Differential debilitation with peer and adult evaluators. *Developmental Psychology,* 1976, *12,* 147–156.

Dweck, C. S., Davidson, W., Nelson, S., & Enna, B. *Sex differences in learned helplessness: (II) The contingencies of evaluative feedback in the classroom and (III) An experimental analysis. Developmental Psychology,* in press.

Dweck, C. S., & Gilliard, D. Expectancy statements as determinants of reactions to failure: Sex differences in persistence and expectancy change. *Journal of Personality and Social Psychology,* 1975, *32,* 1077–1084.

Dweck, C. S., Goetz, T. E., & Strauss, N. *Sex differences in learned helplessness: (IV) An experimental and naturalistic study of failure generalization and its mediators.* Unpublished manuscript, 1977.

Dweck, C. S., & Reppucci, N. D. Learned helplessness and reinforcement responsibility in children. *Journal of Personality and Social Psychology,* 1973, *25,* 109–116.

Eisenberger, R., Kaplan, R. M., & Singer, R. D. Decremental and nondecremental effects of noncontingent social approval. *Journal of Personality and Social Psychology,* 1974, *30,* 716–722.

Enzle, M. E., Hansen, R. D., & Lowe, C. A. Causal attributions in the mixed-motive game: Effects of facilitory and inhibitory environmental forces. *Journal of Personality and Social Psychology,* 1975, *31,* 50–54.

Etaugh, C., & Harlow, H. *School attitudes and performance of elementary school children as related to teacher's sex and behavior.* Paper presented at the meeting of the Society for Research in Child Development, Philadelphia, March 1973.

Feather, N. T. Effects of prior success and failure on expectations of success and subsequent performance. *Journal of Personality and Social Psychology,* 1966, *3,* 287–298.

Gottman, J. M. The effects of modeling film on social isolation in preschool children: A methodological investigation. *Journal of Abnormal Child Psychology,* in press.

Gottman, J., Gonso, J., & Schuler, P. Teaching social skills to isolated children. *Journal of Abnormal Child Psychology,* 1976, *4*(2), 179–197.

Hollander, E. P., & Marcia, J. E. Parental determinants of peer-orientation and self-orientation among preadolescents. *Developmental Psychology,* 1970, *2,* 292–302.

Keller, M. F., & Carlson, P. M. The use of symbols modeling to promote social skills in preschool children with low levels of social responsiveness. *Child Development,* 1974, *45,* 912–919.

Kelley, H. H. *Attribution in social interaction.* Morristown, N.J.: General Learning Press, 1971.

Maccoby, E. E., & Jacklin, C. N. *The psychology of sex differences.* Stanford, Calif.: Stanford University Press, 1974.

McCandless, B., Roberts, A., & Starnes, T. Teachers' marks, achievement test scores, and aptitude relations with respect to social class, race, and sex. *Journal of Educational Psychology,* 1972, *63,* 153–159.

Nicholls, J. G. Causal attributions and other achievement-related cognitions: Effects of task outcomes, attainment value, and sex. *Journal of Personality and Social Psychology,* 1975, *31,* 379–389.

O'Connor, R. D. Modification of social withdrawal through symbolic modeling. *Journal of Applied Behavior Analysis,* 1969, *2,* 15–22.

O'Connor, R. D. Relative efficacy of modeling, shaping, and the combined procedures for modification of social withdrawal. *Journal of Abnormal Psychology,* 1972, *79,* 327–334.

Oden, S. L., & Asher, S. R. Coaching children in social skills for friendship-making. *Child Development,* 1977, *48,* 495–506.

Seligman, M. E. P., & Maier, S. F. Failure to escape traumatic shock. *Journal of Experimental Psychology,* 1967, *74,* 1–9.

Seligman, M. E. P., Maier, S. F., & Geer, J. The alleviation of learned helplessness in the dog. *Journal of Abnormal and Social Psychology,* 1968, *73,* 256–262.

Spivak, G., & Shure, M. B. *Social adjustment of young children.* San Francisco: Jossey–Bass, 1974.

Stevenson, H. W., Hale, G. A., Klein, R. E., & Miller, L. K. Interrelations and correlates in children's learning and problem solving. *Monographs of the Society for Research in Child Development,* 1968, *33* (7, Serial No. 123).

Veroff, J. Social comparison and the development of achievement motivation. In C. P. Smith (Ed.), *Achievement-related motives in children.* New York: Russell Sage, 1969.

Warren, V. L., & Cairns, R. B. Social reinforcement satiation: An outcome of frequency or ambiguity? *Journal of Experimental Child Psychology,* 1972, *13,* 249–260.

Weiner, B. *Theories of motivation.* Chicago: Markham, 1972.

Weiner, B. *Achievement motivation and attribution theory.* Morristown, N.J.: General Learning Press, 1974.

Rudyard Kipling

BAA BAA, BLACK SHEEP

Baa Baa, Black Sheep,
Have you any wool?
Yes, Sir, yes, Sir, three bags full.
One for the Master, one for the Dame —
None for the Little Boy that cries down the lane.

Nursery Rhyme.

THE FIRST BAG

When I was in my father's house, I was in a better place.

They were putting Punch to bed — the *ayah* and the *hamal* and Meeta, the big *Surti* boy with the red and gold turban. Judy, already tucked inside her mosquito-curtains, was nearly asleep. Punch had been allowed to stay up for dinner. Many privileges had been accorded to Punch within the last ten days, and a greater kindness from the people of his world had encompassed his ways and works, which were mostly obstreperous. He sat on the edge of his bed and swung his bare legs defiantly.

"Punch-*baba* going to bye-lo?" said the *ayah* suggestively.

"No," said Punch. "Punch-*baba* wants the story about the Ranee that was turned into a tiger. Meeta must tell it, and the *hamal* shall hide behind the door and make tiger-noises at the proper time."

"But Judy-*baba* will wake up," said the *ayah*.

"Judy-*baba* is waked," piped a small voice from the mosquito-curtains. "There was a Ranee that lived at Delhi. Go on, Meeta," and she fell fast asleep again while Meeta began the story.

Never had Punch secured the telling of that tale with so little opposition. He reflected for a long time. The *hamal* made the tiger-noises in twenty different keys.

" 'Top!" said Punch authoritatively. "Why doesn't Papa come in and say he is going to give me *put-put?*"

"Punch-*baba* is going away," said the *ayah*. "In another week there will be no Punch-*baba* to pull my hair any more." She sighed softly, for the boy of the household was very dear to her heart.

"Up the Ghauts in a train?" said Punch, standing on his bed. "All the way to Nassick where the Ranee-Tiger lives?"

"Not to Nassick this year, little Sahib," said Meeta, lifting him on his shoulder. "Down to the sea where the cocoanuts are thrown, and across the sea in a big ship. Will you take Meeta with you to *Belait?*"

"You shall all come," said Punch, from the height of Meeta's strong arms. "Meeta and the *ayah* and the *hamal* and Bhini-in-the-Garden, and the salaam-Captain-Sahib-snake-man."

There was no mockery in Meeta's voice when he replied — "Great is the Sahib's favour," and laid the little man down in the bed, while the *ayah*, sitting in the moonlight at the doorway, lulled him to sleep with an interminable canticle such as they sing in the Roman Catholic Church at Parel. Punch curled himself into a ball and slept.

Next morning Judy shouted that there was a rat in the nursery, and thus he forgot to tell her the wonderful news. It did not much matter, for Judy was only three and she would not have understood. But Punch was five; and he knew that going to England would be much nicer than a trip to Nassick.

* * *

Papa and Mamma sold the brougham and the piano, and stripped the house, and curtailed the allowance of crockery for the daily meals, and took long council together over a bundle of letters bearing the Rocklington postmark.

"The worst of it is that one can't be certain of anything," said Papa, pulling his moustache. "The letters in themselves are excellent, and the terms are moderate enough."

"The worst of it is that the children will grow up away from me," thought Mamma: but she did not say it aloud.

"We are only one case among hundreds," said Papa bitterly. "You shall go Home again in five years, dear."

"Punch will be ten then — and Judy eight. Oh, how long and long and long the time will be! And we have to leave them among strangers."

"Punch is a cheery little chap. He's sure to make friends wherever he goes."

"And who could help loving my Ju?"

They were standing over the cots in the nursery late at night, and I think that Mamma was crying softly. After Papa had gone away, she knelt down by the side of Judy's cot. The *ayah* saw her and put up a prayer that the Memsahib might never find the love of her children taken away from her and given to a stranger.

Mamma's own prayer was a slightly illogical one. Summarised it ran: "Let strangers love my children and be as good to them as I should be, but let *me* preserve their love and their confidence for ever and ever. Amen." Punch scratched himself in his sleep, and Judy moaned a little.

Next day they all went down to the sea, and there was a scene at the Apollo Bunder when Punch discovered that Meeta could not come too, and Judy learned that the *ayah* must be left behind. But Punch found a thousand fascinating things in the rope, block, and steam-pipe line on the big P. and O. steamer long before Meeta and the *ayah* had dried their tears.

"Come back, Punch-*baba,*" said the *ayah.*

"Come back," said Meeta, "and be a *Burra Sahib*" (a big man).

"Yes," said Punch, lifted up in his father's arms to wave good-bye. "Yes, I will come back, and I will be a *Burra Sahib Bahadur!*" (a very big man indeed).

At the end of the first day Punch demanded to be set down in England, which he was certain must be close at hand. Next day there was a merry breeze, and Punch was very sick. "When I come back to Bombay," said Punch on his recovery, "I will come by the road — in a broom-*gharri.* This is a very naughty ship."

The Swedish boatswain consoled him, and he modified his opinions as the voyage went on. There was so much to see and to handle and ask questions about that Punch nearly forgot the *ayah* and Meeta and the *hamal,* and with difficulty remembered a few words of the Hindustani, once his second-speech.

But Judy was much worse. The day before the steamer reached Southampton, Mamma asked her if she would not like to see the *ayah* again. Judy's blue eyes turned to the stretch of sea that had swallowed all her tiny past, and said: "*Ayah!* What *ayah?*"

Mamma cried over her, and Punch marvelled. It was then that he heard for the first time Mamma's passionate appeal to him never to let Judy forget Mamma. Seeing that Judy was young, ridiculously young, and that Mamma, every evening for four weeks past, had come into the cabin to sing her and Punch to sleep with a mysterious rune that he called "Sonny, my soul," Punch could not understand what Mamma meant. But he strove to do his duty; for, the moment Mamma left the cabin, he said to Judy, "Ju, you bemember Mamma?"

" 'Torse I do," said Judy.

"Then *always* bemember Mamma, 'r else I won't give you the paper ducks that the red-haired Captain Sahib cut out for me."

So Judy promised always to "bemember Mamma."

Many and many a time was Mamma's command laid upon Punch, and Papa would say the same thing with an insistence that awed the child.

"You must make haste and learn to write, Punch," said Papa, "and then you'll be able to write letters to us in Bombay."

"I'll come into your room," said Punch, and Papa choked.

Papa and Mamma were always choking in those days. If Punch took Judy to task for not "bemembering," they choked. If Punch sprawled on the sofa in the Southampton lodging-house and sketched his future in purple and gold, they choked; and so they did if Judy put her mouth up for a kiss.

Through many days all four were vagabonds on the face of the earth — Punch with no one to give orders to, Judy too young for anything, and Papa and Mamma grave, distracted, and choking.

"Where," demanded Punch, wearied of a loathsome contrivance on four wheels with a mound of luggage atop — "*where* is our broom-*gharri?* This thing talks so much that *I* can't talk. Where is our *own* broom-*gharri?* When I was at Bandstand before we comed away, I asked Inverarity Sahib why he was sitting in it, and he said it was his own. And I said, 'I will *give* it you,' — I like Inverarity Sahib, — and I said, 'Can you put your legs through the pully-wag loops by the windows?' And Inverarity Sahib said No, and laughed. *I* can put my legs through the pully-wag loops. I can put my legs through *these* pully-wag loops. Look! Oh, Mamma's crying again! I didn't know I wasn't not to do *so.*"

Punch drew his legs out of the loops of the four-wheeler; the door opened, and he slid to the earth, in a cascade of parcels, at the door of an austere little villa whose gates bore the legend "Downe Lodge." Punch gathered himself together and eyed the house with disfavour. It stood on a sandy road, and a cold wind tickled his knickerbockered legs.

"Let us go away," said Punch. "This is not a pretty place."

But Mamma and Papa and Judy had left the cab, and all the luggage was being taken into the house. At the doorstep stood a woman in black, and she smiled largely, with dry, chapped lips. Behind her was a man, big, bony, gray, and lame as to one leg — behind him a boy of twelve, black-haired and oily in appearance. Punch surveyed the trio, and advanced without fear, as he had been accustomed to do in Bombay when callers came and he happened to be playing in the verandah.

"How do you do?" said he. "I am Punch." But they were all looking at the luggage — all except the gray man, who shook hands with Punch, and said he was "a smart little fellow." There was much running about and banging of boxes, and Punch curled himself up on the sofa in the dining-room and considered things.

"I don't like these people," said Punch. "But never mind. We'll go away soon. We have always went away soon from everywhere. I wish we was gone back to Bombay *soon.*"

The wish bore no fruit. For six days Mamma wept at intervals, and showed the woman in black all Punch's clothes — a liberty which Punch resented. "But p'raps she's a new white *ayah,*" he thought. "I'm to call her Antirosa, but she doesn't call *me* Sahib. She says just Punch," he confided to Judy. "What is Antirosa?"

Judy didn't know. Neither she nor Punch had heard anything of an animal called an aunt. Their world had been Papa and Mamma, who knew everything, permitted everything, and loved everybody — even Punch when he used to go into the garden at Bombay and fill his nails with mould after the weekly nail-cutting, because, as he explained between two strokes of the slipper to his sorely tried Father, his fingers "felt so new at the ends."

In an undefined way Punch judged it advisable to keep both parents between himself and the woman in black and the boy in black hair. He did not approve of them. He liked the gray man, who had expressed a wish to be called "Uncleharri." They nodded at each other when they met, and the gray man showed him a little ship with rigging that took up and down.

"She is a model of the *Brisk* — the little *Brisk* that was sore exposed that day at Navarino." The gray man hummed the last words and fell into a reverie. "I'll tell you about Navarino, Punch, when we go for walks together; and you mustn't touch the ship, because she's the *Brisk*."

Long before that walk, the first of many, was taken, they roused Punch and Judy in the chill dawn of a February morning to say Good-bye; and, of all people in the wide earth, to Papa and Mamma — both crying this time. Punch was very sleepy and Judy was cross.

"Don't forget us," pleaded Mamma. "Oh, my little son, don't forget us, and see that Judy remembers too."

"I've told Judy to bemember," said Punch, wriggling, for his father's beard tickled his neck. "I've told Judy — ten — forty — 'leven thousand times. But Ju's so young — quite a baby — isn't she?"

"Yes," said Papa, "quite a baby, and you must be good to Judy, and make haste to learn to write and — and — and ——"

Punch was back in his bed again. Judy was fast asleep, and there was the rattle of a cab below. Papa and Mamma had gone away. Not to Nassick; that was across the sea. To some place much nearer, of course, and equally of course they would return. They came back after dinner-parties, and Papa had come back after he had been to a place called "The Snows," and Mamma with him, to Punch and Judy at Mrs. Inverarity's house in Marine Lines. Assuredly they would come back again. So Punch fell asleep till the true morning, when the black-haired boy met him with the information that Papa and Mamma had gone to Bombay, and that he and Judy were to stay at Downe Lodge "for ever." Antirosa, tearfully appealed to for a contradiction, said that Harry had spoken the truth, and that it behooved Punch to fold up his clothes neatly on going to bed. Punch went out and wept bitterly with Judy, into whose fair head he had driven some ideas of the meaning of separation.

When a matured man discovers that he has been deserted by Providence, deprived of his God, and cast, without help, comfort, or sympathy, upon a world which is new and strange to him, his despair, which may find expression in evil-living, the writing of his experiences, or the more satisfactory diversion of suicide, is generally supposed to be impressive. A child, under exactly similar circumstances as far as its knowledge goes, cannot very well curse God and die. It howls till its nose is red, its eyes are sore, and its head aches. Punch and Judy, through no fault of their own, had lost all their world. They sat in the hall and cried; the black-haired boy looking on from afar.

The model of the ship availed nothing, though the gray man assured Punch that he might pull the rigging up and down as much as he pleased; and Judy was promised free entry into the kitchen. They wanted Papa and Mamma gone to Bombay beyond the seas, and their grief while it lasted was without remedy.

When the tears ceased the house was very still. Antirosa had decided that it was better to let the children "have their cry out," and the boy had gone to school. Punch raised his head from the floor and sniffed mournfully. Judy was nearly asleep. Three short years had not taught her how to bear sorrow with full knowledge. There was a distant, dull boom in the air — a repeated heavy thud. Punch knew that sound in Bombay in the Monsoon. It was the sea — the sea that must be traversed before any one could get to Bombay.

"Quick, Ju!" he cried, "we're close to the sea. I can hear it! Listen! That's where they've went. P'raps we can catch them if we was in time. They didn't mean to go without us. They've only forgot."

"Iss," said Judy. "They've only forgotted. Less go to the sea."

The hall-door was open, and so was the garden-gate.

"It's very, very big, this place," he said, looking cautiously down the road, "and we will get lost; but *I* will find a man and order him to take me back to my house — like I did in Bombay."

He took Judy by the hand, and the two ran hatless in the direction of the sound of the sea. Downe Villa was almost the last of a range of newly-built houses running out, through a field of brick-mounds, to a heath where gypsies occasionally camped and where the Garrison Artillery of Rocklington practised. There were few people to be seen, and the children might have been taken for those of the soldiery who ranged far. Half an hour the wearied little legs tramped across heath, potato-patch, and sand-dune.

"I'se so tired," said Judy, "and Mamma will be angry."

"Mamma's *never* angry. I suppose she is waiting at the sea now while Papa gets tickets. We'll find them and go along with. Ju, you mustn't sit down. Only a little more and we'll come to the sea. Ju, if you sit down I'll *thmack* you!" said Punch.

They climbed another dune, and came upon the great gray sea at low tide. Hundreds of crabs were scuttling about the beach, but there was no trace of Papa and Mamma, not even of a ship upon the waters — nothing but sand and mud for miles and miles.

And "Uncleharri" found them by chance — very muddy and very forlorn — Punch dissolved in tears, but trying to divert Judy with an "ickle trab," and Judy wailing to the pitiless horizon for "Mamma, Mamma!" — and again "Mamma!"

THE SECOND BAG

Ah, well-a-day, for we are souls bereaved!
Of all the creatures under Heaven's wide
scope
We are most hopeless, who had once most
hope,
And most beliefless, who had most believed.

The City of Dreadful Night.

All this time not a word about Black Sheep. He came later, and Harry the black-haired boy was mainly responsible for his coming.

Judy — who could help loving little Judy? — passed, by special permit, into the kitchen, and thence straight to Aunty Rosa's heart. Harry was Aunty Rosa's one child, and Punch was the extra boy about the house. There was no special place for him or his little affairs, and he was forbidden to sprawl on sofas and explain his ideas about the manufacture of this world and his hopes for his future. Sprawling was lazy and wore out sofas, and little boys were not expected to talk. They were talked to, and the talking to was intended for the benefit of their morals. As the unquestioned despot of the house at Bombay, Punch could not quite understand how he came to be of no account in this his new life.

Harry might reach across the table and take what he wanted; Judy might point and get what she wanted. Punch was forbidden to do either. The gray man was his great hope and stand-by for many months after Mamma and Papa left, and he had forgotten to tell Judy to "bemember Mamma."

This lapse was excusable, because in the interval he had been introduced by Aunty Rosa to two very impressive things — an abstraction called God, the intimate friend and ally of Aunty Rosa, generally believed to live behind the kitchen range because it was hot there — and a dirty brown book filled with unintelligible dots and marks. Punch was always anxious to oblige everybody. He therefore welded the story of the Creation on to what he could recollect of his Indian fairy tales, and scandalised Aunty Rosa by repeating the result to Judy. It was a sin, a grievous sin, and Punch was talked to for a quarter of an hour. He could not understand where the iniquity came in, but was careful not to repeat the offence, because Aunty Rosa told him that God had heard every word he had said and was very angry. If this were true, why didn't God come and say so, thought Punch, and dismissed the matter from his mind. Afterwards he learned to know the Lord as the only thing in the world more awful than Aunty Rosa — as a Creature that stood in the background and counted the strokes of the cane.

But the reading was, just then, a much more serious matter than any creed. Aunty Rosa sat him upon a table and told him that A B meant ab.

"Why?" said Punch. "A is a and B is bee. *Why* does A B mean ab?"

"Because I tell you it does," said Aunty Rosa, "and you've got to say it."

Punch said it accordingly, and for a month, hugely against his will, stumbled through the brown book, not in the least comprehending what it meant. But Uncle Harry, who walked much and generally alone, was wont to come into the nursery and suggest to Aunty Rosa that Punch should walk with him. He seldom spoke, but he showed Punch all Rocklington, from the mud-banks and the sand of the back-bay to the great harbours where ships lay at anchor, and the dockyards where the hammers were never still, and the marine-store shops, and the shiny brass counters in the Offices where Uncle Harry went once every three months with a slip of blue paper and received sovereigns in exchange; for he held a wound-pension. Punch heard, too, from his lips the story of the battle of Navarino, where the sailors of the Fleet, for three days afterwards, were deaf as posts and could only sign to each other. "That was because of the noise of the guns," said Uncle Harry, "and I have got the wadding of a bullet somewhere inside me now."

Punch regarded him with curiosity. He had not the least idea what wadding was, and his notion of a bullet was a dockyard cannon-ball bigger than his own head. How could Uncle Harry keep a cannon-ball inside him? He was ashamed to ask, for fear Uncle Harry might be angry.

Punch had never known what anger — real anger — meant until one terrible day when Harry had taken his paint-box to paint a boat with, and Punch had protested. Then Uncle Harry had appeared on the scene and, muttering something about "strangers' children," had with a stick smitten the black-haired boy across the shoulders till he wept and yelled, and Aunty Rosa came in and abused Uncle Harry for cruelty to his own flesh and blood, and Punch shuddered to the tips of his shoes. "It wasn't my fault," he explained to the boy, but both Harry and Aunty Rosa said that it was, and that Punch had told tales, and for a week there were no more walks with Uncle Harry.

But that week brought a great joy to Punch.

He had repeated till he was thrice weary the statement that "the Cat lay on the Mat and the Rat came in."

"Now I can truly read," said Punch, "and now I will never read anything in the world."

He put the brown book in the cupboard where his school-books lived, and accidentally tumbled out a venerable volume, without covers, labelled "Sharpe's Magazine." There was the most portentous picture of a griffin on the first page, with verses below. The griffin carried off one sheep a day from a German village, till a man came with a "falchion" and split the griffin open. Goodness only knew what a falchion was, but there was the Griffin, and his history was an improvement upon the eternal Cat.

"This," said Punch, "means things, and now I will know all about everything in all the world." He read till the light failed, not understanding a tithe of the meaning, but tantalised by glimpses of new worlds hereafter to be revealed.

"What is a 'falchion'? What is a 'e-wee lamb?' What is a 'base *uss*urper'? What is a 'verdant me-ad'?" he demanded with flushed cheeks, at bedtime, of the astonished Aunty Rosa.

"Say your prayers and go to sleep," she replied, and that was all the help Punch then or afterwards found at her hands in the new and delightful exercise of reading.

"Aunty Rosa only knows about God and things like that," argued Punch. "Uncle Harry will tell me."

The next walk proved that Uncle Harry could not help either; but he allowed Punch to talk, and even sat down on a bench to hear about the Griffin. Other walks brought other stories as Punch ranged further afield, for the house held large store of old books that no one ever opened — from "Frank Fairlegh" in serial numbers, and the earlier poems of Tennyson, contributed anonymously to "Sharpe's Magazine," to '62 Exhibition Catalogues, gay with colours and delightfully incomprehensible, and odd leaves of "Gulliver's Travels."

As soon as Punch could string a few pothooks together, he wrote to Bombay, demanding by return of post "all the books in all the world." Papa could not comply with this modest indent, but sent "Grimm's Fairy Tales" and a Hans Andersen. That was enough. If he were only left alone, Punch could pass, at any hour he chose, into a land of his own, beyond reach of Aunty Rosa and her God, Harry and his teasements, and Judy's claims to be played with.

"Don't disturve me, I'm reading. Go and play in the kitchen," grunted Punch. "Aunty Rosa lets *you* go there." Judy was cutting her second teeth and was fretful. She appealed to Aunty Rosa, who descended on Punch.

"I was reading," he explained, "reading a book. I *want* to read."

"You're only doing that to show off," said Aunty Rosa. "But we'll see. Play with Judy now, and don't open a book for a week."

Judy did not pass a very enjoyable playtime with Punch, who was consumed with indignation. There was a pettiness at the bottom of the prohibition which puzzled him.

"It's what I like to do," he said, "and she's found out that and stopped me. Don't cry, Ju — it wasn't your fault — *please* don't cry, or she'll say I made you."

Ju loyally mopped up her tears, and the two played in their nursery, a room in the basement and half underground, to which they were regularly sent after the midday dinner while Aunty Rosa slept. She drank wine — that is to say, something from a bottle in the cellaret — for her stomach's sake, but if she did not fall asleep she would sometimes come into the nursery to see that the children were really playing. Now bricks, wooden hoops, ninepins, and chinaware cannot amuse for ever, especially when all Fairyland is to be won by the mere opening of a book, and, as often as not, Punch would be discovered reading to Judy or telling her interminable tales. That was an offence in the eyes of the law, and Judy would be whisked off by Aunty Rosa, while Punch was left to play alone, "and be sure that I hear you doing it."

It was not a cheering employ, for he had to make a playful noise. At last, with infinite craft, he devised an arrangement whereby the table could be supported as to three legs on toy bricks, leaving the fourth clear to bring down on the floor. He could work the table with one hand and hold a book with the other. This he did till an evil day when Aunty Rosa pounced upon him unawares and told him that he was "acting a lie."

"If you're old enough to do that," she said — her temper was always worst after dinner — "you're old enough to be beaten."

"But — I'm — I'm not a animal!" said Punch, aghast. He remembered Uncle Harry and the stick, and turned white. Aunty Rosa had hidden a light cane behind her, and Punch was beaten then and there over the shoulders. It was a revelation to him. The room-door was shut, and he was left to weep himself into repentance and work out his own gospel of life.

Aunty Rosa, he argued, had the power to beat him with many stripes. It was unjust and cruel, and Mamma and Papa would never have allowed it. Unless perhaps, as Aunty Rosa seemed to imply, they had sent secret orders. In which case he was abandoned indeed. It would be discreet in the future to propitiate Aunty Rosa, but then, again, even in matters in which he was innocent, he had been accused of wishing to "show off." He had "shown off" before visitors when he had attacked a strange gentleman — Harry's uncle, not his own — with requests for information about the Griffin and the falchion, and the precise nature of the Tilbury in which Frank Fairlegh rode — all points of paramount interest which he was bursting to understand. Clearly it would not do to pretend to care for Aunty Rosa.

At this point Harry entered and stood afar off, eying Punch, a dishevelled heap in the corner of the room, with disgust.

"You're a liar — a young liar," said Harry, with great unction, "and you're to have tea down here because you're not fit to speak to us. And you're not to speak to Judy again till Mother gives you leave. You'll corrupt her. You're only fit to associate with the servant. Mother says so."

Having reduced Punch to a second agony of tears, Harry departed upstairs with the news that Punch was still rebellious.

Uncle Harry sat uneasily in the dining-room. "Damn it all, Rosa," said he at last, "can't you leave the child alone? He's a good enough little chap when I meet him."

"He puts on his best manners with you, Henry," said Aunty Rosa, "but I'm afraid, I'm very much afraid, that he is the Black Sheep of the family."

Harry heard and stored up the name for future use. Judy cried till she was bidden to stop, her brother not being worth tears; and the evening concluded with the return of Punch to the upper regions and a private sitting at which all the blinding horrors of Hell were revealed to Punch with such store of imagery as Aunty Rosa's narrow mind possessed.

Most grievous of all was Judy's round-eyed reproach, and Punch went to bed in the depths of the Valley of Humiliation. He shared his room with Harry, and knew the torture in store. For an hour and a half he had to answer that young gentleman's questions as to his motives for telling a lie, and a grievous lie, the precise quantity of punishment inflicted by Aunty Rosa, and had also to profess his deep gratitude for such religious instruction as Harry thought fit to impart.

From that day began the downfall of Punch, now Black Sheep.

"Untrustworthy in one thing, untrustworthy in all," said Aunty Rosa, and Harry felt that Black Sheep was delivered into his hands. He would wake him up in the night to ask him why he was such a liar.

"I don't know," Punch would reply.

"Then don't you think you ought to get up and pray to God for a new heart?"

"Y-yess."

"Get out and pray, then!" And Punch would get out of bed with raging hate in his heart against all the world, seen and unseen. He was always tumbling into trouble. Harry had a knack of cross-examining him as to his day's doings, which seldom failed to lead him, sleepy and savage, into half a dozen contradictions — all duly reported to Aunty Rosa next morning.

"But it *wasn't* a lie," Punch would begin, charging into a laboured explanation that landed him more hopelessly in the mire. "I said that I didn't say my prayers *twice* over in the day, and *that* was on Tuesday. *Once* I did. I *know* I did, but Harry said I didn't," and so forth, till the tension brought tears, and he was dismissed from the table in disgrace.

"You usen't to be as bad as this," said Judy, awe-stricken at the catalogue of Black Sheep's crimes. "Why are you so bad now?"

"I don't know," Black Sheep would reply. "I'm not, if I only wasn't bothered upside down. I know what I *did,* and I want to say so; but Harry always makes it out different somehow, and Aunty Rosa doesn't believe a word I say. Oh, Ju! don't *you* say I'm bad too."

"Aunty Rosa says you are," said Judy. "She told the Vicar so when he came yesterday."

"Why does she tell all the people outside the house about me? It isn't fair," said Black Sheep. "When I was in Bombay, and was bad — *doing* bad, not made-up bad like this — Mamma told Papa, and Papa told me he knew, and that was all. *Outside* people didn't know too — even Meeta didn't know."

"I don't remember," said Judy wistfully. "I was all little then. Mamma was just as fond of you as she was of me, wasn't she?"

"'Course she was. So was Papa. So was everybody."

"Aunty Rosa likes me more than she does you. She says that you are a Trial and a Black Sheep, and I'm not to speak to you more than I can help."

"Always? Not outside of the times when you mustn't speak to me at all?"

Judy nodded her head mournfully. Black Sheep turned away in despair, but Judy's arms were round his neck.

"Never mind, Punch," she whispered. "I *will* speak to you just the same as ever and ever. You're my own own brother, though you are — though Aunty Rosa says you're Bad, and Harry says you're a little coward. He says that if I pulled your hair hard, you'd cry."

"Pull, then," said Punch.

Judy pulled gingerly.

"Pull harder — as hard as you can! There! I don't mind how much you pull it *now.* If you'll speak to me same as ever I'll let you pull it as much as you like — pull it out if you like. But I know if Harry came and stood by and made you do it, I'd cry."

So the two children sealed the compact with a kiss, and Black Sheep's heart was cheered within him, and by extreme caution and careful avoidance of Harry he acquired virtue, and was allowed to read undisturbed for a week. Uncle Harry took him for walks, and consoled him with rough tenderness, never calling him Black Sheep. "It's good for you, I suppose, Punch," he used to say. "Let us sit down. I'm getting tired." His steps led him now not to the beach, but to the Cemetery of Rocklington, amid the potato-fields. For hours the gray man would sit on a tombstone, while Black Sheep read epitaphs, and then with a sigh would stump home again.

"I shall lie there soon," said he to Black Sheep, one winter evening, when his face showed white as a worn silver coin under the light of the lychgate. "You needn't tell Aunty Rosa."

A month later, he turned sharp round, ere half a morning walk was completed, and stumped back to the house. "Put me to bed,

Rosa," he muttered. "I've walked my last. The wadding has found me out."

They put him to bed, and for a fortnight the shadow of his sickness lay upon the house, and Black Sheep went to and fro unobserved. Papa had sent him some new books, and he was told to keep quiet. He retired into his own world, and was perfectly happy. Even at night his felicity was unbroken. He could lie in bed and string himself tales of travel and adventure while Harry was downstairs.

"Uncle Harry's going to die," said Judy, who now lived almost entirely with Aunty Rosa.

"I'm very sorry," said Black Sheep soberly. "He told me that a long time ago."

Aunty Rosa heard the conversation. "Will nothing check your wicked tongue?" she said angrily. There were blue circles round her eyes.

Black Sheep retreated to the nursery and read "Cometh up as a Flower" with deep and uncomprehending interest. He had been forbidden to open it on account of its "sinfulness," but the bonds of the Universe were crumbling, and Aunty Rosa was in great grief.

"I'm glad," said Black Sheep. "She's unhappy now. It wasn't a lie, though. *I* knew. He told me not to tell."

That night Black Sheep woke with a start. Harry was not in the room, and there was a sound of sobbing on the next floor. Then the voice of Uncle Harry, singing the song of the Battle of Navarino, came through the darkness: —

"Our vanship was the Asia —
The Albion and Genoa!"

"He's getting well," thought Black Sheep, who knew the song through all its seventeen verses. But the blood froze at his little heart as he thought. The voice leapt an octave, and rang shrill as a boatswain's pipe: —

"And next came on the lovely Rose,
The Philomel, her fire-ship, closed,
And the little Brisk was sore exposed
That day at Navarino."

"That day at Navarino, Uncle Harry!" shouted Black Sheep, half wild with excitement and fear of he knew not what.

A door opened, and Aunty Rosa screamed up the staircase: "Hush! For God's sake hush, you little devil. Uncle Harry is *dead!"*

THE THIRD BAG

Journeys end in lovers' meeting,
Every wise man's son doth know.

"I wonder what will happen to me now," thought Black Sheep, when semi-pagan rites peculiar to the burial of the Dead in middle-class houses had been accomplished, and Aunty Rosa, awful in black crape, had returned to this life. "I don't think I've done anything bad that she knows of. I suppose I will soon. She will be very cross after Uncle Harry's dying, and Harry will be cross too. I'll keep in the nursery."

Unfortunately for Punch's plans, it was decided that he should be sent to a day-school which Harry attended. This meant a morning walk with Harry, and perhaps an evening one; but the prospect of freedom in the interval was refreshing. "Harry'll tell everything I do, but I won't do anything," said Black Sheep. Fortified with this virtuous resolution, he went to school only to find that Harry's version of his character had preceded him, and that life was a burden in consequence. He took stock of his associates. Some of them were unclean, some of them talked in dialect, many dropped their h's, and there were two Jews and a negro, or some one quite as dark, in the assembly. "That's a *hubshi,*" said Black Sheep to himself. "Even Meeta used to laugh at a *hubshi*. I don't think this is a proper place." He was indignant for at least an hour, till he reflected that any expostulation on his part would be by Aunty Rosa construed into "showing off," and that Harry would tell the boys.

"How do you like school?" said Aunty Rosa at the end of the day.

"I think it is a very nice place," said Punch quietly.

"I suppose you warned the boys of Black Sheep's character?" said Aunty Rosa to Harry.

"Oh, yes," said the censor of Black Sheep's morals. "They know all about him."

"If I was with my father," said Black Sheep, stung to the quick, "I shouldn't *speak* to those boys. He wouldn't let me. They live in shops. I saw them go into shops — where their fathers live and sell things."

"You're too good for that school, are you?" said Aunty Rosa, with a bitter smile. "You ought to be grateful, Black Sheep, that those boys speak to you at all. It isn't every school that takes little liars."

Harry did not fail to make much capital out of Black Sheep's ill-considered remark; with the result that several boys, including the *hubshi,* demonstrated to Black Sheep the eternal equality of the human race by smacking his head, and his consolation from Aunty Rosa was that it "served him right for being vain." He learned, however, to keep his opinions to himself, and by propitiating Harry in carrying books and the like to get a little peace. His existence was not too joyful. From nine till twelve he was at school, and from two to four, except on Saturdays. In the evenings he was sent down into the nursery to prepare his lessons for the next day, and every night came the dreaded cross-questionings at Harry's hand. Of Judy he saw but little. She was deeply religious — at six years of age Religion is easy to come by — and sorely divided between her natural love for Black Sheep and her love for Aunty Rosa, who could do no wrong.

The lean woman returned that love with interest, and Judy, when she dared, took advantage of this for the remission of Black Sheep's penalties. Failures in lessons at school were punished at home by a week without reading other than school-books, and Harry brought the news of such a failure with glee. Further, Black Sheep was then bound to repeat his lessons at bedtime to Harry, who generally succeeded in making him break down, and consoled him by gloomiest forebodings for the morrow. Harry was at once spy, practical joker, inquisitor, and Aunty Rosa's deputy executioner. He filled his many posts to admiration. From his actions, now that Uncle Harry was dead, there was no appeal. Black Sheep had not been permitted to keep any self-respect at school: at home he was of course utterly discredited, and grateful for any pity that the servant-girls — they changed frequently at Downe Lodge because they, too, were liars — might show. "You're just fit to row in the same boat with Black Sheep," was a sentiment that each new Jane or Eliza might expect to hear, before a month was over, from Aunty Rosa's lips; and Black Sheep was used to ask new girls whether they had yet been compared to him. Harry was "Master Harry" in their mouths; Judy was officially "Miss Judy"; but Black Sheep was never anything more than Black Sheep *tout court.*

As time went on and the memory of Papa and Mamma became wholly overlaid by the unpleasant task of writing them letters, under Aunty Rosa's eye, each Sunday, Black Sheep forgot what manner of life he had led in the beginning of things. Even Judy's appeals to "try and remember about Bombay" failed to quicken him.

"I can't remember," he said. "I know I used to give orders and Mamma kissed me."

"Aunty Rosa will kiss you if you are good," pleaded Judy.

"Ugh! I don't want to be kissed by Aunty Rosa. She'd say I was doing it to get something more to eat."

The weeks lengthened into months, and

the holidays came; but just before the holidays Black Sheep fell into deadly sin.

Among the many boys whom Harry had incited to "punch Black Sheep's head because he daren't hit back" was one, more aggravating than the rest, who, in an unlucky moment, fell upon Black Sheep when Harry was not near. The blows stung, and Black Sheep struck back at random with all the power at his command. The boy dropped and whimpered. Black Sheep was astounded at his own act, but, feeling the unresisting body under him, shook it with both his hands in blind fury and then began to throttle his enemy, meaning honestly to slay him. There was a scuffle, and Black Sheep was torn off the body by Harry and some colleagues, and cuffed home tingling but exultant. Aunty Rosa was out: pending her arrival, Harry set himself to lecture Black Sheep on the sin of murder — which he described as the offence of Cain.

"Why didn't you fight him fair? What did you hit him when he was down for, you little cur?"

Black Sheep looked up at Harry's throat and then at a knife on the dinner-table.

"I don't understand," he said wearily. "You always set him on me and told me I was a coward when I blubbed. Will you leave me alone until Aunty Rosa comes in? She'll beat me if you tell her I ought to be beaten; so it's all right."

"It's all wrong," said Harry magisterially. "You nearly killed him, and I shouldn't wonder if he dies."

"Will he die?" said Black Sheep.

"I dare say," said Harry, "and then you'll be hanged, and go to Hell."

"All right," said Black Sheep, picking up the table-knife. "Then I'll kill *you* now. You say things and do things, and — and *I* don't know how things happen, and you never leave me alone — and I don't care *what* happens!"

He ran at the boy with the knife, and Harry fled upstairs to his room, promising Black Sheep the finest thrashing in the world when Aunty Rosa returned. Black Sheep sat at the bottom of the stairs, the table-knife in his hand, and wept for that he had not killed Harry. The servant-girl came up from the kitchen, took the knife away, and consoled him. But Black Sheep was beyond consolation. He would be badly beaten by Aunty Rosa; then there would be another beating at Harry's hands; then Judy would not be allowed to speak to him; then the tale would be told at school, and then ———

There was no one to help and no one to care, and the best way out of the business was by death. A knife would hurt, but Aunty Rosa had told him, a year ago, that if he sucked paint he would die. He went into the nursery, unearthed the now disused Noah's Ark, and sucked the paint off as many animals as remained. It tasted abominable, but he had licked Noah's Dove clean by the time Aunty Rosa and Judy returned. He went upstairs and greeted them with: "Please, Aunty Rosa, I believe I've nearly killed a boy at school, and I've tried to kill Harry, and when you've done all about God and Hell, will you beat me and get it over?"

The tale of the assault as told by Harry could only be explained on the ground of possession by the Devil. Wherefore Black Sheep was not only most excellently beaten, once by Aunty Rosa and once, when thoroughly cowed down, by Harry, but he was further prayed for at family prayers, together with Jane, who had stolen a cold rissole from the pantry and snuffled audibly as her sin was brought before the Throne of Grace. Black Sheep was sore and stiff, but triumphant. He would die that very night and be rid of them all. No, he would ask for no forgiveness from Harry, and at bedtime would stand no questioning at Harry's hands, even though addressed as "Young Cain."

"I've been beaten," said he, "and I've done other things. I don't care what I do. If you speak to me to-night, Harry, I'll get out and try to kill you. Now you can kill me if you like."

Harry took his bed into the spare room, and Black Sheep lay down to die.

It may be that the makers of Noah's Arks know that their animals are likely to find their way into young mouths, and paint them accordingly. Certain it is that the common, weary next morning broke through the windows and found Black Sheep quite well and a good deal ashamed of himself, but richer by the knowledge that he could, in extremity, secure himself against Harry for the future.

When he descended to breakfast on the first day of the holidays, he was greeted with the news that Harry, Aunty Rosa, and Judy were going away to Brighton, while Black Sheep was to stay in the house with the servant. His latest outbreak suited Aunty Rosa's plans admirably. It gave her good excuse for leaving the extra boy behind. Papa in Bombay, who really seemed to know a young sinner's wants to the hour, sent, that week, a package of new books. And with these, and the society of Jane on board-wages, Black Sheep was left alone for a month.

The books lasted for ten days. They were eaten too quickly in long gulps of twelve hours at a time. Then came days of doing absolutely nothing, of dreaming dreams and marching imaginary armies up and down stairs, of counting the number of banisters, and of measuring the length and breadth of every room in handspans — fifty down the side, thirty across, and fifty back again. Jane made many friends, and, after receiving Black Sheep's assurance that he would not tell of her absences, went out daily for long hours. Black Sheep would follow the rays of the sinking sun from the kitchen to the dining-room and thence upward to his own bedroom until all was gray dark, and he ran down to the kitchen fire and read by its light. He was happy in that he was left alone and could read as much as he pleased. But, later, he grew afraid of the shadows of window-curtains and the flapping of doors and the creaking of shutters. He went out into the garden, and the rustling of the laurel-bushes frightened him.

He was glad when they all returned — Aunty Rosa, Harry, and Judy — full of news, and Judy laden with gifts. Who could help loving loyal little Judy? In return for all her merry babblement, Black Sheep confided to her that the distance from the hall-door to the top of the first landing was exactly one hundred and eighty-four handspans. He had found it out himself.

Then the old life recommenced; but with a difference, and a new sin. To his other iniquities Black Sheep had now added a phenomenal clumsiness — was as unfit to trust in action as he was in word. He himself could not account for spilling everything he touched, upsetting glasses as he put his hand out, and bumping his head against doors that were manifestly shut. There was a gray haze upon all his world, and it narrowed month by month, until at last it left Black Sheep almost alone with the flapping curtains that were so like ghosts, and the nameless terrors of broad daylight that were only coats on pegs after all.

Holidays came and holidays went, and Black Sheep was taken to see many people whose faces were all exactly alike; was beaten when occasion demanded, and tortured by Harry on all possible occasions; but defended by Judy through good and evil report, though she thereby drew upon herself the wrath of Aunty Rosa.

The weeks were interminable, and Papa and Mamma were clean forgotten. Harry had left school and was a clerk in a Banking-Office. Freed from his presence, Black Sheep resolved that he should no longer be deprived of his allowance of pleasure-reading. Consequently when he failed at school he reported that all was well, and conceived a large contempt for Aunty Rosa as he saw how easy it was to deceive her. "She says I'm a little liar when I don't tell lies, and now I do, she doesn't know," thought Black Sheep. Aunty Rosa had credited him in the past with petty cunning and stratagem that had never entered into his head. By the light of the sordid knowledge that she had revealed to him he paid her back full tale. In a household where the most innocent of his motives, his natural yearning for a little affection, had been interpreted into a desire for more bread and jam or to ingratiate himself with strangers and so put Harry into the background, his work was easy. Aunty Rosa could penetrate certain kinds of hypocrisy, but not all. He set his child's wits against hers, and was no more beaten. It grew monthly more and more of a trouble to read the school-books, and even the pages of the open-print story-books danced and were dim. So Black Sheep brooded in the shadows that fell about him and cut him off from the world, inventing horrible punishments for "dear Harry," or plotting another line of the tangled web of deception that he wrapped round Aunty Rosa.

Then the crash came and the cobwebs were broken. It was impossible to foresee everything. Aunty Rosa made personal enquiries as to Black Sheep's progress, and received information that startled her. Step by step, with a delight as keen as when she convicted an underfed housemaid of the theft of cold meats, she followed the trail of Black Sheep's delinquencies. For weeks and weeks, in order to escape banishment from the book-shelves, he made a fool of Aunty Rosa, of Harry, of God, of all the world! Horrible, most horrible, and evidence of an utterly depraved mind.

Black Sheep counted the cost. "It will only be one big beating, and then she'll put a card with 'Liar' on my back, same as she did before. Harry will whack me and pray for me, and she will pray for me at prayers and tell me I'm a Child of the Devil and give me hymns to learn. But I've done all my reading, and she never knew. She'll say she knew all along. She's an old liar too," said he.

For three days Black Sheep was shut in his own bedroom — to prepare his heart. "That means two beatings. One at school and one here. *That* one will hurt most." And it fell even as he thought. He was thrashed at school before the Jews and the *hubshi,* for the heinous crime of bringing home false reports of progress. He was thrashed at home by Aunty Rosa on the same count, and then the placard was produced. Aunty Rosa stitched it between his shoulders and bade him go for a walk with it upon him.

"If you make me do that," said Black Sheep very quietly, "I shall burn this house down, and perhaps I'll kill you. I don't know whether I *can* kill you — you're so bony — but I'll try."

No punishment followed this blasphemy, though Black Sheep held himself ready to work his way to Aunty Rosa's withered throat, and grip there till he was beaten off. Perhaps Aunty Rosa was afraid, for Black Sheep, having reached the Nadir of Sin, bore himself with a new recklessness.

In the midst of all the trouble there came a visitor from over the seas to Downe Lodge, who knew Papa and Mamma, and was commissioned to see Punch and Judy. Black Sheep was sent to the drawing-room and charged into a solid tea-table laden with china.

"Gently, gently, little man," said the visitor, turning Black Sheep's face to the light slowly. "What's that big bird on the palings?"

"What bird?" asked Black Sheep.

The visitor looked deep down into Black Sheep's eyes for half a minute, and then said suddenly: "Good God, the little chap's nearly blind!"

It was a most business-like visitor. He gave orders, on his own responsibility, that Black Sheep was not to go to school or open a book until Mamma came home. "She'll be here in three weeks, as you know of course," said he, "and I'm Inverarity Sahib. I ushered you into this wicked world, young man, and a nice use you seem to have made of your time. You must do nothing whatever. Can you do that?"

"Yes," said Punch in a dazed way. He had known that Mamma was coming. There was a chance, then, of another beating. Thank Heaven, Papa wasn't coming too. Aunty Rosa had said of late that he ought to be beaten by a man.

For the next three weeks Black Sheep was strictly allowed to do nothing. He spent his time in the old nursery looking at the broken toys, for all of which account must be rendered to Mamma. Aunty Rosa hit him over the hands if even a wooden boat was broken. But that sin was of small importance compared to the other revelations, so darkly hinted at by Aunty Rosa.

"When your Mother comes, and hears what I have to tell her, she may appreciate you properly," she said grimly, and mounted guard over Judy lest that small maiden should attempt to comfort her brother, to the peril of her soul.

And Mamma came — in a four-wheeler — fluttered with tender excitement. Such a Mamma! She was young, frivolously young, and beautiful, with delicately flushed cheeks, eyes that shone like stars, and a voice that needed no appeal of outstretched arms to draw little ones to her heart. Judy ran straight to her, but Black Sheep hesitated.

Could this wonder be "showing off"? She would not put out her arms when she knew of his crimes. Meantime was it possible that by fondling she wanted to get anything out of Black Sheep? Only all his love and all his confidence; but that Black Sheep did not know. Aunty Rosa withdrew and left Mamma, kneeling between her children, half laughing, half crying, in the very hall where Punch and Judy had wept five years before.

"Well, Chicks, do you remember me?"

"No," said Judy frankly, "but I said, 'God bless Papa and Mamma,' ev'vy night."

"A little," said Black Sheep. "Remember I wrote to you every week, anyhow. That isn't to show off, but 'cause of what comes afterwards."

"What comes after? What should come after, my darling boy?" And she drew him to her again. He came awkwardly, with many angles. "Not used to petting," said the quick Mother-soul. "The girl is."

"She's too little to hurt any one," thought Black Sheep, "and if I said I'd kill her, she'd be afraid. I wonder what Aunty Rosa will tell."

There was a constrained late dinner, at the end of which Mamma picked up Judy and put her to bed with endearments manifold. Faithless little Judy had shown her defection from Aunty Rosa already. And that lady resented it bitterly. Black Sheep rose to leave the room.

"Come and say good-night," said Aunty Rosa, offering a withered cheek.

"Huh!" said Black Sheep. "I never kiss you, and I'm not going to show off. Tell that woman what I've done, and see what she says."

Black Sheep climbed into bed feeling that he had lost Heaven after a glimpse through the gates. In half an hour "that woman" was bending over him. Black Sheep flung up his right arm. It wasn't fair to come and hit him in the dark. Even Aunty Rosa never tried that. But no blow followed.

"Are you showing off? I won't tell you anything more than Aunty Rosa has, and *she* doesn't know everything," said Black Sheep as clearly as he could for the arms around his neck.

"Oh, my son — my little, little son! It was my fault — *my* fault, darling —— and yet how could we help it? Forgive me, Punch." The voice died out in a broken whisper, and two hot tears fell on Black Sheep's forehead.

"Has she been making you cry too!" he asked. "You should see Jane cry. But you're nice, and Jane is a Born Liar — Aunty Rosa says so."

"Hush, Punch, hush! My boy, don't talk

like that. Try to love me a little bit — a little bit. You don't know how I want it. Punch-*baba,* come back to me! I am your Mother — your own Mother — and never mind the rest. I know — yes, I know, dear. It doesn't matter now. Punch, won't you care for me a little?"

It is astonishing how much petting a big boy of ten can endure when he is quite sure that there is no one to laugh at him. Black Sheep had never been made much of before, and here was this beautiful woman treating him — Black Sheep, the Child of the Devil and the inheritor of undying flame — as though he were a small God.

"I care for you a great deal, Mother dear," he whispered at last, "and I'm glad you've come back; but are you sure Aunty Rosa told you everything?"

"Everything. What *does* it matter? But" — the voice broke with a sob that was also laughter — "Punch, my poor, dear, half-blind darling, don't you think it was a little foolish of you?"

"*No*. It saved a lickin'."

Mamma shuddered and slipped away in the darkness to write a long letter to Papa. Here is an extract: —

> . . . Judy is a dear, plump little prig who adores the woman, and wears with as much gravity as her religious opinions — only eight, Jack! — a venerable horse-hair atrocity which she calls her Bustle! I have just burnt it, and the child is asleep in my bed as I write. She will come to me at once. Punch I cannot quite understand. He is well nourished, but seems to have been worried into a system of small deceptions which the woman magnifies into deadly sins. Don't you recollect our own upbringing, dear, when the Fear of the Lord was so often the beginning of falsehood? I shall win Punch to me before long. I am taking the children away into the country to get them to know me, and, on the whole, I am content, or shall be when you come home, dear boy, and then, thank God, we shall be all under one roof again at last!

Three months later, Punch, no longer Black Sheep, has discovered that he is the veritable owner of a real, live, lovely Mamma, who is also a sister, comforter, and friend, and that he must protect her till the Father comes home. Deception does not suit the part of a protector, and, when one can do anything without question, where is the use of deception?

"Mother would be awfully cross if you walked through that ditch," says Judy, continuing a conversation.

"Mother's never angry," says Punch. "She'd just say, 'You're a little *pagal*'; and that's not nice, but I'll show."

Punch walks through the ditch and mires himself to the knees. "Mother, dear," he shouts, "I'm just as dirty as I can pos-*sib*-ly be!"

"Then change your clothes as quickly as you pos-*sib*-ly can!" Mother's clear voice rings out from the house. "And don't be a little *pagal!*"

"There! 'Told you so," says Punch. "It's all different now, and we are just as much Mother's as if she had never gone."

Not altogether, O Punch, for when young lips have drunk deep of the bitter waters of Hate, Suspicion, and Despair, all the Love in the world will not wholly take away that knowledge; though it may turn darkened eyes for a while to the light, and teach Faith where no Faith was.

35 Mark Twain

from THE ADVENTURES OF HUCKLEBERRY FINN

EDITOR'S NOTE: *The Adventures of Huckleberry Finn* takes place along the Mississippi River in the early 1800s. Having run away from home, Huck escaped to Jackson's Island where he discovered Jim, the runaway slave of Miss Watson, a lady who had previously taken Huck into her home and tried to reform him. Jim and Huck live together for many days and become good friends. After Huck learns that there is a reward on Jim's head, he and Jim begin an escape down the Mississippi River. In the following passage, Huck argues with himself about helping a runaway slave to escape.

. . . Jim said it made him all over trembly and feverish to be so close to freedom. Well, I can tell you it made me all over trembly and feverish, too, to hear him, because I begun to get it through my head that he *was* most free — and who was to blame for it? Why, *me.* I couldn't get that out of my conscience, no how nor no way. It got to troubling me so I couldn't rest; I couldn't stay still in one place. It hadn't ever come home to me before, what this thing was that I was doing. But now it did; and it stayed with me, and scorched me more and more. I tried to make out to myself that *I* warn't to blame, because *I* didn't run Jim off from his rightful owner; but it warn't no use, conscience up and says, every time, "But you knowed he was running for his freedom, and you could 'a' paddled ashore and told somebody." That was so — I couldn't get around that no way. That was where it pinched. Conscience says to me, "What had poor Miss Watson done to you that you could see her nigger go off right under your eyes and never say one single word? What did that poor old woman do to you that you could treat her so mean? Why, she tried to learn you your book, she tried to learn you your manners, she tried to be good to you every way she knowed how. *That's* what she done."

I got to feeling so mean and so miserable I most wished I was dead. I fidgeted up and down the raft, abusing myself to myself, and Jim was fidgeting up and down past me. We neither of us could keep still. Every time he danced around and says, "Dah's Cairo!" it went through me like a shot, and I thought if it *was* Cairo I reckoned I would die of miserableness.

Jim talked out loud all the time while I was talking to myself. He was saying how the first thing he would do when he got to a free state he would go to saving up money and never spend a single cent, and when he got enough he would buy his wife, which was owned on a farm close to where Miss Watson lived; and then they would both work to buy the two children, and if their masters wouldn't sell them, they'd get an Ab'litionist to go and steal them.

It most froze me to hear such talk. He wouldn't ever dared to talk such talk in his life before. Just see what a difference it made in him the minute he judged he was about free. It was according to the old saying, "Give a nigger an inch and he'll take an ell." Thinks I, this is what comes of my not thinking. Here was this nigger, which I had as good as helped to run away, coming right out flat-footed and saying he would steal his children — children that belonged to a man I didn't even know; a man that hadn't ever done me no harm.

I was sorry to hear Jim say that, it was such a lowering of him. My conscience got to stirring me up hotter than ever, until at last I says to it, "Let up on me — it ain't too late yet — I'll paddle ashore at the first light and tell." I felt easy and happy and light as a feather right off. All my troubles was gone. I went to looking out sharp for a light, and sort of singing to myself. By and by one showed. Jim sings out:

"We's safe, Huck, we's safe! Jump up and crack yo' heels! Dat's de good ole Cairo at las', I jis knows it!"

I says:

"I'll take the canoe and go and see, Jim. It mightn't be, you know."

He jumped and got the canoe ready, and put his old coat in the bottom for me to set on, and give me the paddle; and as I shoved off, he says:

"Pooty soon I'll be a-shout'n' for joy, en I'll say, it's all on accounts o' Huck; I's a free man, en I couldn't ever ben free ef it hadn't ben for Huck; Huck done it. Jim won't ever forgit you, Huck; you's de bes' fren' Jim's ever had; en you's de *only* fren' ole Jim's got now."

I was paddling off, all in a sweat to tell on him; but when he says this, it seemed to kind of take the tuck all out of me. I went along slow then, and I warn't right down certain whether I was glad I started or whether I warn't. When I was fifty yards off, Jim says:

"Dah you goes, de ole true Huck; de on'y white genlman dat ever kep' his promise to ole Jim."

Well, I just felt sick. But I says, I *got* to do it — I can't get *out* of it. Right then along comes a skiff with two men in it with guns, and they stopped and I stopped. One of them says:

"What's that yonder?"

"A piece of raft," I says.

"Do you belong on it?"

"Yes, sir."

"Any men on it?"

"Only one, sir."

"Well, there's five niggers run off tonight up yonder, above the head of the bend. Is your man white or black?"

I didn't answer up promptly. I tried to, but the words wouldn't come. I tried for a second or two to brace up and out with it, but I warn't man enough — hadn't the spunk of a rabbit. I see I was weakening; so I just give up trying, and up and says:

"He's white."

"I reckon we'll go and see for ourselves."

"I wish you would," says I, "because it's pap that's there, and maybe you'd help me tow the raft ashore where the light is. He's sick — and so is mam and Mary Ann."

"Oh, the devil! we're in a hurry, boy. But I s'pose we've got to. Come, buckle to your paddle, and let's get along."

I buckled to my paddle and they laid to their oars. When we had made a stroke or two, I says:

"Pap'll be mighty much obliged to you, I can tell you. Everybody goes away when I want them to help me tow the raft ashore, and I can't do it by myself."

"Well, that's infernal mean. Odd, too. Say, boy, what's the matter with your father?"

"It's the — a — the — well, it ain't anything much."

They stopped pulling. It warn't but a mighty little ways to the raft now. One says:

"Boy, that's a lie. What *is* the matter with your pap? Answer up square now, and it'll be the better for you."

"I will, sir, I will, honest — but don't leave us, please. It's the — the — Gentlemen, if you'll only pull ahead, and let me heave you the headline, you won't have to come a-near the raft — please do."

"Set her back, John, set her back!" says one. They backed water, "Keep away, boy —

keep to looard. Confound it, I just expect the wind has blowed it to us. Your pap's got the smallpox, and you know it precious well. Why didn't you come out and say so? Do you want to spread it all over?"

"Well," says I, a-blubbering, "I've told everybody before, and they just went away and left us."

"Poor devil, there's something in that. We are right down sorry for you, but we — well, hang it, we don't want the smallpox, you see. Look here, I'll tell you what to do. Don't you try to land by yourself, or you'll smash everything to pieces. You float along down about twenty miles, and you'll come to a town on the left-hand side of the river. It will be long after sunup then, and when you ask for help you tell them your folks are all down with chills and fever. Don't be a fool again, and let people guess what is the matter. Now we're trying to do you a kindness; so you just put twenty miles between us, that's a good boy. It wouldn't do any good to land yonder where the light is — it's only a woodyard. Say, I reckon your father's poor, and I'm bound to say he's in pretty hard luck. Here, I'll put a twenty-dollar gold piece on this board, and you get it when it floats by. I feel mighty mean to leave you; but my kingdom! it won't do to fool with smallpox, don't you see?"

"Hold on, Parker," says the man, "here's a twenty to put on the board for me. Good-by, boy; you do as Mr. Parker told you, and you'll be all right."

"That's so, my boy — good-by, good-by. If you see any runaway niggers you get help and nab them, and you can make some money by it."

"Good-by, sir," says I; "I won't let no runaway niggers get by me if I can help it."

They went off and I got aboard the raft, feeling bad and low, because I knowed very well I had done wrong, and I see it warn't no use for me to try to learn to do right; a body that don't get *started* right when he's little ain't got no show — when the pinch comes there ain't nothing to back him up and keep him to his work, and so he gets beat. Then I thought a minute, and says to myself, hold on; s'pose you'd 'a' done right and give Jim up, would you felt better than what you do now? No, says I, I'd feel bad — I'd feel just the same way I do now. Well, then, says I, what's the use you learning to do right when it's troublesome to do right and ain't no trouble to do wrong, and the wages is just the same? I was stuck. I couldn't answer that. So I reckoned I wouldn't bother no more about it, but after this always do whichever come handiest at the time. . . .

* * *

EDITOR'S NOTE: After many adventures and separations, Huck finds that Jim has been captured. Huck and his friend Tom Sawyer decide to help Jim escape. Huck wants to do it easily and just open the door of the shack where Jim is. But Tom wants to plan a "proper escape." In the following passage, Tom and Huck plan the escape. Their obedience to the "rules" is typical of the older child.

We stopped talking, and got to thinking. By and by Tom says:

"Looky here, Huck, what fools we are to not think of it before! I bet I know where Jim is."

"No! Where?"

"In that hut down by the ash hopper. Why, looky here. When we was at dinner, didn't you see a nigger man go in there with some vittles?"

"Yes."

"What did you think the vittles was for?"

"For a dog."

"So 'd I. Well, it wasn't for a dog."

"Why?"

"Because part of it was watermelon."

"So it was — I noticed it. Well, it does beat all that I never thought about a dog not eating watermelon. It shows how a body can see and don't see at the same time."

"Well, the nigger unlocked the padlock when he went in, and he locked it again when he came out. He fetched uncle a key about the time we got up from table — same key, I bet. Watermelon shows man, lock shows prisoner; and it ain't likely there's two prisoners on such a little plantation, and where the people's all so kind and good. Jim's the prisoner. All right — I'm glad we found it out detective fashion; I wouldn't give shucks for any other way. Now you work your mind, and study out a plan to steal Jim, and I will study out one, too; and we'll take the one we like the best."

What a head for just a boy to have! If I had Tom Sawyer's head I wouldn't trade it off to be a duke, nor mate of a steamboat, nor clown in a circus, nor nothing I can think of. I went to thinking out a plan, but only just to be doing something; I knowed very well where the right plan was going to come from. Pretty soon Tom says:

"Ready?"

"Yes," I says.

"All right — bring it out."

"My plan is this," I says. "We can easy find out if it's Jim in there. Then get up my canoe tomorrow night, and fetch my raft over from the island. Then the first dark night that comes steal the key out of the old man's britches after he goes to bed, and shove off down the river on the raft with Jim, hiding daytimes and running nights, the way me and Jim used to do before. Wouldn't that plan work?"

"*Work?* Why, cert'nly it would work, like rats a-fighting. But it's too blame' simple; there ain't nothing *to* it. What's the good of a plan that ain't no more trouble than that? It's as mild as goosemilk. Why, Huck, it wouldn't make no more talk than breaking into a soap factory."

I never said nothing, because I warn't expecting nothing different; but I knowed mighty well that whenever he got *his* plan ready it wouldn't have none of them objections to it.

And it didn't. He told me what it was, and I see in a minute it was worth fifteen of mine for style, and would make Jim just as free a man as mine would, and maybe get us all killed besides. So I was satisfied, and said we would waltz in on it. I needn't tell what it was here, because I knowed it wouldn't stay the way it was. I knowed he would be changing it around every which way as we went along, and heaving in new bullinesses wherever he got a chance. And that is what he done.

Well, one thing was dead sure, and that was that Tom Sawyer was in earnest, and was actuly going to help steal that nigger out of slavery. That was the thing that was too many for me. Here was a boy that was respectable and well brung up; and had a character to lose; and folks at home that had characters; and he was bright and not leather-headed; and knowing and not ignorant; and not mean, but kind; and yet here he was, without any more pride, or rightness, or feeling, than to stoop to this business, and make himself a shame, and his family a shame, before everybody. I *couldn't* understand it no way at all. It was outrageous, and I knowed I ought to just up and tell him so; and so be his true friend, and let him quit the thing right where he was and save himself. And I *did* start to tell him; but he shut me up and says:

"Don't you reckon I know what I'm about? Don't I generly know what I'm about?"

"Yes."

"Didn't I *say* I was going to help steal the nigger?"

"Yes."

"*Well,* then."

That's all he said, and that's all I said. It warn't no use to say any more; because when he said he'd do a thing, he always done it. But *I* couldn't make out how he was willing to go into this thing; so I just let it go, and never bothered no more about it. If he was bound to have it so, *I* couldn't help it.

When we got home the house was all dark and still; so we went on down to the hut by the ash hopper for to examine it. We went through the yard so as to see what the hounds would do. They knowed us, and didn't make no more noise than country dogs is always doing when anything comes by in the night. When we got to the cabin we took a look at the front and the two sides, and on the side I warn't acquainted with — which was the north side — we found a square window hole, up tolerable high, with just one stout board nailed across it. I says:

"Here's the ticket. This hole's big enough for Jim to get through if we wrench off the board."

Tom says:

"It's as simple as tit-tat-toe, three-in-a-row, and as easy as playing hooky. I should *hope* we can find a way that's a little more complicated than *that,* Huck Finn."

"Well, then," I says, "how'll it do to saw him out, the way I done before I was murdered that time?"

"That's more *like,*" he says. "It's real mysterious, and troublesome, and good," he says; "but I bet we can find a way that's twice as long. There ain't no hurry; le's keep on looking around."

Betwixt the hut and the fence, on the back side, was a lean-to that joined the hut at the eaves, and was made out of plank. It was as long as the hut, but narrow — only about six foot wide. The door to it was at the south end, and was padlocked. Tom he went to the soap kettle and searched around, and fetched back the iron thing they lift the lid with; so he took it and prized out one of the staples. The chain fell down, and we opened the door and went in, and shut it, and struck a match, and see the shed was only built against a cabin and hadn't no connection with it; and there warn't no floor to the shed, nor nothing in it but some old rusty played-out hoes and spades and picks and a crippled plow. The match went out, and so did we, and shoved in the staple again, and the door was locked as good as ever. Tom was joyful. He says:

"Now we're all right. We'll *dig* him out. It'll take about a week!"

Then we started for the house, and I went in the back door — you only have to pull a buckskin latchstring, they don't fasten the doors — but that warn't romantical enough for Tom Sawyer; no way would do him but he must climb up the lightning rod. But after he got up half-way about three times, and missed fire and fell every time, and the last time most busted his brains out, he thought he'd got to give it up; but after he was rested he allowed he would give her one more turn for luck, and this time he made the trip.

In the morning we was up at break of day, and down to the nigger cabins to pet the dogs and make friends with the nigger that fed Jim — if it *was* Jim that was being fed. The niggers was just getting through breakfast and starting for the fields; and Jim's nigger was piling up a tin pan with bread and meat and things; and whilst the others was leaving, the key come from the house.

This nigger had a good-natured, chuckleheaded face, and his wool was all tied up in little bunches with thread. That was to keep witches off. He said the witches was pestering him awful these nights, and making him see all kinds of strange things, and hear all kinds of strange words and noises, and he didn't believe he was ever witched so long before in his life. He got so worked up, and got to running on so about his troubles, he forgot all about what he'd been a-going to do. So Tom says:

"What's the vittles for? Going to feed the dogs?"

The nigger kind of smiled around graduly over his face, like when you heave a brickbat in a mud-puddle, and he says:

"Yes, Mars Sid, *a* dog. Cur'us dog, too. Does you want to go en look at 'im?"

"Yes."

I hunched Tom, and whispers:

"You going, right here in the daybreak? *That* warn't the plan."

"No, it warn't; but it's the plan *now*."

So, drat him, we went along, but I didn't like it much. When we got in we couldn't hardly see anything, it was so dark; but Jim was there, sure enough, and could see us; and he sings out:

"Why, *Huck!* En good *lan'!* ain' dat Misto Tom?"

I just knowed how it would be; I just expected it. *I* didn't know nothing to do; and if I had I couldn't 'a' done it, because that nigger busted in and says:

"Why, de gracious sakes! do he know you genlmen?"

We could see pretty well now. Tom he looked at the nigger, steady and kind of wondering, and says:

"Does *who* know us?"

"Why, dis-yer runaway nigger."

"I don't reckon he does; but what put that into your head?"

"What *put* it dar? Didn't he jis' dis minute sing out like he knowed you?"

Tom says, in a puzzled-up kind of way:

"Well, that's mighty curious. *Who* sung out? *When* did he sing out? *What* did he sing out?" And turns to me, perfectly ca'm, and says, "Did *you* hear anybody sing out?"

Of course there warn't nothing to be said but the one thing; so I says:

"No; *I* ain't heard nobody say nothing."

Then he turns to Jim, and looks him over like he never see him before, and says:

"Did you sing out?"

"No, sah," says Jim; "*I* hain't said nothing, sah."

"Not a word?"

"No, sah, I hain't said a word."

"Did you ever see us before?"

"No, sah; not as *I* knows on."

So Tom turns to the nigger, which was looking wild and distressed, and says, kind of severe:

"What do you reckon's the matter with you, anyway? What made you think somebody sung out?"

"Oh, it's de dad-blame' witches, sah, en I wisht I was dead, I do. Dey's awluz at it, sah, en dey do mos' kill me, dey sk'yers me so. Please to don't tell nobody 'bout it sah, er ole Mars Silas he'll scole me; 'kase he say dey *ain't* no witches. I jis' wish to goodness he was heah now — *den* what would he say! I jis' bet he couldn' fine no way to git aroun' it *dis* time. But it's awluz jis' so; people dat's *sot,* stays sot; dey won't look into noth'n' en fine it out f'r deyselves, en when *you* fine it out en tell um 'bout it, dey doan' b'lieve you."

Tom give him a dime, and said we wouldn't tell nobody; and told him to buy some more thread to tie up his wool with; and then looks at Jim, and says:

"I wonder if Uncle Silas is going to hang this nigger. If I was to catch a nigger that was ungrateful enough to run away, *I* wouldn't give him up, I'd hang him." And whilst the nigger stepped to the door to look at the dime and bite it to see if it was good, he whispers to Jim and says:

"Don't ever let on to know us. And if you hear any digging going on nights, it's us; we're going to set you free."

Jim only had time to grab us by the hand and squeeze it; then the nigger come back, and we said we'd come again some time if the nigger wanted us to; and he said he would, more particular if it was dark, because the witches went for him mostly in the dark, and it was good to have folks around then.

* * *

It would be most an hour yet till breakfast, so we left and struck down into the woods; because Tom said we got to have *some* light to see how to dig by, and a lantern makes too much, and might get us into trouble; what we must have was a lot of them rotten chunks that's called fox fire, and just makes a soft kind of a glow when you lay them in a dark place. We fetched an armful and hid it in the weeds, and set down to rest, and Tom says, kind of dissatisfied:

"Blame it, this whole thing is just as easy and awkward as it can be. And so it makes it so rotten difficult to get up a difficult plan. There ain't no watchman to be drugged — now there *ought* to be a watchman. There ain't even a dog to give a sleeping mixture to. And there's Jim chained by one leg, with a ten-foot chain, to the leg of his bed: why, all you got to do is lift up the bedstead and slip off the chain. And Uncle Silas he trusts everybody; sends the key to the punkin-headed nigger and don't send nobody to watch the nigger. Jim could 'a' got out of that window hole before this, only there wouldn't be no use trying to travel with a ten-foot chain on his leg. Why, drat it, Huck, it's the stupidest arrangement I ever see. You got to invent *all* the difficulties. Well, we can't help it; we got to do the best we can with the materials we've got. Anyhow, there's one thing — there's more honor in getting him out through a lot of difficulties and dangers, when there warn't one of them furnished to you by the people who it was their duty to furnish them, and you had to contrive them all out of your own head. Now look at just that one thing of the lantern. When you come down to the cold facts, we simply got to *let on* that a lantern's resky. Why, we could work with a torchlight procession if we wanted to, *I* believe. Now, whilst I think of it, we got to hunt up something to make a saw out of the first chance we get."

"What do we want of a saw?"

"What do we *want* of a saw? Hain't we got to saw the leg of Jim's bed off, so as to get the chain loose?"

"Why, you just said a body could lift up the bedstead and slip the chain off."

"Well, if that ain't just like you, Huck Finn. You *can* get up the infant-schooliest ways of going at a thing. Why, hain't you ever read any books at all? — Baron Trenck, nor Casanova, nor Benvenuto Chelleeny, nor Henri IV, nor none of them heroes? Who ever heard of getting a prisoner loose in such an old-maidy way as that? No; the way all the best authorities does is to saw the bed leg in two, and leave it just so, and swallow the sawdust, so it can't be found, and put some dirt and grease around the sawed place so the very keenest seneskal can't see no sign of its being sawed, and thinks the bed leg is perfectly sound. Then, the night you're ready, fetch the leg a kick, down she goes; slip off your chain, and there you are. Nothing to do but hitch your rope ladder to the battlements, shin down it, break your leg in the moat — because a rope ladder is nineteen foot too short, you know — and there's your horses and your trusty vassles, and they scoop you up and fling you across a saddle, and away you go to your native Langudoc, or Navarre, or wherever it is. It's gaudy, Huck. I wish there was a moat to this cabin. If we get time, the night of the escape, we'll dig one."

I says:

"What do we want of a moat when we're going to snake him out from under the cabin?"

But he never heard me. He had forgot me and everything else. He had his chin in his hand, thinking. Pretty soon he sighs and shakes his head; then sighs again, and says:

"No, it wouldn't do — there ain't necessity enough for it."

"For what?" I says.

"Why, to saw Jim's leg off," he says.

"Good land!" I says: "why, there ain't *no* necessity for it. And what would you want to saw his leg off for, anyway?"

"Well, some of the best authorities has done it. They couldn't get the chain off, so they just cut their hand off and shoved. And a leg would be better still. But we got to let that go. There ain't necessity enough in this case; and, besides, Jim's a nigger, and wouldn't understand the reasons for it, and how it's the custom in Europe; so we'll let it go. But there's one thing — he can have a rope ladder; we can tear up our sheets and make him a rope ladder easy enough. And we can send it to him in a pie; it's mostly done that way. And I've et worse pies."

"Why, Tom Sawyer, how you talk," I says; "Jim ain't got no use for a rope ladder."

"He *has* got use for it. How *you* talk, you better say; you don't know nothing about it. He's *got* to have a rope ladder; they all do."

"What in the nation can he *do* with it?"

"*Do* with it? He can hide it in his bed, can't he? That's what they all do; and *he's* got to, too. Huck, you don't ever seem to want to do anything that's regular; you want to be starting something fresh all the time. S'pose he *don't* do nothing with it? ain't it there in his bed, for a clue, after he's gone? and don't you reckon they'll want clues? Of course they will. And you wouldn't leave them any? That would be a *pretty* howdy-do, *wouldn't* it! I never heard of such a thing."

"Well," I says, "if it's in the regulations, and he's got to have it, all right, let him have it; because I don't wish to go back on no regulations; but there's one thing, Tom Sawyer — if we go to tearing up our sheets to make Jim a rope ladder, we're going to get into trouble with Aunt Sally, just as sure as you're born. Now, the way I look at it, a hickry-bark ladder don't cost nothing, and don't waste nothing, and is just as good to load up a pie with, and hide in a straw tick, as any rag ladder you can start; and as for Jim, he ain't had no experience, and so *he* don't care what kind of a — "

"Oh, shucks, Huck Finn, if I was as ignorant as you I'd keep still — that's what *I'd* do. Who ever heard of a state prisoner escaping by a hickry-bark ladder? Why, it's perfectly ridiculous."

"Well, all right, Tom, fix it your own way; but if you'll take my advice, you'll let me borrow a sheet off of the clothes line."

He said that would do. And that gave him another idea, and he says:

"Borrow a shirt, too."

"What do we want of a shirt, Tom?"

"Want it for Jim to keep a journal on."

"Journal your granny — *Jim* can't write."

"S'pose he *can't* write — he can make marks on the shirt, can't he, if we make him a pen out of an old pewter spoon or a piece of an old iron barrel hoop?"

"Why, Tom, we can pull a feather out of a goose and make him a better one; and quicker, too."

"*Prisoners* don't have geese running around the donjon-keep to pull pens out of, you muggins. They *always* make their pens out of the hardest, toughest, troublesomest piece of old brass candlestick or something like that they can get their hands on; and it takes them weeks and weeks and months and months to file it out, too, because they've got to do it by rubbing it on the wall. *They* wouldn't use a goose quill if they had it. It ain't regular."

"Well, then, what'll we make him the ink out of?"

"Many makes it out of iron rust and tears; but that's the common sort and women; the best authorities uses their own blood. Jim can do that; and when he wants to send any little common ordinary mysterious message to let the world know where he's captivated, he can write it on the bottom of a tin plate with a fork and throw it out of the window. The Iron Mask always done that, and it's a blame' good way, too."

"Jim ain't got no tin plate. They feed him in a pan."

"That ain't nothing; we can get him some."

"Can't nobody *read* his plates."

"That ain't got anything to *do* with it, Huck Finn. All *he's* got to do is to write on the plate and throw it out. You don't *have* to be able to read it. Why, half the time you can't read anything a prisoner writes on a tin plate, or anywhere else."

"Well, then, what's the sense of wasting the plates?"

"Why, blame it all, it ain't the *prisoner's* plates."

"But it's *somebody's* plates, ain't it?"

"Well, spos'n it is? What does the *prisoner* care whose — "

He broke off there, because we heard the breakfast horn blowing. So we cleared out for the house.

Along during the morning I borrowed a sheet and a white shirt off the clothes line; and I found an old sack and put them in it, and we went down and got the fox fire, and put that in too. I called it borrowing, because that was what pap always called it; but Tom said it warn't borrowing, it was stealing. He said we was representing prisoners; and prisoners don't care how they get a thing so they get it, and nobody don't blame them for it, either. It ain't no crime in a prisoner to steal the thing he needs to get away with, Tom said; it's his right; and so, as long as we was representing a prisoner, we had a perfect right to steal anything on this place we had the least use for to get ourselves out of prison with. He said if we warn't prisoners it would be a very different thing, and nobody but a mean, ornery person would steal when he warn't a prisoner. So we allowed we would steal everything there was that come handy. And yet he made a mighty fuss, one day, after that, when I stole a watermelon out of the nigger patch and eat it; and he made me go and give the niggers a dime without telling them what it was for. Tom said that what he meant was, we could steal anything we *needed*. Well, I says, I needed the watermelon. But he said I didn't need it to get out of prison with; there's where the difference was. He said if I'd 'a' wanted it to hide a knife in, and smuggle it to Jim to kill the seneskal with, it would 'a' been all right. So I let it go at that, though I couldn't see no advantage in my representing a prisoner if I got to set down and chaw over a lot of gold-leaf distinctions like that every time I see a chance to hog a watermelon.

Well, as I was saying, we waited that morning till everybody was settled down to business, and nobody in sight around the yard; then Tom he carried the sack into the lean-to whilst I stood off a piece to keep watch. By and by he come out, and we went and set down on the woodpile to talk. He says:

"Everything's all right now except tools; and that's easy fixed."

"Tools?" I says.

"Yes."

"Tools for what?"

"Why, to dig with. We ain't a-going to *gnaw* him out, are we?"

"Ain't them old crippled picks and things in there good enough to dig a nigger out with?" I says.

He turns on me, looking pitying enough to make a body cry, and says:

"Huck Finn, did you *ever* hear of a prisoner having picks and shovels, and all the modern conveniences in his wardrobe to dig himself out with? Now I want to ask you — if you got any reasonableness in you at all — what kind of a show would *that* give him to be a hero? Why, they might as well lend him the key and done with it. Picks and shovels — why, they wouldn't furnish 'em to a king."

"Well, then," I says, "if we don't want the picks and shovels, what do we want?"

"A couple of case knives."

"To dig the foundations out from under that cabin with?"

"Yes."

"Confound it, it's foolish, Tom."

"It don't make no difference how foolish it is, it's the *right* way — and it's the regular way. And there ain't no *other* way, that ever *I* heard of, and I've read all the books that gives any information about these things. They always dig out with a case knife — and not through dirt, mind you; generly it's through solid rock. And it takes them weeks and weeks and weeks, and for ever and ever. Why, look at one of them prisoners in the bottom dungeon of the Castle Deef, in the harbor of Marseilles, that dug himself out that way; how long was *he* at it, you reckon?"

"I don't know."

"Well, guess."

"I don't know. A month and a half."

"*Thirty-seven year* — and he come out in China. *That's* the kind. I wish the bottom of *this* fortress was solid rock."

"*Jim* don't know nobody in China."

"What's *that* got to do with it? Neither did that other fellow. But you're always a-wandering off on a side issue. Why can't you stick to the main point?"

"All right — *I* don't care where he comes out, so he *comes* out; and Jim don't, either, I reckon. But there's one thing, anyway — Jim's too old to be dug out with a case knife. He won't last."

"Yes he will *last,* too. You don't reckon it's going to take thirty-seven years to dig out through a *dirt* foundation, do you?"

"How long will it take, Tom?"

"Well, we can't resk being as long as we ought to, because it mayn't take very long for Uncle Silas to hear from down there by New Orleans. He'll hear Jim ain't from there. Then his next move will be to advertise Jim, or something like that. So we can't resk being as long digging him out as we ought to. By rights I reckon we ought to be a couple of years; but we can't. Things being so uncertain, what I recommend is this: that we really dig right in, as quick as we can; and after that, we can *let on,* to ourselves, that we was at it thirty-seven years. Then we can snatch him out and rush him away the first time there's an alarm. Yes, I reckon that 'll be the best way."

"Now, there's *sense* in that," I says. "Letting on don't cost nothing; letting on ain't no trouble; and if it's any object, I don't mind letting on we was at it a hundred and fifty year. It wouldn't strain me none, after I got my hand in. So I'll mosey along now, and smouch a couple of case knives."

"Smouch three," he says; "we want one to make a saw out of."

"Tom, if it ain't unregular and irreligious to sejest it," I says, "there's an old rusty saw blade around yonder sticking under the weatherboarding behind the smokehouse."

He looked kind of weary and discouraged-like, and says:

"It ain't no use to try to learn you nothing, Huck. Run along and smouch the knives — three of them." So I done it.

V ADOLESCENCE

A period of great physical change and emotional turbulence, adolescence is also a time when the child's thought processes undergo fundamental reorganization. No longer concerned merely with the workings of the everyday, actual world, the adolescent begins to ponder what is logically possible, to consider various hypothetical possibilities, and to confront the full range of options in every situation. For the first time the real world is seen as merely one of many possible alternatives: the adolescent becomes concerned with philosophical and theoretical issues.

The excerpts from Inhelder's and Piaget's book describe the reorganization of thought during adolescence and portray the interrelatedness of the cognitive and affective realms. Adolescents build systems — general patterns of knowledge — and their emotions are heavily engaged in this activity.

Various ramifications follow from these new levels of thought. David Elkind examines one aspect of the adolescent's thought. As Elkind portrays it, adolescents spend a great deal of time thinking about themselves. This peculiar kind of egocentrism, at a time when the kind of egocentrism revealed in the experiment with visual displays has long since waned (page 229), is epitomized in the youth's erroneous belief that others are constantly concerned with his or her appearance and behavior, that he or she is always on display. Elkind believes that this egocentrism greatly influences the feelings and the personality development of the adolescent, accounting for the self-consciousness and the volatility of temper that adolescents often show. Again, we find evidence of the intimate relatedness of cognitive and affective development.

Another change is that the adolescent confronts new and different issues. Among these are moral and ethical topics, discussed by Lawrence Kohlberg. But there is more than merely a heightened interest in questions of values. Rather, Kohlberg believes that reasoning about moral issues follows a developmental sequence, with certain *forms* of argument dominating for a time, then giving way to others. Indeed, the content, the adolescent's judgment about the right or wrong of a course of action, is not what determines the level of morality; what matters instead is the argument presented. Kohlberg believes that only with the advent in adolescence of formal reasoning (in Piaget's sense) does a high level of reasoning about moral issues become possible. And he presents evidence from experimental studies in the United States and other cultures to support his claim that the sequence of development of moral reasoning is universal.

Kohlberg's theory refers to the way adolescents *reason* about ethical issues. Carol Gilligan and John Murphy go beyond thought about ethical issues to *actions* which embody these dilemmas. The discovery that categories of thought cannot adequately encompass the facts of their experience presents adolescents with a conflict situation which can lead to development. This dialectic pull between feelings and thoughts on one side and actions and their consequences on the other leads to a synthesis which Gilligan believes characterizes the beginnings of adulthood.

The cognitive and emotional changes during these adolescent years accompany the physical, hormonal changes of puberty. Deborah Waber's study grouped adolescents by their age at the onset of puberty and found that early maturers performed better on tests of verbal abilities than on tests of spatial abilities. This difference was previously believed to be a sex difference, with boys typically better with spatial abilities. Waber's results suggest that rate of maturation is an important variable for understanding higher cortical organization.

Various pathologies can appear at any age, but adolescent girls are especially vulnerable to anorexia nervosa. In the case study by Hilda Bruch, we witness the distintegration of a seemingly delightful, almost "perfect" young lady. The dynamic forces within the adolescent as well as within her family are highlighted in this poignant story.

Finally, the paper by Zick Rubin summarizes the ultimate concerns of developmental psychology. During each of the stages of development, we have noted a double focus: we want to understand the child as he or she is at the moment, and we want to know what can be predicted about the future from the present (or, correlatively, what we can explain of the present by the past). What remains the same and what changes are basic issues that have been addressed by many of the articles from Werner's and Kessen's in the introduction to our final selection, where Zick Rubin suggests that the coherence of the self might well account for constancy even while specific behaviors or attitudes are capable of seemingly dramatic change.

36

Bärbel Inhelder and Jean Piaget

ADOLESCENT THINKING

. . . As opposed to the child who feels inferior and subordinate to the adult, the adolescent is an individual who begins to consider himself as the equal of adults and to judge them, with complete reciprocity, on the same plane as himself. But to this first trait, two others are indissolubly related. The adolescent is an individual who is still growing, but one who begins to think of the future — *i.e.,* of his present or future work in society. Thus, to his current activities he adds a life program for later "adult" activities. Further, in most cases in our societies, the adolescent is the individual who in attempting to plan his present or future work in adult society also has the idea (from his point of view, it is directly related to his plans) of changing this society, whether in some limited area or completely. Thus it is impossible to fill an adult role without conflicts, and whereas the child looks for resolution of his conflicts in present-day compensations (real or imaginary), the adolescent adds to these limited compensations the more general compensation of a motivation for change, or even specific planning for change.

Furthermore, seen in the light of these three interrelated features, the adolescent's adoption of adult roles certainly presupposes those affective and intellectual tools whose spontaneous development is exactly what distinguishes adolescence from childhood. If we take these new tools as a starting point, we have to ask: what is their nature and how do they relate to formal thinking?

On a naïve global level, without trying to distinguish between the student, the apprentice, the young worker, or the young peasant in terms of how their social attitudes may vary, the adolescent differs from the child above all in that he thinks beyond the present. The adolescent is the individual who commits himself to possibilities — although we certainly do not mean to deny that his commitment begins in real-life situations. In other words, the adolescent is the individual who begins to build "systems" or "theories," in the largest sense of the term.

The child does not build systems. His spontaneous thinking may be more or less systematic (at first only to a small degree, later, much more so); but it is the observer who sees the system from outside, while the child is not aware of it since he never thinks about his own thought. For example, in an earlier work on the child's representation of the world, we were able to report on a number of systematic responses. Later we were able to construct the systems characterizing various genetic stages. But *we* constructed the system; the *child* does not try to systematize his ideas, although he may often spontaneously return to the same preoccupations and unconsciously give analogous answers.[1] In other words, the child has no powers of reflection — *i.e.,* no second-order thoughts which deal critically with his own thinking. No theory can be built without such reflection.

In contrast, the adolescent is able to analyze his own thinking and construct theories. The fact that these theories are oversimplified, awkward, and usually contain very little originality is beside the point. From the functional standpoint, his systems are significant in that they furnish the cognitive and evaluative bases for the assumption of adult roles, without mentioning a life program and projects for change. They are vital in the assimilation of the values which delineate societies or social classes as entities in contrast to simple interindividual relations.

Consider a group of students between 14–15 years and the *baccalaureat*.[2] Most of them have political or social theories and want to reform the world; they have their own ways of explaining all of the present-day turmoil in collective life. Others have literary or aesthetic theories and place their reading or their experiences of beauty on a scale of values which is projected into a system. Some go through religious crises and reflect on the problem of faith, thus moving toward a universal system — a system valid for all. Philosophical speculation carries away a minority, and for any true intellectual, adolescence is the metaphysical age *par excellence,* an age whose dangerous seduction is forgotten only with difficulty at the adult level. A still smaller minority turns from the start toward scientific or pseudo-scientific theories. But whatever the variation in content, each one has his theory or theories, although they may be more or less explicit and verbalized or even implicit. Some write down their ideas, and it is extremely interesting to see the outlines which are taken up and filled in in later life. Others are limited to talking and ruminating, but each one has his own ideas (and usually he believes they are his own) which liberate him from childhood and allow him to place himself as the equal of adults.

If we now step outside the student range and the intellectual classes to look at the reactions of the adolescent worker, apprentice, or peasant, we can recognize the same phenomenon in other forms. Instead of working out personal "theories," we would find him subscribing to ideas passed on by comrades, developed in meetings, or provoked by reading. We would find fewer family and still fewer religious crises, and especially a lower degree of abstraction. But under different and varied exteriors the same core process can easily be discerned — the adolescent is no longer content to live the interindividual relations offered by his immediate surroundings or to use his intelligence to solve the problems of the moment. Rather, he is motivated also to take his place in the adult social framework, and with this aim he tends to participate in the ideas, ideals, and ideologies of a wider group through the medium of a number of verbal symbols to which he was indifferent as a child.

But how can we explain the adolescent's new capacity to orient himself toward what is abstract and not immediately present (seen from the outside by the observer comparing him to the child), but which (seen from within) is an indispensable instrument in his adaptation to the adult social framework, and as a result his most immediate and most deeply experienced concern? There is no doubt that this is the most direct and, moreover, the simplest manifestation of formal thinking. Formal thinking is both thinking about thought (propositional logic is a second-order operational system which operates on propositions whose truth, in turn, depend on class, relational, and numerical operations) and a reversal of relations between what is real and what is possible (the empirically given comes to be inserted as a particular sector of the total set of possible combinations). These are the two characteristics — which up to this point we have tried to describe in the abstract language appropriate to the analysis of reasoning — which are the source of the living responses, always so full of emotion, which the adolescent uses to build his ideals in adapting to society. The adolescent's theory construction shows both that he has become capable of reflective thinking and that his thought makes it possible for him to escape the concrete present toward the realm of the abstract and the possible. Obviously, this does not mean that formal structures are first organized by themselves and are later applied as adaptive instruments where they prove individually or socially useful. The two processes — structural development and everyday application — both belong to the same reality, and it is *because* formal thinking plays a fundamental role from the functional standpoint that it can attain its general and logical structure. Once more, logic is not isolated from life; it is no more than the expression of operational coordinations essential to action.

But this does not mean that the adolescent takes his place in adult society merely in terms of general theories and without personal involvement. Two other aspects of his entrance into adult society have to be considered — his life program, and his plans for changing the society he sees. The adolescent not only builds new theories or rehabilitates old ones; he also feels he has to work out a conception of life which gives him an opportunity to assert himself and to create something new (thus the close relationship between his system and his life program). Secondly, he wants a guarantee that he will be more successful than his predecessors (thus the need for change in which altruistic concern and youthful ambitions are inseparably blended).

In other words, the process which we have followed through the different stages of the child's development is recapitulated on the planes of thought and reality new to formal operations. An initial failure to distinguish between objects or the actions of others and one's own actions gives way to an enlargement of perspective toward objectivity and reciprocity. Even at the sensori-motor level, the infant does not at first know how to separate the effects of his own actions from the qualities of external objects or persons. At first he lives in a world without permanent objects and without awareness of the self or of any internal subjective life. Later he differentiates his own ego and situates his body in a spatially and causally organized field composed of permanent objects and other persons similar to himself. This is the first decentering process; its result is the gradual coordination of sensori-motor behavior. But when symbolic functioning appears, language, representation, and communication with others expand this field to unheard-of proportions and a new type of structure is required. For a second time egocentrism appears, but this time on another plane. It still takes the form of an initial relative lack of differentiation both between ego's and alter's points of view, between subjective and objective, but this time the lack of differentiation is representational rather than sensori-motor. When the child reaches the stage of concrete operations (7–8 years), the decentering process has gone far enough for him to be able to structure relationships between classes, relations, and numbers objectively. At the same stage, he acquires skill in interindividual relations in a cooperative framework. Furthermore, the acquisition of social cooperation and the structuring of cognitive operations can be seen as two aspects of the same developmental process. But when the cognitive field is again enlarged by the structuring of formal thought, a third form of egocentrism comes into view. This egocentrism is one of the most enduring features of adolescence; it persists until the new and later decentering which makes possible the true beginnings of adult work.

Moreover, the adolescent manifestation of egocentrism stems directly from the adoption of adult roles, since . . . the adolescent not only tries to adapt his ego to the social environment but, just as emphatically, tries to adjust the environment to his ego. In other words, when he begins to think about the society in which he is looking for a place, he has to think about his own future activity and about how he himself might transform this society. The result is a relative failure to distinguish between his own point of view as an individual called upon to organize a life program and the point of view of the group which he hopes to reform.

In more concrete terms, the adolescent's egocentrism comes out in a sort of Messianic form such that the theories used to represent the world center on the role of reformer that the adolescent feels himself called upon to play in the future. To fully understand the adolescent's feelings, we have to go beyond simple observation and look at intimate documents such as essays not written for immediate public consumption, diaries, or simply the disclosures some adolescents may make of their personal fantasies. For example, in the recitations obtained by G. Dumas from a high-school class on their evening reveries, the most normal students — the most retiring, the most amiable — calmly confessed to fantasies and fabulations which several years later would have appeared in their own eyes as signs of pathological megalomania. Without going into the details of this group, we see that the universal aspect of the phenomenon must be sought in the relationship between the adolescent's apparently abstract theories and the life program which he sets up for himself. Then we see that behind impersonal and general exteriors these systems conceal programs of action whose ambitiousness and naïveté are usually immoderate. We could also consider the following sample taken from the dozen or so ex-pupils of a small-town school in Romansch Switzerland. One of them, who has since become a shopkeeper, astonished his friends with his literary doctrines and wrote a novel in secret. Another, who has since become the director of an insurance company, was interested among other things in the future of the theater and showed some close friends the first scene of the first act of a tragedy — and got no further. A third, taken up with philosophy, dedicated himself to no less a task than the reconciliation of science and religion. We do not even have to enumerate the social and political reformers found on both right and left. There were only two members of the class who did not reveal any astounding life plans. Both were more or less crushed under strong "superegos" of parental origin, and we do not know what their secret daydreams might have been.

Sometimes this sort of life program has a real influence on the individual's later growth, and it may even happen that a person rediscovers in his adolescent jottings an outline of some ideas which he has really fulfilled since. But in the large majority of cases, adolescent projects are more like a sort of sophisticated game of compensation functions whose goals are self-assertion, imitation of adult models, participation in circles which are actually closed, etc. Thus the adolescent takes up paths which satisfy him for a time but are soon abandoned. M. Debesse has discussed this subject of egotism and the crisis of juvenile originality. But we believe that, in the egocentrism found in the adolescent, there is more than a simple desire to deviate; rather, it is a manifestation of the phenomenon of lack of differentiation which is worth a further brief discussion.

Essentially, the process, which at any one of the developmental stages moves from egocentrism toward decentering, constantly subjects increases in knowledge to a refocusing of perspective. Everyone has observed that the child mixes up subjective and objective facts, but if the hypothesis of egocentrism did nothing more than restate this truism it would be worth next to nothing.[3] Actually, it means that learning is not a purely additive process and that to pile one new learned piece of behavior or information on top of another is not in itself adequate to structure an objective attitude. In fact, objectivity presupposes a decentering — *i.e.,* a continual refocusing of perspective. Egocentrism, on the other hand, is the undifferentiated state prior to multiple perspectives, whereas objectivity implies both differentiation and coordination of the points of view which have been differentiated.

But the process found in adolescence on the more sophisticated plane of formal structures is analogous. The indefinite extension of powers of thought made possible by the new instruments of propositional logic at first is conducive to a failure to distinguish between the ego's new and unpredicted capacities and the social or cosmic universe to which they are applied. In other words, the adolescent goes through a phase in which he attributes an unlimited power to his own thoughts so that the dream of a glorious future or of transforming the world through Ideas (even if this idealism takes a materialistic form) seems to be not only fantasy but also an effective action which in itself modifies the empirical world. This is obviously a form of cognitive egocentrism. Although it differs sharply from the child's egocentrism (which is either sensori-motor or simply representational without introspective "reflection"), it results, nevertheless, from the same mechanism and appears as a function of the new conditions created by the structuring of formal thought.

There is a way of verifying this view; namely, to study the decentering process which later makes it possible for the adolescent to get beyond the early relative lack of differentiation and to cure himself of his idealistic crisis — in other words, the return to reality which is the path from adolescence to the true beginnings of adulthood. But, as at the level of concrete operations, we find that decentering takes place simultaneously in thought processes and in social relationships.

From the standpoint of social relationships, the tendency of adolescents to congregate in peer groups has been well documented — discussion or action groups, political groups, youth movements, summer camps, etc. Charlotte Bühler defines an expansive phase followed by a withdrawal phase, although the two do not always seem clearly distinguishable. Certainly this type of social life is not merely the effect of pressures towards conformity but also a source of intellectual decentering. It is most often in discussions between friends, when the promoter of a theory has to test it against the theories of the others, that he discovers its fragility.

But the focal point of the decentering process is the entrance into the occupational world or the beginning of serious professional training. The adolescent becomes an adult when he undertakes a real job. It is then that he is transformed from an idealistic reformer into an achiever. In other words, the job leads thinking away from the dangers of formalism back into reality. Yet observation shows how laborious and slow this reconciliation of thought and experience can be. One has only to look at the behavior of beginning students in an experimental discipline to see how long the adolescent's belief in the power of thinking endures and how little inclined is the mind to subjugate its ideas to the analysis of facts. (This does not mean that facts are accessible without theory, but rather that a theoretical construction has value only in relation to empirical verification.)

From this standpoint, the results of . . . [our investigations of adolescent thought] raise a problem of general significance. The subjects' reactions to a wide range of experimental situations demonstrate that after a phase of development (11–12 to 13–14 years) the preadolescent comes to handle certain formal operations (implication, exclusion, etc.) successfully, but he is not able to set up an exhaustive method of proof. But the 14–15-year-old adolescent does succeed in setting up proofs (moreover, spontaneously, for it is in this area that academic verbalism is least evident). He systematically uses methods of control which require the combinatorial system — *i.e.,* he varies a single factor at a time and excludes the others ("all other things being equal"), etc. But, as we have often seen, this structuring of the tools of experimental verification is a direct consequence of the development of formal thought and propositional logic. Since the adolescent acquires the capacity to use both deduction and experimental induction at the same time, why does he use the first so effectively, and why is he so late in making use of the second in a productive and continuous task (for it is one thing to react experimentally to an apparatus prepared in advance and another to organize a research project by oneself)? Furthermore, the problem is not only ontogenetic but also historical. The same question can be asked in trying to understand why the Greeks were limited (with some exceptions) to pure deductive thought[4] and why modern science, centered on physics, has taken so many centuries to put itself together.

We have seen that the principal intellectual characteristics of adolescence stem directly or indirectly from the development of formal structures. Thus, the latter is the most important event in the thinking found in this period. As for the affective innovations found at the same age, there are two which merit consideration; as usual, we find that they are parallel to intellectual transformations, since affectivity can be considered as the energetic force of behavior whereas its structure defines cognitive functions. (This does not mean either that affectivity is determined by intellect or the contrary, but that both are indissociably united in the functioning of the personality.)

If adolescence is really the age at which growing individuals take their place in adult society (whether or not the role change always coincides with puberty), this crucial social adjustment must involve, in correlation with the development of the propositional or formal operations which assure intellectual structuring, two fundamental transformations that adult affective socialization requires. First, feelings relative to ideals are added to interindividual feelings. Secondly, personalities develop in relation to social roles and scales of values derived from social interaction (and no longer only by the coordination of exchanges which they maintain with the physical environment and other individuals).[5]

Naturally, this is not the place for an essay on the psychology of affects; still, it is important to see how closely these two essential affective aspects of adolescence are interwoven with the transformations of behavior brought on by the development of formal structures.

First, we are struck by the fact that feelings about ideals are practically nonexistent in the child. A study of the concept of nationality and the associated social attitudes[6] has shown us that the child is sensitive to his family, to his place of residence, to his native language, to certain customs, etc., but that he preserves both an astonishing degree of ignorance and a striking insensitivity not only to his own designation or that of his associates as Swiss, French, etc., but toward his own country as a collective reality. This is to be expected, since, in the 7–11-year-old child, logic is applied only to concrete or manipulable objects. There is no operation available at this level which would make it possible for the child to elaborate an ideal which goes beyond the empirically given. This is only one among many examples. The notions of humanity, social justice (in contrast to interindividual justice which is deeply experienced at the concrete level), freedom of conscience, civic or intellectual courage, and so forth, like the idea of nationality, are ideals which profoundly influence the adolescent's affective life; but with the child's mentality, except for certain individual glimpses, they can neither be understood nor felt.

In other words, the child does not experience as social feelings anything more than interindividual affects. Even moral sentiments are felt only as a function of unilateral respect (authority) or mutual respect. But, beginning at 13–15 years, feelings about *ideals* or *ideas* are added to the earlier ones, although, of course, they too subsist in the adolescent as well as the adult. Of course, an ideal always exists in a person and it does not stop being an important interindividual element in the new class of feelings. The problem is to find out whether the idea is an object of affectivity because of the person or the person because of the idea. But, whereas the child never gets out of this circle because his only ideals are people who are actually part of his surroundings, during adolescence the circle is broken because ideals become autonomous. No commentary is needed to bring out the close kinship of this affective mechanism with formal thought.

As for personality, there is no more vaguely defined notion in psychological vocabulary, already so difficult to handle. The reason for this is that personality operates in a way opposite to that of the ego. Whereas the ego is naturally egocentric, personality is the decentered ego. The ego is detestable, even more so when it is strong, whereas a strong personality is the one which manages to discipline the ego. In other words, the personality is the submission of the ego to an ideal which it embodies but which goes beyond it and subordinates it; it is the adherence to a scale of values, not in the abstract but relative to a given task; thus it is the eventual adoption of a social role, not ready-made in the sense of an administrative function but a role which the individual will create in filling it.

Thus, to say that adolescence is the age at which adolescents take their place in adult society is by definition to maintain that it is the age of formation of the personality, for the adoption of adult roles is from another and necessarily complementary standpoint the construction of a personality. Furthermore, the life program and the plans for change which we have just seen as one of the essential features of the adolescent's behavior are at the same time the changing emotional force in the formation of the personality. A life plan is above all a scale of values which puts some ideals above others and subordinates the middle-range values to goals thought of as permanent. But this scale of values is the affective organization corresponding to the cognitive organization of his work which the new member in the social body says he will undertake. A life plan is also an affirmation of autonomy, and the moral autonomy finally achieved by the adolescent who judges himself the equal of adults is another essential affective feature of the young personality preparing himself to plunge into life.

In conclusion, the fundamental affective acquisitions of adolescence parallel the intellectual acquisitions. To understand the role of formal structures of thought in the life of the adolescent, we found that in the last analysis we had to place them in his total personality. But, in return, we found that we could not completely understand the growth of his personality without including the transformations of his thinking; thus we had to come back to the development of formal structures.

NOTES

1. For an example, see *Play, Dreams and Imitation in Childhood,* Chap. IX.

2. *Translators' note: baccalaureat* — a French examination taken at the end of secondary school or about 18–19 years of age. Although, in its details, the analysis of the adolescent presented below fits the European better than the American pattern, one might suggest that even if metaphysical and political theories are less prominent, the American dating pattern and other phenomena typical of youth culture are a comparable "theoretical" or "as if" working out of types of interpersonal relations which become serious at a later point; thus the difference is one of content but not of structure.

3. *Translators' note:* This passage refers to an opinion more prevalent in Europe than in America, namely that the authors' work simply demonstrates a normative view of the child as an irrational creature. In the United States, where problems of mo-

tivation are more often given precedence over purely intellectual functions both from the normative standpoint and in psychological research, another but parallel misinterpretation has sometimes been made; namely, that in maintaining that the child is egocentric, the authors have neglected the fact that he is capable of love. It should be made clear in this section that egocentrism, best understood from its root meaning — that the child's perception is cognitively "centered on his own ego" and thus lacks a certain type of fluidity and ability to handle a variety of perspectives — is not to be confused with "selfish" or "egoistic."

4. No one has yet given a serious explanation of this fact from the sociological standpoint. To attribute the formal structures made explicit by the Greeks to the contemplative nature of one social class or another does not explain why this contemplation was not confined to metaphysical ideologies and was able to create a mathematical system.

5. *Translators' note:* "Interindividual" and "social" are used as oppositional terms to a greater extent in French than in English. The first refers to face-to-face relationships between individuals with the implication of familiarity, and the second to the relationship of the individual to society as a whole, to formal institutional structures, to values, etc. Here the meaning is that the child relates only to small groups and specific individuals while the adolescent relates to institutional structures and to values as such.

6. J. Piaget and A. M. Weil, "Le développement chez l'enfant de l'idée de Patrie et des relations avec l'etranger," *Bulletin international des Sciences sociales* (UNESCO), Vol. III (1951), pp. 605–621.

David Elkind

EGOCENTRISM IN ADOLESCENCE

ABSTRACT: This paper describes the different forms of egocentrism characteristic of each of the major stages of cognitive growth outlined by Piaget. Particular attention is paid to the egocentrism of adolescence which is here described as the failure to differentiate between the cognitive concerns of others and those of the self. This adolescent egocentrism is said to give rise to 2 mental constructions, the imaginary audience and the personal fable, which help to account for certain forms of adolescent behavior and experience. These considerations suggest, it is concluded, that the cognitive structures peculiar to a given age period can provide insights with respect to the personality characteristics of that age level.

Within the Piagetian theory of intellectual growth, the concept of egocentrism generally refers to a lack of differentiation in some area of subject-object interaction (Piaget, 1962). At each stage of mental development, this lack of differentiation takes a unique form and is manifested in a unique set of behaviors. The transition from one form of egocentrism to another takes place in a dialectic fashion such that the mental structures which free the child from a lower form of egocentrism are the same structures which ensnare him in a higher form of egocentrism. From the developmental point of view, therefore, egocentrism can be regarded as a negative by-product of any emergent mental system in the sense that it corresponds to the fresh cognitive problems engendered by that system.

Although in recent years Piaget has focused his attention more on the positive than on the negative products of mental structures, egocentrism continues to be of interest because of its relation to the affective aspects of child thought and behavior. Indeed, it is possible that the study of egocentrism may provide a bridge between the study of cognitive structure, on the one hand, and the exploration of personality dynamics, on the other (Cowan, 1966, Gourevitch & Feffer, 1962). The purpose of the present paper is to describe, in greater detail than Inhelder and Piaget (1958), what seems to me to be the nature of egocentrism in adolescence and some of its behavioral and experiential correlates. Before doing that, however, it might be well to set the stage for the discussion with a brief review of the forms of egocentrism which precede this mode of thought in adolescence.

Preparation of this paper was supported in part by grant No. 6881 from the Office of Education. . . .

SOURCE: From David Elkind, "Egocentrism in Adolescence," *Child Development* 38 (1967), 1025–1033.

FORMS OF EGOCENTRISM IN INFANCY AND CHILDHOOD

In presenting the childhood forms of egocentrism, it is useful to treat each of Piaget's major stages as if it were primarily concerned with resolving one major cognitive task. The egocentrism of a particular stage can then be described with reference to this special problem of cognition. It must be stressed, however, that while the cognitive task characteristic of a particular stage seems to attract the major share of the child's mental energies, it is not the only cognitive problem with which the child is attempting to cope. In mental development there are major battles and minor skirmishes, and if I here ignore the lesser engagements it is for purposes of economy of presentation rather than because I assume that such engagements are insignificant.

Sensori-motor Egocentrism (0–2 Years)

The major cognitive task of infancy might be regarded as *the conquest of the object.* In the early months of life, the infant deals with objects as if their existence were dependent upon their being present in immediate perception (Charlesworth, 1966; Piaget, 1954). The egocentrism of this stage corresponds, therefore, to a lack of differentiation between the object and the sense impressions occasioned by it. Toward the end of the first year, however, the infant begins to seek the object even when it is hidden, and thus shows that he can now differentiate between the object and the "experience of the object." This breakdown of egocentrism with respect to objects is brought about by mental representation of the absent object.[1] An internal representation of the absent object is the earliest manifestation of the symbolic function which develops gradually during the second year of life and whose activities dominate the next stage of mental growth.

Pre-operational Egocentrism (2–6 Years)

During the preschool period, the child's major cognitive task can be regarded as *the conquest of the symbol.* It is during the preschool period that the symbolic function becomes fully active, as evidenced by the rapid growth in the acquisition and utilization of language, by the appearance of symbolic play, and by the first reports of dreams. Yet this new capacity for representation, which loosed the infant from his egocentrism with respect to objects, now ensnares the preschool children in a new egocentrism with regard to symbols. At the beginning of this period, the child fails to differentiate between words and their referents (Piaget, 1952b) and between his self-created play and dream symbols and reality (Kohlberg, 1966; Piaget, 1951). Children at this stage believe that the name inheres in the thing and that an object cannot have more than one name (Elkind, 1961a, 1962, 1963).

The egocentrism of this period is particularly evident in children's linguistic behavior. When explaining a piece of apparatus to another child, for example, the youngster at this stage uses many indefinite terms and leaves out important information (Piaget, 1952b). Although this observation is sometimes explained by saying that the child fails to take the other person's point of view, it can also be explained by saying that the child assumes words carry much more information than they actually do. This results from his belief that even the indefinite "thing" somehow conveys the properties of the object which it is used to represent. In short, the egocentrism of this period consists in a lack of clear differentiation between symbols and their referents.

Toward the end of the pre-operational period, the differentiation between symbols and their referents is gradually brought about by the emergence of concrete operations (internalized actions which are roughly comparable in their activity to the elementary operations of arithmetic). One consequence of concrete operational thought is that it enables the child to deal with two elements, properties, or relations at the same time. A child with concrete operations can, for example, take account of both the height and width of a glass of colored liquid and recognize that, when the liquid is poured into a differently shaped container, the changes in height and width of the liquid compensate one another so that the total quantity of liquid is conserved (Elkind, 1961b; Piaget, 1952a). This ability, to hold two dimensions in mind at the same time, also enables the child to hold both symbol and referent in mind simultaneously, and thus distinguish between them. Concrete operations are, therefore, instrumental in overcoming the egocentrism of the preoperational stage.

Concrete Operational Egocentrism (7–11 Years)

With the emergence of concrete operations, the major cognitive task of the school-age child becomes that of *mastering classes, relations, and quantities.* While the preschool child forms global notions of classes, relations, and quantities, such notions are imprecise and cannot be combined one with the other. The child with concrete operations, on the other hand, can nest classes, seriate relations, and conserve quantities. In addition, concrete operations enable the school-age child to perform elementary syllogistic reasoning and to formulate hypotheses and explanations about concrete matters. This system of concrete operations, however, which lifts the school-age child to new heights of thought, nonetheless lowers him to new depths of egocentrism.

Operations are essentially mental tools whose products, series, class hierarchies, conservations, etc., are not directly derived from experience. At this stage, however, the child nonetheless regards these mental products as being on a par with perceptual phenomena. It is the inability to differentiate clearly between mental constructions and perceptual givens which constitutes the egocentrism of the school-age child. An example may help to clarify the form which egocentrism takes during the concrete operational stage.

In a study reported by Peel (1960), children and adolescents were read a passage about Stonehenge and then asked questions about it. One of the questions had to do with whether Stonehenge was a place for religious worship or a fort. The children (ages 7–10) answered the question with flat statements, as if they were stating a fact. When they were given evidence that contradicted their statements, they rationalized the evidence to make it conform with their initial position. Adolescents, on the other hand, phrased their replies in probabilistic terms and supported their judgments with material gleaned from the passage. Similar differences between children and adolescents have been found by Elkind (1966) and Weir (1964).

What these studies show is that, when a child constructs a hypothesis or formulates a strategy, he assumes that this product is imposed by the data rather than derived from his own mental activity. When his position is challenged, he does not change his stance but, on the contrary, reinterprets the data to fit with his assumption. This observation, however, raises a puzzling question. Why, if the child regards both his thought products and the givens of perception as coming from the environment, does he nonetheless give preference to his own mental constructions? The answer probably lies in the fact that the child's mental constructions are the product of reasoning, and hence are experienced as imbued with a (logical) necessity. This "felt" necessity is absent when the child experiences the products of perception. It is not surprising, then, that the child should give priority to what seems permanent and necessary in perception (the products of his own thought, such as conservation) rather than to what seems transitory and arbitrary in perception (products of environmental stimulation). Only in adolescence do young people differentiate between their own mental constructions and the givens of perception. For the child, there are no problems of epistemology.

Toward the end of childhood, the emergence of formal operational thought (which is analogous to propositional logic) gradually frees the child from his egocentrism with respect to his own mental constructions. As Inhelder and Piaget (1958) have shown, formal operational thought enables the young person to deal with all of the possible combinations and permutations of elements within a given set. Provided with four differently colored pieces of plastic, for example, the adolescent can work out all the possible combinations of colors by taking the pieces one, two, three and four, and none, at a time. Children, on the other hand, cannot formulate these combinations in any systematic way. The ability to conceptualize all of the possible combinations in a system allows the adolescent to construct contrary-to-fact hypotheses and to reason about such propositions "as if" they were true. The adolescent, for example, can accept the statement, "Let's suppose coal is white," whereas the child would reply, "But coal is black." This ability to formulate contrary-to-fact hypotheses is crucial to the overcoming of the egocentrism of the concrete operational period. Through the formulation of such contrary-to-fact hypotheses, the young person discovers the arbitrariness of his own mental constructions and learns to differentiate them from perceptual reality.

ADOLESCENT EGOCENTRISM

From the strictly cognitive point of view (as opposed to the psychoanalytic point of view as represented by Blos [1962] and A. Freud [1946] or the ego psychological point of view as represented by Erikson [1959]), the major task of early adolescence can be regarded as having to do with *the conquest of thought.* Formal operations not only permit the young person to construct all the possibilities in a system and construct contrary-to-fact propositions (Inhelder & Piaget, 1958); they also enable him to conceptualize his own thought, to take his mental constructions as objects and reason about them. Only at about the ages of 11–12, for example, do children spontaneously introduce concepts of belief, intelligence, and faith into their definitions of their religious denomination (Elkind, 1961a; 1962; 1963). Once more, however, this new mental system which frees the young person from the egocentrism of childhood entangles him in a new form of egocentrism characteristic of adolescence.

Formal operational thought not only enables the adolescent to conceptualize his thought, it also permits him to conceptualize the thought of other people. It is this capacity to take account of other people's thought, however, which is the crux of adolescent egocentrism. This egocentrism emerges because, while the adolescent can now cognize the thoughts of others, he fails to differentiate between the objects toward which the thoughts of others are directed and those which are the focus of his own concern. Now, it is well known that the young adolescent, because of the physiological metamorphosis he is undergoing, is primarily concerned with himself. Accordingly, since he fails to differentiate between what others are thinking about and his own mental preoccupations, he assumes that other people are as obsessed with his behavior and appearance as he is himself. *It is this belief that others are preoccupied with his appearance and behavior that constitutes the egocentrism of the adolescent.*

One consequence of adolescent egocentrism is that, in actual or impending social situations, the young person anticipates the reactions of other people to himself. These anticipations, however, are based on the premise that others are as admiring or as critical of him as he is of himself. In a sense, then, the adolescent is continually constructing, or reacting to, *an imaginary audience.* It is an audience because the adolescent believes that he will be the focus of attention; and it is imaginary because, in actual social situations, this is not usually the case (unless he contrives to make it so). The construction of imaginary audiences would seem to account, in part at least, for a wide variety of typical adolescent behaviors and experiences.

The imaginary audience, for example, probably plays a role in the self-consciousness which is so characteristic of early adolescence. When the young person is feeling critical of himself, he anticipates that the audience — of which he is necessarily a part — will be critical too. And, since the audience is his own construction and privy to his own knowledge of himself, it knows just what to look for in the way of cosmetic and behavioral sensitivities. The adolescent's wish for privacy and his reluctance to reveal himself may, to some extent, be a reaction to the feeling of being under the constant critical scrutiny of other people. The notion of an imaginary audience also helps to explain the observation that the affect which most concerns adolescents is not guilt but, rather, shame, that is, the reaction to an audience (Lynd, 1961).

While the adolescent is often self-critical, he is frequently self-admiring too. At such times, the audience takes on the same affective coloration. A good deal of adolescent boorishness, loudness, and faddish dress is probably provoked, partially in any case, by a failure to differentiate between what the young person believes to be attractive and what others admire. It is for this reason that the young person frequently fails to understand why adults disapprove of the way he dresses and behaves. The same sort of egocentrism is often seen in behavior directed toward the opposite sex. The boy who stands in front of the mirror for 2 hours combing his hair is probably imagining the swooning reactions he will produce in the girls. Likewise, the girl applying her makeup is more likely than not imagining the admiring glances that will come her way. When these young people actually meet, each is more concerned with being the observed than with being the observer. Gatherings of young adolescents are unique in the sense that each young person is simultaneously an actor to himself and an audience to others.

One of the most common admiring audience constructions, in the adolescent, is the anticipation of how others will react to his own demise. A certain bittersweet pleasure is derived from anticipating the belated recognition by others of his positive qualities. As often happens with such universal fantasies, the imaginary anticipation of one's own demise has been realized in fiction. Below, for example, is the passage in *Tom Sawyer* where Tom sneaks back to his home, after having run away with Joe and Huck, to discover that he and his friends are thought to have been drowned:

> But this memory was too much for the old lady, and she broke entirely down. Tom was snuffling, now, himself — and more in pity of himself than anybody else. He could hear Mary crying and putting in a kindly word for him from time to time. He began to have a nobler opinion of himself than ever before. Still, he was sufficiently touched by his aunt's grief to long to rush out from under the bed and overwhelm her with joy — and the theatrical gorgeousness of the thing appealed strongly to his nature too — but he resisted and lay still.

Corresponding to the imaginary audience is another mental construction which is its complement. While the adolescent fails to differentiate the concerns of his own thought from those of others, he at the same time over-differentiates his feelings. Perhaps because he believes he is of importance to so many people, the imaginary audience, he comes to regard himself, and particularly his feelings, as something special and unique. Only he can suffer with such agonized intensity, or experience such exquisite rapture. How many parents have been confronted with the typically adolescent phrase, "But you don't know how it feels. . . ." The emotional torments undergone by Goethe's young Werther and by Salinger's Holden Caulfield exemplify the adolescent's belief in the uniqueness of his own emotional experience. At a somewhat different level, this belief in personal uniqueness becomes a conviction that he will not die, that death will happen to others but not to him. This complex of beliefs in the uniqueness of his feelings and of his immortality might be called *a personal fable,* a story which he tells himself and which is not true.

Evidences of the personal fable are particularly prominent in adolescent diaries. Such diaries are often written for posterity in the conviction that the young person's experiences, crushes, and frustrations are of universal significance and importance. Another kind of evidence for the personal fable during this period is the tendency to confide in a personal God. The search for privacy and the belief in personal uniqueness leads to the establishment of an I-Thou relationship with God as a personal confidante to whom one no longer looks for gifts but rather for guidance and support (Long, Elkind, & Spilka, 1967).

The concepts of an imaginary audience and a personal fable have proved useful, at least to the writer, in the understanding and treatment of troubled adolescents. The imaginary audience, for example, seems often to play a role in middle-class delinquency (Elkind, 1967). As a case in point, one young man took $1,000 from a golf tournament purse, hid the money, and then promptly revealed himself. It turned out that much of the motivation for this act was derived from the anticipated response of "the audience" to the guttiness of his action. In a similar vein, many young girls become pregnant because, in part at least, their personal fable convinces them that pregnancy will happen to others but never to them and so they need not take precautions. Such examples could be multiplied but will perhaps suffice to illustrate how adolescent egocentrism, as manifested in the imaginary audience and in the personal fable, can help provide a rationale for some adolescent behavior. These concepts can, moreover, be utilized in the treatment of adolescent offenders. It is often helpful to these young people if they can learn to differentiate between the real and the imaginary audience, which often boils down to a discrimination between the real and the imaginary parents.

THE PASSING OF ADOLESCENT EGOCENTRISM

After the appearance of formal operational thought, no new mental systems develop and the mental structures of adolescence must serve for the rest of the life span. The egocentrism of early adolescence nonetheless tends to diminish by the age of 15 or 16, the age at which formal operations become firmly established. What appears to happen is that the imaginary audience, which is primarly an anticipatory audience, is progressively modified in the direction of the reactions of the real audience. In a way, the imaginary audience can be regarded as hypothesis — or better, as a series of hypotheses — which the young person tests against reality. As a consequence of this testing, he gradually comes to recognize the difference between his own preoccupations and the interests and concerns of others.

The personal fable, on the other hand, is probably overcome (although probably never in its entirety) by the gradual establishment of what Erikson (1959) has called "intimacy." Once the young person sees himself in a more realistic light as a function of having adjusted his imaginary audience to the real one, he can establish true rather than self-interested interpersonal relations. Once relations of mutuality are established and confidences are shared, the young person discovers that others have feelings similar to his own and have suffered and been enraptured in the same way.

Adolescent egocentrism is thus overcome by a twofold transformation. On the cognitive plane, it is overcome by the gradual differentiation between his own preoccupations and the thoughts of others; while on the plane of affectivity, it is overcome by a gradual integration of the feelings of others with his own emotions.

SUMMARY AND CONCLUSIONS

In this paper I have tried to describe the forms which egocentrism takes and the mechanisms by which it is overcome, in the course of mental development. In infancy, egocentrism corresponds to the impression that objects are identical with the perception of them, and this form of egocentrism is overcome with the appearance of representation. During the preschool period, egocentrism appears in the guise of a belief that symbols contain the same information as is provided by the objects which they represent. With the emergence of concrete operations, the child is able to discriminate between symbol and referent, and so overcome this type of egocentrism. The egocentrism of the school-age period can be characterized as the belief that one's own mental constructions correspond to a superior form of perceptual reality. With the advent of formal operations and the ability to construct contrary-to-fact hypotheses, this kind of egocentrism is dissolved because the young person can now recognize the arbitrariness of his own mental constructions. Finally, during early adolescence, egocentrism appears as the belief that the thoughts of others are directed toward the self. This variety of egocentrism is overcome as a consequence of the conflict between the reactions which the young person anticipates and those which actually occur.

Although egocentrism corresponds to a negative product of mental growth, its usefulness would seem to lie in the light which it throws upon the affective reactions characteristic of any particular stage of mental development. In this paper I have dealt primarily with the affective reactions associated with the egocentrism of adolescence. Much of the material, particularly the discussion of the *imaginary audience* and the *personal fable* is speculative in the sense that it is based as much upon my clinical experience with young people as it is upon research data. These constructs are offered, not as the final word on adolescent egocentrism, but rather to illustrate how the cognitive structures peculiar to a particular level of development can be related to the affective experience and behavior characteristic of that stage. Although I have here only considered the correspondence between mental structure and affect in adolescence, it is possible that similar correspondences can be found at the earlier levels of development as well. A consideration of egocentrism, then, would seem to be a useful starting point for any attempt to reconcile cognitive structure and the dynamics of personality.

NOTES

1. It is characteristic of the dialectic of mental growth that the capacity to represent internally the absent object also enables the infant to cognize the object as externally existent.

REFERENCES

Blos, P. *On adolescence.* New York: Free Press, 1962.

Charlesworth, W. R. Development of the object concept in infancy: methodological study. *American Psychologist,* 1966, *21,* 623. (Abstract)

Cowan, P. A. Cognitive egocentrism and social

interaction in children. *American Psychologist,* 1966, *21,* 623. (Abstract)

Elkind, D. The child's conception of his religious denomination, I: The Jewish child. *Journal of Genetic Psychology,* 1961, *99,* 209–225. (a)

Elkind, D. The development of quantitative thinking. *Journal of Genetic Psychology,* 1961, *98,* 37–46. (b)

Elkind, D. The child's conception of his religious denomination, II: The Catholic child. *Journal of Genetic Psychology,* 1962, *101,* 185–193.

Elkind, D. The child's conception of his religious denomination, III: The Protestant child. *Journal of Genetic Psychology,* 1963, *103,* 291–304.

Elkind, D. Conceptual orientation shifts in children and adolescents. *Child Development,* 1966, *37,* 493–498.

Elkind, D. Middle-class delinquency. *Mental Hygiene,* 1967, *51,* 80–84.

Erikson, E. H. Identity and the life cycle. *Psychological issues.* Vol. 1, No. 1. New York: International Universities Press, 1959.

Freud, Anna. *The ego and the mechanisms of defense.* New York International Universities Press, 1946.

Gourevitch, Vivian, & Feffer, M. H. A study of motivational development. *Journal of Genetic Psychology,* 1962, *100,* 361–375.

Inhelder, Bärbel, & Piaget, J. *The growth of logical thinking from childhood to adolescence.* New York: Basic Books, 1958.

Kohlberg, L. Cognitive stages and preschool education. *Human Development,* 1966, *9,* 5–17.

Long, Diane, Elkind, D., & Spilka, B. The child's conception of prayer. *Journal for the Scientific Study of Religion,* 1967, *6,* 101–109.

Lynd, Helen M. *On shame and the search for identity.* New York: Science Editions, 1961.

Peel, E. A. *The pupil's thinking.* London: Oldhourne, 1960.

Piaget, J. *The child's conception of the world.* London: Routledge & Kegan Paul, 1951.

Piaget, J. *The child's conception of number.* New York: Humanities Press, 1952. (a)

Piaget, J. *The language and thought of the child.* London: Routledge & Kegan Paul, 1952. (b)

Piaget, J. *The construction of reality in the child.* New York: Basic Books, 1954.

Piaget, J. *Comments on Vygotsky's critical remarks concerning "The language and thought of the child" and "Judgment and reasoning in the child."* Cambridge, Mass.: M.I.T. Press, 1962.

Weir, M. W. Development changes in problem solving strategies. *Psychological Review,* 1964, *71,* 473–490.

Lawrence Kohlberg

THE CHILD AS A MORAL PHILOSOPHER

How can one study morality? Current trends in the fields of ethics, linguistics, anthropology and cognitive psychology have suggested a new approach which seems to avoid the morass of semantical confusions, value-bias and cultural relativity in which the psychoanalytic and semantic approaches to morality have foundered. New scholarship in all these fields is now focusing upon structures, forms and relationships that seem to be common to all societies and all languages rather than upon the features that make particular languages or cultures different.

For 12 years, my colleagues and I studied the same group of 75 boys, following their development at three-year intervals from early adolescence through young manhood. At the start of the study, the boys were aged 10 to 16. We have now followed them through to ages 22 to 28. In addition, I have explored moral development in other cultures — Great Britain, Canada, Taiwan, Mexico and Turkey.

Inspired by Jean Piaget's pioneering effort to apply a structural approach to moral development, I have gradually elaborated over the years of my study a typological scheme describing general structures and forms of moral thought which can be defined independently of the specific content of particular moral decisions or actions.

The typology contains three distinct levels of moral thinking, and within each of these levels distinguishes two related stages. These levels and stages may be considered separate moral philosophies, distinct views of the socio-moral world.

We can speak of the child as having his own morality or series of moralities. Adults seldom listen to children's moralizing. If a child throws back a few adult clichés and behaves himself, most parents — and many anthropologists and psychologists as well — think that the child has adopted or internalized the appropriate parental standards.

Actually, as soon as we talk with children about morality, we find that they have many ways of making judgments which are not "internalized" from the outside, and which do not come in any direct and obvious way from parents, teachers or even peers.

MORAL LEVELS

The *preconventional* level is the first of three levels of moral thinking; the second level is *conventional,* and the third *postconventional* or autonomous. While the preconventional child is often "well-behaved" and is responsive to cultural labels of good and bad, he interprets these labels in terms of their physical consequences (punishment, reward, exchange of favors) or in terms of the physical power of those who enunciate the rules and labels of good and bad.

This level is usually occupied by children aged four to ten, a fact long known to sensitive observers of children. The capacity of

SOURCE: From Lawrence Kohlberg, "The Child as a Moral Philosopher." Reprinted by permission of *Psychology Today* Magazine.

"properly behaved" children of this age to engage in cruel behavior when there are holes in the power structure is sometimes noted as tragic (*Lord of the Flies, High Wind in Jamaica*), sometimes as comic (Lucy in *Peanuts*).

The second or *conventional* level also can be described as conformist, but that is perhaps too smug a term. Maintaining the expectations and rules of the individual's family, group or nation is perceived as valuable in its own right. There is a concern not only with *conforming* to the individual's social order but in *maintaining*, supporting and justifying this order.

The *postconventional* level is characterized by a major thrust toward autonomous moral principles which have validity and application apart from authority of the groups or persons who hold them and apart from the individual's identification with those persons or groups.

MORAL STAGES

Within each of these three levels there are two discernable stages. At the preconventional level we have:

Stage 1: Orientation toward punishment and unquestioning deference to superior power. The physical consequences of action regardless of their human meaning or value determine its goodness or badness.

Stage 2: Right action consists of that which instrumentally satisfies one's own needs and occasionally the needs of others. Human relations are viewed in terms like those of the marketplace. Elements of fairness, of reciprocity and equal sharing are present, but they are always interpreted in a physical, pragmatic way. Reciprocity is a matter of "you scratch my back and I'll scratch yours" not of loyalty, gratitude or justice.

And at the conventional level we have:

Stage 3: Good-boy — good-girl orientation. Good behavior is that which pleases or helps others and is approved by them. There is much conformity to stereotypical images of what is majority or "natural" behavior. Behavior is often judged by intention — "he means well" becomes important for the first time, and is overused, as by Charlie Brown in *Peanuts*. One seeks approval by being "nice."

Stage 4: Orientation toward authority, fixed rules and the maintenance of the social order. Right behavior consists of doing one's duty, showing respect for authority and maintaining the given social order for its own sake. One earns respect by performing dutifully.

At the postconventional level, we have:

Stage 5: A social-contract orientation, generally with legalistic and utilitarian overtones. Right action tends to be defined in terms of general rights and in terms of standards which have been critically examined and agreed upon by the whole society. There is a clear awareness of the relativism of personal values and opinions and a corresponding emphasis upon procedural rules for reaching consensus. Aside from what is constitutionally and democratically agreed upon, right or wrong is a matter of personal "values" and "opinion." The result is an emphasis upon the "legal point of view," but with an emphasis upon the possibility of *changing* law in terms of rational considerations of social utility, rather than freezing it in the terms of Stage 4 "law and order." Outside the legal realm, free agreement and contract are the binding elements of obligation. This is the "official" morality of American government, and finds its ground in the thought of the writers of the Constitution.

Stage 6: Orientation toward the decisions of conscience and toward self-chosen *ethical principles* appealing to logical comprehensiveness, universality and consistency. These principles are abstract and ethical (the Golden Rule, the categorical imperative); they are not concrete moral rules like the Ten Commandments. Instead, they are universal principles of *justice,* of the *reciprocity* and *equality* of human rights, and of respect for the dignity of human beings as *individual persons.*

UP TO NOW

In the past, when psychologists tried to answer the question asked of Socrates by Meno "Is virtue something that can be taught (by rational discussion), or does it come by practice, or is it a natural inborn attitude?" their answers usually have been dictated, not by research findings on children's moral character, but by their general theoretical convictions.

Behavior theorists have said that virtue is behavior acquired according to their favorite general principles of learning. Freudians have claimed that virtue is superego-identification with parents generated by a proper balance of love and authority in family relations.

The American psychologists who have actually studied children's morality have tried to start with a set of labels — the "virtues" and "vices," the "traits" of good and bad character found in ordinary language. The earliest major psychological study of moral character, that of Hugh Hartshorne and Mark May in 1928–1930, focused on a bag of virtues including honesty, service (altruism or generosity), and self-control. To their dismay, they found that there were *no* character traits, psychological dispositions or entities which corresponded to words like honesty, service or self-control.

Regarding honesty, for instance, they found that almost everyone cheats some of the time, and that if a person cheats in one situation, it doesn't mean that he *will* or *won't* in another. In other words, it is not an identifiable character trait, *dis*honesty, that makes a child cheat in a given situation. These early researchers also found that people who cheat express as much or even more moral disapproval of cheating as those who do not cheat.

What Hartshorne and May found out about their bag of virtues is equally upsetting to the somewhat more psychological-sounding names introduced by psychoanalytic psychology: "superego-strength," "resistance to temptation," "strength of conscience," and the like. When recent researchers attempt to measure such traits in individuals, they have been forced to use Hartshorne and May's old tests of honesty and self-control and they get exactly the same results — "superego strength" in one situation predicts little to "superego strength" in another. That is, virtue-words like honesty (or superego-strength) point to certain behaviors with approval, but give us no guide to understanding them.

So far as one can extract some generalized personality factor from children's performance on tests of honesty or resistance to temptation, it is a factor of ego-strength or ego-control, which always involves non-moral capacities like the capacity to maintain attention, intelligent-task performance, and the ability to delay response. "Ego-strength" (called "will" in earlier days) has something to do with moral action, but it does not take us to the core of morality or to the definition of virtue. Obviously enough, many of the greatest evil-doers in history have been men of strong wills, men strongly pursuing immoral goals.

MORAL REASONS

In our research, we have found definite and universal levels of development in moral thought. In our study of 75 American boys from early adolescence on, these youths were presented with hypothetical moral dilemmas, all deliberately philosophical, some of them found in medieval works of casuistry.

On the basis of their reasoning about these dilemmas at a given age, each boy's stage of thought could be determined for each of 25 basic moral concepts or aspects. One such aspect, for instance, is "Motive Given for Rule Obedience or Moral Action." In this instance, the six stages look like this:

1. Obey rules to avoid punishment.
2. Conform to obtain rewards, have favors returned, and so on.
3. Conform to avoid disapproval, dislike by others.
4. Conform to avoid censure by legitimate authorities and resultant guilt.
5. Conform to maintain the respect of the impartial spectator judging in terms of community welfare.
6. Conform to avoid self-condemnation.

In another of these 25 moral aspects, the value of human life, the six stages can be defined thus:

1. The value of a human life is confused with the value of physical objects and is based on the social status or physical attributes of its possessor.
2. The value of a human life is seen as instrumental to the satisfaction of the needs of its possessor or of other persons.
3. The value of a human life is based on the empathy and affection of family members and others toward its possessor.
4. Life is conceived as sacred in terms of its place in a categorical moral or religious order of rights and duties.
5. Life is valued both in terms of its relation to community welfare and in terms of life being a universal human right.
6. Belief in the sacredness of human life as representing a universal human value of respect for the individual.

I have called this scheme a typology. This is because about 50 per cent of most people's thinking will be at a single stage, regardless of the moral dilemma involved. We call our types *stages* because they seem to represent an *invariant developmental sequence.* "True" stages come one at a time and always in the same order.

All movement is forward in sequence, and does not skip steps. Children may move through these stages at varying speeds, of course, and may be found half in and half out of a particular stage. An individual may stop at any given stage and at any age, but if he continues to move, he must move in accord with these steps. Moral reasoning of the conventional or Stage 3–4 kind never occurs before the preconventional Stage-1 and Stage-2 thought has taken place. No adult in Stage 4 has gone through Stage 6, but all Stage-6 adults have gone at least through 4.

While the evidence is not complete, my study strongly suggests that moral change fits the stage pattern just described. (The major uncertainty is whether all Stage 6s go through Stage 5 or whether these are two alternate mature orientations.)

HOW VALUES CHANGE

As a single example of our findings of stage-sequence, take the progress of two boys on the aspect "The Value of Human Life." The first boy Tommy, is asked "Is it better to save the life of one important person or a lot of unimportant people?" At age 10, he answers "all the people that aren't important because one man just has one house, maybe a lot of furniture, but a whole bunch of people have an awful lot of furniture and some of these poor people might have a lot of money and it doesn't look it."

Clearly Tommy is Stage 1: he confuses the value of a human being with the value of the property he possesses. Three years later (age 13) Tommy's conceptions of life's value are most clearly elicited by the question, "Should the doctor 'mercy kill' a fatally ill woman requesting death because of her pain?" He answers, "Maybe it would be good to put her out of her pain, she'd be better off that way. But the husband wouldn't want it, it's not like an animal. If a pet dies you can get along without it — it isn't something you really need. Well, you can get a new wife, but it's not really the same."

Here his answer is Stage 2: the value of the woman's life is partly contingent on its hedonistic value to the wife herself but even more contingent on its instrumental value to her husband, who can't replace her as easily as he can a pet.

Three years later still (age 16) Tommy's conception of life's value is elicited by the same question, to which he replies: "It might be best for her, but her husband — it's a human life — not like an animal; it just doesn't have the same relationship that a human being does to a family. You can become attached to a dog, but nothing like a human you know."

Now Tommy has moved from a Stage 2 instrumental view of the woman's value to a Stage-3 view based on the husband's distinctively human empathy and love for someone in his family. Equally clearly, it lacks any basis for a universal human value of the woman's life, which would hold if she had no husband or if her husband didn't love her. Tommy, then, has moved step by step through three stages during the age 10–16. Tommy, though bright (I.Q. 120), is a slow developer in moral judgment. Let us take another boy, Richard, to show us sequential movement through the remaining three steps.

At age 13, Richard said about the mercy-killing, "If she requests it, it's really up to her. She is in such terrible pain, just the same as people are always putting animals out of their pain," and in general showed a mixture of Stage-2 and Stage-3 responses concerning the value of life. At 16, he said, "I don't know. In one way, it's murder, it's not a right or privilege of man to decide who shall live and who should die. God put life into everybody on earth and you're taking away something from that person that came directly from God, and you're destroying something that is very sacred, it's in a way part of God and it's almost destroying a part of God when you kill a person. There's something of God in everyone."

Here Richard clearly displays a Stage-4 concept of life as sacred in terms of its place in a categorical moral or religious order. The value of human life is universal, it is true for all humans. It is still, however, dependent on something else, upon respect for God and God's authority; it is not an autonomous human value. Presumably if God told Richard to murder, as God commanded Abraham to murder Isaac, he would do so.

At age 20, Richard said to the same question: "There are more and more people in the medical profession who think it is a hardship on everyone, the person, the family, when you know they are going to die. When a person is kept alive by an artificial lung or kidney it's more like being a vegetable than being a human. If it's her own choice, I think there are certain rights and privileges that go along with being a human being. I am a human being and have certain desires for life and I think everybody else does too. You have a world of which you are the center, and everybody else does too and in that sense we're all equal."

Richard's response is clearly Stage 5, in that the value of life is defined in terms of equal and universal human rights in a context of relativity ("You have a world of which you are the center and in that sense we're all equal"), and of concern for utility or welfare consequences.

THE FINAL STEP

At 24, Richard says: "A human life takes precedence over any other moral or legal value, whoever it is. A human life has inherent value whether or not it is valued by a particular individual. The worth of the individual human being is central where the principles of justice and love are normative for all human relationships."

This young man is at Stage 6 in seeing the value of human life as absolute in representing a universal and equal respect for the human as an individual. He has moved step by step through a sequence culminating in a definition of human life as centrally valuable rather than derived from or dependent on social or divine authority.

In a genuine and culturally universal sense, these steps lead toward an increased *morality* of value judgment, where morality is considered as a form of judging, as it has been in a philosophic tradition running from the analyses of Kant to those of the modern analytic or "ordinary language" philosophers. The person at Stage 6 has disentangled his judgments of — or language about — human life from status and property values (Stage 1), from its uses to others (Stage 2), from interpersonal affection (Stage 3), and so on; he has a means of moral judgment that is universal and impersonal. The Stage-6 person's answers use moral words like "duty" or "morally right," and he uses them in a way implying universality, ideals, impersonality: He thinks and speaks in phrases like "regardless of who it was," or ". . . I would do it in spite of punishment."

ACROSS CULTURES

When I first decided to explore moral development in other cultures, I was told by anthropologist friends that I would have to throw away my culture-bound moral concepts and stories and start from scratch learning a whole new set of values for each new culture. My first try consisted of a brace of villages, one Atayal (Malaysian aboriginal) and the other Taiwanese.

My guide was a young Chinese ethnographer who had written an account of the moral and religious patterns of the Atayal and Taiwanese villages. Taiwanese boys in the 10–13 age group were asked about a story involving theft of food. A man's wife is starving to death but the store owner won't give the man any food unless he can pay, which he can't. Should he break in and steal some food? Why? Many of the boys said, "He should steal the food for his wife because if she dies he'll have to pay for her funeral and that costs a lot."

My guide was amused by these responses, but I was relieved: they were of course "classic" Stage-2 responses. In the Atayal village, funerals weren't such a big thing, so the Stage-2 boys would say, "He should steal the food because he needs his wife to cook for him."

This means that we need to consult our anthropologists to know what content a Stage-2 child will include in his instrumental exchange calculations, or what a Stage-4 adult will identify as the proper social order. But one certainly doesn't have to start from scratch. What made my guide laugh was the difference in form between the children's Stage-2 thought and his own, a difference definable independently of particular cultures.

Illustrations number 1 and number 2 indicate the cultural universality of the sequence of stages which we have found. Illustration number 1 presents the age trends for middle-class urban boys in the U.S., Taiwan and Mexico. At age 10 in each country, the order of use of each stage is the same as the order of its difficulty or maturity.

In the United States, by age 16 the order is the reverse, from the highest to the lowest, except that Stage 6 is still little-used. At age

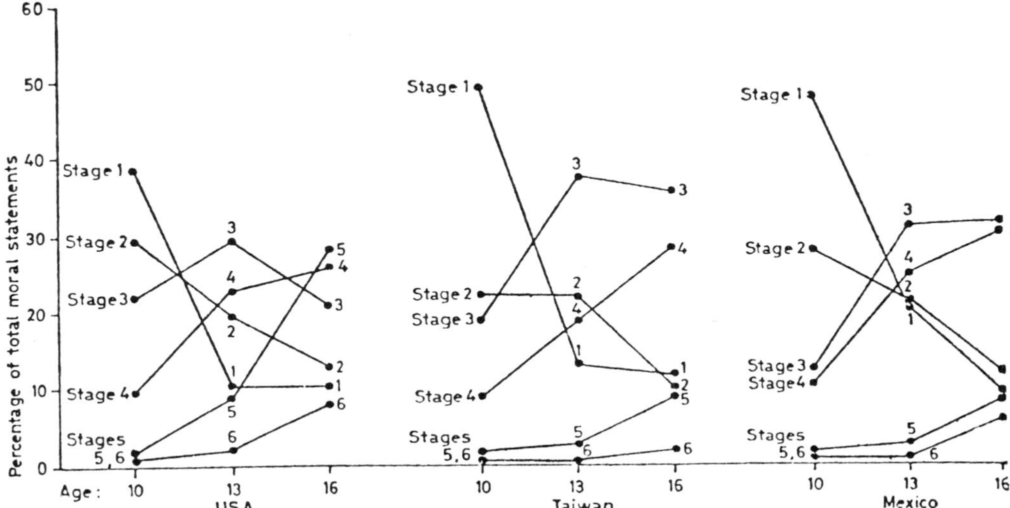

Figure 1. Middle-class urban boys in the U.S., Taiwan and Mexico (*above*). At age 10 the stages are used according to difficulty. At age 13, Stage 3 is most used by all three groups. At age 16 U.S. boys have reversed the order of age 10 stages (with the exception of 6). In Taiwan and Mexico, conventional (3–4) stages prevail at age 16, with Stage 5 also little used.

Figure 2. Two isolated villages, one in Turkey, the other in Yucatan, show similar patterns in moral thinking. There is no reversal of order, and preconventional (1–2) thought does not gain a clear ascendancy over conventional stages at age 16.

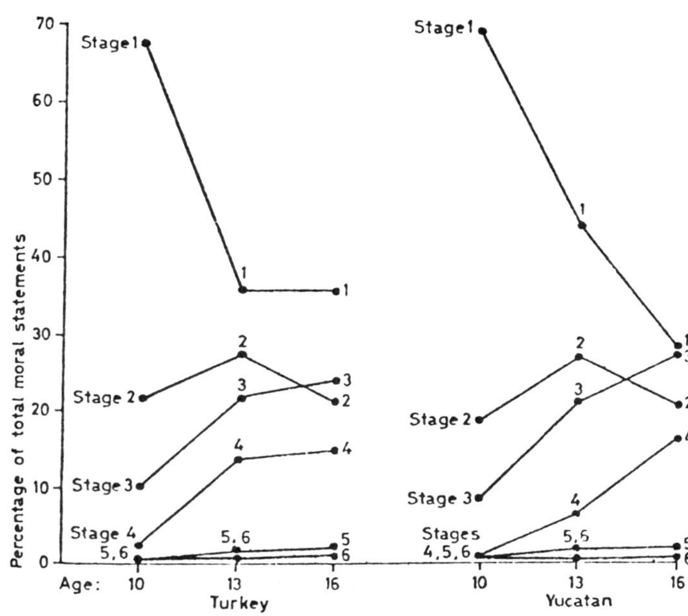

13, the good-boy, middle stage (Stage 3), is not used.

The results in Mexico and Taiwan are the same, except that development is a little slower. The most conspicuous feature is that at the age of 16, Stage-5 thinking is much more salient in the United States than in Mexico or Taiwan. Nevertheless, it *is* present in the other countries, so we know that this is not purely an American democratic construct.

Illustration 2 shows strikingly similar results from two isolated villages, one in Yucatan, one in Turkey. While conventional moral thought increases steadily from ages 10 to 16 it still has not achieved a clear ascendency over preconventional thought.

Trends for lower-class urban groups are intermediate in the rate of development between those for the middle-class and for the village boys. In the three divergent cultures that I studied, middle-class children were found to be more advanced in moral judgment than matched lower-class children. This was not due to the fact that the middle-class children heavily favored some one type of thought which could be seen as corresponding to the prevailing middle-class pattern. Instead, middle-class and working-class children move through the same sequences, but the middle-class children move faster and farther.

This sequence is not dependent upon a particular religion, or any religion at all in the usual sense. I found no important differences in the development of moral thinking among Catholics, Protestants, Jews, Buddhists, Moslems and atheists. Religious values seem to go through the same stages as all other values.

TRADING UP

In summary, the nature of our sequence is not significantly affected by widely varying social, cultural or religious conditions. The only thing that is affected is the *rate* at which individuals progress through this sequence.

Why should there be such a universal invariant sequence of development? In answering this question, we need first to analyze these developing social concepts in terms of their internal logical structure. At each stage, the same basic moral concept or aspect is defined, but at each higher stage this definition is more differentiated, more integrated and more general or universal. When one's concept of human life moves from Stage 1 to Stage 2 the value of life becomes more differentiated from the value of property, more integrated (the value of life enters an organizational hierarchy where it is "higher" than property so that one steals property in order to save life) and more universalized (the life of any sentient being is valuable regardless of status or property). The same advance is true at each stage in the hierarchy. Each step of development then is a better cognitive organization than the one before it, one which takes account of everything present in the previous stage, but making new distinctions and organizing them into a more comprehensive or more equilibrated structure. The fact that this is the case has been demonstrated by a series of studies indicating that children and adolescents comprehend all stages up to their own, but not more than one stage beyond their own. And importantly, *they prefer this next stage.*

We have conducted experimental moral discussion classes which show that the child at an earlier stage of development tends to move forward when confronted by the views of a child one stage further along. In an argument between a Stage-3 and Stage-4 child, the child in the third stage tends to move toward or into Stage 4, while the Stage-4 child understands but does not accept the arguments of the Stage-3 child.

Moral thought, then, seems to behave like all other kinds of thought. Progress through the moral levels and stages is characterized by increasing differentiation and increasing integration, and hence is the same kind of progress that scientific theory represents. Like acceptable scientific theory — or like *any* theory or structure of knowledge — moral thought may be considered partially to generate its own data as it goes along, or at least to expand so as to contain in a balanced, self-consistent way a wider and wider experiential field. The raw data in the case of our ethical philosophies may be considered as conflicts between roles, or values, or as the social order in which men live.

THE ROLE OF SOCIETY

The social worlds of all men seem to contain the same basic structures. All the societies we have studied have the same basic institutions — family, economy, law, government. In addition, however, all societies are alike because they *are* societies — systems of defined complementary roles. In order to *play* a social role in the family, school or society, the child must implicitly take the role of others toward himself and toward others in the group. These role-taking tendencies form the basis of all social institutions. They represent various patternings of shared or complementary expectations.

In the preconventional and conventional levels (Stages 1–4), moral content or value is largely accidental or culture-bound. Anything from "honesty" to "courage in battle" can be the central value. But in the higher postconventional levels, Socrates, Lincoln, Thoreau and Martin Luther King tend to speak without confusion of tongues, as it were. This is because the ideal principles of any social structure are basically alike, if only because there simply aren't that many principles which are articulate, comprehensive and integrated enough to be satisfying to the human intellect. And most of these principles have gone by the name of justice.

Behavioristic psychology and psychoanalysis have always upheld the Philistine view that fine moral words are one thing and moral deeds another. Morally mature reasoning is quite a different matter, and does not really depend on "fine words." The man who understands justice is more likely to practice it.

In our studies, we have found that youths who understand justice act more justly, and the man who understands justice helps create a moral climate which goes far beyond his immediate and personal acts. The universal society is the beneficiary.

Carol Gilligan and John Michael Murphy

DEVELOPMENT FROM ADOLESCENCE TO ADULTHOOD: THE PHILOSOPHER AND THE DILEMMA OF THE FACT

"Reason alone is sufficient to govern a rational creature," says one of the Houyhnhnms in *Gulliver's Travels* and, like Gulliver, we are tempted to agree. Accustomed by the myriad studies of Piaget to trace the growth of intelligence in the progression from the charming fallacies of childhood explanation to the irrefutable logic of adolescent thought, we readily equate cognitive development with the growth of logical thinking and see the formal operations of propositional logic as the apogee of human thought. "No person can disobey reason, without giving up his claim to be a rational creature," warn the Houyhnhnms, and this inexorable logic becomes ever more compelling as Gulliver witnesses the order it sustains.

For in this land to which he has come, these amazing horses, whose self-chosen name proclaims them to be "the perfection of nature," have a rational solution for all of life's problems. Correcting the random disorder of nature with the measured constancy of reason, they rearrange children to make families alike, replacing loss, accepting death, and eliminating disagreement by decisions so rational as to be beyond dispute. Among these creatures "who cultivate reason," inequality vanishes and moral problems disappear, except of course for that of Gulliver — the "wonderful Yahoo that could speak like a Houyhnhnm" — who, being at once both rational and human, defies the categories of Houyhnhnm thought and so, in the end, is expelled from their land.

In this chapter, we describe a similar encounter that occurs in the course of human development when adolescents discover that the categories of their reason cannot encompass the facts of their experience. This is the time in cognitive development that Inhelder and Piaget (1958) describe as "the return to reality," the shift from a metaphysical to an empirical truth that charts the "path from adolescence to the true beginnings of adulthood" (1958, p. 346). Then the contradictory pulls of logic and affect, and the difficulty of their integration, call into question

This research was supported by grants from the Spencer Foundation, the Milton Fund, and the small grants section of the National Institute of Mental Health. We would like to thank Terry Deacon, John Gibbs, Donna Hulsizer, and Dennis Norman for their comments. Deanna Kuhn provided excellent editing suggestions through several drafts of this chapter and merits our special thanks.

SOURCE: Reprinted with permission of the author and publisher. Originally published by Jossey-Bass Inc., Publishers in 1979. Gilligan, C., and Murphy, J. M., "Development from Adolescence to Adulthood: The Philosopher and the Dilemma of the Fact." In D. Kuhn (Ed.), *New Directions for Child Development: Intellectual Development Beyond Childhood,* no. 5. San Francisco: Jossey-Bass, 1979. An expanded version of this article will appear in *Beyond Formal Operations: Alternative Endpoints to Human Development,* edited by Charles N. Alexander and Ellen Langer (Oxford University Press).

the equation of reason with logic, giving rise to a conflict that can be the occasion for further development.

FORMAL LOGIC AND INTELLECTUAL MATURITY: THE STRUCTURE OF ADOLESCENT AND ADULT THOUGHT

> Now, as we have come to see more clearly through Gödel but knew long before, the ideal of a structure of all structures is unrealizable (Piaget, 1971, p. 142).

While Piaget (1967, 1971, 1972; Inhelder and Piaget, 1958) stresses the difference between the adolescent's egocentric belief in the omniscient capacity of formal logic and the adult's more equilibrated "reason which reunites intelligence and affectivity" (1967, p. 80), the nature of this transformation has not been systematically explored. Thus it remains unclear how the structures of formal operations that permit bright twelve-year-olds to solve the pendulum problem are transformed by the return to reality that Piaget claims is brought about by the responsibility of adult work.

The increased interest in the nature of cognitive development in adulthood that has occurred during the past ten years, however, promises — as Piaget saw — not only to fill in this gap by "elucidating from a cognitive point of view the passage from adolescence to adulthood" but also to "retroactively throw light on what we already think we know about earlier stages" (Piaget, 1972, pp. 9–10).

Questions about the nature of formal operations and questions about the structural qualities of mature thought are thus conjoined. According to Labouvie-Vief, "the ideal form of [development] has been seen in the operative functioning of logical and mathematic group structures. The use of mathematico-logical tasks in the assessment of 'mature' cognition has been derived, in turn, from these forms" (Labouvie-Vief, 1979, pp. 3–4). This raises the question of whether "the Piagetian emphasis on formal logic as a criterion of adaptive maturity does not virtually guarantee the observation of adaptive failure and regression on either side of the adolescent apogee" (Labouvie-Vief, 1979, p. 2).

There is one line of research that points to a way out of this dilemma. Instead of assuming that the definition of mature cognition is already known and fully operationalized, a number of researchers have attempted to elucidate the structures of cognition used by adults in everyday life (Kitchener and King, 1979; Riegel, 1973; Sinnot, 1975; Youniss, 1974), with an eye toward describing the particular adaptiveness they may have. It is in this approach that our own work is grounded. Labouvie-Vief argues that "although the picture of intellectual maturity derived from [Inhelder and Piaget's] tests may be particularly germane in a school setting and at that stage of life, it may lack validity if applied to more mature adults and to new, nonacademic situations" (1979, p. 16).

Thus, although it may be possible to generate "all possible combinations of propositions" (Piaget, 1967, p. 358) to Inhelder and Piaget's formal reasoning tasks in the laboratory or even to solve all the logical problems encountered in the classroom, in the real-life situations faced by most adults such full formalism may be inadequate and even maladaptive. As Flavell suggests, "Real problems with meaningful content are obviously more important in everyday human adaptation [than abstract, wholly logical problems], and it is possible that these are the kinds of problems our cognitive apparatus has evolved to solve" (1977, p. 117).

Thus, the demand for formalization in reasoning may be a false standard for development. Such an interpretation is supported by a finding in the field of logic:

> The most important theorems limiting the formalization of logical thought are due to Gödel. They are based on the fact that within any deductive system which includes arithmetic . . . it is possible to construct formulae — i.e., sentences — which are demonstrably undecidable within that system, and that such a sentence — the famous Gödelian sentence — may say of itself that it is undecidable within the system (Polanyi, 1958, p. 259).

According to Quine (1976), Gödel's proof legitimates contradiction within the study of formal logic and is, because of its proof of formal undecidability, a "veridical paradox." Thus, Polanyi observes that:

> This uncertainty can be eliminated for any particular deductive system by shifting it onto a wider system of axioms, within which we may be able to prove the consistency of the original system. But any such proof will still remain uncertain, in the sense that the consistency of the wider system will always remain undecidable (Polanyi, 1958, p. 259).

Such considerations have a direct bearing on research attempting to measure the attainment of formal operations, and in fact Gödel's work was central to Piaget's elaboration of the dialectical implications of his basic "structuralism."

> Since Gödel . . . the idea of a formal system of abstract structures is thereby transformed into that of the construction of a never completed whole, the limits of formalization constituting the grounds for incompleteness, or as we saw earlier, incompleteness being a necessary consequence of the fact that there is no "terminal" or "absolute" form because any content is form relative to some inferior content and any form the content for some higher form (Piaget, 1970, p. 140).

The incompleteness of formal structures thus introduces a new element into the research on formal operations. The closed-system INRC logic that could generate all possible combinations is now qualified by a "certain openness," and a dialectic with "new knowledge," other legitimate points of view, and empirical reality is now required to demonstrate adequacy. These observations about the structure of formal systems lead Piaget to open his definitions of the structure of knowledge as well:

> From Gödel's conclusions there follow certain important insights as to the limits of formalization in general; in particular, it has been possible to show that there are, in addition to formalized levels of knowledge, distinct "semi-formal" or "semi-intuitive" levels which wait their turn so to say for formalization (Piaget, 1971, p. 35).

Or, as Polanyi observes, "In the Gödelian process we add to a formally undecided statement of ours a tacit interpretation of our own . . . we establish something new by an inescapable act of our own, induced — but not performed — by formal operations" (1958, p. 260).

Thus the incompleteness of formal systems leads to an irremediable gap between the logical deduction and the tacit assent of the person who chooses to affirm it. The adequacy of a system of formal logic depends, then, as much on an awareness of the need to ground it within the context of the "next 'higher' theory" (Piaget, 1971, p. 34) as on the demonstration of its completeness. Thus it would seem that the appropriate evaluation of a formal judgment would lie less in the elegance of its formal justification than in a more open and dialectical process involving contextualization and an openness to reevaluation.

The implications of Gödel's work for a theory of adult cognition have recently been examined by Labouvie-Vief (1979). She links this proof of the limits of a single perspective and the need for continued empirical verification in logic to the questions raised at the outset of this paper about individual cognitive development. In doing so, she sketches a two-step progression of continuing cognitive development past the adolescent attainment of formal operations which begins with "a cognitive differentiation, namely a realization that logic is merely a necessary condition and becomes a sufficient element of adult life only if subordinated to a hierarchically higher goal: social system maintenance. It is important then to distinguish between logic as a *goal* and logic as a *tool.* We propose that it is exactly this cognitive differentiation which brings with it the second step, the adult concerns with commitment, generativity, and social responsibility" (Labouvie-Vief, 1979, pp. 19–20).

She argues that the general outline of this progression is to be found in Piaget's discussions of the reconciliation between formal thought and reality (Inhelder and Piaget, 1958; Piaget, 1967, 1972). The importance of the concern with social system maintenance, or in Erikson's sense, with generativity, is apparent there as well, she claims, citing Piaget's observation that "[adult] personality . . . results from the submission or rather the autosubmission of the self to some kind of discipline . . . In this sense the person and the social relationships he engenders and maintains are interdependent" (Piaget, 1967, p. 65).

While the adult concern with generating and maintaining interdependent systems of social relationships has been studied by theorists of ego development, this concern has implications for cognitive psychology as well — ones that are manifest particularly in the area of moral development.

> The adult's commitment towards social system maintenance raises the most provocative question of extensions to other areas of cognitive development — in particular, moral development. Adulthood has sometimes been said to bring a return to a more conventional level of morality. Yet, we may ask, are there not genuine structural differences between an assertion of authority-qua-authority and a complex cognitive realization of the genuine multiple embeddedness of social system interweaving? If so, one might argue that moral development in adulthood brings a spiral-like but progressive recurrence of the polarity of earlier social-cognitive structures . . . [but] raised to a higher level of cognitive differentiation in adulthood . . . Few empirical studies are available at present to demonstrate this hypothesized structural feature of an autonomous submission to social roles but Perry's (1970) has emphasized the hierarchical integration of commitment vis-a-vis relativity (Labouvie-Vief, 1979, pp. 21–22).

In his empirical study of the *Forms of Intellectual and Ethical Development in the College Years,* Perry (1968) found evidence for a sequence of development through nine "Positions" from the early absolutism of adolescent logic, through its full flowering in the forms of multiplicity and relativism, to the development of a new equilibrium of epistemological commitment within contextual relativism. Perry views these post-relativistic positions of commitment (6–9) as adding "an advanced 'period' to Piaget's outline," or in other terms, a post-formal-operational stage to the sequence of cognitive development.

For Perry, an individual's attainment of this advanced period is dependent on a single epistemological paradigm shift beginning with the realization of the contextual relativism of all knowledge. This, in turn, is based on an understanding of the limits of formal logic, which Perry refers to as reason:

> Reason reveals relations within any given context; it can also compare one context with another on the basis of metacontents established for this purpose. But there is a limit. In the end, reason itself remains reflexively relativistic, a property which turns

> reason back upon reason's own findings. In even its farthest reaches then reason will leave the thinker with several legitimate contexts and no way of choosing among them — no way at least that he can justify through reason alone. If he is still to honor reason he must now also transcend it; he must affirm his own position from within himself in full awareness that reason can never completely justify him or assure him (Perry, 1968, pp. 135–136).

Thus, for Perry, the formally undecidable nature of human choice leads to an acknowledgment of the tacit component of thought referred to by Polanyi and Piaget. In Perry's scheme, Polanyi's tacit assent becomes affirmation, an act of commitment which "ushers in the period of responsibility" (1968, p. 205).

Perry's scheme operationalizes the more dialectical notion of post-formal intellectual and ethical development for which we have argued here. In contrast, Kohlberg's (1971, 1976) approach to the study of moral reasoning operationalizes a formal logical model of cognitive and moral development. In Kohlberg's conception, each Piagetian cognitive stage provides a necessary but not sufficient condition for a parallel moral stage. Moral Stages 1 and 2 in Kohlberg's theory are based on advancing substages of concrete operations, while moral Stages 3, 4, and 5 are based on substages of formal operations (Kohlberg and Gilligan, 1971). Principled moral reasoning (Stage 5 and beyond) in particular depends on the attainment of consolidated formal operations. Kohlberg claimed it was possible to assess moral reasoning in terms of its correspondence to a system of internal logic whose highest point relied on the propositional operations of logically reversible and universalizable "justice structures" (Kohlberg, 1976).

While this conception may be useful in research on moral development in children and younger adolescents, it encounters difficulties when applied to samples of older adolescents and adults, where there has been a persistent finding of late adolescent regression from the highly logical Stage 5 to mixed (4/5) or conventional (Stage 4 or Stage 3) scores in adulthood. The problem was first noted by Kohlberg when he followed his adolescent sample longitudinally into early adulthood. In 1969 he reported with Kramer the anomolous finding that 20 percent of Kohlberg's subjects seemed to have turned away from the compelling formal logic of his highest stages and regressed to less complex forms of judgment. This finding led Kohlberg to undertake the complete revision of his scoring system (Kohlberg and others, 1978) in an effort to correct what he assumed was a confusion of content with form.

Rather than relaxing the formal requirements of his highest stages, however, he has, if anything, increased them. Thus while the rescoring of his own data by his revised system has virtually eliminated regression, it has also eliminated Stage 6 and drastically reduced the incidence of Stage 5 (Kohlberg, 1979). The situation with respect to moral development is thus analogous to that in cognitive development: by strict formal criteria, very few adults appear to be mature. In a different longitudinal sample of very bright subjects, scored by the same coders according to the revised manual, more than half of the twenty-six subjects scored at the fully principled level at one of the longitudinal testing points. Most of these subjects, however, later regressed from Kohlberg's highest stages, thus repeating with the new scoring system the particular violation of sequence that it was designed to correct (Murphy and Gilligan, in press).

However, when the same data were scored according to a different scoring system based on Perry's scheme, longitudinal progression through a sequence was clear. Since Perry's scheme is based on a progression from early formal operations (Positions 3 and 4 in Perry's scheme — Multiplicity) through a transitional crisis (Position 5 — Relativism) to a post-formal operational equilibrium in which the structures of cognition have been transformed (Positions 6 and beyond — Commitment in Relativism), the Murphy and Gilligan findings of developmental sequence in Perry's system can be viewed as empirical support of a model of cognitive development that postulates progression in late adolescence towards more dialetical or contextual structures of thought.

Our use of Perry's theory as a way of making sense of late adolescent development stemmed from our attempt to analyze the way in which individuals at Kohlberg's highest stages applied their reasoning to the solution of their own real moral dilemmas. Our research began in 1970 when the senior author set out to investigate the development of thinking about real life experiences of moral conflict and choice. The study that resulted was designed to describe the ways in which thinking about actual dilemmas differed from thinking about hypothetical dilemmas and to investigate the role of life experience in the process of moral development. By asking college students to describe the moral dilemmas they encountered and the ways in which they had come to resolve them, Gilligan began to identify the universe of dilemmas encountered by these students and to see the role that such encounters played in the evolution of their thought. The students' association of changes in their thinking with real experiences of conflict and choice then led to a naturalistic study of people who were facing a moral decision. Gilligan (1977) and Belenky (1978) interviewed women deciding whether to continue or abort a pregnancy and described the different forms of thinking that were brought to bear on the construction and resolution of that dilemma. In addition, Belenky and Gilligan (1979) described changes in thinking that were manifest on a one-year follow-up interview, addressing the natural history and sequence of developmental transition and the conditions likely to precipitate or impede its occurrence.

The same transitional processes that appeared in the naturalistic study of abortion decisions were also found among subjects in the college sample referred to previously. While a number of the subjects in that sample did seem to meet or even exceed Kohlberg's rigorous criteria of formal logical structure at age nineteen, at ages twenty-two and twenty-seven they began to indicate dissatisfaction with this logic as an adequate basis for understanding their own personal dilemmas of moral conflict and choice. Instead, their reasoning began to show some different structural qualities which, according to their self-reports, emerged from experiences that had revealed to them the limitations of their earlier perspectives.

In sum, these longitudinal data suggest that moral reasoning in its real-life contexts relies on cognitive structures other than those deriving solely from formal logic. In particular, the second author's reinterviews of the college subjects at age twenty-seven indicates that a developmental evolution can be traced from the perfection of logical systems as a basis for moral reasoning in adolescence to the placing of these formal logical systems within the broader context of a more differentiated and dialectical moral understanding in adulthood. The present chapter, then, describes aspects of our ongoing longitudinal study designed to elucidate the developmental passage from adolescence to adulthood by analyzing the nature of thinking about "the reality of things" (Piaget, 1967) and the ways in which the growing experience of this reality can affect the development of thought.

THE PHILOSOPHER AND THE DILEMMA OF THE FACT

> Friendship and benevolence are the two principal virtues among the Houyhnhnms and these are not confined to particular objects, but universal to the whole race, for a stranger from the remotest part, is equally treated with the nearest neighbor, and wherever he goes, looks upon himself as at home (Swift, *Gulliver's Travels*).

> Because I know that time is always time
> And place is always and only place
> And what is actual is actual only for one time
> And only for one place
> I rejoice that things are as they are . . .
> And pray to God to have mercy upon us
> (T. S. Eliot, *Ash Wednesday*)

The two adolescent "philosophers" we will discuss were college seniors at the time that they agreed to participate in our interview. They were part of a group of students who were chosen for study because they had shown particular interest in the study of morality, electing as sophomores to take a course on moral and political choice. At the time of the course, their moral judgments were assessed by Kohlberg's standard method. We have chosen these two students for comparison here because they typify a pattern of developmental divergence that was evident in the sample as a whole.

Both students were philosophy majors whose judgments had, in their senior year, reached the highest level of Kohlberg's stage sequence. Philosopher One's judgments of hypothetical dilemmas reflected a principled moral understanding that was scored at the highest of Kohlberg's stages (Stage 5 by the 1978 manual) both in his sophomore and senior years. At the beginning of his sophomore year, the judgments of Philosopher Two were scored as transitional between conventional and principled morality (4(5)) but by the end of his senior year they too had reached the fully principled stage. Thus, in the senior-year interviews, these two philosophers applied their principles of justice to the solution of Kohlberg's hypothetical dilemmas, proclaiming unequivocally the moral rightness of stealing a drug to save a life and earning for their principled certainty the unequivocal score of Stage 5.

However, our interview went beyond the standard Kohlberg procedure of assessing judgment of hypothetical dilemmas and posed questions about moral conflicts that the students had experienced in the course of their lives, asking them to describe their thinking about these events. In this open-ended section of the interview on life experience, both students recounted involvement in dilemmas of sexual fidelity, and told of their difficulty in judging their actions. Philosopher One had broken a "mutual expectation" of honesty and fidelity in his relationship with "Girl A" by not acknowledging to her that he had fallen in love with "Girl B." Philosopher Two's dilemma stemmed from the fact that the husband of the woman with whom he was involved had not been told about the affair. While each subject raised questions about the morality of his actions, and their apparent discrepancy with his principles of justice, the questions in each case were different and therein lies the basis for our comparison.

Philosopher One seems never to have questioned his belief that there was a right way to judge his dilemma. His problem stemmed rather from his uncertainty as to whether or not he was judging it correctly. Unclear as to whether he had "violated" his principles in acting toward Girl A as he did, he explains that:

> Falling in love with Girl B made it hard for me to honor all of my commitments to Girl A, and it made it harder for me to always be as attentive to her as I really

> wanted to be, because I was preoccupied with somebody else. So, *it is difficult to sort out whether or not I was violating something.* I could make a case that I might believe (and I don't know whether I have, unconsciously or consciously) that I hadn't really grossly transgressed my principles, and then again I could construct another case that I maybe had in a few respects.

Attempting to reconstruct the facts of the dilemma in accordance with the principles of trust, he suggests that he might possibly at least have respected the spirit of the agreement whose letter he had broken.

> How do I prevent myself from violating this first girl's trust, and I did that partly, and I didn't do it completely successfully . . . it was a question of her wanting not to be displaced in my feelings, and I think in some kind of a sense I didn't do that, so I sort of honored her essential expectations, which was not that I tell her the truth so much as I not displace her with somebody else. *It's hard to know whether I did or not,* and sometimes I think I did and if I did, that would be a case where I could perhaps feel that I acted unjustly, if I did displace her, but I think that thinking about it, it is the kind of thing that had to end. And we were not doing that. And then it came time to do it, and I sort of had an extra impetus to do it because there was something else happening to me. And yet it did not seem to alter in an important way the course of things between the first girl and me. It did alter my treatment of her a little bit.

To resolve his quandary concerning the judgment of this dilemma, he turns away from the contradictions that arise in his description of the event and focuses instead on questions of principle, asking: "What are her legitimate expectations of me and how do you define trust in principled terms?" He attributes the limitation of his current judgment in assessing the legitimacy of her expectations to his incomplete understanding of the principle of trust. Having initially endorsed the mutuality of trust, he nevertheless had acted "according to my estimation of where her interests lay instead of what her expectations were." Upon reflection, however, he seemed to feel that something was amiss in the expectation itself and questioned whether "the sort of trust and understanding we had was *the right one* to have" (emphasis added).

This student's philosophy, clearly at odds with the "facts" of his dilemma, is stretched to provide the judgment he seeks. Convinced that a right answer exists and that eventually he will find the complete definition of trust, he believes that this discovery ultimately will determine the legitimacy of interpersonal expectations, establishing the logical priorities to guide a just solution to this dilemma. Throughout his discussion his concern remains with the internal consistency of his principles of justice, allowing him to reconstruct both his action and her expectations in his search for justification. The almost exclusive concern with logical consistency at the expense of empirical verification suggests a lack of cognitive maturity of the type described by Piaget and Labouvie-Vief and the kind of closed formal structures discussed earlier in relation to Gödel's theorem.

Philosopher Two, in contrast, begins with a clear acknowledgment of moral violation. His principle was one of "obligation and if I see some kind of ongoing unjust situation, I have some kind of obligation to correct it in whatever way I see." Clearly in his mind the husband of the woman with whom he was involved "should be told," since "otherwise he was not getting the information he needed to judge what his best interests should be in the situation . . ." Putting himself in the husband's place, Philosopher Two had no difficulty in recognizing that "I would have wanted to know." The injustice consisted in "his not knowing the full truth . . . I think that truth is an ultimate thing."

However, the complexity of the situation from the woman's perspective complicated his judgment and confronted him with a dilemma. Overwhelmed by exams at school and illness in her family, she said she was unable to face the additional stress of informing her husband about the affair. Although she did intend to tell him, she was waiting for a more opportune time and thus resisted Philosopher Two's requests that she inform him. In the interim, however, the husband discovered the affair. This unintended outcome, in fact, resolved the dilemma, but the experience itself had a profound impact on Philosopher Two, shaking the foundations of his "moral system."

> So my dilemma was whether I should call the guy up and tell him what the situation was. I didn't, and the fact that I didn't has had a tremendous impact on my moral system. It did. It shook my belief and my justification of the belief that *I couldn't resolve the dilemma of the fact* that I felt that someone should tell him . . . I did feel that there was some kind of truth issue involved here, higher than the issue of where the truth comes from. The kind of thing that no matter what happens the other person should have full knowledge of what is going on, is fair. And I didn't tell him.

Left with a sense of moral compromise in not having acted in accordance with his principles but realizing the uncertainty of the possible consequences of such action for the woman for whom he cares, he seeks neither to alter the facts of the dilemma nor to abandon his principles of responsibility. Instead he begins to reexamine the premises underlying these principles. In doing so, he begins to question whether "somehow there is a sense in which truth is relative, or is truth ever relative? That is an issue I have yet to resolve."

Asked what he thought he had learned from the situation, he says:

> What I learned was I became much less absolute. I was always aware of the kind of situation in which truth was not absolute. If a person comes up to me with a gun in his hand, in that situation I never thought that the truth was that absolute. But with interpersonal situations that dealt with psychological realities and with psychological feelings, with emotions, I felt that the truth should win out in most situations. Then after that situation, I became more relativistic about it. As you can tell, right now, I have not worked out a principle that is satisfactory to me that would resolve that issue if it happened again tomorrow.

However, unlike Philosopher One, he no longer is convinced that such a principle could ever be worked out:

> I try to work out a system that would be fair to all persons involved . . . and I suppose the dilemma I have is in the fact that — Rawls calls it the Blanket of Ignorance — the Veil of Ignorance — is not down. It is very difficult for me to completely withdraw from the situation and say if I was K. or if I were T., I would certainly want to know the truth. I feel there is no question on that. But if I were K., would I see what I wanted to do as being the right thing to do? And was her right to sanity, which I think was being jeopardized, less important than his right to know? That is a good moral dilemma. Now you figure it out.

Thus, the relativism that has begun to erode his former claim to absolute knowledge of the "right thing to do" arises from his incipient awareness of the possible legitimacy of a different point of view.

As he begins to imagine alternative constructions of the dilemma which also have a claim to truth, his conception of truth itself begins to change, becoming, as he says, "more relativistic." No longer can he unequivocally defend the single "high-handed" perspective of his former moral judgments, and in the absence of this support, the Rawlsian "Veil of Ignorance" falls, removing the basis in Kohlberg's terms for a principled moral resolution. As his experience leads him to see the moral legitimacy of other people's perspectives, Philosopher Two begins to understand how the experience of others might lead them to the discovery of different truths. Finding the problem now in his former construction of the dilemma itself, he reconstructs it more broadly as a conflict of rights, but one that now no longer reduces to a logically deductive moral solution.

Five years later at age twenty-seven, this contextual relativism has invaded his hypothetical moral reasoning as well, causing his Kohlberg score to fall from the principled to the transitional level. His discovery that "experiences in my life tend to make simple solutions a lot more difficult to accept," colors his responses to Kohlberg's dilemmas. The problem of judgment now occurs in two contexts that frame different aspects of the moral problem: the context of justice in which he articulates the universal logic of fairness and reciprocity and the context of compassion in which he focuses instead on the particularity of consequence for the actual participants. His resolution combines the absolute logic of a system of moral justification with a probabilistic contextual assessment of the likely consequences of choice. Thus, the right solution from a justice perspective that might be right "in an ideal world" might not in fact be the best solution in the actuality of time and place. The contextual morality of responsibility for the actual consequences of choice thus enters into dialogue with the abstraction of rights, resulting in a judgment whose contradictory normative statements are scored as a mixture of Kohlberg's Stages 4 and 5.

Our interpretation that Philosopher Two's apparent regression is an artifact of a new, more encompassing perspective is supported by his retrospective reflection at age twenty-seven on the dilemma he had reported five years earlier. Now the moral discussion "about who tells the truth and who doesn't" appears to him in a "very different perspective": as legitimate to "the justice approach" but ancillary to "the more fundamental issue" of the causes and consequences of infidelity. Focusing his discussion at age twenty-seven on his understanding of why the situation arose in the first place and the problem of life choice its occurrence presented, he attributes his previous unawareness of these issues to "an incredible amount of immaturity on my part" which he sees reflected in his "justice approach."

> The justice approach was really blinding me to a lot of issues. And, in a sense, I was trying to make it a justice issue, and it really blinded me to a lot of the realities of the problem. And now, being in a situation where, you know, married for a few years . . . it's a very different perspective to have on it. That it really wasn't a moral issue, that it was a moral issue, that part of it was, but that there were other things that I was not considering. [What was the moral issue?] I think that the moral issue was simply the matter of honesty and truth in the relationship. But even if that had been fulfilled, we would have been left with the interpersonal dilemma of life choices, of what kind of relationship you want in your life. It could have been just as easily that [she] told her husband. So what? [You are] still left with the choice. And morality won't do you one bit of good in that decision.

Equating morality with "the justice approach," he now sees its illumination to have been "blinding," concealing from him the "realities of the problem" — the unresolved dilemma of choice. The perceived disparity between the justice solution (telling the truth to honor respect) and the remaining problems of responsibility and consequence leads him to the further realization that while the problem was at once both moral and not moral, the "moral" solution wouldn't solve the problem. Then the question becomes one of definition as to what is included in the moral domain, since the justice approach does not adequately address the responsibilities and obligations that ensue from "life choices."

In our full sample, the shift to a dual-context form of reasoning was prominent in a number of subjects between twenty-two and twenty-seven. Its appearance was repeatedly tied to the experience of the "dilemma of the fact": that in the experience of life choices, no single perspective could adequately encompass the problem. It was precisely this problem of multiple contexts that made the right answer no longer seem right, giving rise to such seemingly contradictory realizations as "I had violated my first principle of moral behavior, but I had made the right decision" (Subject T).

The addition of this second context for judgment has been consistently mistaken (as Labouvie-Vief has pointed out) for a retreat from the adolescent cognitive apogee — in this case from the principled morality of Kohlberg's highest stages. According to Kohlberg's view that there were objective criteria of logical justification that made the moral principle of justice "best," adult reasoning that took into account the facts of contextual relativism was considered to be the same as the moral equivocation that sometimes occurs in the transition between Stages 4 and 5. Thus in the case of Philosopher Two, his contextual judgments at age twenty-seven received a lower score in Kohlberg's system than his "principled" judgments at age twenty-two.

CONCLUSION

In this chapter we have argued that intellectual development continues beyond adolescence and into adulthood through the shift from the metaphysics of logical justification to the empirical discovery of the consequences of choice. Our data are compatible with the interpretation that this discovery requires a cognitive transformation from a formal to a dialectical mode of reasoning that can encompass the contradictions out of which moral problems themselves arise. While formal logic and principles of justice can release adolescent judgment from the binding constraints of a conventional mode of moral reasoning, the choices that arise in adulthood impose a new context for moral decision that changes the dimensions of the problem. Then, the realization of the special obligations and the responsibilities that commitments engender restructures the understanding of moral choice from a problem of formal justification to a problem of what Perry calls "commitment in relativism." Since this restructuring is based on the epistemological recognition of the fallibility of all knowledge, it forms the basis for an expanded ethic that encompasses compassion, tolerance, and respect.

In the world of the Houyhnhnms, where the operation of reason is not "discoloured by passion or interest" ("they have no fondness for their colts or foles but the care they take in educating them proceedeth entirely from the dictates of reason"), the rationality of the justice approach operates "[in entire agreement] with the sentiments of Socrates" (Swift, pp. 165–166). The social order of that world, however, is maintained by breaking the tie to Gulliver, expelling the contradiction that he represents and the threat that it poses to the order of the land. In the human world, however, when the bonds of attachment threaten to upset the order of reason and to compromise the operation of justice, a more inclusive understanding can be brought to bear.

In our attempt to reconnect a cognitive stage theory of development with data on late adolescent and adult thinking about real problems of moral conflict and choice, we found it necessary to posit a different notion of maturity to account for the transformations in thinking that we observed. These transformations arise out of recognition of the paradoxical interdependence of self and society, which then overrides the false simplicity of formal reason and replaces it with a more encompassing form of judgment. The structure of this judgment is able to sustain the irreducible tension between justice and care. Thus, as Piaget had envisioned, "reason which expresses the highest form of equilibrium reunites intelligence and affectivity," embracing the problem of contradiction rather than expelling it from the cognitive domain.

REFERENCES

Beckett, S. *Endgame.* New York: Grove Press, Inc., 1958.

Belenky, M. "Conflict and Development: A Longitudinal Study of the Impact of Abortion Decisions on Moral Judgments of Adolescents and Adult Women." Unpublished doctoral dissertation, Harvard University, 1978.

Belenky, M., and Gilligan, C. "Predicting Clinical Outcomes: A Longitudinal Study of the Impact of the Abortion Crisis on Moral Development and Life Circumstance." Unpublished manuscript, Harvard University, 1979.

Eliot, T. S. *Ash Wednesday.* New York: Putnam and Sons, 1978/1930.

Erikson, E. H. (Ed.). *Adulthood.* New York: W. W. Norton, 1978.

Flavell, J. H. *Cognitive Development.* Englewood Cliffs, N.J.: Prentice-Hall, 1977.

Gilligan, C. "In a Different Voice: Women's Conceptions of Self and of Morality." *Harvard Educational Review,* 1977, *47,* 481–517.

Gilligan, J. "Beyond Morality: Psychoanalytic Reflections on Shame, Guilt, and Love." In T. Lickona (Ed.), *Moral Development and Behavior.* New York: Holt, Rinehart and Winston, 1976.

Inhelder, B., and Piaget, J. *The Growth of Logical Thinking from Childhood to Adolescence.* New York: Basic Books, 1958.

Kitchener, K., and King, P. "Reflective Judgment: Patterns in Post-Adolescent Formal Operations, and Verbal Reasoning." Unpublished manuscript, University of Minnesota, 1979.

Kohlberg, L. "From Is to Ought." In T. Mishel (Ed.), *Cognitive Development and Epistemology.* New York: Academic Press, 1971.

Kohlberg, L. "Continuities in Childhood and Adult Moral Development Revisited." In P. Baltes and K. W. Schaie (Eds.), *Life-Span Developmental Psychology: Personality and Socialization.* New York: Academic Press, 1973.

Kohlberg, L. "Moral Stages and Moralization: The Cognitive-Developmental Approach." In T. Lickona (Ed.), *Moral Development and Behavior.* New York: Holt, Rinehart and Winston, 1976.

Kohlberg, L. "The Meaning and Measurement of Moral Development." *Heinz Werner Memorial Lectures.* Clark University, Worcester, Mass., April 1979.

Kohlberg, L., and others. "Assessing Moral Stages: A Manual." Unpublished manuscript, Harvard University, 1978.

Kohlberg, L., and Gilligan, C. "The Adolescent as a Philosopher: The Discovery of the Self in a Post Conventional World." *Daedalus,* 1971, *100,* 1051–1086.

Kohlberg, L., and Kramer, R. "Continuities and Discontinuities in Childhood and Adult Moral Development." *Human Development,* 1969, *12,* 93–120.

Labouvie-Vief, G. "Uses of Logic in Life-Span Development: A Theoretical Note on Adult Cognition." *Human Development,* 1979, in press.

Murphy, J. M., and Gilligan, C. "Moral Development in Late Adolescence and Adulthood: A Critique and Reconstruction of Kohlberg's Theory." *Human Development,* in press.

Nagel, E., and Newman, J. R. *Gödel's Proof.* New York: New York University Press, 1958.

Perry, W. B. *Forms of Intellectual and Ethical Development in the College Years.* New York: Holt, Rinehart and Winston, 1968.

Piaget, J. *Six Psychological Studies.* New York: Random House, 1967.

Piaget, J. *Structuralism.* New York: Basic Books, 1970.

Piaget, J. *Biology and Knowledge.* Chicago: University of Chicago Press, 1971.

Piaget, J. "Intellectual Evolution from Adolescence to Adulthood." *Human Development,* 1972, *15,* 1–12.

Polanyi, M. *Personal Knowledge.* Chicago: University of Chicago Press, 1958.

Quine, W. V. *The Ways of Paradox and Other*

Essays. Cambridge: Harvard University Press, 1976.

Riegel, K. "Dialectic Operations: The Final Period of Cognitive Development." *Human Development,* 1973, *16,* 346–370.

Sinnot, J. D. "Everyday Thinking and Piagetian Operativity in Adults." *Human Development,* 1975, *18,* 430–443.

Swift, J. *Gulliver's Travels.* Chicago, Encyclopedia Britannica, Inc., 1952.

Youniss, J. "Operations and Everyday Thinking." *Human Development,* 1974, *17,* 386–391.

Deborah P. Waber

SEX DIFFERENCES IN COGNITION: A FUNCTION OF MATURATION RATE?

ABSTRACT: Regardless of sex, early maturing adolescents performed better on tests of verbal than spatial abilities, the late maturing ones showed the opposite pattern. Those maturing late were more lateralized for speech than those maturing early. Sex differences in mental abilities, it is argued, reflect differences in the organization of cortical function that are related to differential rates of physical maturation.

Discussions about the origins of sex differences in behavior have usually focused on obvious dichotomies, such as nature versus nurture and male versus female. However, the sexes can also be arrayed along continuous biological dimensions. Examining data from this point of view might yield more information about the mechanisms of sex differences than do dichotomous comparisons of male and female.

One such dimension is maturational rate; females generally attain physical maturity at an earlier age than males (*1, 2*). Therefore, I hypothesized that this biological variable would be systematically related to mental abilities for which sex differences have been repeatedly demonstrated: (i) verbal ability (fluency, articulation, and perceptual speed), at which females have been reported to excel, and (ii) spatial ability, at which males have been reported to excel (*3*).

Several authors have proposed relationships between verbal and spatial ability and the organization of higher cortical functions. Buffery and Gray (*4*) have argued that earlier and stronger lateralization of language in females facilitates verbal ability and that bilateral representation of space in males facilitates spatial ability. Alternatively, Levy (*5*) has postulated that intraindividual differences between these abilities reflect differences in the degree of specialization of language in the left cerebral hemisphere. That is, bilateral mediation of language increases the probability that language will interfere with spatial processing, which is presumed to be the province of the right hemisphere. Recent data indicating that speech is more lateralized among adult males than females (*6*) are consistent with the Levy hypothesis (*5*).

In this study, both verbal and spatial performance and lateralization of linguistic pro-

Supported by a grant-in-aid from Sigma Xi, the Scientific Research Society of North America, and PHS grants HD-03008 and HD-01994. I thank E. Zigler, V. Seitz, M. Genel, M. Studdert-Kennedy, and P. H. Wolff for their assistance in various phases of the execution of the study and the preparation of this report.

SOURCE: From Deborah P. Waber, "Sex Differences in Cognition: A Function of Maturation Rate?", *Science,* Vol. 192, pp. 572–574, 7 May 1976.

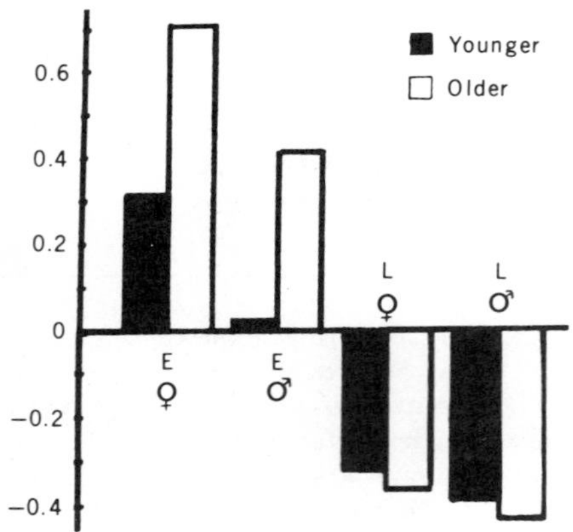

Figure 1. Mean values of difference scores for each grouping of sex, maturation, and age level. Positive values indicate that the verbal score is greater than the spatial score, and negative values indicate that the spatial score is greater than the verbal score.

cessing were examined in relation to sex and maturational rate. Two hypotheses were tested. Along a continuum of rate of maturation, and regardless of sex, (i) so-called early maturers perform better at verbal than spatial ability, and so-called late maturers perform better at spatial than verbal ability; and (ii) early maturers are less lateralized for speech perception than late maturers. The results of the study support these two hypotheses.

A sample of early and late maturing adolescents was selected at two age levels, which were chosen to maximize the observable physical variability and so differed for boys and girls. Girls 10 and 13 years old and boys 13 and 16 years old from a middle-class Caucasian population were examined medically and rated according to the Tanner criteria for staging secondary sexual characteristics, which are a good indicator of general physical growth (*2*). From this population, individuals were selected as early maturers if their chronological age was at least 1 standard deviation below the mean age for their stage of sexual development, and as late maturers if their chronological age was at least 1 standard deviation above, according to norms reported by Marshall and Tanner (*2*). Subjects in the final sample of 80, which comprised ten early and ten late maturing girls and boys at both age levels, were given psychological testing in school (*7*).

Tests for which sex differences in the appropriate direction had previously been reliably reported were used to assess mental abilities (*3*). The Digit Symbol subtest of the Wechsler Intelligence Scale for Children (WISC) (*8, 9*), the Color-Naming subtest of the Stroop Color Word test (*10*), and the Word Fluency subtest of the Primary Mental Abilities (PMA) test (*11, 12*) measured verbal ability; the Block Design subtest of the WISC (*9, 13*), the Embedded Figures test (*14*), and the Spatial Abilities subtest of the PMA (*12, 15*) measured spatial ability.

A dichotic test of phoneme identification measured lateralization (*16*). The stimuli were all possible pairs of the six consonant-vowel syllables, bæ, dæ, gæ, pæ, tæ, and kæ. There were 60 presentations given in two random orders on two different tapes. Subjects heard each tape twice (counterbalanced for ear and channel) and were asked to record the sound they had heard after each presentation. An index of ear advantage was computed for each subject on each tape (*17*).

The scores from the six ability tests were transformed to *z*-scores within each age grouping to permit comparisons between tests and age groupings. Factor analysis for the entire sample indicated that the tests could be assumed to measure separate verbal and spatial factors. Therefore, the mean of the three verbal scores and the mean of the three spatial scores were used for further computations. A difference score, the verbal score minus the spatial score, represented intraindividual strengths and weaknesses independent of overall intelligence. The correlation between difference scores and IQ was very small ($r = -.14$). Two scores were used in the analysis of the dichotic listening data. The mean of the index scores on the two tapes indicated both the direction and magnitude of lateralization, and the mean of the absolute values of the index scores indicated magnitude independent of direction. A three-way, sex by maturation by age level, analysis of variance was computed for the verbal, spatial, difference, and lateralization scores.

As was predicted, within individuals and regardless of sex, early maturers scored better on verbal than spatial tasks, and late maturers scored better on spatial than verbal tasks ($P < .001$) (Fig. 1). The earliest maturing group (early maturing girls) and the latest maturing group (late maturing boys) showed the greatest differences ($P < .001$). However, the difference score represented a dissociation between the spatial scores, which were systematically related to rate of maturation ($P < .001$), and the verbal scores, which showed no relationship to rate of maturation. Sex differences, although in the predicted direction, did not reach a conventional level of significance.

To control for the possible effect of chronological age, a two-way, sex by maturation, analysis of variance was computed for the 13-year-old group only. Again, the difference scores were systematically related to maturational rate ($P < .03$), and sex differences, although in the predicted direction, did not reach a conventional level of significance.

Late maturers showed larger ear advantages than early maturers in the older but not in the younger group for both dichotic measures ($P < .02$; Fig. 2), and there were no sex differences. The extreme-groups design did not permit a valid correlation between scores of degree of lateralization and those of mental ability to be computed; however, that the group showing a greater degree

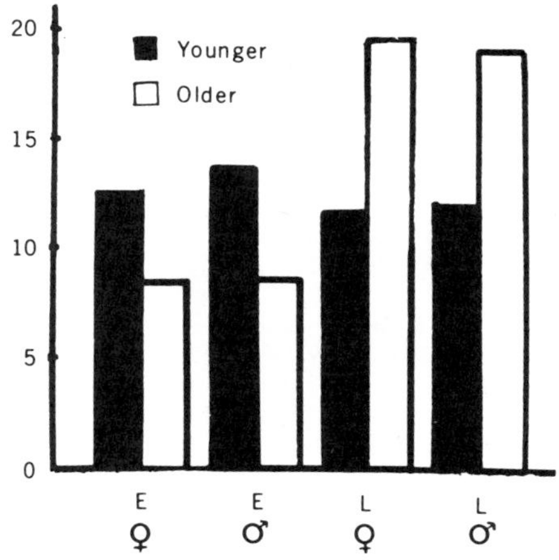

Figure 2. Absolute values of mean percent ear advantage (lateralization) scores for each grouping of sex, maturation, and age level.

of lateralization was also superior in spatial ability supports the Levy position (*5*) against that of Buffery and Gray (*4*).

The striking relation between rate of physical maturation (independent of sex) and spatial ability, verbal-spatial patterns, and lateralization has several important implications. First, sex accounted for only a very small proportion of the variance in comparison to maturational rate. Therefore, reported sex differences in these behaviors probably reflect the differential distribution of the sexes along a physiological continuum more than a categorical difference between male and female. This concept might also apply to other behaviors not examined in this study. Second, since maturational rate was shown not to be related to verbal ability, the sex differences in verbal and spatial abilities may have very different etiologies and cannot be explained by a common set of causes, whether environmental or constitutional. Finally, rate of maturation (or its implicit physiological correlates) may play an important role in the organization of higher cortical functions.

REFERENCES AND NOTES

1. J. M. Tanner, *Growth at Adolescence* (Blackwell, London, 1962).

2. W. A. Marshall and J. M. Tanner, *Arch. Dis. Child. 44,* 291 (1969); *ibid. 45,* 13 (1970).

3. E. E. Maccoby, in *The Development of Sex Differences,* E. E. Maccoby, Ed. (Stanford Univ. Press, Stanford, Calif., 1966), pp. 25–55.

4. A. W. H. Buffery and J. A. Gray, in *Gender Differences: Their Ontogeny and Significance,* C. Ounsted and D. C. Taylor, Eds. (Churchill Livingstone, London, 1972), pp. 123–158.

5. J. Levy, *Nature (London) 224,* 614 (1969).

6. J. McGlone and W. Davidson, *Neuropsychologia 11,* 105 (1973); J. McGlone and A. Kertesz, *Cortex 9,* 313 (1973); R. Remington, S. Krashen, R. Harshman, paper presented at the 86th Annual Meeting, Acoustical Society of America, Los Angeles, Calif., 30 October to 2 November 1973.

7. Although the two WISC subtests, the Embedded Figures test, and the Stroop subtest were administered individually by an experimenter who was aware of the child's maturational status, the PMA subtests and the dichotic listening test were administered to groups of early and late maturers mixed together. Since the pattern of results was similar under both conditions, it is assumed that experimenter bias was minimal.

8. The child is instructed to draw an appropriate code symbol under each of a series of random numbers as quickly as possible.

9. D. Wechsler, *Wechsler Intelligence Scale for Children* (Psychological Corporation, New York, 1949).

10. J. R. Stroop, *J. Exp. Psychol. 18,* 643 (1935). The child is instructed to name a series of 100 patches of five common colors as rapidly as possible.

11. The child is told to list as many words as possible beginning with the letter S in 2 minutes.

12. L. L. Thurstone and T. C. Thurstone, *SRA Primary Mental Abilities Test for Ages 11–17* (Science Research Associates, Chicago, 1947).

13. The child is given a set of blocks and instructed to copy a design with them in a limited time period (*9*).

14. H. A. Witkin, *J. Pers. 19,* 1 (1950). The child must find a simple design hidden in a complex one and time to solution is recorded.

15. The child is asked to indicate which of a series of figures can be rotated to match a stimulus figure (*12*).

16. Dichotic listening is a technique in which two sounds are presented simultaneously, one to each ear. These, however, are not perceived as simultaneous and it is assumed that the discrepancy is a function of lateralization. The sound presented contralaterally to the dominant hemisphere tends to be perceived first. See also D. Kimura [*Can. J. Psychol. 15,* 166 (1961)].

17. The number of correct identifications of stimuli presented to the right (R) and left (L) ears are entered into the formula $(R - L)/(R + L) \times 100$. as described by M. Studdert-Kennedy and D. Shankweiler [*J. Acoust. Soc. Am. 48,* 579 (1970)].

41

Hilde Bruch

SPARROW IN A CAGE

When Ida went home for the summer vacation after her freshman year at college, she was in considerably better health than when she came to me for treatment a year ago. Her weight had risen from a low of sixty-eight pounds to about ninety pounds, still considerably below her normal weight. She enjoyed being home but missed the fuss they had made about her in the past, when everybody was acutely concerned about her poor health and had treated her "like a nine-day wonder"; now they took her for granted. For the first few days she felt she did not belong, had nothing to contribute. She began to worry again about her weight, and felt she was too heavy and suffered from the old feeling of hating herself. One afternoon while walking on the beach with the sun behind her, she had a definite feeling that she would be happy if she looked like her shadow, narrow and elongated. She was so unhappy about not looking that thin that she began to cry. She began thinking about her whole life, how it had developed.

Even as a child Ida had considered herself not worthy of all the privileges and benefits that her family offered her, because she felt she was not brilliant enough. An image came to her, that she was like a sparrow in a golden cage, too plain and simple for the luxuries of her home, but also deprived of the freedom of doing what she truly wanted to do. Until then she had spoken only about the superior features of her background; now she began to speak about the ordeal, the restrictions and obligations of growing up in a wealthy home. She enlarged on the image, that cages are made for big colorful birds who show off their plumage and are satisfied just hopping around in the cage. She felt she was quite different, like a sparrow, inconspicuous and energetic, who wants to fly around and take off on its own, who is not made for a cage.

Many anorexics express themselves in similar ways, even in much the same imagery, that their whole life had been an ordeal of wanting to live up to the expectations of their families, always fearing they were not good enough in comparison with others and, therefore, disappointing failures. This dramatic dissatisfaction is a core issue in anorexia nervosa, and it precedes the concern with weight and dieting. The underlying anguish and discontent stand in contrast to the fact that these girls come from homes that make a good first impression. Everything a girl can need for her physical well-being and intellectual development has been provided. The parents described their marriages as stable and there are few broken homes. In the last fifty cases I have observed, there were only two divorces before the onset of the anorexia and one couple spoke of marital difficulties. In one family the mother had died several years before the onset of the illness, and in another the father (both his wife and daughter spoke in idolizing terms of their happiness before his death).

Most anorexic girls come from upper-middle-class and upper-class homes; financial achievement and social position are often high. The relatively few homes of lower-middle-class or lower-class rating were upwardly mobile and success-oriented. The anorexic daughter of a postal clerk had two older brothers, one a physician, the other a lawyer, who felt they owed their accomplishments to the driving encouragement from their mother. Another girl, the daughter of a blue-collar worker, was the only child in an extended family group, and everybody had contributed to prepare her for a special career.

These families were of small size; in my last fifty cases, the average number of children was 2.8. The age of the parents at the time of birth of the anorexic child was rather high: thirty-eight years the average for the fathers, the oldest being fifty-four; and thirty-two for the mothers, with forty-three as the highest age. The few only children had parents who married late and who were well along in middle age when their one child was born. Sexual relations were often at low ebb or had ceased altogether.

A conspicuous feature of these families was the paucity of sons. More than two thirds of these families had daughters only. Most denied that this posed any problems, though one mother became so depressed for having given birth to a fourth daughter, having disappointed her husband by not giving him a son, that the father had to take care of the little girl; he raised her with the precision of his professional training as an electrical engineer. In another case the patient was convinced that not having a son had not been a problem for her father, that he took pride in his daughters, that he treated them intellectually as sons; he was particularly proud that they all knew how to throw a ball "correctly" (namely, like a boy). The anorexic girls who had brothers were often the youngest child, a few times with two or three older brothers; throughout childhood they had tried to keep up with their brothers' activities. Other anorexic girls were considerably older than a late-born brother. It is significant that the fathers value their daughters for their intellectual brilliance and athletic achievements; rarely if ever do they pay attention to their appearance as they grow into womanhood, though they will criticize them for becoming plump.

The question is what goes on in these seemingly well-functioning and well-off families so that the girls grow up deficient in self-esteem, unable to meet and enjoy the new opportunities of adolescence and adulthood? A common feature is that these children believe they must prove something about their parents, that it is their task to make them feel good, successful, and superior. Yet the very success of the parents, their lavish style of living and all the material and cultural advantages, are experienced by these children as excessive demands. In talking about the obligations of growing up in a wealthy family, Ida of the golden cage used the image, "If you are born the son of a king, then you are condemned to be very special — you, too, have to become a king." She spoke with anguish about the burden of privilege: "If you are given much, much is expected of you."

Information about the early care of these youngsters reveals that their mothers were usually conscientious and devoted, felt that they had done well and that the child had thrived under their care. Only a few had been cared for by a nurse or governess. In contrast to many modern uncertain parents, those of anorexics are rather self-assured. They stress how well they did everything and how their way of handling the child had been better than that of their friends and neighbors. Until she became sick, the child had done so well, never giving any trouble, that she was a living proof of her parents' superior method. These parents may well be described as good, devoted, and ambitious. For subtle personal reasons the particular child was overvalued. But the child felt that too much was expected in return.

The mothers had often been career women, who felt they had sacrificed their aspirations for the good of the family. In spite of superior intelligence and education, practically all had given up their careers when they married. Quite recently several mothers expressed dissatisfaction with having done so and were now, in their early forties, studying to prepare themselves for some independent work. They are submissive to their husbands in many details and yet do not truly respect them. The fathers, despite social and financial success, often considerable, feel in some sense "second-best." They are enormously preoccupied with physical appearance, admiring fitness and beauty, and expecting proper behavior and measurable achievement from their children. This description probably applies to many success-oriented middle-class families, but the traits appear more pronounced in the families of anorexics. In spite of their emphasis on their normality and happiness, underlying strain can be easily discerned.

To give an example: Alma . . . had parents who were deeply devoted, child-oriented, and who had provided the best in every respect. Her father was a successful businessman who played a prominent role in the financial and political life of a midwestern city, and her mother was a leader in many social activities. However, both parents felt in some way defeated; the father had wanted to pursue a professional career, but circumstances had not permitted it. The mother felt that she had sacrificed her dream of a theatrical career. The parents were proud that they could offer their children the best educational opportunities. The older daughter was only average, and her mediocre behavior and achievement were a bitter disappointment to the parents. Great things were expected of Alma, who excelled not only academically but also in sports and the arts and who was popular. She went along with everything her parents wanted until it became too much, and her establishment of excessive control over the body, and aggressive negativistic behavior, seemed like an escape from this overwhelming situation.

Quite often these mothers are unusually weight-conscious and preoccupied with dieting. Other mothers are obsessively preoccupied with some flaw in the perfection of their bodies. Gertrude's mother, who had been nearly forty when she gave birth, became increasingly concerned with her tissues not being firm and smooth enough. She followed many advertised remedies to undo these signs of aging and had her daughter, from the age of about twelve to fourteen, inspect her thighs and buttocks to evaluate whether the latest cure was restoring her youth. In other families the father is obsessed with dieting, in even more absolute and dictatorial terms. Jill's father, seventy-two years old, reported with pride that his weight was exactly the same as when he left college, and that he had weighed himself every single morning; when there was the slightest increase he would adjust his diet. When Jill became somewhat plump in early adolescence, he persuaded her to reduce and praised her for her lower weight. The problem was that she did not stop dieting but remained in the desert of self-starvation.

Karla, too, recalled that her deceased father had been extremely diet-conscious. There was an absolute prohibition against snacks. Food was eaten at mealtimes and nothing was allowed in between. She expressed a peculiar mixture of feelings about her weight loss: she had done it in an effort to please him, but at the same time she felt that she had out-smarted him, that he couldn't make her eat now even if he were alive, that she had got even with him.

THE PARENTS WILL SPEAK with pride of having given a happy and harmonious home to their children. But this may not be what the anorexic girl herself has experienced. She may have been the one who was aware of the strain and felt it to be her obligation to make up to the parents for what was lacking in their relationship.

As an example I give the story of Laura, the second daughter of parents of prominent status in a northwestern state. The older sister had been considered emotionally unstable, rather troublesome. There was a younger sister who went quietly about her business. Laura had lived her whole life as "the shadow" of her older sister, imitating her in every possible way except in causing trouble. The sister was often cruel and aggressive toward Laura. To some extent the mother was aware of this, but she didn't interfere because she dreaded the temper tantrums of the older girl. Since her sister had done so, Laura also decided to spend the last year of high school in France. She was acutely unhappy and returned home before the end of the term. She had lost a considerable amount of weight and continued to lose. Until then she had been always close to her mother. In contrast to the demands the older sister made, she had tried to be "a comfort" to her mother. Now she became annoyed about certain mannerisms of her mother, her indecisiveness, her difficulty with being anywhere on time. Then she became critical of both parents, though she continued to admire her father as the "most perfect" man she knew.

The father was a successful financier who was involved in several important enterprises and also took active part in the cultural development of his city; in a way he had adjusted to his position of being the only man in a four-woman family by seeking satisfaction outside the home. In spite of all her admiration for him, Laura felt he was emotionally detached. There was never any criticism from him; on the contrary, he was lavish with praise and encouragement. But Laura was convinced that it meant nothing, that her father never showed his true feelings, that he was patient and considerate because that was a father's job. She was desperately anxious that she could never know what he really felt. As the anorexia persisted, she also expressed concern about the quality of her parents' marital relationship. She felt her mother maintained what only looked like harmony by being always conforming and obedient to what the father wanted. Now she was impatient with her mother because she saw in her what she dreaded would be her own fate — to be a nothing, to be devoted to a husband, to be devoted to her children, but without a life of her own.

Many other girls express a feeling of having a special responsibility for their mother; sometimes this is openly expressed, in others only implied. For Mabel it had always been a basic rule to be considerate of her mother. Whatever plan came up, her first concern was, "What will Mommy say?" When she was fourteen years old a nearby university offered a summer course in modern mathematics for gifted high-school students. She was dying to attend but decided against it because she was afraid her mother, who was engaged in an artistic career, might feel left out or even feel stupid in comparison. The mother had expressed in many subtle ways that she considered the sciences to be less creative than the arts, and she had admonished her daughter not to waste her time on mathematics or science.

This excessive concern with her parents' feelings convinced Mabel that she did not have the right to express her own feelings or to act on them. At nine years old she was sent to a camp in the French Alps, to give her a healthy summer in the mountains and to help her learn to speak French. Mabel was miserably unhappy and looked wan and was rather quiet when she returned home, but she told her parents that she had had a marvelous time. The following year, outguessing her parents' plans, Mabel asked to go back to France, though she dreaded another summer of misery; she felt it was her duty not to disappoint her parents. She was sure that they would feel they had made a mistake if she told them how unhappy she was, and she had to prevent this.

In her college years Mabel studied psychology. One day she was rather excited when she came to her session with me because she had found in one of her texts an exact description of her mother. She was referring to some family studies on schizophrenia where the egotistical behavior of the mother is described in detail, that she raises her children in a way that fulfills *her* needs and wishes. Mabel gave many details how in her family life had been arranged according to the way mother wanted it, according to her tastes and interests and preferences for *her* friends. All this had applied as much to her father, but he could escape into his very active business career, whereas she had been tied to her mother and had been molded by her mother's wishes, dreams, and ambitions. This realization helped her also to understand why she had a relapse each time she went home on vacation; regardless of how much progress she had made, the mother was unstinting in her criticism that she had not developed in the right way. Her mother was critical of her friends, most of whom she didn't know in person, but she was convinced they were not the type of friends she would have chosen. Her father, too, had great ambitions for her and, like his wife, was critical of her friends, though in a different, more sarcastic way.

Not only the parents but the patients too, when first seen, are apt to give a glowing picture of the blessings and happiness of their home, that the anorexia is the only flaw in what otherwise would be a perfect life. Some of this is a direct denial of facts, or a fear of being put in the position of saying something critical. It is also an expression of overconformity: what the parents said was always right and they blamed themselves for not being good enough. Nancy had lost an enormous amount of weight just before graduating from high school. This was one of the few families with an early divorce, and she had lived alone with her mother since age three. Though Nancy's cadaverous appearance was a living accusation that something was painfully wrong, her description made everything in her life appear perfect, particularly the relationship to her mother, of whom she said repeatedly, "I am very happy with my mother." The only trouble between them was caused by the illness. "She tries to be patient but it's hard for her to see what I am doing to myself and not say anything. She gets very upset and angry and tired." This made Nancy feel guilty; she was also guilty that mother worked very hard to provide her with so many privileges. When a question was raised about expressing anger, she answered with bitterness, "I'm never allowed to! My mother wouldn't stand for it. I'm not allowed to talk back or anything like that." Then she became silent, as if she had revealed a forbidden secret.

Polite behavior was emphasized in all the families I saw, and the parents were proud of their perfect child who never showed common childish misbehavior such as talking back, stubbornness, or anger. As a matter of fact, nonexpression of feelings, particularly negative feelings, is the general rule, until the illness becomes manifest and the former goodness turns into undiscriminating negativism. Many patients carry this repression on after the illness starts and resist suggestions to express feelings openly. A self-important attitude of "but this isn't done" pervades whatever they say and express.

There is much preoccupation with what it will look like, what people would think, and with the image they must maintain. This applies to the patient as well as to the families.

Many of these youngsters are troubled by the question of what their parents truly feel and think, but they are exceedingly reluctant to acknowledge that there is a problem. Everything Olga had to say about her family was the highest praise, that they had offered the best to her, though she had not felt worthy of it. Her childhood had been a continuous effort to please her parents, never to warrant any blame or criticism. As she remembered it, she never was punished, but she lived in constant fear of punishment because she never knew what her parents really thought behind their pleasant and approving front. There was never any argument between them, and they seemed to get along well enough, but as a child Olga was continuously worried about what they felt, in particular her father, who never expressed emotions; she knew this had also puzzled the older children. Olga's solution was to be more perfect than any parent could possibly expect a child to be, and to hide all signs of anger and rebelliousness. She formed a completely unrealistic picture of what her life should be like, was preoccupied with what people thought about her, and dreaded society's verdict. Her parents were loving and deeply devoted to their late-born child, and had encouraged her in all her interests. Although puzzled by her lack of self-assertion, they were still not sufficiently concerned to recognize it as abnormal submission.

APPEARANCES AND GOOD BEHAVIOR are not the only areas in which too much is expected from these youngsters. There is also much emphasis on academic achievement, and they are sent to the best schools and given broad cultural exposure. They are taken to concerts and museums at an early age, are included to some extent in the active social life of their parents, and many travel abroad. The parents take pride in their children's achievements. One girl could list on her college application a whole page of rewards for special activities; each one, be it social work, athletics, or artistic achievement, had been pursued in an effort to please her father. Another remembered her father's teasing as painful, in his sarcastic remarks that she did not bring home as many prizes as her older brother had.

Karla had this rather touching memory. Her father had not been involved in the details of the children's education, though he took a benevolent interest in their doing well in school. Karla remembered, with affection and sadness, the expression of great satisfaction and pride on her father's face when her brother received the highest prize from his demanding school. Toward her very good report card he showed his usual kind interest. It became Karla's absorbing ambition that one day she would do something so outstanding that it would elicit the same expression of great satisfaction — only she never achieved it, because her father died a year later. Throughout her treatment she emphasized, "If he had lived, I wouldn't have needed to become sick. I could have felt his pride in me in other ways."

The describable problems leading up to the illness which the parents might have recognized as warning signs are of a rather subtle nature. In recent years parents often have read popular reports on anorexia nervosa which emphasize the importance of family problems. Fortunately most go along with the need for exploring and clarifying the hidden, underlying problems that lead them to expect too much from at least one of their children. A common feature is that the future patient was not seen or acknowledged as an individual in her own right, but was valued mainly as someone who would make the life and experiences of the parents more satisfying and complete. Such expectations do not preclude a relationship of great warmth and affection. Usually clinging attachment and a peculiarly intense sharing of ideas and feelings develop. When seen together as a family, it is rare that any one member speaks in direct terms about his or her own ideas and feelings. Each one seems to know what the other feels and truly means, at the same time disqualifying what the other has said. I have called this style of communication a "confusion of pronouns" because one never knows in whose name anyone is speaking. Father will explain what mother really means, and mother is sure that she must correct what daughter says she thinks, and daughter in turn will explain the parents. Siblings usually manage to stay out of this enmeshment, finding satisfaction among each other or outside the home, but leaving the anorexic child, whom they generally dislike as the goody-goody she is, isolated, a sacrifice to the parents' needs.

The question is what makes parents use a child in this way. It is important for the therapist to expose their concealed dissatisfactions and disappointments. Some will deny, or even violently protest, that such factors could have played a role in their family. The whole evaluation is complicated by the fact that the illness has such an enormous disruptive impact on a family. Parents refuse to be blamed and expect the patient to feel guilty for causing them so much unhappiness and worry. Paula's father opened the first interview by pointing to his daughter: "She has the anorexia, let her explain why she has it." When certain marital problems came into the open, he brushed their importance aside: "I can't see that has anything to do with her being sick." Actually it was clearer than in most cases that they were related to Paula's abnormal development. Even as a child she had felt that her parents were "different." They were older than most, and she had learned quite early that it was her task in life to give her mother the satisfaction she seemed to be missing in her marriage. When very young, Paula took pride in being so close to her mother that they both knew at all times what the other was thinking. She had received much love, attention, and stimulation from her parents and their many friends.

Through kindergarten and school Paula was afraid of the other children. She became more outgoing in the second grade and felt on an equal footing with her friends, though none could ever be as close as she and mother had been. Then she became aware that something had gone wrong between her parents, because her mother suddenly changed back to the way she used to behave when Paula was much younger, re-creating the former closeness. She made many claims on Paula's time and acted as if she felt left out when Paula did things on her own. Instead of encouraging her to have friends, she would criticize or belittle them and their families, and Paula again began to feel different from the other girls. She became anorexic at age fifteen, after her parents had shown their disapproval of her last remaining friend.

Once the anorexia has developed, parents complain that their whole life and every relationship have changed. Instead of quiet harmony there is now open fighting, angry outbursts, mutual blame and recrimination. Few conditions evoke such severe emotional reactions as voluntary and defiant food refusal; the coercive strength of hunger strikes is well known. A characteristic power struggle develops, with the parents trying to force the child to eat; she responds with angry refusal or deceitful manipulations, such as pretended eating, secretly disposing of the food, or vomiting what has been forced down.

Actually this stressful and noisy struggle after the illness has become manifest is only an exaggeration of what was there all the time. An imbalance of power has existed throughout the child's life. The child's agreeable compliance conceals the fact that she had been deprived by her parents of the right to live her own life. The parents had taken it for granted that it was their task to make all plans and decisions, to direct the child in every respect. These parents speak with conviction of their approach to life as right, normal, and desirable, and of their being entitled to expect that this child will fulfill their dreams and wishes. The child's inability for constructive self-assertion and the associated deficits in personality development are the outcome of interactional patterns that began early in life. The parents' unawareness that they have exercised such excessive control over the child and their inability to let go of it are part of the on-going pattern that sustains the illness.

42

Zick Rubin

DOES PERSONALITY REALLY CHANGE AFTER 20?

"In most of us," William James wrote in 1887, "by the age of 30, the character has set like plaster, and will never soften again." Though our bodies may be bent by the years and our opinions changed by the times, there is a basic core of self — a personality — that remains basically unchanged.

This doctrine of personality stability has been accepted psychological dogma for most of the past century. The dogma holds that the plaster of character sets by one's early 20s, if not even sooner than that.

Within the past decade, however, this traditional view has come to have an almost archaic flavor. The rallying cry of the 1970s has been people's virtually limitless capacity for change — not only in childhood but through the span of life. Examples of apparent transformation are highly publicized: Jerry Rubin enters the 1970s as a screaming, war-painted Yippie and emerges as a sedate Wall Street analyst wearing a suit and tie. Richard Alpert, an ambitious assistant professor of psychology at Harvard, tunes into drugs, heads for India, and returns as Baba Ram Dass, a long-bearded mystic in a flowing white robe who teaches people to "be here now." And Richard Raskind, a successful ophthalmologist, goes into the hospital and comes out as Renée Richards, a tall, well-muscled athlete on the women's tennis circuit.

Even for those of us who hold on to our original appearance (more or less) and gender, "change" and growth" are now the bywords. The theme was seized upon by scores of organizations formed to help people change, from Weight Watchers to est. It was captured — and advanced — by Gail Sheehy's phenomenally successful book *Passages,* which emphasized people's continuing openness to change throughout the course of adulthood. At the same time, serious work in psychology was coming along — building on earlier theories of Carl Jung and Erik Erikson — to buttress the belief that adults keep on developing. Yale's Daniel Levinson, who provided much of Sheehy's intellectual inspiration, described, in *The Seasons of a Man's Life,* an adult life structure that is marked by periods of self-examination and transition. Psychiatrist Roger Gould, in *Transformations,* wrote of reshapings of the self during the early and middle adult years, "away from stagnation and claustrophobic suffocation toward vitality and an expanded sense of inner freedom."

The view that personality keeps changing throughout life has picked up so many adherents recently that it has practically become the new dogma. Quantitative studies have been offered to document the possibility of personality change in adulthood, whether as a consequence of getting married, changing jobs, or seeing one's children leave home. In a new volume entitled *Constancy and Change in Human Development,* two of the day's most influential behavioral scientists,

---

SOURCE: From Zick Rubin, "Does Personality Really Change After Twenty?" *Psychology Today,* 15 May 1981. Reprinted from *Psychology Today* Magazine.

sociologist Orville G. Brim, Jr., and psychologist Jerome Kagan, challenge the defenders of personality stability to back up their doctrine with hard evidence. "The burden of proof," Brim and Kagan write, "is being shifted to the larger group, who adhere to the traditional doctrine of constancy, from the minority who suggest that it is a premise requiring evaluation."

And now we get to the newest act in the battle of the dogmas. Those who uphold the doctrine of personality stability have accepted the challenge. In the past few years they have assembled the strongest evidence yet available for the truth of their position — evidence suggesting that on several central dimensions of personality, including the ones that make up our basic social and emotional style, we are in fact astoundingly stable throughout the course of adult life.

THE 'LITTER-ATURE' ON PERSONALITY

Until recently there was little firm evidence for the stability of personality, despite the idea's intuitive appeal. Instead, most studies showed little predictability from earlier to later times of life — or even, for that matter, from one situation to another within the same time period — thus suggesting an essential lack of consistency in people's personalities. Indeed, many researchers began to question whether it made sense to speak of "personality" at all.

But whereas the lack of predictability was welcomed by advocates of the doctrine of change through the life span, the defenders of stability have another explanation for it: most of the studies are lousy. Referring derisively to the "litter-ature" on personality, Berkeley psychologist Jack Block estimates that "perhaps 90 percent of the studies are methodologically inadequate, without conceptual implication, and even foolish."

Block is right. Studies of personality have been marked by an abundance of untested measures (anyone can make up a new "scale" in an afternoon), small samples, and scattergun strategies ("Let's throw it into the computer and get some correlations"). Careful longitudinal studies, in which the same people are followed over the years, have been scarce. The conclusion that people are not predictable, then, may be a reflection not of human nature but of the haphazard methods used to study it.

Block's own research, in contrast, has amply demonstrated that people *are* predictable. Over the past 20 years Block has been analyzing extensive personality reports on several hundred Berkeley and Oakland residents that were first obtained in the 1930s, when the subjects were in junior high school. Researchers at Berkeley's Institute of Human Development followed up on the students when the subjects were in their late teens, again when they were in their mid-30s, and again in the late 1960s, when the subjects were all in their mid-40s.

The data archive is immense, including everything from attitude checklists filled out by the subjects to transcripts of interviews with the subjects, their parents, teachers, and spouses, with different sets of material gathered at each of the four time periods.

To reduce all the data to manageable proportions, Block began by assembling separate files of the information collected for each subject at each time period. Clinical psychologists were assigned to immerse themselves in individual dossiers and then to make a summary rating of the subject's personality by sorting a set of statements (for instance, "Has social poise and presence," and "Is self-defeating") into piles that indicated how representative the statement was of the subject. The assessments by the different raters (usually three for each dossier) were found to agree with one another to a significant degree, and they were averaged to form an overall description of the subject at that age. To avoid potential bias, the materials for each subject were carefully segregated by age level; all comments that referred to the person at an earlier age were removed from the file. No psychologist rated the materials for the same subject at more than one time period.

Using this painstaking methodology, Block found a striking pattern of stability. In his most recent report, published earlier this year, he reported that on virtually every one of the 90 rating scales employed, there was a statistically significant correlation between subjects' ratings when they were in junior high school and their ratings 30 to 35 years later, when they were in their 40s. The most self-defeating adolescents were the most self-defeating adults; cheerful teenagers were cheerful 40-year-olds; those whose moods fluctuated when they were in junior high school were still experiencing mood swings in midlife.

'STILL STABLE AFTER ALL THESE YEARS'

Even more striking evidence for the stability of personality, extending the time frame beyond middle age to late adulthood, comes from the work of Paul T. Costa, Jr., and Robert R. McCrae, both psychologists at the Gerontology Research Center of the National Institute on Aging in Baltimore. Costa and McCrae have tracked people's scores over time on standardized self-report personality scales, including the Sixteen Personality Factor Questionnaire and the Guilford-Zimmerman Temperament Survey, on which people are asked to decide whether or not each of several hundred statements describes them accurately. (Three sample items: "I would prefer to have an office of my own, not sharing it with another person." "Often I get angry with people too quickly." "Some people seem to ignore or avoid me, although I don't know why.")

Costa and McCrae combined subjects' responses on individual items to produce scale scores for each subject on such overall dimensions as extraversion and neuroticism, as well as on more specific traits, such as gregariousness, assertiveness, anxiety, and depression. By correlating over time the scores of subjects tested on two or three occasions — separated by six, 10, or 12 years — they obtained estimates of personality stability. The Baltimore researchers have analyzed data from two large longitudinal studies, the Normative Aging Study conducted by the Veterans Administration in Boston and the Baltimore Longitudinal Study of Aging. In the Boston study, more than 400 men, ranging in age from 25 to 82, filled out a test battery in the mid-1960s and then completed a similar battery 10 years later, in the mid-1970s. In the Baltimore study, more than 200 men between the ages of 20 and 76 completed test batteries three times, separated by six-year intervals. Less extensive analyses, still unpublished, of the test scores of women in the Baltimore study point to a similar pattern of stability.

In both studies, Costa and McCrae found extremely high correlations, which indicated that the ordering of subjects on a particular dimension on one occasion was being maintained to a large degree a decade or more later. Contrary to what might have been predicted, young and middle-aged subjects turned out to be just as unchanging as old subjects were.

"The assertive 19-year-old is the assertive 40-year-old is the assertive 80-year-old," declares Costa, extrapolating from his and McCrae's results, which covered shorter time spans. For the title of a persuasive new paper reporting their results, Costa and McCrae rewrote a Paul Simon song title, proclaiming that their subjects were "Still Stable After All These Years."

Other recent studies have added to the accumulating evidence for personality stability throughout the life span. Gloria Leon and her coworkers at the University of Minnesota analyzed the scores on the Minnesota Multiphasic Personality Inventory (MMPI) of 71 men who were tested in 1947, when they were about 50 years old, and again in 1977, when they were close to 80. They found significant correlations on all 13 of the MMPI scales, with the highest correlation over the 30-year period on the scale of "Social Introversion." Costa and McCrae, too, found the highest degrees of stability, ranging from .70 to .84, on measures of introversion-extraversion, which assess gregariousness, warmth, and assertiveness. And Paul Mussen and his colleagues at Berkeley, analyzing interviewers' ratings of 53 women who were seen at ages 30 and 70, found significant correlations on such aspects of introversion-extraversion as talkativeness, excitability, and cheerfulness.

Although character may be most fixed in the domain of introversion-extraversion, Costa and McCrae found almost as much constancy in the domain of "neuroticism," which includes such specific traits as depression, anxiety, hostility, and impulsiveness. Neurotics are likely to be complainers throughout life. They may complain about different things as they get older — for example, worries about love in early adulthood, a "midlife crisis" at about age 40, health problems in late adulthood — but they are still complaining. The less neurotic person reacts to the same events with greater equanimity. Although there is less extensive evidence for its stability, Costa and McCrae also believe that there is an enduring trait of "openness to experience," including such facets as openness to feelings, ideas, and values.

Another recent longitudinal study of personality, conducted by University of Minnesota sociologist Jeylan Mortimer and her coworkers, looked at the self-ratings of 368 University of Michigan men who were tested in 1962–63, when they were freshmen, in 1966–67, when they were seniors, and in 1976, when they were about 30. At each point the subjects rated themselves on various characteristics, such as relaxed, strong, warm, and different. The ratings were later collapsed into overall scores for well-being, competence, sociability, and unconventionality. On each of these dimensions, Mortimer found a pattern of persistence rather than one of change. Mortimer's analysis of the data also suggested that life experiences such as the nature of one's work had an impact on personality. But the clearest message of her research is, in her own words, "very high stability."

IS EVERYBODY CHANGING?

The high correlations between assessments made over time indicate that people in a given group keep the same rank order on the traits being measured, even as they traverse long stretches of life. But maybe *everyone* changes as he or she gets older. If, for example, everyone turns inward to about the same extent in the latter part of life, the correlations — representing people's *relative* standing — on measures of introversion could still be very high, thus painting a misleading picture of stability. And, indeed, psychologist Bernice Neugarten concluded as recently as five years ago that there was a general tendency for people to become more introverted in the second half of life. Even that conclusion has been called into question, however. The recent longitudinal studies have found only slight increases in introversion as people get older, changes so small that Costa and McCrae consider them to be of little practical significance.

Specifically, longitudinal studies have shown slight drops over the course of adulthood in people's levels of excitement seeking, activity, hostility, and impulsiveness. The Baltimore researchers find no such changes in average levels of gregariousness, warmth, assertiveness, depression, or anxiety. Costa summarizes the pattern of changes as "a mellowing — but the person isn't so mellowed that you can't recognize him." Even as this mellowing occurs, moreover, people's relative ordering remains much the same — on the average, everyone drops the same few standard points. Thus, an "impulsive" 25-year-old may be a bit less impulsive by the time he or she is 70 but is still likely to be more impulsive than his or her agemates.

The new evidence of personality stability has been far too strong for the advocates of change to discount. Even in the heart of changeland, in Brim and Kagan's *Constancy and Change in Human Development,* psychologists Howard Moss and Elizabeth Susman review the research and conclude that there is strong evidence for the continuity of personality.

PEOPLE WHO GET STUCK

The new evidence has not put the controversy over personality stability and change to rest, however. If anything, it has sharpened it. Although he praises the new research, Orville Brim is not convinced by it that adults are fundamentally unchanging. He points out that the high correlations signify strong associations between measures, but not total constancy. For example, a .70 correlation between scores obtained at two different times means that half of the variation (.70 squared, or .49) between people's later scores can be predicted from their earlier scores. The apostles of stability focus on this predictability, which is all the more striking because of the imperfect reliability of the measures employed. But the prophets of change, like Brim, prefer to dwell on the half of the variability that cannot be predicted, which they take as evidence of change.

Thus, Costa and McCrae look at the evidence they have assembled, marvel at the stability that it indicates, and call upon researchers to explain it: to what extent may the persistence of traits bespeak inherited biological predispositions, enduring influences from early childhood, or patterns of social roles and expectations that people get locked into? And at what age does the plaster of character in fact begin to set? Brim looks at the same evidence, acknowledges the degree of stability that it indicates, and then calls upon researchers to explain why some people in the sample are changing. "When you focus on stability," he says, "you're looking at the dregs — the people who have gotten stuck. You want to look at how a person grows and changes, not at how a person stays the same."

Brim, who is a president of the Foundation for Child Development in New York, also emphasizes that only certain aspects of personality — most clearly, aspects of social and emotional style, such as introversion-extraversion, depression, and anxiety — have been shown to be relatively stable. Brim himself is more interested in other parts of personality, such as people's self-esteem, sense of control over their lives, and ultimate values. These are the elements of character that Brim believes undergo the most important changes over the course of life. "Properties like gregariousness don't interest me," he admits; he does not view such traits as central to the fulfillment of human possibilities.

If Brim is not interested in some of the personality testers' results, Daniel Levinson is even less interested. In his view, paper-and-pencil measures like those used by Costa and McCrae are trivial, reflecting, at best, peripheral aspects of life. (Indeed, critics suggest that such research indicates only that people are stable in the way they fill out personality scales.) Levinson sees the whole enterprise of "rigorous" studies of personality stability as another instance of psychologists' rushing in to measure whatever they have measures for before they have clarified the important issues. "I think most psychologists and sociologists don't have the faintest idea what adulthood is about," he says.

Levinson's own work at the Yale School of Medicine (see "Growing Up with the Dream," *Psychology Today,* January 1978) has centered on the adult's evolving life structure — the way in which a person's social circumstances, including work and family ties, and inner feelings and aspirations fit together in an overall picture. Through intensive interviews of a small sample of men in the middle years of life — he is now conducting a parallel study of women — Levinson has come to view adult development as marked by an alternating sequence of relatively stable "structure-building" periods and periods of transition. He has paid special attention to the transition that occurs at about the age of 40. Although this midlife transition may be either smooth or abrupt, the person who emerges from it is always different from the one who entered it.

The midlife transition provides an important opportunity for personal growth. For example, not until we are past 40, Levinson believes, can we take a "universal" view of ourselves and the world rising above the limited perspective of our own background to appreciate the fullest meaning of life. "I don't think anyone can write tragedy — real tragedy — before the age of 40," Levinson declares.

DISAGREEMENT OVER METHODS

As a student of biography, Levinson does not hesitate to take a biographical view of the controversy at hand. "To Paul Costa," he suggests in an understanding tone, "the most important underlying issue is probably the specific issue of personality stability or change. I think the question of *development* is really not important to him personally. But he's barely getting to 40, so he has time." Levinson himself began his research on adult development when he was 46, as part of a way of understanding the changes he had undergone in the previous decade. He is now 60.

Costa, for his part, thinks that Levinson's clinical approach to research, based on probing interviews with small numbers of people, lacks the rigor needed to establish anything conclusively. "It's only 40 people, for crying out loud!" he exclaims. And Costa doesn't view his own age (he is 38) or that of his colleague McCrae (who is 32) as relevant to the questions under discussion.

Jack Block, who is also a hard-headed quantitative researcher — and, for the record, is fully 57 years old — shares Costa's view of Levinson's method. "The interviews pass through the mind of Dan Levinson and a few other people," Block grumbles, "and he writes it down." Block regards Levinson as a good psychologist who should be putting forth his work as speculation, and not as research.

As this byplay suggests, some of the disagreement between the upholders of stability and the champions of change is methodological. Those who argue for the persistence of traits tend to offer rigorous personality-test evidence, while those who emphasize the potential for change often offer more qualitative, clinical descriptions. The psychometricians scoff at the clinical reports as unreliable, while the clinicians dismiss the psychometric data as trivial. This summary oversimplifies the situation, though, because some of the strongest believers in change, like Brim, put a premium on statistical, rather than clinical, evidence.

When pressed, people on both sides of the debate agree that personality is characterized by *both* stability and change. But

they argue about the probabilities assigned to different outcomes. Thus, Costa maintains that "the assertive 19-year-old is the assertive 40-year-old is the assertive 80-year-old . . . *unless something happens to change it.*" The events that would be likely to change deeply ingrained patterns would have to be pretty dramatic ones. As an example, Costa says that he would not be surprised to see big personality changes in the Americans who were held hostage in Iran.

From Brim's standpoint, in contrast, people's personalities — and especially their feelings of mastery, control, and self-esteem — will keep changing through the course of life . . . *unless they get stuck.* As an example, he notes that a coal miner who spends 10 hours a day for 50 years down the shaft may have little opportunity for psychological growth. Brim believes that psychologists should try to help people get out of such ruts of stability. And he urges researchers to look more closely at the ways in which life events — not only the predictable ones, such as getting married or retiring, but also the unpredictable ones, such as being fired or experiencing a religious conversion — may alter adult personality.

At bottom, it seems, the debate is not so much methodogical as ideological, reflecting fundamental differences of opinion about what is most important in the human experience. Costa and McCrae emphasize the value of personality constancy over time as a central ingredient of a stable sense of identity. "If personality were not stable," they write, "our ability to make wise choices about our future lives would be severely limited." We must know what we are like — and what we will continue to be like — if we are to make intelligent choices, whether of careers, spouses, or friends. Costa and McCrae view the maintenance of a stable personality in the face of the vicissitudes of life as a vital human accomplishment.

Brim, however, views the potential for growth as the hallmark of humanity. "The person is a dynamic organism," he says, "constantly striving to master its environment and to become something more than it is." He adds, with a sense of purpose in his voice, "I see psychology in the service of liberation, not constraint."

Indeed, Brim suspects that we are now in the midst of "a revolution in human development," from a traditional pattern of continuity toward greater discontinuity throughout the life span. Medical technology (plastic surgery and sex-change surgery, for example), techniques of behavior modification, and the social supports for change provided by thousands of groups "from TA to TM, from AA to Zen" are all part of this revolution. Most important, people are trying, perhaps for the first time in history, to change *themselves.*

Some social critics, prominent among them Christopher Lasch in *The Culture of Narcissism,* have decried the emphasis on self-improvement as a manifestation of the "Me" generation's excessive preoccupation with self. In Brim's view, these critics miss the point. "Most of the concern with oneself going on in this country," he declares, "is not people being selfish, but rather trying to be better, trying to be something more than they are now." If Brim is right in his reading of contemporary culture, future studies of personality that track people through the 1970s and into the 1980s may well show less stability and more change than the existing studies have shown.

THE TENSION IN EACH OF US

In the last analysis, the tension between stability and change is found not only in academic debates but also in each of us. As Brim and Kagan write, "There is, on the one hand, a powerful drive to maintain the sense of

one's identity, a sense of continuity that allays fears of changing too fast or of being changed against one's will by outside forces. ... On the other hand, each person is, by nature, a purposeful, striving organism with a desire to be more than he or she is now. From making simple new year's resolutions to undergoing transsexual operations, everyone is trying to become something that he or she is not, but hopes to be."

A full picture of adult personality development would inevitably reflect this tension between sameness and transformation. Some aspects of personality, such as a tendency to be reclusive or outgoing, calm or anxious, may typically be more stable than other aspects, such as a sense of mastery over the environment. Nevertheless, it must be recognized that each of us reflects, over time, both stability and change. As a result, observers can look at a person as he or she goes through a particular stretch of life and see either stability or change or — if the observer looks closely enough — both.

For example, most people would look at Richard Alpert, the hard-driving psychology professor of the early 1960s, and Ram Dass, the bearded, free-flowing guru of the 1970s, and see that totally different persons are here now. But Harvard psychologist David McClelland, who knew Alpert well, spent time with the Indian holy man and said to himself, "It's the same old Dick!" — still as charming, as concerned with inner experience, and as power-oriented as ever. And Jerry Rubin can view his own transformation from Yippie to Wall Streeter in a way that recognizes the underlying continuity: "Finding out who I really was was done in typical Jerry Rubin way. I tried everything, jumped around like crazy with boundless energy and curiosity." If we look closely enough, even Richard Raskind and Renée Richards will be found to have a great deal in common.

Whether a person stays much the same or makes sharp breaks with the past may depend in large measure on his or her own ideas about what is possible and about what is valuable. Psychological research on adult development can itself have a major impact on these ideas by calling attention to what is "normal" and by suggesting what is desirable. Now that researchers have established beyond reasonable doubt that there is often considerable stability in adult personality, they may be able to move on to a clearer understanding of how we can grow and change, even as we remain the same people we always were. It may be, for example, that if we are to make significant changes in ourselves, without losing our sense of identity, it is necessary for some aspects of our personality to remain stable. "I'm different now," we can say, "but it's still me."

As Jack Block puts it, in his characteristically judicious style: "Amidst change and transformation, there is an essential coherence to personality development."